Books by the Boston Women's Health Book Collective

OUR BODIES, OURSELVES
OURSELVES AND OUR CHILDREN
OUR JOBS, OUR HEALTH
THE NEW OUR BODIES, OURSELVES

OURSELVES, GROWING OLDER

Women Aging with Knowledge and Power

———————————————

Paula Brown Doress and Diana Laskin Siegal
and the Midlife and Older Women Book Project
in cooperation with the Boston Women's Health Book Collective

ILLUSTRATIONS BY ROSELAINE PERKIS

A TOUCHSTONE BOOK
PUBLISHED BY SIMON AND SCHUSTER
NEW YORK • LONDON • TORONTO • SYDNEY • TOKYO

Simon and Schuster/Touchstone Books,
Published by Simon & Schuster, Inc.
Simon & Schuster Building
Rockefeller Center
1230 Avenue of the Americas
New York, New York 10020

SIMON AND SCHUSTER, TOUCHSTONE and colophons are
registered trademarks of Simon & Schuster, Inc.

Designed by C. Linda Dingler
Manufactured in the United States of America

1   3   5   7   9   10   8   6   4   2
1   3   5   7   9   10   8   6   4   2   Pbk.

Library of Congress Cataloging in Publication Data
Doress, Paula Brown.
Ourselves, growing older.

"Written in collaboration with the Boston Women's
Health Book Collective . . ."—Pref.
Bibliography: p.
Includes index.
1. Aged women—United States—Psychology.
2. Aged women—Health and hygiene—United States.
I. Siegal, Diana Laskin.   II. Midlife and Older
Women Book Project.   III. Boston Women's Health
Book Collective.
HQ1064.U5D67   1987   305.4   87-12898

ISBN: 0-671-50501-7
0-671-64424-6   Pbk.

DISCOUNT FOR LOW-INCOME, OLDER WOMEN'S GROUPS:

Ourselves, Growing Older is available at $4.79 per paperback copy (plus $1.00 shipping costs) to organizations and groups that are either licensed by a state to operate as a clinic, health counseling service, or service center for older, low-income women. Orders must be for 12 or more copies with payment and a document verifying health or social service status and your IRS number for tax exemption enclosed. The document must be a copy of a statement filed with a state or federal agency indicating health or social services as a primary purpose of your group. Make your check payable to Simon and Schuster and send to: Special Sales Department, Simon and Schuster, 1230 Avenue of the Americas, New York, NY 10020.

COPIES SO PURCHASED MAY NOT BE OFFERED FOR RESALE.

DEDICATION

To my mother, Ethel Brown. Like so many older women, she deserved a much better old age than she got. Despite the ravages of Parkinson's disease, she always enjoyed a good party, and, until her death at age eighty-two, never allowed pain or discomfort or difficult travel accommodations to keep her away from a celebration. It is a great personal sadness that her death came just after Diana and I signed the contract for this book and before our opening meeting/celebration. I regret that she was not able to participate, yet her spirit inspires me daily and has contributed immeasurably to the carrying of this project to its conclusion.

To my father, Abraham Brown. As one of the small but growing minority of caregiving husbands, he cared for my mother with unfailing devotion, risking his own health in doing so. Despite the many difficulties and strains of caregiving, he has never been too burdened to be supportive to his children's and grandchildren's projects. From my dad, I learned that if I keep putting one foot in front of the other I will eventually reach my goal.

To Allen Worters, my new husband, who read early drafts of chapters, made incisive comments, brought flowers at particularly stressful times, was generous when the project overran its advance, and believed me each time I said the book was very nearly done.

Paula Brown Doress

To my parents, Ann and George Laskin, whose outlooks and styles, though very different from each other, combined to inspire me with the desire and the zeal to produce this book. My mother, always the idealist who believes that the world should be a better place for everyone, is the inspiration for the reformer in me. She exemplifies the strength of older women in the way she has continued to grow and rise to new challenges. She gave her full support to this project, including reading chapters, contributing experiences, and providing contacts and clippings. My father started his own business at midlife, demonstrating that one's earlier, seemingly unrelated work may be the necessary preparation for later accomplishment. His sense of humor and his attitude that "of course" I can do anything I want is the reason I have done what I wanted to do.

To my older, loving, enthusiastic women friends (you know who you are) who kept me going with laughs, parties, meals, movies, and hugs.

To Dick, whose memory will always be with me.

Diana Laskin Siegal

We both thank Ann and George Laskin, who put up with The Invasion of the Book Project—its staff and its visitors. Ann frequently fed us, George repaired lamps, toaster ovens, and various other items. Together they provided a beautiful garden where we enjoyed our lunch and rested our weary eyes whenever we needed a break from the computer screen.

To our respective children and stepchildren, Naomi Siegal, John Siegal, Hannah Doress, Benjamin Doress, David Worters, and Susan Worters, with our support for the goals and paths they have chosen for their lives, and with our hope that in their older years they will see the results of our efforts.

PBD & DLS

ACKNOWLEDGMENTS

Ruby Abrahams
Alice Adams
Marie Adams
Rita Addison
Jeffrey Ahlin
John Albright
Anna C. Alden
Susan Allein
Kathleen Allen
Anne Alpert
Mark D. Altschule
Alzheimer's Disease and
   Related Disorders
   Association, Boston and
   Chicago
Alzheimer's Disease Support
   Group, Eliot Mental
   Health Center, Concord,
   Massachusetts
Donna Ambrogi
Leslie Antokolsky
Arthritis and Health
   Resource Centres, Inc.,
   Wellesley, Massachusetts
Esther Atlas
Ellie Atlee
Abigail Avery
Billye Avery
Elizabeth Badger
Mildred L. Badnek
Agnes Barr
Lorraine Baugh
Connie Bean
Susan Bell
Otilia Bengsston
George Beram
Irma Sue Berkelhammer
Peg Bevins
Catherine M. Bishop
Mary Blackburn
Lillian Blacker
Robin Blatt
Joanne Baxter Bluestone
Barbara Bolduc
Louise Bonar
Christine Bond

Alice Bonis
Deanne Bonner
Joan Borysenko
Boston Public Library,
   General and Humanities
   Reference Services
Miriam Pass Botnick
Stamata Bouloukes
Ursula Bowring-Trenn
Arminta Bradley
Barbara Bradley
Lydia Bragger
Elizabeth Bredin
Mimi Breed
Brookline Public Library,
   Main Reference
   Department
Kathy Brooks
Kay Brooks
Susan Brown
Vivienne Brown
Suzanne Butterfield
Yetta Butters
Cathy Cade
Blake Cady
Jessica Callahan
Susan Calloway
Peg Cameron
Caroline Campanella
Cancer Information Service,
   Dana-Farber Cancer
   Center
Norma Canner
Gloria Cartwright
Florence Charlton
Otta Chase
Aparna Chattoraj
Joyce Betries Chediac
Helen Cheeks
Eleanor Chilson
Bunny Clapper
Thelma Clapper
Mary Clark
Vidal Clay
Nora Coffey
Mabel Cohen

Michael David Cohen
Carola Cohn
Stuart Cohn
Louise Collier
Eleanor Collins
Mimi Conklin
Thelma Cooper
Louise Corbett
Sarah Corman
Naomi Cotter
Hildreth Coulter
Countway Library
Selma L. Crevoshay
Rosamund Critchley
Mary Ann Cromer
Sue Crook
Linda Crossman
Thelma Crowley
Cornelia Curtis
Jaffray Cuyler
Dorothy Dana
Jessica Daniels
Pamela Daniels
Elizabeth Deady
Hadwig Dertouzos
Tobey Deutsch
Lena DeVincent
Miriam Diamond
Bruce Ditzion
William Docken
Lorraine C. Doherty
Caroline Jo Dorr
Mildred Dreeszen
Buffy Dunker
Hannah Dupasse
Tess Durfee
Frances M. Dwyer
Naomi Emmerling
Carol Englender
Johanna Erickson
Frederica Erlenmeyer
Chavela Esparza
Nancy Eustis
Kathy Fabiszewski
Jean Fairfax
Sally Feather

Stephen Feldman
Marie Feltin
Libby Fennel
Judith Ferber
Cindy Ferguson
Mary Ann Ferguson
Paul Ferguson
Norma Finkelstein
Judy Fischbach
Anne Fishbain
Libby Fishbane
Mary Flaherty
Jean Fleming
Edith Fletcher
Carmen Flores
George Foord
Inge Fowlie
Robin Ann Fradkin
Denise Frangules
Elsie Frank
Elizabeth Freeman
Roberta Freeman
Mike Freidman
Jeanette French
Kathie French
Mary French
Stella Friml
Mary Gaffney
Lillian Gallivan
Sally Gardner
Patricia Loring Garrity
Penny Gay
Ruth Gay
Natalie Gelbert
Tobin Gerhart
Jean Gilfillan
Frances Gill
Luke Gillespie
Sofia Gitter
Leonard Glantz
Pat Glasgow
Gena S. Glicklich
Janet Goldberg
Barbara Goldmuntz
Lillian Golovin
Joan Kendall Gordon

Priscilla Grace
Tova Green
Harriet Ford Griswold
Vera Gropper
Sarah Grosberg
Teri Guido
Lee Hadley
Pearle Hadley
Jane Halliburton
Christina Halkett
Eleanor Hamilton
Helen Hanchett
Elizabeth Harris
Marian Harris
Susan Harris
Ruth Haugen
Faith Hawkins
Alice Ryerson Hayes
Leonard Hayflick
Margaret Healy
Regina Healy
Renée Hecht
I. Craig Henderson
Jeanne Henderson
Charles H. Hennekens
Eileen Henry
Jan Keil Hernandez
Ruth Edmonds Hill
Lillian Holcomb
Tippie Holmes
Norma Holt
Charlotte Horblit
Betty Hoskins
Wanda Howard
Gudrun Howe
Constance Hsia
Jeanne Hubbuch
Joan Hughes
Virginia Huhndorf
Demetria Iazzeto
Ann Irwin
Beryl Jackson
Bill Jackson
Ellen Jackson
Margie Dixon Jackson
Celia Jacobs
Celene Jacobson
Claradine Moore James
Patricia Jean
Judith S. Jenkins
Janyce Jennings
Pat Jerabek
Judy Johannet
Anna Johnson
Alice Jones
Helen Makie Jones
Janet Jones
Sallie M. Jones
Jini Jordan
Hilda Kahne
Barbara Kahwaty
Gertrude Kaplan
Helen Kaplan
Liselotte Karplus-Wissing
Judith N.M. Kass

Seymour Kass
Geri Kassirer
Cynthia P. Keefe
Janet Keep
Justine Kelliher
Dorothy Kemp
Monika Kehoe
JoAnn Kerrick-Mack
Elana Klugman
Edna Knox
Richard A. Knox
Hazel Krantz
Gisela Krause
Maggy Krebs
Maggie Kuhn
Mildred Kuusisto
Anita Landa
Frances Landry
Joseph Lane
Virginia Lanzkron
Barbara M. LaRoche
Phyllis Larrabee
Patricia LaRue
Lorraine Laverriere
Marie Lavine
Rosemary Lawson
Mabel G. Leavitt
Marie T. Lee
Ruth Lee
Delores LeGrand
Teresa Leitner
Eleanor Lenke
Mary Leno
Clare Lesser
Rhoda Levinson
Roberta Levinson
Bess Levitt
Mary A. Lewis
Myrna Lewis
Frederic Li
Debbie Lieberson
Midge Lillis
Sophie Linkin
Deborah Little
Patricia Lockwood
Lucile Shuck Longview
Susan M. Love
Sonja M. McKinlay
Elizabeth MacMahon
Isabel MacMahon
Diane Mahoney
Mary Jane Maloof
Laura E. Manning
Phyllis Mansfield
Thomas Manzelli
Julie V. Marsteller
Nancy H. Martin
Massachusetts College of
    Pharmacy, Drug
    Information Line
Massachusetts Nutrition
    Resource Center
Carol Mathieson
Arthur Mazer
Kathleen Harrington Mazer

Ethel McFerson
Janet Meacham
Margaret Vance Hay Means
Cathy Meecham
Jean Meggison
Nellie Kenick Meras
Barbara Merchant
Thelma Miles
Priscilla Mitchell
Fran Moira
Michael Moore
Anna Morgan
Susanne Morgan
Amadea Morningstar
Marion Morra
Winn Morrell
Ruth Moy
Freda Mulkern
Agnes Murphy
Dorothy Murphy
Alf Nachemson
Eva Naiherseg
Anita Nardini
Helen Nearing
Janet Neuman
Sue Newell
Margaret S. Nichols
Peggy Nickman
Elizabeth Noble
Agnes Norsigian
Loraine Obler
Judy Olmstead
Frances Olrich
Gloria C. Ortiz
Annabelle Osterberg
Elizabeth T. Palmunen
Florence Parker
Gloria J. Parker
Urada Parnell
Ginger Parsons
Dorothy Patten
Bradford Patterson
Cicely Payne
Roselaine Perkis
Helen Perry
Marguerite Pfeiffer
Robbie Pfeufer-Kahn
Minna Plotkin
Alonzo Plough
Elinor Polansky
Fran Pollner
Judith G. Poole
Mary Pogoryiliki
Mary Pratt
Gena Prenowitz
Helane Press
Avis Pretzler
Joanne Prince
Alice Quinlan
Agnes V. Quinn
Marguerite Ramedell
Myra Ramos
Tania Rash
Eloise Rathbone-McCuan
Shirley Renfrew

Beth E. Rhude
Miriam Rice
Sharon Rich
Janet Richards
Aldean Richardson
Joyce Richardson
Doris Richman
Georgie Ridlon
Martha Robbins
Harriet Robey
Virginia Robinson
Geogorita Rodriguez
Judy Rogers
Annette Rosen
Sandra Rosenthal
Alice Rossi
Anita Rossien
Grace Rossien
Mary Rovner
Lydia Roy
Jane Royse
Thelma Rutherford
Sally Rynne
Florence Sacarob
Dorothy Saccoccia
Rose Safran
Miriam Salomé-Haven
Judy Salzman
Dorothy Sanborn
Ethel Sanders
Shirley Sartori
Norma Satten
Marian Saunders
Marnette Saz
Loretta Schalk
Jane Schaller
Toni Schiff
Irene A. Schmeid
Mildred Schuckstes
Hilda Schwartz
Hilda Scott
Mary Scott
Judith Seixas
Sarah Semerjian
Annie Senhouse
E. Mary Shannon
Jody Shaw
Beth Sheffel
Barbara Sher
Susan Sherry
Louise B. Shrieves
Rose L. Sidman
Naomi Siegal
Winifred Siegel
Irene Siegler
Phyllis Rolfe Silverman
Ethan A.H. Sims
Geraldine Sindut
Gladys Singman
Claudia M. Sisson
Lucy Skinner
Connie Slater
Joanne Small
Nancy Smart
Pearl Smith

Louise Snipes
Muriel Snowden
Jan Solet
Mickey Spencer
Ellen Sue Spivack
Erna Sporer
Betty Stanco
Marie Steinmeyer
Arlene Stern
Betsy Steven
Irene Stewart
Larry Stiffler
Greta Stone
Marian G. Stoodley
Janet Stout
Julia Sutton
Lillian R. Suvalle
Karyl Sweeney
Sharon E. Sweet
Carolyn Ruth Swift
Pauline Swift

Lois Swingler
Doris Tanner
Mary Taschner
Louise Taub
James Taylor
Jo Tempesto
Toni Tenette
Richard Thal
Elizabeth Theriault
Wendy Thurber
Olive Tiffany
Ruth M. Tinsley
Thelma Tisdale
Jean Tock
Frances Toy
Dorothy Tollifson
Anne Tremearne
Rona Troderman-King
Lonie Troub
Suzanne Tufts
Eleanore Tupper

Blanche Aurora Turner
Gladys Vanderbelt
VISION, Inc.
Joy Vronsky
Mary Waggener
Nancy Wagman
Judith S. Wallerstein
Lila Wallis
Janet M. Walther
Adeline Wanatee
Deborah Ward
Marjorie Waters
Liz Watson
Cassandra Batson Way
Ursula Weimersheimer
Ira Weinberg
Marlena Weinstein
Marya Weinstock
Sandra Weintraub
Fran Weisse
Rosemary Whiting

Sally Wilkins
Esther Wilson
Mollie Wilson
Gertrude Winchell
Bernice Winer
Richard Wolff
Bruce Wood
Irene Wood
Josephine Worrell
Frances Worters
Peggy Ann Wright
Sarah Yarrington
Marilyn M. Young
Aileen Zahn
J. Carolyn Zavarine
Geraldine Zetzel
Irving K. Zola
Michael Zucker
Cecile Zunner

CONTENTS

UNDERSTANDING, PREVENTING,
AND MANAGING
MEDICAL PROBLEMS

FOREWORD

We are all aging. The pioneers of the second wave of feminism are advancing into middle age or beyond. In fact, the whole postwar baby-boom generation is moving into midlife, which means that this will be an age group to reckon with in every sense.

Yet the specific concerns of older women are just coming to the fore. There were so many women's issues to be dealt with, and in the 1970's, women of the new wave of feminists were usually quite young. In the area of health, reproductive rights and childbirth issues understandably took precedence. While these remain important to all women because they deal so basically with control of our bodies, there are other concerns which can no longer be ignored.

This book examines the neglected health concerns of middle-aged and older women. The basic principle—that we must know our own bodies and ourselves in order to be free from mistaken notions, the legacy of the patriarchal culture in which we live—continues after reproductive functions have ended. We remain females to the end of our days, and our status as women affects us as long as we live.

Like its predecessor, *Our Bodies, Ourselves,* this book is a collaborative effort. Many women have participated in its writing, and it is based on common experience. It reveals the impact of ageism, compounded with sexism, on all of us. It opens up new ways to free ourselves of both of these, not only in our own minds but also in the society around us. Insights both from the older women's advocacy movement and the women's health movement are encompassed within it. For older women it is a milestone.

Some of us who have been advocates for older women's issues for a long time are delighted to observe this spread of consciousness. The circle of concern is widening; there are now many approaches, not one; and there is greater organizational and personal interest in the problems of the growing-older female. This book should be a landmark in speeding up that process of consciousness-raising.

A work like this encourages confidence and creativity and the acceptance of self-worth at

Janet Beller

xiii

any age. It should help women release the internal brakes we have applied so long and help us take off in any direction we would like to go. The idea is to enjoy life in later years, to make the most of this most precious season of our lives. This health and living handbook will also increase women's ability to stay well, thereby expanding the growing force of active middle-aged and older women. More women will participate in the Older Women's League and other advocacy organizations to make things easier for the next generation coming along. For older women *can* change the circumstances of aging for all women, and men as well.

Such efforts expand the concept of sisterhood across generations, with women in midlife providing a crucial bridge. Together we are building a new road to aging, and at the same time that road is building us. Young women have as great a stake in our efforts as older women do, for their turn is coming.

When we finally bridge the generation gap, women will be a magnificent force for positive change in society. For we are the compassion experts—we've been socialized in that direction. Humanizing the social fabric is our special domain. We're the nurturers and informal healers, even though professionals of both sexes have medicalized the process, leaving only the unpaid part for us.

At present we're caught within the confines of an impossible health care system, filled with absurdities and based upon an economic underpinning that distorts it into grotesque shapes. But given a long view, and our involvement, that, too, can be changed. Knowledge is the first step. The second is taking more control over whatever aspects of our own health that we can.

From dependency on "experts" we must move toward greater independence, which means taking on a greater degree of responsibility for our own bodies, as well as for the policies which affect us.

I do believe that women will take the lead in remodeling the health care system of the future, and those of us in midlife or older will play an important part of that eventual transformation. Why? Not only because we are the compassion experts—and healing is intimately connected with compassion—but also because we have the least to lose and the most to gain by that transformation. Women of all ages, by changing their own health habits and affecting others around them, by speaking up and then becoming involved with all aspects of health care delivery, will, I predict, have far greater influence than we now can imagine in redesigning the whole system. But first we must start with ourselves. Then we should move on to try to understand the forces that drive the present system, its costs, its distribution of services and where we fit in—or don't fit in. Then we will be able to join with others to create a health care system worthy of the name.

Taking control of our own lives and of our bodies is the most basic feminist principle there is. This book moves us in that direction, for it breaks down that formidable barrier in our minds—the fear of growing old. It helps us to see that midlife and old age are stages of life, as important as any other. Since we cannot beat aging, we had better learn how to join it. That is what this book is about. I'm very glad to have been a part of it.

Tish Sommers

PROJECT COORDINATORS' PREFACE

The contributors to this book comprise a rich mosaic of women whose life experiences span the length of the century, who come from a variety of religious, economic, and ethnic backgrounds, and who live in a wide range of housing and living situations. We came together to address the special opportunities and challenges of living in a time of ever-increasing longevity for women.

This book was written in collaboration with the Boston Women's Health Book Collective, and began out of the process of producing a chapter on "Women Growing Older" for *The New Our Bodies, Ourselves*. Writing that chapter pre-

sented challenges; the task of squeezing the health and living issues of four or five decades of life into one chapter seemed insurmountable. In a meeting, the coordinator of that chapter exclaimed, "Do you realize that we are trying to write a mini-*Our Bodies, Ourselves* for the second half of life?" With that awareness the idea of a new book was born.

Forty-five women participated in writing, rewriting, and editing this book, while over three hundred participated as readers, consultants, contributors of experiences and information, and links with sources of new information. Several of the women who contributed to *The*

Janet Knott/The Boston Globe

Project coordinators (*seated*) with some of the project participants at a meeting of the Greater Boston Older Women's League.

xv

New Our Bodies, Ourselves contributed to this book as well. Other contributors came to us through the growing network of women's health and older women's organizations. Most of the project writers were based in the Boston area and rural New England, but a number of women participated who lived in other parts of the country—California, the Southwest, the Midwest, New York, and Pennsylvania. Those who could travel to Boston met a number of times during the life of the project to exchange mutual support and ideas about writing our chapters and to enjoy good company and delicious potluck dinners. Our more far-flung writers had to be content with coming together in spirit, communicating by mail and telephone, with occasional lucky opportunities to meet while someone was traveling. Networks were created and firm friendships forged, which we know will continue beyond the life of the project.

While most of the writers who coordinated chapters ranged in age from their mid-forties to early seventies, none of the most long-lived women were willing to take on such a task. As one woman put it:

I enjoy contributing my ideas to an intellectual discussion, but I find in my eighties that I no longer have the energy to coordinate a project. The time for that is past. Yet I enjoy putting my ideas into the pot with everyone else's. I continue to feel a valued part of many organizations and projects by participating in this way.

Special thanks are due to the oldest women who did contribute to the book project through sharing their experiences, attending group discussions, interviewing friends, and reviewing chapters, often while fighting increasing physical limitations. We especially want to thank the following women who contributed so much to the book: Lois Harris (age eighty-two), Lucy Mitchell (eighty-five), Faire Edwards (seventy-nine), Elsie Reethof (ninety), and Beth Rosenbaum (eighty). Their spirit, wisdom, and breadth of life experience enriched this book in so many ways. Their courage and optimism inspire us to carry on.

As project coordinators, we cannot possibly give adequate acknowledgment to the writers of the chapters for the hard work, maturity, and cooperation which the task we undertook together required. Many of the women who worked on the project donated hours of labor beyond what we were able to compensate. We hope they will enjoy the satisfaction of seeing the book in print.

We would especially like to thank Mary C. Allen, our project editor, who carefully and painstakingly edited each chapter and contributed immeasurably to the complex task of weaving them into a coherent whole. Our thanks to Barbara Williams, Henry Ferris, and the many others at Simon and Schuster who contributed to the editing, design, and production of this book.

Special thanks are also due to members of the Boston Women's Health Book Collective for their collaboration and support in carrying out this project. Judy Norsigian, Esther Rome, Pamela Morgan, Sally Whelan, Norma Swenson, and Jan Brin constantly fed us information from the files of the Collective's Women's Health Information Center. Jane Pincus and Norma Swenson between them read and critiqued the entire book and Judy and Esther read substantial sections. Wendy Sanford and Nancy Hawley read and commented on important chapters. Special appreciation goes to Vilunya Diskin, whose support was critical at an early stage.

Many lesbians participated actively in this book from the very beginning as writers, readers, and consultants, as contributors of experiences, photographs, and poems. Some attended small discussion groups to share their concerns, their lives, and relationships. We especially appreciate their openness in view of the homophobic pressures which make it risky for lesbians to reveal their sexual preference.

We are grateful to the secretaries and office workers who typed the manuscript, kept our files organized, and often were our first critics: Mary Ann McCarthy, Carola Cohn, Chris Crandall, Barbara Connell, Laura Last, Felice Katz, Jasmine Loisell, Wendy Levine, and Bill Russell. While typing our manuscript, one woman stopped smoking and another reevaluated her eating patterns. We hope the book will have a similar effect on our readers.

A book such as this one would not be possible without the help of many women sending experiences, information, poetry, photos, and drawings, and women and men reading chapters and offering comments. The names of all those who helped are listed in the Acknowledgments. Many of those listed offered constructive criticism, and inclusion of their names does not mean that they agreed with the final product.

This book is not an anthology of individual statements, but a compilation of many women's ideas from a feminist perspective. To achieve this end, the project coordinators in dialogue with the writers deleted material that repeated other chapters, worked on contradictions between chapters and moved material from one writer's chapter to another when that seemed to improve the flow of the book. The project coordinators retained and exercised final editorial control and thus are responsible for omissions, errors, and inclusion of controversial material. We hope others, women and men, will write more about the experience of growing older. We want this book to have plenty of company.

The death of Tish Sommers (author of the Foreword and the concluding chapter) in October 1985 was one of the saddest events that occurred during the writing of this book. She and her colleague and close friend Laurie Shields, co-founders of the Older Women's League, were among the first to urge us to expand *The New Our Bodies, Ourselves* chapter on "Women Growing Older" into a book of its own, and both generously encouraged the project. We felt privileged to work with Tish, to have the benefit of her empowering vision of older women's political potential. In her last years she accomplished what many would be proud to accomplish in a lifetime. Tish undertook the task of writing a chapter and a foreword for this book, making it clear that she would work as long as she was able, but that when her condition worsened she would bow out and trust us to do the final editing and provide the resource list for her chapter. Indeed, that is just what happened. Tish met all of her deadlines with characteristic optimism, directness, and flair. When she was no longer able to work, she let us know without delay. Her clarity, courage, and honesty with herself and others continue to inspire us.

Paula Brown Doress
Diana Laskin Siegal

THE POTENTIAL OF THE SECOND HALF OF LIFE

by Paula Brown Doress and Diana Laskin Siegal with
help from Caroline T. Chauncey, Robin Cohen,
Marilyn Bentov, and Lois Harris

This book grows out of our conviction that the decades after forty can be rich and fulfilling, a time when we as women can come into our own. One in eight Americans is now over sixty-five. Older women are survivors, living an average of eight years longer than men, enjoying longer lifespans than we might as young women have expected to or planned for. Life expectancy for women is seventy-eight years; for those already over sixty-five it is eighty-three and a half years. We can and do use our added years in ways that please us—learning new skills, traveling, and living out long-delayed dreams. Yet, as survivors, women are also likely to face more of the challenges of aging: chronic health conditions; inadequate income; caregiving responsibilities; lack of care when we need it;* and perhaps most devastating of all, the deaths of family members and friends. In this book, we have tried to give equal attention to both the promise and the challenge of the later years.

WHY A BOOK ABOUT BOTH MIDDLE-AGED AND OLDER WOMEN?

The economic problems of older women grow out of women's early experience of sex discrimi-

---

*We cannot rely on family ties for care. By the age at which most women need care the majority of those who had married are widowed; many others have never married; and 25 percent of women over seventy have no living children.

nation in the workplace and the prejudicial belief that women do not need to earn enough money to support themselves. The two poorest groups in the U.S. today are women raising children alone and women over sixty-five living alone. Whether we have been poor all our lives or have experienced downward mobility in our middle or later years, many of us find that we do not have adequate financial resources for the second half of our lives. A feminist analysis is an important tool to help us become aware of the ways that we women are programmed from our earliest years toward financial and emotional dependency. At midlife, we can begin to make changes in order to avoid the isolation, poverty, and ill health that mar the later years of so many older women.

In the role of traditional caregivers, women at midlife are in closer contact than any other group, except for the aging themselves, with the problems that arise when public policy fails to meet needs such as elder housing, long-term care, and in-home care. When such needs go unmet by public services, it is middle-aged women who are expected to give their unpaid labor to provide the services required. Frequently, our personal aspirations and careers suffer when we do so. Also, our future security suffers if we fail to earn pension and Social Security credits in those crucial middle years. Policies that require women to care for the elderly for free at home are short-sighted. Such policies sow the seeds for another generation of impoverished older women. We must demand the resources for respite care, long-term care, and

AGING AND AGEISM

Whole
Woman of the ∧ Year.

Have you ever known a woman named "November"?
Neither have I.
Now "May" and "June" and "April" have their
    namesakes—
Ever ask why?

We rarely picture woman as autumnal;
Female is spring.
Please, someone, name a newborn girl "October"
And hear her sing

Of harvest cut and growth complete and fruit
    mature,
Not just of birth.
Oh, let a woman age as seasons do;
Love each time's worth!

Miriam Corcoran

Ellen Shub

Ageism—the belief that a person's worth and abilities are determined solely by chronological age—is the enemy that threatens the creative, growing future we envision for ourselves. Research shows that intellectual capacity remains stable throughout life—the ability to learn new things continues unabated and, when actively exercised, enhances our well-being.[1] Yet ageism declares us obsolete at a socially defined deadline. At age sixty we find ourselves on our community's senior-citizen list, and at sixty-five many companies expect us to retire even though mandatory retirement has been abolished by federal law.

In a youth-oriented society, both middle-aged and older women struggle with ageism. Because of the double standard, women are labeled "old" at an earlier age than men are.[2] The sexist beliefs that relegate women to child rearing and domestic work exclusively seem to mark us as obsolete when children leave home and our childbearing potential is at an end. Such archaic beliefs are irrelevant to most contemporary women, yet we continue to suffer the discrimination which is their legacy, especially when we enter or reenter the work force or change jobs in our middle years.

We live in a society that values the quick fix and the slick package. As one woman put it, "I'm a lot more interesting than I was at twenty-five or thirty-five, but it's a lot harder to get anyone to pay attention." We can fight such attitudes by

housing and support services that will provide alternatives to the limited choices of unsupported independent living vs. a nursing home.

Many of us become so habituated to caring for others and helping others achieve that we lose sight of our own goals or never get around to formulating any. In the second half of life, many of us have an opportunity to pay attention to ourselves and our own needs and aspirations, perhaps for the first time. The added years we gain with increased longevity can be ours to grow spiritually and intellectually. Midlife is often spoken of by women in metaphors of birth and rebirth, a time to nurture our own talents, casting off the external criteria by which we may have devalued ourselves and blossoming in new ways.

If we think of our future years as providing an opportunity to develop our creativity, our passions, and our activism, we can look forward to our older years with confidence and enthusiasm.

The Boston Globe

UNITY AND DIFFERENCE AMONG WOMEN

When you read the experiences of the women quoted in this book, do not automatically picture a white, middle-class, heterosexual, able-bodied woman. We reached out to and heard from a great variety of women—white women and women of color, middle-aged and old women, heterosexual and lesbian and bisexual women, able-bodied women and women with disabilities. Because the book is primarily about aging, we identified the speakers by age alone unless another characteristic was significant to her story and not apparent in what she said.

Sexual Preference

At least 10 percent of women, perhaps more, are lesbian. It is sad that homophobia, the irrational fear and hatred of homosexuality and bisexuality, is still so prevalent that many lesbian women are reluctant to openly acknowledge their preference. Many women who have found a way to survive and thrive in a woman-centered community still hide this important part of themselves from their heterosexual friends and colleagues.

In gathering personal experiences for this book, we found that the lesbians (mostly middle-aged) who are part of an organization or network with other lesbians welcomed an opportunity to discuss the satisfactions of living a woman-centered way of life. We were less successful in reaching the oldest and most isolated lesbians who grew up and lived in even more repressive circumstances. Their fear of exposure and learned discomfort with openness has rendered them understandably reluctant to share their experiences and even keeps them isolated from all but a few of their lesbian sisters. This is a loss to all of us who could learn from their life experiences as women surviving on their own.

We must unite as women to fight against the ageism, sexism, racism, homophobia, and discrimination against persons with disabilities that blight all our lives, especially in our later years. Our unity will be more powerful and effective if we can honor our differences and work toward inclusiveness of all groups. Each of us, whether heterosexual, lesbian, or bisexual, can examine our own attitudes and practices. We may be able in our own social circles to build a

actively reaching out and valuing one another. At a social or community gathering, if you seek out one of the oldest women and get acquainted with her, you will be amply rewarded.

I went to a women's brunch where most of the women ranged from the mid-thirties to the mid-fifties. I was curious about one much older woman who turned out to be a sculptor in her seventies. She invited me to visit her at her studio near the shore. I drove down with a photographer friend, bringing a picnic lunch, and enjoyed a delightful afternoon viewing her recent work, each of us sharing her experiences as a woman trying to do creative work at different times in the life cycle. [a forty-four-year-old woman]

At a wedding where I did not know many people I noticed an older woman in her seventies who seemed to have a visual disability. No one was speaking with her, so I struck up a conversation. I found out she was a founding member of a self-help organization for people with low vision and did counseling on the telephone from her home for others with low vision. It was fun to meet and talk with such a gutsy lady. [a forty-eight-year-old woman] climate of inclusiveness and openness that will make every woman feel accepted and affirmed for who she is.

Aging and Disability

It is a mistake to equate disability with a particular age. Some women have lived with severe limitations from birth or an early age, while others become disabled later in life as a result of an accident or disease. Even the longest-lived women may remain free of limiting disabilities, but a number of women must learn to manage a disability in the middle and later years. If that happens to us, we may have to learn about adapting our living space, demanding access to buildings, and a whole host of other situations we may never have had to deal with before. In that situation, there is much we can learn from other women with disabilities and from the disabled people's movement. Yet advocacy groups representing elders rarely communicated with those representing the disabled, at least until a recent conference on aging and disability in 1986.[3] We hope this communication will be the beginning of a dialogue about aging and disability.

In the past, when it was more common for people to die at earlier ages, many people feared that premature death would close off the chance of accomplishing their life's goals. But today, many people fear pain, illness, and dependency more than death—a fear of "dying socially" before biological death occurs—or they fear "living too long."[4] Much of the fear of aging and the ageism that results is our own fear of disability. If we can work for a society in which disability does not mean social death, we can make it a better society in which to grow old.

HEALTH AND AGING

Experts on aging have described a phenomenon they have tagged with the unlikely name of "youth creep." As life expectancy lengthens, people stay youthful longer. Thus, those over seventy-five used to be called "old-old," but now this term refers to those over eighty-five, as the group from seventy-five to eighty-four stays healthier and lives more independently than before. Some use the term old-old to refer only to those who are ill or disabled, while those who are in good health and independent even in

their eighties and nineties are counted as young-old.

Most of the health and medical problems we face in our later years are chronic rather than acute, and require innovative approaches to people's needs for personal support, caregiving, and housing. However, our health care delivery system and health insurance specifically for the elderly—even Medicare—is geared to medical intervention for acute medical problems, and is frequently at a loss in responding to the chronic conditions more common in our later years. Aging is part of the life span and should not be turned into a medical event. We can help ourselves and one another in maintaining our good health, and in other situations in which we have been taught to turn to professionals for answers.

WOMEN AND POLICY FOR THE ELDERLY

Women make up the majority of the over-sixty-five population, and outnumber men in the over-eighty population by two to one. Therefore, the needs of older women should be central to public policy for the elderly. While poverty has been reduced in the overall elderly population to nearly the average for the population as a whole,* it continues to be higher for older women—17 percent, compared to 10 percent for men. Of older women living alone, one fourth are poor, with a median annual income only $620 above the poverty level. Women outlive men an average of eight years, so nearly all once-married women experience widowhood for some part of their later years. Eighty-five percent of surviving spouses are women.[5] Once widowed, we are much less likely than men to remarry. Men over age sixty-five are seven times more likely to begin a new marriage—and they usually marry younger women.[6] Although most older men are married, most older women are

---

*An important statistical inconsistency makes it difficult for us to know just how many older people are poor. The Villers Foundation report, *On the Other Side of Easy Street: Myths and Facts About the Economics of Old Age*, notes that the Census Bureau applies a different poverty standard to elders than to other adult age groups on the assumption that an adult sixty-five years of age or older needs less income than an adult sixty-four or younger. Tacit acceptance of this double standard reinforces the inaccurate assumption that few older persons are poor.

Jerry Howard/Positive Images

income elders, still it has not been enough to assure that all elders can live above the poverty line. It is important to keep these significant economic differences in mind when we hear pronouncements about how well older Americans today are doing. Single older women must have strong community ties and substantial family support just to maintain an adequate standard of living.

The growth in numbers of older women gives us greater political clout. We have a lot to contribute to society and to ourselves. We know what the world felt like before the nuclear bomb made apocalypse a grim possibility. We won the vote, worked to feed families in the Depression, ran factories when men went off to war, raised children who in adulthood brought fresh winds of change to our society, and learned to confront racism and sexism. Now we are learning to confront ageism.

The supports we build for ourselves through organizing, community building, networking, and political activity can help change negative stereotypes of age, of women, of the powerless—and those we have of ourselves. Our friendships with women can be lifelong relationships as important as family, often outlasting family ties. Being open to meeting new people and building

not. And older women living alone are more likely to be poor than those living with a partner or others.

The poverty rate of Hispanic women is 24 percent, and that of Black women over sixty-five is 42 percent;[7] for Black women over eighty-five and living alone, it is 73 percent.[8] Black women now live nearly as long as white women, both reaching an average age of over seventy-five years, so the needs of the elderly must be an interracial issue. Though Black women are socialized to be financially self-supporting, their earnings are the lowest of any group. Because of racism, Black women often worked as laundry workers and domestics, where they were paid low wages and were not covered by Social Security. Thus, older women of color continue to have the most serious and devastating economic problems of all. While programs such as SSI have raised the income level of the lowest-

Jerry Howard/Positive Images

on old and new friendships are important ways to counter the isolation that can occur as we sustain losses in our later years.

The Older Women's League, the Gray Panthers, and other activist organizations provide plenty of opportunities on a local and on a national level to improve the status and image of older people. We can establish a safer, healthier environment for women in and through women's political organizations, in any way that opens—or resists the closing of—doors to more and better jobs, pay, education, and status for all women. We can band together, we middle-aged and older women, as allies to agitate for social change and to improve the prospects for our own not-so-distant future. In doing this work, we fight for ourselves, our mothers, our grandmothers, and the well-being of the generations of women who will grow old after us.

NOTES

1. K. Warner Schaie and Sherry Willis, "Can Decline in Adult Intellectual Functioning Be Reversed?" *Developmental Psychology*, Vol. 22, No. 2, 1986, pp. 223–32.

2. Susan Sontag, "The Double Standard of Aging." *Saturday Review*, Vol. 95, No. 39, September 23, 1972.

3. Irving Kenneth Zola, "Toward a Unifying Agenda: Some Major Issues Cross-cutting Policies and Programs Concerning Aging and Disability." Paper presented at the Sixth Pew Health Policy Fellows Conference, to be published in a forthcoming volume of the American Enterprise Institute for Public Policy Research, 1150 Seventeenth St., N. W., Washington, DC 20036.

4. Matilda White Riley and John W. Riley, Jr., "Longevity and Social Structure: The Added Years." *Daedalus: Journal of the American Academy of Arts and Sciences*, Winter 1986, pp. 51–75.

5. Coalition of Women on the Budget, "Inequality of Sacrifice: The Impact of the Reagan Budget on Women," March 1984. Distributed by National Women's Law Center, 1616 P St., N. W., Washington, DC 20036.

6. *Older Women: The Economics of Aging*, Women's Studies Program and Policy Center at George Washington University, 1980.

7. U. S. Department of Commerce, Bureau of the Census, "Characteristics of the Population Below the Poverty Level: 1983." *Current Population Reports*.

8. Alan L. Otten, "U.S. Agencies Awaken to the Need for More Data on Nation's Elderly." *Wall Street Journal*, December 9, 1986.

AGING WELL

1

AGING AND WELL-BEING

by Marilyn Bentov, Dori Smith, Diana Laskin Siegal,
and Paula Brown Doress, with help from Eve Nichols

Special thanks to Joleen Bachman, Ruth Hubbard, Jane Jewell,
and Faith Nobuko Barcus
Massage by Sylvia Pigors, Marilyn Bentov, and Diana Laskin Siegal

At My Age

Last summer our vegetable garden yielded small
bounty: round pink tennis ball tomatoes ripening
among the marigolds in an inferno of sun, captives
of ninety degree days, of unwavering heat, fitful
squalls of rain that released, not a drenching cool,
but drops of water that glanced off tight shiny skins
the way globules hiss from a sizzling fry pan.

One day I looked into the patch and there was one
tomato seamed and split, a deeper fruitier juicier
red inside, but with a frayed and largely open look.

I wanted to cup it into my hands and not lose a drop.

Doris Panoff

A PLAN FOR
AGING WELL

Many of us want to live long lives, but fear the
infirmities or disabilities that may come with
advancing age. In this chapter we will emphasize that aging well is more than the absence of
disease. It is a harmony of mind, body, and
spirit. Each of us can take an active role in our
well-being as we age—a holistic approach that
involves sharing with others, reducing stress,
and participating in community, among other
methods.

*The reason wellness is so important to me is that I have
so many things I want to do, and I have to be well to do
them. I don't want to live to be eighty or ninety unless I*
*am well enough to be active. I don't want quantity of
life without quality. [a fifty-seven-year-old woman]*

*Whether I am healthy because I can be busy and happy
or whether I am busy and happy because I am healthy
is a question. I can do many things that I never had
time to do before. Among my activities, I play the recorder in two groups, make ceramics, take part in a
book group and a financial-planning group, go to concerts, plays and lectures, garden with the help of a
young man, and volunteer at a food collection center.
For the good of my somewhat achy leg, I swim three or
four times a week, take a yoga class, and sometimes
bicycle. Life gets somewhat hectic but there's nothing I
want to stop because I really enjoy the things I do very
much. [a seventy-four-year-old woman]*

At any age, we may have disease or disability
to contend with, but we can still be as healthy
and active as possible.

*I am multiply disabled—legally blind, with chronic
pain syndrome from head and neck injuries. I am very
sold on the pain program at my local hospital. Instead
of drugs (I was using narcotics), much of my pain can
be relieved by physical therapy, particularly the aerobic treadmill, jogging, and the stationary-bicycle
program. Every day, in addition to the aerobics, I do
forty-five minutes or so of muscle stretching and isome-
trics, push-ups, sit-ups, etc. I am taught that these
changes I am making in my life-style must be permanent, daily, lifelong. [a forty-one-year-old woman]*

The self-care necessary to be well begins with
self-value. *Deciding* on wellness reflects and fos-

Randy Dean/VNA of San Francisco's Adult Day Health Care Center

The best way I know to stay healthy and alive is to stay away from pills and out of the rocking chair. [a ninety-year-old woman]

To keep involved and growing, we must recognize and fight ageism in all of its manifestations. We can deal with ageism more effectively if we have energy and strength.

I realized that in another year I'll be on the senior citizens' list for my town, because once you turn sixty you automatically get the mailings. And you know, this is silly, but my mailman is someone I know personally, and I feel it's none of his business how old I am, but he would see those mailings.

AGING IS NOT OLD AGE

There is a difference between "aging" and "getting old." "Aging" encompasses all the biological changes that occur over a lifetime—for example, increase and decrease in height, onset and cessation of menstruation, and shaping of the young-adult and middle-aged body. Changes in thymic hormones are sometimes used as a sign of the aging process because the thymus gland, a pyramid-shaped gland beneath the breastbone involved in regulation of the immune system, begins to shrink slowly after the age of two.[2] The pace of biological aging differs among individuals. In all people, some organs age faster than others. The impact of genetic and environmental factors on biological aging are just beginning to be understood.

"Getting old," on the other hand, is a social concept, and our feelings about it may only be slightly related to the biological processes of "aging."

It is not surprising that women have such feelings about being identified as aging; our culture has a strong prejudice against older women. Traditional cultures often hold their elders in high regard, seeing them as storehouses of wisdom to be transmitted to the next generation; older women, especially, are often seen as healers. The Pueblo Indians, for example, believe their elders' rituals help the sun to rise each morning. Imagine how it would feel to believe oneself so vital to life itself!

For as long as I can remember, I've cherished an image of my future self as a "wise old woman." I can see myself now—my silver hair provides softness around my

ters that self-value. We can prolong our healthy, active years by paying attention to good nutrition, activity and movement, solitude and rest, good relationships, and our links to the communities in which we live and work.

I'd been depressed and anxious and using sleeping pills for a number of years. With the help of a friend who was a therapist, I became aware of a lot of anger I'd been holding toward my mother and father—and toward my husband. I started adopting some new habits—like taking care of myself physically. I was all out of shape—I started jogging and I took yoga to learn to relax. Feeling better physically bolstered my self-esteem and gave me the courage to confront my husband about the inequities in our relationship and to push for changes. [a woman in her fifties]

Studies show that older people who give themselves a better health rating than their physician does frequently prove, in time, the greater accuracy of their own intuitive feelings about the state of their health.[1]

Norma Holt

face. I live in a log cabin by a stream, and my fireplace walls are decorated with well-used iron skillets and copper pots. I'm preparing to receive young guests who come regularly to visit me. I find my fulfillment in teaching them the wisdom gained over my lifetime. This image has sustained me through many dark hours in which I feared I would never make a contribution to life. [a forty-three-year-old woman]

It is especially important to distinguish physiological aging from the capacity for intellectual growth and social participation. Even very ill or frail old people can continue to learn and to be socially involved. If aging well is our goal, it is important to view health as the World Health Organization defined it in 1946: "A state of complete physical, mental, and social well-being, not just the absence of disease or infirmity."[3] Continued engagement and productivity is the best way of delaying the onset of frailty in the older years. Robert Butler argues that "health and productivity are interacting conditions: the unproductive human is at higher risk of illness and economic dependency and the sick person is limited in productivity and is, therefore, at higher risk of dependency."[4]

Scientists have learned a great deal about senescence, the biological changes that occur in different cells and tissues over time, but they still have fundamental questions about how and why these changes come about. Some think that aging is controlled by a genetically programmed "biological clock," but others think that aging results from cumulative damage to certain systems in the body. It may be many years before we know which theory or combination of theories explains biological aging.

Research is currently exploring factors that seem associated with longevity in the hope of finding a formula for extending human life expectancy or minimizing conditions associated with aging. We must be careful to differentiate between test results in the laboratory and what happens in our own bodies. For example, rats and mice placed on a diet containing 30 to 50 percent fewer calories than the normal diet for caged laboratory rodents but containing essential vitamins and minerals live longer than control animals.[5] But studies of the relationship between longevity and weight in humans have produced conflicting results.[6]

Commercial manufacturers sometimes take advantage of highly publicized laboratory results to promote products that have no proven value. Superoxide dismutase (SOD) supplements sold in stores are a good example of this. Research has discovered that SOD, an enzyme involved in the repair of cellular damage, is found at higher levels in animals with long lifespans than in those with shorter ones. Advertisements now tout SOD as an anti-aging drug, but in fact, SOD is broken down during digestion and cannot be reassembled in the body.[7] Thus, these diet supplements have no effect on human longevity and are a waste of money.

Laboratory studies of the effects of vitamin and mineral supplements on the aging process also must be evaluated carefully. The possible anti-cancer action of vitamins A and C and the anti-aging actions of the mineral selenium deserve further investigation, but the evidence available does not support the contention that these supplements either prevent cancer or extend life.[8]

It is unlikely that researchers will find a single intervention to stop aging. Indeed, any promise of extraordinary benefit probably indicates something of which the buyer should beware. In the future, scientific advances in many areas may delay specific aging processes, such as the decline in immune function, but until then, caution should be used in assessing claims for the life-extending or rejuvenating properties of any anti-aging agents or regimens.[9]

The term "life expectancy," refers to the average number of years of life expected for an individual in a given population. "Life span" is the maximum number of years of life possible for a species. Researchers involved in efforts to increase understanding of the aging process have found ways to increase both the life expectancies and the life spans of experimental animals.[10]

The average life expectancy in developed countries has increased steadily during the past two hundred years as a result of improvements in housing, nutrition, health care, and sanitation. In the United States today, the average life expectancy at birth is seventy-eight years for a girl; for a boy it is seventy-one years. More people are living to an old age than in past centuries, but the human life span has remained fixed at about 115 years for all of recorded history.

Although the prospect that the life span might be increased is exciting, we believe that the present focus of aging research should be to improve the quality of life for all members of society. One of the ways to do this is by perfecting techniques for the prevention and treatment of disease (including illnesses previously thought to be unavoidable signs of aging) and by changing the view that old age is a sure predictor of declining function.

Women and Research

The major problem with most clinical studies on aging is that until recently very few of them have involved women. For example, the Baltimore Longitudinal Study of Aging, which began in 1958, did not admit women volunteers until 1978. This omission was due to the traditional tendency to view males as the norm for the species. Processes that occur only in women have generally attracted less interest than male-related processes. In addition, studies focusing on one gender are less expensive, recruitment of subjects is easier, and data analysis is less complex.

Researchers have now begun to recognize that comparisons of women and men can contribute significantly to knowledge about age-related diseases and the aging process in general. For example, premenopausal women are less prone to cardiovascular disease than men. A better understanding of the reasons for this difference and of the changes that occur after menopause could lead to new preventive and therapeutic measures for both women and men. Similarly, studies comparing bone loss in men and women could lead to new ways to maintain our muscles, bones, and tendons over time and to prevent fractures from osteoporosis.

Health statistics indicate that life expectancy at birth is greater for women than for men in most parts of the world, but that the length of time varies significantly depending on the country. For example, both women and men live longer in Sweden than they do in the United States, but the longevity gap between the genders is much smaller in Sweden. Research designed to help us understand the reasons for these differences could help improve the quality of life for all people.

CHANGING HEALTH HABITS

Science is developing information about the aging process which strongly suggests that our health choices—positive or negative—greatly affect how we age. Growing old well—maintaining, even improving, physical and emotional health—is something over which today's women in midlife and beyond have more control than ever before.

There are no magic wands or potions for good health, no fountains of youth, no products that cure all ills, no vitamins that prevent all ailments. A wellness program requires effort, planning, and persistence, but it is an investment that pays back with unbelievably high interest. When we feel good we are more likely to exercise, eat well, and take care of ourselves, all of which in turn are likely to make us feel better. Thus we create a "virtuous cycle."

Habits are like the "backbones" of our lives—the firm structures upon which we can rely. It helps not to have to think about every step we take—to have comfortable routines in our lives. But as we grow older, some habits may no longer serve us well. The morning mad rush routine that helped us get ourselves and a whole family off to school and work may no longer be necessary. We may be happier and calmer with fifteen minutes of quiet meditation before starting our day. Illness may require us to change from a vigorous exercise program to a more gentle one. Or we may be inspired by new information or changes in our lives to pay better attention to ourselves, to pursue renewed health and vitality by dramatically altering our pattern of health habits.

It is not true that as we grow older, we become less flexible, less able to change. Change and renewal are possible at any age.

In my later years, my concept of time has changed, as has my use of it. In my late sixties, I was pleased that I was active and showed no sign of slowing down. I thought that slowing down was something to be avoided; it would show that I was getting old. While I had never aspired to fourteen-thousand-foot mountains, I had hiked up medium-sized peaks. Then in my seventies I went with the Appalachian Mountain Club on a week's camping and hiking trip. That summer, I found I was going up more modest elevations and enjoying them and my companions on the way thoroughly. As I left to come back to civilization, I heard a voice (and it was very distinct) saying, "Today you can stop running and start walking."

So I began to go slower. Because I have considerable vitality, I am far from stopping. In fact, I sometimes still rush but the overall result has been freeing, there's less reason to have to redo or undo mistakes caused by dashing. As I go slower, I am more aware of my companions. I can look at situations with greater calm. I am becoming more interested in the quality of time rather than the quantity of it. [a woman in her seventies]

Learning Kung Fu [a martial art] has really made a dramatic change in my life. During the two months I was away from home learning it, my life-style was markedly different—I ate only fresh fruits, vegetables, and grains—no sugar, dairy products, or meat. I was walking nearly ten miles a day and spending one to two hours a day on Kung Fu. The extra pounds fell away, my body became lithe, and my overall health was the best of my life. Now I can easily recognize problems immediately if I neglect my diet or cut back on my walking. When I stay very physically active and eat right, I always feel happy, ambitious, and have lots of energy. [a fifty-year-old woman]

A "clean slate" approach may be your style of change, and can be very helpful when you're ready.

Gaye Hilsenrath with Julie Durlester

I got in the habit, over a number of years, of "needing" a variety of legal drugs: coffee, six to eight cups a day, to keep my spirits up; alcohol before bedtime to calm me down; a couple of aspirin to make sure I didn't wake up with a headache; then in the morning I really needed that coffee to get going. Eventually, I was exhausted all the time and prone to illnesses. My doctor suggested that all these bad habits supported each other, and she was right. I was able to quit after some good introspection about getting my real needs met. I went on a one-week "cleansing fast"* of fruit juices and spring water. I rested, walked, and watched clouds. Two months later, I had dropped all my unhealthful habits and I began to know what my own energy feels like—and I like it! It feels great to depend on myself, not on all those stimulants and depressants. [a forty-two-year-old woman]

A gradual approach may be more successful for many of us. You may want to begin with a single change. Identify the roots of the problem. Ask yourself these questions: When did I first establish the habit? What need did it serve then? Does it now? Can other habits provide more satisfaction? Become aware of your *real* needs—for example, when you reach for a cigarette or coffee, you may be looking for a relaxing break or sociability. Fulfill them directly and in healthier ways.

Make changes in small, manageable steps. Many habits interact, so changing one may help you change others that are harder to break. For example, if you are trying to quit smoking, drink milk, fruit or vegetable juice, or herbal tea instead of coffee to break the coffee-and-cigarette association.

No matter which approach to change you choose, take on a habit when you feel strong and have no other major issues pressing on you. But watch out for procrastination. When you feel overwhelmed, call a friend, change environments if possible, or change your activity. Get support from others to help you change. Form a partnership with a friend to support each other's new habits.

I spent a vacation at a lake with my college roommate swimming, canoeing, and eating the macrobiotic style

*Some holistic health practitioners believe that fasting—going without food and taking only water and juices for a very brief time—is helpful in making the transition to a natural diet. See for example, Dori Smith, "Guidelines for a Cleansing Fast" in Shepard Bliss, ed., *The New Holistic Health Handbook*. Lexington, Mass: The Stephen Greene Press, 1985, pp. 144–5. Get guidance from a health practitioner, especially if you are older or have physical problems.

of food combinations and preparation which she has studied. I knew I didn't want to change my meals so drastically but enjoyed sampling her cooking. I also realized I felt better with more activity. A year later I am still following the changes I made. I am walking more, eating more whole grains and less fat in my meals than before the visit. [a fifty-four-year-old woman]

If your budget allows, find a supportive retreat or spa, and change attitudes, diet, and exercise all at once. These are more common in Europe, where they are less expensive. The best ones take into consideration all aspects of health—physical, emotional, and spiritual—to help you experience a deep change.

Certain devices may help you, such as a "wellness contract" with yourself or a friend that spells out what you want to achieve, and how you plan to achieve it. Keeping a record such as a journal or a progress report may help. Note obstacles and triumphs, but don't blame yourself for backsliding. Instead, reward yourself for each accomplishment.

As we become older, it is vital not only to break harmful habits but to develop new activities and establish new habits of living.

Mental-health researchers recommend that elders "flex their mental as well as physical muscles for better health" and offer suggestions such as working crossword puzzles or playing word games for inductive reasoning, or doing woodworking, assembling objects, reading maps, or doing needlework for spatial orientation. Most important is to do something you really like and are interested in.[11]

At sixty, I used to say to myself, "Whatever you were supposed to do in this world you've already done. There's nothing more." But at sixty-eight I discovered drawing and a whole new world opened up. [a seventy-five-year-old woman]

Flexibility ranks high with me as an important quality to cultivate throughout the life span. I feel that there are three characteristics important to flexible personality: the first is capacity for learning and interest in pursuing it; the second is imagination; the third is a realistic working philosophy of life. Since I have turned eighty I have had to slow down physically so I have developed new interests and taken more time for old ones. I write more poetry. I reread more books and seek out new ones. I have seen a therapist for the first time in my life to help me through some temporary difficulties. I tried massage and liked it. I plan to keep on growing. [an eighty-two-year-old woman]

Enjoying Life with Less Energy

by Paula Brown Doress, Lois Harris, Jane Hyman, and Dori Smith. Special thanks to Lucy Mitchell, Beth Rosenbaum, and Elsie Reethof.

Finding ourselves with physical limitations can bring frustration, sadness, and a strong sense of loss. We miss the things we are no longer able to do.

If you have anything wrong with you it makes all the difference in the world. Six years ago I was trying out lots of new things and the world was more or less my oyster. I had fun with music, I had fun with painting, and I was having fun with poetry. Anything seemed possible to me. Then I got rheumatoid arthritis, and I got it badly. I had three major operations in five months, and two new shoulders and one new knee. And at age seventy-three, three major operations take a lot of getting over. I still have the disease and feel lousy a great deal of the time. I don't quite feel that the world is my oyster anymore. [a seventy-nine-year-old woman]

We resent health problems when they are painful, make us feel weak and tired, and restrict our movements and our lives. We get angry with our bodies because we want to do everything the way we used to and we can't.

When joints ache, I calculate each step. I don't automatically get up to get a drink of water, or to put something away...I wait and take these steps in conjunction with some other necessary steps. I don't do things on the spur of the moment anymore....Will our eyesight grow worse? Will we become increasingly hard of hearing? Will the arthritis be harder to control? and so on....It makes no sense to let our thoughts wander in this direction, but inevitably they do. [a woman in her late eighties][1]

Usually, the first change we make is to reorganize our environment as much as possible to accommodate our conditions. Basically, this means keeping all regularly used objects in the same place and within easy reach, and finding new ways to accomplish daily chores.

I always put my glasses and keys on a very attractive plate that I keep in the center of my apartment so I'm not always hunting for them. This is a way I conserve my energy. [an eighty-two-year-old woman]

Learn about ways you can adapt your environment to make the most of your abilities and reduce the impact of physical changes (see Housing chapter, p. 145). The disability rights movement is redefining the term "disability" as an improper fit between a person and an environment rather than a fault of the person.[2] In other words, if you can no longer get out of a chair by yourself, you get a chair that helps you get up. Social-service agencies and medical-supply companies have catalogs with helpful gadgets and appliances.

Support from others becomes a necessity. We may need the help of friends and family as everyday activities we took for granted —fixing a meal, doing the laundry, shopping—become difficult. We also need moral support. We want others to believe in us, that we can do it, that we can fight weaknesses. We need to believe it too.

The mind is terribly important. If I really believed I was ninety, I would think I couldn't do anything. But I'm still interested in many things and can make people happy. [a woman who maintains a high level of involvement living in a continuing care community]

For most women, energy eventually becomes an issue, whether they have health problems or not. If, through most of our sixties and seventies, we have been "the marvelous old woman" whose vitality everyone admired, we may feel we are letting people down as well as letting go of a valued image of ourselves.

I have reached a stage in my life that I had not given much thought to. Somehow I had thought that I would continue as active as I had been in the past. This is not so. I am now eighty-one and I think something is happening to me that may happen at an earlier or a later age for many women. It's a new stage—one that can be looked upon as negative, or it can be looked at simply as a continuation of the life span. [a woman in her eighties]

The first step in self-help is what many women with illnesses and disabilities had to learn earlier in life—to stop blaming themselves for limited energy and to plan realistically for it. If you have been very active on a professional or volunteer basis it

(continued)

may be necessary to reassess your activities and cut out those that tax your strength too much or are no longer personally rewarding.

After I retired, I was often asked to serve on committees. After a while, I learned to refuse to be a token old person on a committee and accepted only those appointments which seemed to value what I uniquely had to offer. I do not feel that I can continue attending as many meetings as I have in the past. There are other aspects in my life now to which I need to give more time and attention. [an eighty-two-year-old woman]

Look at your assumptions about what you *have* to do, and see how much isn't essential. You will feel better if you can pare down obligations while keeping up the pleasurable part of your commitments.

Everything I do takes so much longer—just getting dressed—I have to choose how to spend my time. I choose not to cook anymore because my back won't take it; all our family celebrations are now in my children's homes. My grandchildren have to accept that when they visit me they won't get chicken soup and potato pancakes anymore. [a seventy-nine-year-old woman]

When I think about packing and moving I feel overwhelmed. I can't do at seventy-eight what I could do at seventy-two. For the first time I am considering letting my son help me or paying the movers to do the packing.

Think of energy-conserving ways in which you can handle your needs.

The grocery store is about fifteen or twenty minutes away. I wouldn't think of going out to shop without my cart. I am experimenting with taking along a small folding chair and a book, so I'll sit down and rest when I get tired and also have a chance to read something. [an eighty-one-year-old woman]

Regular physical activity and exercise help improve energy and increase stamina and endurance, but don't assume that you have to continue your leisure activities at the same pace, or give them up entirely. Try walking, gardening, swimming, and exercising at a slower pace, or for shorter periods of time. Women often find they enjoy these activities more when they ignore any feelings of haste or need for achievement.

Thinking, meditating, watching, and listening are as worthwhile as more strenuous activities. In our younger years, we were often too busy and rushed for reflection. Now that we cannot rush, we can turn to these quieter pursuits if we wish.

I wonder if sometimes we who are concerned about stereotypes don't fall into the trap of using one ourselves, and that is talking about "getting out of the rocking chair" and looking askance at a person sitting in one. I don't know what we can do about the impression that when you sit in a rocking chair, you are really not "doing" anything. I want to save time for meditation, reflection, and just some plain ordinary thinking. In protecting our free time, we will be free to use it, not to think we have to be physically active. I hope that we can reinstitute a rocking chair as a valuable complement to our other activities. [an eighty-one-year-old woman]

Life Review

Reflecting on the past is a natural process that helps us gain perspective on our lives and count our contributions and our blessings. We can also look at our mistakes and disappointments, but it is vital to do this in a positive framework, letting go of guilt or sense of loss. We can arrive at a conviction of the utter rightness of our lives.[3]

I've had a wonderful life. Tell me, what could I have changed? There's nothing I could have made any different. Everything was the way it had to be. [a ninety-eight-year-old woman]

This is the time of life to write about your life's journeys, share experiences with others, and do the work of integrating past, present, and future. Your children or other loved ones will appreciate the legacy of your autobiography. Writing it—or tape-recording it—can motivate you to reflect on your life, and on the events you've witnessed or taken part in. Be sure to include rich detail to bring the picture to life—what you wore, what the furniture looked like, the sounds and smells. This can be a way of maintaining links between generations, so much needed in our life today.

One custom worth adapting for the twentieth century is the "ethical will." In medieval times, parents wrote extensive letters to their children and grandchildren advising them on the morals and values which had given meaning to their own lives.[4] You may wish to look back on your life, and write about the most important thing about you that you'd like your friends and family to remember after you're gone. What about you has made a difference in the world?[5] What are you most satisfied and proud of?

You can also relive the high points of your life. Think back to a peak experience —a time when you were in love, or viewing a beautiful sunset, or had a creative insight. Relive that experience. Then ask yourself, what are the essential qualities of that experience? How can you give that to yourself in your life *now*?[6]

There are many ways to reflect on your experiences. One is called the "Stepping-stones" process.[7] In it, you review your life and identify specific events that stand out as signposts. Reflect and write about each one, using these words: "It was a time when..." If you read what you've written out loud in a group of friends or write letters to family members, you may find added significance. Courses in autobiography or life review are sometimes offered in senior centers or adult education programs. If you can't find one, get together with your friends and create your own.

Craftswoman

See, she threads with bleeding feelings
The jagged shards of her shattered past.

From that which was tragedy
Or at best, a grim joke

Will she, can she weave
A design of grace?

Gittel Simon[8]

1. Janet Neuman, "Old Age: It's Not Funny." *Perspective on Aging*, November/December 1982, published by the National Council on Aging.

2. Irving Kenneth Zola, "Toward a Unifying Agenda: Some Major Issues Cross-cutting Policies and Programs Concerning Aging and Disability." Paper presented at the Sixth Pew Health Policy Fellows Conference, to be published in a forthcoming volume of the American Enterprise Institute for Public Policy Research, 1150 Seventeenth St., N. W., Washington, DC 20036.

3. Based on Erik Erikson's theory of adult development, in Erik H. Erikson, "Eight Ages of Man." *Childhood in Society*, New York: W. W. Norton & Co., 1963, pp. 268–69.

4. "Ethical Wills: Twelfth and Fourteenth Centuries", pp. 311–16 in Jacob R. Marcus, ed., *The Jew in the Medieval World*, New York: Atheneum, 1974.

5. Adapted from Janette Rainwater, *You're in Charge: A Guide To Becoming Your Own Therapist*. Marina del Rey, CA: DeVorss and Co., 1985, p. 203.

6. Ibid., p. 44.

7. Ira Progoff, *At a Journal Workshop*. New York: Dialogue House Library, 1975, pp. 119–130.

8. In *Late Harvest: Poems from Lifetime Learning of Newton*. The Coalition for Newton Community Education, Inc., of Newton Community Schools, 492 Waltham St., West Newton, MA 02165, 1982.

DISARMING STRESS

Old Age Must Be Like This

Alone and sick at three in the morning
She relives each mistake
wonders if there's enough money in the bank
But it's her life that's overdue
She's made too many plans
Who did she think she was
in those hectic days of health—
magic legs moving from sink to stove
from barn to the woodpile
—and the telephone lifting itself so easily
off the hook
the throat making all those intricate movements
in order to speak
Now simple tasks
laundry
dinner
fetching the mail—
can't be done
Dishes pile up in the sink
wood stays in the barn
She turns the electric blanket higher
wonders who will feed her birds—

Marilyn Zuckerman

Cathy Cade

How we manage the stress in our lives is an important component of whatever disease-prevention and health-promotion regimen we undertake. In a dangerous situation, our bodies go "on alert," ready to take immediate action—to fight the threat, or to run away. This is called the "stress response" and is normal and evolutionarily significant in humans as in other animals. However, in modern society the threats we experience are not often direct physical dangers, but are more generalized and ongoing, such as the pressures of a job, or the lack of one, sex and age discrimination, losses of relationships, and global dangers such as the threat of nuclear war. Sometimes, stress occurs when we feel emotionally threatened—such as when we perceive a neutral event or situation as threatening, or exaggerate a danger in our minds. There is a profound connection between thinking, feeling, behavior, and what happens inside our bodies.

Stress can become a problem when it is continuous or ongoing, because the body does not return to its normal, non-aroused state. Chronic triggering of the fight-or-flight response has been shown to lead to many health problems, including hypertension,[12] elevated sugar levels, an overworked endocrine system, and possibly brain-cell loss.[13] By adopting new habits to reduce stress and reverse its harmful effects, we can prevent the damage that can result from continual or chronic exposure.

Signs of Stress

How can you tell that you are under stress? Our bodies usually send us warning signals, but we may ignore them or cover them up with pills or minimize their importance. Sometimes we are not even aware that we are under stress.

The first time I realized that feelings affect my health was during a routine physical exam. I was worrying, just a little, about a decision I'd made. But my blood pressure was up—so much higher than usual that I knew I was anxious, terribly so, more than I wanted to believe. [a fifty-six-year-old woman]

Signs of stress that we all experience include muscle tightening, clenching, shallow breathing, headaches, and digestive disturbances. We may feel driven to compulsive behavior such as excessive eating, drinking, smoking, or talking. We may turn to alcohol, drugs, caffeine, or tranquilizers. Depression, difficulty in sleeping, sleeping too much, lack of concentration, or irritability—even getting a fair number of irritable responses from other people—are all signs that we are not handling stress effectively.

Special Stresses of Middle-aged and Older Women

As middle-aged and older women, we face special stresses caused by sexism and ageism. We women face sexism throughout our lives. But we face ageism earlier than men do, sometimes even before forty, because of the double standard of aging. This compounding of ageism and sexism brings with it added stresses. Each experience of prejudice—each rebuff, dismissal, act of condescension—is new and painful. Poverty and inadequate funds deepen all other stresses and contribute to a feeling of despair. Each chips away at our self-esteem. Growing older in a society that has few respected roles for elders can bring a multiplicity of stressful experiences.

Caregiving is a role that frequently falls to women in the midlife and older years and can be extremely exhausting, isolating, and stressful. Bereavement, one of life's most painful experiences, occurs most often in the second half of life. Sometimes we face a series of losses in quick succession.

It seems like everything happened at once. I had to put my mother in a nursing home, where she suddenly died. I didn't have time to grieve, because I had to work for weeks to settle her affairs. About then, my seventeen-year-old daughter was preparing to leave home. I now had the freedom to move where I wanted to but I had a hard time leaving my home. What could I let go of? Every little thing had meaning for me. I had to go slow in packing—I kept injuring myself and my skin kept breaking out. I'm still grieving, months later. Healing from my mother's death will take a long time. [a forty-nine-year-old woman]

Life Events Rated for Stressfulness[14]	Stress Rating*
Death of a spouse	100
Divorce	73
Death of a close family member	63
Personal injury or illness	53
Marriage	50
Retirement	45
Change in financial status	38
Death of a close friend	37
Children leaving home	29
Beginning or finishing school	26
Christmas	12

*Participants were asked to rate each life event on a scale of 0 to 100, where marriage was rated 50.

In the above scale, adapted from the research of psychologists T. H. Holmes and R. H. Rahe, a series of life events were rated by 394 persons according to the amount of "social readjustment" they required. Among the life events ranked most stressful are those that are frequently faced by middle-aged and older women, sometimes in close succession.

As older women, our lifelong socialization as nurturers can contribute to our feeling stressed. When we allow ourselves to be too generous to others with our time and energy, we risk overextending ourselves with too many commitments, some of which are neither vital nor beneficial. Thus we may damage our own well-being.

We are taught from early childhood to control our aggressiveness and suppress our anger. In fact, most of us don't even admit having aggressive feelings. Behind the mask of "being nice" often lurk anger, lack of self-esteem, and a frustrated sense of entitlement. When we repeatedly suppress our negative feelings out of fear or concern for others, we turn our accumulated anger and frustration against ourselves, and the chronic stress can damage our health.

I tried meditation, but my suppressed rage was so intense that nothing seemed to alleviate my health problems. When I was forty-seven, I finally woke up to the fact that I had been a doormat. I read that Tae Kwon Do [a Korean martial art] was good for assertiveness training for submissive women. To my surprise, yelling, hitting, and kicking at an imaginary opponent for an hour did wonders for my mind and body. My stress-related health problems began to disappear one by one. Today, at age fifty-nine, I have no pills in my medicine cabinet.

Learning to use our anger in appropriate and constructive ways helps us preserve ourselves, prevent stress, and make needed changes. Organizing to change society's laws and attitudes as well as making use of organizational resources can help us counteract the stress that comes from feeling powerless and anxious.

Most of the time we react automatically to stressors with feelings, words, thoughts, behaviors, and attitudes that we learned a long time ago—things which worsen the stress. An important part of coping with stress is learning to become less automatic in our responses. "Rule No. 1 is, don't sweat the small stuff. Rule No. 2 is, it's all small stuff. And if you can't fight and you can't flee, flow."[15] Some people find that sharp-

Norma Holt

ening their conscious awareness of stress and how it affects them helps them interrupt harmful patterns and adopt more constructive ways of coping. You can learn about your patterns through keeping a journal, talking with your friends, or seeing a psychotherapist. You can achieve a sense of *real* control by understanding what makes you tense, knowing what you can and cannot do to change or avoid those things, and knowing you can discharge the tension in various short-term and long-term ways.

• Paying attention to yourself, your desires, aspirations, and needs is a first step toward identifying who or what might be causing stress.
• Elicit the help of the people around you. Develop, cherish, and nurture friendships. Take care to maintain multiple friendships and roles. These can be a buffer when one relationship or role is in conflict. In times of stress, friendships are especially important.
• When the cause of our stress is too big and powerful to tackle alone, you can join together with friends, co-workers, neighbors, and others to work for change in movements and organizations.
• Laughter actually has stress-reducing effects on the body. Read funny stories and watch comedies on TV.[16]
• Catch yourself when you notice you are dwelling on negative thoughts without working toward problem-solving. Concentrate on your strengths and accomplishments.

• In many situations, you can clearly express your dissatisfaction and work out a mutually satisfactory solution. For example, people respond better to "I" statements than to "you" statements. Don't say, "*You* are giving me a headache with that darn radio." Instead, say, "*I* can't think when the radio is so loud."[17] The idea is to clearly express your own discomfort and to avoid blaming anyone for it. Thus you enlist cooperation in solving a problem. Blaming passes your stress on to others—and it may bounce back.
• Scientists have proved what pet lovers already know—pets can be very beneficial to human health. Pets give and receive affection and touch.
• Eating well, especially foods that are high in vitamin B complex and vitamin C, can help you manage stress better. Avoid beverages containing caffeine (coffee, chocolate, tea, and carbonated soft drinks) because too much caffeine can cause nervousness, irritability, and problems with digestion and sleep.
• Getting enough sleep is very important. Many people report needing less sleep as they age, so if this is true for you, allow time for rest and quiet instead. Don't try to solve problems at night or when you are tired.
• Have fun. Develop hobbies that you enjoy. Gardening, photography, amateur theater, and pottery all provide many hours of pleasure. Take advantage of adult-education programs, in which you can learn and meet people at the same time.

I draw and paint. It gives me a sense of accomplishment. When you are all alone and living on a fixed income like I am, you have to find things to keep you occupied without spending a lot of money. I go to public auctions, local fairs, museums, or I window shop. I also like to keep my mind stimulated and work crossword puzzles and read novels, mysteries, and history. I watch basketball games on TV. I do sitting-in-the-chair exercises while watching TV. [a sixty-three-year-old woman]

• Exercise helps reduce the effects of stress by bringing blood to the muscles and brain, and by stimulating production of chemicals called endorphins and enkephalins that give you a sense of well-being. Any expressive body movement can help make creative use of the pain of anger, fear, grief, or depression. Try dancing to a favorite record and using rhythm and strong movement to say what you feel. Any prolonged regular movement will loosen you up, such as a fast walk, a long swim, jumping rope, or simply stretching hard while doing rhythmic breathing.

The Relaxation Response

The Relaxation Response[18] is a simple meditation technique that synthesizes Eastern teachings with Western knowledge. The basic components are:

- A quiet environment and uninterrupted time
- A sound, word, or short phrase of your own choosing repeated silently. The word "one" is suggested—or a word from a prayer or meditation that is consistent with your culture or belief system.[19]
- A receptive attitude (the most important element). Clear your mind and visualize nothing. Keep your palms up as if you were open to whatever would happen.

Follow these simple steps:

1. Sit or kneel quietly in a comfortable position.

2. Close your eyes.

3. Deeply relax all your muscles, beginning with your feet and progressing up to your face. Keep them relaxed.

4. Breathe through the nose. Become aware of your breathing. As you breathe out, silently say the word or phrase you have selected. Breathe slowly and naturally.

5. Continue for ten to twenty minutes. When you finish, sit quietly for several minutes with your eyes closed and then for a few more with them open. (It is better to open your eyes when you feel the need to check the time than to use an alarm.)

6. Do not worry about whether you are successful in achieving a deep level of relaxation. *Permit relaxation to occur at its own pace.* If distracting thoughts occur, acknowledge them and let them go. Return to repeating your word or phrase.

Practice the technique once or twice daily, but not within two hours after any meal.[20] Once you are comfortable with it, you can utilize the technique in a waiting room, in an empty classroom, or almost any place you wish. You will feel quiet inside, mentally clear, alert, and in charge.

A second relaxation method is Progressive Relaxation[21]:

1. Lie comfortably on your back in a quiet place. Allow yourself to relax.

2. Begin by taking a few deep breaths and then relaxing into your natural breathing rhythm.

3. Tense and release groups of muscles, one group at a time, beginning with your toes. Tense the muscles; hold for a count of five and then release. Do this same thing to each group of muscles until you reach the top of your head.

4. Notice what the tension feels like as you contract each muscle group. Focus on the experience of *letting go* of this tension as you progressively relax parts of your body. You might imagine the *letting go* as a warm sun that's melting your icy body, or as water flowing around whatever part of your body you're relaxing. Allow the tension to float out of your muscles as you let them go as limp as you can. You are gradually relaxing yourself into a state that is almost bodiless until you feel that you are floating in space.

Music and Imagery

Music and imagery can help you reach either a relaxed or an energized state, and can even help heal stress-related illnesses.[22] Try various kinds of music to see what states of awareness or mental pictures they encourage.

I put on Beethoven's Pastorale Symphony, lie down, and imagine myself in my favorite spot—a high mountain meadow. I notice the freshness of the air, the light on the peaks. Sometimes I invite an imaginary friend. As the music progresses, I move through its moods. Birds sing as I frolic in a cool pond, then warm myself in the sun. I run through wildflowers, enjoy a glorious thunderstorm, then rest as a rainbow arches across the sky. When the music is over, I feel as refreshed as if I'd spent a week in the Rockies. [a forty-three-year-old woman]

I put on Dixieland jazz or Chopin for energy to start the day. There's a reggae [Jamaican] music program on the radio at 5:30 P.M. that freshens me when I'm tired. [a fifty-four-year-old woman]

Self-Hypnosis or Self-Talk

After you master deep breathing and relaxation, you can learn to achieve a meditative state using self-hypnosis, sometimes called autogenesis. With self-hypnosis you can suggest relaxation (or other desired states such as alertness or joy) to your unconscious mind, which then causes your body to respond appropriately. You can practice it in any environment—at your desk, waiting in line, or trying to fall asleep at night. To practice, sit or lie down. Loosen clothing (ties, belts); become comfortable. Allow gentle concentration. Let your day's experiences pass through and out of you. Concentrate on a sensation and suggest it to yourself. Repeat it three times and take it to each part of your body as you say it; for example, if you say, "I am at peace," imagine an area of tension and fill it with peace; peace may be a color, sensation, image, or something that conveys deep peace to you.

To relieve a migraine, try decreasing blood flow in the head by saying to yourself, "Blood is flowing away from my head and down through my body." Concentrate on making that happen. Imagine a cool breeze going through your head; imagine the vessels dilating, expanding, and letting the blood flow rapidly.

I could not sleep because of all the noise outside. I decided that there was nothing I could do except not make it worse. If I couldn't sleep, I would rest. I just told myself things that would relax me. "I am healing. I will be better tomorrow. This rest is worth more than sleep." I relaxed each part of my body, thinking, "I am sinking into a profound state of rest that is even deeper than sleep." I told myself that if the noise stopped I might doze off for only a few minutes before being awakened again but in those few moments I would have several hours of rest and would feel refreshed. The next day I felt fine and gave one of the best classes I have ever given. [a fifty-five-year-old woman]

Prayer and Meditation

As we grow older, many of us find the spiritual aspects of our lives becoming more important. As our consciousness of our own mortality increases, we ask ourselves the meaning of our lives and of our places in the world. This can be especially true for women with physical limitations. As energy wanes and our movements are restricted, the pleasures of the mind and the spirit grow stronger. Some women continue an earlier bent for religion, philosophy, science, or literature, finding that their lives' experiences make study richer and more meaningful than ever before; some develop new interests.

Meditation and prayer can help you find spiritual strength and achieve a state of physical and emotional calm. Whether you choose meditation or prayer or a combination of the two will depend on your beliefs.

Some women find that, as they grow older, their religious beliefs and practices change. Some leave established religious groups, others renew their faith or find a new spiritual community. A growing literature on spirituality and its relation to well-being, healing[23], and feminism[24] is available in libraries and bookstores.

SHARING TOUCH—MASSAGE

As we get older, some of us fear that if we are not in a sexual relationship we may never be touched or held. We touch to express nonsexual tenderness and affection, to acknowledge each other's presence nonverbally, to comfort, to support, and to soothe. The misconception that touching always involves sex and is only appropriate in a sexual context causes real deprivation. People need to touch and be touched throughout their lives.

Some of us worry about touching or hugging others, especially other women, and so deny ourselves pleasure, comfort, and closeness. Some of us come from families where touching is limited to ritual holiday kisses. Intergenerational or homophobic taboos may make it hard to exchange hugs with friends or family members. But if we are able to free ourselves of these constrictions, we open ourselves to a whole array of rich experience.

Those of us who are disabled or very ill continue to need touching. Family members, friends, and staff members must recognize that patients in hospitals and residents in nursing homes need friendly touching every day. The wish for emotional intimacy and physical touching of another caring person is inseparable from other needs. Providing massage, allowing and encouraging patients to touch one another, and affectionate hugs and nonsexual touching on the part of staff members should all be part of the life of nursing-home residents. Staff members must be sensitive to individual and cultural differences in residents' acceptance of touch.

Since we never outgrow the need for warm physical touch, we may experience "skin hunger"[25] if we rarely touch or are touched. One way to meet this need is through giving and receiving massage.

Massage has had a bad reputation in the

United States because of the tendency to equate pleasurable touching with genital sexual arousal and the association of massage parlors with prostitution. Yet most massage is not sexual. Massage has a respected history in both the East and West as a form of physical therapy. Massage

Marianne Gontarz

offers many physical benefits, such as lowering blood pressure and stimulating circulation. In addition to its physical benefits, massage is one of the most pleasurable ways to relax. It is energizing yet relaxing to both the giver and the receiver.

Connecting with each other through caring touch is deeply affirming and fun. We can form "touch partnerships" with one or more friends and exchange massages regularly.

I enjoy sensuality. I gathered a group of women with whom I could do massage. Our group members would call each other up and exchange massages—twenty minutes each. We took lessons and learned techniques. We became fast friends. [a sixty-five-year-old woman]

Giving and receiving warmth and caring is healthy and imparts a sense of being connected with your own body. The message given by caring massage is, "I care about you just as you are."

Massage makes me feel re-created; it's so pleasant. When I look in the mirror, I'm lean and gaunt-looking, but I don't feel like that when I'm being massaged. [a seventy-seven-year-old woman]

It is also possible to use similar techniques to massage yourself, communicating your caring for your own body.

Keep conversation to a minimum during the massage. Silence deepens the experience, allowing both giver and receiver to pay more attention to what's happening. It is important for the person receiving massage to give feedback on what feels good and what doesn't. Often the clearest feedback comes without words in a sigh of relaxation or in a slight contraction against pressure that's too hard or too sudden.

Before starting a massage, be sure to ask about injured areas to be avoided. Do not massage a blood clot, or areas that are swollen, inflamed, or tender.

If you or the person you are massaging feels shy, start with foot and hand rubs, or head, neck, and face. A rapping motion with sides of hand, cupped palms, or loosely closed fists feels great on the arms, legs, back, and shoulders— try it on yourself first, then with each other. Finger-tapping feels good on the head and face. Kneading, squeezing, and rolling or rocking can be done over loose clothing. In order to glide smoothly over skin, use a lubricant such as light vegetable oil with or without perfume, or a bar of cocoa butter. Do not use mineral oil or products that contain it, such as baby oil. Hand lotions and creams are too quickly absorbed and do not provide enough lubrication, but cream may work well for facial massage.

The person receiving the massage will be most relaxed if she lies on a firm, comfortable surface, but you can also work on her as she sits. The person giving the massage should always work in a comfortable position. Deepen your own breathing as you remind the person you are massaging to deepen hers. When finishing a particular area, use long, light brushing strokes with fingertips. To finish the massage session, place your hands gently on the head or feet for a long moment, visualizing the person as healed

17

and perfect. See Resources for books that illustrate various massage techniques.

Technique is less important than transmitting a sense of caring through your hands. Remember that you are touching a person, not just skin. As you touch, allow yourself to be fully attentive and aware of the uniqueness of the person you are massaging. The experience of giving massage is as heartwarming as receiving it.

I learned to be a massage therapist at the age of fifty-six, as a second career. Conditioned as a "proper Bostonian" to be extremely cautious and doubtful of my own sensuality and sexuality, it took me a long time to feel comfortable with saying that I like to touch people.

This touching is inward as well as outward. Massage deepens my connections with people. It offers a way to drop my judgments and expectations so I am able to accept and affirm someone exactly as she or he is. And in creating that acceptance and affirmation of the other person, I am creating the same for myself. [a fifty-nine-year-old woman]

Many adult-education centers offer classes in massage. There you can find people interested in massage and find out about the different techniques. There are several: Swedish massage, Heller work, Soma, Rolfing, myotherapy, and Trigger Point therapy deeply penetrate muscles and joints. Polarity therapy, Acupressure, Shiatsu, Trager, reflexology, Jin Shin Jitsu, Therapeutic Touch, and Reiki concentrate on energy balancing. Aston-patterning and Rolf movement combine massage and movement reeducation. There are also techniques specifically tailored for athletes, infants, and pregnant women. A woman experiencing Therapeutic Touch for the first time described it this way:

I had driven over 2,000 miles in under three days, and my head was tight and buzzing. The therapist had me sit in a chair, fully clothed, telling me to close my eyes and deepen my breathing. She kept her hands for several minutes, motionless, on different parts of my body; sometimes she'd make long sweeps downwards, either not touching me, or only very lightly. "How can this help?" I thought. But 45 minutes later, all the tightness had gone out of my head. I felt calm and I was ready to deal with the world again. [a fifty-two-year-old woman]

I always enjoy massage, whether from friends or from massage therapists. I tend to hold all my tensions in my back and so suffer from stiffness and pain. Exercise and relaxation techniques, including massage, help. When I visited my daughter, who is a massage therapist, she gave me a Trigger Point [deep muscle work] treatment

that kept me pain-free for several months. I found someone where I live who is helping me on a regular basis so the pain won't start again. [a fifty-four-year-old woman]

You may, as you are being massaged, feel an opening awareness of emotion, as massage is more than just physical manipulation. It is your decision whether the person giving the massage is the person with whom to discuss the feelings that come up during a massage. Alternatively, you may want to think through these issues yourself, write in a journal, talk with a friend, or discuss them with a psychotherapist.

Jerry Howard/Positive Images

GETTING IN TOUCH WITH OTHERS— FRIENDS AND SUPPORT GROUPS

We have the power to enrich our lives and those of others through our personal relationships. Research has shown that those who maintain strong bonds with family, friends, or neighbors actually have lower death and illness rates. When we feel isolated, it takes courage and initiative on our part to reach out to make new friends. A ten-year study of seven thousand people across the nation found that the mortality rate among people with poor social bonds was 2.5 times higher than among people with a good support system of friends and relatives.[26]

One thing that American society lacks, from my point of view, is that people don't have groups of friends. You have one individual friend. And if something happens to him or her, you have no one to talk to. And you wind up at the psychiatrist....I have friends who let me talk

Norma Holt

things out. Through the talking, I realize what I must do. [a Chinese-American woman, age eighty][27]

When we were younger, neighborhood women often gathered to talk over coffee, discussing child rearing, sharing homemaking tips, and enjoying the pleasure of conversation. At work, coworkers band together to help each other survive the pressures of the job. Now that we are older, these natural groups may have fallen away. And as society becomes more mobile and fragmented, with family members often far away, there's a vital social gap to be filled. Friends become our family of choice on whom we depend.[28]

Though many groups meet for specific purposes, simple friendship can be a sufficient reason for gathering. One group of women of all ages, fearing a future alone, call themselves "Just Friends." They meet not only for the enjoyment of being in a group of women of all ages, but also to help each other. Another group who talk together while working on handcrafts call themselves "The Stitch and Bitch Club."

The Stream

bubbles
below the falls
rush complete small circles
most float on like raindrops each one
alone

many
dash from side to
side striking out hectic
until they disappear from sight
dissolved

there are
a few that move
toward some others
they touch they blend then they go on
growing

Lois Harris

19

Self-Help Groups

Specific shared issues can be a good catalyst for bringing people together. You, perhaps with a friend, may wish to form a self-help group of women who share a common problem, such as a troubled relationship with an adult child, arthritis, allergies, or urinary incontinence. You can also join a short-term group such as Widow-to-Widow, or a hospice group that supports you after the death of a loved one.

Self-help groups often have practical results. A good example is the effect an older women's group had in helping older people stay in their homes. The group organized a pool of younger volunteer and paid workers who helped with housekeeping, repairs, transportation, companionship, and a variety of other personal services.[29]

Self-help groups are different from old-style authoritarian groups, and it takes some adjusting and patience to get one working well. Here are some pointers:

A self-help group sets its own goals. Begin by discussing, in democratic fashion, what the group members' needs are. It is assumed that each member is an expert on her own problems, needs, and goals. Avoid letting one member take over; encourage those members with professional expertise to participate as equals, without reference to credentials.

Leaderless self-help groups insure that each woman's needs, goals, and experiences are equally respected. The results are well worth the time and trouble. Another approach is to rotate leadership among group members, or to appoint one member as a facilitator to keep the group focused. Whoever leads the group has the same needs as the other members and must be given time to air her concerns while another member fills in as leader. In such groups, we learn new skills of openness and flexibility, and

Elana Freedom

develop our natural leadership and communication abilities.

I was a member of a support group that had started off with a leader. When we became independent, I sometimes felt frustrated, so I thought, "What would Ann [the former leader] say if she were here?" and then I would try it. Now we all share the responsibility of keeping the group moving. [a woman in her fifties]

In my women's group we divide up the tasks of leadership and take turns doing them. At each meeting one woman is "watch witch," keeping track of the time allowed for each person to speak. Another woman is responsible for keeping the discussion on track, so that as each woman speaks she is free to concentrate solely on what she is saying. [a forty-seven-year-old woman]

NOTES

1. Asenath LaRue, et al., "Health in Old Age: How Do Physicians' Ratings and Self-ratings Compare?" *Journal of Gerontology*, Vol. 34, No. 5, 1979, pp. 687–91.

2. Marc E. Weksler, "Genetic and Immunologic Determinants of Aging." In *Proceedings of the Second Conference on the Epidemiology of Aging*. Bethesda, Maryland: U.S. Department of Health and Human Services, National Institutes of Health, 1980, pp. 15–22.

3. Robert N. Butler, "Health Productivity and Aging: An Overview." In Robert N. Butler and Herbert P. Gleason, eds., *Productive Aging: Enhancing Vitality in Later Life*. New York: Springer, 1985, p. 8.

4. Ibid., p. 12.

5. Mary Anne Kurz, "Theories of Aging and Popular Claims of Extending Life." *News and Features from NIH*, Vol. 85, No. 4, 1985, pp. 8–10.

6. Edward L. Schneider and John D. Reed, Jr., "Life Extension." *New England Journal of Medicine*, Vol. 312, No. 18, May 2, 1985, pp. 1159–68.

7. Kurz, op. cit.

8. Schneider and Reed, op. cit., p. 1161.

9. Ibid., p. 1165.

10. Gene Bylinsky, "Science Is on the Trail of the Fountain of Youth." *Fortune*, July 1974, p. 134.

11. K. Warner Schaie and Sherry Willis, "Can Decline in Adult Intellectual Functioning Be Reversed?" *Developmental Psychology*, Vol. 22, No. 2, 1986, pp. 223–32.

12. B. Folkow and E. H. Rubinstein, "Cardiovascular Effects of Acute and Chronic Stimulations of the Hypothalmic Defense Area in the Rat." *Acta Physiologica Scandinavica*, Vol. 68, 1966, pp. 48–57. Quoted in Herbert Benson, *The Relaxation Response*. New York: Avon Books, 1976, p. 70.

13. R. M. Sapolsy, et al., "Hippocampal Neuronal Loss During Aging: Role of Glucocorticoids." Paper given at Conference on Aging and the Dementias, Montefiore Centennial Series, Rockefeller University, New York, October 24, 1984.

14. Excerpted from T. H. Holmes and R. H. Rahe, "The Social Readjustment Rating Scale." *Journal of Psychosomatic Research*, Vol. 11, 1967, p. 213.

15. Robert Eliot, a Nebraska cardiologist, quoted in Claudia Wallis, "Stress: Can We Cope?" *Time* magazine, June 6, 1983, p. 48.

16. Norman Cousins, *Anatomy of an Illness*. New York: W. W. Norton and Co., 1979.

17. Thomas Gordon, *Parent Effectiveness Training*. New York: P. H. Wyden, 1970.

18. Herbert Benson, *The Relaxation Response*. New York: Avon Books, 1976.

19. Herbert Benson, *Beyond the Relaxation Response*. New York: Times Books, 1984. How to harness the power of faith and personal belief in the healing process.

20. Benson, *The Relaxation Response*, p. 163.

21. Steve Kravette, *Complete Relaxation*. Rockport, Massachusetts: Para Research, 1979, pp. 21–37.

22. Carolyn Latteier, "Music as Medicine." *Medical Self Care*, Issue No. 31, November/December 1985, pp. 48–52.

23. Benson, *Beyond the Relaxation Response*, op. cit.

24. *Ms.*, December 1985, special issue on women and spirituality. See also Resources—Feminism, Religion, and Spirituality.

25. Flora Davis, "Skin Hunger—An American Disease." *Woman's Day*, September 27, 1978, p. 156.

26. Lisa Berkman and S. Leonard Syme, cited in Judy Foreman, "Friends: As Vital as Family." *Boston Globe*, February 3, 1982.

27. Grace Chu, in Jane Seskin, ed. *More Than Mere Survival: Conversations with Women Over 65*. New York: Newsweek, 1980, p. 223.

28. Karen Lindsey, *Friends as Family*. Boston: Beacon Press, 1982.

29. Mike Samuels and Nancy Samuels, *Seeing with the Mind's Eye*. New York: Random House, 1975, pp. 56–64.

2

HABITS WORTH CHANGING

by Dori Smith, Diana Laskin Siegal, and Paula Brown Doress

Alcohol by Sandra T. Bierig and Ruth L. Fishel

Dealing with Pain with special thanks to Sylvia Pigors

We live in a substance-abusing society. We are surrounded by billboards, store displays, and ads in all the media touting alcohol, over-the-counter drugs, cigarettes, soft drinks, coffee—all promoting a glamorous and happy life. The message is, "Reach for a [whatever it is] and all your problems will be solved." Physicians are also bombarded by drug-company salespeople and medical-journal ads offering drugs for every symptom. But these substances—tobacco, caffeine, alcohol, and drugs—when turned into habits are so common and damaging that they warrant special attention. They also interact with each other in ways that increase their dangers.

SMOKING

Cigarette smoking is the chief avoidable cause of death in our society, and the most important health issue of our time.[1] Smoking is on the rise for women. Since World War II, women have been smoking in large numbers and now our smoking-related disease patterns are beginning to resemble men's. In fact, our favorable advantage in life span over men (78.3 years to men's 71 years, as of 1983) may change for the worse as a result.[2] Lung cancer is now the number one cancer killer of women, exceeding both breast cancer and colorectal cancer.[3]

The dangers of "passive smoking"—smoke inhaled from other people's cigarettes—are also very high. "Secondhand smoke" contains thousands of chemical compounds, including some deadly ones. It contains fifty times more ammonia, five times more carbon monoxide, and *twice as much tar* as the smoker inhales.[4] Awareness of the rights of nonsmokers has been heightened in recent years by the efforts of activist groups such as ASH (Action on Smoking and Health). Local groups such as GASP (Group Against Smoking Pollution) in Massachusetts and other states support efforts to create no-smoking areas in public places and the workplace and to ban both the sale of cigarettes in hospitals and the distribution of cigarettes to minors.

The risks of smoking increase with age and with the number of years you've smoked. These risks include osteoporosis, glaucoma, a full range of cardiovascular and respiratory diseases, and many more kinds of cancer than the obvious lung cancer. Smoking accounts for about 30 percent of all cancer deaths.[5] There is an increased danger of cardiovascular disease among users of oral contraceptives who smoke, and an increased risk of cancer of the mouth, pharynx, larynx, and esophagus among people who both drink and smoke. Smoking also increases wrinkles.

Nicotine is by no means the only dangerous ingredient in cigarettes. We must also count carbon monoxide (in an amount eight times greater than the amount industry is allowed to release into the air), tars, and even the heat itself. Chemical additives and modern tobacco-curing processes apparently add to cigarette-smoking's deadly results.

The good news is that smoking is avoidable. The highest mortality rates are among current smokers, and quitting *at any age* causes the mortality rate to drop. In the case of coronary heart disease, quitting causes a 50 percent drop in death rate within twelve months, and after a decade or more of not smoking the mortality rate from coronary heart disease approaches that of nonsmokers.[6]

How to Celebrate a Twenty-fifth Smokeless Anniversary

by Beth Rosenbaum

It is now twenty-five years since I smoked my last cigarette. In 1960 I inhaled the last nicotine-laden draft into my then fifty-four-year-old lungs. For thirty-four years a cigarette had been my constant companion, my picker-upper, my relaxer, and my security blanket. "Put me in a padded cell," I told my family, "if you want me to stop smoking."

In the Roaring Twenties the cigarette was the flapper's logo of sophistication. "Cigarette me, big boy," said Joan Crawford, and we all bought carved ivory holders. "Be nonchalant, light a Murad," said the elegant smokers on the billboards.

Now the Government, doctors, and health organizations warn, cajole, raise consciousness, modify behavior, hypnotize, segregate, and abuse smokers—with questionable success.

But in my twenty-fifth Smokeless Anniversary year, I offer my method free to all nicotine addicts. No coupons to clip. No salesperson will call. No obligations.

First: Build up a strong guilt feeling. Guilt can be very productive if used constructively. How can one feel guilty about smoking? Many ways. You don't want to give your children and grandchildren unhealthy habits, do you? More children of smoking parents become smokers than the lucky offspring of nonsmoking parents. No children? Think of all the money you could give to your favorite charity; at today's cigarette prices, several hundred dollars a year. Besides, don't you feel uneasy about all the air you're polluting? Your loved ones are breathing it, not to mention innocent strangers. So, pick the guilt that suits your situation and dwell on it.

Second: Choose a day with a spiritual, mystical, or sentimental association for you. I chose Yom Kippur—the Jewish Day of Atonement—after reading in the service: "This day...I have set before you life and death, blessing and curse; therefore choose life, that you and your descendants may live" (Deuteronomy 30:19). Good advice, I decided, from an authorized source. Or choose your birthday, surely a symbolic day. You came into this world with clean, rosy-pink lungs. Do you really want to go out with dirty black lungs? Don't choose New Year's Eve. Decades of bad jokes about New Year's resolutions have conditioned us to break the ones we make.

Third: Think upbeat. Make a little ceremony around smoking that last cigarette. Tell yourself, out loud: "This is the last time in my life I'll smoke. I am not giving anything up. I'm starting something new." You, yourself, built the habit of smoking. You can build a new habit. After you eat anything, even a snack, use a toothpick vigorously. Keep that toothpick in your mouth or put it in an ashtray. You'll find your own substitute habit. Sweets and coffee won't help. They tend to make you want to eat and smoke...a never-ending cycle. Concentrate on something—like a Double Crostic. Occupy your mind and hands. It works.

Fourth: Enjoy. It's a great ego-booster. Feel superior to all those lily-livered, black-lunged weaklings who think their very lives depend on a tiny, dangerous, expensive paper tube stuffed with straw.

Fifth: Declare a victory. A poet and soldier described the First World War as "damned dirty, damned dull, and damned dangerous." *You* have just won a war, also dirty, dull, and dangerous. Congratulations. You deserve a medal to pin on your healthier chest.

Take heart in knowing that a high percentage of those who try to quit succeed, even if it takes several attempts. The "frontal attack" on the smoking habit—going "cold turkey"—may work. But there's a risk: if you don't succeed, the habit may grow stronger, and you may feel less powerful in relation to it. If you make a slip—take one cigarette—you may feel like a failure and go into a full-scale relapse. The motto of Alcoholics Anonymous, "One day at a time," can be helpful to anyone trying to quit. Many quit on their own, assisted by self-help literature. For others, self-help groups and cessation programs (the cost of which may be covered by insurance if prescribed by a doctor) are essential.

Smokers reach for cigarettes to relieve boredom, to fill time, to do something when feeling tense or anxious. One reaction to tension is to hold your breath or to take little, shallow breaths. If you smoke, inhaling a cigarette may be your only way to take a full, deep breath. Try taking three deep breaths when you crave a cigarette. You may actually crave oxygen.

Smoking a cigarette may be the only socially accepted way of taking a break at your workplace. You may have to fight for acceptance of a more healthful break, like going for a short walk, or just to the door or window for air, or getting up to stretch.

Some women are working to create a smoke-free environment where they are employed. One woman wrote to tell us how she fought and won such a struggle:

Over the past eight years I have worked in an office with no ventilation system, no windows that opened, and no source of fresh air except the front door. I got so angry about having to endure all the smoke that I even filed a union grievance and went through all the steps. The union said that I was the problem and that perhaps I should just get another job.

I tried the fire department. The chief inspected and, though sympathetic, said that he could not ban smoking since there were no volatile gases or flammable materials in the worksite.

I started going to GASP meetings, and I read and brought their literature to the office. I decided that I was willing to sue for a smoke-free work environment. After being turned down by many law firms that would not take the case on a pro bono *basis,* we finally found *a lawyer whose wife was an oncologist (a physician who specializes in treating cancer).*

I was jubilant when the judge issued a ten-day restraining order against smoking in the office. The office was divided on the issue. A few people said the air was better after the smoking stopped. Others were angry and sarcastic. People told me I would never be promoted and might even lose my job.

The case went on for a year. The hardest thing was being portrayed in court as a maladjusted woman. I was indignant because there was plenty of evidence available about the hazards of smoking. I felt it was a public health issue, just like having a clean water supply.

The outcome was that when our office moved into new space it was divided up. Four addicted smokers chose a room with a separate ventilation system; the rest of the space is smoke-free. The other smokers chose to work in a smoke-free environment and do not smoke at their desks.

Three years later, the tension has subsided and some of my co-workers have even thanked me. Other offices are pleading for smoke-free work areas but so far the agency hasn't done anything about it. They only did it in my office because of my court case. [a fifty-eight-year-old woman]

Smoking is a hard habit to break, and for various reasons women have a harder time quitting than men. Stopping smoking often requires that we confront these obstacles:

- Tobacco manufacturers spend millions on special advertising efforts to expand their markets among women. The financial clout of the tobacco industry inhibits the flow of anti-smoking information while assuring that the prosmoking messages remain in the media—a serious infringement of freedom of the press.[7] Earlier advertising attempted to link smoking with sexiness. Now the ads play on a caricature of feminism that links smoking to women's struggles for equality and feeling "tough" and "cool." The only way smoking helps you to "come a long way, baby" is by catching up to men's lung-cancer rates.
- Nicotine is a physiological addictor. When you smoke, you reward yourself for smoking, and when you try to quit, it feels like you are punishing yourself. You can reverse this by developing a reward system for every cigarette you do *not* smoke. One suggestion is to set aside the money you spend on cigarettes for a

From pro bono publica, *a Latin phrase meaning "for the public good." In English usage, this means legal work done for free or at reduced rates in order to bring certain issues before the courts.

*Two years later, the agency has ruled that smoke-free offices must be provided at every site.

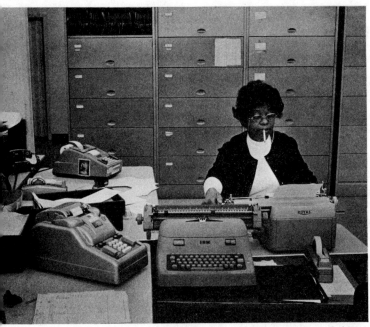
Cathy Cade

present for yourself. By *not* smoking you can spend the money on something you will enjoy longer than a cigarette.

- Smoking is higher among groups stressed by job pressures and economic concerns— women (especially very young women), people of color, blue-collar workers.* Much of the material on the dangers of smoking is in publications that reach high-income persons; much of the advertising promoting smoking is in media reaching lower-income persons.

- Women learn to suppress anger, and some of us tend to reach for a cigarette when feeling angry.

It took me eight years to stop smoking completely. The last cigarettes I gave up were the ones I "bummed" at work when I didn't feel free to say what I really thought. My close co-workers would ask me after the meeting, "What didn't you like?" [a fifty-four-year-old woman]

- Many women use cigarette smoking to reduce calorie intake, picking up a cigarette instead of a dessert. We fear gaining weight if we quit. Cigarette manufacturers play on such fears through advertising and use of such names as

*Even among health professionals, smoking continues to be a problem when job pressures go hand-in-hand with the lack of authority to make changes in the workplace. Doctors and nurses are equally aware of the health risks of smoking, but approximately 35 percent of nurses still smoke, whereas only 20 percent of doctors smoke.

Virginia Slims. Food will taste and smell better without cigarettes, but weight gain is not inevitable. Instead, try noncaloric or low-calorie substitutes like gum or carrot sticks rather than resorting to high-calorie foods to sate your reawakened appetite. Try chewy, satisfying whole grains like brown rice to restore the B vitamins lost in smoking. Drink extra fruit and vegetable juices to speed elimination of nicotine from your system. Increase your walks or other exercise. Try swimming; nobody smokes in a swimming pool.

When you resolve to quit, prepare for your new adventure. You can expect to feel rocky for a period of time, so get support from family and friends. Other helpful supports are self-help manuals and "stop smoking" groups. A good "stop smoking" program will help you confront your individual smoking patterns.

Some immediate rewards of quitting smoking are an increase in endurance, an end to "smoker's cough," and regaining your senses of taste and smell. Some long-term rewards are better health, longer life, and the pride of being in control.

CAFFEINE

Coffee is the "drug of choice" for millions of Americans. We use coffee as fuel for our industry and business, making typists type faster and executives work longer hours.

Caffeine and related compounds are found in coffee, colas, caffeinated teas, and chocolate. Partly as a result of public awareness, coffee consumption is slipping, and caffeine-free colas are now available. The coffee industry has gone on the offensive, asking us to become "coffee achievers" again.

What caffeine in fact achieves is partial responsibility for a wide range of disorders: panic attacks,[8] chronic nervousness and irritability; digestive difficulties, including heartburn, indigestion, and ulcers; fibrocystic breast lumps; migraine headaches; and low blood sugar. It can lead to increased risk of pancreatic and bladder cancers,[9] and, as a heart stimulant, is linked to blood-pressure abnormalities and myocardial infarction. In a 1973 study of 440 patients with acute myocardial infarction, the disease was seen 60 percent to 120 percent more frequently in coffee drinkers.[10]

Norma Holt

"Decaffeinated" coffee is only half decaffeinated! It still contains about 3 percent caffeine, compared to regular coffee's 6 percent, as well as other substances such as tars, acids, and oils that may be part of the coffee/disease picture. If you drink several cups of decaf, you are still getting a lot of caffeine. The safest way to remove caffeine from coffee is the water-processed method. Specialty shops and health-food stores may sell water-processed decaf. Chemically processed decaf has been specifically implicated in pancreatic cancer.[11]

The "coffee klatsch," which developed among neighborhood women to inject a little sociability in a day filled with chores and isolation, is often just an excuse to sit down together. You can still have the sociability without the dangers of caffeine.

What can you do if you want to switch? Cut down gradually. When you feel like having a cup of coffee, find other ways to increase circulation and oxygen to the brain, such as aerobic exercise. Drinking milk, vegetable juices, unsweetened fruit juices, herbal beverages, and grain-based coffee substitutes (iced or hot) may add a new flavor dimension to your life. Don't forget your need for water. Evaluate your priorities, and see if you are pushing yourself harder than necessary using coffee as a whip.

ALCOHOL

During their middle and later years, women undergo significant life changes and cultural pressures. Trying to cope with these changes and pressures is very difficult, and a drink or a tranquilizer may seem like an easy way to cope. Women can often trace changes in their drinking habits to upsetting events in their lives.[12] But drinking opens a door to a nightmare of alcohol abuse and possible addiction.

If we are having trouble sleeping, we may be tempted to have a drink before bed to encourage sleep. To add to this danger, physicians may prescribe drugs that can eventually control us physically, mentally, and spiritually, and can interact dangerously with alcohol.[13]

If we have already spent several decades using alcohol as an accompaniment to life, it is difficult to imagine that it can suddenly take over completely. Yet it can do just that!

When I was living alone with no car, I felt really alone. I had a morbid fear: suppose I lost my mind or something? I'd open a can of beer and make a gin and tonic, and have a sip of one and then a sip of the other. It was so warm and soothing. But it was dangerous. [an eighty-eight-year-old woman]

Are we overstating the case, being alarmist? After all, most Americans drink. It is a customary part of our social life. Sometimes there is social pressure to drink. We are more apt to drink, or to drink more than we usually do, in a group, for the sake of sociability. It is important to remember that we have the right to abstain.

When I was going through menopause I found that any alcohol triggered severe hot flashes and so asked for seltzer water or juice. I was amazed at the pressure from people (not from my close friends) who were unrelenting in trying to get me to drink alcohol. I finally started to lie and told them I was taking medication that could not be taken with alcohol. Then they were sympathetic and stopped pressuring—until the next time. [a fifty-five-year-old woman]

Relatively little is known about the effects of alcohol on women of any age because most research on alcohol and drug abuse is still being done with men as subjects. We do know that women's average body weights are lower than men's, so the same quantity of alcohol hits us harder. Even at the same weight, alcohol enters our bloodstreams faster because of our higher proportion of body fat, which doesn't absorb alcohol. Twenty-five percent of women who become alcoholics do so between the ages of forty and fifty-five,[14] and anywhere from 1 to 5 percent succumb to the disease after age sixty.[15]

My family and friends knew there was something wrong with me, but they just couldn't put a finger on it. The changes had been too subtle. They could see that I was drinking a little too much, now and again. What they did not know, because I went to great pains to hide it from them, was that the times I drank had become more and more frequent, and the times between shorter. [a woman in her fifties]

Many women fall prey to problem drinking without realizing it is happening. If alcohol becomes a problem for you, will you realize it? Will you know how to handle it? Will you want to do so? We owe it to ourselves to be aware of certain telltale signs of problem drinking in ourselves or in others close to us.

No one starts life with the goal of becoming an alcoholic. There are no sure ways to predict who will or will not become one. The onset of alcohol abuse is usually very slow and insidious.

Ellen Shub

My tolerance to alcohol grew so that I had to drink more to achieve the same effect. My daily activities began to be planned around my drinking time, and more and more often, drinking became my main activity. My dependence on the alcohol was growing as my addiction took hold. I could manage to rationalize anything if it meant defending my right to drink. At that point, of course, my "right" was a synonym for my physical and emotional need. [a fifty-one-year-old woman]

While it is not possible to predict exactly who will or will not become an alcoholic, the following questions can provide some early clues. Are you, for example:

- Drinking faster or more frequently? Are you gulping your drinks or trying to maintain the feeling drinking gives you, while looking for more opportunities to drink and feel okay about it?
- Changing your daily pattern of drinking? Has a nightcap been expanded to include a before-dinner drink?
- Changing companions? Are you breaking dates with old friends and trying to find new ones who drink as you do?
- Having trouble maintaining your activity level at work or at home? Do lunches include an alcoholic beverage when tea or coffee used to be enough? Is it increasingly difficult to return to work afterward? Have you lost interest in activities that used to make you happy but did not include drinking?
- Becoming unable to resist when you want to drink, even at times you would normally consider inappropriate? Are you planning ahead to insure your supply? Finding reasons to justify drinking? Can you rationalize almost anything if it means you can drink when you want to do so?
- Denying that anything has changed? Are you lying to yourself and others about the frequency of your drinking and your need to continue it? Are your friends and family members making excuses for you? Is your relationship with them changing for the worse?
- Experiencing blackouts? Are you beginning to have times when you cannot remember things you did while drinking?

"The quality of life returns as we learn a day at a time how not to drink." As these words were spoken at an A.A. meeting recently, there flashed before me the scene of a Christmas morning in my living room—and the faces of my husband and son—as I stood shakily before

them following what I hope is my last drunken black-out, seven years ago. [a seventy-two-year-old woman]

· Having more accidents? Are you falling more, or getting burns or cuts without being able to explain how?

Until I almost fall down, or become ill, or wake up the next day with a massive hangover, I don't truly recognize how drunk I am. [a fifty-year-old woman]

Facing Problem Drinking

Drinking is considered to be inappropriate behavior for women, especially for older women. Women who drink to excess are judged harshly, their value as people and women challenged. Those of us who grew up during the times when women were more restricted socially may feel this prejudice more keenly, but few of us are free of it entirely.

I called A.A. at least three times over my last five years of heavy drinking. Each time I called with a different story, a different lie! Once I said I was calling because my son drank too much. I don't remember the other lies. I even disguised my voice because I felt so ashamed. [a forty-nine-year-old woman]

As well as robbing women who drink too much of their self-esteem and security, this attitude keeps many from getting help. Most women are reluctant to seek treatment, even privately, because of the stigma attached. Seventy percent of women who drink to excess hide their drinking for as long as possible.[16] Some women can hide the extent of their drinking or drug abuse better than others. Women who live by themselves or with partners who are absent frequently can do so more easily. Women in higher income brackets may also be able to hide problems more easily because expense is less of an issue and because they rarely come to the attention of social workers or the criminal justice system.

However, no one is exempt from addiction. Although it often seems as if no one wants to admit it, the woman alcoholic or problem drinker can be anyone—a next-door neighbor, a co-worker, or a close relative. She can be a lesbian, a member of an ethnic minority, a strict churchgoer, a professional, an eighty-five-year-old great-grandmother, or you.

Alcohol and the Lesbian

Most women over thirty-five did not know the freedom growing up that our younger sisters have today. The experiences of older lesbians involved the painful conflict of fear of being found out versus a deep need to socialize. The situation was made more complex by the fact that social life in past years centered around bars.

Too many older lesbians still feel isolated, guilty, ashamed, and have low self-esteem because of society's homophobia. Alcohol, first used as a temporary relief from those pressures, grew to be a constant need for almost one third of all lesbians.[17]

I so deeply suppressed my homosexual feelings that I was no longer aware that they existed. Married at twenty-three, I lived the role of a traditional mom and wife. I had always felt different from my friends, and I thought that something must really be wrong with me. Having a drink before supper was a nightly event for my husband and me. Gradually, however, this one drink became two or three for me. I really looked forward to those drinks because they were the only times that I felt able to relax. Gradually, over the years, I lost control of my drinking and became an alcoholic.

Fortunately, at forty-two, I found A.A. and began my road to recovery. In the process, my old feelings began to resurface and I could no longer deny that I was both emotionally and sexually attracted to other women. While these feelings frightened me, I could no longer suppress them. Instead, I began to actively seek out other women like me. While I had been afraid that going to bars would be my only way to find them, I discovered that the A.A. meeting book actually listed several gay meetings.

Nervous and frightened, I went to my first meeting. I was so paranoid that I thought everyone from my small town had followed me. I sat in a chair close to the door so I could make a quick escape if necessary. But when I heard an attractive young woman on the podium say, "Welcome. My name is Kathy and I am an alcoholic and a lesbian," tears of relief streamed down my face. [a forty-nine-year-old woman]

New organizations for older lesbians provide opportunities for socializing in an alcohol-free environment.

I was in A.A. and alcohol-free for some years when I found an older-lesbian group of more than two hundred women over the age of forty. The group sponsors an activity each month plus two weekends a year. All of the group's activities are alcohol-free, and even smoking is confined to a separate area. Our members have started small groups to read books, play cards, and other activities. Alcohol had been such an integral part of my lifestyle back in the 1940s and '50s, when the only place to socialize was the gay bars. Perhaps life would have unfolded differently for me if we had had other places then. How wonderful for all of us now, but especially for the younger women, to have sane and safe places free from the dangers of alcohol and police raids in the bars. [a sixty-two-year-old woman]

Social Effects of Alcohol Abuse

A long list of social troubles can be the outcome of problem drinking and alcoholism. Choosing to take a mood or mind-altering substance instead of dealing with issues that come up in daily life also causes problems. We can lose friends and lovers, see our marriages break up, lose jobs, run up debts by spending money to insure our supply rather than paying our bills, be picked up for drunk driving violations, and so on.

As I began to drink more, I began to be late to work. At first it was just once in a while, and then more frequently. Finally I started missing days completely. When I was at work, the quality of my work was becoming more uneven. At first my friends covered up for me, but eventually they were less and less willing to do so. Finally my boss began to notice. I was warned a number of times, and people bent over backward to help me, but I was unable to see what was happening to me. When I lost that job I rationalized that it hadn't been much of a job anyway, and I would be happier without it. [a fifty-one-year-old woman]

Health Hazards of Alcohol Abuse

Heavy alcoholism over a period of years adversely affects every organ and system of the body. Some of these damaging effects can be reversed, but many cannot.[18] When we drink, we might like to think that any long-term effects will happen only to others, but they can happen to us. The possibilities include:

- Memory loss caused by brain atrophy
- Digestive problems, including inflammation of the pancreas, gastritis, fatty liver, hepatitis, and cirrhosis. Heavy drinking can impair the absorption of vitamin B_1 (thiamine), which can contribute to both brain damage and many problems of the intestinal system.
- High blood pressure and cardiac arrhythmia (irregular heartbeat), coronary artery disease and alcohol cardiomyopathy (heart muscle damage)
- Nerve and muscle disorders resulting in weakness, the gradual wasting of muscles, and even paralysis
- An increased susceptibility to infection. Alcohol suppresses the production of white blood cells and impairs their ability to get to the site of an infection quickly.
- An increase in the effect of carcinogens (cancer-causing substances) such as tobacco. Alcoholics with cancer have a poorer chance of survival and a greater chance of developing another primary tumor than do nonalcoholics with the same cancer.
- Malnutrition. Alcoholics often neglect their nutrition, leading to anemia and increased tendency to bleed.

It cannot be overstated that, in addition to the above, there can be severe, sometimes fatal, effects as a result of combining alcohol with other drugs, even those drugs which are necessary for various health problems.

My friend Margo had a serious thyroid problem which was controllable with medication. She was also one of those unfortunate people who suffered from long- and short-term memory loss related to alcohol use. Over the years of heavy drinking, her thyroid condition worsened because she would forget to take her medication, increasing the burden on her overworked heart. Ultimately her heart did give out and Margo died when she was just fifty-two years old. The death certificate stated that she died of heart failure, but it was her alcoholism which was the real cause.

Getting Help

If you cannot stop drinking when you want to; if, on any given occasion, you find you are taking drugs more than you want to; or if you know deep inside that drinking or drugs are affecting any part of your life in a negative way, help is as close as your telephone. Even if you are only beginning to wonder if you have a problem, it is never too early to seek help, nor is it ever too late.

Finally, after twenty years of drinking, I went to a psychiatrist to whom I confessed out loud for the first time that I couldn't stop drinking. In his ignorance of the disease of alcoholism, he said, "There, there, dear. You are just a little neurotic. A few pills and a few more visits and you should be all right in a few months." In my own ignorance and desperation, I actually believed this man. He started me on Librium and then when that didn't work, Valium. And then Elavil and then lithium. Two and one-half years later he had tried thirty-one different drugs on me, including Artane because I shook so much from the combination of all these drugs. I now know that Artane is particularly dangerous when used in combination with alcohol. When he gave it to me, this doctor knew that I had not stopped drinking. I had always told the truth about that.

At last I told this doctor that I felt I was wasting my time and money, and that I planned to go to A.A. Though he had been unable to help me, he did not encourage me to go. He subscribed to the stereotype that A.A. is only for people who are down and out and he told me that I would never find a group in which I could be comfortable. Instead, I found hope and love and warmth from my first A.A. meeting. I have been sober for several years now, and my life has changed dramatically for the better. [a forty-nine-year-old woman]

You no longer have to be alone, feel guilty, or hide. Help and support are available in every state, town, and neighborhood. Your anonymity will be protected.

You must first get sober and stay sober. You may need a detoxification program* to get sober, and A.A. to keep sober. Once you are sober, you may want to work on your problems. If you choose to work with a therapist, it is important to find someone who has a clear understanding of A.A. and can help you to use both systems effectively.[19] Many therapists will urge an alcoholic to go to A.A. if she is not already doing so.

Helping Someone We Care About

When someone we care about has a drinking or drug problem, it is not easy to find the best way to help. Helping a friend or family member acknowledge that she or he has a problem can be one way to make a difference.

My best friend became an alcoholic and was progressively getting worse. She was raised in a teetotaling family, and I knew how the dichotomy between her upbringing and her secretive drinking was tearing her apart, in addition to the physical destruction of alcoholism. I assumed she would deny any accusation with vigor, and was very fearful that she might be so angry she would terminate our friendship, an outcome I would find intolerable. So time dripped by and I did nothing. After three years, I knew that I could no longer call myself a friend if I continued to ignore what she was doing. I arranged a day's outing and confronted her. She was so relieved! Nobody in her family had acknowledged what she was doing and she had concealed it from her therapist. As always, with confrontation, my only regret was that it took me so long to be able to do it. [a fifty-seven-year-old woman]

*There is a serious shortage of treatment programs for alcoholic women throughout the country. *The New York Times,* June 14, 1987, p. 51.

When we are closely involved with alcoholics —whether our spouses, lovers, parents, or children—we tend to become caught up in the illness as well. We spend prolonged periods of time trying to change our loved ones and convince them that they are destroying themselves by continuing to drink. We find ourselves fighting a losing battle to maintain some semblance of normalcy, unable to believe that the presence of alcoholism in our lives is permanent. The sooner we get help for ourselves from Alanon or, for our teenaged children, from Alateen, the sooner we will learn how to live our own lives, how to put the responsibility on the alcoholic for her or his own behavior, and not shoulder the blame ourselves.

We women are such good nurturers that we are usually loyal to our relationships even when we suffer as a result. Alcoholism is one disease in which the effort to smooth over and solve problems all by ourselves is misplaced. We can become what has been called a co-alcoholic or para-alcoholic, exhibiting the same denial, guilt, and blame as the alcoholic. The responsibility for alcoholism should rest squarely on the alcoholic—where it belongs. Even after many years of unhappy marriages and other close relationships with alcoholics, women have been able, through Alanon and other organizations, to reconstruct their own lives.

OVER-THE-COUNTER AND PRESCRIPTION DRUGS

Though persons over the age of sixty-five constitute 11 percent of the total population, they take about 25 percent of all the drugs dispensed in the United States, both prescription and over-the-counter (OTC).[20] In the United States in 1986, consumers spent an estimated $21.3 billion on 1.51 million prescription drugs[21] and more than $8 billion on the 200,000 nonprescription medicinal products available. Many of these drugs may be needed, even life-saving, but many are not. Often old prescriptions are not reevaluated for continued need and for interactions with new prescriptions and with OTC preparations. "Polypharmacy" is the term used to describe taking too many, or excessive amounts of, drugs at a time. It is common among older women who may be seeing several physicians for different conditions.

Drug companies, in business for profit, have offered new products to the market while sometimes failing to report adverse and life-threatening reactions to drugs.[22] The U.S. Food and Drug Administration continues to permit drugs on the market that later prove harmful and have to be withdrawn. Do not agree to use a drug which has been on the market for less than four years unless you are willing to be part of an experiment.[23]

Harmful effects from drug interactions are too numerous to list here, so always inform your physician of everything you are using (prescriptions, OTC, and vitamin supplements) and always double-check with your pharmacist. OTC drugs and vitamins, herbs, and supplements from health-food stores can be just as potent and dangerous as prescription drugs. Do not take leftover or other people's medicines.

Most drug dosages should be adjusted to the size and the age of the person taking the drug. Women at any age may require lower drug dosages than men because of women's lower body weight and mass. We become even more sensitive to drugs over time because, as we age, drugs are metabolized more slowly, the kidneys and the liver excrete them more slowly, and so they remain in the body longer. Also as we age, some muscle mass turns to fat, so many drugs that can be stored in fat tissue, such as Valium, stay in the body a longer time, increasing the likelihood of addiction even from low, infrequent doses. Drug companies have only recently started testing the effects of drugs on older people and still do not distinguish the more severe effects of drugs on people over the age of seventy from the effects on the whole group over fifty. Drugs may be harmful or may be taken in too high doses if individual adjustments and frequent reevaluations are not made. One study of older persons admitted to a state mental hospital found that 15 percent were actually suffering from drug toxicities rather than from dementia or other mental illness.[24] There are similar findings in the rest of the older population.

Over half the adult women in this country have used tranquilizers, sedatives, and amphetamines (stimulants often used in "diet pills"). These drugs are legally available and are the most commonly abused classes of drugs among older women. The practice of some physicians freely to write prescriptions for these types of controlled drugs has declined in those states which require monitoring of physicians' prescription-writing habits. This policy of monitoring, with the penalty of withdrawing medical licensure for physicians who overprescribe these drugs, should be adopted in all states.

Since these drugs tend to be chemically and emotionally addictive and don't cure anything by themselves, they seem to be a nonproductive treatment for stress or fatigue. Their use is an attempt to treat medically what is really a social problem—the stress and isolation of many older women's lives. Taken in combination with alcohol, they can cause permanent damage, even death. Still, millions of dollars are devoted to promoting tranquilizers as the solution to women's depression and anxiety; and too many doctors who recommend exercise for men under stress prescribe drugs to their female patients with the same symptoms.

We do not know the long-term effects of illegal recreational drugs. We do know, though, that marijuana can damage the respiratory system and that cocaine is addictive and can cause sudden death through its action on the heart. The continued use of such substances will compound the health problems of future generations of older women who started using such drugs when they were young.

Some physicians do not realize how they help to create drug problems. When women ask them for help with complaints, many doctors are apt to treat the symptom rather than to probe a little deeper to find the source of the complaint.

On my frequent trips to my family doctor for treatment of recurring bouts with bronchitis, he did not seem to attach significance to the facts that I was putting on weight, that my blood pressure had begun to rise, and that I was generally sluggish. I told the doctor that I was just having trouble sleeping so he gave me a prescription for some sleeping pills, and told me to cut back on my activities a little. He knew I had an alcohol problem but he never asked if I was drinking more than usual. He never asked me to check back with him after I had tried the pills. [a fifty-one-year-old woman]

This woman might have died from the combination of pills and alcohol in her system.

It is imperative that medical schools include more courses on alcohol and drug abuse and related illnesses. Pharmacists need more legal power to write warnings on bottles and to caution their customers. Despite the fact that these addictions are national problems with enormous impact on the public, only a few medical schools teach their students anything at all about them. Physicians often assume we do not feel satisfied with our visit unless we come away with a prescription. One study, however, showed that 72 percent of the patients surveyed preferred a nondrug remedy when it and a drug were both offered and fully explained.[25] We might benefit more from explanations, answers to our questions, support, and sound practical advice than from drugs. Unfortunately, training of physicians in these approaches is even weaker than their training in pharmacology.

It is important to know what the drugs we take can do for us and to us. Antihistamines, for instance, frequently cause drowsiness. Some other cold medicines contain drugs to clear stuffy noses (vasoconstrictors), which may make you feel jumpy, and caffeine to keep you active when you probably should be resting in bed. Most liquid cold preparations and mouthwashes contain alcohol; many preparations and vitamins contain sugar. Be forewarned: the advertising for many products never mentions that the drugs they contain could cause dependency or undesirable interactions with other drugs.

When considering any medication, consult your health care provider and your pharmacist. Bring a list of all the prescription and nonprescription preparations you are using. Report any allergies or reactions to medication you suffered in the past. Seek the answers to the following questions:[26]

1. What are both the brand name and the scientific (generic) name of the medication, and what is it supposed to do?

2. How do I store it and take it, and for how long? What should I do if I miss a dose?

3. What foods, drinks, other medicines, and activities should I avoid while taking this medicine? What do I especially need?

4. What other effects might I have while taking this drug, and what should I do if they occur?

5. Is there any written information available about this medicine?

If you decide to take a medication, save money by requesting the generic drug. Find out as much as you can so you can take the medication in the most beneficial way. Do not, for example, crush a coated tablet, for the coating has been put on to protect you or to improve the drug's absorption.

Two common problems for which too many women habitually use harmful drugs are insomnia and constipation. Both are better dealt with by nonpharmaceutical methods.

Dealing with Insomnia

Some changes in sleep patterns may occur as we get older but at any age we need adequate, deep sleep for good health. Do not assume you have a problem just because you get less sleep than you used to. Judge by how you feel, not just by the number of hours you sleep. Some women have problems falling asleep; others may readily fall asleep, but wake up after only a few hours and have trouble going back to sleep. There are many things we can do to sleep better.

Worries and depression can cause sleeplessness. Many women will focus on the sleeplessness rather than on the causes of the worries and depression. If you seek and find the right kind of help for the underlying cause of the problem, you may be able to sleep better. Labeling the problems as insomnia will not solve either the problems or the insomnia, and may make it worse by starting a cycle in which you go to bed each night worrying about whether your "insomnia" will keep you awake.

Many activities can interfere with sleep. Among them are eating late at night (especially sugar); having unsuspected caffeine in soft drinks, cocoa and chocolate, and tea; taking vitamin B or C before bed; not getting enough protein in your diet. Tryptophan is an amino acid which induces drowsiness. Since many tryptophan-rich foods are high in protein (milk, turkey, fish, meat), many persons who avoid these foods may have trouble sleeping and may be helped by taking tryptophan.

Drugs are a common cause of sleep problems. Caffeine is not the only one. The complete list of prescription and over-the-counter drugs that interfere with sleep is too long to include here. Just a few are: nicotine in cigarettes; pain relievers and cold remedies that contain caffeine or antihistamines; appetite suppressants; decongestants; drugs for asthma, high blood pressure, heart rhythm, and thyroid problems; and many others. Antihistamines (contained in cold remedies and over-the-counter sleeping pills) and alcohol cause drowsiness initially but interfere with later sleep and can cause early awakening. The insomnia caused by certain conditions such as an overactive thyroid will be relieved when treated appropriately—not by sleeping pills.

Medications formulated to help you sleep, including sleeping pills, tranquilizers, and anti-anxiety drugs, can cause sleeplessness after their use is discontinued. They can also be addictive. Sleeping pills may make older people less alert, aggravate memory loss, and have other adverse effects, all which may be confused with dementia. Their use increases the likelihood of falls, and resultant broken hips or other broken bones. Chloral hydrate, commonly prescribed, interferes with rapid eye movement sleep (REM, the time when we dream), which is vital for mental health. While you might choose to use sleeping pills for a few nights in some special situation, you should be especially cautious as you get older. Smaller than usual doses will probably suffice.

Sleeping pills slow down respiratory function in some people and are particularly dangerous for people with sleep apnea (the sudden cessation of breathing during sleep) or heavy snoring. Sleep apnea may occur from a few times to several hundred times a night with or without heavy snoring. If your bed-partner or roommate tells you that your breathing seems to stop during sleep, you should seek medical advice, preferably at a hospital sleep center, because this behavior often signals a more serious problem.

To deal with sleeplessness:

- Try to go to sleep and arise at regular hours in whatever pattern suits you best. You may want to avoid daytime naps in order to sleep more hours at night, or you may feel better sleeping fewer hours at night and taking a daytime nap.
- Exercise during the day, not just before bed.
- Soak in a hot tub before bed, unless you have diabetes.
- Don't go to bed hungry but avoid eating a huge meal before bed. Being too full may disturb sleep. Try milk before bed, warm if you like. The tryptophan in milk will help you sleep.
- Try relaxation techniques. If something is on your mind, make a note to deal with the problem the next day and then try to forget it.
- Make your surroundings as comfortable as possible, including the bed, temperature and humidity, sound and light.
- Develop the association between bed and sleep. Follow the same rituals every night be-

fore going to bed. Do not read or write in bed. If you cannot sleep, get out of bed and go back later.
- Keep a journal of your sleep patterns to help you identify problems and the success of changes you try.

I have a tape of the sound of ocean waves on a cassette by my bed. If I wake up in the middle of the night, I reach over and turn on the tape. It seems to crowd out distracting thoughts and lulls me back to sleep. [a fifty-five-year-old woman]

Dealing with Constipation

Laxatives are another commonly overused medication. Many of us were taught that we were supposed to have a bowel movement each and every day. In fact, though two thirds of the women in a survey claimed one bowel movement per day, the normal variation was between three times a day and twice a week.[27] Consider yourself constipated only if your customary pattern changes or if you have hard, difficult-to-pass stools.

Changes in diet can alleviate constipation. White flour products with or without sugar are the most common culprit. Add more natural fiber by eating plenty of vegetables, fruit, and whole grains as well as breads and cereals that contain bran. Drink eight to ten glasses of fluid each day, more on very hot days or if you are sweating heavily from work or exercise. Fresh fruit and fruit juices, especially prune juice, can have a laxative effect. Additional fluids are necessary if you add bran to your diet in order to prevent the stool from becoming too bulky and hard. Large amounts of caffeine usually cause diarrhea but in some women may cause constipation. Withdrawing from coffee may also cause constipation temporarily.

Activity is needed to keep the bowels active. A little exercise each day, especially walking, does wonders. Exercise also alleviates stress, anxiety, and depression, which can all cause constipation. Strengthening weak abdominal and pelvic muscles can help elimination. It is particularly important to keep the stool soft if you have a weakening in the wall of the rectum (a rectocele) in which the feces can collect.

Many women become constipated because they are too busy to take time in the bathroom. They may "hold it" too long, just as they hold urine too long, losing awareness of their need to "go." (See Urinary Incontinence chapter.) Go to the toilet at regular times but do not strain. Holding the breath while pushing can raise blood pressure. If you can't move your bowels, relax and try later.

Common medications and vitamins can affect bowel movements. You will have to make the decision for yourself. For example, magnesium-aluminum antacids are the most effective for persons who suffer from gas and other problems that might be relieved by an antacid. However, milk of magnesia can cause diarrhea, so the aluminum is added to, counteract it.[28] Aluminum antacids interfere with the absorption of calcium. Iron supplements often cause constipation. Taking vitamin C increases the absorption of the iron and also helps alleviate the constipation. Many other drugs, especially painkillers, slow down the bowels.

One of the most common causes of chronic constipation is the use of laxatives. The body can become habituated to the laxatives and lose the ability to function normally without them. Laxatives also interfere with the body's absorption of vitamins, minerals, and many medications. If you are used to laxatives, try tapering off gradually while improving your eating habits and exercising regularly.

While you are tapering off, use the type of laxative most suitable for your problems. Read the labels so you will know what you are taking. Bulk laxatives (such as psyllium seed) add bulk to the stool. Lubricants (such as docusate sodium) encourage water to enter the stool, thereby increasing its bulk and softness. Salt laxatives (such as milk of magnesia) also hold water, making the stool softer and bulkier, but are not recommended for those on low-salt diets. Irritant drugs (such as castor oil or senna) stimulate the intestinal nerves, thus increasing bowel activity. Glycerin suppositories stimulate the bowel muscle and lubricate the stool already in the rectum. Mineral oil helps lubricate stools higher in the intestines but prevents absorption of many needed nutrients. If it is necessary to use mineral oil, take it at 6 A.M. and take a supplement of fat-soluble vitamins at 6 P.M.

Dealing with Pain

Many people overuse and misuse pain medication. They may become addicted to pain medication and continue its use long after the pain has stopped. Others suffer needlessly from pain because they fear reliance on medication, or addiction. Our instinct to pull away from something painful—such as a hot stove—has great survival value. Pain can be a signal to protect ourselves or a warning for us to pay attention. Ignoring pain can put us in great danger, and even cause death. People vary in how they interpret and tolerate pain signals, and there are as yet few ways to measure how much pain people feel. Understanding our bodies will help us know when to seek help.

We have to cope not only with pain, but with what the pain means to us—usually our fear of what we think might be causing the pain, or fear that the pain will not end. Sometimes we ignore pain that could easily be helped because we fear a more serious cause. Stress and pain have a close relationship. It's easy to understand that being in pain stresses us. But stress can also cause or intensify pain. When pain does not have a clear-cut cause or, worse, is interpreted as signaling a dangerous illness, it can feel more intense. Factors such as tension or tightening up, anxiety, depression, and fatigue can modulate the pain threshold.

There are many pains for which no specific cause can be found, or for which there is no single effective cure. That does not mean that our pain is imaginary or should be dismissed. Unfortunately, many doctors believe that much of women's pain is imaginary or a device for getting attention. All pain is real. We should not be told that we must just learn to live with pain; we should be given specific suggestions on how to do it.

Traditional healing methods, many from Eastern medicine and philosophy, approach pain as if it were blocked energy. The practitioner of such methods should be our partner in exploring the possible connections between our present pain and our entire life-style—day-to-day habits of eating, exercise, emotional patterns, social relationships, occupation, creative and spiritual connections—as well as possible disease. We can learn to use deep breathing and relaxation exercises to control and manage pain. Some of us have used the techniques learned in childbirth classes throughout our lives. Techniques such as relaxation, meditation, massage, yoga, and acupuncture are helpful for managing pain. Although these techniques seem to work particularly well with chronic pain (pain lasting more than six months), they can also help us with acute pain. In a situation of acute, even life-threatening, pain that requires immediate emergency medical care, such as a heart attack, techniques learned from relaxation, meditation, and self-hypnosis can help us avoid panic and cope with pain.

Western medicine tends to see pain as an enemy, to be destroyed as soon as possible. The focus is on the specific body parts that hurt: what is the cause, what is the cure? The physician is the expert and has the primary responsibility for finding the cure. But Western medicine is beginning to combine Eastern mind-body concepts with modern technology to develop techniques—such as biofeedback—which can be useful in pain control. Other new methods include TENS and PCA. TENS (transcutaneous electrical nerve stimulation) sends measured pulses of electric current to the pain sites through electrodes attached to the skin, providing significant but temporary relief for up to 70 percent of the users. Some researchers think TENS causes the body to release natural opiates called endorphins; others think it interferes with the transmission of pain signals. Patient-controlled analgesia (PCA) is an innovation that provides individualized pain control. This technique utilizes a device that permits intravenous self-administration of narcotic drugs within limits of dose and frequency established with the physician.[29]

Pain clinics, which now exist in many cities, focus on the whole person and may use both Western and traditional techniques appropriate to the individual. As one client in a pain-relief clinic said, "It's a relief to be treated as a person, instead of as a hip problem." This approach, which should be used by all health care providers, invites us to be more active on our own behalf, befriending those parts of us that have hurt for so long that we may have given up on them—our bum knees, miserable back, perpetual headaches.

I've changed my attitude toward pain. I don't think of my foot that's hurting as a separate, bad part of me—something to be angry at. I now try to take a more caregiving approach, to see what kind of special attention it wants. I massage my feet and calves every night. The trouble with having the doctor be the only one who can fix you is that, if he can't do it, then you're a goner. It's good I've found some things I can do for myself to help myself feel better. [a thirty-five-year-old woman]

Once we adopt a body-befriending approach to pain management, we can create many self-help techniques. There are many things that alleviate pain, such as exhaling or panting rather than holding the breath while we do physical work, thinking about something else more pleasant while the dentist drills, stopping negative self-talk, soothing painful areas with Therapeutic Touch (see Massage, p. 16). Many others are well known: taking a hot bath or a cold shower, taking a walk, distracting ourselves by doing some favorite thing. It's difficult to feel depressed when we are singing or to feel anxious while we are taking slow, deep breaths.

There are many painkilling drugs, including aspirin, acetaminophen, acetophenetidin, codeine, and morphine. All pain-relieving drugs have undesirable and potentially harmful effects. They may cloud our consciousness at the very time when we might wish to get as much out of life as possible.

On the other hand, many of us are so fearful of pain medication that we deprive ourselves of comfort and help when we could most use it. Pain is very tiring; pain can use up the energy we need for caring for ourselves and managing the condition causing the pain. Many times a moderate and careful use of pain medication can help us have the strength we need for dealing with the cause. Using the nondrug pain-relief methods already described can reduce our need for medication. Smaller, more frequent doses of pain medication may keep us comfortable and result in use of less medication than if we wait until the pain becomes so severe that we need massive doses to feel relief. Avoid drugs or combinations of pain-relieving drugs that make you sleepy without reducing pain.[30]

When faced with severe pain, we should be able to choose the extent of pain relief that suits us. Each woman has her own level of pain tolerance. When death is imminent, we need not fear addiction. Especially at that time we should be able to remain in control and be able to choose among all options.

NOTES

1. U.S. Office of the Assistant Secretary for Health and Surgeon General, *The Health Consequences of Smoking: The Changing Cigarette. A Report of the Surgeon General.* Rockville, Md.: U.S. Department of

Health and Human Services, Public Health Service, 1981.

2. G. H. Miller and D. R. Gerstein, "The Life Expectancy of Nonsmoking Men and Women." *Public Health Reports*, Vol. 98, 1983, pp. 343–9, quoted in Jonathan E. Fielding, "Smoking: Health Effects and Control;" *The New England Journal of Medicine*, Vol. 313, No. 8 (August 22, 1985), p. 491.

3. American Cancer Society, *1985 Cancer Facts and Figures*, p. 9.

4. Massachusetts Department of Public Health/ Massachusetts Hospital Association brochure, "Are You Really a Non-Smoker?"

5. American Cancer Society, op. cit., p. 17.

6. Miller and Gerstein, op. cit.

7. Susan Okie, "The Press and Cigarette Ads: Smoke Gets in Their Eyes." *HealthLink*, March 1986, pp. 54–5.

8. Paul Raeburn, "Caffeine Tied to Panic Attacks in Over 2 Million People." Associated Press, printed in *The Boston Globe*, October 19, 1986, p. 23.

9. Frances Sheridan Goulart, *The Caffeine Book: A User's and Abuser's Guide*. New York: Dodd, Mead and Co., 1984. Thorough coverage of health effects of caffeine-containing foods and beverages.

10. Hershel Jick, et al., "Coffee and Myocardial Infarction: A Report from the Boston Collaborative Drug Surveillance Project." *The New England Journal of Medicine*, Vol. 289, No. 2 (July 12, 1973), pp. 63–7.

11. Goulart, op. cit.

12. Jean Kinney and Gwen Leaton, *Loosening the Grip*. St. Louis, Mo.: C. V. Mosby Co., 1978, p. 223.

13. Barbara Gordon, *I'm Dancing as Fast as I Can*. New York: Harper & Row, 1979, pp. 304–5.

14. *Report on the White House Mini-Conference on Older Women*, Alcoholism and Drug Abuse Section, 1980, p. 36.

15. Jacob A. Brody, "Aging and Alcohol Abuse," in *Nature and Extent of Alcohol Problems Among the Elderly*. Presented at the White House Conference on Aging, Washington, DC, 1981, p. 305.

16. Jonica D. Homiller, *Women and Alcohol: A Guide for State and Local Decision Makers*. Washington, DC: The Council of State Authorities, Alcohol and Drug Problems Association of North America, 1977, p. 15.

17. Nancy Taylor, *Alcohol Abuse Prevention Among Women: A Community Approach*. Presented at the National Council on Alcoholism, Washington, DC, 1982, p. 1.

18. C. Samuel Mullin, *Medical Consequences of Chronic Alcohol Abuse*. Boston: Massachusetts Department of Public Health, Division of Alcoholism, 1983.

19. Alvin Rosen, "Psychotherapy and Alcoholics Anonymous. Can They Be Coordinated?" *Bulletin of the Menninger Clinic*, Vol. 45, No. 3 (1981), pp. 229–46.

20. Annabel Hecht, "Medicine and the Elderly." *FDA Consumer*, September 1983, p. 20.

21. Estimate obtained by Carlos Ortiz of CVS from Prescription Drug Services of Phoenix, AZ.

22. "Prescription Drug Pushers" and "Five Dangerous Drugs." *Health Letter*, Vol. 3, July–August 1986, pp. 1, 12.

23. "Another Dangerous Drug." *Health Letter*, Vol. 2, No. 1 (March–April 1986), p. 1.

24. "Report of the Public Health Service Task Force on Women's Health Issues." *Public Health Reports*, Vol. 100, No. 1 (January–February 1985), p. 96.

25. Gail Povar, et al., "Patients' Therapeutic Preferences in an Ambulatory Care Setting." *American Journal of Public Health*, Vol. 74, No. 12 (December 1984), pp. 1395–7.

26. Adapted from the National Council on Patient Information and Education.

27. Marie Feltin, *A Woman's Guide to Good Health After 50*. An AARP Book. Glenview, IL: Scott, Foresman and Company, 1987, p. 174.

28. "Gas, Heartburn and Antacids." *Living Healthy*, Vol. 3, No. 3 (August 1980), pp. 1–12.

29. National Institutes of Health, "The Integrated Approach to the Management of Pain." *Consensus Development Conference Statement*, Vol. 6, No. 3 (May 19–21, 1986).

30. Kathleen M. Foley, "The Treatment of Cancer Pain." *The New England Journal of Medicine*, Vol. 313, No. 2 (July 11, 1985), pp. 84–95.

3

WHO NEEDS COSMETIC SURGERY?
REASSESSING OUR LOOKS
AND OUR LIVES

by Jane Hyman

Herstory—in a Plate

Her face reminds me of my
  grandmother's antique plate—
    cracked with fine-lined patterns
    of living.
I can see either the beauty or the imperfection—
  Usually I see the beauty,
    except when she irritates me, or my
    fears of my own mortality block my vision.
We are both—mortal and perfect—
  beautiful and imperfect—
    a crazed pattern of sanity
    in a cracked world—
  a throwback to another time,
    and a vision yet
      to be.

Molly Smith Strong

Marianne Gontarz

As we get older, we have to come to terms with our changing appearance and others' reactions to it. We wrinkle, our hair turns gray, and our body weight changes and is redistributed. Chronic diseases or disabling conditions can also affect the way we see our bodies. Such challenges require fresh sources of strength and a reassessment of our interests, abilities, and needs.

Looking Older—What It Means to Us

Those of us who grew up knowing and loving our grandparents or other older people probably remember loving their wrinkled faces. In the years before we learned to think of the signs of aging as "unattractive," a wrinkled face was often the most loving and the most beloved face

we knew. However, as adults we live in an environment in which standards of beauty are important, narrow, and restricted to the young.

I have no passion to look eighteen forever, but I still have vanity. I rather hate looking at that reticulated network of wrinkles that looks like downtown Schenectady traffic—but there it is! What can you do about it? [a sixty-nine-year-old woman]

Looking older can be hard on us, since as women we are raised to please others rather than ourselves, and to value ourselves by how pleasing we are to others. This makes us especially vulnerable to the idea that through makeup, hair dyes, face-lifts, diets, and clothes we can—and must—live up to a certain ideal of beauty. Many of us were very hard on ourselves in our younger years, not beginning to accept or like our faces or bodies until we were in our late thirties or early forties. We may have hardly overcome early prejudices against ourselves—hips too large, nose too small—when we are faced with another: ageism.

When I was thirty-eight I looked at my naked body in the mirror, and for the first time in my life thought, "Gee, nice!" And then I started aging. [a fifty-two-year-old woman]

The quest for physical perfection may be taken more seriously by women in the United States than by women in other countries. America is a young and powerful country and it admires the young and powerful. The message is that we only count if we are white, slender, attractive, able-bodied—and young. For some women, especially in midlife, this narrow standard of acceptability leads to a period of grieving over the loss of "peak" years. Barbara MacDonald (age sixty-nine), co-author of a book on ageism, reflects on her own aging:

Sometimes lately...I see my arm with the skin hanging loosely from my forearm and cannot believe that it is really my own. It seems disconnected from me; it is someone else's. It is the arm of an old woman. It is the arm of such old women as I myself have seen, sitting on benches in the sun with their hands folded in their laps; old women I have turned away from. I wonder now how and when these arms I see came to be my own—arms I cannot turn away from.[1]

Middle-aged men are a possible exception to the generally narrow standard of looks. According to one study, they are considered even more attractive than young men. This same study showed that middle-aged women are considered less attractive than young women, and that old men and women are both considered less attractive than the young or middle-aged. Some researchers think that middle-aged men gain in attractiveness because others see them as being at the peak of success in their social roles. Conversely, middle-aged women, seen primarily as mothers, are considered to be past their social usefulness because they are no longer bearers of children.[2] If looks are associated with usefulness and power, it may be that the looks of old age are considered unattractive because the elderly are seen as useless and powerless. As middle-aged and older women become more powerful, others may see them as more attractive. We may see ourselves as more attractive as well.

Sometimes I think of the alternatives to looking older, and I wonder what it would be like to have my face

frozen the way it was in my thirties, and I think—that would be ridiculous! That's not me, that doesn't reflect the years I've lived and all the things I've experienced. I don't want to deny my experiences and I feel that if I dislike my aging looks I'm denying all the wonderful parts of my life. I don't want to do that. [a forty-eight-year-old woman]

Women's responses to looking older vary greatly. Women who grew up in warmly affectionate families where they were hugged, kissed, and cuddled, for example, tend to accept their bodies as they are. There are indications that women whose families provided opportunities for physical activity or who were athletes in high school and college feel more positive about their looks than women without such experiences.[3] In general, warm, close family relationships and physical activity foster self-confidence and high self-esteem. When self-esteem is high, body image is often positive. Considering the importance of athletics and self-esteem, it is no surprise that studies show that men (always encouraged to participate in sports) *over*rate their body image, thinking that others have a higher opinion of their looks than they actually do, while women *under*rate their body image, thinking others have a lower opinion of their looks than they do.[4]

If you were considered unusually attractive as a younger woman, looking older may be more difficult for you than for a woman who never set great store by her looks. A woman who is constantly praised for being pretty may come to believe that her worth as a person depends on her looks. A woman who never considered herself pretty, however, has already dealt with that issue and gone beyond it.

Marianne Gontarz

Women who are concerned about looking older seem to experience this concern during midlife up to their middle or late sixties. In fact, many women in midlife like *getting* older; they feel freer and more confident. What they don't like is *looking* older.[5]

I'm forty-three now and this whole past year I've felt a sense of getting older which I never did before. When I look in the mirror, I don't like what I see, so I don't look at myself. When I go someplace I try to forget about what I look like, and that isn't the way it used to be. I used to think, "Today I look good!"

In later years, this concern tends to disappear. It seems that the anticipation of looking older is more distressing than the actual experience. Perhaps with the years we learn to place greater value on our inner qualities. Also our own or our partner's health and energy become more important, and losses or other concerns can become paramount.[6]

Body changes as a result of health problems can also cause a temporary or permanent difference in the way we see ourselves. Skin diseases, scaly dryness or chapping of the skin, a stoop due to osteoporosis, and swelling of the joints as a result of arthritis are all visible changes.

I am trying to recognize that my hands are indeed a part of me, and a part of me that I love. Because I do a great deal with my hands, of course, and they are very capable despite the fact that they have these configurations [arthritic swelling]. And I realize that I have indeed been taken in by what a woman's hands should look like, and mostly they're supposed to look pretty useless. My hands don't look useless at all. In fact they look as though they've been used a great deal. [a sixty-four-year-old woman]

Appliances such as a hearing aid, pacemaker, cane, or walker can change our body image, especially when we first begin to wear or use them. They often seem much larger and more conspicuous to us than to anyone else. The effects of drugs, scars or a limp from operations or accidents, and amputated limbs or organs can profoundly influence our body image. Integrating such changes into our self-image is an important factor in feeling whole again despite the loss.

Marianne Gontarz

In a bathing suit I'm not so hot because there is a huge gouge where one hip was taken out, and the incision got infected. That is hard for small children to have to look at so I wear very matronly bathing suits. So my image of myself as a sexy-looking woman went, and I decided to be quaint—a quaint old lady. [a sixty-nine-year-old woman]

As we grow older we may become slightly shorter due to the gradual drying of the discs of the spine or compression fractures caused by osteoporosis. Otherwise, most of the visible changes associated with age occur in the skin, hair, and underlying muscles and fatty tissue.

Since the skin is susceptible to influences from inside and outside the body, it is hard to distinguish between "normal" signs of aging and those caused by environmental damage, such as overexposure to sunlight. Skin changes which normally occur with time can be accelerated by exposure to the elements, especially radiation from the sun. Black and olive-skinned women experience a slower rate of change with age, partly because of the larger amounts of melanin (pigment) in their skin. Some women find as they age that they sunburn more easily. All women can protect themselves against skin damage and skin cancer by avoiding tanning and sunburning.*

Skin cells grow more slowly with age, and the outer layer of skin is not shed and replaced at the same rate as in younger years. Changes in a protein called collagen make the skin stiffer and less pliable, and some sebaceous glands which provide oil for the hair and skin become less active. With age, cells lose some of their ability to retain water, causing dryness. Some women relieve dryness and itching by patting themselves dry after washing, and applying cream or oil while the skin is still moist. It can also help to bathe less often and to use only a mild or creamy soap or no soap at all on trouble areas.

As the skin loses tone and elasticity it sags and wrinkles, especially in areas where there is frequent movement, such as the face, neck, and joints. Sagging is also caused by the pull of gravity over the years. The underlying muscles and fatty tissue undergo similar changes. Small blood vessels become more fragile due to thinning of the vessel walls, and can cause frequent black-and-blue marks. "Age spots" (also called

*See pages 60–61 on need for obtaining vitamin D from sunlight.

"liver spots") may appear. They would be more appropriately called sun spots, since they are caused by exposure to sunlight over the years. Hair becomes thinner as hair follicles decrease their activity, and grayer as cells stop producing a color-determining pigment. These gradual changes are a part of the cycle of life, and everyone who lives long enough will experience some of them.

How Weight Influences The Way We See Ourselves

As we grow older, many of us tend to gain weight. Since our metabolism slows down, our bodies need fewer calories, yet we often consume the same amount of food as in our younger years (see Weighty Issues chapter). Many of us get less exercise or have disabling conditions that keep us sedentary. Weight gain in our older years can be particularly hard to accept because we are also trying to come to terms with other changes in our bodies.

I went to Weight Watchers and lost eight pounds. But I gained them right back. Then last summer I fractured my shoulder. I was home a lot. It was a terribly hot summer. The only exercise I got was a little walk every day. That walk always included a stop at the ice cream parlor. Now I look in the mirror and I say: "You are fat!" and I don't like it. [a seventy-three-year-old woman]

Studies have shown that the value placed on thinness in advertising has a strong impact on us. Many women live in constant fear of gaining another pound. We tend to see ourselves as overweight even when we are within what is generally considered a desirable weight range. Women want to be even thinner than men want them to be.[7] The influence of advertising is also evident in the growing incidence of eating disorders such as anorexia and bulimia in middle-aged women.[8]

It isn't easy to fight the effects of advertising single-handedly. Through body-image workshops, reading, or exercise, we can make our image of ourselves more positive. It is worth trying to accept our size rather than using our energy disliking our bodies and going on unnecessary diets.

When I swim or walk regularly I feel stronger and more energetic and my body is more limber. My weight stays the same but people say to me, "You've lost weight!" as if only pounds mattered. [a fifty-three-year-old woman]

Some women think that if they learn to accept and love their bodies they will just eat everything and gain more weight. Only punishment through diet can work, they believe. But, in fact, many women have found that if you punish your body you cannot lead it to a positive, healthy state. "You have to love your body *before* you can change it—if indeed you wish to change it once you love it."[9]

Belly dancing is an example of an exercise only weighty women can do well. The movements make you feel sensuous, not heavy. Belly dancers love their bellies, have fun "throwing their weight around," and benefit from the exercise.

THE "BEAUTY" BUSINESS

As they grow older, many women attempt to mask or alter their physical appearance. Even the poorest women spend money on cosmetics and beauty parlors.* Some of us wear makeup, or more of it, and dye our hair. According to one survey, most women who color their hair do so to cover the gray. This is most common among women in their forties and fifties, 45 percent of whom dye their hair.[10]

It is hard to resist the temptation to alter our appearances, since in every store we see bottles, tubes, and jars containing cosmetics advertised to make us more attractive and younger-looking. The cosmetics industry makes millions of dollars by reinforcing the message that we need not, dare not, look older. As the population ages, advertisements abound for products which are said to prevent or hide wrinkles.

Advertisements for skin care preparations and advice columns in the women's magazines spell out an impossible prescription: clear, fresh, firm, and youthful [skin] ... in short, a skin that shows no sign of physical maturity, hard work, aggravation, exhaustion, hormonal changes, the effects of pregnancy, or the normal wear and tear of daily living.[11]

*There are signs that more and more men, new victims of the youth culture, are becoming intensely concerned about looks and aging. More men buy cosmetics and undergo plastic surgery and hair transplants than ever before. Shari Miller, "A New Image." *Vogue,* January 1985, p. 243.

Cosmetics manufacturers are not required to obtain FDA approval before putting their products on the market. Responsible manufacturers test their products for safety before marketing. Still, many cosmetics contain dangerous substances.* One hundred cosmetic ingredients are suspected chemical hazards, according to the National Institute of Occupational Safety and Health.[12] Many of these hazardous substances can be absorbed through the skin, including the scalp. Be wary of cosmetics that list hormones in the ingredients. They usually contain estrogen, which can affect the body's hormonal balance. Reported effects of hormonal cosmetics include vaginal bleeding in women over sixty-five.[13] Lipstick enters the body through the throat along with food and drink. Many lipsticks and other cosmetics contain color additives that cause cancer in laboratory animals. These colors include reds 3, 8, 9, 19, and 37, and orange 17.[14] Petroleum-based hair dyes, mostly in dark shades, cause cancer in laboratory animals. If you do color your hair, a hair crayon, available from a beauty-supply store, can help you use less hair dye by extending the time between hair-dyeing applications.

For a small but growing number of women, the need to look young or thin may be so strong that they choose to undergo surgical procedures such as face or eyelid lifts, or surgery that slenderizes the abdomen, thighs, or buttocks, or de-wrinkles hands.† Women seem to be choosing such operations earlier, between forty and fifty—even in their thirties. Some women hope that plastic surgery will lead to a major life change, but surgery is no guarantee that a woman will get or keep a partner or a job, nor is it a cure for low self-esteem.

Plastic surgery increased 61 percent between 1981 and 1984, making it one of the fastest-growing medical specialties in the country.[15]

The risks of plastic surgery include scarring, severing of a facial nerve, infection, hemorrhage, and blockage of a blood vessel in the lung or brain. The latter three risks can cause severe impairment and, in rare cases, even death.[16]

*You can work for greater cosmetic safety by writing your representative in Congress and demanding that the Food, Drug, and Cosmetics Act of 1938 be amended to include required testing and FDA approval of cosmetics *before* marketing.

†Wrinkles, sags, and fat deposits are called "deformities" in medical literature on cosmetic surgery.

Other complications include blindness caused by bleeding behind the eyes. High blood pressure can cause excessive bleeding during surgery. Women who take large amounts of aspirin should stop five to seven days prior to surgery, since the drug interferes with clotting. A recent study showed that 10 percent of people who had face-lifts experienced skin slough, the death of skin from inadequate blood supply, after surgery. The majority of those who experienced skin slough smoked more than one pack of cigarettes a day.

At a time in life when our risks of medical complications are going up, why expose ourselves to the additional hazards of unnecessary surgery and anesthesia?

THE SOCIAL IMPACT OF LOOKING OLDER

Relationships with Men

Many women fear that looking older means losing the power to attract men. This can mean losing the excitement of sexual attraction and the warmth of physical intimacy. For many women, men have played the role of the great critics of their lives. Men's opinions of our outward appearances, their acceptance or rejection of us based on our looks, have strongly influenced the way we see ourselves.

Last year when a much younger man I was very attracted to told me that what he really wanted was friendship, I felt shattered. I assumed that he rejected me sexually because of my age, and that started a whole train of bad feelings about myself—about growing older and not having anybody love me anymore—especially men. That blow has been repaired by the love and attention of another man, which is wonderful. Yet it bothers me that I seem to be so reliant on the opinions of men, as though I didn't have it within me just to care about myself. It's amazing—since I met this other man I feel much, much better about myself. It's as though I look in the mirror and see a different person—as though my whole outward appearance changes in my own eyes, to be built up or torn down by someone else. [a forty-five-year-old woman]

Unattached women seeking a sexual partner are often more concerned with signs of age than those who feel secure in a marriage or relationship.[17] Midlife divorce can heighten a woman's sense of competition, throwing her back into the "dating game."

Women who feel sexually dissatisfied in long-standing marriages or relationships may be frustrated because they believe that their age makes it impossible to have new sexual experiences.

I have tried to talk about sexuality with my husband but it's been a long time, a long marriage, and it's very hard to change things. Then when I read The Hite Report I suddenly found myself validated. I hadn't known that I had any sexual rights and that the desires that I had were normal desires of a so-called normal woman. It made me feel a lot better, but also it made me feel that I'd been cheated. I was fifty or so and I felt that I could not retrieve some of these things or start over again because I was not sexually attractive enough anymore. I thought that these are privileges of the young. You have to have a smooth body, no wrinkles—be "juicy," as I call it. This voice kept telling me, "You're too old for that; who would want you?" And I was angry, at being "too old." [a sixty-one-year-old woman]

Some women who are in generally unsatisfactory marriages or relationships may stay in the relationship, afraid that they are too old to find another partner.[18]

With the years we may feel that our partners turn away from us, and this can cause or reinforce negative feelings about our looks. It helps to realize that low self-esteem can cause us to perceive rejection when none was intended.[19] Finding a new relationship or a new source of self-esteem can help us overcome negative feelings.

It's nice to be appreciated. I can tell by the way he looks at me that he loves my face and my body, as old as it is. [a sixty-eight-year-old woman, remarried five years]

Now, I feel I have to press ahead in the world out of some inner sense of myself rather than with the help of my looks. And that's exciting because it makes me more adventurous. I'm working on my Ph.D. and preparing for a life of teaching and scholarly writing. As a younger woman I wouldn't have had the courage to embark on such a challenging career. [a forty-three-year-old woman]

I'm no longer the completely lonely person I was before because I have established an inner strength. I find new patience and compassion with others. I had always thought that the emptiness in me could only be filled by someone else. I'm finally discovering that I can be a complete and happy person through my own inner resources. [a sixty-eight-year-old woman]

Some women have found their relationships unsatisfactory and burdensome, and are not concerned about looking young for men.

Now that I'm fifty-two—who needs an old man around! And he'll be retired pretty soon and sitting around all day. It's different when a woman retires because she has friends and can get around with other women. But when a man retires you've still got to cook for him and wash. He doesn't have any friends—he just sits there, in the way.

Relationships with Women

Some lesbian women may be less concerned with weight gain and aging than heterosexual women. Loving another woman can change the way a woman sees her body.

When I came out as a lesbian at thirty-seven, my body image changed. My lover's body was like mine, with breasts and curves, yet different. Our love was based on mutual respect and caring, bodies came second. I remember looking in the mirror a couple of years after we met and noting that my body seemed to have changed. My breasts hung lower, were less prominent. But mostly it was the feeling inside me that had changed. My breasts were part of a whole, not something to be leered at or mauled. I found myself looking at my breasts and body with pleasure. I liked what I saw. I claimed my body. [a forty-two-year-old woman]

Although I do have difficulty with aging, I believe that it is easier as a lesbian. I am less self-conscious about cosmetic perfection, about weight gain and wrinkles— and feel that I have more sexual/romantic opportunities than a straight woman of my age. I cannot say that I love getting older. However, I am more comfortable with myself than I have ever been before. And peaceful. I feel confident, for the most part, attractive and assured. My life is rich, full, adventurous and really quite wonderful. [a fifty-year-old woman]

But many lesbian women feel a strong pressure to look young and see themselves at a disadvantage in finding partners.

I cannot say that I am unselfconscious or not preoccupied at times with aging. Most of my self-esteem as a young woman was based on my looks and it has been a shock and an adjustment to have wrinkles and look older, especially when I feel so young inside. I am self-conscious about approaching younger women, worry about being inappropriate and question what younger women see in me in terms of my looks. My lovers have all been much younger than me, which is a concern. I worry that I will not remain attractive to them and what their reactions will be to my aging and possibly declining health. [a fifty-year-old woman]

Work

For many of us, our main concerns about looking older center on our power to earn money and to be valued as workers. As we look for jobs, or want to change from an unsatisfactory job, we become aware that looking older can mean being unemployable.

I do free-lance work in a young business. All the people I deal with are my age or younger, and each time I have a new project interview I go thinking, "Do I look young enough, do I look young?" I'm afraid people will stop hiring me, because you don't hire fifty-year-old women to do this kind of stuff. I'm scared about what it means for me professionally. [a thirty-nine-year-old woman]

Sometimes we can counteract employers' or colleagues' ageist attitudes with the help of our own strong self-esteem and/or the support of other older workers.

At first it seemed strange to me that everyone in the department is about thirty-five years younger than I am. But then I thought, if they have trouble dealing with a colleague old enough to be their mother, that's their problem! [a sixty-nine-year-old woman]

If you use your beauty to get a job, a man, then you are always indebted to it. You're always chasing it, looking in the mirror to see if it is still there. Once you stop that and realize you can use your head, your whole person, nobody can take that from you! You are powerful if you realize you have a brain and can use it. Society says: "You are no longer valuable because you aren't gorgeous." We say we are valuable, because we think and do. [a sixty-five-year-old woman]

Some women find that being older brings more respect and power on the job. Looking older increases our credibility and authority. Being older brings better judgment and wisdom. We can speak more freely and be listened to. These advantages depend on the kind of work we do, and seem to be greater in the professional world.[20]

As a therapist, my age really is an advantage. I have a much larger store of experiences and understanding of what makes people tick and of what kinds of things happen to people, just because I've lived so much longer. [a seventy-nine-year-old woman]

Being older has helped me in my profession. I have much more authority: the fact that I'm known, that I've published, my experience in running a department. With my students I don't have to prove that I know something; they take that for granted. Certainly it would be much more difficult at twenty-five to be the authority I am. It would be impossible! Whatever my fears may be, whatever my private problems, what my students see is a woman of power. [a fifty-six-year-old woman]

AGE AND IDENTITY

We live in a culture that rejects us for our looks just when we have the most to offer. Some women feel betrayed by such a society. Some of us, however, feel sorry for those who cannot see through our wrinkles and gray hair to our talents and abilities.

When I was younger I was considered more attractive than I am now. I no longer feel as though people look at me and say "Oh, wow, what an attractive woman," which they did when I was younger. And I feel sorry for them because I am really a much more interesting person now than I was then. But that's their problem. [a sixty-five-year-old woman]

Our culture's view of how older women should look and behave is constricting to them and detrimental to society as a whole. Many women refuse to be confined by set images of what they should look like, be, and do. We dress and move according to our tastes and our personalities. We are as emotionally and physically involved with life as our wishes and our health allow. We see aging as a new experience for which we are setting the pace.

Getting old can be wonderful if you're not imposed on by other people's rules about how you should be when you're old. I consciously break as many as I can because then I'm breaking through oppression. [a sixty-five-year-old woman]

Life's less confusing for me now, things are falling into place. In a way I feel happier than I did at thirty—I like myself much better. And I think that's a key point—to like oneself, to be your own best friend. [a fifty-seven-year-old woman]

We can choose whether or not to use the technology—cosmetics, plastic surgery—offered us to look younger. And, in fact, many women find that instead of wanting to look different they see an inner and outer beauty in themselves and other older women that they didn't see before. Some of us find that we like signs of aging and that they make a face more interesting than the smoothness of youth. We respond to other, last-

Mikki Ansin

ing qualities of appearance, such as bone structure, or an alert, lively expression.

I know a lot of handsome older women. They have character! They're people! They've lived! One friend my age has the most animated, humorous, charming face. She would really beguile anybody! [a seventy-nine-year-old woman]

Self-confidence brings us a freedom many of us never felt in our younger years; we no longer feel obliged to be youthfully "feminine" sex objects. We feel free to be ourselves, to be honest and outspoken, and are relieved and relaxed with this freedom.

You can make conscious efforts to change your own and others' ideas of beauty. Older women can learn, from the impact of the phrase "Black is beautiful," how to raise self-esteem. One way to do so is to tell your older friends how good they look, how alive and interesting. Tell them how fine and handsome are the visible signs of

Marianne Gontarz

years, experiences, and character. This is an important way women can help each other deal with our culture's negative attitude toward age.

NOTES

1. Barbara MacDonald and Cynthia Rich, *Look Me in the Eye*. San Francisco: Spinsters, Ink., 1983, p. 14.

2. Gwendolyn T. Sorell and Carol A. Nowak, "The Role of Physical Attractiveness as a Contributor to Individual Development," in Richard M. Lerner and Nancy A. Busch Rossnagel, eds., *Individuals as Producers of Their Own Development: A Life-Span Perspective*. New York: Academic Press, 1981, pp. 389–446.

3. Jan Benowitz Eigner, "Interaction and Building of Body Concept and Self Concept Over the Lifespan: A Study of 20 Women Age 40 to 60." Unpublished dissertation, Saint Louis University, 1984.

4. Daniel Goleman, "Dislike of Own Body Found Common Among Women." *The New York Times*, March 19, 1985, pp. C1, C5.

5. Diane White, "An Age-Old Problem." *The Boston Globe*, October 26, 1983.

6. Carol A. Nowak, "Does Youthfulness Equal Attractiveness?" in Lillian E. Troll, Joan Israel, and Kenneth Israel, eds., *Looking Ahead: A Woman's Guide to the Problems and Joys of Growing Older*. New York: Prentice Hall, 1977.

7. Jennifer Robinson, "Body Image in Women over Forty." *The Melpomene Report*, Melpomene Institute for Women's Health Research, 316 University Ave., St. Paul, MN 55103, October 1983, pp. 12–4.

8. While eating disorders are epidemic among adolescent women, their incidence, although small, is growing alarmingly among middle-aged women.

9. Marcia Germaine Hutchinson, author of *Transforming Body Image*, quoted in "Body Hatred." *McCall's*, April 1985, p. 136.

10. Clairol, 1983, as cited in Robin Marantz Henig, *How a Woman Ages*. New York: Ballantine Books, 1985, p. 61.

11. Susan Brownmiller, *Femininity*. New York: Fawcett, 1985.

12. Jane E. Brody, "Personal Health." *The New York Times*, September 19, 1984.

13. *The Medical Letter on Drugs and Therapeutics*, June 21, 1985.

14. *Health Facts*, Center for Medical Consumers, Inc., New York, October 1985.

15. Report of the American Society of Plastic and Reconstructive Surgeons, cited in *Newsweek*, May 24, 1985.

16. Robin Marantz Henig and the editors of *Esquire*, *How a Woman Ages—Growing Older: What to Expect and What You Can Do About It*. New York: Ballantine Books, 1985, p. 28.

17. Cleo S. Berkun, "Changing Appearance for Women in the Middle Years of Life," in Elizabeth W. Markson, ed., *Older Women*. Lexington, MA: D. C. Heath/Lexington Books, 1983, p. 24.

18. Berkun, op. cit., p. 28.

19. Troll, Israel, and Israel, op. cit., p. 51.

20. Berkun, op. cit., p. 24.

4

WEIGHTY ISSUES

by Jane Hyman, Diana Laskin Siegal,
and Elizabeth Volz

Special thanks to Esther Rome, Robin Cohen, and Mary P. Clarke

In this country we are preoccupied with weight. Every women's magazine has articles on diets and "fitness." In the general mania for thinness, many of us think we are overweight when we really are not.

Many women avoid healthful foods they think are fattening and skip meals in an effort to lose weight. "Fat phobia"—the fear of being fat—can interfere with proper nutrition. We can feel well and strong without being exploited by the multimillion-dollar weight-loss and fitness industries. Our money is better spent on healthful foods and activities that are fun, sociable, and cause no injury.

ANOTHER LOOK AT DIETING AND WEIGHT

Each of us has a unique size, shape, and body chemistry strongly determined by heredity.[1] How much we weigh is a function of energy input (food), energy used (activity), our own body's rate of using energy (metabolism), and other factors that are not well understood. The amount of energy we use to perform tasks, including sedentary activities such as office work and reading,[2] can vary from woman to woman. Studies show that fat women generally do not eat more nor are they less physically active than thin women.[3] The difference is in the fat woman's naturally larger build and in her rate of metabolism.

Because of the constant pressure to be thin,

many women try sporadically or constantly to lose weight by reducing the calories they consume. This is so common that to most of us the term "diet," which in its original meaning simply refers to what we eat, has come to mean a plan to lose weight. Dieting to lose weight can become a way of life. Most dieters never learn healthful food habits. When you go on a low-calorie diet, your body reacts as if it were being starved and tries to preserve as much energy as possible by decreasing its rate of metabolism. Your rate of metabolism may slow down more with each diet and remain slower once you return to your usual eating habits. Ironically, this means that after each diet, unless you drastically increase your exercise, you may gain weight more easily than before, since your body adds more fat to protect itself in case you deprive it of food again. This partially explains why 90 to 99 percent of dieters regain their weight within five years, or even regain more than they lost.[4] It also explains why some researchers say that repeated low-calorie dieting may be a major cause of weight gain.[5]

Women are frequently encouraged to lose weight not only because "thin is in" but because medical authorities believe that being "overweight" puts us at risk for a variety of diseases and even death. But studies done on weight and health contradict each other, and many are faulty. Some studies find a relationship between high weight and early death, and others do not. Many studies do not take into account other known health risks such as cigarette smoking,

Rachel Perkis

upper bodies have significantly more hypertension, diabetes, and gallbladder disease than women with fat predominantly on their lower bodies. Relatively more fat from the waist up (as compared to hips) is associated with higher rates of these diseases even among women with comparable total body fat. Arthritis is associated with fat on the hips in some women. In the case of arthritis, factors such as added weight on the joints or the effects of fat tissue on posture and motion appear to be more important than the metabolic activity of the fat tissue.[7] Thin women who jog may be stressing their joints just as much as fat women who walk.

Moreover, our bodies' needs change with age. Some research shows that the ratio of weight to height associated with long life rises with age. Therefore, healthy people should not be concerned if they gain some weight as they move from early adult years to late middle age. The weights in the often-quoted Metropolitan Life Insurance Height and Weight Chart were increased in 1983 but are still too restrictive for women in their fifties and sixties. There are advantages for women in being a little heavier than previously thought—gaining a pound a year is apparently healthy.[8]

As we grow older, some lean muscle tissue is replaced with fatty tissue. Even if we stay the same weight, we will have more fat proportionately at eighty than we did at forty. Since it takes less energy to maintain fat tissue than to maintain muscle tissue, we would have to cut our calories* by 10 to 15 percent from age twenty to age sixty just to maintain the same weight.[8] But if we cut our intake, we may not get adequate nutrition.

Emphasis on "ideal" weight dictated by weight charts masks the damage caused by the constant pressure on women to be thin. Fat women suffer more from discrimination against fat than from any weight-related health problems. Many dieters experience emotional disturbances due to the effects of starvation on the body. Studies show that weight-related emotional disturbances are related to overeating, disparagement of body image, and the complications of dieting. Eating at night, insomnia, and skipping morning meals are associated with stressful life circumstances and often related to

repeated dieting, or hereditary factors, and most studies do not include women. One study which included women (but did not ask if they repeatedly dieted) did find an increase in death rates among women who for many years were 55 percent to 65 percent over the average weight charts.[6] But this means that, depending on your height and build, you would have to be about 65 to 110 pounds "overweight" for many years to be adversely affected.

One of the problems in interpreting weight studies is knowing what the term "overweight" means. We tend to read weight charts with the assumption that "overweight" is bad no matter how old we are, what kind of body tissue we have, and where it is located on the body. But weight can mean many things. Poundage by itself is not a measure of fat; skin-fold measurements and water-immersion tests are better indicators. The weight we add as a result of exercise and body conditioning is not a hazard to our health. Increasing our weight by increasing our muscle mass will strengthen our bones and help prevent osteoporosis.

In addition, recent research shows that when studying the association between weight and disease, not only fat mass but the distribution of fat has to be considered. Fat tissue that was once considered an inert mass on the body is apparently involved in a number of metabolic functions that vary in different parts of the body. Women ages forty to fifty-nine with fat distribution predominantly on their waists and

*A calorie is simply a way of estimating the energy available in a particular food.

depression,[10] perhaps made worse by fruitless dieting attempts.

The following "diets" have dangers in addition to the general hazards mentioned above.

• The use of "diet pills." Just because a drug is prescribed by a doctor doesn't mean that it is either effective or safe. Many prescription "diet pills" contain amphetamine, a stimulant that speeds up the body's processes and can cause insomnia and diarrhea. It is addictive, toxic, and can even cause violent behavior and death. Also, don't assume that, because something is sold over the counter (OTC) without a prescription, it is harmless. Most OTC diet pills contain phenylpropanolamine (PPA), which is chemically similar to amphetamine. PPA raises blood pressure and alters brain function, but is not a proven aid to weight loss. It is also used as a nasal decongestant and is found in many cold remedies. Many diet pills and cold remedies also contain caffeine, which heightens the effect of PPA. Even recommended doses can cause confusion and hallucinations; high doses can cause heart damage, seizures, strokes, and even death. **A person can easily overdose by combining diet pills and cold remedies.**

• High-protein/low-carbohydrate, and sometimes high-fat diets. These raise triglycerides (fats) in the blood, promote dangerously high levels of ketones in the blood, increase calcium loss, and trigger carbohydrate "binges." Very low carbohydrate intake can cause fainting spells and depression.

• Grapefruit, banana, egg, or other limited-food diets. No single food is a "magic" way to reduce weight. No enzymes in them melt away or otherwise remove fat from our bodies. High-egg diets are also high in cholesterol. These diets lack the nutrients you can obtain only by eating a variety of foods.

• Powdered-protein or high-protein liquid diets. These products (also called protein-sparing) are supposed to protect the lean body mass. They have many adverse effects, such as causing irregular heartbeats and even sudden death.[11] They should be used only under the close supervision of a research physician skilled in weight loss.

• Special supplement combinations, such as vinegar, lecithin, kelp, and vitamin B_6. These substances by themselves do not cause weight loss. Rather, weight loss is achieved through the limited-calorie diet which is supposed to accompany the supplements.

An increase in two severe eating problems which primarily affect women, anorexia nervosa and bulimia, reflects the general tendency in society to promote thinness at all costs. Anorexia is a form of severe and initially deliberate self-starvation; bulimia is an eating pattern of bingeing and then purging, usually by vomiting or laxative usage. Anorexia is more common among young women, but it is increasing among older women. Bulimia seems to be found among all age groups. Anorexia and bulimia can result from severe psychological distress as well as cause it. Both create many physical problems, including loss of tooth enamel (from regurgitated stomach acid), loss of ability to absorb food properly, loss of the gag reflex, and imbalances in the body's fluids severe enough to cause death. Even some best-seller diets encourage these methods as ways to lose weight.[12]

Therapists who treat people with eating problems agree with the feminist critics who first pointed out that anorexia and bulimia affect women more than men because of women's lack of power in society and because of the constant messages that women should be thin.

I felt out of control in my life. This was the one place where I could exert control—over my eating—and I did. Ultimately, however, I didn't have control of it—it had control of me. I could not stop when I wanted to. [a forty-five-year-old woman]

Being Thin

With all the emphasis on thinness, we may be so proud of ourselves if our weight is low that we do not realize when we are malnourished. Thin people are more susceptible to certain diseases, including lung diseases, fatal infections, ulcers, and anemia.[13] Studies show that older people who are "significantly underweight" die sooner than those who are not.[14] But the term "underweight" is just as controversial as the term "overweight."* Many weight studies do not take into account smoking and preexisting diseases that might have caused both the thinness and the early death.

Being thin is just as natural for some women

*Underweight is usually defined as 10 to 15 percent below the Metropolitan Life Insurance weight-for-height charts.

as being heavy is for others. However, as older women, we frequently lose weight simply because we fail to eat enough. This may be a consequence of depression or loneliness, lack of interest in preparing or eating food, physical conditions that make preparing food or chewing difficult, not being able to afford enough to eat, and changes in the ability to taste food as we age. Certain drugs and certain illnesses, such as Type I diabetes, overactive thyroid, and cancer, can also cause weight loss. If you lose weight and are not sure why, or if you have no appetite, you should see your health care provider to make sure there is not an underlying problem.

FEELING WELL: ACHIEVING A HEALTHFUL FOOD/ACTIVITY BALANCE

The entire concept of an "ideal" weight for any woman or group of women should be abandoned.[15] Instead, we should focus on getting plenty of good food and exercise. We need to create new patterns for dealing with food and activity if old patterns are not serving us well. Here are some suggestions.

- *Listen to your own body's feelings of hunger and fullness.* Years of dieting and bingeing can cause us to lose awareness of our body's signals. Eat when you are hungry and stop when you are full.
- *Learn good nutrition.* Basically, this means cutting down on high-fat foods and replacing them with whole grains, vegetables, fruits, and legumes. If you ate four candy bars a day you would get 1600 calories but you wouldn't be feeding your body what it needs.
- *Exercise.* Begin slowly. Don't do more than feels comfortable, or you won't keep it up. Statistics from many studies show that if you use 300 to 350 calories a day in exercise (2100 to 2500 per week), you will feel happier, more energetic, and stronger. Some people take two or more years to work up to that level. In 20 minutes you consume about 90 calories in light housework, 100 calories in brisk walking, and 240 calories in swimming. In one study, weighty women who simply added a half-hour walk to their daily routines without changing their calorie intake lost twenty pounds in a year.[16]

Months of pain and inactivity had seriously limited my ability to move. I love to swim, but at first I could only walk the length of the pool, though the support of the water made it easier. When I felt well enough to swim one length, I had to rest until my heart stopped pounding. It took twenty months, with setbacks from illnesses which meant I had to work up slowly again, for me to be able to do thirty lengths in one hour. Now with swimming, some walking, and stair-climbing, I've reached my goal of 2000 calories of exercise a week. [a sixty-one-year-old woman]

- *If your caloric intake is too low, try to eat more.* This is usually best accomplished by eating small, frequent snacks that are high in nutrition and calories, such as ice cream, puddings, milk shakes, cheese, nuts, nut butters, and whole-grain cookies, crackers, and muffins. Choose the vegetables and fruits that have the most calories. Use the fortified instant breakfast drinks and meal-in-a-can drinks *in addition to* your regular foods. Flavor your food with herbs and spices. Arrange to eat with others when you do not feel like eating.
- *Keep records.* Keep daily records of exercise, and of what and how much you eat (written within fifteen minutes of eating). If you discover you are gaining or losing more weight than you wish, a review of accurately kept records can be enlightening. One woman thought she should cut calories by giving up bread. Keeping a record showed her that eating bread helped her avoid overeating. Consider the records over a period of a week rather than for each day.
- *Set goals for success.* Unrealistic food and exercise goals set you up to fail. Sometimes the only achievable goal seems small (one day a week I'll carry a piece of fruit to work instead of cookies), but the fact that you *do* achieve it helps you take the next step.
- *Control your environment.* Make your meals as attractive, tasty, and fun as possible. Try moving your TV into the bedroom and take your planned snack with you to enjoy during late-night watching. Don't skip parties and celebrations because you want to avoid food. Enjoy yourself and choose nutritious food—or bring your own.
- *Enjoy what you choose to do or to eat.* For example, when choosing among several kinds of cookies, remember that an oatmeal-raisin cookie gives you more nutrients than a chocolate cookie. A glass of skim milk and a potato

Jane Jewell

have approximately the same number of calories as the same size glass of Coke and ten to fifteen potato chips. But the first two provide protein, calcium, vitamins A and D, and other nutrients while the latter provide calories and little else. If you decide on the chocolate cookie or the potato chips, enjoy them. When you decide to treat yourself to a favorite food, whatever it may be, this is an informed choice, not a "failure."

Last night at a restaurant I chose fried shrimp and French fried potatoes because I wanted them. I didn't fool myself by ordering broiled fish and a baked potato which I really didn't want and then pretending I wasn't adding extra butter. I felt satisfied and know I won't binge the way I used to when I felt deprived. [a fifty-eight-year-old woman]

I have developed such a sweet tooth in my old age. I just can't resist candy or sweets when I have them in the house. My neighbor told me about a wonderful substitute: frozen banana slices. You freeze the banana peeled and wrapped in foil, then slice as many slices as you want with a sharp knife and rewrap the rest. It's amazing how much a banana tastes like candy when it is frozen. [a seventy-five-year-old woman]

I keep my favorite nutritious snacks in the refrigerator —low-fat cole slaw, cold boiled potatoes, and steamed broccoli—to counter the conditioned siren-call to high-fat foods that fills TV, magazines, and newspapers. Sometimes I feel the whole world is out to get my money, and to hell with my health. [a sixty-one-year-old woman]

NOTES

1. Albert J. Stunkard, et al., "An Adoption Study of Human Obesity." *The New England Journal of Medicine*, Vol. 314, No. 4 (January 23, 1986), pp. 193–8. Though the title mentions only obesity, the study showed that the relationship between biological parents and adoptees was not confined to the obesity weight group but was present across the whole range of fatness—from very thin to very fat. The conclusion was that family environment alone has no apparent effect. Obesity is usually defined as at least 20 percent over the "ideal weight" according to life insurance weight tables.

2. Susan C. Wooley, O. W. Wooley, and Susan R. Dyrenforth, "Theoretical, Practical, and Social Issues in Behavioral Treatments of Obesity." *Journal of Applied Behavior Analysis*, Vol. 1, Spring 1979, p. 8.

3. Susan C. Wooley and O. W. Wooley, "Obesity and Women—I. A Closer Look at the Facts." *Women's Studies International Quarterly*, Vol. 2, 1979, pp. 69–79.

4. W. Bennett and J. Gurin, "Do Diets Really Work?" *Science*, Vol. 82, March 1983, p. 43.

5. Wooley and Wooley, op. cit.

6. Artemis Simopoulos and T. Van Itallie, "Body Weight, Health, and Longevity." *Annals of Internal Medicine*, Vol. 100, No. 2 (February 1984), pp. 285–95.

7. Arthur J. Hartz, David C. Rupley, and Alfred A. Rimm, "The Association of Girth Measurements with Disease in 32,856 Women." *American Journal of Epidemiology*, Vol. 119, No. 1 (1984), pp. 71–80.

8. Reubin Andres, "Impact of Age on Weight Goals." *Health Implications of Obesity*, Program and Abstracts, National Institutes of Health Consensus Development Conference, February 11–23, 1985, pp. 77–80. More complete information is available in Reubin Andres, et al., eds., *Principles of Geriatric Medicine*. New York: McGraw-Hill, 1985, pp. 311–8.

9. Daphne A. Roe, *Geriatric Nutrition*. Englewood Cliffs, N. J.: Prentice-Hall, 1983, p. 64.

10. Albert Stunkard and Thomas A. Wadden, "The Adverse Psychological Effects of Obesity." *Health Implications of Obesity*, NIH Consensus Development Conference, February 11–13, 1985, pp. 59–62.

11. Rafael A. Lantigua, et al., "Cardiac Arrhythmias Associated with a Liquid Protein Diet for the Treatment of Obesity." *The New England Journal of Medicine*, Vol. 303, No. 13 (September 25, 1980), pp. 735–8.

12. O. Wayne Wooley and Susan Wooley, "The Beverly Hills Eating Disorders: The Mass Marketing of Anorexia Nervosa." *International Journal of Eating Disorders*, Vol. 1, No. 3 (1982), pp. 57–69.

13. Paul Ensberger, "Fat and Thin Not Black and White." *Radiance*, Vol. III, Spring 1986, pp. 21–2.

14. Simopoulos and Van Itallie, op. cit.

15. T. R. Knapp, "A Methodological Critique of the 'Ideal Weight' Concept." *Journal of the American Medical Association*, Vol. 250, 1983, pp. 505–10.

16. G. Gwinup, "Effects of Exercise Alone on the Weight of Obese Women." *Archives of International Medicine*, Vol. 135, 1975, pp. 676–80.

5

EATING WELL

by Elizabeth Volz and Diana Laskin Siegal with help from Mary P. Clarke

Special thanks to Kathleen I. MacPherson

Food is important to us on many levels. What we eat is connected to our health, our feelings about ourselves, our social and family ties, our ethnic backgrounds, and our roles as women.

When I was sick with the flu as a little girl, my mother would fix me chicken soup. To this day I never smell chicken soup but what I don't remember how much better it made me feel then. Even now when I'm feeling bad, I'll want some soup like my mother made for me. This canned stuff is not a good substitute. [a sixty-eight-year-old woman]

Many of us are experienced in meal planning and preparing food. We may have spent many hours clipping and trying out new recipes or preparing our family's favorites over and over again. Being responsible for one to three meals a day, seven days a week, however, can sometimes dampen our enthusiasm for cooking. Many of us are more familiar with taking care of others than with taking care of ourselves. It may be hard to prepare a nice meal for ourselves when we feel lonely. Or we may enjoy the freedom from fixed schedules and complicated meals but fail to pay attention to our nutritional needs.

Since my husband died and my youngest daughter left home, I find it hard to prepare real meals for myself. If I haven't planned ahead, I'll stand at the refrigerator and eat whatever is handy—pickles, ice cream, cold weenies, whatever. [a fifty-five-year-old woman]

I gained ten pounds after my husband died. I like sweets, but he had so many restrictions on what he could eat when he was ill, and I just ate what I prepared for him. When it was over, I felt a certain release and indulged myself in eating all those "forbidden" goodies.

Now I plan more what I am going to eat. I cook ahead and freeze small portions in packets that can be dropped into boiling water when I am ready to use them. I bake a large sheet cake, freeze half and keep half

in the refrigerator, so it will be there when I want it, but I won't be tempted to eat it all at once. [a woman in her eighties]

Mass advertising promotes high-profit processed foods and soft drinks, promising fun and eternal youth but delivering only empty calories. Health-food stores and food co-ops are good sources of foods not easily found in supermarkets, but in a growing number of communities, supermarket managers are responding to increased consumer sophistication about nutrition by stocking whole-grain breads and crackers, tofu,* and a wider variety of fruits and vegetables. Stores now also contain a variety of ethnic and new foods which can improve our food selections and broaden our pleasures. A good tip for supermarket shopping is to begin by going around the edges of the market where the unprocessed food is—dairy, meat, fish, and produce. Use the center aisles mainly to restock staples and paper products.

Eating in healthier ways usually means deciding to change and then doing it slowly. One way to start is to learn more about what a healthy diet is. Healthy unprocessed foods can be flavorful and interesting. One woman who suffered from gastritis and constipation reports:

I decided to put into practice some of the nutritional advice which I'd been reading. I stopped eating white sugar in any form. No more processed food, including white bread, noodles, and spaghetti; in came more fresh vegetables and grains. That was five years ago and

*Tofu is a bland, custardlike food from East Asia. Made from soybeans, it is high in protein and calcium, low in calories and carbohydrates, and has no cholesterol. Tofu is available in East Asian food markets and health food stores, and increasingly in supermarkets as its popularity grows in the U.S.

Norma Holt

today all the ailments I mentioned earlier are completely gone. No more of that headachy feeling from constipation. I count my blessings for being freed from this condition from which I suffered so long. [a fifty-seven-year-old woman]

MAKING EATING SOCIABLE AND EASY

The company of others can seem particularly important at mealtime. Try to make eating a happy sociable event. Plan to share a meal or two a week with friends. Consider going out to lunch—food is generally cheaper then and sometimes it is easier to schedule time with friends at midday. For people over sixty-five, most senior centers provide one hot meal a day. In some areas, nursing homes, schools, and churches serve as meal sites.

Though some women avoid the meal sites because they mistakenly perceive them as only for the economically needy or because they don't want to be associated with "old people," those who do go enjoy it a lot and frequently become "regulars."

I live alone but I am rarely by myself, due to a steady stream of family, friends, and international visitors, and many activities. I enjoy eating at the local senior meal site. This is how I solve my problem of thinking of a meal as a true communion. I urge others to try it. [an eighty-seven-year-old woman]

Not all of us are able to travel or live in a group setting, but we can certainly make our home or apartment a place where people want to be—and then ask them over! Potlucks are popular, economical, and fun.

You can eat well more easily if you simplify the storing and cooking of food. For example, if you have freezer space, cook food ahead of time, divide it into meal-size packages, and freeze it. You don't have to make a complicated meal to have nutritious foods. Fresh or frozen vegetables can be cooked in five to ten minutes in a steamer (for under five dollars you can buy one that fits any saucepan). Small pieces of chicken, fish, or meat can be broiled in a short amount of time. Low-fat dairy products such as skim milk, cottage cheese, and yogurt can make convenient, nutritious snacks. In addition to cooking grains such as brown rice, whole grains can be eaten in cereals (shredded wheat, oatmeal, wheat germ, bran cereal) or by eating whole-grain bread, crackers, and pasta.

Other circumstances can affect how we eat. For instance, living too far from a market or having too many stairs to climb can limit the amount of food you can get into the house. Apartments or houses may have too little storage space, or refrigerators or stoves that don't function properly. Poorly fitting dentures can be an impediment to good nutrition. Sometimes help can be found in the form of a friend or neighbor to shop or eat with, a senior center that serves meals, a neighborhood health center that provides dental care or social services, or a legal-services agency for housing problems.

Eating Well for Less Money

For many of us, the kind and amount of food we eat is influenced by the cost. Most families spend an average of 15 to 20 percent of their income on food. Poor older women may have to spend 30 percent or more of their income on food.[1] For these women, the choice may come down to paying the rent or buying food.

Some suggestions that may help those on a limited budget are:

1. Buy only as much as you can use or store. Split cheaper "economy size" packages with a friend.

2. Buy foods that are "nutrient dense"—in other words, unprocessed foods that give you the most nutrition per dollar. For instance, eggs, low-fat cottage cheese, dried beans, whole chickens, protein-enriched spaghetti products, peanut butter, oatmeal, low-fat milk, whole-grain cereal, catfish and other inexpensive fish, and hamburger.

3. Avoid highly processed foods when possible. They seem economical but aren't. For instance, a bologna sandwich, a cup of canned beef-noodle soup or a frozen creamed chicken dinner are in about the same price range as the foods mentioned above. Their percentage of protein, however, is far less.

4. Fresh vegetables and fruits are cheapest in season. Frozen vegetables are often less expensive than fresh and have approximately the same nutritional value. Avoid frozen vegetables packed in sauces because they cost more and contain more salt and fat. Canned vegetables can be quite inexpensive although there is some nutritional loss. For instance, four ounces of canned green beans contain one third the amount of vitamin C of fresh or frozen beans.

5. Meals at a senior nutrition center or meal site are inexpensive. You can also save cooking time and meet new friends.

6. Don't hesitate to apply for food stamps and surplus foods at your local welfare office. If you qualify, you are entitled to them.

Food in Institutions

People in nursing homes and hospitals often don't have much choice about what they eat. Institutional food is often high in refined carbohydrates and fats and low in fresh fruits and vegetables. This can be a very difficult situation to deal with. If you, a friend, or relative is in this situation and find the food lacking in nutrition or taste, one solution is to bring in or have brought in small amounts of food from the outside. Another is to put pressure on the institution to provide better food. Discussing this with your doctor or dietitian can often be useful. If that doesn't improve the situation, talk with other residents informally and then bring it up in the residents' council, if you have one, or contact one of the nursing-home reform organizations (see Nursing Homes in Resources).

WHAT IS A GOOD FOOD PLAN?

No single food program is right for everyone. We all have different nutritional needs as well as different physical and economic limitations. Advertisements, books, magazines, and television all present conflicting information on what to eat.

I still don't know what I should eat or how much. I try to keep up with nutrition through magazines and newspapers, but I am never sure I'm getting what I need. [a fifty-five-year-old woman]

The purpose of this chapter is to help us evaluate what we read and hear so that we can eat healthier food.

Little solid research has been done in the area of nutrition for older women. The U.S. Department of Agriculture's (USDA) Human Research Center for Aging is currently studying the nutrition of healthy older people. After this research is done, we may have more answers about diet and aging, but we will still have questions about the different dietary needs of older women and men.

Nutrients—carbohydrates, fats, proteins, vitamins, water, and minerals—work together in our bodies to provide heat and energy, regulate bodily processes, and provide material for repair and growth. Each nutrient has its own functions, so the food we eat must contain all of the nutrients for our bodies to function really well.

Most labels on food packaged in the United States contain information on the United States Recommended Daily Allowances (USRDA) for certain nutrients. These are recommendations set by the Food and Drug Administration and are derived from the guidelines provided by the National Academy of Sciences. The Academy sets its guidelines within a range from the minimum amount needed to prevent deficiencies (MDA) to the amount that would cause an overdose. The USRDA is usually close to the minimum amount. Also, the guidelines do not include all known essential nutrients.[2] So while the USRDAs can be used to compare one product with another, getting your USRDA will not necessarily assure you of good nutrition.

More useful are the dietary goals published by the Senate Select Committee on Nutrition and Human Needs. The committee concluded that we as a country are not particularly well nourished. We know that the poor of this country, a large proportion of whom are older women, have a hard time meeting their nutritional needs. But even among middle-class Americans, the committee found that 40 to 50 percent suffer from at least one nutritional deficiency.[3] The committee also found that although we as a country have far more than our share of agricultural resources, our nutrition has suffered as a result of the extent to which processed food has become an ever-increasing part of our diets.

Our food supply has changed from reliance on whole, unrefined foods such as fresh fruits, vegetables, meats, dairy products, and whole grains to highly processed, "fortified," preserved, synthetically manufactured "convenience" foods. The latter take up at least half the space in any supermarket and an ever-larger percentage of space in convenience stores. Our use of fats and oils increased by 50 percent from 1910 to 1980.

Our use of sugar and other sweeteners has increased by one third since 1909, largely because of the use of hidden sugars in processed foods and beverages.[4]

The following suggestions are adapted from the goals set by the senate committee and from the *Dietary Guidelines for Americans* published jointly by the U.S. Department of Agriculture and the U.S. Department of Health and Human Services.

1. *Increase consumption of complex carbohydrates.* This category includes fruits and vegetables; nuts; legumes such as split peas, lentils, chick peas, lima beans, and navy and other beans; whole grains such as brown rice, bulgur, and buckwheat; and whole-grain products such as whole-wheat bread, whole-grain crackers, bran cereals, non-instant oatmeal and oat bran, and shredded wheat.

2. *Reduce consumption of refined sugars.* This category includes processed foods that list sugars as first, second, or third ingredients. Sugars may have a variety of names, such as corn syrup or corn sweetener, sucrose, dextrose, maltose, lactose, fructose, or levulose. "Natural" sugars such as honey, barley malt, maple syrup, apple concentrate, and molasses are only slightly better for you and should be eaten only in small quantities.

3. *Reduce overall fat consumption.* Foods to cut down on include fatty cuts of meat, processed meats (cold cuts, sausages), deep-fried foods, butter, margarine, mayonnaise, high-fat cheeses, pastries, chips, and other "snack" foods. Good substitutes for some of these foods are lower-fat animal products such as fish, poultry without the skin, low-fat dairy products, and vegetable proteins such as grains and beans. Unbuttered popcorn is an excellent snack.

4. *Change the ratio of saturated to unsaturated fats, reducing the use of saturated fats.* Saturated fats are generally solid at room temperature and include animal fats, hydrogenated (hardened) vegetable fats, and coconut and palm oils. Unsaturated fats are liquid at room temperature and include vegetable or nut oils such as safflower, sunflower, soy, corn, linseed, and walnut oils. Saturated fats raise cholesterol levels while unsaturated fats lower them. Mono-unsaturated fats, like peanut or olive oil, are liquid at room temperature but solidify easily with refrigeration. Mono-unsaturates have no effect on or may lower cholesterol levels and can be

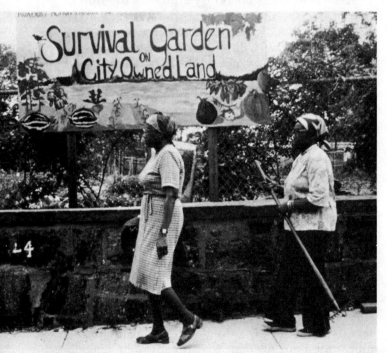

Ellen Shub

Carbohydrates

Carbohydrates should provide 50 percent or more of our energy needs and supply the glucose necessary for brain function. Adequate carbohydrate intake keeps the body from using protein as an energy source, so that protein can be conserved for body-building functions.

Carbohydrates are usually divided into two categories—simple and complex. Simple carbohydrates are sugars such as table sugar, honey, and the sugar in fruits (glucose and fructose). Complex carbohydrates are starches such as grains, starchy vegetables, fruits, and beans. All sugars and starches are converted by digestion into a simple sugar called glucose, which is released into the bloodstream. However, the glucose from starches is digested and absorbed more slowly than that from sugar, avoiding the rapid rise and fall of blood sugar that can come from eating too many simple sugars at one time. Whole foods with complex carbohydrates such as grains also furnish essential nutrients and fiber, while simple carbohydrates such as sugar and refined flour tend to be "empty calorie" foods—they supply too many calories for the nutrients they provide. White flour loses most of twenty-three of its vitamins and minerals in the refining process and is then labeled "enriched" when only four are replaced.

used in cooking, as they remain stable at high temperatures. The fats in fish (including shellfish, the cholesterol levels of which were previously overestimated) contain omega-3 fatty acids, which actually lower cholesterol and triglyceride levels in the blood (see the chapters on arthritis, hypertension and heart disease).

5. *Reduce sodium consumption.* Eat only small quantities of salt-cured foods, most condiments, salty snack foods, soy sauce, foods containing monosodium glutamate (MSG), most canned vegetables and soups, and any processed food in which salt or sodium is high on the list of ingredients. Keep track of your use of salt in cooking and at the table. Be aware that some water softeners work by adding salts. Avoid over-the-counter medications high in sodium, including many antacids. However, some sodium is essential for our well-being and cutting intake too low for our needs can result in weakness.

Choosing Our Food

What should we eat on a daily basis for the nutrition we need? Nutritionists traditionally dealt with this question by dividing food into four groups: (1) fruits and vegetables; (2) dairy products; (3) breads and cereals; and (4) meats and other protein foods. Since these groups don't take into account such things as levels of saturated fat or different ethnic eating habits, we have changed the groups somewhat to make the recommendations a little more flexible. However, if you ate all of the minimums, for every group, you would be eating too little; if you ate all of the maximums, you would be eating too much in total calories.

- *Vegetables*—2 to 5 servings (one serving is ½ cup cooked). Includes all fresh, frozen, or canned vegetables. Generally, the deeper the color of the vegetable, the more nutritious it is in vitamin A, so tip the balance in favor of dark green leafy and yellow/orange vegetables. Also include starchy vegetables such as corn, peas, and potatoes.
- *Fruit*—1 to 4 servings (one serving is one average-size fruit, or approximately ½ cup). Includes all unsweetened fruit—fresh, frozen, canned, dried, or juiced. Whole, raw fruit is generally the most nutritious. Include a vitamin C fruit or vegetable source daily.
- *Dairy products*—1 to 3 servings (one serving is approximately one cup of liquid like milk or yogurt, or 1 to 1½ ounces of cheese). Includes milk, yogurt, all cheeses, ice milk, or ice cream. Be sure to include low-fat dairy products such as skim milk, low-fat yogurt, and low-fat cottage cheese.
- *Whole grains, including bread and cereal*—3 to 6 servings (one serving is ½ cup of grain or cereal, or one slice of bread). Includes all whole grains—rice, barley, millet, cracked wheat, corn; whole-grain breads and cereals—oatmeal, bran, shredded wheat; whole-grain crackers, pasta, and tortillas. If you are not used to whole grains, start gradually to substitute them for white-flour products and eat only as much as your digestive system can comfortably handle. For example, you can

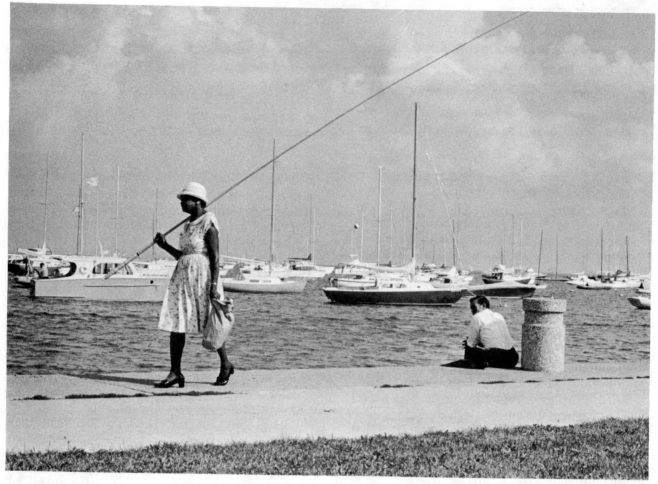

Cathy Cade

cook a combination of brown rice and enriched white rice, gradually shifting toward more of the whole grain.

- *Protein*—2 to 3 servings (one serving is approximately 3 ounces of cooked lean meat, chicken, or fish, 5 ounces of tofu, 2 large eggs, 1 cup cooked beans, or combinations such as ⅓ cup beans with ⅔ cup rice). Many women over age seventy do not eat enough protein.

Protein is the second most plentiful substance in the body. It is important for the growth, development, and repair of all body tissues. Proteins are composed of units called amino acids. The body requires approximately twenty-two amino acids to make human protein. All but nine of these can be produced by the body. These nine are called "essential amino acids" and must come from the food we eat. Animal proteins from foods such as meat, poultry, fish, dairy products, and eggs contain all of the amino acids in adequate amounts and are therefore called "complete proteins."

Many vegetables, grains, beans, nuts, seeds, and other complex carbohydrates contain proteins but are "incomplete" by themselves and have to be combined in order to have sufficient amounts of all of the amino acids. Combined vegetable proteins have the advantage of being lower in fat, higher in fiber and minerals, and generally lower in cost than complete proteins.

Many traditional food combinations yield complete protein—such combinations as grains and beans, beans and nuts or seeds, grains and nuts or seeds, and any vegetable protein with any animal protein such as potatoes with dairy products. For more information on combining foods to make complete protein, see *Diet for a Small Planet* by Frances Moore Lappé.

- *Essential fatty acids*—approximately 1 to 2 tablespoons per day in salad dressing or cooking. This is not really a food group, but we do need small amounts of oil and fat in our diet for good health. Fats are part of the basic structure of every cell. Furnishing more than twice the number of calories per gram as carbohydrates and proteins, they provide the most concentrated form of energy in the diet. Fats act as carriers for fat-soluble vitamins (A, D, E, and K) and provide insulation and protection for our organs and the skeleton. Oils high in essential fatty acids (in descending order) are fish oils, linseed, walnut, soy, safflower, sunflower, and corn oils. If you eat a diet which is high in fatty fish, whole grains, seeds, and nuts, you may not have to add extra oil.

• *Water*, although it is not a nutrient, is the most important element for life and is frequently overlooked. Our bodies are made mostly of water, which is vital to maintain life and health. Water is essential for proper functioning of both the kidneys and the bowels, and is an important vehicle for disposing of poisonous substances. It is the basic transport system of the body, moving all nutrients, hormones, blood cells, waste products, and oxygen through the body.

As we age, our mechanisms for controlling fluid balance become less efficient. Most of us need six to eight cups of water daily, and more in some circumstances. Water can also be obtained from soups, juices, beverages, fruits, and vegetables. Coffee and other beverages containing caffeine actually push fluids and minerals out of the system and should be avoided.

• *Fiber*, although not a nutrient, is nonetheless a necessary component of a well-balanced diet. Fiber serves primarily as a vehicle for holding water, binding both toxic and essential nutrients, and providing the soft bulk that absorbs body waste. Because of these properties, fiber helps our intestines work more smoothly. This is particularly important as we grow older and our intestines lose some of their elasticity and mobility, increasing the tendency toward constipation. Adequate fiber intake may also help prevent such conditions and diseases as diverticulosis, gallbladder disease, colitis, colon cancer, and high cholesterol.[5]

Different forms of fiber have different functions; for instance, oat bran lowers cholesterol, whereas wheat bran does not. Pectins from foods such as apples and beans prevent diarrhea and help excrete cholesterol. Cellulose and other fibers from whole grains help prevent constipation and colon cancer. It is therefore important to eat a variety of fibrous foods, including whole grains, beans, fruits, vegetables, nuts, and seeds. Beware of fiber-enriched white breads. Some contain harsh sawdust products. Fiber has its negative side as well. High fiber intake can cause gas and bloating. More seriously, it can interfere significantly with calcium, iron, and zinc absorption.[6] So far, there are no established recommendations for fiber intake for older women. A prudent course is to have enough fiber (and adequate fluid) to make our bowel movements soft and easily passed.

• *Vitamins* are organic compounds found in living things. Their function is to act as catalysts for chemical reaction. Some chemical processes require the presence of several vitamins simultaneously. Vitamins themselves do not furnish energy, as they have no calories, but they are necessary for metabolism.

Vitamins are soluble in either fat or water. The fat-soluble vitamins—A, D, E, and K—require fat in order for the body to absorb them from the intestinal tract. They are also easily stored in the body and can become toxic at high doses. This is particularly true for vitamins A and D. Water-soluble vitamins are the B complexes and vitamin C. Because they are water-soluble, unneeded amounts can be disposed of easily in the urine. And because they are not stored easily in the body, we need to be more careful to get them on a daily basis. They are generally not toxic except at very high levels.

• *Minerals* are inorganic compounds that originate in soil, rocks, and water. Approximately seventeen minerals are necessary for human nutrition; several others are thought to have at least a minor role in body processes.

Like vitamins, minerals act as catalysts for many chemical reactions in the body. These include regulation of muscle contractions, transmission of messages through the nervous system, and aiding the digestion and metabolism of foods. Certain minerals also constantly adjust our internal water balance and regulate the flow of substances in and out of cells. They control the acid balance in our blood and tissues. The essential "macrominerals," those present in relatively high amounts in the body, are sodium, potassium, calcium, magnesium, and phosphorus. The essential "trace minerals," those present in only very small amounts, are iron, copper, zinc, manganese, chromium, selenium, vanadium, and molybdenum.

Should We Take Nutrient Supplements?

Unfortunately, there is no simple way to know how well nourished you are. One technique, hair analysis, is useful in discovering toxic levels of minerals such as lead, arsenic, and mercury. It does not, however, give accurate information about the nutritional condition of various tissues of the body. It can even give false readings about nutritional status if, for example, certain shampoos are used before testing. Whereas zinc in hair can be low if a diet is deficient, it can also be normal if hair is slow-growing because of semistarvation.[7]

There are some conditions under which you may want to consider taking a supplement: when you don't have control over the food you eat (for instance, in a nursing home); when you are on a medication which can interfere with absorbtion of nutrients; if you indulge in cigarettes, alcohol, or caffeine; if you haven't yet changed to healthful food habits.

Remember that supplements are supposed to do just that—supplement your diet. You cannot use them to replace food or to make up for a nutritionally unsound diet. A good vitamin-mineral supplement is low in the fat-soluble vitamins A and D (A—15,000 IUs or less, D—400 IUs or less), contains a complete B complex (B_1, B_2, B_6, B_{12}, biotin, folate, niacin, pantothenic acid, choline, inositol, and PABA), vitamin C, vitamin E, and minerals such as magnesium, iron, selenium, chromium, manganese, and zinc. If you feel you need more than a general supplement or are confused about what to take, you can consult a nutritionist, dietitian, or a medical professional who has knowledge and experience in clinical nutrition.

SPECIAL NEEDS FOR WOMEN OVER FORTY

The specific nutritional needs of older women have not been determined. The nutritional levels of the healthiest of the elderly—those who are largely free of disease and are mobile—are remarkably similar to those of younger peo-

ple. Unfortunately, what is clear is that as many as 50 percent of women over the age of sixty-five are malnourished because they consume too few calories, proteins, and essential vitamins and minerals for good health.[8] Specifically, many do not get enough thiamine (B_1), riboflavin (B_2), vitamins B_6, B_{12}, C, D, K, folic acid, magnesium, zinc, and iron, as well as calcium.[9]

Adequate daily calcium intake is vital throughout our life span. The USRDA for adult women remains at 800 mg. per day, but surveys show that most women consume barely half that amount.[10] The 1984 Osteoporosis Consensus Conference recommended increases in calcium for women taking estrogens and for postmenopausal women. But the National Academy of Sciences, which met in 1985, did not change their RDAs for calcium. The following chart, compiled from several sources, lists recommendations higher than 800 mg. per day.

CALCIUM NEEDS OF WOMEN

Age	Milligrams per Day
9–19	1200
If pregnant	1500–2000
If breastfeeding	2200
20–50 (premenopausal)	1000
Postmenopausal or for early natural or surgical menopause	1500

A thousand milligrams of calcium can be obtained in one day by eating all of the following: two half-cup servings of cooked green vegetables, one ounce of cheese, and two cups of skim milk. Adding a corn muffin, a serving of sardines or yogurt, and increasing the two green vegetables to one-cup servings will increase the calcium to 1500 mg. for the day.

All dairy products are rich in calcium. Skim or fat-free milk is commonly recommended,[11] but one recent book states that small amounts of fat improve calcium absorption because the absorption of calcium and fat is interrelated.[12] Whole milk contains only about 3 percent fat. You can drink one or even three glasses of whole milk daily and still keep your cholesterol level low. You can add additional low-fat powdered milk to muffins, pancakes, soups, custards, puddings, and casseroles.

You can still obtain calcium if you are lactose intolerant. Try consuming small amounts of

GOOD CALCIUM SOURCES

Food	Portion Size	Mg. of Calcium
Whole milk	1 cup	290
Low-fat (2%) or skim milk	1 cup	300
Buttermilk	1 cup	285
Nonfat dry milk	¼ cup powder	377
Cheddar cheese	1 oz.	205
Cottage cheese	½ cup	77
Parmesan cheese	1 oz.	320
American cheese	1 oz.	175
Yogurt, plain lowfat	1 cup	290
Ice cream	½ cup	90
Collard greens, cooked	1 cup	350
Parsley	3½ oz.	203
Kale, cooked	1 cup	200
Spinach, cooked	1 cup	150
Broccoli, cooked	1 cup	130
Sardines (with bones)	¼ lb.	300
Salmon (canned with bones mashed in)	¼ lb.	225
Oysters (fresh)	¼ lb.	210
Shrimp	1 cup	147
Brazil nuts	¼ cup	140
Almonds	¼ cup	80
Tofu made with calcium sulfate	4 oz.	145
Corn tortilla	6" diameter	60
Kelp	½ oz.	150
Blackstrap molasses	1 tablespoon	135

dairy products and note how you feel. Most people can tolerate half a glass of whole milk with each meal and can eat yogurt, cheese, and buttermilk without discomfort.[13] Tablets containing the enzyme required to digest milk and lactose-free milk are now available in some large supermarkets and in health-food stores.

Many magazines now carry ads for calcium supplements, playing on our fears of bone fractures. Because of these ads, some women may now be adding *too much* calcium to their diets. This may interfere with the absorption of iron and other nutrients, and may cause imbalances in calcium metabolism. Adding a calcium supplement to bring the total daily intake from food and the supplement up to 800 mg. on days when we can only eat less than 800 mg. of calcium is certainly safe, but high-dose supplementation should probably be reserved for women with established osteoporosis or a high risk of osteoporosis. If you have a history of kidney stones, check with your physician about calcium levels that are safe for you. For most women, however, a maximum calcium intake from *food and supplements* of 2000 mg. a day is considered safe. Make sure to divide your intake throughout the day and save the final for bedtime, as the body tends to lose calcium during sleep. Calcium before bed may prevent leg cramps during the night. A glass of milk before bed also contains tryptophan (which will help you sleep), protein, and vitamins.

If calcium supplements are desirable for public health then they should be sold at reasonable prices. Instead, prices keep climbing. The labels on some calcium supplements now list the percentage of elemental calcium in the supplement based on the assumption that 1000 mg. per day

How Much Calcium Is in the Supplements?

- Calcium carbonate · · · · · · · 40%
- Tricalcium phosphate · · · · · 39%
- Calcium chloride · · · · · · · · 36%
- Calcium phosphate · · · · · · · 23%
- Calcium lactate · · · · · · · · · 13%
- Calcium gluconate · · · · · · · 9%
- Bone meal* · · · · · · · · · · · · 31%
- Dolomite* · · · · · · · · · · · · · 22%

To find the actual amount of calcium contained in each tablet, multiply the percentage of calcium contained in that particular form by the number of milligrams of the entire tablet. For instance, a 500 mg. calcium carbonate tablet actually contains only 200 mg. of elemental calcium (500 mg. of calcium carbonate × .40 = 200 mg. of calcium).

*Taken in small amounts as an occasional supplement to a healthful diet, the traces of toxic minerals reported in these sources of calcium are not harmful.

is the recommended amount. If the label lists 200 mg. of elemental calcium, then that is the actual amount in the supplement.

The question is not only how much calcium you are eating, but how your body is using it. It is doubtful that the calcium in these supplements is absorbed as well as the calcium in food. Calcium carbonate is not water-soluble and is not absorbed well, especially as we get older. Water-soluble calcium in calcium citrate, gluconate, aspartate, and lactate is more readily absorbed. Do not use calcium lactate if you have lactose intolerance. Many women, nevertheless, prefer to use calcium carbonate, which can be purchased at drugstores in an inexpensive powdered form. Calcium carbonate is also found in antacid tablets such as Tums, which, however, also contain sugar. Be careful not to use an antacid containing aluminum as it can cause calcium to leave the bones. In addition, all calcium supplements are harder on the stomach than the calcium in food. For some women, calcium carbonate causes constipation, gas, or "acid rebound" with heartburn. If you have an insufficient amount of hydrochloric acid in your stomach, which is common in

Marianne Gontarz

older people, these products may make digestion difficult and can interfere with the absorption of other nutrients.

Vitamin D and magnesium are two important nutrients necessary for calcium absorption and utilization. Because vitamin D is formed on the skin in the presence of light, vitamin D deficiency can occur when we are not often exposed to sunlight. Although only one-half hour of sun-

---

Factors That Decrease Calcium Absorption

- Foods containing oxalic acid in combination with calcium interfere with calcium absorption. These are spinach, rhubarb, Swiss chard, sorrel, parsley, beet greens, and unhulled sesame seeds. None of these foods should be used as a main source of calcium, but can and should be added to a diet that is varied.

- Foods containing phytates (a substance found in the outer layers of grain seed, such as wheat bran) may also make calcium unavailable for absorption. Sprouted-grain breads contain no phytates, but unprocessed bran does. Phytates may be broken down more in breads baked with yeast than in unleavened breads and crackers. If your general calcium intake is varied, however, you do not need to worry about phytates.

- The absorption of calcium and that of fat are interrelated. Small amounts of fat improve calcium absorption. As we have al-

ready discussed, too much fat is unhealthy.

- High stress levels decrease absorption.

- Calcium absorption tends to decrease with age in both women and men.

- Caffeine and alcohol act as diuretics and can cause loss of calcium in the urine. Alcohol also directly interferes with calcium absorption.

- Drugs that impede calcium absorption include tetracycline, laxatives, corticosteroids, Dilantin, diuretics, heparin, caffeine, antacids containing aluminum, and nicotine.

- There is a direct relationship between high salt intake and loss of calcium in the urine.

- Foods high in phosphorus (red meat, cola drinks, and processed foods that have phosphorus additives) prevent calcium absorption.

light daily on 20 to 30 percent of the skin is needed, getting enough sunlight can be a problem for women who are housebound or institutionalized, or who spend the winter months in cold climates.[14] Vitamin D is not found in many foods. Cod-liver oil and other fish oils contain the highest amounts. You may be vitamin D deficient if you have reduced your consumption of egg yolks, butter, liver, and vitamin D-fortified dairy products in order to reduce saturated fats and avoid lactose.[15] If you need to supplement your diet with vitamin D, 400 IUs per day is a reasonable amount. Magnesium is plentiful in green leafy vegetables, whole grains, nuts, seeds, and fruits. If you take a dietary supplement with

calcium, it is a good idea to increase magnesium intake to half the level of your calcium intake.

Chronic diseases as well as changes in cardiac, respiratory, liver, and kidney functions can affect our nutritional needs. In addition, many medications interfere with the absorption or utilization of nutrients. Eating well will help us stay healthy and resistant to disease.

Drug Effects on Nutrient Absorption

Drug	Effect
Over the Counter	
Aspirin	iron loss
Antacids	phosphate loss, thiamine deficiency
Laxatives	decrease in potassium, calcium, magnesium, zinc, vitamins A, D, and E
Prescription	
Antibiotics	can decrease riboflavin, vitamin C, and calcium absorption and destroy the bacteria in the intestinal tract that produce vitamin K
Phenytoin (Dilantin)	decreases vitamins D, K, and folic acid
Phenobarbital	decreases vitamin D
Indomethacin (Indolin) and other antiinflammatory drugs	iron loss
Chlorpromazine hydrochloride (Thorazine) and Thioridazine (Mellaril)	decrease in riboflavin
Tricyclic antidepressants	weight gain or loss

And many others. Check with your pharmacist.

NOTES

1. Agriculture Research Service, *Family Economics Review.* Washington, DC: U.S. Department of Agriculture, No. 1, 1983, p. 31.

2. Jeffrey Bland, *Nutraerobics.* San Francisco: Harper & Row, 1983, p. 54.

3. Rudolph Ballantine, *Diet and Nutrition.* Honesdale, Pa.: Himalayan International Institute, 1978, p. 10.

4. Bland, op. cit., p. 59.

5. C. W. Suitor and M. F. Crowley, *Nutrition: Principles and Applications in Health Promotion*, 2nd ed. Philadelphia: J. B. Lippincott Co., 1984, p. 152.

6. Ballantine, op. cit.

7. K. M. Hambidge, "Hair Analysis: Worthless for Vitamins, Limited for Minerals." *American Journal of Clinical Nutrition*, Vol. 36, November 1982, pp. 943–9.

8. Erik Eckholm, "Malnutrition in the Elderly: Widespread Health Threat." *The New York Times*, August 13, 1985.

9. Jeffrey B. Blumberg, "Nutrient Requirements for the Healthy Elderly." *Contemporary Nutrition*, Vol. 11, No. 6 (1986); Janet R. Mahalko et al., "Nutritional Adequacy in the Elderly." *The American Journal of Clinical Nutrition*, Vol. 42, September 1985, pp. 542–53; and Institute of Food Technologists' Expert Panel on Food Safety and Nutrition, "Nutrition and the Elderly." *Food Technology*, Vol. 40, No. 9 (September 1986), pp. 81–8.

10. USDA National Food Consumption Survey, 1977–78, quoted in the NIH *Osteoporosis Consensus Development Conference Statement*, Vol. 5, No. 3 (1984).

11. Jane Fonda, *Women Coming of Age.* New York: Simon and Schuster, 1984, p. 195.

12. Betty Kamen and Si Kamen, *Osteoporosis: What It Is, How to Prevent It, How to Stop It.* New York: Pinnacle Books, 1984.

13. Jeanne Goldberg and Jean Mayer, "Milk Isn't Natural for Everybody." *The Boston Globe*, May 2, 1984.

14. M. L. Freedman and Judith C. Ahronheim, "Nutritional Needs of the Elderly: Debate and Recommendations." *Geriatrics*, Vol. 40, No. 8 (August 1985), pp. 45–62.

15. Daphne A. Roe, *Geriatric Nutrition.* Englewood Cliffs, NJ: Prentice-Hall, 1983, p. 127.

6

MOVING FOR HEALTH

by Elizabeth DuBois, Marilyn Bentov,
Diana Laskin Siegal, and Dori Smith

Many women walk, lift, bend, and stretch daily in their work. Increasingly, however, we are becoming more sedentary. Our desk jobs offer us little relief for the strain and inactivity imposed on our bodies. The washing machine and the car have replaced arm and leg power. Decreased energy, illness, age-related problems, and partial immobilization also make it easy to slip into sedentary habits.

Marianne Gontarz

There is strong evidence that appropriate levels of physical activity not only safeguard health, but improve it at any age, even if you have disabilities. In an experimental exercise program at the University of Southern California, sixty- and seventy-year-old women and men became as fit and energetic as people twenty to thirty years younger. The older people in that program who improved the most had been in the poorest shape![1]

I was having back pain, so I started to swim at the Y. When I began, I was forty-six. I thought twenty-five lengths a day was terrific for my age. Now I'm fifty-four and I swim almost a mile (seventy-two lengths). My resting heart rate is fifty-three. That's the rate for a young male athlete.

After stopping exercises for one year for personal reasons, I got stiff, sluggish, flabby, and had aches and pains. I felt old and tired all the time. My spirit was low, too. When I started a regular regime again three times a week, I improved after three months. I felt alive again, got my stamina and good spirits back. [a seventy-five-year-old woman]

People who are active and who exercise tend to suffer less from headaches, chronic back pain, stiffness, painful joints, irregularity, and insomnia. Women often report renewed sexual energy and enjoyment, and the alleviation of hot flashes. Inactivity causes depression, poor circulation, weak muscles, stiff joints, shortness of breath, loss of bone mass, and "that tired feeling."[2] It's hard to get started if you're tired all the time.

But where to begin? We have to overcome the societal prejudice against women being physically active, especially in their later years.

My son told me that he's embarrassed to have a mother who dances at seventy-five. He thinks I ought to be rocking and knitting.

When we exercise as hard as our bodies allow us to, we're actually being kind to ourselves. Joints develop or regain flexibility, muscles become strong, blood pressure lowers, bone density improves, our cardiovascular system becomes more efficient, and food digests better. We have more, rather than less, energy for everyday living. Feelings of alertness, well-being, and energy from exercise provide us, in turn, with reasons to stay active.[3]

I run several miles a week and I try to work out on a Nautilus machine twice a week. If I'm feeling depressed or tired, just having a half-hour run really helps. I know that if I'm feeling blue or down, I have a way out, running, and it really does help. It increases my energy level. [a forty-three-year-old woman]

Age is not the crucial factor in determining and improving fitness. More important are our general state of health and, to some extent, inherited characteristics. Patterns of activity adopted today will affect the strength and agility of our bodies tomorrow and in the years to come. Regardless of what we did in the past, today is the time to start living healthier, more active lives.

GETTING STARTED

Shedding

My skin scares me. It feels tight.
I envy the snake who sheds his. Mine
binds me in limited space.
I circle, move more slowly, less,
a running-down top.

taking three deep breaths I
soar   make
spirals that sweep
add more space
am alive

Lois Harris

Unless you've been consistently exercising, start your new activities slowly and gradually. For example, find ways to increase the amount of time you spend walking each day. Try parking a block or two away from your destination or getting off the bus a few stops from where you're going, and walking the rest of the way. Add a few stairs whenever possible. Find reasons to walk instead of using your car.

No matter where you are, you can begin moving by stretching your fingers and toes, rotating your ankles, wrists, and shoulders, stretching out your arms and legs, and breathing deeply.

My idea of a woman in motion is me: I walk instead of riding; I climb stairs instead of using the escalator or elevators. I do these in addition to normal lifting, bending, carrying, stretching. [a seventy-two-year-old woman]

There are hundreds of daily opportunities to move—look for them! Try tightening abdominal and pelvic muscles while waiting for a bus, or swinging arms and legs while watching TV.

While daily activities keep us moving, they are usually not sufficient to promote and maintain the degree of fitness that promotes radiant health. Unless we do them correctly, many movements such as vacuuming, making beds, lifting, and even standing actually put added strain on the body, especially the lower back. To counteract inactivity or movements that potentially tire or strain our bodies, we need a complete exercise program which includes stretching, strengthening, corrective posture, and cardiovascular conditioning. Among the activities that help achieve these are folk dancing, ballroom dancing, ballet, belly dancing, walking, running, biking, camping, boating, yoga, Tai Chi, jogging, hiking, weight training, swimming, skating, skiing, tennis, bowling, racquetball, golf, squash, volleyball, and—you name it!

Some activities promote contact with other people. You can cultivate new friendships while

Cathy Cade

you get fit at community and senior centers, parks, continuing-education centers, YW and YMCAs, community schools, and colleges. Folk dancing and square dancing traditionally attract people of all ages. Hundreds of clubs exist for middle-aged and older people who like swimming, walking, bowling, golfing, bicycling, or cross-country skiing.

If you can't find the activity or kinds of people you enjoy, you can always start something yourself. Many older women are seeking adventurous outdoor activities such as hiking and backpacking, wilderness camping, rock climbing, and white-water rafting.

I celebrated my fiftieth birthday by flying from Pennsylvania to Vermont to snowshoe ten miles to a campsite. I carried a fifty-pound backpack and learned how to pitch a tent at night in ten-degree temperatures and snow. Through the tent flap, I watched the sky at night, the moonlight on snow and ice covering the branches. This was a birthday I'll never forget!

For years I had been an active member of the Appalachian Mountain Club, hiking in this country and abroad. Then, at seventy-eight, came difficulties with walking. I had to carry a cane. Would I have to give up active interaction with nature? I needed to find out. I decided to try a two-week camping trip in the Virgin Islands. Mountains are not essential props in this particular stage of my life. I learned that strolls on beaches and quiet rambles over other near-horizontal terrain will do nicely to keep me feeling connected with nature. [an eighty-two-year-old woman]

Your movement program should be varied and should be compatible with your preferences and physical limitations.

When my mother was in her seventies and wheelchair-bound with Parkinson's disease, she was very excited and proud of learning to play "basketball"—aiming the ball at a wastebasket in the center of a circle of fellow players in wheelchairs. My mother came from a very traditional community in Poland, where girls' sports were virtually nonexistent, so she was learning to play for the first time. [a forty-eight-year-old woman]

I am blessed with quite good health. I have arthritis, which I ignore.* I have a bike and ride whenever I can, but every morning I take a standing-still ride on the contraption I have in my bedroom. I also have a series

*In fact, she is not ignoring her arthritis but is helping it with exercise (see Joint and Muscle Pain, Arthritis and Rheumatic Disorders chapter).

of exercises which I do each morning to get my bones moving. I live very close to the center of the city, and can walk practically anywhere I want to go. [a seventy-five-year-old woman]

Finding time for exercise despite all the demands of jobs and a busy home life can be difficult but empowering.

Anna Alden

A good plan of exercise will allow for improvement in the four areas that comprise total fitness: flexibility, cardiovascular endurance, muscular strength, and body composition (ratio of body fat to lean body mass). We can set realistic and achievable goals for ourselves.

Randy Dean/VNA of San Francisco's Adult Day Health Care Center

Keeping Our Joints Limber

Flexibility is the ability of a joint to move freely about its axis. Chronic joint stiffness can lock us into painful fixed positions and keep us immobile and unable to do what we want to do. Gentle activity warms the gel that surrounds joints and that acts as a fluid lubricant. It's a good idea to exercise in the morning to liquefy the gel and lubricate the joints. Always warm up with about five minutes of walking, light jogging in place, stationary biking, or any activity that gently accelerates heart rate, breathing, and circulation. Try gentle swinging motions of arms and legs, circling of the wrists and ankles, and shoulder shrugs.

When I wake up I take a warm shower, run up and down the stairs a few times, ride a stationary bike while my cereal is cooking, and then am "warmed up" enough to do my stretches before I eat. [a fifty-year-old woman]

Once the body is warmed up, do stretches by holding each one for ten to twenty seconds, letting gravity gently increase the stretch. Breathing should be continuous and normal. This is called static stretching, which helps increase the space between joints and keeps the spine flexible. Do not do the bouncing, pulsing kind of stretches (called ballistic stretching), which can tear connective tissue, and do not stretch "cold" muscles without sufficient warmup.

Be *especially gentle* when doing the following: (1) bending or rotating the head (it is best to go forward and side to side—not back); (2) dropping the head and body over the legs from a standing position (don't lock your knees when doing this); (3) extending the legs (lift, don't kick); (4) standing knee bends (always keep the knees over the toes and do not bend lower than 90 degrees); (5) arching the lower back (always be cautious: don't do "donkey kicks" on your hands and knees, bringing the knee to the chest and then lifting the leg straight back, and don't do "fire hydrants" on hands and knees, lifting the leg like a dog peeing); (6) don't do forced two-person stretches or bouncing stretches.

Putting Your Heart into It: Aerobic Exercise

The lungs, heart, and blood vessels, working together to carry oxygen to every cell in the body

Pam White

by means of the blood, comprise the cardiovascular system.

Aerobic (meaning "in the presence of oxygen") exercise is any physical activity which uses the major muscle groups of the body in a rhythmic manner and which is performed at an intensity that raises the heart rate to between 60 percent and 85 percent of its maximum capacity for twelve or more minutes. At this rate, the heart and lungs can keep up with the body's demand for oxygen and a conditioning effect takes place.

The benefits of such conditioning are a lowered pulse rate both at rest and during exercise, due to a larger and stronger heart muscle which allows more blood to be pumped with each beat, decreased blood pressure because of more elastic and stronger blood vessels, and more efficient removal of carbon dioxide—the end or waste product of breathing. Such conditioning can lengthen life.

Anaerobic exercise is any activity done so vigorously that the heart and lungs cannot keep up

How to Determine Your Heart Rate

1. Resting Heart Rate: Take your pulse for sixty seconds. Most people will get a 60, 70, 80, or 90. Take your pulse several times during the day to determine your average.

2. Maximum Heart Rate: Subtract your age from 220. This is the fastest your heart can beat. DO NOT EXERCISE AT THIS RATE!!!

3. Training Heart Rate, or Target Zone: Subtract your resting heart rate from your maximum heart rate; multiply by .60 and by .85; add to each your resting heart rate; the result is your training heart rate, or target zone, per minute. To find the rate for ten seconds, divide by six.

Example: A fifty-five-year-old woman has a resting heart rate of 85 beats per minute. To calculate the target zone (or range of heartbeats per minute within which she should carry on an aerobic activity):

$220 - 55$ (age) $= 165$ (Maximum Heart Rate)
$165 - 85$ (Resting Heart Rate) $= 80$
$80 \times .60 + 85 = 133$ beats per minute
$80 \times .85 + 85 = 153$ beats per minute
$133 \div 6 = 22.2$ (22 beats per 10 seconds)
$153 \div 6 = 25.5$ (26 beats per 10 seconds)

When this woman exercises, she should maintain a heart rate of 133 to 153 beats per minute (22 to 26 beats per 10 seconds).

Those on beta-blockers, blood-pressure medications, or other medications that may affect heart rate should check with their physician about computing their maximum heart rate and about the percentage they should use in calculating their target zone.

Once you have calculated your target zone, take ten-second pulse checks at regular intervals (every five or ten minutes) during aerobic activity. Keep moving as you count, as heart rate drops rapidly when exercise is stopped. All you have to remember are the two ten-second figures—don't go below or above those numbers. It's also best to work near the lower or middle end of your target zone. The beneficial results are the same, and you are running no risk of injury if you are in normal health.

with the body's demand for oxygen and cannot carry away the chemical byproducts of exercise. Anaerobic exercise cannot be done continuously for long periods of time. Examples are sprinting and weight lifting.

Naturally, a beginner must get into aerobic exercise gradually. Start with three to five minutes of stationary biking, walking, or simple dance steps. Take your pulse count for ten seconds at rest, and then several minutes into your exercise routine. A pulse count is your only way of monitoring aerobic progress. In time, the aerobic portion of your exercise routine can last thirty minutes or longer, three times a week—or more. The safe way is to warm up, stretch, do your aerobic workout, then to cool down with slow walking or another gentle movement.

I have a series of yoga-type stretches I have done every morning for years that stretch every part of my body. They take ten minutes to do. Then I go out for a brisk thirty-minute walk. When I come in from my walk I am ready for my breakfast and feel energetic enough to face the day's work. [a sixty-year-old woman]

A second advantage to aerobic activity is that it causes excess fat to burn more efficiently than by any other means. A well-designed aerobic-exercise program combined with proper eating may actually *increase weight* by increasing muscle and bone mass, but will *decrease fat*.

The Strength Factor

In order to perform many of our daily activities and to be able to bear the weight involved in many forms of aerobic exercise, our bodies must be strong. That's where muscles enter the picture. When a gradually increasing demand is placed upon muscles, they respond, given sufficient rest between exercise sessions (at least forty-eight hours), by becoming larger and stronger. Also, as muscles contract during exercise, they act beneficially on the bones, causing calcium to be properly deposited within them to make them denser and stronger.[4] This reduces chances of brittle, easily breakable bones—the condition known as osteoporosis.

Conventionally, girls and women have not been encouraged to be strong. Fortunately, that picture is changing.

I train people of all ages on Nautilus and on free weights. At least 50 percent are women and they love the results. They stand taller and are stronger and have more endurance and muscle strength for walking, danc-

ing, aerobics, skiing, and swimming. I'm a living example. My posture is great and I have a resting heart rate of 51. So—it can *be done!* (And I am fifty-one years old!)

Initially, and perhaps predictably, weights were considered a man's domain. After all, men were the more muscled of the species. Though men tend to develop greater muscle mass than women do, this does not mean that women cannot or should not develop their muscular potential to the fullest. Society has stereotyped women as soft, round, weak, and submissive. We can and must break that image. Our very health and survival depend on it.

Making gains in the development of muscular strength need not be difficult. Each day find ways to use your leg, arm, chest, back, and buttock muscles to lift, carry, support or move weight. When lifting, always bend your knees, use your leg not your back muscles, and keep objects close to your body. You can add weights to your home exercise program by holding objects such as small cans of food or by purchasing a set of light hand and ankle weights with instructions. Some women make weights from mattress ticking filled with sand.

If you have experienced bone fractures because of osteoporosis, check with your physician before working out with weights. Other exercises to strengthen the muscles and bones should be done first.[5]

Posture: Standing Tall

Posture? We'd all like it to be good; but, aside from appearance, does it matter that much? Yes, it does, because posture profoundly affects physical and mental health.

Simply sitting for hours at a job, even slightly bent over, can induce high states of anxiety. The reason is that in this position the lungs are constricted, oxygen intake is reduced, and thus the amount of glucose (fuel for brain cells) that reaches the brain cells is greatly diminished. Sitting bent over can contribute to round shoulders, which can reduce breathing capacity, elevate blood pressure, and contribute to the formation of a dowager's hump.

Poor posture can affect digestion and elimination, contribute to hernias, hemorrhoids, intestinal diverticuli,[6] and bladder-control problems. With prolonged poor posture, some muscles

67

shorten while others lengthen and weaken. A ripple effect takes place: one disturbed set of muscles, especially around a joint, affects others, and they, in turn, affect still others. Gradually, posture becomes increasingly faulty and injurious.[7]

Good posture permits free movement and offers the best starting point for any physical work or exercise. Since posture affects us all the time, it is advisable to pay attention to body alignment and body coordination while walking, standing, sitting, stooping, lifting, or doing more complicated movements. You can begin to change poor postural habits by strengthening abdominal, back, and chest muscles.

As one whose posture was poor all of my life, I speak from experience. No amount of urging me to "stand up straight" on my mother's part or my own efforts to do so ever improved my posture one iota. At fifty-plus years of age I stand taller and prouder than ever before in my life. I owe it all to weight training. We have to be aware of what is holding the body upright. It's not bone. It's not fat. It's not water or blood. It's muscle—the active tensing of moving muscle tissue pulling upwards against the downward pull of gravity.

DESIGNING OUR OWN FITNESS PROGRAM

The major muscles of the body that we need to strengthen are the abdominal muscles, the chest

Norma Holt

and back muscles, and the muscles of the legs and arms. Without fancy equipment and expensive clubs, we can use the most effective method of strengthening muscles—moving against the force of gravity. Walking, swimming, bicycling, and dancing strengthen our muscles and improve the cardiovascular system. At any age, these are the most all-round beneficial, easily accessible, and least expensive kinds of activity.

In planning your activities, consider safety factors. Dress comfortably, wear proper shoes and a bicycle helmet when biking outdors. Campaign with others for bike paths, safe streets, snow removal, and swimming lessons for the disabled and other adults in your community.

Walking

Vigorous walking helps accelerate blood flow: the veins in the legs get squeezed with every step, sending the blood back to the heart. Brisk walking, including a few hills, can be an effective aerobic exercise. Keep your target zone in mind and calculate your pace. You might begin with ¼- to ½-mile walks or even shorter ones daily. When that distance becomes easy, increase it gradually. When you can walk a mile without tiring, try walking that same distance a little faster. Then add a little more distance. Then more speed, etc. Walking provides the same benefits as jogging without the extra stress on joints.

Swimming

Swimming sets off a reflex action that enlarges the heart, causing it to pump more blood than it does in land sports, and also increases flexibility. Swimming does increase bone density, especially in the upper body, which is not strengthened by walking.

In swimming, as in other aerobic activities, when you hit your stride, your mind is free to wander, plan, solve problems, imagine.

I've learned to keep my pencil and a pad of paper in my locker so I can write down all the solutions that come pouring into my head after I've done about a third of my laps in the pool. [a fifty-four-year-old woman]

Bicycling

Bicycling is an excellent exercise for the cardiovascular system. There are adult three-wheeled

68

bicycles that are easier to balance than two-wheelers. Stationary bicycles are also convenient for those who never learned to ride and for exercising while watching television, reading, or listening to music.

Dancing

Dancing is perhaps second only to walking as the most beneficial form of exercise. Besides developing flexibility and strength, it gives a natural "high" and a feeling of well-being. Moving to a beat or to music is one of the oldest activities on earth.

As I dance, I affirm the beauty of my rounded belly that birthed two babies who are now adults, of my heavy hips that carried them, the beauty of my breasts that nursed them, of my skin that is hard from years of heat and cold. As I dance, I affirm the strength of these legs that have labored up fifty-six years of steps. I insist that my asthmatic lungs still work for my pleasure, and my curved back still supports my desire. As I dance, I reach out to other women and say, "Look, we are beautiful; no one need tell us so; we know it; and we love each other."

Furthermore, you can dance alone in the privacy of your own home to a record or the radio, as well as socially at gatherings, clubs, dance groups, and parties.

I learned how important it was for me to do some kind of movement as I got older. I developed an exercise and yoga program for the elderly people who ate lunch at a nutrition site. Our movement leader was an enthusiastic fifty-nine-year-old dance therapist. At first, people were reluctant to get up from the lunch tables. But a seventy-eight-year-old Chinese woman got up, smiling and dancing, and gradually others joined her. (She told us later that old people in China are very active. She was feeling depressed about being old in America before she discovered us.)

People came regularly for about three months. We saw women begin to unbend locked elbows and to twist heads and torsos that had stiffened into one piece. Once after a two-hour session, they didn't want to leave. So we did circle dances with tambourines, castanets, drums, ribbons, and scarves for another half an hour. While we were dancing, one woman, in her late eighties, turned to me and said: "My husband would never believe this if he saw me." Another, who always carried a cane, left and forgot it. The therapist joked: "And the lame shall walk." But she had tears in her eyes. So did I. [a fifty-four-year-old woman]

Hatha Yoga

Hatha Yoga is one of the best exercises for attaining total body flexibility. Its fringe benefits can include inner peace, relaxation, help with insomnia, decreased blood pressure, and relief from anxiety and stress.

Hatha Yoga has a great calming effect. It's good for stress reduction and flexibility. I was immobilized at age fifty-two by an arthritis attack. My yoga exercises helped me return to being as flexible as anyone.

Yoga is particularly useful as we age because its stretches keep joints flexible. Yoga positions help strengthen abdominal muscles and foster good posture—both areas that are vital to the health of older women.

Tai Chi

Tai Chi is a beautiful exercise and "martial art" developed in ancient China. In modern China, it is considered especially appropriate for the old. Tai Chi is a continuous sequence of forms that includes gently moving all the joints and paying attention to the effect of breathing on the ebb and flow of energy. Tai Chi is becoming increasingly popular and available in this country because it has such positive effects on physical and emotional fitness.

In some countries, inner or spiritual growth through exercise is considered to be a major aspect of an aging person's daily life. The disciplines from the East, such as yoga and Tai Chi, not only develop flexibility and strength, but also inner awareness and concentration.

I learned once, in a dance class, that it's important to talk to your body. It's like mothering a child. Instead of getting upset or angry because it isn't behaving the way you'd wish, you praise your body for small achievements, comfort it when it hurts, promise it pleasure, and encourage it to push just a little harder. In this way, I've learned that my body and I, though we feel separate, are different parts of the same being. [a fifty-four-year-old woman]

Methods to Change How We Move

Several movement/awareness approaches, such as the Feldenkrais method and the Alexander technique, use movement for improving both physical and emotional health. These methods are especially useful for learning how to move easily without pain despite disabilities and physical restrictions.

Some forms of psychotherapy also use the body to diagnose and treat emotional problems. The two best known, bioenergetics and psychomotor therapy, attempt to break through chronic muscle tensions developed early in life in response to emotionally disturbing situations. These methods can also improve coordination.

How Much of a Good Thing?

The average woman should start slowly and work up to three to five hours a week in a combination of flexibility, cardiovascular, and muscle-strengthening exercises to create and maintain fitness. Let your body be your guide. It helps to keep a journal for several months after starting a movement plan to clarify needs, expectations, and feelings about the program you've started.

WHEN MOVEMENT IS LIMITED

There are times when we can't be active—during illness, or when recuperating from an illness or an operation. Some of us suffer from disabilities that greatly restrict movement. If you have a disability, you can still benefit from exercise. Even if you are bed- or wheelchair-bound, you can improve lung capacity, muscle strength, and flexibility with consistent daily exercise tailored for you. Few conditions require total rest or immobility. Encourage your health care providers to guide you in designing a medically sound movement program.

It's difficult and discouraging to exercise when we're feeling weak or in pain. But there is no question about the importance of exercise in rehabilitation. A moderate and regular exercise program helps many problems.

A massive stroke impaired my ability to function independently. The effects seriously damaged my physical and emotional stability. Learning to swim was one of

Elana Freedom

Deborah Kahn

my most effective coping techniques. Two swimming sessions (forty-five minutes each) weekly increased my strength and endurance. The encouragement from the therapist and members of the group for even a small accomplishment was a tremendous morale booster. We adopted the motto "Press on regardless." The formation of new friendships was essential in helping to develop emotional security. [a thirty-eight-year-old woman]

Close to 100 percent of persons responding to a survey of women with arthritis mentioned that regular exercise decreased their pain.[8]

If you are confined to a chair or bed, exercise can help maintain strength and flexibility of joints and muscles, good digestion and bowel movements, good blood circulation, and a better mental outlook. It can prevent bedsores, and it makes things easier for the caregiver as well. Home health aides and nursing home personnel should be trained to provide exercises for persons in beds or chairs.

Here is a list of things you can do at your own pace. Try them for a few days and experience the relaxation and the gentle glow of energy that simple movement can give you. Do the exercises with energy and concentration to enhance their effectiveness. Start slowly and do more each day. *Many of these exercises are the same ones that women in more fit condition will find useful also.*

1. Breathe deeply.

2. Contract and relax any muscle group you can control. While breathing regularly, tighten the muscles for several seconds, and then slowly release. Be aware of the relaxation that follows.

3. Kegel exercises and "tummy blops" (see page 73).

4. Exercise your face muscles by making "funny faces." Move your lower jaw from side to side and forward and back. Open eyes wide, then scrunch shut. Wiggle your ears if you can.

5. Stretch and limber the neck slowly, carefully. In bed your neck is protected from bending too far backward. Rotate the head in wide circles, in both directions. Alternately look slowly to the ceiling, stretching the front of the neck, then look slowly down, being aware of a stretch in the back of the neck ("Yes"). Then turn the head from side to side ("No").

6. Placing hands on shoulders or by your sides, rotate shoulders in both directions.

7. Stretching arms out to your sides, twist them in both directions. Make small circles with your hands and then with your arms. Then open and close fists. Alternately stretch each arm upward from the shoulder as if picking apples.

8. Circle wrists as far as they can go. Quickly open and close fists several times, stretching fingers. Circle your ankles in both directions. Flex feet backward and forward, then clench toes and release.

9. Tie a rope to the foot of your bed (or have someone do this for you) and slowly pull yourself to sitting position, then lower again.

10. "Walk" against the footboard of the bed.

11. If you can, pull your knee to your chest; then the other knee; then both.

12. If you can stand, hold on to the back of a chair while rotating your legs, one at a time, from the hip. Rotate in both directions. Then extend your leg forward and slowly swing your lower leg backward and forward.

AVOIDING INJURY

The best way to avoid injury is to get a medical checkup before you start an exercise program. The examination should make you aware of potential problem areas and possible limiting factors, and help you to set realistic goals. Particularly if you decide to undertake demanding movement programs like tennis, racquetball, cross-country skiing, use of Nautilus or other weight-lifting equipment, or if you have physical disabilities, it's best to get a medical evaluation to prevent injury, to get the maximum benefit from what you do, and to set realistic goals. Your physician may recommend a stress test, which monitors your heart while you are performing an ever-increasing work load on a treadmill, to discover and make you aware of any hidden heart disease. It isn't infallible, however, especially for women, and may be too stressful (p. 319).

In the long run, only you can choose how much caution (or precaution) to use before starting your exercise plan. Most important, always pay close attention to how you feel.

Normal Reactions to Exercise:
  Increased depth and rate of breathing
  Increased heart rate
  Feeling/hearing your heart beat
  Mild to moderate perspiration
  Mild muscle aches and tenderness at first

Abnormal Reactions to Exercise—STOP IMMEDIATELY:
  Severe shortness of breath
  Wheezing, coughing, difficulty in breathing
  Chest pain, pressure, or tightness
  Lightheadedness, dizziness, confusion, word slurring, fainting
  Cramps, severe pain, severe muscle ache
  Nausea

Severe, prolonged fatigue or exhaustion after exercising

If these symptoms recur with further exercise, check with your physician. You might need special guidance.[9]

Some General Precautions

1. Lubricate *all* joints with gentle bending and swinging (shoulders, elbows, wrists, knees, ankles), contraction and release (fingers, toes, arches, spine), and stretches.

2. Don't hold your breath; coordinate full breathing with each movement.

3. Drink fluids before and after exercising. It is common as we age not to feel thirsty, even when dehydrated.

4. When ill, do only mild stretches, joint lubrication, and deep breathing. Gentle movement that doesn't cause you to tire will allow your body to use its energy for rehabilitation. This is a good time to practice deep breathing and meditation.

5. No two bodies are alike. Achieve what is possible for yourself; do not compare yourself to others.

6. Wear any comfortable clothing that breathes (natural fibers like cotton are best), that doesn't bind in the crotch, around the shoulders, or at the waist. There's no need to spend money on expensive sportswear unless you want to. *Never* wear rubberized or plastic sweat suits. They can cause high internal temperatures (hyperthermia), dehydration, and even death. Supportive shoes with arches are necessary to soften impact on your organs and spine. If you decide to jog, buy running shoes; if you do aerobic dancing, buy aerobic shoes. They are not the same. Running shoes have more support in the heel and aerobic shoes have more support under the ball of the foot.

EXERCISES FOR ALL WOMEN

Two problems that are special issues for women are very much affected by exercise. These are:

• Bladder control to prevent loss of urine, particularly when we cough, sneeze, or laugh. The strength of the muscles in the pelvic floor, abdomen, and back is very important.

• Loss of bone density due to inactivity, resulting in osteoporosis and bone fractures.

MUSCLES OF THE PELVIC FLOOR

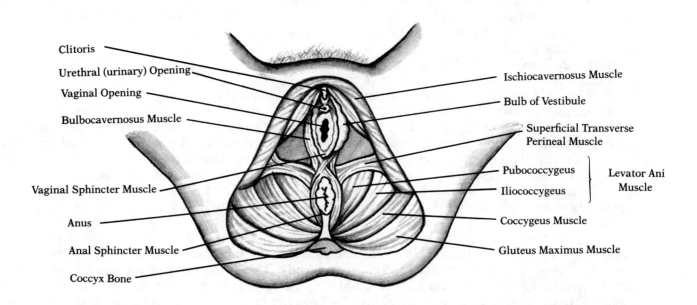

Clitoris
Urethral (urinary) Opening
Vaginal Opening
Bulbocavernosus Muscle
Vaginal Sphincter Muscle
Anus
Anal Sphincter Muscle
Coccyx Bone

Ischiocavernosus Muscle
Bulb of Vestibule
Superficial Transverse Perineal Muscle
Pubococcygeus
Iliococcygeus
Levator Ani Muscle
Coccygeus Muscle
Gluteus Maximus Muscle

Kegel and Other Exercises to Develop Your Own "Girdle"

Dr. Arnold Kegel, after whom this exercise is named, first began his pioneering research in the 1940s, in response to women's complaints of leaking urine.[10] He later demonstrated how strengthening the pubococcygeal muscle (also called the levator ani muscle) not only improves bladder control, but also contributes to increased sexual satisfaction and more comfortable childbirth.

When you exercise the pubococcygeal muscle you will become aware of your vagina. A surprising number of adult women have to be taught how to locate this muscle and how to exercise it; they have been living for years with a kind of inertness or numbness in this region. Others, even at an advanced age, still do not know that there are three separate openings in the pelvis of the female body. One woman in her seventies wanted to use tampons in her vagina to absorb urine leakage.

There are several sets of muscles that run across the abdomen that act like a mat, keeping the intestines in place and protecting and keeping pressure on the uterus and bladder, helping to maintain their correct position. When women use cloth and elastic girdles, they are trying to compensate for the loss of control over these muscles. Keeping these muscles in shape not only improves the contours of the body, but also contributes to the support of the internal organs and the back.

A good way to locate the muscles that support the bladder and uterus is to spread your legs apart and start and stop the flow of urine. Other methods are to tighten around one or two fingers inserted into the vagina or around a man's erect penis during intercourse. Your ability to do these indicates how strong your muscles are.

Start these exercises by lying down, as there will be less pressure on the pelvic floor from the weight of the pelvic organs. If you cannot feel the muscle working in this position, raise your buttocks on a pillow and use gravity to assist. As you progress and the pelvic floor strengthens, you will be able to do your exercises while lying, sitting, or standing.

As you should with all exercises, breathe naturally when doing them. You may combine these exercises, but in order not to strain or overwork your pelvic floor, do no more than fifty contractions a day.[11]

Exercise 1: Contract or draw up the pelvic

floor, hold for three seconds, and relax. Repeat five times. Repeat the series occasionally during the day, building up to ten groups of five contractions. If the muscle feels sore, reduce the number of contractions or stop for a day or two until this temporary soreness disappears, and then increase gradually.

Exercise 2: Think of your bladder and uterus as an elevator which you are trying to raise to a higher floor, and visualize pulling them up into the abdominal cavity toward your stomach. When you reach the top, go down floor by floor again, gradually relaxing the muscles in stages. When you reach the basement, let go of all the tension and think release. Then come back up again to the first floor, so the pelvic floor is slightly tense and able to hold the organs firmly in place.

Exercise 3: Raise the entire pelvic area, as though sucking water into the vagina. Relax and repeat five times. This series of five contractions may be repeated four to six times a day, building up to twenty to thirty contractions a day.

The following exercises will strengthen the upper and lower abdominal muscles. In order to do them effectively and protect your back, tighten your abdominal muscles before you start rather than doing them with your abdomen sticking out.

For the upper abdominals, do modified bent-knee sit-ups. Lying on your back with knees bent and feet flat on a bed or the floor, lift the head and shoulders while reaching forward with the hands to touch the knees, then lie back again, keeping eyes looking up and shoulders off the bed or floor. Reach for your left knee with your right hand as you twist your waist slightly, then do the same with the right knee and left hand. As you become stronger, you can do these sit-ups with your hands behind your head (do not pull up on your head—use hands only to support your head on the way down), reaching your elbows toward your knees. Do not do sit-ups with straight legs.

For the lower abdominals, lie on your back with legs extended straight up overhead. You may find this easier to do with your buttocks against a wall. "Walk" your feet in the air in place or toward your head. "Bicycling" with legs as high as possible also strengthens the lower abdominals.[12] Also while standing, tighten your abdominal muscles with tummy "blops." On an empty stomach only, inhale fully, exhale fully,

then tighten and release stomach muscles three or four times. Then inhale, and repeat the cycle several times. Another way is to lie on your side with your knees drawn up. Contract your belly muscles so that you pull your knees and head closer together.

Exercising for Strong Bones

Remember that when we are physically active, the body uses calcium efficiently for bone growth and maintenance. When we are inactive, calcium is not absorbed well into the bones but is "dumped" and excreted in the urine. The depletion of bone cells (osteoporosis) can lead to a dowager's hump and to bone fractures. Many physicians now treat osteoporosis with special exercises.[13]

For older women, fast walking is the best exercise to increase bone density in the lower body. If you have no spinal or skeletal problems, jogging may be all right, but it is more stressful on the joints. Exercise the upper body as well so calcium will be deposited in all the bones. Weight training, which develops muscle, is especially beneficial because it also increases the strength of the connective tissues, tendons, and ligaments. Exercise also improves balance and coordination so we are less likely to fall or, if we do fall, more likely to fall safely.

"GOING FORMAL": CHOOSING A MOVEMENT FACILITY

If you want to undertake a conditioning program that requires special facilities or instructions, take time to find the best place. Any facility or program should provide safety, well-trained instructors, and personal attention. It should be reasonably priced, easily accessible, and suited to your personal needs. In considering whether you can afford instruction, keep in mind the intangibles that aren't price-tagged: better health can give you time otherwise spent in illness; you will feel better about yourself and life; better fitness can bring down your medical costs.

What should you look for in a fitness center or program?[14] First, find the facilities that have the activities you want. Next, check further about each: Are their hours convenient? Can you get

C. Pratt

there easily? If you have special needs, will they be met there? Are the costs reasonable?

Then, arrange a tour of centers that meet your criteria, and ask questions. What credentials does the staff have? (Look for college degrees in and certification in applied anatomy and physiology, physical education, nutrition, and exercise physiology and current CPR certification.) Try to visit at the busiest time of day, or at a time you will want to use the center. Ask some of the clients how they like the center and what some of the problems are. Look to see whether equipment is in good condition and whether showers and other wet areas are clean. Beware of places that push "lifetime contracts." A life membership lasts only as long as the life of the facility or organization unless another facility or new management agrees to honor it. Buy the shortest-term package to try out before committing a lot of money. Does the center take a medical history? Do they take blood pressure and pulse rate before, during, and after exercise? Can you get personal guidance in the use of equipment? Some centers have special rates for club usage during the midday hours, when it is least busy. If those hours are convenient for you, this may be an ideal arrangement, as it benefits both you and the club.

Don't make a decision on your first visit. Beware of high-pressure salespeople who offer you bargains if you "make a decision today," or who refuse to allow you to take the contract home to review before signing. The right choice can make a big difference in whether you use the center regularly, consistently, and safely.

Finally, guard against giving up instead of accepting limits and going on.

I used to like to go mountain climbing. When I couldn't do that, I went hill climbing. Now I walk on more level ground. You don't have to give up your dream. You just shape it differently. [an eighty-two-year-old woman]

NOTES

1. Herbert A. deVries with Diane Hales, *Fitness After Fifty.* New York: Charles Scribner's Sons, 1974, pp. 9–11.

2. James Blumenthal and R. Sanders Williams, Duke University Center for the Study of Aging. *Center Reports,* Vol. 6, No. 3 (December 1982), p. 4.

3. Robert S. Brown, et al., "The Prescription of Exercise for Depression." *The Physician and Sports Medicine,* Vol. 6, No. 12 (December 1978), pp. 52-8.

4. A. Chamay and P. T. Schantz, "Mechanical Influences in Bone Remodeling: Experimental Research on Wolff's Law." *Journal of Biochemistry,* Vol. 5, 1972, pp. 173–80; and E. L. Smith, Jr., et al., "Bone Involution Decrease in Exercising Middle-Aged Women." *California Tissue International,* Vol. 36, Supplement 1 1984, pp. 129–38.

5. Joseph Lane, "Post Menopausal Osteoporosis: The Orthopedic Approach." *The Female Patient,* Vol. 6, November 1981, p. 54.

6. Gerda Hinrichsen, *Body Shop: Scandinavian Exercises for Relaxation.* New York; Taplinger Publishing Co. Inc., 1976, p. 46.

7. Joseph T. Freeman, "Posture of the Aging and Aged Body," in *Health Aspects of Aging.* American Medical Association Committee on Aging, Chicago, 1965, pp. 49–55.

8. *Hot Flash,* Vol. 3, No. 2 (Winter 1984), p. 1.

9. Stephanie Fall Creek and Mollie Mettler, *A Healthy Old Age: A Source Book for Health Promotion with Older Adults.* Wallingford Wellness Project, Seattle, Wash.: University of Washington School of Social Work, 1979; and Henry C. Barry, "Exercise Prescriptions for the Elderly." *American Family Physician,* Vol. 34, No. 3 (September 1986), pp. 155–62.

10. Arnold Kegel, "The Physiologic Treatment of Poor Tone and Function of the Genital Muscles and of Urinary Stress Incontinence." *Western Journal of Surgery, Obstetrics, and Gynecology,* Vol. 57, 1949, pp. 527–35.

11. With thanks to the Adelaide Women's Commu-

nity Health Centre, North Adelaide, Australia, for their instructions, "Exercising and Strengthening the Pelvic Floor, Kegel Exercises"; and Sheila Kitzinger, *Woman's Experience of Sex*. New York: Penguin Books, 1985, pp. 48–50.

12. Personal communication from Maggie Lettvin.

13. Lane, op. cit., p. 54.

14. Adapted from Gretchen M. Von Mering, *The Fitness Directory: A Guide to Exercise, Nutrition, and Recreation Programs and Services in the Greater Boston Area*. Boston: The Medical Foundation, Inc., 1983, pp. 5–15.

LIVING WITH OURSELVES AND OTHERS AS WE AGE

7

SEXUALITY IN THE SECOND HALF OF LIFE

by Aurelie Jones Goodwin
with Lynn Scott

Special thanks to Mary C. Allen, Sarah F. Pearlman,
and Wendy Sanford

Letter to My Children*

If we
could start again
You, newbegotten, I
A clean stick peeled
of twenty paper layers of years
I'd tell you only what you know,
Teach one commandment,
"Mind the senses and the soul
Will take care of itself
Being five times blessed."

Anne Wilkinson

We affirm ourselves as we experience plea-sure through our senses. Now that we are older, if we attend to the wisdom of our minds and bodies, we can enhance our sexual pleasure. The pleasures of the body, and specifically sexual pleasures, provide us with release, shared inti-macy, communion with our inner selves and with our partners, and a chance to express our-selves physically. We can give ourselves pleasure through masturbation, whether or not we are in a sexual relationship with another person. Sex allows us intimate connection with someone we love, or adventure with a new partner. Our senses provide us with pleasure and our thoughts and feelings give meaning to our expe-rience.

Almost all of us who are middle-aged or older grew up in an environment where attitudes to-ward sexuality were more rigid than they are

*From *Collected Poems of Anne Wilkinson*, A. Smith, ed., Macmillan Co. of Canada Ltd., 1968, p. 94.

today. We may have learned that we should not talk about sex and that women do not or should not enjoy sex as much as men, or that men should always initiate sex. Because of this early training, we may still feel embarrassed or ashamed over sexual issues. Paradoxically, we may believe that because of the "sexual revolu-tion" we shouldn't be uncomfortable, or that we ought to have more sex than we do. A double standard of sexual behavior still exists, particu-larly among middle-aged and older people. This chapter is intended to affirm and support our sexuality and to help all of us enjoy our sexual-ity more fully.

Two misconceptions occur when women are stereotyped by ageist thinking. Older women are considered neither sexually attractive nor sexually active. Those men who are available often choose younger women or women who look young as partners. Things are changing slowly in this respect. According to a recent ar-ticle in *Time*, "The average age of desirability in American women seems to have risen by a dozen years or more."[1] Yet we are still expected to project a youthfully glamorous image. These stereotypes make it hard for us to fully accept our sexuality. Believing the stereotypes leads to fear and denial of aging, and takes a toll on our self-esteem when we see the signs of aging in ourselves and in those we love.

As we age, some physical changes occur which may affect our sexual activity. But there is no physical reason based on age alone why we can-not continue to enjoy sex for as long as we live. Despite social pressures, many of us are accept-

79

ing and enjoying our sexuality more freely than ever. One way we can help ourselves in this respect is to break through the barrier of silence and talk with each other about sexuality. Although it may be hard to talk openly with other women about sex if you have never done so, it is such a positive experience that it is worth the effort. By listening to older women in our families or in women's groups, we can recognize negative messages about sex which we received as children, and then reevaluate our attitudes. Talking to family members about sex can be especially difficult; yet it is often liberating.

Women's groups in which we talk about sexual experiences and feelings have developed since the late sixties as an outgrowth of the women's movement. There are women's groups at most women's centers and some churches and other community organizations. It is common to hear women exclaim, "I never knew anyone else felt the way I do!" One long-married woman, age fifty, who had complained of lack of sexual interest, returned to a women's group to say, "After our discussion last week I went home and talked with my husband and we had an absolute orgy!"

MYTHS AND REALITIES ABOUT WOMEN, SEX, AND AGING

Sexism, ageism, homophobia, and Victorianism all interact to create a pervasive mythology about sex and the older person. These myths do the most damage when we ourselves accept and act on them, and in so doing give up pleasures that are an important and valuable part of our humanity. Consider the following:

Myth 1: Older people are no longer interested in sex and sexuality and no longer engage in sexual activity. Sex is for the young.

This myth has its roots in several notions that link sex and youthfulness. Since society equates attractiveness with youth, it follows that, according to the myth, when you are no longer young, you are no longer desirable.

This myth also connects sexuality with romantic love. In the media, in stories, songs, and the general folklore of our culture, romantic love is the exclusive province of young heterosexual women and men.[2]

The reality is that if you are interested in sex and want to act on that interest, you are just like many other people your age. A recent study of people sixty to ninety-one years old revealed that 91 percent enjoyed sex for a variety of reasons: it reduces tension, makes women feel more feminine, helps people sleep, and provides a physical outlet for emotion. The people studied engaged in sexual relations an average of 1.4 times a week—about what they averaged when they were in their forties.[3] Both the Kinsey research and Masters and Johnson found that women and men continue their accustomed sexual patterns throughout their later years. If you led an active sexual life when you were younger, you can look forward to continuing to do so. If you found sex a burden, you may decide to cease sexual activity as you grow older. Masters and Johnson's research confirmed what many women have discovered for themselves: that there is no time limit on women's sexual capacity. Although our responses may slow down, we can continue to enjoy sex and orgasm throughout our lives.[4]

It is often especially difficult for adult daughters and sons to accept us as sexual beings—they continue to see us as asexual, as they did during childhood.

Myth 2: Changes in hormone levels which occur during and after menopause create a "deficiency disease" that causes women to find sex uncomfortable and unpleasant.

Menopause has been the subject of many fallacious myths, several created and perpetuated by physicians, psychiatrists, and drug companies. The notion that menopause produces a deficiency disease[5] has, among other things, fostered widespread use of hormonal supplements. In fact, menopause is a normal life transition, not a disease. Women continue to feel sexual and enjoy sex until very late in life.

Myth 3: Women who are beyond childbearing years lose their desire and their desirability.

Sexuality and sex appeal are not the same as fertility. For many older women and men sex is actually *better* in the later years. Many women experience a reawakening of sexual interest when pregnancy is no longer a worry. Couples often have more time to relate to each other sexually after children are grown. A divorce or other life change which has nothing to do with fertility may also contribute to a reawakening of sexual interest.

Myth 4: In order to have a full and complete sex life, a woman must have a male partner.

Although the majority of women do have relationships with men, we can be sexual in a variety of ways—with a man or a woman or by pleasuring ourselves alone. The choice is ours to make.

Myth 5: The only truly satisfying and acceptable sex is through intercourse, culminating in mutual orgasm. All other sexual activity is "foreplay" and doesn't count.

While sex is sometimes defined in terms of intercourse, it is not true that intercourse is the only satisfying form of lovemaking. As we age, our experience of intercourse changes. Older women and men need more time for sexual stimulation before they are ready for intercourse. Once we learn that gratifying sexual experience without penetration is a possible choice, we can feel free to explore the variety of other caresses that can provide pleasure.

Older people report in several studies that oral sex is a favorite activity.[6] Cuddling, caressing, and manual stimulation are also satisfying. Lovemaking may continue to be satisfying whether one, both, or neither party has an orgasm.

SEX AND AGING: SOME WOMEN'S EXPERIENCES

People have this idea that sex is somehow naughty for older people. They picture serene and wise grandparents. Older people are not supposed to be feeling and passionate. But at fifty I thought, "Hey, I'm old enough to do as I damn well please."

There is a current of sexuality in everyday life. I find him a very attractive man and he finds me a desirable woman and we tell each other that without words all the time. There's a kind of flow. [a fifty-eight-year-old woman whose husband is seventy-five]

After I came out as a lesbian I danced more than I had in the previous thirty-five years. People ask if I feel foolish—not at all! It's good for the young to know you can keep right on doing, and not pay attention to the wrinkles. [a woman in her eighties]

When searching for a new partner, I often felt discouraged about looking older and worried that I would no longer be appealing to men. Once I was in a relationship, the years I've lived became a plus; I felt proud of my experience and skill as a lover, something I did not have as a younger woman. [a forty-eight-year-old divorced woman]

I've worked at learning to let go of rational thinking during sex. I say I'm going to experience the moment. Here is a wonderful experience I'm going to have, a dedicated time and place. I'm going to live it fully. I soak up the feelings, immerse myself in the sensation and plea-

sure. The more I do it, the better it gets, like turning a golden key. It is very beautiful to me. [a single woman in her late fifties]

At seventy-three, being sexual feels right, comfortable, and just plain satisfying, but it wasn't always like this. Growing up with Victorian spinster aunts, the family disgrace of a flapper cousin who "had to get married," and baffling warnings to always be careful on infrequent dates left me with feelings of being ugly and unwanted. Where I am today is one stage in a constant process of growing. I learned to love and be loved, helped by friends and lovers. I bore a child at age thirty-eight and raised him, developing my own changing value system.

When I was growing up women worried about being thought bossy or willful when we were outspoken or assertive. Now my husband has become more nurturing and accepting of my assertiveness. Our relationship is more balanced. [a woman in her sixties]

We could be equals. We could be friends. I didn't need anything from him and I was free to be me. We were like two kids playing in a sandbox. Oh Lord. A chance to play! [a divorced woman in her fifties]

Now I can just enjoy it. I don't have to be such a good citizen. When I was younger I worried so much for my partner that I never got much real pleasure for myself. [a woman in her fifties]

I have earned the right to express what I like and expect to get it. I want pleasure, joy, fun, and passion during sex for the rest of my life. My contribution to a partner is to give her the same. [a woman in her fifties]

I feel more accepting than I used to—if I don't have an orgasm, if he doesn't have an orgasm, if we stop in the middle, or if we just go to bed and hold each other—it's much more all right than it was when I was younger. [a fifty-five-year-old divorced woman]

Last year I spent several months without sex. I masturbated occasionally, but I even stopped that after a while. I simply didn't miss it; it didn't seem terribly important. I was working pretty hard. Now I'm enjoying it again, but I could do without it. I don't find myself with that rush about sex any more—that feeling of getting hit in the stomach—none of that passion. I still have orgasm, but I seem to have lost my passion, lust. In a way, that's restful. [a fifty-five-year-old woman]

I used to enjoy masturbation and orgasm. But now I don't have any desire for that or a sexual relationship. [an eighty-year-old woman]

Sex was fine but it was only a part of our marriage and I was happily married for thirty years. Since my husband died I've never looked at another man. I masturbate occasionally, but it's not important to me. Knowing another person—that is what matters. I get as much pleasure from my work as I might get from sex. [a sixty-year-old woman]

I miss the intimacy, the love letters, but I'm back solidly celibate. I never could masturbate. It's not the orgasm I crave, but the intimacy—the candles, the flowers, the feeling of another body. [a seventy-two-year-old woman commenting on the ending, several years ago, of a relationship with a woman]

PLEASURING OURSELVES*

Masturbation is one way of giving ourselves pleasure. Most of us enjoy a variety of sensual pleasures and view pleasure as a good thing, yet many of us were taught to believe that giving ourselves *sexual* pleasure is bad. Whether we masturbate or not is our choice. Pleasuring ourselves through masturbation can be a satisfying alternative to sex with a partner. If you have lost a partner with whom you enjoyed good lovemaking, you may not be ready to start over with someone new.

After my divorce masturbation was an important part of my life that made it very nice to go to bed. It's still a special occasion. [a seventy-eight-year-old woman]

If you do have a partner, masturbation can be a good way to learn about your own sexual responses—what fantasies you enjoy, what kinds of touch arouse you and please you—without having to worry about your partner's needs and opinions. Then, if and when you choose, you can tell or show your partner what you've learned. Some of us incorporate masturbation into our lovemaking with a partner as a way to enhance pleasure and to reduce pressure on both partners to "satisfy" the other.

If you have never masturbated but would like to try, it may take some time to adjust to the idea and to find the way that gives you the most pleasure. The Resources section lists some excellent books that offer specific suggestions. Deliberately setting the mood in much the same way you would with a partner—candles, incense, and music—can enhance the experience. A soothing bath or a glass of wine may help you relax and focus on yourself for an interlude of

---

*The expression "pleasuring ourselves" as an alternative for the word "masturbation" was suggested to us by Eleanor Hamilton, a seventy-five-year-old pioneer in sex education who has written a great deal about cultural biases against pleasure and sex. Hamilton objects to the word "masturbation," which is derived from the Latin meaning "to pollute with the hand."

personal sexual pleasure. You may enjoy the feelings of arousal whether or not you have an orgasm.

Those of us for whom masturbation is not an acceptable choice can still enjoy sensuality—luxuriating in a bubble bath, feeling the sun on our skin, exchanging a massage with a friend. These body experiences can enrich our lives and help us feel alive and vital.

FANTASIES

Sexual fantasy can help arouse, maintain, and increase sexual excitement. It is particularly helpful to women who lose their concentration during sex. A fantasy can be a story or stories, or a series of erotic images. Sometimes partners share their fantasies.

We have a wide variety of scenes. I am the rampaging female who leaps into bed in a comical way. Or when I'm very tired he says, "You rest, I'll do all the work." Or we play who gets to be the baby—or other psychological conditions—we play with them and we don't feel threatened. [a woman in her late fifties]

We may feel disloyal to a partner if we fantasize while lovemaking, or worry that something we imagine is bad or "sick." Yet creating erotic images is just a way of allowing ourselves to experiment without risk. It may take a while to accept our fantasies and understand that we can enjoy them without having to act on them.

SEXUALITY AND RELATIONSHIPS

During the second half of life, we face major physical and emotional changes affecting our sexuality. Many long-time partners feel increasingly more comfortable over time as they learn how to give sexual pleasure to each other.

In a long-term relationship, lovemaking provides a way to express our deepest feelings of tenderness and mutual caring. Lovemaking can also provide comfort during times of loss and change.

We were feeling so troubled and unhappy we just went to bed and made love to give each other some solace from this terrible sadness. [an eighty-two-year-old woman]

Marianne Gontarz

A loving partner who understands and accepts us and is willing to compromise is an important element in a satisfying sexual relationship.

We have a generalized sexual relationship. We're very sexy with each other in a continuous way. It doesn't show a lot...just through little things like touching fingers in the movies. [a fifty-eight-year-old woman]

There are several factors that can diminish interest in sexual activity between long-term partners. Recent research shows that the sexual activity of married women seventy or older is directly influenced by physical disability, illness, or loss of their male partners.[7] In many instances, when a male partner loses his interest in sex, his self-confidence, or his ability to have an erection, all sexual activity ends. Sometimes when both partners retire they feel they are spending too much time together; each person feels emotionally crowded. Women in long-term lesbian relationships often share the same activities and friends; they may be even more likely to find themselves struggling with this problem. For all couples, having some separate interests, activities, and friends can help keep each

partner and their mutual relationship vital and interesting.

Sometimes sadness, unresolved anger, or disappointment with a partner can block sexual feeling. Allowing your feelings to surface, acknowledging them, and discussing them with your partner may renew sexual desire.

A number of studies suggest that in marriage, satisfaction increases after child rearing is finished and children leave home.[8]

We didn't have choice of time when the kids were young. Now we have time during the day. We seldom make love at nighttime. Now we can choose. It might be 10 A.M., or 2 P.M.—whenever we're feeling turned on. [a sixty-five-year-old woman]

Because of the double standard in aging, some women as they grow older worry about losing their partner to a younger woman.

My husband is going through some kind of change—he's on a strict diet and runs several miles a day. I have to admit to myself he looks fifty. Me, I look my age. He's got this young woman at work—says she's like a daughter and he's helping her—she keeps calling for this and that. Joe wants me to invite her to dinner but I'm not fooled by this daughter business. I think he's trying to hold on to youth. I keep suggesting things we can do together. We joined a theater group and sometimes we go out dancing with another couple. [a sixty-five-year-old woman, married forty years]

Because women on average have a longer life expectancy than men, most of us will experience the loss of a partner through death. If your relationship has ended with your partner's death, you may not feel sexual for some time while you mourn the loss.

After he died I was celibate for a long while and then went through a long stretch of mourning and masturbation, always with a tremendous sense of grief. [a seventy-eight-year-old woman speaking of a time when she was in her fifties]

After a time of grieving most of us redefine ourselves as survivors with continuing needs for love, affection, and sexual expression. Then we may be ready to consider a new sexual partner.

When partners separate, some of us—particularly those who didn't initiate the breakup—may also lose interest for a while in expressing ourselves sexually as we grieve over the end of the relationship. Our self-esteem may be low and it may take us a while to regain sexual confidence. Or we may be ready to resume sexual activity right away. We may be surprised or even embarrassed by unexpected feelings of sexual desire.

Whereas married people sometimes take sex for granted, single people face continuing decisions about their sexuality, including the choice of being sexual with one person or with more than one.

I have been single for ten years and had many lovers. I like sex a lot; I went through what I call my sport fucking phase. I didn't have to love him—if I felt like having sex I had sex. Now I have two lovers. Sex is very nice with both these men. In fact it's better than it's been for a long time. [a fifty-five-year-old woman]

Many women want more emotional intimacy than can be found in a casual sexual encounter. Some of us have difficulty finding male partners who care about intimacy as much as we do.

It's hard to get emotional closeness and great sex to come together in one relationship. I had an affair and enjoyed it but we didn't have commitment as I did with my husband. It's true what the books say: sexuality goes on all your life. But you can't split sexuality from emotion. To me sexuality means intimacy. [a seventy-year-old woman]

If we are dating again for the first time in many years, we may feel awkward and unsure of what to expect. How far will my date expect me to go? Can I get by with a goodnight kiss? Often, both men and women would be happy to have a friendly, nonsexual relationship, but feel pressured by certain expectations.

After I got divorced at forty-eight, I expected to have a man courting me like my husband did when I was a teenager in Venezuela. I was very naive, so I had some surprises. I went out with a man and then he asked me to go up to his apartment to listen to music. So I said, "We just came from listening to music!" I was naive, but I wasn't stupid! I wanted someone to hold my hand and say nice things, not to jump into bed with someone I didn't really know. [a fifty-nine-year-old woman]

Now I enjoy flirtations; when I don't worry about whether we'll have sex, it's totally fun. [a forty-eight-year-old divorced woman]

After about two years of brief and unsatisfactory relationships, I met a wonderful, warm, caring man, with a surprisingly developed feminist consciousness. How delightful to find that in bed he was exciting, passionate, and playful. [a forty-four-year-old divorced woman]

The man shortage, a hot topic among women of every age, can become critical in the second half of life. Today one out of every five middle-aged women is single,[9] whether out of choice, widowhood, or divorce. Among older women, the majority are unmarried; in fact, older women are twice as likely to be unmarried as older men.[10] Men over sixty-five are seven times more likely to remarry than women over sixty-five, and when they do, they usually marry younger women.[11]

Whenever I have been between relationships I have prided myself on being independent and not needing a man in my life. But now that I have no man in my life—now that I am not even casually dating, now that I have cut my ties with my long-distance lover—I realize that what I miss most is the physical contact. I am not even necessarily talking about sex, although that is very important to me. I miss the cuddling and holding and touching with affection. [a woman in her fifties]

Being single I miss that flow in marriage—when I was married if we didn't make love one day there was always tomorrow. [a divorced woman in her fifties]

What the hell. I'm really nicer than I used to be and now no one's looking. [a divorced woman in her sixties]

I wasn't only mourning my husband, I was mourning that there might never be someone else. [a seventy-eight-year-old widow]

Women who have lost a partner find many different solutions to the problem. Some marry again. Others choose a less formal although not necessarily less committed relationship, dating one male or female partner exclusively but maintaining separate living quarters, or living with a partner without marrying. Some women who are having trouble finding suitable sexual partners are learning to initiate both social and sexual interactions more often. Some of us, even some who never dreamed we would choose an unconventional life-style, are considering or trying out new kinds of relationships.

I keep wondering—is this the end of lovers? I can't really believe that. Yet in my experience few men my age are interesting and vital. Younger men? Sure, why not. But not too much younger or the experience gap becomes too much. I meet lots of interesting women and I am enlarging my circle of women friends. If I really connected with someone would I consider a lesbian relationship? Maybe. In the meantime, I am accepting myself in a new and different way. I am learning to treat and to nurture myself by doing the things I want to do and not doing what I don't want in a more honest way than ever before. [a woman in her fifties]

I feel such intense body hunger—for touching and stroking and for good old-fashioned sex. Sometimes I get together with an old friend. Neither of us wants it to be more than what it is now—good old friends with sex sometimes. [a forty-nine-year-old divorced woman]

I met a man fourteen years younger. We can laugh and talk and it feels so relaxed. He is very uninhibited sexually. We spend our time laughing and doing fun things. I relate so much better to younger men; they are less rigid about sex roles than older men. I like their values. [a forty-eight-year-old divorced woman]

I know a woman who is fifty-two who has a forty-year-old lover. She told me I have a hang-up about age, but I'm fifty-three, I'm afraid of getting hurt. Still, there's something to what she said: "If you're alive and beautiful inside, with all the experience and patience older women have, no twenty-two- or thirty-year-old can really compete. A fascinating older woman can be irresistible for certain types of younger men." I'm thinking about this and loosening up.

Sexuality between two women can be deeply satisfying. Some middle-aged or older women are, for the first time, considering or having sexual relationships with women.

I had an orgasm during a nonsexual massage which another woman was giving me. I thought, "What difference does it make what gender the hands are?" [a woman in her fifties]

My first sexual experience with a woman was at age forty. I found myself very suddenly and very intensely turned on to a good friend who was gay. No sexual involvement was possible since she was in a long-term relationship with another woman, but the feeling was clearly there. That summer I began to seek out women as sexual partners while on vacation. I was absolutely captivated by the sensations of holding and physically loving another woman. The combination of delicacy and strength was thrilling. And the softness...that double twofold softness of two women together. [a fifty-year-old woman]

I spent years trying to make it in the heterosexual world because my sexual identity was "wrong." When I finally allowed myself to love another woman fully, it was like coming home—home at last. [a woman in her sixties]

I grew up loving women—the way they walk, smell, feel; wanting to touch them, cherish them, love them passionately and overtly, but it was not until years later that I actually fell in love with a woman. I found it extremely liberating and also a wonderful way to develop deep friendships and associations in one's old age. I am part of a group of women who are developing mutual interests and commitments. [a seventy-eight-year-old woman]

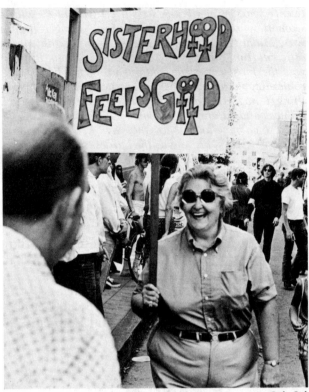

Cathy Cade

Although it is sometimes suggested that heterosexual women would be more sexually active if they would consider women as partners, a recent survey of one hundred lesbians aged sixty to eighty-six found that 53 percent had had no sexual contact in the past year. One-third of the 53 percent consider themselves celibate, but three-quarters of that number are not celibate by choice.[12] It may be that the issue is not the gender of our partners, but our own socialization, which conditions us to wait for someone else to initiate a sexual relationship.[13] Another study of twenty-five lesbians over sixty found none had casual sex after sixty, but most had sex an average of three times a month, which is comparable to or more frequent than lesbian couples of all ages.[14] It is difficult to know how to interpret findings such as these because research on older lesbians is very limited.

Early in my life I knew that I never wanted to have children and I never wanted to marry. I had crushes on camp counselors and some girl friends, but I also had boy friends. At forty-five for the first time in my life I suddenly wanted to get married. My menopausal crisis! My lover was willing but then I realized that while it was a good relationship for a weekend in another city, I couldn't imagine being married to him. I decided marriage was not right for me and then I was celibate for twenty years. When I was sixty-five I fell in love with a woman who was twenty-three years younger than I was. Making love with a woman was not that much different from experiences I had had with men. But this was the most complete relationship of my life. It was romantic, passionate, sharing, intellectual. It was everything I had read about but never experienced—such fullness and balance. When the relationship ended I decided to go back to celibacy, the way I had lived happily for twenty years, but it was the hardest thing I ever did. Maybe I'm into twenty-year cycles and can look forward to another love when I'm eighty-five. That would be nice. [a seventy-two-year-old woman]

Many middle-aged and older women are celibate. Some lack the opportunity to meet partners, others prefer to be celibate rather than change a lifetime pattern of being involved in one special relationship.

Whether you are celibate out of necessity or by choice, you can still lead a happy and satisfying life, enjoying affection, the company of friends, and sensual pleasures.

SEX AND AGING: PHYSIOLOGICAL AND EMOTIONAL CHANGES

As we age, we experience changes in our bodies that affect our sexuality. It's important to distinguish between the effects of the aging process itself, temporary hormonal changes we undergo during and after menopause, and the effects of illness, disability, and relationship difficulties. We don't need to resign ourselves to sexual problems as a natural, irreversible part of aging. As women, we have learned to come to terms with changes in our bodies; we can understand and accommodate ourselves to the changes of aging just as we did during menstruation and pregnancy. If you connect your sexual identity with the ability to have children, after menopause you may experience a sense of loss and a *temporary* drop in sexual desire. Some women report a need to mourn the ending of fertility, although such feelings are usually short-lived.

I know I wouldn't ever want to get pregnant again. Yet I'm aware that we derived great satisfaction from the thought that we could get pregnant if we wanted to. Sometimes we fantasize that we are making a baby, but it's not the same. [a fifty-one-year-old woman]

Many women in their fifties experience a reawakening of sexual interest once they no longer

need to prevent pregnancy and once the pressures of child rearing are past.[15]

It's wonderfully freeing. I always hated the mess and the interruption of birth control. I was always anxious about getting pregnant and that put a damper on sex. [a forty-nine-year-old woman]

At times, hot flashes during menopause can interfere with sexual enjoyment.

My lover and I have had to be very creative to find suitable positions for lovemaking which take into account that one of us is bound to have a hot flash in the middle of it all. We discovered that lying next to each other, toes to head, gives us a good vantage point for genital play (toes are good for sucking too) without overwhelming each other with our wacky temperature controls. We'll be damned if such a thing can slow down our sexual pleasuring. [a lesbian in her fifties]

Orgasm

For many women, clitoral stimulation leads to orgasm. Yet until the mid 1960s, medical texts and marriage manuals followed Freud's famous dictum that the "mature" woman had orgasms only when her vagina, not her clitoris, was stimulated. Then sex researchers found that much of the sexual pleasure women experience occurs because of direct or indirect stimulation of the clitoris.[16] This information electrified the newly developing women's movement and contributed to a revolution in women's understanding of ourselves as sexually autonomous beings rather than sexual objects.[17] More recent research indicates that orgasm may occur as the result of clitoral stimulation, vaginal[18] and uterine stimulation, or a combination of both.

For many women, continuous clitoral stimulation is what most surely brings orgasm. Some women enjoy orgasms brought on by penetration of the vagina which they describe as feeling "deep" or "uterine," and may find clitoral stimulation distracting if continued during vaginal penetration. In addition, increasing attention is being given to those women who report a loss of sexual feeling after hysterectomy;[19] they may miss the jiggling of the pelvic muscles and cervix which they had formerly felt during deep penetration. These new understandings lend further support to the idea that women's sexuality is complex and multifaceted. The main thing to remember is that you are the expert about yourself, and you can adjust your sexual pleasures to meet your changing needs.

Women who have uterine contractions during orgasm sometimes find that after menopause these are less intense, more spasmodic and irregular, and fewer in number. A few older women experience painful contractions, somewhat like menstrual cramps, during orgasm. This is more likely to occur if orgasm is infrequent. If this happens to you, try not to get into a cycle of worrying about it, because this condition is similar to the discomfort we experience when any seldom-used muscle is exercised and is less likely to continue if you have orgasms more frequently. If you have sex with a partner infrequently, or if the anxiety about the contractions interferes with your orgasm with a partner, you can help yourself by masturbating to orgasm until you feel more relaxed and the contractions go away or become less painful.

Slower Arousal Time

As a result of aging, both women and men become aroused more slowly.

You know you are middle-aged when a "quickie" takes forty-five minutes. [a fifty-one-year-old woman]

It's true that I need more time to be turned on, but everything balances out because I enjoy sex more once I do get aroused. [a forty-nine-year-old woman]

I've never been quick to have an orgasm and now it takes longer and I can't always count on it. I choose to make love because I want to be touched and stroked. [a fifty-five-year-old woman]

The slowing of sexual responses is similar to other ways in which our bodies slow down physically. If we believe social attitudes that "virility" or "sexual allure" means instant arousal, we may become alarmed as our bodies respond more slowly. This may lead to further anxiety and affect our confidence in ourselves. However, slower arousal time has its compensations.

When Jay used to lose his erection I would think that I had failed as a woman because I couldn't keep him aroused. But now I see that it can mean more time to play around and a chance to start over again so that lovemaking lasts longer. [a forty-nine-year-old woman]

Vaginal Changes

As we age, the lips of the vagina, or the labia, become less firm, and less fatty tissue covers the mons, or pubic bone. This reduction in fatty tissue may decrease the pleasurable sense of fullness that was formerly part of your sexual response. The length of the vaginal canal may seem shorter, since the tissues are less elastic. The stretching of these delicate tissues may hurt on penetration or deep thrusting. In addition, thinner vaginal walls offer less protection to the bladder and urethra during intercourse and may result in bladder irritation or infection. Drinking a glass of water before sex and urinating after sex, as well as washing your genitals before and after sex, may help this condition. A hot bath feels good and helps relieve irritation after lovemaking.

The lower estrogen levels that accompany middle age may cause dryness or itching of the vagina, making intercourse less comfortable or even painful. You may need more stimulation before you are lubricated enough for penetration. Dryness can also make it uncomfortable to have the vulva or clitoris caressed. Changing your lovemaking to allow more time to get aroused and expanding your repertoire to include more caresses—especially oral sex, which provides its own lubrication—before or instead of penetration may be all that is necessary.

A lot of hand play is wonderful because it does start the juices flowing. [a woman in her seventies]

I've always loved sex and I could make love for hours. Now, even though I'm excited, my vagina doesn't have enough juice. It's so frustrating—I want to, but it hurts. We have found that after penetration if he just waits and doesn't move for a while it stops hurting and then it's fine. [a fifty-one-year-old woman]

We can incorporate lubricants into our lovemaking now even if we never used them earlier in our lives. Try an over-the-counter product. Knowing that you are already lubricated may help you to relax and let your feelings of arousal build until your natural lubrication takes over. Artificial lubricants should not be expected to replace natural lubrication, since without some of her own lubrication a woman is neither physically nor psychologically ready for intercourse.[20]

If a woman feels pressured by her partner for rapid penetration, she may experience even less lubrication. Susanne Morgan notes that "lubrication is more than wetness: it is the first indication of arousal."[21]

There are several safe and effective lubricants on the market today, such as massage oils (with or without a variety of fragrances), vitamin E oil, apricot kernel oil, sesame oil, coconut oil, cocoa butter, and wheat germ oil. You can order Trans-lube or Kama Sutra oils through ads in magazines like *Ms.* or *Cosmopolitan*. Some authorities, however, suggest using only water-based lubricants because oil-based lubricants don't flush out of the system as readily, and in older women they may cause vaginal infection.[22] Do not use petroleum products such as Vaseline for lubrication. Perfumes may be irritating to many women. Koromex, K-Y Jelly, and Ortho II are all sterile, water-based vaginal jellies available in drug stores. Astroglide and Senselle are smooth, slippery, long-lasting lubricants that can be ordered through the mail (see Resources). Aci-gel, for vaginal itching, is available with a prescription. It is a medication that changes the pH of the vagina. When itching stops, go back to a nonmedicated lubricant.

After my hysterectomy I started to experience discomfort with intercourse; my vagina was becoming very dry. There was no longer any pleasure in the activity; sex became something to avoid. Early on I started to use a personal lubricant with unsatisfactory results. Being a resourceful person, I dug deep into my past experience and remembered that the introduction of the spermicidal jelly with an applicator (which I used to use with my diaphragm) always produced the side advantage of easier intercourse. So I dug out my old plastic plunger-type applicator and filled it with the lubricant as in days gone by. The result was tremendous! My husband and I instantly noticed the improvement. The problem of getting the lubricant where I needed it the most was resolved. [a woman in her late thirties]

Some physicians prescribe estrogen for a dry vagina. This is a powerful drug which should not be taken without first considering all of its potential effects. (See chapter on Menopause and p. 268.) An alternative to taking estrogen orally is the use of low-dose estrogen cream. It is important to note that estrogen is absorbed even more quickly when used vaginally than when taken orally. Because estrogen cream bypasses the liver, the risk of liver and gallbladder problems is reduced. However, the risk of cancer of the uterine lining (endometrium) and the risk of other effects of estrogen are still present. If nothing else helps and you feel you must try estrogen cream, use as little as possible for as short a time period as is necessary to get the desired results. Apply the cream

to the area which is most sore, usually the entrance to the vagina. A week of such treatment will usually relieve soreness. English researchers found that only one-eighth of the dosage usually recommended by American doctors is enough to plump up vaginal tissues.[23] The cream comes with an applicator with rings on the side which measure out four grams. You can measure a one-eighth dose if you use only enough cream to fill one of the small rings marked on the plastic applicator. If you can't use estrogen, androgen cream (which is made of 1 to 2 percent testosterone in a water-soluble cream) is another way to treat vaginal soreness and is used in the same fashion as estrogen cream (see p. 297 for the risks of using testosterone). These powerful substances are medications. They should never be used as lubricants at the time of lovemaking.

Clitoral Changes

The clitoris is always highly sensitive and grows even more so as we age. The hood of skin that covers the clitoris may pull back, so that the clitoris is fully exposed. If your clitoris becomes hypersensitive, you may not be able to tolerate having it directly touched or rubbed without lots of lubrication. Touching the mons, the clitoral hood, and the labia will stimulate the clitoris indirectly and provide pleasure.

Men Also Change

Men as well as women undergo changes in their sexuality as they age. Lower testosterone levels are sometimes a factor in loss of sexual interest for some men. Their sexual responses may slow down, and they may need a longer time of nondemanding genital stimulation before they attain a full erection. Once lost, the erection may take longer to regain.

A woman can help her partner to gain a full erection by putting pressure on the base of his penis, and massaging it away from his abdomen. This will press against the major blood vessels and hold the blood in the penis, creating an erection. It is important not to pull it up toward the abdomen, since this will drain the blood from the penis and diminish the erection. Another technique which some men like is to

EXTERNAL GENITALIA

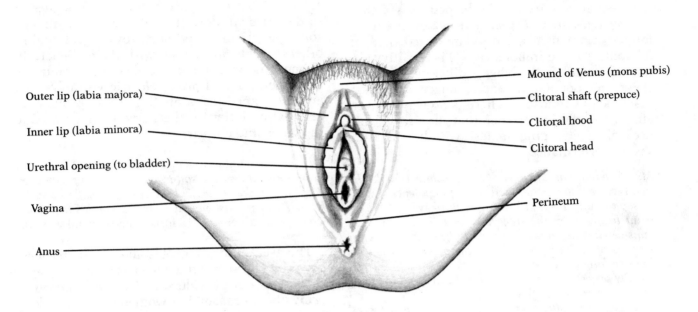

Outer lip (labia majora)

Inner lip (labia minora)

Urethral opening (to bladder)

Vagina

Anus

Mound of Venus (mons pubis)

Clitoral shaft (prepuce)

Clitoral hood

Clitoral head

Perineum

stuff a partially erect penis into the vagina and then the woman tightens her vaginal muscles rhythmically as a form of stimulation for both partners.[24]

Middle-aged and older men also experience changes in orgasm. They often don't need to ejaculate at the end of each sexual experience and may opt for orgasm every two or three episodes rather than every time they make love. Older men also need a longer time to renew their sexual energy after an orgasm before they can have another erection. But by delaying ejaculation and not pushing for orgasm after each lovemaking session, an older man can often rapidly become erect again. This means that both partners can enjoy frequent lovemaking and have orgasms when it feels right.[25]

My lover's divorce had left him feeling sexually rejected and vulnerable. When our relationship grew intimate, I made it clear that I didn't regard sex as a competition, but as a way for two people to express warmth and caring. My friend's "problem," delayed ejaculation, allowed us to prolong our lovemaking until both of us were ecstatically exhausted. Instead of the conventional problem of "would I come?" I worried at first when he didn't come, but he assured me that he didn't need to come every time. Sometimes we would resume our lovemaking in the morning and then he would have his orgasm, while I would sometimes have another. As we grow to love each other more, our delight in giving each other pleasure deepens. [a forty-seven-year-old woman]

Now there is longer playing around...and without fussing about whether it's going to be regular intercourse. We can bring each other to orgasm at any time. It's no longer goal oriented, so it's wonderful. [a woman in her late seventies]

Impotence is the inability to maintain an erection long enough to have intercourse. It is usually temporary. Sudden onset of impotence is usually the result of some unusual stress. Once the stress is removed, potency often returns.

I was getting angry because he seemed to be giving up sex. I was being solicitous—doing oral sex because I wanted it to work the first time after his operation. Then oh! It worked just like it used to! [a sixty-eight-year-old woman]

We enjoy each other. As far as sex is concerned, he is sensible. He understands he can't do what he used to do. Some men can't admit this and blame the woman, but not him. [a sixty-eight-year-old woman in a second marriage of thirty years]

He can't maintain an erection, so we mutually masturbate and it's very satisfying. [a sixty-five-year-old woman]

Although there is a sharp upward turn in male impotence after age fifty, a high percentage of men who become impotent after years of normal sexual activity can be helped by sex therapy. Worries about career and money or illness, fatigue, heavy meals, and too much to drink can all contribute to impotence. "This sensitivity to mental fatigue is the biggest difference between the aging population and younger men," say Masters and Johnson. "There is no way to overemphasize the importance that the 'fear of failure' plays in aging males' withdrawal from sexual performance."[26]

My husband was anxious about prostate trouble. He had been very ill and had a history of impotence. I want to say to him, "Relax, it's going to be okay," but I don't want to touch on the subject because I'm afraid he'll consider it a demand. He seems to be getting back his feelings of sexiness, but it's a slow process. When it's been so long [since we had sex] that I'm taking it personally or feel far away from him, I initiate it by doing something romantic. I dress up and do a dance, or I arrange a sexy situation of some sort—and it works. But he prefers to get it going himself because he's never sure if he's going to have an erection. [a sixty-five-year-old woman]

Recent evidence has shown that up to 50 percent of male impotence (more than was suspected) may be caused by physical problems such as arteriosclerosis.[27] But when a partner has sexual problems or slows down sexually, whether because of physiological or psychological problems, we may interpret it as rejection, or fear that it has something to do with our diminished "attractiveness."

Social stereotypes that men are "supposed" to have stronger sex drives than women and that women are "supposed" to be passive but alluring recipients of sex only aggravate the situation.

My husband became impotent. One of the grimmest things was the sense of helplessness and guilt. I wondered what I could do differently but was not able to speak about it openly because it was a big bad sad problem. We went months without sex and every time I would realize this I became enraged that he didn't want it. I thought maybe I should take the initiative, but he saw that as aggressive and as a demand, and he wouldn't even play around. I found that painful—we couldn't be physically intimate in any way without his seeing it as a threat. When we became preoccupied with his erections, I didn't have orgasm any more. I was left hanging in the air. [a woman in her fifties]

Sexual Aids

Many older women are enjoying sex aids which are available through mail-order catalogues or in department stores (see Resources). Although some people may find such toys objectionable, others delight in playing with them. Generally, women find vibrators more effective stimulation than men do, and prefer electric vibrators that are not shaped like a phallus. These provide intense stimulation to the nerve endings around the vulva and clitoris.

I'd never be without one again! Sometimes I just want to be soothed and the sound and continuing vibration does that. Other times if I want to get really excited I know I can if I use my vibrator. For me it's a sure-fire way to have an orgasm. [a forty-nine-year-old woman]

The weak vibration of some small, battery-powered vibrators often advertised in sex magazines does not provide sufficient stimulation to bring about orgasm, but women who enjoy deep penetration may prefer them.

Many women report that they like a sensation of fullness inside the vagina, and use dildoes for this purpose. You can order dildoes from sex magazines or you can make your own from candles or vegetables (either raw or partially cooked). It is important never to use glass objects or anything which might hurt you or break. Always wash anything which has been in the anus before inserting it in the vagina.

Some couples like to look at erotic films, magazines, or books, or to listen to sexy music or relaxing tapes or records of environmental sounds such as surf, forest sounds, or falling water. "White noise" such as the hum from a fan or air conditioner can block distracting noises and allow you to concentrate on your intimate environment.

Accommodations in Lovemaking

Illness may bring about a temporary loss of sexual interest or ability to engage in sexual activity. Most illnesses do not mean the end of sexual activity but may require different ways of giving and receiving pleasure. With problems such as arthritis or back pain, fear of causing pain or being hurt can affect spontaneity. If a partner holds back in lovemaking or rarely initiates sex, her or his concern about illness may be misinterpreted as rejection. In fact, good sex can actually help relieve pain. It is distracting, and sexual stimulation releases neurotransmitters in the brain which block pain and produce pleasure.[28]

People sometimes fear returning to sexual activity after an illness or surgery. Through masturbation, you can rediscover your sexual self in private communication with your own body, trying out degrees of arousal that feel safe and comfortable. Once you feel reassured that your body is still capable of responding with pleasure, you may be ready to ask your partner to join you. Satisfying intimacy can hasten the healing process. Many women find they are more comfortable with a gradual resumption of lovemaking—touching, hand-holding, and caressing at first as a way to express closeness until they feel ready to resume full sexual relations.

If one person is unavailable sexually because of illness, it is always possible to lie together and hold each other and let feelings flow in a warm and close embrace. The most important thing to remember is that if you are open to trying new ways of making love you *will* be able to continue having sex. Even when you can't enjoy penetration or intercourse, you can still give and receive pleasure using a variety of techniques.

My husband had a series of operations last year—a penile implant—and he's still unable to enjoy sex. That doesn't matter so much to me. We still make love and hold and kiss. [a sixty-five-year-old woman, married forty years]

The following ideas may help when one of the partners is having physical problems.

Sex researchers encourage exercising sexual organs through Kegel exercises, masturbation, or lovemaking to help maintain muscle tone and lubrication. If you have not been sexual in a while, you may feel tight or dry at first, but you can overcome this with Kegel exercises (see p. 73) followed by gentle and slow resumption of sexual activity.

Let your partner know what feels good and what hurts during sex. You may want to do this by talking or by guiding your partner's hand away from tender areas, or toward places that feel especially good. Tell your partner what your present sensations feel like. Once you feel secure about being understood, you will be better able to relax and surrender to sexual pleasure without fear of pain.

Before making love, agree on a clear signal which you both know is a sign to stop if something hurts you. If a favorite position has become uncomfortable because of temporary or permanent aches and pains, experiment to find a position that feels better.

Ask for what you want in a positive way. Offering an alternative sexual activity which you enjoy is easier on your partner's ego. Some women find it easier to discuss sexual issues during nonsexual times together. Look for a private time when you won't be interrupted.

Communication is important between partners regardless of gender. We cannot assume that a woman partner will know what we want and enjoy—women have to make the effort to be clear and explicit with each other. It's easy to hide our own embarrassment or reluctance to ask for what we want behind the assumption that "She must know, for, after all, she is a woman like me." It's important to understand that every woman is different.

Choose a time of day when you are both feeling comfortable. Making love in the morning when you are rested can help if you tire easily. Men are more likely to have an erection in the morning. Time lovemaking to coincide with maximum effectiveness of pain medications. Turn up the thermostat; a warm room helps you feel limber.

Creating a relaxed sexy mood with your partner can be a way to increase intimacy and release sexual energy. Changing the time and place for sex may keep it from seeming routine. The setting can make a big difference in whether you feel a surge of desire—an attractive, tidy bedroom free of reminders of illnesses can be an asset. Simply moving all the pill bottles into the bathroom may lift our spirits and put us in the mood for lovemaking.[29]

Mild exercise, yoga, massage, breathing and relaxation exercises, meditation, and prayer all reduce stress, counteract stiff muscles, and can be good preludes to making love. Taking a bath or shower together, listening to music, sharing a relaxing meal or quiet talk can help you and your partner feel close and connected.

Getting Help

Usually sexual difficulties can be resolved by talking things through in a spirit of mutual cooperation, but at times it may be necessary to

The "spoon position," where both partners lie on their sides and one has her back to the other, is excellent for cuddling and for lovemaking with or without intercourse. You can stimulate your own clitoris and breasts in this position or ask your partner to do so.

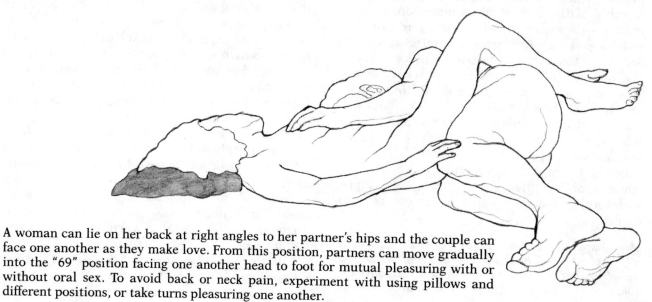

A woman can lie on her back at right angles to her partner's hips and the couple can face one another as they make love. From this position, partners can move gradually into the "69" position facing one another head to foot for mutual pleasuring with or without oral sex. To avoid back or neck pain, experiment with using pillows and different positions, or take turns pleasuring one another.

Use a low hassock or stool to lean on while kneeling, and your partner can hold you from behind; or stand and lean forward against a sturdy piece of furniture such as a bureau, and your partner can caress you.

Having one partner on top of the other may be too stressful if either partner is having physical problems. Partners can caress one another or have intercourse in a sitting or reclining position. It can be comfortable to sit in an armless chair where one person sits in the chair and the second person sits on her partner's lap. Make sure the chair is sturdy. Sit so that both partners' feet touch the ground; this way neither person bears too much weight.

Change positions to allow for fatigue. The person who is ill or tired can lie on her or his back while the other partner kneels above. Several pillows can be used to advantage to support a back or be placed under the knees.

SAFE SEX GUIDELINES FOR WOMEN AT RISK FOR AIDS TRANSMISSION*

If you believe that you or your sex partner(s) may be infected with the AIDS virus, or you are not sure, avoid sexual activity that involves contact with body fluids, infected blood, semen, urine, feces, and possibly vaginal secretions. Body fluids can be exchanged through needle-sharing, or through *unprotected* sexual contact with a person who is infected.

Specific Guidelines for Sexual Activity

SAFE
   Massage
   Hugging
   Body-to-body rubbing
   Social (dry) kissing
   Voyeurism, exhibitionism,
      fantasy
   Masturbation

POSSIBLY SAFE
   Vaginal or anal intercourse with
      a condom
   Fellatio/blow jobs/oral sex on a
      man with a condom
   Cunnilingus/oral sex on a woman
      with a barrier
   Hand/finger-to-genital contact
      with a latex or rubber glove or
      finger cot
   French (wet) kissing
   Water sports/sex play involving
      urination (external only)

POSSIBLY UNSAFE
   Cunnilingus/oral sex without a
      barrier
   Hand/finger-to-genital contact
      without a latex or rubber glove
      or finger cot

UNSAFE
   Vaginal or anal intercourse
      without a condom
   Fellatio/blow jobs without a
      condom
   Semen or urine in the mouth
   Blood contact of any kind
      (including menstrual blood and
      sharing IV needles)
   Rimming (oral-anal contact)
   Fisting (hand in rectum/vagina)
   Sharing sex toys that have
      contact with body fluids

IN ANY SITUATION, SEXUAL OR OTHERWISE,
SHARING NEEDLES IS UNSAFE.

*Reprinted from *The Network News*, Vol. 11, No. 6, November/December 1986.

PREVENTIVE MEASURES

CONDOMS: Recently, studies have shown that condoms block the transmission of the AIDS virus in the laboratory. Therefore, most researchers believe that condoms, carefully used, will offer some protection from the AIDS virus. A small amount of spermicide or a water soluble lubricant (not Vaseline) inside of the tip of the condom increases sensitivity for the male partner but too much could cause the condom to slip off.

SPERMICIDES: Nonoxynol-9, the active ingredient in most spermicides, has been found to kill the AIDS virus in some laboratory situations. Many researchers believe, therefore, that it is a good idea to use a spermicide containing nonoxynol-9 as a backup in case the condom splits or breaks. CAUTION: Some people are allergic to nonoxynol-9. Test the spermicide on the inside of your wrist before using it. If it stings or you get another reaction, try changing brands.

DISPOSABLE LATEX OR RUBBER GLOVES AND FINGER COTS: If you have cuts, scratches or hangnails on your fingers or hands, physicians' disposable latex or rubber gloves, or finger cots, will prevent contact with the AIDS virus during hand-genital or hand-anal contact.

LATEX OR RUBBER BARRIERS ("RUBBER DAMS"): Some sexologists have suggested that cunnilingus may be safe if done using a barrier that prevents the exchange of fluids between the tongue and vulva. Rubber dams are a thin piece of latex that comes in various sizes and is about the same thickness as a physician's disposable glove. Latex barriers come in rolls or sheets and can be purchased at dental and surgical supply houses. At this time, no research has been done on whether or not they provide protection. People who have tried to use them find them fairly awkward. However, they should be considered if there is a significant risk to transmitting the AIDS virus.

DISCLAIMER

Condoms, spermicides, latex gloves, and other barriers can prevent the transmission of the AIDS virus in ideal conditions. However, real life is often not ideal and they may not work in all instances.

For more information call a local AIDS hotline; the SF AIDS Foundation Hotline at 415/863-AIDS; or COYOTE at 415/552-1849.

Compiled by the Women's AIDS Network, Coyote,
Project Aware and the Lesbian Insemination Project

consult a sex therapist or counselor specially trained to understand sexual problems.

Sex therapy usually takes less than six months. Clients are given sexual "homework assignments" which they carry out at home and then discuss with the therapist at the following meeting. Lists of qualified sex therapists are available through women's health or resource centers, SIECUS, or AASECT (see Resources), or you can ask your physician for a referral.

Getting information from physicians can be a problem if either you or the doctor is reluctant to discuss sexual matters. Some doctors are comfortable with sexuality and are aware that older people have sex lives. Most, however, have little or no training in issues related to sexual functioning in general and many are ignorant or embarrassed about sex or have ageist attitudes. If you encounter a doctor who shifts the focus of your questions about sex into other areas or ignores or trivializes them, you may want to find another doctor.

The medical history your physician takes should include sexual problems in the past, changes in genital organs, and present sexual functioning. Your physician should also question you not only about the prescription drugs you take, but also about vitamin and mineral supplements and over-the-counter preparations.

Physicians rarely initiate a discussion about how an illness or medical procedure will affect sexuality, so you will have to introduce this topic yourself. Find out when you can resume sexual relations. Ask which activities you can resume and when. Be *very* specific in your questions and insist on explicit answers.

I accompanied my partner to the hospital where he was to have a prostate biopsy. The doctor gave a rapid-fire list of instructions on self-care for the days and weeks following surgery. When he mentioned sex, he said, "Sex, the same." I stopped him and asked, "Do you mean abstain from sex the same number of days as the previous instruction, or the same as usual, or what?" "Oh, two days" was the reply.

As instructed, we obediently abstained. When the two days were up we were eager to resume lovemaking. Proceeding in a gingerly fashion, we were gratified to find everything in good working order and had a lovely time. The following day, we began to feel turned on and started playing around. I was masturbating him with my hand, whereupon we were shocked to see a stream of bright red blood shoot forth from his penis. Since we had not yet heard the good news that the biopsy was negative, we were particularly frightened and upset. We

called the HMO and spoke with a nurse on call who finally reached the doctor and relayed his new instructions to us. No sex for two weeks! Either he had misstated the original instruction, or he was changing it based on changed circumstances. When my partner returned for his follow-up visit, the young doctor was terribly embarrassed, as much out of surprise that we were "so active" at our age as for his error. [this woman and her partner are both in their late forties]

A nurse tells of a woman in her seventies who seemed inexplicably depressed after being told she could go home following a successful colostomy.* The staff had been impressed with the closeness between this woman and her husband and were surprised at her lack of anticipation about going home. Finally, she confided to the nurse, "I'm not the same as I was." She was concerned that the operation would make her unable to have sexual relations. Neither the doctor nor any of the nurses had reassured her or her husband that they could have sexual relations, assuming they were "too old" to care about sexuality.

Also ask your doctor how prescribed drugs will affect your sexuality. For example, antidepressant and anti-anxiety drugs may either increase or decrease your usual level of sexual desire. Some anti-hypertension medications interfere with blood entering the penis, causing problems with erection. Without exception, all drugs have a variety of effects in addition to the effect intended. Since pharmacists frequently know more than physicians about the effects of drugs, you may want to ask a pharmacist. See the chart in Helen Singer Kaplan's *The New Sex Therapy*, or check the *Physicians' Desk Reference* to discover the effects of drugs on sexual functioning.

Residents of nursing homes may have somewhat changed sexual needs due to illness or frailty, yet most still have sexual needs. Many nursing homes do not allow residents sexual privacy. All of us need privacy regardless of whether we are part of a couple, a single person, or whether we are heterosexual or lesbian. This human right is ours by law. Federal regulations state: "The patient may associate and communicate privately with persons of her choice ...unless medically contraindicated (as documented by his physician in the medical records)."[30]

*See Cancer chapter for a description of colostomy (p. 341).

Resuming Sex After A Heart Attack

After a heart attack, fear of having another may cause people to delay sexual activity. Yet the incidence of death occurring during intercourse is less than 0.3 percent.[31]

Be sure your physician understands your interest in resuming sexual activity as soon as you safely can. People who have had a heart attack are usually able to have sex two to four weeks afterward, while bypass patients may reach this point in one to three weeks after they leave the hospital.[32] People who have been in the hospital for ten days, and have had a treadmill test, can have sex on the first day home, because a treadmill test is more strenuous than sex. If you can climb two flights of stairs without chest pain, palpitations, or shortness of breath, you can engage in lovemaking safely. If you suffer from angina, you may be able to take a nitroglycerin pill for the pain before lovemaking and then proceed.

Wait one to three hours after eating a full meal. Digesting your food takes an increased amount of blood. Your heart would have to work harder to provide blood during sex.

If you experience angina or pains in the jaw, neck, chest, or stomach, shortness of breath, and rapid or irregular heartbeats, tell your partner, rest, and take medicine if prescribed. When the symptoms disappear, you can resume sexual activity. If the symptoms do not stop, or if they start again, you need to get medical help.

After Surgery

Our culture trains us to believe that "bodily perfection" is a prerequisite for good sex.* If a part of your body has been surgically removed, you need time to come to terms with the changes in order to feel ready to be sexual again. A partner's attitude is of prime importance in helping you to complete the healing process and regain sexual intimacy.

When I came home from the hospital after my mastectomy, my husband literally had to force me to remove my blouse before we made love. My scar did not turn

*See The New Our Bodies, Ourselves for a more extensive discussion and bibliography on sex and disability.

him off, as I was afraid it would, and our lovemaking was good, and healing.

Many hospitals offer counseling to their patients after surgery; this has proved helpful to many people in the past,[33] especially to women who have had mastectomies or who must wear appliances as a result of ostomy surgery.

I "practiced" talking about my breast surgery with two of my best friends because I didn't see how I could tell a man I wasn't intimate with; yet how would I ever get that far if I didn't tell him? Saying the words helped me get familiar with the language I would be comfortable using. Then I did meet a man, and when I managed to tell him, he was very easy about it. I think I was more nervous than I needed to be, because afterwards it seemed to fall into place so easily. He likes me for me!

CONCLUSION

In 1979, Betty Friedan said we must "create new patterns of intimacy and growth, love, and work in the third of life that most women now hope to enjoy...after fifty."[34] We have the experience and wisdom to manage changes, problems, and losses, and to find ways to continue to meet our needs for pleasure. We are in a position to refine and enhance what we already know. We have learned to both give and receive, and to appreciate the fleeting moment and its pleasures. Our sexual selves become more integrated with our emotional and spiritual selves. We know how to value ourselves and our intimate loved ones and we can share our bodies as it best suits our desires. As long as we want it, sex can be a part of our lives.

NOTES

1. Lance Morrow, "Women and Aging." *Time*, Vol. III, No. 17, April 24, 1978, p. 99.

2. Ivor Felstein, *Sex in Later Life*. Harmondsworth, Middlesex, England: Penguin Books, 1973.

3. Bernard Starr and Marcella Weiner, *Starr-Weiner Report*. New York: Stein & Day, 1981, p. 35.

4. Timothy H. Brubaker, *Later Life Families*. Beverly Hills, CA: Sage Publications, Inc., 1985, pp. 36–45.

5. This idea appeared in *Feminine Forever* by Robert Wilson (New York: M. Evans & Co., Inc., 1966), and was common in many magazine articles a decade ago. See Menopause chapter.

6. Starr and Weiner, op. cit.; and Edward Brecher,

Love, Sex and Aging. Boston: Little, Brown & Co., 1984.

7. Ewald Busse and Eric Pfeiffer, eds., *Behavior and Adaptation in Later Life.* Boston: Little, Brown & Co., 1968.

8. Reported in Jane Porcino, *Growing Older, Getting Better: A Handbook for Women in Later Life.* Reading, Massachusetts: Addison-Wesley Pub. Co., 1983, p. 15.

9. Joan Cohen, Karen Coburn and Joan Pearlman, *Hitting Our Stride: Good News About Women in Their Middle Years.* New York: Delacorte Press, 1980, p. 168.

10. In 1979, 36.9 percent of older women were married compared with 74.6 percent of older men. U.S. Bureau of the Census, Current Population Reports, Series P-23, No. 59 and Series P-20, No. 349.

11. Women's Studies Program and Policy Center, *Older Women: The Economics of Aging.* Washington, D.C.: George Washington University, 1980.

12. Monica Kehoe, "Lesbians over Sixty: A Triply Invisible Minority," in Monica Kehoe, ed., *Historical, Literary and Erotic Aspects of Lesbianism.* New York: Haworth Publications, Inc., 1986.

13. Personal communication from Sarah F. Pearlman, a therapist specializing in counseling couples.

14. Marcy Adelman, as reported in JoAnn Loulan, *Lesbian Sex.* San Francisco: Spinsters', Ink, 1984, pp. 194–5.

15. William Masters and Virginia Johnson, "Human Sexual Response in the Aging Female," in Bernice Neugarten, ed., *Middle Age and Aging.* Chicago: University of Chicago Press, 1968, pp. 260–70.

16. William Masters and Virginia Johnson, *Human Sexual Response.* Boston: Little, Brown & Co., 1966.

17. Wendy Sanford, et al., "Sexuality," in Boston Women's Health Book Collective, *The New Our Bodies, Ourselves.* New York: Simon and Schuster, 1984, and earlier editions, as well as other feminist writing on sexuality. See Anne Koedt, "The Myth of the Vaginal Orgasm" in *Liberation Now: Writings from the Women's Liberation Movement.* New York: Dell, 1971, pp. 311–20.

18. Alice Ladas, Beverly Whipple and John Perry, *The G Spot.* New York: Dell, 1982. The G spot is the name given to a part of the anterior wall of the vagina which may be especially sensitive to stimulation.

19. L. Zussman, S. Zussman, R. Sunley and E. Bjornson, "Sexual Response after Hysterectomy-Oophorectomy: Recent Studies and Reconsideration of Psychogenesis." *American Journal of Obstetrics and Gynecology,* Vol. 140, No. 7, August 1, 1981, pp. 725–9.

20. Boston Women's Health Book Collective, op cit.; and F. Bellview and L. Richter, *Understanding Human Sexual Inadequacy.* Boston: Bantam Books, 1970, p. 196.

21. Susanne Morgan, *Coping with Hysterectomy.* New York: Dial Press, 1982, p. 163.

22. Personal communication, Myrna Lewis, co-author of *Sex After Forty* (see Resources.)

23. G. I. Dyer, et al., "Dose-Related Changes in Vaginal Cytology After Topical Conjugated Equine Oestrogens." *British Medical Journal,* Vol. 284, March 13, 1982, p. 789.

24. Robert Butler and Myrna Lewis, *Sex After Sixty.* New York: Harper & Row, 1976, p. 156.

25. Masters and Johnson, *Human Sexual Inadequacy.* Boston: Little, Brown & Co., 1970, p. 323.

26. Masters and Johnson, "Human Sexual Response in the Aging Male," in Neugarten, ed., op. cit., pp. 277–8.

27. Thomas P. Hackett, *Sexual Activity in the Elderly.* Clinical Perspectives on Aging, No. 4. Philadelphia: Wyeth Laboratories, Dr. Irwin Goldstein of the N.E. Reproductive Center, University Hospital, Boston, quoted in *The Boston Globe,* September 22, 1985, p. 34.

28. Barry Komisarik and Beverly Whipple, "Evidence that Vaginal Stimulation in Women Suppresses Experimentally Induced Finger Pain." Paper presented at June 1984 conference in Boston, Society for the Scientific Study of Sex.

29. Masters and Johnson, "Human Sexual Response in the Aging Male," in Neugarten, ed., op. cit., pp. 148–53.

30. U.S. Dept. of Health Education and Welfare, "Skilled Nursing Facilities," *Federal Register.* Vol. 39, No. 193, part 2, October 3, 1974.

31. Lee Scheingold and Nathaniel Wagner, *Sound Sex and the Aging Heart.* New York: Pyramid Books, 1975, p. 82; Herman Hellerstein and Emanuel Friedman, "Sexual Activity and the Post-coronary Patient." *Archives of Internal Medicine,* Vol. 125, 1970, pp. 987–99.

32. "Sex and Heart Disease," 1983. Available from American Heart Association, National Center, 7320 Greenville Ave., Dallas, TX 75231.

33. Mary Reid Gloeckner, "Partner Reaction Following Ostomy Surgery." *Journal of Sex and Marital Therapy,* Vol. 9, No. 3, Fall 1983, pp. 182–90.

34. Betty Friedan, "Feminism Takes a New Turn." *The New York Times Magazine,* November 18, 1979, p. 102.

8

BIRTH CONTROL
FOR WOMEN IN MIDLIFE

by Paula Brown Doress, Edie Butler, and Trudy Cox

Special thanks to Susan Bell, Judy Norsigian, and Suzanne Ollivier

Women continue to need up-to-date, reliable contraceptive information until they are sure they are well past their fertile years. This brief discussion of birth control is meant to highlight special contraception issues that affect women in midlife.

If you do not already have a basic familiarity with reproductive anatomy and birth control and would like to, we encourage you to turn to other resources, such as the Birth Control and Anatomy chapters in *The New Our Bodies, Ourselves*,[1] for more comprehensive information. A women-run health clinic or family-planning clinic is another good source of instruction and contraceptive services in many states. In general, nurse-practitioners and certified nurse-midwives who specialize in family planning are more thorough and knowledgeable than most gynecologists and will take much more time with each woman.

Women who are sexually active with men must continue to use birth control until they are past menopause. Middle-aged women often look forward to being free of the need for birth control, yet they may stop believing in their fertility before it is reliably at an end. As early as our late thirties or early forties, our periods may become quite irregular, and those of us who are sexually active with a male partner may worry about whether a missed period means a pregnancy. Keeping track of the patterns in our menstrual cycles and paying attention to other body changes we experience can help us to distinguish them from signs of pregnancy. It can help

Nancy Press Hawley

us to talk with other women who are going through or have gone through menopause and to become familiar with the signs (see Menopause chapter). Women sometimes ovulate months or even over a year after menstruation appears to have stopped. If you are certain you do not want to become pregnant, it is crucial to continue contraception until two years past the last menstrual period. It is certainly no less true at midlife that control of our fertility is essential to control over the rest of our lives.

CHOOSING A BIRTH-CONTROL METHOD

Choosing a birth-control method is a very personal matter. We must weigh a lot of factors in making a decision. Each method's safety and effectiveness should be taken into consideration. Unfortunately, no contraceptive exists which is 100 percent effective and 100 percent safe. The most accepted measure of effectiveness is the failure rate—the number of pregnancies per 100 women using the contraceptive for one year, most often the first year, as in the chart below. In evaluating a contraceptive's effectiveness for any group of women, it is important to know the failure rate for typical users (usually called the actual or use-failure rate) and the failure rate when a method is used carefully and consistently (sometimes called the theoretical failure rate).[2] Actual failure rates are strongly influenced by age, education, and socioeconomic status. Women under twenty-two are much more likely to experience contraceptive failure than women thirty and over. With barrier methods, very young women have failure rates 17 to 22 percent higher than women thirty and over.[3] Because older women are more likely to have the experience and confidence to use a method carefully and consistently, the theoretical failure rate may actually be closer to our own.

A variety of studies in the United States and Great Britain have shown diaphragm failure rates ranging from a low of 2 to a high of 23 pregnancies per 100 women per year. The fact that a large study involving more than 70,000 months of diaphragm use reported a pregnancy rate of 2 per 100 women per year illustrates the high theoretical effectiveness of a properly fitted diaphragm when used regularly with a spermicide by a conscientious woman. On the other hand, a pregnancy rate of 12 to 19 per 100 women per year illustrates the wide discrepancy possible between theoretic- and use-effectiveness of the diaphragm. Some feel that a failure rate of 2 or 3 per 100 women per year is a sound reflection of the overall effectiveness for married women who are long-term users of a properly used diaphragm.[4]

First Year Failure Rates of Selected Birth Control Methods[5]

Method	Lowest Observed Failure Rate	Failure Rate in Typical Users
Combined estrogen and progestin birth-control pills	.5%	2.0%
Progestin-only pill	1.0%	2.5%
IUD	1.5%	5.0%
Diaphragm	2.0%	19.0%
Cervical cap	2.0%	13.0%
Condom	2.0%	10.0%
Foams, creams, jellies, and vaginal suppositories	3.0 to 5.0%	18.0%
Contraceptive sponge	9.0 to 11.0%	10.0 to 20.0%

The Pill and the IUD

By their middle years, many women have found a birth-control method which they consider convenient and effective. It may come as a nasty shock to many of them, then, to discover that two of the most popular methods, the Pill and the IUD (intrauterine device), pose special hazards to middle-aged women.

Oral contraceptives (or birth-control pills) contain one or a combination of artificial hormones which prevent pregnancy by suppressing ovulation. **Women over thirty-five and women over thirty who smoke are strongly advised *not to use* the Pill because of the increased risk of**

Judy Norsigian

heart attack and stroke. The Pill is the most frequently used and the most effective method of reversible birth control. Even so, Pill use declined in the late 1970s from a high of 10 million to 6 million users because of growing awareness among women of its hazards and risks. Since then, we have witnessed a "reselling of the Pill,"[6] part of a new effort on the part of drug companies and population-control "experts" to convince the public that the Pill is no longer risky and may even be beneficial. Yet there were five hundred Pill-related deaths as late as 1982, when the number of prescriptions dispensed had climbed back up to 8.5 million.[7]

As a woman gets older, she is more likely to have a Pill-related heart attack or stroke. One study found that among women thirty to thirty-five years old who take oral contraceptives, the risk of a fatal heart attack is almost three times as great as for women who do not. For women forty to forty-four years old, the risk is almost five times as great.[8]

The risk of heart disease and stroke for Pill users increases with age:

Age	Cases of heart disease or stroke
Under 25	4 per 100,000
25 to 34	13 per 100,000
35 and over	54 per 100,000[9]

Smoking while on the Pill is dangerous for women of any age. Women age forty to forty-nine who use the Pill and smoke have fifteen times as many fatal coronary and circulatory disorders as women who do neither, and thirty-nine times the risk of acute myocardial infarction (heart attack).[10] If no women thirty-five and over used the Pill, deaths from Pill use would be reduced by over one half. If, in addition, no smokers used the Pill, Pill-related deaths per year would be reduced from five hundred to seventy.[11]

Birth-control pills can cause a number of unintended effects and complications of varying degrees of severity. These effects may range from discomforts such as nausea, weight gain, depression, and increased susceptibility to urinary-tract and yeast infections to serious and potentially life-threatening complications[12] such as the following:

• Blood clots
• Heart attack and stroke
• Liver tumors
• Sickle-cell anemia

• High blood pressure
• Gallbladder disease
• Malignant melanoma (a type of skin cancer)[13]

It is dangerous for a woman at any age to use the Pill if she already has any of the above conditions, a history of bile-flow blockage during pregnancy, or a past leg injury. Pill use is discouraged as well within four weeks of any surgical procedure. Also, women with diabetes are advised to avoid the Pill.

An estimated 9,400 women are hospitalized each year as a result of diseases brought about by use of the Pill. Heart disease, stroke, and deep vein and pulmonary embolism are the main causes of such hospitalizations. Any woman who takes the Pill should see a health-care practitioner at least once a year for a complete well-woman gynecological exam, including a heart and blood-pressure examination. Women in their thirties should consider discontinuing use of the Pill as early as possible.

Some women who have intercourse very infrequently may be tempted to use the "morning-after pill" as birth control. This is not advisable because of the very high amount of hormones in this pill and the dangers associated with them, especially for women over forty (or heavy smokers over thirty). Never use the "morning-after pill" without supervision from an experienced doctor or other health-care practitioner. It is not FDA approved.

The IUD is a small plastic or copper device designed to be inserted through the vagina into the uterus and left in place indefinitely. It is not known exactly how the IUD works. The most widely accepted theory is that the IUD causes an inflammation or chronic low-grade infection in the uterus. This causes the body to produce a higher number of white cells, which may hinder the buildup of the uterine lining, thus preventing implantation.[14] This does not preclude the possibility of conception, however, and may increase the risk of ectopic or "tubal" pregnancy [outside the uterus], a life-threatening condition.[15]

Because of increasing numbers of lawsuits (and probably increasing evidence of IUD-related infections), the manufacturers of most IUDs have voluntarily stopped selling them. By early 1986, virtually all IUDs had been removed from the market in the United States.

Three of the most dangerous are the Dalkon Shield, the Majzlin Spring, and the Birnberg Bow. If you have any one of these IUDs, you should have it removed right away, because it could be life-threatening. All of these have been off the market for several years, and the manufacturer will probably pay for its removal.

The Progestasert IUD is one of the few still available. It contains synthetic progesterone and is sometimes prescribed to middle-aged women to control heavy bleeding occasionally caused by another IUD or by the menstrual irregularity of the perimenopausal years (see pp. 118–20). The Progestasert IUD must be changed annually and is thought to cause a higher-than-usual rate of ectopic pregnancy.

One major risk of the IUD is infection. IUD-related infections can lead to damage to the fallopian tubes and/or uterus, sterility, and sometimes even death. Most doctors no longer recommend the IUD for younger women who may want to have children in the future. However, some middle-aged women may want to have a child, and no woman wants to risk a potentially life-threatening infection. There are other reasons that the IUD may not be an appropriate choice for women in midlife. Mid-cycle bleeding, common among IUD users, can also be a symptom of certain types of reproductive cancer such as cancer of the uterus and uterine lining. While these cancers are not common, they are found most often in women over forty. Such bleeding in IUD wearers may be either disregarded or misdiagnosed, thus delaying important treatment. IUDs are not recommended for women who have uterine fibroids, a condition also most common in women over forty. In addition, as women approach menopause, the uterus becomes smaller and the IUD can become deeply embedded and difficult to remove.[16]

The other most serious risk of the IUD is that it will perforate the uterus and travel partially or completely through the uterine wall. This is a serious emergency requiring immediate medical attention.

If the IUD has been your chosen mode of contraception and you plan to continue using it, it is critical to have regular examinations to check on the condition of the uterus around it, especially as you approach menopause, or if you experience increased bleeding. Any pelvic pain also needs to be evaluated immediately. Aspirin and antibiotics may interfere with the IUD's effectiveness so use an additional method of birth control when you take these.

The IUD and pregnancy constitute a potentially dangerous combination. If you have an IUD in place and you become pregnant, have the IUD removed *whether or not* you intend to continue the pregnancy. If you remove the IUD, your chances of miscarriage are about 25 percent, while if you do not have it removed, the chance of miscarriage rises to 50 percent. If you do not remove it, you run the risk of an infected miscarriage, sometimes called a septic abortion. In extreme cases, this can cause the death of the woman as well as the fetus, and in most cases it is serious enough to require hospitalization. Women with IUDs should check out every missed period to be sure they are not pregnant or having a septic abortion. Of course, missing periods is fairly usual in the years prior to menopause, so this is yet another reason that the IUD is not a desirable method of contraception for women in midlife.

Barrier Methods

The diaphragm and other barrier methods are the birth-control practices most often recommended for women in midlife. See *The New Our Bodies, Ourselves* for detailed descriptions, pictures, and diagrams. In our thirties, forties, and fifties, many of us find that we use barrier methods more successfully than when we were younger because we have grown more knowledgeable and comfortable with our bodies over the years. We more often have the confidence and assertiveness to *use* whatever birth-control method we select. For those of us who feel less comfortable with our bodies than we would like, using a vaginal barrier method is an opportunity to expand our self-knowledge and sexual confidence. Also, for women experiencing vaginal dryness, an increasingly common problem at midlife, contraceptive foam, cream, or jelly can provide additional lubrication. For women who are not in a long-term sexual relationship, barrier methods are advantageous because they do not have to be in place all the time. Barrier methods also provide some protection against sexually transmitted diseases.*

When the diaphragm is fitted properly and its

*Condoms and spermicides containing nonoxynol-9 are among the contraceptives which offer some protection against sexually transmitted diseases (STDs) and which may be effective in preventing the transmission of the AIDS virus, which is affecting more women. See box pp. 94–5; and Jane Sprague Zones, "AIDS: What Women Need to Know," *The Network News* (Publication of the National Women's Health Network, see General Resources), Vol. 11, No. 6, November/December 1986, p. 1.

use taught carefully, it can be up to 98 percent effective when used with spermicidal cream or jelly.[17] There is a tenfold difference in failure rate between typical users and those who receive thorough instruction as described above.[18] Choose a health care practitioner or clinic that allows enough time for you to practice inserting and removing the diaphragm several times. Too many practitioners omit this crucial step.

Two recent studies implicated the diaphragm as a risk factor for woman who suffer from recurrent urinary infections.[19] Pelvic conditions such as a prolapsed uterus, a bladder that protrudes through the vaginal wall (called a cystocele), or any other openings in the vagina (called fistulas) are somewhat more common in midlife. If you have any of these conditions you may not be able to use the diaphragm, the cervical cap, or the contraceptive sponge. However, your partner can use a condom, and you can add foam for additional protection. Some women find it convenient to purchase and keep a supply of condoms to offer to a partner who may not have one available. *Used together, the condom and contraceptive foam offer almost 100 percent effectiveness and no dangerous side effects.*

Toxic Shock Syndrome (TSS)

As women in midlife, we are apparently less susceptible to TSS, but we are not entirely protected either. TSS is a rare but serious disease (see *The New Our Bodies, Ourselves* for more information), which primarily strikes menstruating women under thirty who are using tampons, especially high-absorbency tampons. However, a number of cases have been related to postsurgical complications or to use of barrier contraceptives, especially the contraceptive sponge, during menstruation, or to leaving a contraceptive in place for much longer than the recommended amount of time.

Every woman should be aware of the symptoms of TSS:

- A high fever, usually over 102 degrees
- Vomiting
- Diarrhea
- A sudden drop in blood pressure, which may lead to shock
- A sunburnlike rash

If you have these symptoms, remove the tampon or contraceptive at once and get medical attention immediately.

BIRTH CONTROL WITHOUT CONTRACEPTIVES

Abstinence is not the only alternative to the Pill, the IUD, or barrier methods. Sex without intercourse is an important birth-control option when we do not have access to safe and effective contraception as well as an important variation in lovemaking. Fertility observation, or "natural birth control," involves learning from an experienced teacher to monitor and understand the hormonal changes in our bodies by observing the amount and quality of vaginal discharge, noting changes in the texture and position of the cervix, and keeping track of body temperature. In the years approaching menopause, however, menstrual cycles are apt to be erratic, making fertility observation ineffective as birth control.* However, it can be a useful and interesting—even exciting—tool for monitoring premenopausal hormonal changes, and for women who are trying to get pregnant at midlife.

Sterilization

Sterilization, a *permanent and irreversible* method of birth control through surgery, is now widely available, and for married couples over thirty, it is the most commonly used method of contraception.[20] Sterilization is a highly reliable method of birth control; the theoretical and actual failure rate for both tubal ligation (sterilization of the woman) and vasectomy (sterilization of the man) is 0.4 percent.

A growing number of women and men in midlife choose sterilization because they are very sure they will not want to have more children. However, too many women still choose sterilization without adequate information and in desperation over the limited safety and effectiveness of other contraceptive methods. There is a deplorable history of sterilization abuse in the United States against middle-aged women,† poor women, women of color, and women who speak a language other than Eng-

---

*Younger women with regular cycles may be able to monitor their fertility in this way accurately enough to use this as a birth-control method.

†Middle-aged women have been the chief victims of unnecessary and inappropriate hysterectomies. Too many doctors still regard a middle-aged or older woman's uterus as expendable.

lish. Primarily as a result of pressure from minority and women's groups, regulations were enacted in March 1979 to protect women obtaining federally funded sterilizations.[21] For example, the regulations require that a woman be provided information in her preferred language (orally and in writing) about the risks, negative effects, and irreversibility of sterilization, as well as alternative methods of reversible birth control. The regulations also prohibit overt or implicit threat of loss of welfare or Medicaid benefits if a woman doesn't consent to sterilization. The regulation especially relevant to middle-aged women is the one prohibiting a hysterectomy for the sole purpose of sterilization. **Hysterectomy—removal of the uterus—is major surgery, and should not be considered a method of birth control or sterilization.** (See the Hysterectomy and Oophorectomy chapter for more information.) Even now, after Federal legislation has eliminated the worst abuses, too many women, especially non-English-speaking women, are not adequately informed of either the permanence of sterilization or its possible risks and side effects.[22]

Sterilization Procedures

Tubal ligation, popularly called "tying the tubes," blocks the woman's fallopian tubes so that eggs cannot pass through them into the uterus. It may be done either abdominally or vaginally, often through a laparoscope (see p. 305). Serious complications are rare and the death rate is low (3.6 deaths per 100,000 procedures) compared with other surgery. The risk of death is greater when general anesthesia is used.[23] The skill of both the anesthesiologist and the surgeon is very important; be sure to inquire about the number of tubal ligations the surgeon has performed. Complications of laparoscopic sterilization may include puncturing of the intestine, bowel burns (with cauterization), perforation, hemorrhage, infection, and cardiac arrest. Some women experience a postlaparoscopic syndrome including heavy irregular bleeding and increased menstrual pain, which may create the need for repeated D&Cs or, in some cases, lead to hysterectomies.[24]

Vasectomy, or male sterilization, is a much simpler and less expensive procedure with fewer possible complications than female sterilization. It can be done in a doctor's office in a half hour under local anesthesia. However, a vasectomy is not immediately effective, so use another means of birth control for the first fifteen days after the procedure or until after ten ejaculations. Tests should then be done on samples of semen.[25] The man is considered sterile after two negative sperm counts.

MISSED PERIODS AND PREGNANCY SCARES

If you miss a period when you are not trying to get pregnant, consider whether it is a sign of pregnancy or a sign of menopause (see p. 119). If you continue to be uncertain, it is important to have a pregnancy test early, so you can begin prenatal care if you decide to have a child, or make plans for an early abortion if you decide to terminate the pregnancy. If your periods have become irregular, you may want to wait until you have skipped two months before testing, but do not wait until a third month or you will not be able to have a less traumatic first-trimester abortion.

Many of the commonly used pregnancy laboratory tests cannot distinguish the hormonal changes of pregnancy from those of menopause; one test that can is a blood test called the Beta Subunit. In large cities it may be possible to have this test done at a drop-in clinic; however, in many localities you will be charged for an office visit each time you want the test done. (Medicaid and some insurance companies cover lab tests, including pregnancy testing.)

ABORTION

Middle-aged women who are routinely in good health have no special medical problems associated with abortion. A thorough medical history should be taken *before* an abortion and your physician should check for certain conditions. For example, fibroid tumors or a bladder that protrudes into the vagina may necessitate performing the abortion in a hospital.

Abortion is a vital option in controlling our fertility—and, therefore, our lives. Whether or not abortion is any one woman's personal choice, safe, legal, and accessible abortion must continue to be available to all women who choose it. As the generation that fought for repro-

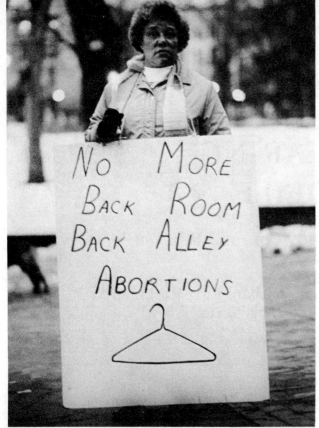

Ellen Shub

ductive freedom, today's middle-aged women recognize the threat anti-choice forces pose to the progress of women in every walk of life. Entering our post-reproductive years does not weaken our resolve to defend the right to choice and control over our bodies for ourselves, our daughters, and future generations of women.

NOTES

1. Boston Women's Health Book Collective, *The New Our Bodies, Ourselves*. New York: Simon and Schuster, 1984.

2. Robert A. Hatcher, et al., *Contraceptive Technology: 1986–1987, 13th Revised Edition*. New York: Irvington Publishers, 1986, p. 101.

3. Howard W. Ory, *Making Choices: Evaluating the Health Risks and Benefits of Birth Control Methods*, 1983. The Alan Guttmacher Institute, 1360 Park Avenue South, New York, NY 10010.

4. Stephen L. Corson, et al., *Fertility Control*. Boston: Little, Brown & Company, 1985, p. 225.

5. Hatcher et al., op. cit., 13th Revised Edition, p. 102.

6. Alice Wolfson, "The Reselling of the Pill." *Second Opinion*, Coalition for the Medical Rights of Women, June–July 1983.

7. "Special Report: The Pill After 25 Years." *Contraceptive Technology Update*, Vol. 6, No. 1, January 1985, pp. 1–3.

8. Dennis Slone, et al., "Risk of Myocardial Infarction in Relation to Current and Discontinued Use of Oral Contraceptives." *The New England Journal of Medicine*, Vol. 305, No. 8, August 20, 1981, pp. 420–4.

9. Ory, op. cit., p. 43.

10. Charles H. Hennekens, et al., "Oral Contraceptive Use, Cigarette Smoking and Myocardial Infarction." *British Journal of Family Planning*, Vol. 5, 1979 pp. 66–7.

11. Ory, op. cit., p. 42.

12. "New Studies of Malignant Melanoma, Gallbladder and Heart Disease Help Further Define Pill Risk." *International Family Planning Perspectives*, Vol. 8, No. 2, June 1982, pp. 76–8; and Dennis Slone, op. cit.

13. Boston Women's Health Book Collective, op. cit., pp. 240–1.

14. Boston Women's Health Book Collective, op. cit., p. 250.

15. Boston Women's Health Book Collective, op. cit., p. 427.

16. Bernard M. Kaye, et al., "Long-Term Safety and Use-Effectiveness of Intra-Uterine Devices." *Fertility and Sterility*, Vol. 28, No. 9, September 1977, 937–42.

17. Mary Lane, et al., "Successful Use of the Diaphragm and Jelly in a Young Population: Report of a Clinical Study." *Family Planning Perspectives*, Vol. 8, No. 2, 1976, pp. 81-6.

18. Robert A. Hatcher, et al., *Contraceptive Technology: 1984–1985: 12th Revised Edition*. New York: Irvington Publishers, 1985, p. 108.

19. Betsy Foxman and Ralph R. Frerichs, "Epidemiology of Urinary Tract Infection: Diaphragm Use and Sexual Intercourse," *American Journal of Public Health*. Vol. 75, No. 11, November 1985, pp. 1308–13; and Larianne Gillespie, "The Diaphragm: An Accomplice in Recurrent Urinary Infections." *Urology*, Vol. 24, No. 1, July 1984, pp. 25–30, quoted in Kathleen O'Brien, "Lifestyle Factors and Urinary Tract Infections," *The Network News*, Vol. 12, No. 1, January/February 1987.

20. Boston Women's Health Book Collective, op. cit., p. 256.

21. See *The New Our Bodies, Ourselves* for more information and for resources on sterilization abuse.

22. See *The New Our Bodies, Ourselves*, pp. 256–7, for details and for organizations working on this issue.

23. Hatcher, et al., op. cit., 13th Revised Edition, p. 287.

24. Boston Women's Health Book Collective, op. cit., p. 258.

25. Hatcher, et al., op. cit., 12th Revised Edition, p. 213.

9

CHILDBEARING
IN MIDLIFE

by Paula Brown Doress, Trudy Cox, and Edie Butler

Special thanks to Judy Norsigian, Barbara Katz-Rothman,
Phyllis Greenleaf, and Jane Pincus

More women today are choosing to have children in their middle years. Because we live longer and stay healthier longer, we can concentrate on other areas of our lives in our young adult years, and still choose parenthood even into our forties. Despite some of the added pressures of the middle years, such as more stressful and challenging jobs, new relationships, and aging parents, older women often have more experience at balancing life's demands.

I'm forty-three and becoming aware of the issues of old age, as I help my baby start his life. The advantage of having my children at thirty-five and forty-three is that I know myself; I knew I really wanted children. I know some things about what I need, what contributions I can make in addition to raising the children. I've made a commitment to photography and have a number of projects that I'm working on or looking forward to. Some of them are about lesbian family life.

At times I do feel a bit out of sync—with friends my age whose children are grown, with friends who have children the age of mine who are ten or fifteen years younger than I; or when I feel myself hitting my stride in photography and need to move at a slower pace partly because of the family commitments.

I've noticed that when I'm with friends in their fifties and sixties I envy their clean, quiet rooms. I tell myself, I've had this before and some day again this will be mine. I'm grateful to be intimately in touch with the stages and cycles of life. I asked the babies, "Is this too abstract?" They said, "Ba, Ba, Ba, Ba."

The best thing in my life is the joy of actually having a child. Eleven years ago when I was pregnant with my son, my marriage was in such terrible shape I almost

Lyn Stirewalt

had an abortion because I couldn't envision living my life with that much dissension. My husband wasn't supportive of me and so I figured he wouldn't be supportive of a child either. A sister had even made all the arrangements. Then the morning the abortion was scheduled, I decided not to have it, because I was thirty-four and I thought, I may not have the opportunity to become pregnant again. And with all the pressures and difficulties I have faced, some of my greatest joys have come from being a mother. The doctors referred to me as an "elderly primip," which made me laugh. I was healthy as a horse.

What saved my sanity when I was raising my youngster alone was that my mother lived next door to me. I never had to concern myself with finding a baby-sitter. My mother, like so many Black grandmothers and aunts, provided care without my asking her and I could work whatever schedules I was asked to work. In fact, my son came home once and asked me what a baby-sitter was. [a forty-five-year-old woman]

For me, having children in my forties while raising two step-children seemed natural and appropriate. My age seemed irrelevant to me and to my husband, though sometimes it seemed to concern others when they found out. What is it like now to be fifty-eight and have a sixteen- and eighteen-year-old? Well, we do worry about getting it together for their college and our retirement, but other than that we don't feel very deviant and our kids don't seem to mind having "older parents." At least they don't seem to have much to say about it.

I was a forty-one-year-old first-time mother married to a fifty-three-year-old father of three children. In what some called an "advanced maturity" marriage, we needed time to be alone together as well as time to spend with our newborn, as well as time for his children from his former marriage and time for our dependent parents.

The difficulty of orchestrating all this with time alone for spiritual stretching and meditating seemed to increase with age. The demands on our energy and creativity were titanic. We felt we needed a minimum of one evening out per week and one weekend away alone together every six weeks because we would be sixty and seventy before there would be an "empty nest."

We might have managed this if we had forfeited privacy and hired live-in help, or had not moved when our newborn was a year old, leaving a network of friends built up during our adult years. Our marriage did not survive the stress. Paying attention to time alone and time together is a major challenge in combining midlife childbearing and midlife marriage.

Lisa Roper

CONCEPTION AND MIDLIFE FERTILITY

Women who plan a pregnancy in their thirties or forties may worry if they do not conceive right away. Some women's bodies continue to produce eggs regularly up until menopause, while other women in their thirties gradually begin to produce fewer eggs, and thus have fewer opportunities for conception. The reduced fertility of women over thirty compared with younger women may be partly attributable to less frequent intercourse among longer-married couples.[1] So it is wise to be patient and allow enough time and opportunity for conception before assuming that there is a fertility problem.

Infertility is usually defined as the inability to conceive after a year or more of sexual intercourse without contraception.[2] One study found that it takes an average of 3.8 months for women ages thirty-five to forty-four to conceive, compared with about 2 months for women ages fifteen to twenty-four.[3] Medical and lay media reports that exaggerate the degree to which fertility decreases with age have contributed to women's worries about their fertility.[4]

Infertility is becoming increasingly common at all ages due to environmental hazards and pelvic infections resulting from sexually transmitted diseases (STDs) and/or IUDs. If you have been trying to conceive for more than a year, you may want to read some of the feminist literature on infertility and new reproductive technologies (see Resources) before going to see a health-care practitioner.

If you have taken a long time to conceive, you may be at risk for the "medicalization" of your pregnancy and birth. Doctors often intervene unnecessarily in midlife pregnancies with procedures such as Cesareans in order to "safeguard" the pregnancy of a woman who has taken a long time to conceive.[5] This is a concern because every medical intervention brings its own set of risks and complications. In considering the risks of midlife pregnancy, we must keep in mind that low fertility is a problem of conception, not of pregnancy. Once we are pregnant, we do not need to be treated a special way because we took a long time conceiving. However, a history of repeated miscarriages may require exercising special care during pregnancy.

CHILDBEARING FOR WOMEN IN MIDLIFE

A major change over the past ten years has been the extension of women's "fertility deadline" from the early thirties to the early forties. What has brought about this change? Several factors stand out:

- Improved health and extended longevity of women
- Reliable birth control
- The women's movement, which has encouraged us to decide for ourselves whether and when we will have children
- More sophisticated prenatal testing and the availability of legal abortion
- New research which shows that some of the earlier assumptions and concerns about pregnancy and age have been incorrect or overstated

Phyllis Kernoff Mansfield, a health educator at Pennsylvania State University, has challenged established beliefs about maternal age and risk during pregnancy. Mansfield examined all the studies ever published in the United States that relate the age of the mother to seven pregnancy complications. She found in her review of the literature that the vast majority of studies published before 1970 did not pass the simplest tests for methodological soundness. The most glaring deficiency was the lack of a control group; that is, no comparison was made between older and younger women. The "problems" of older women were simply assumed to be related to their age, without accounting for other factors such as fertility history, general health, or number of previous pregnancies. Mansfield's research revealed that when other factors were held constant, only Cesarean sections showed a definite increase in risk with age —and a C-section is not a complication but an intervention. Mansfield and her associates concluded that the general health and nutritional habits of the mother had far more influence than age on the outcome of a pregnancy.[6]

A 1982 report from the National Center for Health Statistics concluded that contemporary women who first became pregnant in their thirties and forties have good results because they do not have a history of delayed childbearing due to pregnancy-related problems.[7] These

Marianne Gontarz

women have *chosen* to begin childbearing in their thirties and forties when they have found the right partner, when their job or career is going well—when they feel ready.

Other studies have also found that some of the risks formerly associated with childbearing in midlife have on more careful examination turned out to be associated with diseases or chronic conditions.[8] As we get older, we are at higher risk of developing such chronic diseases as diabetes, hypertension, and heart disease, as well as fibroid tumors, endometriosis, and scarring from operations and infections in the pelvic area, all of which can complicate conception and pregnancy. But these conditions affect only a relatively small number of women and do not warrant intervention in the majority of pregnancies in healthy older women. *Older women who do not have such conditions have no higher risk of a difficult pregnancy than younger women.*

The following is a list of factors that can complicate pregnancy and childbirth:

- Toxemia, or the presence of toxic substances in the blood, can lead to a much more serious condition called eclampsia, which in turn leads to convulsions and coma. Research has found the risk of this disease to be associated not with age, but with diabetes.[9] Diabetes is also linked to many other pregnancy and childbirth complications.
- Unnecessary Cesareans. Doctors tend to intervene more readily in a prolonged labor when the mother is over thirty-five. They perform Cesarean sections more often and use painkillers and anesthetics sooner and in greater amounts. The use of anesthetics during childbirth has been associated with low blood pressure in the mother and respiratory problems

in the newborn. And if a woman is apprehensive that she will have a difficult delivery because she is older, she may be more easily influenced to accept or to ask for drugs.[10]

My doctor was certain that my slow labor meant I had a "sluggish uterus," which he thought typical of older women. He was already preparing for a C-section when I went into transition. I later found out that my mother and sister had had similar labors. It was a family pattern. [a fifty-eight-year-old woman reporting on a first childbirth at forty]

• Low birth weight tends to be a problem affecting babies born to the youngest (teenage) and the oldest (over thirty-five) mothers, but in the years since 1970, low birth weight has declined as a problem for the oldest mothers. The evidence suggests that the older mothers of today are more highly educated and more likely to be well informed about pregnancy, nutrition, and exercise. They are more highly motivated to take good care of themselves and to seek prenatal care; therefore they are more likely to have heavier, healthier babies.[11]

• Socioeconomic status, not age of the mother, is the most significant factor in predicting infant mortality in the U. S.* Women who have higher incomes have better access to a wide choice of good prenatal care and a wider choice of facilities. They can more easily purchase the additional food and vitamins they need during pregnancy. Recent funding cuts in health and nutrition programs and in prenatal care services threaten to deepen the shocking disparity between the middle class and the poor in infant mortality and to slow the gradual decline in the national infant-mortality rate.[12]

• Maternal and infant mortality are more likely to be related to disease than to age. In one study, two-thirds of maternal deaths reported were among Black women with hypertension[13] (more common in Black women than white women). Cardiovascular disease in the mother, not her age, is the factor that most increases the risk of infant mortality.[14] A recent study eliminated those with hypertension from the

study sample and found that healthy Black women over thirty-five had successful outcomes in pregnancy and birth.[15]

• Placental hemorrhage and other complications of the placenta have been linked to cardiovascular diseases such as hypertension.[16]

• Down's syndrome is sometimes associated with the age of the mother. However, the father's age plays a role in one kind of Down's syndrome,[17] and another kind of Down's syndrome is hereditary—the age of neither parent is a factor.

The risk of bearing a child with Down's syndrome, a form of mental retardation in varying degrees of severity, increases gradually with each year of age, rather than rising sharply at five-year intervals, the way the conventional mode of reporting would lead us to believe. Thus, it is helpful for women to see the figures year by year. We do not dramatically increase the risk when we reach "magic numbers" in age such as thirty-five or forty.[18]

Estimated Rates of Down's Syndrome in Live Births by One-Year Maternal-Age Intervals, Based on Upstate New York Birth Certificate Data[19]

Maternal Age	Number of Down's Syndrome Babies per Number of Live Births
(20)	(1/1923)
(25)	(1/1205)
30	1/885
31	1/826
32	1/725
33	1/592
34	1/465
35	1/365
36	1/287
37	1/225
38	1/177
39	1/139
40	1/109
41	1/85
42	1/67
43	1/53
44	1/41
45	1/32

Tables such as this one will need to be revised to account for the father's age. This table

*See "Some Facts About the Lack of Prenatal Care for Poor Women and Women of Color" in *The New Our Bodies, Ourselves*, p. 331.

was compiled prior to the widespread use of amniocentesis. The rates are much lower now.[20]

Nutrition

Everything in the chapter under Aging Well deserves double emphasis if you are pregnant. Stay away from smoking, alcohol,[21] and drugs, and avoid caffeine. See *The New Our Bodies, Ourselves* for a more in-depth discussion of the effects of harmful substances on pregnancy. While age itself is not a risk, the chances of developing a chronic disease increase with age. Taking care of yourself often prevents disease, thus improving the outlook for a healthy pregnancy.

It is essential that you eat nutritiously while you are pregnant. Unfortunately, most obstetrician-gynecologists know little about nutrition and pregnancy, so you may want to talk to a nutritionist. Ask your health care provider about her or his background in nutrition.

A Suggested Daily Diet for Pregnancy[22]

1. A quart of milk (whole, skim, buttermilk) or milk equivalents (cheese, yogurt, cottage cheese). Once we are over thirty-five, our bodies do not absorb calcium and protein as well as when we were younger (see Eating Well chapter).

2. Two to four servings of meat, fish, poultry, cheese, tofu, eggs, or nut-grain-bean-dairy combinations for protein. If you do not drink one quart of milk a day (or eat its equivalent in milk products), add additional protein foods.

3. A serving of fresh, leafy green vegetables—spinach, dark leaf lettuce, broccoli, cabbage, Swiss chard, kale, alfalfa sprouts, or collard, mustard, or beet greens.

4. One or two vitamin-C-rich foods—potato with the skin, grapefruit, orange, melon, green pepper, cabbage, strawberries, fruit, orange juice.

5. A yellow or orange vegetable or fruit for vitamin A.

6. Four to five slices of whole-grain bread, pancakes, tortillas, corn bread, or a serving of whole-grain cereal or pasta. Use wheat germ and brewer's yeast to fortify other foods.

7. Moderate amounts of butter, fortified margarine, vegetable oil. (You need some fat in your diet, but in controlled amounts.)

8. Salt to taste. (Avoid table salt and foods and drinks with needless sodium.)

9. Six to eight glasses of liquid—fruit and vegetable juices, water, and herb teas. Avoid sugar-sweetened juices and colas.

10. For snacks, choose dried fruits, nuts, pumpkin and sunflower seeds, popcorn.

Eating well will ensure that you and your baby will be able to meet the demands of pregnancy, labor, and childbirth, and help ensure that your baby will have an adequate birth weight. Low-birth-weight babies are more susceptible to complications at birth. Eating well also lowers the risk of complications such as anemia and toxemia, and reduces the risk of mental retardation in your baby. During pregnancy your body stores fats and fluids you will need if you breastfeed. Older women are a little more likely to have twins, creating an extra need for nourishment (an additional 100 grams of protein per day is recommended).[23]

In the past, doctors put a great deal of emphasis on gaining as little weight as possible during pregnancy. Pregnancy, however, *increases* your body's need for calories and protein; *it is not the time to diet*.[24] Monitor your weight to avoid a *sudden* increase in weight. This can be a sign of toxemia. It is best to eat as healthfully as you can and let your weight take care of itself. If you have a very low income, you may be eligible for the WIC (Women, Infants, and Children) program, a supplemental food program for pregnant and lactating women sponsored by the Government. If you are on welfare, you may be eligible for a higher food allowance.[25]

Physical Activity and Exercise

Staying active is an important part of good prenatal care. You can swim, run, walk, dance, do yoga, whatever feels comfortable and does not tire you out too much. Physicians sometimes advise pregnant women not to "overdo it." They may be even more cautious with older pregnant women. Such advice can cause stress to women who are accustomed to exercise. It is important to keep up exercise at your accustomed level. If you have been sedentary, find ways to move more, beginning with walking and gentle exercise.

I noticed that although I was one of the oldest women in my prenatal exercise class, I was in much better physical condition than the majority. Perhaps my regular swimming and dance made the difference. Clearly, one's emotional/physical condition rather than one's age is most important. [a forty-one-year-old woman]

The Kegel exercises (see page 73 for description and instructions) can help during pregnancy to strengthen the muscles in the pelvic area, which can make the entire delivery process easier. See Resources for books on exercise during pregnancy and childbirth-preparation exercises.

Getting Support

At any age, we want our pregnancy to include solid emotional support from our partners, friends, and families. That support can be especially important as we press through the maze of medical decisions and pressures that often accompany a midlife pregnancy. We may also be dealing with stressful situations, such as older children going through a turbulent adolescence or aging parents depending on us for support; we may have demanding jobs or careers; we may be worried about how pregnancy will change a relationship. Talking with other women often can be an important source of support.

When I first learned that I was pregnant, I was delighted, joyful, excited. And I assumed that people close to me would share my joy. Not so. My mother, my teenaged daughter, and my closest woman friend openly disapproved because I was unmarried. However, there were others—my sister, a close older woman friend and mentor, a male peer counselor, and other old friends who were happy for me. It was real important to my well-being to have warm support from people around me during my pregnancy. My prenatal exercise classes, besides readying my body for giving birth, also serve as an open forum for sharing concerns, thoughts, and resources with other pregnant women. It's always such a relief to suddenly step into a room where everyone is pregnant. The feelings of isolation immediately vanish. [a divorced woman in her forties]

An important source of support during pregnancy is a prenatal-care practitioner who will view you and your pregnancy as normal and healthy, while carefully monitoring any special medical conditions you may have. Although a late pregnancy can be as safe as an early one if a woman is healthy, older mothers run a high risk of having their pregnancies "medicalized by health care practitioners," causing worry and stress which can take a toll on pregnancy out-

Ilene S. Hauck

come. Thus, feeling optimistic and keeping stress at a minimum is an advantage medically as well as psychologically.[26]

In general, a midwife or a family-practice physician may be more likely to view midlife pregnancy as healthy and normal than an obstetrician. Obstetrical training is more intervention-oriented. The Pregnancy chapter in *The New Our Bodies, Ourselves* includes a detailed discussion of the kinds of care available and the issues involved.

A new law passed in Massachusetts requires hospitals to disclose their track record in perinatal (occurring during the period immediately preceding and following birth) care, so that a pregnant woman can find out the Cesarean rate as well as other birth practices at that hospital before signing up for childbirth care. Women are urged to find out as much as possible about prenatal-care providers and the facilities they practice in before making a choice. "We think the way change is going to occur is by parents' having more information and taking more responsibility for their own birth experiences," commented Beth Shearer of Cesarean Support, Education, and Concern, one of the fifteen consumer health groups who worked together to pass this bill, which they hope will be a model for health activists in other states.[27]

Prenatal Testing

Prenatal tests such as ultrasonography, amniocentesis, and chorionic villi sampling offer older women the option of choosing motherhood by reducing their risk of bearing a child with certain congenital disorders. However, several writers on midlife parenthood have observed that the process of testing, waiting for test results to come back, and deciding on a course of action delays a woman's or a couple's emotional commitment to the pregnancy,[28] in addition to raising several difficult moral and ethical issues that each woman must consider carefully. For women, the right to reproductive choice is central to all other rights in life.

I felt I had to make the decision, before we knew the results, that if we got a diagnosis of Down's I would have an abortion. We talked to a genetics counselor before the test. She was very helpful—all the medical support staff were helpful; they made all the difference in my thinking of it as a positive thing we were doing. [a thirty-eight-year-old first-time mother]

I chose not to have an "amnio" because, after much soul-searching, I decided that I would be open to having a Down's child. My personal experience with adults who have Down's syndrome is that they are among the most loving people around. Though Down's children take more care, work, and commitment, they can develop into contributing creative adults. They play a very humanizing role in our society. [a forty-one-year-old woman with a long-delayed second pregnancy]

Because of my age, I was considered a high-risk pregnancy, but I did not consider myself one. I was healthy and ate well and had a strong family history. At this point in my life I wanted a child very much and felt prepared to accept whatever happened in terms of [the baby's] health. I also had had a miscarriage and felt the risk of another miscarriage, though slight, with amniocentesis, was great enough to warrant not *having any unnecessary intervention.* [a thirty-eight-year-old woman]

Though prenatal tests have their place, women are increasingly concerned about the way testing has become routine for women over thirty-five and increasingly pushed upon women as young as thirty. Practitioners overdo testing to protect themselves against the possibility of a lawsuit if a child is born with an abnormality which could have been detected by testing. Those who administer the tests often fail to ask whether the woman would consider abortion in the event of an abnormality. If not, is it worth the risk of a possible miscarriage that the test entails? Medical interventions and procedures always carry risks. Let your prenatal-care prac-

titioner know if you want to minimize intervention in your pregnancy.

Ultrasound

Ultrasound is used in conjunction with amniocentesis for one or more of the following: to help pinpoint the exact location and position of the fetus; to help determine the age and size of the fetus; and to check for structural abnormalities in the fetus. It uses intermittent high-frequency sound waves to create pictures of the body's inner organs by measuring the length of time it takes for an echo to be returned.

If you have an ultrasound test, you will be asked to drink several glasses of water just before the procedure is done. A technician or physician will run a transducer, a hand-held instrument resembling a microphone, over your abdomen. A computer then translates the echoes picked up by the transducer into pictures of the fetus on a video screen. The pictures are then "read" by a radiologist. The results are usually available in a matter of hours.

Though ultrasound appears to be one of the safest tests and can provide important information, its long-term effects are still unknown. Because of this, women are cautioned to use the test only when necessary. For example, physicians sometimes want to use ultrasound to test for twins. Consider whether you really need to have this information early in your pregnancy.

Amniocentesis

Amniocentesis can detect approximately eighty chromosomal abnormalities as well as certain biochemical and metabolic disorders; it is most often used to test for Down's syndrome. Amniocentesis does not detect every possible disorder and is not a guarantee of a healthy infant.

The test involves withdrawing a small amount of fluid from the amniotic sac by way of a large needle and is usually performed between the fifteenth and sixteenth weeks of pregnancy, when there is enough amniotic fluid to give an adequate sample but the least risk of damaging the fetus. It takes approximately four weeks to obtain results.

The risk of miscarriage associated with the test is estimated at between one in 250 and one in 66 procedures, depending on the skill of the doctor.[29] There is also the risk of damage to the fetus: women have reported a variety of problems, including damaged, missing, or underdeveloped limbs, dating from approximately the time of the test.[30]

The accessibility of amniocentesis is still somewhat limited. While the fluid can be drawn in a doctor's office, only specially equipped laboratories can analyze it. The cost can also be prohibitive: it ranges from $600 to over $1,000. Many insurance companies, Medicare,* and Medicaid will pay for this test if a doctor states that it is necessary.

For women over forty, the chance of finding a defect is greater than the risk of miscarriage. Between ages thirty-five and forty, the odds are about even, and under age thirty-five, the risk of miscarriage is greater than the chance of finding a problem.[31]

A major drawback of amniocentesis is that it must be done too late in the pregnancy to allow for abortion during the first trimester. When you add on the four-week waiting period, it would be not much earlier than twenty weeks into the pregnancy, and may be as late as twenty-four weeks, before a woman could make a decision. If she chooses abortion, an instillation (saline or prostaglandin) procedure would have to be done.

Chorionic Villi Sampling

Chorionic villi sampling is a new alternative to amniocentesis which can detect chromosomal and other genetic abnormalities between the eighth and tenth weeks of pregnancy. The chorion, the tissue that grows around the developing embryo, eventually becomes the placenta. Scientists in China discovered that the tiny projections, called villi, which cover the chorion have a genetic composition similar to the embryo. By analyzing these villi, genetic information about the fetus may be obtained. To perform the test, a physician inserts a catheter through the vagina and into the uterus, guided by ultrasound equipment. A small sample of the villi is then aspirated and tested immediately.

CVS is still being studied in this country. Potential risks include spontaneous abortion, infection, maternal bleeding, and birth defects. A major drawback to the procedure is its relative

*For persons under sixty-five on Medicare, such as disabled women.

inaccuracy. Sometimes chromosomal abnormalities in the placental tissue are not present in the fetus, and vice versa. If this test can be made safe and accurate it would be preferable to amniocentesis, since it is performed when a first-trimester abortion would still be possible.

Prenatal testing is a special skill. The risk of complications is reduced when the physician performing the tests is experienced. Some women go to a specialist for these tests, but choose a less interventionist style of routine prenatal care.

ALTERNATIVES TO MIDLIFE CHILDBEARING

As menopause approaches, some women speak of an urge to become pregnant before it is "too late." One woman, divorced when her first child was young, and approaching her fortieth birthday, spoke of her wish to have another baby.

My son is sixteen and I suddenly have a strong urge to have a baby. I still want a family with children in it. I wonder if I'm really wanting a baby or if I just want to be part of a family, and it feels like a baby would give me that.

If you decide that having a child of your own is not central to your wish for a family, you may want to explore alternatives such as communal living or foster parenthood. Another increasingly popular alternative is adoption. A forty-five-year-old single woman, determined to have her own child, decided on adoption because of her infertility.

I had a total hysterectomy, so that settled it as far as giving birth to my own child was concerned. At that point I was forty-two and realized that I couldn't fool around any more—I needed to go ahead—and I was very fortunate that a friend of mine worked for an international adoption-counseling center. One evening she told me there was a four-year-old girl available and asked, "Are you interested?" Something told me, "This is it, now or never." I was able to fly down and meet her first so I could get to know her and then decided to go ahead.

Be prepared for the possibility of bias against older women at state-run agencies. The unwritten rule is that a woman should not be more than forty years older than her adopted child. In addition, we deplore the discriminatory practices of state and private agencies that make it virtually impossible for an openly lesbian woman or couple to adopt children or to be foster parents.

While it is true that there is often a long waiting period (as much as seven years) to adopt a healthy white infant, social service agencies have many older children and children with some medical problems who can be adopted immediately.

I didn't seem to have that need to have an infant. I felt I was older, so I wanted an older child! I felt it would work better for me economically, having to work and not earning enough to pay for day care. The adoption itself took all my savings. [a woman in her forties]

There are also many adoptable children of color of all ages within the United States and from Third World countries. If you are considering adopting a child of a racial group different from your own, it is important to learn about the child's cultural background so that you will be better able to support your child's sense of identity and to cope with racial prejudices.[32]

I took Spanish lessons for four months before she came. I was okay—I could get by. She was very kind—she didn't make fun of my Spanish, and that was all we spoke the first two or three months. [a woman in her forties]

It helps to have friends of the same background as the child's who can be part of a racially diverse support system or extended family. Many support groups have formed in response to the multiple problems and challenges facing adoptive parents, especially those who adopt children from abroad (see Resources). Such a group will put you in touch with other adults who are dealing with similar issues and also provide playmates for your child.

Adopting a child can be exhilarating and demanding.

Being a mother is wonderful. It's exhausting, challenging, fulfilling. I feel complete. There's no more of this nagging feeling that there's something missing in my life. I feel like I'm home. But she's a real challenge of a person to be with. Our cultures are different. We're very different people. Yet we've definitely made a bond. She wants very much to be close but at the same time she is testing a lot. She hits or bites or teases. She wants her way and has a hard time with no's. In the beginning she was more into pleasing but I think that she was raised in a strict environment and this is a much more permissive, loving environment. It's been hard for her to adjust to the change and it's been hard for me to get

stronger in setting limits. But she's happy and I feel very lucky to have found such a lively and caring soul, too. Just a real good person. She's a challenge, she tests every area where I'm weak. It's good for me! We're both growing a lot in the process. [a woman in her forties who adopted a four-year-old child]

NOTES

1. A. F. Guttmacher, "Factors Affecting Normal Expectancy of Conception." *Journal of the American Medical Association*, Vol. 161, 1956, pp. 855–60.

2. Boston Women's Health Book Collective, *The New Our Bodies, Ourselves.* New York: Simon and Schuster, 1984, p. 419.

3. Guttmacher, op. cit.

4. Alan H. DeCherney and Gertrud S. Berkowitz, "Female Fecundity and Age." An editorial in *The New England Journal of Medicine*, Vol. 306, No. 7, pp. 424–6; Bayard Webster, "Study Finds Female Fertility Drops Sharply After Age of 31." *The New York Times*, February 18, 1982.

5. Phyllis Kernoff Mansfield, *Pregnancy for Older Women: Assessing the Medical Risks.* New York: Praeger, 1986.

6. *Ibid.*; see also Donna Kirz, "Advanced Maternal Age: The Mature Gravida." *American Journal of Obstetrics and Gynecology*, Vol. 152, 1985, pp. 7–12. The author criticizes obstetricians' use of pejorative language to describe a middle-aged pregnant woman.

7. S. J. Ventura, "Trends in First Births to Older Mothers, 1970–1979." National Center for Health Statistics, *Monthly Vital Statistics Report*, Vol. 31, No. 2, Supp. (2); DHHS Pub. No. (PHS) 82-1120, Public Health Service, Hyattsville, MD, May 1982.

8. David A. Grimes and Gail K. Gross, "Pregnancy Outcomes in Black Women Age 35 and Older." *Obstetrics and Gynecology*, Vol. 58, No. 5, November 1981, pp. 614–20.

9. Mansfield, op. cit.

10. Mansfield, op. cit.

11. Ventura, op. cit.

12. C. Arden Miller, "Infant Mortality in the U.S." *Scientific American*, Vol. 253, No. 1, July 1985, pp. 31–7.

13. E. O. Horger and A. R. Smythe, "Pregnancy in Women over Forty." *Obstetrics and Gynecology*, Vol. 49, 1977, pp. 257–61.

14. K. R. Niswander and M. Gordon, *The Women and Their Pregnancies*, DHEW Publication (NIH) 73-379, Public Health Service, Washington, DC.

15. Grimes and Gross, op. cit.

16. P. Kajanoja and O. Widholm, "Pregnancy and Delivery of Women Aged 40 and Over." *Obstetrics and*

Gynecology, Vol. 51, 1978, pp. 47–51; and Mansfield, op. cit.

17. L. S. Penrose, "Paternal Age in Mongolism," *Lancet*, Vol. 1, 1962, p. 1101.

18. Pamela Daniels and Kathy Weingarten, *Sooner or Later: The Timing of Parenthood in Adult Lives.* New York: Norton, 1983, p. 186.

19. Daniels and Weingarten, op. cit., p. 186

20. Judith Blackfield Cohen, *Parenthood After 30? A Practical Guide to Personal Choice.* Lexington, MA: D.C. Heath and Company/Lexington Books, 1985.

21. Z. Stein and J. Kline, "Smoking, Alcohol and Reproduction." *American Journal of Public Health*, Vol. 73, 1983, pp. 1154–6.

22. Boston Women's Health Book Collective, op. cit., 330.

23. J. A. Pritchard and P. C. MacDonald, *Williams Obstetrics*, 16th ed. New York: Appleton-Century Crofts, 1976, p. 531.

24. Boston Women's Health Book Collective, op. cit., p. 330.

25. For more information, call your public health nurse at your local health department.

26. Phyllis Kernoff Mansfield and Margaret D. Conn, "Stress and Midlife Childbearing: Key Nursing Interventions." *Maternal-Child Nursing Journal*, Vol. 15, No. 3, Fall 1986, pp. 139–51.

27. Richard A. Knox, "Law Signed Giving Parents Access to Cesarean Data." *The Boston Globe*, January 1, 1986, p. 38.

28. Daniels and Weingarten, op. cit.; and Barbara Katz Rothman, *The Tentative Pregnancy: Prenatal Diagnosis and the Future of Motherhood.* New York: Viking, 1986.

29. Santa Fe Health Education Project, "What Is Amniocentesis?" *Health Letter*, Vol. 4, No. 10.

30. Barbara Katz Rothman, personal communication.

31. Rayna Rapp, "XYLO: A True Story," in Rita Arditti, Renate Duelli Klein and Shelley Minden, eds., *Test Tube Women*. Boston: Pandora Press, Routledge and Kegan Paul, 1984.

32. Joyce Ladner, *Mixed Families: Adopting Across Racial Boundaries*. Garden City, New York: Anchor Press, 1977.

10

MENOPAUSE: ENTERING OUR THIRD AGE

by Diana Laskin Siegal with Judy Costlow,
Maria Cristina Lopez, and Mara Taub
of the Santa Fe Health Education Project
and Fredi Kronenberg

Most of us remember our first menstrual period. We may remember who told us about menstruation, or, if we were not prepared, we remember the shock of our first period. Just as there was a time for our periods to start, there is a time for them to stop. Yet few of us are ever prepared for menopause. We hope this chapter will help change that.

The generation of women approaching menopause today has had more choices about reproduction than did their mothers and grandmothers. Whatever choices we have made about contraception and childbearing in our lives, menopause means the end of our choices about fertility. To the extent that women's lives can be described by fertility, there are three stages: childhood until puberty; the years when we are able to bear children; and the "third age,"[1] the years past menopause.[2] We are, however, more than our fertility and have much to offer throughout our lives regardless of our decisions about reproduction.

While females of some species remain fertile throughout their lives, women live past the end of fertility and truly have a "change of life." As we go through this change, some of us mourn the end of childbearing potential, while many celebrate entering an age of freedom from the concern about pregnancy.

When we are defined as sex objects and breeders, and valued only while young, we may fear menopause as a symbol of the approach of a demeaned old age. We are then vulnerable to societal myths that after menopause we are past our prime. Consider the irony of Sandra Day O'Connor referring to herself as "over the hill" because she was past menopause when appointed as the first woman justice of the U.S. Supreme Court. With the increase in longevity, our "third age" can be as much as half our lives and can be a time of activity and productivity.

Elizabeth Freeman started a business when she was sixty-four years old. She writes:

What a burst of energy women experience as they leave menopause. Putting together a newsletter for an organization called the Older Women's Network (OWN) in the 1970s made me aware of the outpouring of poetry, fiction and thoughts of midlife and older women in all parts of the country. I'm continually impressed and excited by the energy and creativity of older women. At the same time I realized the dearth of publishers available to them. I wanted to print the work of older, feminist women. Using the word "crone," which, though generally derogatory in our society, originally meant "wise old woman," I conceived of a name for my publishing house. Adding the OWN (Older Women's Network), Crones' Own Press came into being. To me this period of my life has been most exciting and creative.

Menopause is a natural event, but doctors in the United States developed, and some still perpetuate, the medical myth that menopausal women suffer a crisis or a "deficiency disease"[3] for which treatment is needed. The myth still persists, fed by drug company advertising and by ridicule from comedians, that we are difficult to live with at menopause.

Researchers are only now beginning to study what affects women's experiences of menopause. Cultural patterns and attitudes may have an influence on these experiences. Yewoubdar Beyene compared the social status of older women, nutrition, and attitudes toward childbearing and menopause of both Mayan and rural Greek women. She found that Mayan women look forward to menopause, eat a diet high in carbohydrates and calcium, but no meat or dairy products, and do not report hot flashes. Rural Greek women report more anxiety about menopause and growing older, eat a diet more like ours than like the Mayan, but although they report hot flashes, they do not seek medical intervention.[4]

The Santa Fe Health Education Project reports that the dominant culture in the United States may be more powerful than its subcultures in shaping the experience of menopause: "Our experience in giving menopause workshops for over eight years to groups of Hispanic, Native American, and other women of a range of ages, economic backgrounds, geographic locations, and professions has led us to the conclusion that the experience of menopause cross-culturally in the United States is much more the same than it is different."

Most women go through "the change," as menopause is often called, with few problems and go on with their lives. Some women, however, do have a very difficult time with menopause. Those who feel isolated and friendless, without others to share their experience, may be unprepared and therefore susceptible to fears and misinformation about menopause. Women are often blamed and are told that their attitudes about themselves are the cause of their problems. It is important to acknowledge that some women who are prepared for menopause, who have support, and are happy with their choices may still experience discomfort as their hormone levels are changing.

New feminist research shows that many women learn to care for others first and only later to care for themselves.[5] Menopause is a time when, if we have not already done so, we should learn to take good care of ourselves.

This time is a rebirth of sorts, an incredible opportunity to rediscover who I am as a human being. The truth is that I have a very long life ahead, and now I can choose how I am going to experience it and what I'm going to do. It's exciting to be making a journey in response to myself rather than in response to the values placed upon me. [a forty-two-year-old woman]

WHAT IS MENOPAUSE?

The word "menopause" is used in a variety of ways. Popularly, "menopause" is used to describe the many years when our bodies are changing from menstrual cycles to a noncyclic stage. More precisely, menopause is defined as the date of our final period. The medical literature distinguishes three time periods: premenopausal, perimenopausal (when we may notice changes), and postmenopausal (after periods have ceased); it combines the peri- and early postmenopausal times into the climacteric. While the average age at the time of the final menstrual period is between ages fifty and fifty-one, the range is very broad—menopause may occur between the late thirties and the late fifties. We do not know that we have had that final period and reached menopause until a year without periods has passed. The common folk expression "change of life" (often condensed to "the change") is a good term to describe the entire process, which takes perhaps twenty years —ten years before and ten years after the cessation of menses.

Signs of Menopause

"Symptoms" is not an appropriate word to describe changes at menopause. A symptom is a change due to disease, while menopause is not a disease. Three "signs" are clearly associated with menopause: cessation of periods, vaginal changes, and hot flashes. Cessation of periods is the only sign experienced by all women. Wrinkles and graying hair, which happen to both women and men as a function of the normal aging process, are not caused by menopause. Likewise, irritability, which is frequently listed as a "symptom" of menopause, may occur at any time in our lives and may also occur as we get older and react to age discrimination, which is so evident in our society today.

Some physicians attribute much of what happens to a woman at midlife to menopause, sometimes overlooking what might be symptoms of gallbladder disease, hypertension, and other serious conditions.[6] For example, profuse sweating, fatigue, and vaginal itching may be symptoms of diabetes;[7] headaches and dizziness may be symptoms of disease.

Because physicians are often not aware that it is normal for women's experiences of menopause to vary widely, they often treat the normal signs of menopause as illness. Rather than offering help in managing those changes which become severe and annoying, they are quick to offer drugs (especially hormones) or hysterectomy. The emphasis of this chapter is on the self-help approaches women have found to deal with menopausal discomforts and to avoid drugs and surgery.

A few years ago this chapter would have been the place for a discussion of physicians' misuse and overuse of estrogens for women at and following menopause. In the late 1970s and early 1980s, the risks of estrogen therapy for menopause were widely publicized so its use dropped and then leveled off. Now in the mid-1980s, we are again seeing a surge in prescriptions—estrogen or a combination of estrogen and progesterone. Some physicians still prescribe hormones when they may not be necessary so the discussion of whether to take them or not is still relevant. Since most drug companies that sell hormones and physicians who prescribe them are now basing their recommendations for hormones on a campaign of fear of broken bones, the discussion of hormones has been placed in the Osteoporosis chapter, pp. 268–71.

The myth that women go mad at menopause persists despite research showing that women are *less* likely to experience mental illness at midlife than in other years. Some women do report temporary depression during the perimenopausal stage when hormone levels are fluctuating and readjusting. While this depression does not happen to many women, the few who do experience it need to know it will likely pass after menstruation ceases, with the coming of menopause.[8]

I searched for the truth about menopause but what I found didn't help me. All the books I read and all the people I talked with told me it was nothing at all. Some said, "Think positively and don't gain weight." Others said, "It's all in the culture." I had to validate my own experience. No one would acknowledge or could explain why I had a hard time whenever my hormones shifted. I thought I was going mad at thirteen, I was depressed when I was pregnant, and I had unexplained depression and mood changes for the nine years between the ages of forty-five and fifty-four when my periods were changing. I was raising a daughter alone but I lived with peo-ple who were supportive and I tried everything: estrogen for two years, jogging, massage therapy, a women's support group, homeopathic remedies. They helped a little but not enough. I even tried an antidepressant, which did not help either, and caused me to gain twenty-five pounds. Once my periods stopped, I not only had an absence of depression but had a lightness and buoyancy, a state of being positively happy. I am fine now but I feel I lost a decade of my life. [a fifty-six-year-old woman]

Some of us may experience premenstrual changes for the first time: swollen, tender breasts, water retention, and some tension or anxiety. Women who have had these and other discomforts severe enough to be considered premenstrual syndrome (PMS) can look forward to relief from their discomforts.* As periods stop and hormone cycles level out, so will PMS. This process may take several years. Even women with only minor water retention and breast tenderness may still be aware of some cycling in their bodies after their periods cease. Those women who suffer from underlying depression in addition to PMS may find their symptoms a little worse during this time. After menopause, PMS will subside, but they still may have to cope with the underlying depression.[9]

Changes in Menstrual Patterns

Our bodies may require years before our well-established pattern of periods stops completely. Some women do not experience menstrual-cycle changes before their periods stop; but most experience some changes in the length, amount, and frequency of menstrual flow, often starting in their forties and sometimes their thirties.

The chart shows the hormonal patterns that result in varying patterns of flow. The heavy period (heavy bleeding or menorrhagia) is the most annoying and worrisome. Sometimes the flow is so heavy that a tampon can be flooded out of the vagina and even heavy pads cannot contain it. We may feel faint momentarily. We

---

*PMS can sometimes be alleviated by a low-salt diet or other dietary changes, natural diuretics, aspirin, and acupuncture. Vitamin B₆, calcium with Vitamin D, and magnesium may help relieve PMS. Some women have found essential fatty acids (specifically linseed oil and/or evening primrose oil), along with some zinc, vitamin C, and vitamin B complex, very helpful. For help with PMS, see Michelle Harrison, *Self-Help for Premenstrual Syndrome*. New York: Random House, 1985; and *The New Our Bodies, Ourselves*. New York: Simon and Schuster, 1984.

may fear or be embarrassed by so much blood. Heavy periods are common but subside as the estrogen level drops.

At age forty-five I was dining in a foreign city when I felt the gush. I wiped myself as well as I could in the bathroom, made a pad out of paper towels, and managed to get back to my hotel. I reminded myself that menstrual blood is normal and that I did not have to worry or be embarrassed. I remembered that one of the first women to run officially in the Boston Marathon had her period the day of the race and had blood flowing down her leg. Everyone near me cheered her on and no one jeered at the blood. But still I felt better that I was in a city where no one was likely to recognize me. I had a few other episodes before my periods stopped. [a fifty-four-year-old woman]

Women have found helpful things to do to control heavy bleeding, such as eating a healthful diet, taking vitamin A in limited quantities, and getting plenty of rest. Also, it is best to avoid alcohol, strenuous activity such as swimming or jogging when the period is beginning, and aspirin and other drugs that slow down blood clotting. Some women report that their periods seemed to be under better control after using techniques such as acupuncture and meditation combined with visualizing a compact uterus. Self-help techniques require months of learning about and observing our bodies' patterns and changes. This is part of the process of taking care of ourselves.

Sometimes the periods become so extended

Progesterone is a hormone secreted by the ovaries, adrenals, and placenta. It is responsible for the changes in the uterine lining in the second half of the menstrual cycle, for development of the maternal placenta after implantation, and development of the breast glands.

Progestin or *Progestogen* are terms for any natural or synthetic hormonal substance which produces effects similar to those produced by progesterone.

Usually the word "progesterone" is used for the body's hormone and "progestin" or "progestogen" for any substance which has the same effects on the body as progesterone. The three words, however, are sometimes used interchangeably.

---

and so close together that we seem to be having one continuous period. You should report repeated heavy and continuous periods to your health care practitioner and may want to undergo tests to assess the status of the lining of the uterus. Beware of pressure to have surgery for bleeding. (see Hysterectomy and Oophorectomy chapter) There are other options. Though heavy bleeding is inconvenient, embarrassing, and scary, the only real health hazard (once a biopsy rules out malignancy) is iron deficiency (anemia). Have your hemoglobin checked and eat iron-rich foods. Take iron supplements, if recommended, but not unless you are actually anemic.

One medical approach to the heavy bleeding caused by the body's prolonged estrogen or reduced progesterone production is the use of a progestin (progestogen). When used at the very beginning of a period, progestins cause the lining of the uterus to slough off more completely than in previous cycles. The next period may then be lighter because the lining has not built up so thickly. Progestins may also be used to interrupt prolonged estrogen production, stimulate a period, and start a new cycle. Some women decide to try small doses of an oral progestin for a very short time, or sporadically, depending on the pattern of their periods. Beware of large doses or injections that stay in the body for several months. Progestins do not alleviate all bleeding problems. IUDs impregnated with a progestin have all the dangers of IUDs plus longer exposure to the progestin.

The occasional "missed" period can be worrisome to women who are heterosexually active and fear they might be pregnant. In spite of scanty periods you can still be fertile, so keep using contraceptives for two years after the final period (see Birth Control for Women in Midlife chapter, p. 99). Become familiar with your pattern by charting your periods and noting other body changes which differ from those of pregnancy.

Pregnancy	*Menopause*
Missed period	Missed period
	May have other signs such as:
Nausea	Hot flashes
Tender breasts	Vaginal dryness

Many women have reported occasional bleeding after they thought their menstrual periods

Patterns of Natural Hormone Levels and
Their Effects on Menstrual Periods

	Estrogen Level	Ovulation	Progesterone Level	Effect on Endometrial Lining	Effect on Period
MENSTRUAL YEARS	Usual cyclic pattern. More estrogen than progesterone before ovulation	Egg produced. Both estrogen and progesterone drop at ovulation, then rise	Usual cyclic pattern. More progesterone than estrogen after ovulation	Estrogen builds up lining. Progesterone causes lining to slough off	Usual period
PREGNANCY	Estrogen level increases after fertilization and during pregnancy	Egg produced and fertilized	Level increases during pregnancy	Endometrium builds up to provide environment for embryo to develop	No period
PERIMENOPAUSAL YEARS Hormone levels may fluctuate from one period to the next causing variations in cycles and in periods. Some cycles may be ovulatory (an egg produced) and some cycles may be anovulatory (no egg produced). Estrogen levels may drop gradually so that periods diminish gradually, may drop suddenly so that periods stop suddenly, may fluctuate so that the flow is heavier, lighter, or skips some months	Usual cyclic pattern and level	Egg produced	Usual cyclic pattern and level	Usual cyclic pattern	Usual period
	Less estrogen	Egg may or may not be produced	Less progesterone	Thin uterine lining	Period may be lighter in flow or last fewer days
	Even less estrogen	No egg produced	Even less progesterone	Thinner uterine lining	No period
	Prolonged estrogen	Probably no egg produced	Less progesterone	Irregular or thick lining. May not slough off completely or evenly. Portion may remain during the next cycle	One period may start, stop, and start again. Period may be longer and heavier and clotting may be present
POSTMENOPAUSAL YEARS	Low estrogen; no cyclic pattern (some estrogen is still produced)	No egg produced	Even less progesterone; no cyclic pattern (production of progesterone virtually ceases)	Thin uterine lining. No cyclic changes	No period

had finally stopped. We now know that stress can affect the level of reproductive hormones in the body. At a workshop on menopause, two women reported experiencing some bleeding long after the cessation of their menses. Each started flowing when she took a sick parent to a hospital emergency room.

Prolonged bleeding or more than a few brief episodes of bleeding after menopause may be a symptom of cancer, and should be checked by your health-care practitioner. Do not agree to hysterectomy unless you have a confirmed diagnosis that warrants it (see Hysterectomy and Oophorectomy chapter).

Vaginal Changes

As we age, there is a tendency for the skin and mucous membranes in various parts of our bodies to become drier. To help with this condition add moisture to the air in your house and drink eight cups of fluid each day. The vaginal membranes become thinner, hold less moisture, lubricate more slowly. Even walking may be uncomfortable. Some women also suffer dry eyes, and some a loss of saliva. For some women vaginal dryness is an early sign of menopause; others do not experience it until many years later, and many never do. Little research has been done on this subject but data from the first surveys of a large number of women to find out how many are bothered by vaginal dryness should be available shortly.[10]

Some prescription and over-the-counter drugs can cause dryness. Antihistamines, for example, dry other tissues as well as nasal tissues. Do not use douches, sprays, and colored or perfumed toilet paper and soaps, which can irritate the tissues of the vulva. If itchiness develops, avoid scratching, which can irritate the delicate tissues and lead to infections and further problems. Aci-gel and other prescription ointments are available to help the itchiness (see Sexuality chapter for more suggestions).

Hot Flashes

It was a freezing December night when I lay in bed, dreading to get up and go down a long cold hall to an even colder bathroom. Then I had a hot flash, and, all of a sudden, it was very easy to leave my warm bed! For the rest of the winter I used my nighttime hot flashes this way. My friends laughed when I told them that hot flashes are not all bad! [a fifty-nine-year-old woman]

Ron Schildknecht/Water Tower Art Association

Women working on the Hot Flash Fan Project. Ann Stewart Anderson, Judy Chicago, and seventy other workers. Photo by Ron Schildnecht

Many of us had flashes during pregnancy or experienced something resembling hot flashes at other times—the red face of blushing or the increased heartbeat and sweating during times of great stress. In folk wisdom and humor, hot flashes are the sign most commonly associated with menopause.

Sometimes our flushing is interpreted as blushing or being flustered. Since sweating from a hot flash reveals age and menstrual status, both of which are supposed to be secrets, we may be subjected to jokes and embarrassed reactions. Also, many older women were taught that "Ladies don't sweat!" Fortunately we are speaking up, supporting each other, and changing many of these attitudes.

Surveys report that anywhere from 47 percent to 85 percent of women will experience hot flashes.[11] Some women never experience hot flashes at all. In one study of one thousand women, 470 had hot flashes but only 155 (15.5 percent of the total) reported that they were bothered by them.[12]

For most, a hot flash or flush means nothing more than a transient sensation of warmth. Many women report their hot flashes are not unpleasant, may even be pleasant, and as in the above example, useful. Some women experience waves of heat and drenching sweats, often followed by chills; some experience chills first. The flashes are often preceded by a brief aura, a

Hot Flash Fan, completed. Photo by L. Suzanne LaValley

Suzanne LaValley/Water Tower Art Association

sense of the coming flash. Feelings of tension, heart palpitations, anxiety, and nausea may also accompany hot flashes or may precede and be relieved by the hot flash.

Hot flashes can begin when menstrual cycles are still regular or when they are becoming irregular. Typically, they continue for less than a year after the final menstrual period; however, for some women they persist for five, ten, or even more years.[13] In some instances, hot flashes first begin many years after menopause. Although they usually last a few minutes, the duration of some hot flashes may be shorter or longer. Their frequency also varies. Hot flashes may occur once a month, or once an hour, or several times an hour. They can occur any time day or night, though one study reports they are more frequent between 6 and 8 A.M. and again between 6 and 10 P.M.[14] Each woman has her own pattern.

At age fifty I skipped a period and had hot flashes at night for the first time during the month I was on jury duty for seven trials including two murder trials! I got my period the day after I finished jury duty and didn't have another hot flash for six more months. [a fifty-five-year-old woman]

We have few clues as to who is most likely to get hot flashes, how intense they might be, or how long the hot flashes might last. Generally the body gradually adjusts to the lower level of estrogen, and for most women the hot flashes stop.[15]

Many women report that their hot flashes are most disturbing at night when they are awakened and may have to change their nightclothes and sheets due to drenching sweats. The loss of sleep over many nights can cause fatigue, irritability, and feelings of inability to cope similar to depression (see Dealing with Insomnia, in Habits Worth Changing chapter, p. 32).

Women whose ovaries are removed before menopause, resulting in a sudden drop in estrogen levels, may experience intense hot flashes often beginning immediately after surgery, and vaginal dryness at an earlier age. Hot flashes occur more frequently and severely in these women (especially for about six months after surgery) than they do in women who go through natural menopause.[16] The ovaries continue to produce estrogen after menopause so a woman may begin to experience hot flashes if she has her ovaries removed after her periods had already stopped.

During a hot flash, the blood vessels most

commonly expand (dilate) and blood flow to the skin increases. Though the skin temperature often rises from four to eight degrees F. during a hot flash, and the sensation is one of heat or blushing, the internal body temperature actually falls.[17] This occurs because the body eliminates heat through increased blood flow to the skin and by sweating. The dilation can clear a stuffy nose, and the rush of blood to the surface can cause dizziness, reddening, and crawly feelings on the skin. The increased heartbeat that often occurs with a hot flash may be accompanied by a feeling of anxiety. Some women experience chills and tingling skin when the blood vessels narrow (constrict).

Since my studio apartment had a patio door, I could easily step outside to cool off when I felt a hot flash coming. I felt shut in and constricted when that source of relief wasn't present in other settings. [a fifty-three-year-old woman]

At my first unexpected hot flashes I was afraid. I had in mind that hot flashes involved a loss of control, but when I paid close attention, I felt half in a dream state, flushed and physically lightheaded. Actually, it seemed like an altered state of consciousness, which wasn't that unfamiliar to me, because I meditate. But I can see that for many women it would be a new experience, one they'd fear and try to suppress. [a forty-two-year-old woman]

Only in the past ten years have researchers begun to study what causes hot flashes. Their occurrence is related to a decline in estrogen levels. However, something else is probably involved in triggering each hot-flash episode. Some researchers speculate that the hypothalamus (that part of the brain which regulates body temperature) is involved in a hot flash, perhaps through the release of some substance which triggers the hot flash. They are looking at the ways hormones interact with the temperature-regulating system.[18]

Physicians and researchers would gain much by listening carefully both to the descriptions that women give of their sensations of hot flashes and to the techniques women have found to minimize and relieve their discomforts. We hope that a better understanding of the mechanism of hot flashes will lead to new approaches and self-help techniques for relief rather than just to new drugs.

Self-Help for Hot Flashes

· Keep Track.

Chart your hot flashes in relationship to your menstrual periods and other events to see if you can find a pattern. The more you know about yourself, the better you'll be able to manage your hot flashes and the better you will feel.

From ages fifty-one to fifty-three I skipped many periods. Whenever I skipped periods I had hot flashes; the months I had periods I had no hot flashes. I began to see a pattern and could predict what to expect. [a fifty-five-year-old woman]

· Keep Healthy.

Some women have found that caffeine (coffee, tea, cola drinks, chocolate), alcohol, sugar, spicy foods, hot soups, hot drinks, and very large meals may trigger hot flashes. Eat well.

Some women find that vitamin E minimizes or eliminates hot flashes. Vitamin E is found in vegetable oils (wheat germ, corn, and soybean), wheat and rice germ, legumes, corn, and almonds. Egg yolks contain vitamin E but also contain very high levels of cholesterol. If you take a supplement, start with 25 milligrams per day and find your effective level by increasing gradually up to, but not more than, 400 IUs per day. Avoid it if you are taking digitalis or are diabetic. Take only water-soluble vitamin E if you have high blood pressure. Some find adding 25 mg. of B complex to be helpful.

Many women report more hot flashes at times of stress. Try the methods described in "Disarming Stress" (p. 12) to relax. If hot flashes disturb your sleep at night, take naps and meditate to avoid fatigue.

· Keep Cool.

Dress in layers. Clothes made of natural fibers may be more comfortable than those made of synthetic materials. When you feel a hot flash starting, take off some clothes. Go to a cooler spot, stand by an open window. Relax, take a few deep breaths. There is no reason to feel embarrassed. Fan yourself with whatever is at hand or collect fans to match your wardrobe

Using Herbs

Over the years women of many cultures have used herbs for menopausal complaints. The following information was compiled by the Santa Fe Health Education Project with help from Amadea Morningstar (nutritionist), Chavela Esparza (herbalist), and Gregorita Rodriguez (curandera-healer). See Resources for other books on using herbs.

Some herbs can be toxic in large quantities, so if you are not familiar with an herb, obtain more information, preferably from someone with experience in their use. Use herbs with caution and start taking them in moderate amounts. Read labels carefully. You can save money and be assured of purity and freshness by growing your own.

Herbs are available from herbalists, health-food stores, herb stores, and farmers' markets. They come in different forms —dried for making teas, or powdered in capsules. Dried herbs may be fresher than capsules. Some people prefer the capsules because not all herbs are soluble in water and it is easier to swallow a capsule than to brew tea. Allow two to six weeks to feel the herbs' effects; do not expect immediate relief.

The most commonly used herbs for complaints of menopause include black cohosh, damiana, dong quai, cramp bark, ginseng, golden seal (used in England), licorice root, red raspberry leaves, sarsaparilla and spearmint (*yerba buena*). These are traditionally taken as teas. Herb mixtures for menopause available in capsules in health-food stores may contain contain false unicorn, blessed thistle, and squaw vine.

Ginseng and black cohosh contain natural estrogen, so precautions about estrogen therapy apply to them also. Ginseng is also not advised for women with high blood pressure or diabetes. Dong quai is also called female ginseng.

The following are herbal tea recipes. Try one for six weeks to see if it helps before trying another. Different combinations of herbs work best for different people.

1. A tea made from the following three Southwestern herbs: skunk weed, snake broom, and lizard tail (*yerba de zorrillo, escoba de la vibora,* and *yerba del manso*). Bring half a gallon of water to a boil. Add two tablespoons of the dried leaves of each herb (or a quarter of a cup of each of the fresh plants—leaves, stem, and roots). Boil two to three minutes. Set aside, covered, for 10 minutes. Strain. Drink a cup three times a day.

2. A tea brewed in the same way from two tablespoons of alfalfa seeds to a pint of water. Drink three times a day with lemon. For economy, the same seeds may be used for a second brewing.

3. A tea brewed from an ounce of wild or sweet marjoram in a pint of hot (not boiling) water. Cover. When cool, strain and add a large glass of port wine. Take one tablespoon before meals, three times a day.

4. A tea brewed from two parts each of motherwort and red sage, and one part each of tansy, pennyroyal, and skullcap. Take one-half teaspoon in a little lukewarm water before meals three times a day.

5. A tea brewed from black cohosh, sweet flag, licorice root, star root (*Aletris farinosa*), black haw, cramp bark (*Viburnum opulus*), squaw weed (false valerian), and motherwort. Take one cup during the day with a meal.

6. Gotu Kola is a high-mineral herb. Drink one cup of tea in the morning for energy before breakfast. This is not recommended for women with overactive (hyper) thyroids.

Especially for Anxiety and/or Insomnia

1. A cup of tea per day brewed from a rounded teaspoon of any one of the following herbs: camomile, spearmint, rosemary, skullcap, passion flower (*Passiflora incarnata*), tilia flowers.

2. A tea brewed from a mixture of catnip, valerian, camomile, skullcap, lady slipper, and peppermint.

3. Sleeping on a pillow stuffed with dried hops.

as our great-grandmothers did. Drink something cool. Place something cool where it feels best—on the wrists, temples, forehead. Shower. Visualize yourself in a cool place such as sitting by a lake with a cool breeze blowing. Lower the thermostat, get a cooler, an electric fan, or an air conditioner. Before bed, put a cup of table salt in a tub of warm water; lie in it until the water cools; rinse with cold water and go right to bed.[19] If you have a bedmate, get dual controls for the electric blanket.

· **Keep Talking.**

Break the taboos against menopause. Stay comfortable by letting people know when you

Cathy Cade

are having a hot flash and reaffirm that it is nothing to be ashamed of. Use positive, not demeaning, humor. Tell household members or co-workers what is happening.

I never felt that I should suffer hot flashes in silence, so my husband and kids called me "Flash." When I told my husband it was the first anniversary of my last period he said, "Congratulations, Flash. You've done it." So we went out to dinner and celebrated that night. [a fifty-one-year-old woman]

Talking with others, sharing our experiences and feelings, acquiring knowledge about how our bodies are changing, and giving each other support eases our "change of life." A group of women coming together in a menopause self-help group or workshop to learn from one another, in a respectful, informative, and supportive setting, can effectively counteract fears

and uncertainties with support and information. Much of the material in this section comes from women who have shared their experiences and their wisdom. An indispensable resource is *Menopause: A Positive Approach* by Rosetta Reitz, a pioneer in menopause self-help groups. By talking with other women we will continue to discover and exchange new self-help methods.

Rondel*

Now that I am fifty-six
Come and celebrate with me.

What happens to song and sex
Now that I am fifty-six?

They dance, but differently.
Death and distance in the mix;
Now that I am fifty-six
Come and celebrate with me.

Muriel Rukeyser

NOTES

1. So-called by the French and Portuguese according to Betty Friedan, "Changing Sex Roles: Vital Aging," in Robert N. Butler and Herbert P. Gleason, eds., *Productive Aging: Enhancing Vitality in Later Life.* New York: Springer Publishing Company, 1985, p. 93.

2. In ancient times women in the three ages were called nymphs, maidens, and crones. See Barbara Walker, *The Crone: Women of Age, Wisdom and Power.* New York: Harper & Row, 1985.

3. Frances B. McCrea, "The Politics of Menopause: The 'Discovery' of a Deficiency Disease." *Social Problems*, Vol. 31, No. 1, October 1983, pp. 111–23.

4. Yewoubdar Beyene, "Cultural Significance and Physiological Manifestations of Menopause: A Biocultural Analysis." *Culture, Medicine and Psychiatry.* Vol. 10, No. 1, March 1986, pp. 10–17.

5. Carol Gilligan, *In a Different Voice: Psychological Theory and Women's Development.* Cambridge, MA: Harvard University Press, 1982.

6. Catherine DeLorey, "Health Care and Midlife Women," in Grace Baruch and Jeanne Brooks-Gunn, eds., *Women in Midlife.* New York: Plenum Press, 1984, pp. 277–301.

7. Jane Porcino, *Growing Older, Getting Better.* Reading, MA: Addison-Wesley Publishing Co., 1983, p. 277.

*"Rondel" by Muriel Rukeyser, from *Breaking Open*. New York: Random House, 1973, p. 18.

8. John B. McKinlay, Sonja M. McKinlay, Donald Brambilla, "The Relative Contributions of Endocrine Changes and Social Circumstances to Depression in Mid-Aged Women." Unpublished paper, 1985, available from the New England Research Institute, 42 Pleasant St., Watertown, MA 02172.

9. Information on PMS at menopause from a conversation with Michelle Harrison, M.D.

10. Sonja M. McKinlay and John McKinlay, New England Research Institute, op. cit.

11. Sonja M. McKinlay & M. Jeffreys, "The Menopausal Syndrome." *British Journal of Preventive & Social Medicine*, Vol. 28, 1974, pp. 108–15; and Bernice L. Neugarten and R. J. Kraines, "Menopausal Symptoms in Women of Various Ages." *Psychosomatic Medicine*. Vol. 27, 1965, pp. 266–73.

12. Jane Haliburton, personal communication about research in progress.

13. Fredi Kronenberg, unpublished data.

14. Ann M. Voda, *Menopause—Me and You.* Salt Lake City: University of Utah College of Nursing, 1984, pp. 7–8.

15. R. Don Gambrell, Jr., and Ann L. Hyatt, "Benefits and Risks of Estrogen Replacement Therapy in the Menopause." *Delaware Medical Journal*, Vol. 56, No. 4, April 1984, p. 20.

16. S. Chakravarti, et al. "Endocrine Changes and Symptomatology After Oophorectomy in Premenopausal Women." *British Journal of Obstetrics & Gynaecology*, Vol. 84, 1977, pp. 769–75.

17. I. V. Tataryn, et al., "Post-menopausal Hot Flushes: A Disorder of Thermoregulation." *Maturitas*, Vol. 2, 1980, pp. 101–7.

18. Fredi Kronenberg, et al., "Menopausal Hot Flashes: Thermoregulatory, Cardiovascular, and Circulating Catecholamine and LH Changes." *Maturitas*, Vol. 6, 1984, pp. 31–43.

19. Gregorita Rodriguez, Santa Fe, New Mexico.

11

RELATIONSHIPS IN MIDDLE AND LATER LIFE*

by Dorothy Frauenhofer, Lynn Scott,
Paula Brown Doress, and Kristine Rosenthal-Keese.
Material on mothers-in-law by Jane Porcino

Women value relationships. For us middle-aged and older women, especially, concern for interpersonal relationships has been a central theme of our lives. Most of us have worked hard to reach out to others, to express feelings of caring and attachment, and to be helpful when friends and family members are troubled. Throughout our lives our "people skills" have helped us get through some of the tough times.

As we move into the later decades of our lives, however, nearly all of us experience losses or changes in many of our most important relationships. When this happens, we fear the loneliness of being "unattached" and the emptiness of not being needed or valued. Many of us from traditional backgrounds were raised on homilies like "Blood is thicker than water," and taught to avoid sharing confidences with "outsiders." Yet long-lived women frequently survive all of their close family members. Though we grieve for the loss of relationships we can never replace, we *can* overcome loneliness and isolation by reweaving and changing family relationships, nurturing old and new friendships, and especially by reaching out to other women to form new connections for support and intimate

friendships. Our middle and later years can be a time of expanding choices and new opportunities.

EXTENDING OUR FAMILIES

This chapter speaks about extending, rather than extended, families, to emphasize our active role in expanding the conventional definition of family. Most women who have lived their younger adult years in a nuclear family with children extend their definition of family to include partners of children and, of course, grandchildren. Particularly in our middle and later years, we may also begin to think of our closest friends as a kind of extended family.

Family is important throughout our lives as a source of intimacy and connection. Whether we choose a family similar to or different from the one we grew up in, most of us continue to value the love, acceptance, and intimacy of family life.

Being the center of a family network goes right on for us anyway, even though the children don't live at home any more. I am still embedded in family. Different people need me and us for different reasons. I've taken on my husband's family as well as my own, and he's taken on mine. I have two children by my first husband and my former mother-in-law is still living. My husband has three children and two of them have families of their own. Also my stepmother and stepfather, the second spouse of each of my parents, are still living and I, for various reasons, am their most responsible child. We have a stable happy marriage and my husband is a doctor, so we attract whoever is ailing. And we are both in

---

*In this chapter we talk about many different life situations. We recognize and even celebrate our diversity as women. We have included in the chapter some material on relatively uncommon situations to extend to women the full range of alternatives that are available to all of us in our middle and later years. We hope this approach will raise consciousness and encourage women to unite across barriers of generation, race, class, and sexual preference that have divided us in the past.

the "support business," it's just how we are emotionally. [a fifty-seven-year-old woman]

I have two sisters who live upstairs. People are always surprised that we get along so well, living in the same house. My sisters never go out without coming by to ask me if they can get me anything. We weren't always like that. We were too busy with our own lives. Now we try hard to help each other. [a seventy-year-old woman, widowed]

Living with Loss

During our middle years, most of us first become aware of signs of advancing age in our parents, aunts, and uncles. We are shocked! These are not the elderly relatives of our grandparents' generation, but the stalwart adults who formed the strong, dependable landscape of our youth. Can it be possible that they are slowing down and needing help from *us?* This process can be a frightening reminder of our own mortality.

My father and all his family died in their late fifties. So, does that mean I have only four more years? I don't really feel morbid about it, but I live with a different perspective. [a fifty-five-year-old woman]

It suddenly hit me last year when my father died, having lived to the ripe old age of ninety-three, that I was now the oldest living member of my family. When you get into your middle years, as long as you can say, "My father or my mother...this or that," as long as you are still somebody's daughter, then you can't be that old. Somehow I can't see myself as the matriarch of the family. [a fifty-nine-year-old woman]

It's scary not to have any parents or grandparents or any relatives except for one sister. I miss the unconditional love and caring—the free caring of someone calling not because they want me to serve on some committee but because they just want to know how I am. I get a little of that from my twelve-year-old daughter. I wish I had more kindness coming my way. I wish I weren't alone so much. [a fifty-year-old married woman who works on crafts at home]

Friends as Family[1]

For all of us, irrespective of marital status or sexual preference, women friends provide the support and continuity that enable us to enjoy new challenges and cope with the changes and losses we face in the second half of life. With this awareness, growing numbers of us are learning to regard our friendships as lifelong relationships to be worked at and cared for "just like family." For those of us who grew up thinking of other women as our competitors, or as less interesting or less valuable than men, it has been rewarding to share our lives and our histories in women's groups and discover that women are, in fact, terrific.

My women friends hand-carried me through my divorce. When my marriage of sixteen years got difficult, my women's group helped me consider what to do. They recommended marriage counselors and therapists. A year later, when it was still clearly not working, my friends helped me find the resources I needed—books on the transition of divorce, referrals to lawyers, poems about women rediscovering themselves after painful losses. Getting hugs and occasionally back rubs from my friends kept me feeling cared for and connected. A friend who had been through a divorce came to the court hearing with me. When I couldn't afford new up-to-date clothes for going out to meet people, the same friend, now remarried and pregnant, suggested I borrow some of her nonpregnant outfits for the season. A single friend invited me to dinner to meet a divorced man she thought I would like. She and another friend loaned me some money so I could get holiday presents for my kids. [a woman in her forties]

Many of us are accustomed to forming primary emotional links with a man. But even when we live in a traditional way with a male partner, there is a high statistical likelihood that we will grow old in the company of other women. The divorce rate is rising and most married women outlive their partners.

Because I was widowed young (in my early thirties), I had a series of short- and long-term relationships with men near my own age over the next twenty years that met my sexual needs pretty well. However, they did not always meet my emotional needs for closeness on a daily basis; they were not live-in arrangements, and in fact, more often than not, the man lived in another city or state. In my fifties, I became aware that even the sexual aspects of this type of relationship were not as satisfying as they had been, as my now middle-aged partner's sexual needs and problems often required that my attention be diverted from my own. At about the same time, a new friendship with another woman developed, with almost daily contact, and I recognized that the closeness and affection it was providing on a regular basis was meeting deeper emotional needs than the more sporadic sex offered by men my own age. [a fifty-four-year-old woman]

It's extremely important for women growing older to have a circle of women friends; there's no other way to

Marianne Gontarz

guard against the inevitable loneliness. [a woman in her eighties]

If we have been raised to form our closest bonds with family members and others within an ethnically homogeneous community, we may be more comfortable having our most intimate friendships with those of similar background. However, it can be a pleasant surprise at times to find a kindred spirit in a more diverse setting.

I have often been shy about making new friends, but I am learning to reach out. I have just made a new friend. Though I am Jewish and she is Methodist, we share so many things in our life experiences that we could almost have been twins. Our ideas about the spirit, about religion, about life are so similar. We even share the experience of being estranged from our own children. We have helped one another and have found in one another sisters, extended family, friends for life. [a fifty-five-year-old woman]

Freda Rebelsky, an expert on adult development, observes, "So many good friendships start at times of our lives when we feel the most need for someone else to understand our pain.... From that we can develop the kinds of friendships that lead to lots of laughter, lots of joy, lots of sharing, and lots of growth."[2]

The greatest pleasure of growing old is remaining in contact with friends from church and in the community. I'm treasurer of the Older Women's League chapter here, and also the Black Caucus on Aging. I kept contact with my friends from childhood. I love people, all kinds of people. I don't give up a relationship easily. I only gave up one in seventy-two years, someone who really, really hurt me. I am friends with my ex-husband's

second wife and went to see her on my vacation. She was so glad to see me. [a seventy-five-year-old woman]

I've just celebrated my seventieth year with a collective celebration of aging, together with friends of all generations, from two to eighty-two. What a warm and wonderful event, with food and drink and song and dance!

Our Children Grow Up

Are You Trapped in a Rusty Stereotype?

The trouble with getting old is
you can't say how shitty it is.
It shocks the young.
They think you don't belong with words like that
because you make your beds
and wax the floor. If not
they say, "She's cracking up."

So stand there. One foot in and one foot out.
Speak out of both sides of your old mouth:
"Oh fiddlesticks!"   "Fuck them!"
And potter through your tidy house
wearing your outer-directed bourgeois apron.
Wave your rolling pin; hum "Tea for Two"
while longing inside for an ashram.

It's hard to learn after fifty not to care
if the pictures hang straight on the walls
learn not to water plants
and people.

Let 'em go, sister,
off to be happy monks
while you practice sitting on a made bed
inviting what's left of your soul.

Alice Ryerson

For those of us who have raised families, being a mother was probably one of our most absorbing, time-consuming, and demanding relationships. We become parents in part because of our own needs to bond with others and to find fulfillment and meaning. Yet once our children are grown up and leave home, we must accept the fact that the daily caregiving part of mothering is done and trust our children to take care of themselves, while we go on to take care of ourselves.

When we have meaningful work and other relationships outside the home—plans and goals to look forward to and other anchors for our identity and self-esteem—it becomes easier to let children go and to relish the freedom and opportunity of the next stage.[3] If we turn the con-

Teri Carsten

cern and energy that we had directed toward our children toward meeting new possibilities, we can be happy and positive about the future, and as a bonus we give our children an optimistic view of growing older.

For some of us, the end of the caregiving years of mothering can present as much of a challenge and be as emotionally demanding as becoming a parent for the first time.[4] Some of us have to work at relinquishing control over our children's choices and giving up the dailiness of the relationship with them.

The way I get along with my kids is to realize that their lives are theirs and mine is mine. So I've learned to leave them alone to make their own decisions. When I was having trouble letting go of my youngest, my oldest daughter helped me. I now let them live their own lives. Actually, that's been my philosophy all along. I felt I had to prepare them to be on their own and make their own way. So I can't cry when they finally get to the point of doing what I had planned for them all along, can I? [a sixty-eight-year-old woman]

I really missed my children when they moved away but you have to "divorce" your children. One way I got over longing for my children was to think about the relation-ship I had with my mother when I was my children's age. I, too, had wanted freedom and control over my own life. Back then I didn't want to have to be with my mother all the time. I had my own friends. When I finally recognized this, the longing disappeared and I didn't worry any more. It's an act of love to want your children to live their own lives. [a sixty-five-year-old woman]

Others of us look forward to the time our parenting obligations will be fulfilled.

I have had this job for twenty-five years and I am looking forward to being "Parent Emeritus." I have never lived alone, never, ever. So it's going to be a whole new experience when the last one leaves. I've been happy when each one left, even my oldest daughter, who was really easy to raise. When I think of sitting across the breakfast table from my ex-husband and trying to find something to talk about, I feel lucky not to be in that situation. Sometimes I think, "Does this mean I'm going to grow old alone?" I don't really look forward to that. On the other hand, I don't want to do a lot of things like accounting for my time, preparing meals, having someone sick. So, I think it's a new challenge! I may end up finding out that I simply hate living alone, and then I'll do something about it. But I hope I'll like it because I want to have the extra space when my four kids come back to visit. [a fifty-year-old woman]

Having children return home or make new demands for support and nurturing after they have left home and been on their own is a prevalent concern of middle-aged women today. Though we may now feel ready to begin a new life of our own, there is always the possibility that we may be called upon to share our resources once more.

My twenty-eight-year-old son moved back into our apartment when he was discharged from the Air Force. It was supposed to be temporary until he could find an apartment, but after a year he's still here. He says he can't afford to pay $400 a month until he finds a steady job. Then my daughter moved back when she and her friends were evicted. I was looking forward to peace and quiet, but here I am. [a sixty-year-old woman]

Some parents find it possible to live with adult children, and sometimes grandchildren, but the transition from the mother/child relationship to one of independent and mutually respectful adults is a very difficult one, and may not be possible for everyone. It requires willingness to compromise, clarity about individual as well as family goals and values, and the weathering of crises.

At the other extreme, some adolescent and

adult children may want to put the maximum possible distance between themselves and their parent(s). It is natural to grieve if your child does not wish to see you or be close. Don't add to your feelings of rejection and loss by perceiving this situation as a personal failure, however. Try to remain warm, understanding, and open to communication while keeping busy with your own life. Chances are that once your child feels more secure in her or his independence, she or he will once again want to be in touch with you. There is little you can do but accept the fact that your child, for whatever reasons, does not want to be close for the time being. Sometimes the closer we have been to a child, the more extreme is the need for separation.

I decided that if my daughter did not want to communicate with me, I would respect her wishes; that in doing so, she would learn that I am indeed a separate person and might become curious about this person who is separate, who respects her, and who is no longer "available mother." And that this separation would help me grow as well as help her grow. [a fifty-three-year-old woman]

I wasn't prepared for the intensity of the changes in my teenage daughter. As I look back on it, I think we were each experiencing hormonal changes at opposite ends of the continuum. She was so changeable—one minute happy, another minute depressed. One moment she needed me and acted like a sweet child again, and another time she's telling me she knows more about everything than I do. Those were stressful years. Now that she's working and has her own apartment, we're great friends and everything seems to be in balance again. [a forty-nine-year-old woman]

Barring serious financial, emotional, or health problems, the parent-child relationship, which was based on dependency, should now be based on mutuality: mutual recognition of each other as separate personalities, mutual respect, and mutual helping.

There may be times when a mother finds herself in need of help from her children. Many women are particularly reluctant to accept help from children even when freely offered.

My son is a doctor but it took me a long time to recognize his skills. I continued to think of him as my little Johnny—messy, awkward, and uncertain. Then some of my friends became his patients and were constantly praising him. I began to see him in a different way, began to ask him questions about my health and to seek his advice. Now I go to one of the doctors in his clinic

and my son takes care of me by consulting with my doctor. [a sixty-eight-year-old woman]

My daughter is always buying me something, even if I need it like a hole in the head. She wants me to look good. She always notices if I don't wear it. My daughter wants to give me something. She wants to take care of me. I think she would like it better if I were more dependent. [a sixty-eight-year-old woman]

Though it is hard for us to give up our role as the helping or caring person within the family, it may help to think of receiving help as part of the mutual exchange of family caring.

I really don't like being dependent on my children, but what can I do? I have to face reality. I'm sure they know that for many years they were dependent on me. I really tried hard to help them, protect them, give them a good education. I suppose it's my time to receive help from them. [a woman in her seventies]

When I was between jobs, my son emptied out his bank account and sent it to me for my birthday. He wrote, "This is for you to use as an interest-free loan. You'll pay me back when you are able to." I hadn't asked for help, but somehow he got the idea. It made me feel that all that nurturing and caring had made an impression. [a fifty-nine-year-old woman]

I never quite had the relationship with my own mother that I now enjoy with my daughters. We travel together, go to movies, plays, and often do our shopping together. I can't explain how it came about, especially when I consider the tumultuous times we went through during all their adolescent years. I was patient and sort of waited for them to grow up—you know, sort of let them scream and yell their way through it. Now, they are well adjusted and successful and great fun to be with. [a sixty-one-year-old woman]

Becoming a Mother-in-Law

Mothers-in-law have been the source of every type of commentary from humor to outright derision. These woman-hating barbs reflect the low regard in which older women are held in our society. The conventional rivalry between a woman and her daughter-in-law, supposedly competitors for the attention of the man, epitomizes the very essence of the intergenerational barrier between women that this book seeks to change.

It is eye-opening to look at the two roles of grandmother and mother-in-law together. It is evident how little the stereotypes conform to the reality of our lives. After all, the sweet, loving, gentle soul that a grandmother is supposed to be and the critical, interfering busybody that is the caricature of a mother-in-law are often the same woman.

Mothers-in-law have traditionally been advised to "mind their own business." This can be in practice a very difficult prescription, because for so many years, your child *was* your business. Yet once your child is grown up, and certainly once she or he is in a serious relationship, you are not expected to offer help unless it is requested, or advice unless it is sought. The in-law relationship is one in which we have no choice at all. Perhaps that is part of its difficulty. Whether we like our son- or daughter-in-law, his or her parents, and the other in-law relatives is almost a matter of chance. We must suspend judgment and simply accept the mate that our child has chosen. This is a way to show love and respect for your child.

It is difficult to see your child make a choice that you disapprove of or consider harmful. It is particularly hard if the choice means that your child will live far away from you, either geographically or emotionally, by choosing a lifestyle which is very different from yours.

The best part of our trip to Australia was getting to know our son-in-law. He and I took long walks on the beach, had breakfast together, and visited with his mother, who told me all about him as a young boy. When he took us sailing for a week, his skills and interest were apparent.

There had been problems between us before, but I approached this trip with a positive attitude. I traveled 6,000 miles to discover that my son-in-law was very lovable. I should have known, since my daughter had been telling me so for years. [a woman in her sixties]

You have had some twenty or more years to transmit your values to your child. The entire family relationship will be strengthened if you can trust that your child has absorbed those values. It would probably help both of you to let your child know that you still love her or him and want to maintain a caring relationship, whether you approve of the chosen partner or not. Resist the temptation to say "I told you so" if their relationship does not work out. Your child and maybe even the former partner may need your continued support. They will feel freer to turn to you if they have not been made to feel defensive.

As if being a mother-in-law were not difficult

enough in itself, many of us now have the additional confusion of being a "something-or-other" to our child's live-in lover. Perhaps a new title would change the whole view of this difficult relationship. Perhaps, just as we talk of love relationships and love children, we should also speak of mothers-in-love.

In traditional cultures, the roles and obligations of the parents of an engaged or married couple are formally defined. Today, however, it may take time to recognize a relationship as serious and lasting. Without guidelines to tell us what our role is during the courtship's progression, we may feel at a loss in determining where we fit in the couple's life.

My daughter has been living with her friend for four years and I'm just beginning to treat him more like a permanent presence. I've begun addressing letters to both of them. He's becoming less like just a boyfriend and more like a son-in-law. [a sixty-one-year-old woman]

My son and Deborah dated in college and since that time have shared an apartment. I like her and she and I have a good relationship, but I don't know the rules. What expectations should I have for holidays and when should I invite them? Last year was the first time I gave Deborah a birthday present. I felt good about acknowledging her relationship with my son. [a fifty-four-year-old woman]

Some of us who considered ourselves openminded and "modern" have surprised our children and even ourselves by being upset over the nontraditional and unexpected choices our grown children may make. We may discover that we unconsciously harbored a fantasy of a partner from a similar religious or cultural background, reflecting a wish to have our children carry on our family traditions into the future. If this happens, or if our children choose not to marry and have children at all, or simply delay these choices,[5] we may find ourselves feeling anxious, guilty, and wondering what we have done wrong.

The issue of children who delay having children or choose not to have them may be a major part of the dilemma for parents of those who choose a partner of the same sex. This can be a problem even for parents who *can* accept their child's sexual preference. There are also many other issues that come up for parents of a gay or lesbian child. Support groups have been formed so that the parents can talk about their feelings and come to understand their children's choices (see Resources).

Our favorite in-law is our daughter's woman friend. They have lived together happily for over four years, and are an important part of all family gatherings. I have found this new member of our family particularly sensitive to both the joys and sorrows in my life. I feel most comfortable to just drop in on them and to share the experiences of their life—but also, to know they want to share my feelings, too. [a sixty-two-year-old woman]

Becoming a Grandmother

One cannot deny the pleasurable feeling of self-renewal that is experienced by grandparents. To see a new generation coming, perhaps carrying on our features, talents, or idiosyncrasies, is most fascinating.

Being a grandmother is one of the great experiences of life, especially today, when we don't take the miracle for granted. There is no question that having a grandchild come to visit is demanding physically, mentally, and emotionally, especially when the grandmother is also working. Our three-year-old granddaughter has just left after a four-week visit. As the wildflowers in the juice glass fade, I try to decide which of the twenty-one crayon and watercolor pictures to keep taped to the banister. I rescue a 1950 miniature trailer truck her father used to play with from under the bed and hear her say proudly, "I'm bigging!" I see the world anew through her eyes and hope I'm still bigging too. [a woman in her seventies]

Ellen Shub

Cathy Cade

Jerry Howard/Positive Images

Jerry Howard/Positive Images

Marianne Gontarz

Some women look forward to having a less stressful relationship with their grandchildren than they did with their children, especially if they were too busy or too unsure of themselves to have fully enjoyed the early years of their children. Women whose economic conditions have improved over the years may take special pleasure in indulging their grandchildren in ways that they were not able to with their own children. Unfortunately, this can become a source of friction, so be sure to discuss treats and presents with your own child in advance.

A new stage in the mother-in-law relationship often follows the birth or adoption of our first grandchild. At that time we become more like colleagues or peers to our daughters or daughters-in-law, and can relate to each other as one mother to another. While we may be able to be closer to them than we were in the earlier honeymoon-couple/in-law phase, it is important to continue to respect the autonomy of our adult children, as well as their authority as parents.

In our culture, which is still too much in the grips of the adoration of youth, becoming a grandmother often bears a stigma for a still-youthful woman.

When my daughter called me from Florida to tell me I was now a grandmother, I was not in the least elated. I had recently remarried and was seeing myself as a

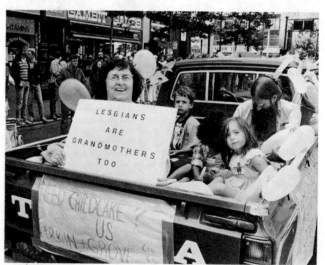

Cathy Cade

134

young, passionate lover. I didn't want to think of myself as a grandmother. That was because of the picture I had of my own grandmother—a fussy, domineering, and strict woman who took care of us when my mother worked. I think when my daughter first informed me of the birth of my grandchild I felt I couldn't fulfill the role expected of me. And I didn't want to. I finally made my own decision about our relationship but sometimes I feel guilty that I'm not a good enough grandmother. [a woman in her fifties]

Today's grandmothers want to define for themselves the specific relationship they have with their grandchildren. Few grandmothers want to baby-sit regularly or be responsible for child care. Most women resist the stereotype of the "doormat" grandmother, always there when anyone needs her.

I have an unwritten understanding with my children: I do not baby-sit my grandchildren. I entertain them. I invite them—but I'm not called in as a baby-sitter. I think baby-sitting damages the relationship. They know when I'm with them I'm there because I want to be and because I enjoy their company. And I invite them on that basis too. I don't want to be considered a baby-sitter because that's not the relationship I want to establish with my grandchildren. [a seventy-four-year-old woman]

Some women, however, enjoy taking care of grandchildren.

I'm going to do my first stint of grandchild care for my nine-month-old grandchild this summer. My daughter is signed up for a four-day course. I really love children and I think it will be fun. I'm looking forward to it. I'm a little ticked off that her husband isn't doing it, but I'm really staying out of that. And it's nice to do something concrete for my oldest daughter. She's just consistently very giving and thoughtful. [a fifty-year-old woman]

Some women care for grandchildren because of the illness, incapacity, or death of the child's parents. Often when we do this we have many mixed feelings and need support. Other grandparents experience anguish at losing contact with their grandchildren after the parents have been divorced or separated. It is important to realize that such things happen and to build good relationships with our children's partners. If you cannot work things out with your child's former partner, it can help to have the advice and support of an organization involved with grandparents' rights (see Resources).

Some women find it easier to ask their older grandchildren for help or companionship than

Peter Lantos

they do their own children. Conversely, a grandparent may offer help in a way that complements what parents can do, or that fits better with what a young person wants.

When one of my grandsons got himself into a jam with jobs during his senior year in high school and couldn't make it home to dinner, I invited him to come have dinner with me. I would set my dinner hour to accommodate the time when he could make it because I thought it was unhealthful for him to be skipping meals.

I don't feel hesitant about asking them to do things that I don't have the strength to do. My sixteen-year-old grandson is very strong and if I have a piece of shrubbery I can't uproot, I call him up and ask him, and he does it. Sometimes I pay them, especially if it is a special skill that they should be paid for. My other grandson services my car and I pay him for it, but when I need someone to pick me up at the airport, he comes and meets me and picks me up and, of course, I don't pay him for that.

I have a very easy relationship with my grandchildren now. I hope that they consider me as a friend and not as an authority figure. That's what I aim for. I'm not the kind of grandmother you put a lap robe over. [a seventy-four-year-old woman]

I want to do something with the money I have left so my children and grandchildren will have memories of me—not just leave it to them and have them buy a car or some material thing, and that's the end of it.

I have two grandchildren here and two in New York. When they were all about eight or nine I started taking them on trips. I usually take one of the Massachusetts grandchildren and one of the New York grandchildren on each trip, because I want them to know each other, too. So, now they have been to lots of places that they will always remember. And we have wonderful pictures, too. [a woman in her seventies]

PARTNERS AND LOVERS

Some of us have stayed married for decades to partners who remain as dear to us as they were when we first fell in love. We can enjoy our joint achievements with no interruptions in our later years.

I am sixty-eight years old and have been married to the same man for almost forty-three years. In earlier periods we had more ups and downs, preoccupied as we were with the ambitions and pressures of work, child raising, and developing our identities as separate persons. We are more capable now of appreciating one another and have a more relaxed and confident view of ourselves and a greater sense of gratitude and contentment that we have each other. I think we have come to have a kind of pride in each other, in the kind of person we each have become.

From the beginning of our much-valued marriage, we agreed that we would each gather gifts of knowledge, skills, and a wide variety of disciplines to bring to our relationship so that it would prosper and serve as a measure of our own growth.

After forty-six years we have learned that we cannot change each other and that it is not weakness but rather strength to be willing to adapt. We have also learned that it is a myth that one member of a long-term relationship is always dominant while the other is a follower. Over the long years, we have taken turns at being leader, in both good times and bad.

Today, as we near our seventies, our daily lives are rich in shared experience and in appreciation of the

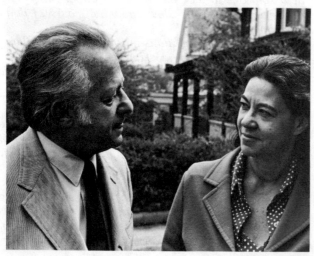

Joan K. Gordon

many aspects of human love. We are both lucky and skillful in maintaining our sexuality as a happy resource in friendship and communication.

For many women, the demands of raising a family have meant delaying or holding back our individual aspirations. After the children have grown, however, the husband's life outside the family often continues as before, while the wife may face a total redefinition of all her roles, even if she has been employed continuously outside the home—but especially if she has not. Most households are arranged around the personality or the employment needs of the husband and the developmental needs of the children. The changes we women go through inevitably make waves in our relationships and challenge us to rework our ways of living with our partners. Some men are flexible, secure, and caring enough to understand and accept the required adjustments, but in many relationships a period of renegotiation may be needed.

My husband didn't like it when I got a studio away from the house to do my art work, but I did it. I don't ask permission any more. When I want to go somewhere, I say, "I'm going," not "Is it all right if I go?" I'm going to travel for a month by myself. That would have been inconceivable ten years ago. So this has been a long slow process of changing myself and my marriage. At first, we had a lot of fights and arguments and we started to say, "Let's call it quits." But somehow the love kept it going and we decided to go to a therapist. After a while, my husband began to appreciate some of my changes. One of the nice things about aging is that after so many years of coping you begin to see that problems aren't insurmountable. You know you've solved them before and so you can see the light at the end of the tunnel. We have finally learned to accept each other as we are. If the positives outweigh the negatives in a relationship, then it is worth saving. No relationship is a bed of roses. [a fifty-seven-year-old woman]

My husband worked in an automotive factory on the line for more than forty years. Sometimes he worked double and triple shifts during the good times. He provided well for me and our six children and all the kids finished college. We had money in the bank and looked forward to the time when he could come home and relax. We never dreamed this would cause any problems, but it did. For about a year after he retired we fussed and fought. Then, even though I hadn't worked since my youngest was in kindergarten, I went out and got a job as a saleswoman in a department store in town. He resented that—wanted to know who would cook and keep the house. I said, "You can." The biggest surprise was that he learned to cook. Every day when I come home he has dinner on the table. We have learned to

Marianne Gontarz

enjoy each other's company and we are both happy with our new life. [a sixty-eight-year-old woman]

When partners carry out the tasks of marriage and family building as "shoulds," putting aside their own needs for growth and development, unmet needs and resentments fill the void left by the children's departure. These may have begun to surface during the children's adolescence. Partners in long-standing marriages need to have individual and shared goals to keep themselves and the relationship vital. A challenge of midlife marriage is to develop new goals once the family-building stage is completed.

There are so many aspects to a marriage: love, children in common, mutual friends, common interests—each a thread that keeps a marriage together. Sometimes only one or two of these threads have remained unbroken, yet the partners are reluctant to separate. Often the transition of grown children starting a life of their own, or the sudden understanding that an unsatisfactory marriage will forever prevent us from achieving our life goals, becomes the needed push toward the dissolution of a long-standing partnership.

After twenty years of marriage my husband and I decided to divorce. We had gotten along badly for many years and whatever was left of our relationship was finished long before we made this decision. The one thing that was hard to give up was our group of friends. We engaged in a very active social life and actually had fun going out often in social groups. Our friends were astounded—many people called us the "golden" couple, always happy and having fun. They never dreamed my husband was an alcoholic—

though still successful in his work—and his drinking and affairs with other women corroded our family life. [a forty-five-year-old woman]

Women who initiate a divorce themselves may feel the exhilaration of a new beginning, or at least the energy of acting on long-repressed feelings. That energy can give us the courage to face the changes of marital separation.

I was trained to be a lifetime servant and didn't believe that life could be fun. Through counseling and group therapy at our battered women's outreach, I have discovered my inner strength, and that I deserve the best life has to offer. I am now divorced from my battering husband. I wrote many poems tracing my experiences from darkness to light, from bondage to freedom. I think this journey of self-discovery is what every woman tries to take. [a thirty-nine-year-old woman]

Leaving my marriage to an abusive husband was a real liberation for me. No more waiting up at night until the wee hours, listening for his footsteps, trying to determine how drunk he would be. No more fighting off his sexual advances when he was too drunk and impotent to do much about that anyway. No more having to take the children's side constantly because I felt I had to make up for his emotional abuse of them. The night I packed everything in the car to leave, he padlocked the gate and slashed the tires. I called a locksmith and AAA and before dawn we were on our way. I was forty-four years old and starting over after twenty years of marriage.

Breaking up a marriage is rarely an impulsive decision for women, and often it is preceded by years of gradual preparation. Preparation for financial self-sufficiency can be a significant step toward emotional readiness to withstand the pain of separation and the challenge of being on your own.

I had tried numerous times to get my husband to move out of the house so I would feel safe, but I did not succeed until I started an internship at a hospital. I guess he finally realized that I meant it when I said I wanted him to get out when he saw that I was preparing to support myself. In addition, I stopped covering up for him: I stopped cleaning up the messes he made smashing things; I stopped the crisis interventions; I stopped trying to act as his therapist. Instead, I went to a divorce and mediation center. Mediation turned out to be impossible since my husband refused to talk. The mediator told me to get a divorce attorney, which I did. [a fifty-two-year-old woman]

When it is our partner who initiates the breakup of a marriage or a long-term relationship, the feelings of pain and rejection can be especially devastating, especially if he or she has left us for a younger lover.

I'm so bitter—I sometimes feel like totally destroying him. I gave twenty-five years to this marriage—making sacrifices, taking care of the children, taking his shit. Now he's with this girl young enough to be his daughter. I have been in therapy for a year trying to cope with it. It's helped me handle my anger. Yet I feel exploited. He took my youth, my beauty—he destroyed that. My innocence, too. I long for that sometimes. [a fifty-year-old woman]

Divorce

Divorce is having
all your teeth out one by one.
First the incisors wear down dull
as your grandfather's carving knife,
then the eye teeth go blind
lose their dogged bite.
The molars cease to grind out love
and then the judge excises
the impacted wisdom of the wedding
and you bleed and bleed.

Jane Bailey-Blood Strete

I had never allowed myself to face the possibility of divorce. I was so fearful at the thought of being on my own. I was in shock, briefly, and then I was sad, frightened, and lonely. For six months I believed I could get my husband to come back. Finally I began to accept what had happened and to look ahead to my own future.

I got my former husband to share in the care of our youngest son so I could go back to school. Then I lived with a group of older people; that created a new home for me and helped me to feel less lonely.

Today I am living on my own as a single person, going to graduate school in a city 800 miles from my former home and building a new life. I see myself as a dependent person acting independently. I'm a risk-taker, that's what's helped me make the changes I've made. [a sixty-year-old woman]

The breakup of a marriage, however devastating it may seem, carries with it the potential for a new life. With age, we grow in maturity, experience, and confidence, qualities which have a beauty and power to attract in their own right. Best of all, these are qualities that reflect how we feel about ourselves and do not depend on the perception of others.

Widowhood or Loss of a Partner

Since women usually live longer than men and are often younger than their mates, widowhood is the experience of the majority of married women. The average age of widowhood in the United States is fifty-six, and the average widow lives for eighteen years after her husband's death.[6]

My youngest son had just decided not to stay in college. I remember driving along thinking that now my husband and I could begin to plan for our old age. When I got home I got a call about my husband. He died suddenly just as I was about to turn fifty-eight. [a seventy-eight-year-old woman]

The experience of widowhood varies according to the time of life in which it occurs. If you have lived with a partner happily for four or five decades, and perhaps raised a family together, your grief may be tempered by an awareness of the good fortune you shared together. Yet, if you are in your seventies or eighties and in failing health yourself, you may have less emotional and physical energy to rebuild your life as a single woman. Women who are widowed young often are devastated by the shock and overwhelmed with the responsibility of raising and educating children on their own, yet the younger you are the more likely you are to eventually recover from your grief.

Many recently widowed women report that they imagine their partner is still there and catch themselves starting to talk to him or her. They worry that they are losing their minds. However, this is not unusual behavior in the early months of widowhood. It may seem inconceivable to many a recently widowed woman that she can ever find happiness again, or comfort, or even peace of mind by herself or with a new love. Gone is the companionship, the sexuality, the economic partnership, the intimacy of many years. Some of these pieces of the lost relationship will never be replaced; for others perhaps only a pale substitute can be found.

I think I'm still depressed. I don't think I've gotten over it—after twenty years I still feel his presence. When I lost my husband I cried and cried even though I had a lot of support. People would talk to me, try to reason with me—still I just wanted to die. But then always my mind would come back to "I have three sons who still need me. I can't just die." [a sixty-five-year-old woman]

In the last four years I have come from the depths of despair to feeling that life is good and that there still is a reason and a need for me to be in this world. At the beginning I continued to live because I felt my children had been through enough and they didn't need any more grief. It took a long time before I started to live for myself. I functioned extremely well most of the time (everyone always said how well I coped) but felt like I was just going through the motions, waiting for my husband to come home. [a woman in her fifties]

Particularly stressful is loss of a partner in a relationship that was not publicly acknowledged. If you have lost a lover and few of your friends and acquaintances knew of the relationship, you may feel quite alone with your grief, and have to carry on without the usual social supports that are mobilized for the widow. Even if you have been open about your relationship, friends may not fully appreciate the depth of your loss.

Recently I vacationed with friends who had been friends also with my deceased partner-in-life. A guest arrived with slides of earlier vacations, including pictures of my lover.

I objected that if I had been a man who had been recently widowed, they surely would have asked if I would object to showing the pictures. One friend responded that she wanted very much to see them. She blanched when I suggested that she might feel differently after the death of her husband. Clearly, she thought that my relationship to Karen differed from her marriage; she evidently also thought my love differed from her friendship with Karen only by degree. Heterosexuals really do not understand what lesbians feel for their partners, even when they know us well. All of these friends had known Karen and me as lovers and had sent me bereavement condolences when Karen died.*

For a few women, the death of a spouse is a relief from a relationship that they may have wanted to leave earlier but for one reason or another were not able to do so. This situation can also be painful, as we grieve for the kind of relationship we might have hoped for when we first married.

For years I stayed in a marriage with an abusive husband because I was always afraid to divorce for economic reasons. After all, where was I to go and how would I be able to support myself? I did miss him for the year following his death. I never minded taking care of him while he was ill. After all, he was family. But I did resent all of the earlier years when he was so dominating and critical. Being a widow is my first freedom. I have a good relationship with my children and with my brothers and sisters. I have friends of long standing. I don't mind being alone at all. No one yells at me ... I do what I want. [a seventy-eight-year-old woman]

It is not uncommon for recently widowed women to continue to receive guidance from their husbands, in dreams, in daydreams, in convic-

*Excerpted from an unpublished manuscript by Carolyn Ruth Swift.

tions that "this is just what he would want me to do." Women who were accustomed to relying on a husband, who have not had a lot of experience making their own decisions, may need time to accept that the ideas they are willing to trust, the advice they consider wise, come from themselves.

I still have dreams—not as often as I did when Bill first died—that he is giving me advice on how to do things. And it is always good advice; I listen to it. If I am ever undecided about something, he seems to come in my dreams and tell me what to do. [a sixty-seven-year-old woman, five years after the death of her husband]

Once a woman experiences some of the satisfactions of doing things for herself, she may begin to realize that she has many of the competencies she formerly ascribed to her husband.

Getting more education or a better-paying job is part and parcel of this process for many widows. Yet some women are reluctant to assume their independence and to feel the possibility of being active and powerful, as if managing for themselves would be disloyal or would diminish the importance of their past relationship.

Eventually, widows must restructure their lives as single women. We appreciate old friends who continue to call, to invite us and include us in their lives, but we may be disappointed in some who maintain the Noah's Ark system of social life: couples only. These friends may simply be afraid to confront the widow's grief. By avoiding her they can deny the possibility that death could disrupt their own relationship.[7]

While well-meaning friends and family may tell a widow to make new friends, find new interests, and create a new life for herself, many recently widowed women may need at first to reminisce about the past relationship, relive its good moments, hold on to the sense of the continuing presence of the lost spouse. If the relationship was a deep and involving one, then a widow's new life must be made out of parts of the old, and some of these parts must now be retrieved from the ended relationship. This is a way that many widows preserve the continuity of their lives.

My children, family, and many friends have been extremely supportive. Contrary to the experiences of many widows, the friends who are couples and who were friends of my husband and myself have continued to include me in their social lives. For the first two years or so it was usually too painful and I preferred not to spend too much time with them, but they were persistent and continued to invite me. In the last several months I have felt more comfortable and it is easier and even pleasant to join them sometimes. Most of my other social life is with women friends and family. I haven't "dated" at all but feel that if the opportunity arises I am ready to consider a new relationship. [a fifty-two-year-old woman]

Married friends, children, and relatives usually find themselves inadequate to the task of comforting a recent widow. Once the apparent emergency and the immediate needs are past, the widow is expected to pick up her own life and take care of herself. This is the time when the grieving person tends to feel most abandoned and helpless. But our lifetime habit of forming friendships and creating extended emotional "networks" contributes, according to researchers, to women's greater ability to survive after widowhood.[8]

Only someone who has actually been through the same experience can fully appreciate and meet the continuing needs of a grieving widow. This is why various kinds of widow-to-widow networks—both the ones that deal with practical matters such as balancing a checkbook and the ones that focus more on emotional issues—have been growing.[9] Being part of a group of women dealing with loss helps us understand that grief is appropriate and normal. In such groups we can feel freer than we do among family and friends to expose the depth of our pain and loss, knowing that we will be understood.

Being Single

Contrary to the prevailing stereotypes, a recent study of fifty single women aged from sixty-five through the mid-nineties found that those women who had never married were as embedded in relationships and social networks as women who were presently, or had been, married. For many women, the world of work was an important source of friends, but in retirement many went on to initiate new friendships with neighbors or members of organizations to which they belonged. Families were also a significant source of important relationships, especially siblings.[10]

These women understand the importance of friendship; they have had the lifelong habit of reaching out to other women and the freedom to do so. Women who have been single all their lives are probably less likely than married women to go through midlife upheavals.

Older single women we spoke with expressed satisfaction with their lives and their choices.

Single? I feel great about what I've seen and what I've passed up. I haven't missed a thing. I have a good many friends. Most of my closest friends have been married, a few single. I made matches but not for myself, even though I did have three different engagement rings which they never would take back. I eluded all attempts to marry. If I had my life to live over again I think I would marry— it's nice to have children. But being single has given me a lot of freedom to do what I want when I want. I help others solve problems, rather than have my own. My relationships have grown richer. My friends and I appreciate each other more. Many of us are still around and we've gone through a lot together. Today, we have a little more in material comfort than we started out with and we have friendships that have lasted a lifetime. [a seventy-two-year-old woman]

In generations past, marriage was the norm for women, and the main concern of their families. Not to marry was to be an outsider. Singleness was a stigma.

I was a pediatrician for forty-odd years, of which I am proud. But do you know what? At family gatherings and in the old neighborhood they still see me as the one who didn't marry. Not as the first in the family to go to college. Not as one of the first Catholics admitted into the fancy medical school I attended. Not as a well-known physician in Philadelphia. No, just as Sally, "the one who never got married."[11]

Often it is only in the middle years, when the supply of potential mates is dwindling and it becomes clear that one's life-style is firmly estab-

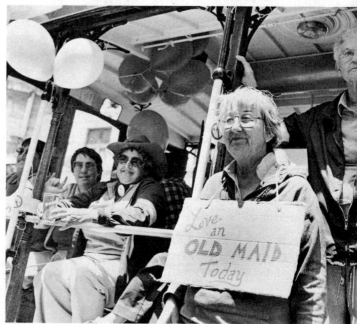

Cathy Cade

lished, that women admit to themselves that they have made a choice and that they are happy with it.[12] Some women for whom sexuality has not been a priority may have truly preferred to be celibate. Others have guarded their personal freedom by making their sexual lives, with men or with women, a small and perhaps temporary part of their lives. Whatever the reason, once the choice is recognized and accepted, it opens up new possibilities for security and comfort. Buying a house, deciding on a new geographical location, joining resources with other women in business or leisure, and providing for old age all complete the life of the single woman.

In later years, loneliness and isolation can be a serious problem for older women who have outlived their friends, spouses, or partners. If you are feeling isolated, if your neighborhood has changed and you find you no longer know many people, senior citizens' centers can be good places to find new activities and to meet people.

I say to them, why don't you just get out and come on up to the center? Everyone misses you there. We're really getting that garden we started in shape. It's beautiful! But we need your help. I know how hard it can be sometimes to get out with all the aches and pains, but we have to keep going. [a sixty-eight-year-old woman]

You can't just sit and wait for someone to come to you. They won't. Let's face it, old people are easy to forget, not through any fault of their own but because everyone is so busy these days. Young people don't have the time to sit around and talk. So we have to make more of an effort ourselves. I call my folks even if they don't call me. I know some people who just sit around all alone and then get mad if nobody calls them. They've got the telephone right there and probably have more time than a lot of people to make the calls and keep in touch. [a woman in her seventies]

For women who've been divorced or widowed after a long marriage, it is not easy to begin again. Perhaps you have spent most of your adult life within a family where you had to expend little energy to maintain comfortable contact with close friends. Close association with your family and your husband's family and with friends who also socialize in couples may have met all your social needs. Now you have to become more assertive in reaching out to others.

I needed a new social life. With older couples, you begin to feel you don't belong with them any more. I looked for single people to be with because they understood my problems. After my divorce I wanted to talk about the hurt

Norma Holt

and disappointment, but my married friends didn't want to hear about it. Perhaps they didn't want to acknowledge that it could happen to them too. So we grew apart.

I had a girlfriend who was a widow. She said, "You can't sit home." We Latin people love to dance and go to parties, so she took me to a party at her church for widowed people. When I protested that I was not a widow, she said, "Who cares?" At first, it was a mixed group of mostly widowed people. Recently, more divorced people have joined the group. [a sixty-year-old woman]

New Partners

Many women are eager to find a new partner, if not immediately after their marriages end, certainly at some point thereafter. This is when the insecurities of aging, of changing values, and of confused expectations come into play. It is perhaps useful to consider that we are not starting over from the beginning, but from where we are right now. The search for love, companionship, and new friendships may take us down some roads we never thought we'd take. Many women try new activities such as community theater, adult education, or political-action groups that suit their talents, interests, and time schedules. Although it's a bit like entering a sweepstakes (the odds for finding true love may not be so good), the fun of new activities and sometimes curiosity about who is "out there" can be very energizing. Consider reaching out beyond your usual circle. You may find new friends who are appropriate to the new person you are in process of becoming.

I want someone like myself, with some education, but not so smart that I would bore him, someone I could get along with. I almost married again. I met someone who took the time to get to know me. I was unhappy and he lifted me out of my unhappiness. He made me feel that I deserved love and respect when I had been feeling that I was "finished" in my forties, an old bag. I was afraid that I would end up living in a rooming house or having to move in with one of my kids, so I was going to marry him. But he was old-fashioned. He wanted to do things a way that I used to like, but that I don't want any more. He didn't want me to work after we were married or to own my own house. We couldn't seem to agree on anything so the relationship fizzled out. But he did me the big favor of making me feel valuable, that I was a mature, beautiful woman, even though I was no longer young. [a fifty-nine-year-old woman]

Some women find someone they care about enough to risk a second marriage. Remarriage can be challenging, yet experience and maturity can make it an easier adjustment than it was the first time around.

My present husband is more supportive and less critical than my first husband. We're very different and that makes this marriage astonishing and full of surprises. If we'd married young the differences between us would have overwhelmed us. In middle age the differences are sort of a lark—they're intriguing. Here's this person who has to watch baseball. In my twenties I would have felt quite critical because I would have thought it reflected on me and my taste in men, but when you're fully formed in your middle years it doesn't bother you. Instead the differences between you keep the relationship surprising and fresh. [a fifty-seven-year-old woman]

Lesbian Partnerships

Over the years, some women who were thought to be single have in fact been in discreet lifelong relationships with other women, which for reasons of public opinion had to be kept secret. Though the social strictures are less severe than

formerly, many women are still understandably reluctant to make their sexual preference known. For other women, however, the relaxation of social attitudes has provided a liberating atmosphere in which to exercise new options. Some women, after years as wives and mothers, turn to a lesbian relationship and become part of a community of women. Whether our friendships with women will also include sexuality is a matter of very personal preference, but knowing that there is such a possibility can be very liberating.

I feel so lucky to have the choice in this period of women's liberation to leave behind society's negative attitude about women and instead be a woman-identified woman. How rich we are in wisdom, experience, talents, and skills! I believe we have within us the necessary balance to turn the society around and I am a part of that movement! [a woman in her fifties]

Elizabeth Furdon

Around the age of forty, I began realizing that I was sexually attracted to women, but I continued to date men until I fell in love with a woman at age forty-five and began a long-term relationship. I was married for sixteen years and have two adult children. I am now in a relationship with a West Indian woman which has presented me, as a Jewish woman, with numerous challenges in terms of cultural and racial differences.

I feel that my life would be far more limiting if I were still heterosexual and erotically dependent on men. I find traditional men of my age sexist, controlling, patronizing, and unable to express emotion...qualities which are unattractive and boring.

Although the stigma and restrictions of homosexuality certainly affect me, I love being a lesbian. I love the companionship of women and a life-style where my re-

lationships are primarily with women. [a woman in her fifties]

The advantage of such a "coming out" is the existence of a ready-made supportive community which the new lesbian can enter. Yet, as the following experience shows, acceptance may take a while.

After twenty-five years as wife and mother, the label I heard when I first mingled with lesbians was that I was not a real lesbian. I didn't understand—after all, wasn't I in love with another woman? I was confused and intrigued at the same time that lesbians expected me to be strong, self-supporting, with a place out there in the world. No one was interested in the passive, unopinionated woman I had been who knew how to use her body seductively for attraction and approval. I had to learn how to be with lesbians—to develop my knowledge and creativity at a deeper level than I had ever before been challenged to do.

Now I realize that I was still acting like a privileged heterosexual princess. Even though lesbians depend emotionally on others, they are usually self-supporting. I had never been trained to be that and I still expected, on some level, that someone would take care of me. I am grateful for the lesbian community's higher expectations. I have discovered a lot of inner strength and know now that I can be financially, emotionally, and mentally self-supporting, and that is freedom! [a fifty-four-year-old woman]

There are, of course, risks in changing sexual orientation. Those who are close and dear to us may find the change too drastic and withdraw, or refuse to accept our newfound selves, friends, or lovers.

I was involved with a woman and my daughter said, "Are you planning to come to Thanksgiving dinner?" and I said, "Oh sure I am, and I'd like to bring Elaine with me too." She said, "I don't think that's a very good idea. The families have talked about it and we thought it would be better if you just come alone." Then she added, "Why don't you come and just try to act like a real grandmother?" That taught me a great deal because I did not want to come to Thanksgiving dinner and act like a real grandmother because I don't know what that is. "What the hell is that? A real grandmother!" I said. "There isn't a model." [a sixty-three-year-old woman]

I remember the morning I greeted my friend of twenty years with the usual hug and kiss, then sat her down to tell her I had become a lesbian. She listened as we talked for hours, and told me she didn't understand at all, but would remain my friend. When she got up to go, and I approached her for a goodbye hug, she put out her hand at arm's length and said, "I cannot hug you anymore." That really hurt. [a fifty-four-year-old woman]

If we come from a social world where women and men mingle, we may long for the comfort and security of social acceptance. We may be fortunate in carrying some friends over from former days, but they, too, now lack our experience. Realizing that we may lose old friends both compels and enables us to embrace a concept of "family" which includes a larger community. Maintaining relationships is an important value of the lesbian community and women who formerly were lovers often remain close and supportive friends.

The lesbian community that we see at women's dances, at concerts, in bars, often seems to have found the key to eternal youth. Already disoriented in many ways, an older woman new to lesbian life may miss the companionship of women her own age. In some large cities, organizations specifically for older lesbians (and gay men) can help you meet other women your age. It is important to find a balance between former friends and new friends who are lesbians, even if you find yourself among women your daughter's age. Changing your sexual preference can make you feel insecure for a while, and you will need other lesbians for support. It is a rare old friend who can talk with you about your new self-discovery without questioning your choice or feeling threatened by it.

As lesbians, we have sharpened our wits and shaped our viewpoints on discrimination and the struggle for survival. We are drawn, as are many women, to the fight for women's rights over our bodies, for our rights not to be abused sexually, emotionally, or physically, for the restoration of health to the earth, for peace and a decent standard of living all over the world, and for the rights of those of our loved ones most vulnerable: children and frail elders. For some of us the work is never done as long as we feel the pinch of discrimination in our own lives. [a fifty-six-year-old woman]

LIVING IN COMMUNITY

It is important for women at any age to overcome the notion that we are somehow incomplete if we are not married or involved in a long-standing sexual relationship. The middle and later years can be a time to achieve a balance between companionship and solitude. It can help to stop thinking of our unpartnered state as aloneness, and to think of ourselves instead as moving into a life community. We have many choices to make in this new way of life. How big a community feels comfortable, and whom do you want to include in it? Do you want to consider a group-living situation? Do you want to see friends more often? Think about what you like to do and which of your friends would enjoy sharing that activity with you. Reaching out to other women in similar circumstances to yours can be a good source of new friendships. Women's and senior organizations, community activist groups, adult-education classes, and exercise and recreational activities are just a few of the many ways to meet new friends.

If you find yourself excited about a new creative pursuit or political agenda, you may find as you join groups or classes that you meet new people who share your passion, a wonderful

basis for new friendships. We are never too old to begin new friendships.[13]

NOTES

1. Heading borrowed from a book of the same title by Karen Lindsey, Boston: Beacon Press, 1981.

2. Freda Rebelsky, "Friends: Who Needs Them? Part II," a lecture reprinted in *The Community Church News*, 565 Boylston St., Boston, MA 02116, November 1986.

3. Lillian B. Rubin, *Women of a Certain Age: The Midlife Search for Self*. New York: Harper & Row, 1979.

4. Zenith Henkin Gross, *And You Thought It Was Over: Mothers and Their Adult Children*. New York: St. Martin's Press, 1985.

5. Susan Christian, "Grandparent Anxiety." *Modern Maturity*, December 1983–January 1984, pp. 32–5.

6. Phyllis R. Silverman, *Helping Women Cope with Grief*. Beverly Hills, California: Sage Publications, 1981.

7. Ibid.

8. Knud Helsing, Moyses Szklo, and George W. Comstock, "Factors Associated with Mortality After Widowhood." *American Journal of Public Health*, Vol. 71, 1981, pp. 802–9.

9. Phyllis R. Silverman, *Widow to Widow*. New York: Springer, 1985; and Silverman, op. cit.

10. Barbara Levy Simon, *Never Married Women*. Philadelphia: Temple University Press, forthcoming 1987.

11. Barbara Levy Simon, "C'est la Vie: Never Married Old Women and Disability, a Majority Experience." In Michelle Fine and Adrienne Asch, eds., *Voices from the Margins: Lives of Disabled Girls and Women*. Philadelphia: Temple University Press, 1987.

12. Nancy L. Peterson, *The Ever-Single Woman: Life Without Marriage*. New York: Morrow, 1982.

13. Rebelsky, op. cit.

Marianne Gontarz

12

HOUSING ALTERNATIVES AND LIVING ARRANGEMENTS

by Mickey Troub Friedman

Material on shelter poverty and the housing shortage
by Caroline T. Chauncey

Special thanks to Elaine Ostroff for help with section
on adaptive environments

Housing is an important issue for everyone, and can be a critical one for middle-aged and older women. Beyond the need for a safe, comfortable, affordable place to live, having a sense of "home" is a vital part of identity, security, and community. Home is the center of life, and, for many women, of work as well. Home, with its treasured mementoes and familiar furnishings, provides a link to the past and a feeling of rootedness.

As younger family members leave to live on their own, we may find ourselves rattling around a once-crowded house or apartment. We may move, alone or with a partner, to a quieter setting or a warmer climate upon retirement. As widowed or divorced women, we may find a for-merly congenial suburb no longer hospitable and seek the companionship of other single women and men in an urban environment. We may revel in a room of our own, perhaps for the first time.

Window Locks

Today I'm installing my condominium window
locks. Measure with the eye, then with scout
knife awl begin the screwhole. Drill. The bit
sticks. Turn the drill backward. It slips
off the bit. Work out the bit, replace it
in the drill. Measure screw against
finger at depth of hole on bit.

I could pay to have this done; but I save
money, enjoy the doing, keep out the cold
and some rampaging man on a ladder.
Til now all my locks were screwed in
by father, carpenter, husband. I searched
out this do-it-myselfing, raced after,
hounded, tackled, captured it
roll ecstatic with it now in my arms.

Try installing your own window locks.
You'll know why carpenters are proud,
insist on cash-in-the-palm. I am my own
journeywoman, nurtured by past lives, taught
by my father in his hobby shop, by handling
my mother's carpenter-father's tools.
I know these locks as I knew my babies'
bodies. The heat of my arms turns the drill.
I can install my own life.

Jane Bailey-Blood Strete

Marianne Gontarz

Whatever our circumstances, as we grow older most of us will experience a multiplicity of changes in health, income, family structure, and way of life, which in turn will influence both our housing preferences and the kind of housing available to us. Where we live and how we live is such an intrinsic part of our daily existence that even thinking about making a change can be unsettling. But once you get started, simply by reaching out for information you begin to make connections with others engaged in the same search. The process itself contributes to creating a support network for the present as well as contacts you can draw upon in the future.

SHELTER POVERTY AND DISPLACEMENT

Maintaining an affordable home that meets our needs is one of the key challenges of our middle and later years. "Shelter poverty" is defined as spending so much money on housing and fuel that not enough is left over to meet other basic needs. Experts estimate that, ideally, no more than 25 percent of one's income should be spent on shelter. But 25 percent of a low income is simply not enough for decent housing, so many people who are technically above the poverty level are in reality "shelter poor." Nearly one third of the population spends more than 25 percent of its income on housing, and in more than two million households, total shelter costs take up a whopping 85 percent of the budget. Many older women live alone, and consequently their per person housing cost is higher than for those who share housing with others.

With incomes either fixed or diminishing and the costs of both owning and renting a home steadily rising, shelter poverty thus becomes a major concern for older women. Housing problems associated with aging are even more difficult for Black and Hispanic women, who are almost twice as likely to live in rental housing as are all other elderly. The National Urban League calls this "double jeopardy." Having more housing options available can help solve many of the problems women face in the second half of life.

The Housing Shortage and Homelessness

To keep up with the escalating demand for new housing, the federal government estimates that the construction industry would have to provide two million new housing units per year. But the gap in reaching that goal continues to widen. The tight housing supply is reflected in the low vacancy rates found in many major cities—often less than 5 percent.

It is also reflected in the vast number of homeless people in the U.S. Estimates range from 500,000[1] to as high as three million, depending on who is describing the problem, but all agree that the numbers are rapidly increasing at the rate of 10 percent to 38 percent per year.[2]

Adding to the problem of homelessness is the disappearance of single-room-occupancy (SRO) hotels in urban areas. Though these hotels are often dirty and dangerous, they are sometimes the only housing option available for many older people. In recent years, such hotels have been remodeled or torn down to make way for urban-development projects, with little thought given to finding new housing for the displaced former tenants. In some large cities as many as half the SRO units have been lost to condominium conversion and other redevelopment projects. Changes in the housing market have resulted in many communities in the loss of lodging houses which formerly provided a convenient housing alternative for some older people.

In New York City, the housing shortage has become so severe that special shelters for the elder homeless have been created. Contrary to

Norma Holt

146

prevailing stereotypes, these shelters serve many elders who are well educated and some who had owned their own homes in the past. Some had been evicted for nonpayment of rent and others lost an apartment when the building they lived in became a cooperative or condominium or was torn down. Some have incomes too low to qualify for market level housing, but too high to qualify for subsidized housing.[3]

A number of activist and advocacy groups are working to end homelessness. The Community for Creative Non-Violence, based in Washington, D.C., studied thirty cities exhaustively and published the results in an excellent book, *Homelessness in America*.[4] Rosie's Place, a drop-in center and emergency shelter in Boston, offers a place for women not only to sleep but also to eat and socialize. Run by a staff of ten and 150 volunteers, it has been offering its unique support for eleven years, working with many civic and church groups and hoping to increase awareness. A local mental hospital has actually told Rosie's that without them its patient population would be above capacity.

Low- or moderate-income housing is only marginally profitable, so the trend is toward building luxury apartments, condominiums, and expensive single-family homes. As the upwardly mobile move into newer and better housing, their former homes become available to lower-income households, but when this filtering process slows down, due to a shortage of new housing at all income levels, the overall quality of affordable housing declines. This presents particular problems for older women. If you are fortunate enough not to have to deal with these issues in your own life, you may want to add your voice and/or contribute money or resources to help address this problem.

When Neighborhoods Change

Gentrification occurs when developers or private investors buy inexpensive homes or buildings in moderate-income neighborhoods and renovate them for resale to more affluent buyers. With gentrification, property values rise —and with them, property taxes, building-code requirements, and rents. Along with the pressure of these added expenses, we may feel abandoned when friends move away or face a significant loss as the corner grocery is replaced with an espresso café. Even though gentrifica-

tion increases the sale price of our homes, that money may not go far enough toward finding us an appropriate or comfortable replacement and it may be difficult for a woman on her own to obtain a mortgage or home-building loan.

Neighborhood deterioration can also make us feel uneasy or isolated. Programs to increase safety may not be reassuring when we feel threatened by street crime and an inadequate police presence. Banks' illegal practice of refusing to invest in low-income or minority neighborhoods, called redlining, may hasten the deterioration process.* There *are* legal ways for residents to preserve services and to press for reform. Tenants can withhold rent and spend it on needed repairs. Neighborhood groups can get together and reclaim abandoned buildings. The National Trust for Historic Preservation (see Resources) has seed money available for qualified nonprofit groups.

IF YOU ARE A RENTER

There is no need to talk here about the many landlords who enjoy good relationships with their tenants. Our concern is with dishonest landlords who use such illegal tactics as verbal harassment, neglect of necessary repairs and safety precautions, reduction in utility service, or even deliberate damage to their own buildings to force out unwanted tenants. Such practices have shortened the lives of many elderly poor, including many women who may find it extremely difficult to defend themselves because of language barriers, lack of education, frailty, fear of retaliation, or because they don't feel comfortable "making a fuss." Don't allow yourself to be coerced. Find out what your rights are. Most tenants are unaware of their rights, as are many social-service professionals who work with them. Laura Monroe, an attorney with Greater Boston Legal Services for the Elderly, stresses that "it is very important to make good use of your day in court. There is nothing trou-

*Banks are beginning to take a new look at the profit-making potential of investing in low-income communities, perhaps in part because city and state governments are demanding that out-of-state banks show that they will make a contribution to the community before a new bank is chartered or a merger approved. Ann Mariano, *The Washington Post*, "Banks See Profit in Housing for Poor," *Maine Sunday Telegram*, December 7, 1986, p. 7a.

Elana Freedom

---

ble-making about exercising your rights. Rights that are unused are like no rights at all."[5]

For those who want to get involved in advocacy, there are several good books available and opportunities at all levels to make an impact on housing policy. Federal cutbacks tightening income requirements and directing less money to large subsidized-housing complexes, coupled with escalating need, make this a time when advocacy is especially crucial.* Get on political-action mailing lists, find out when hearings on housing will be held by your state legislature and by local agencies and organizations that

---

*By 1990 many Federal housing programs will expire, affecting over one million families. Residents of public housing and advocates are alarmed by the Reagan Administration's attempt to sell public housing to private developers. *The New York Times*, June 1, 1985, pp. 1, 46.

Tenants' Rights*

Regulations and ordinances to protect tenants can be complex, and vary so much from state to state that it would be impossible to summarize them here, but legal services for low-income elderly exist in every state and provide free assistance. This kind of help is provided in both urban and rural areas.

These five general principles of landlord–tenant law have nationwide applicability:

1. In most states, there is an implied "warranty of habitability," which means the landlord is required to provide decent housing in exchange for the payment of rent.

2. Most states have protection against evicting tenants in retaliation for their complaints about housing conditions.

3. In almost all states a landlord must use judicial procedures to evict tenants. A landlord cannot physically eject a tenant without a court order.

4. The Federal Fair Housing Act prevents discrimination against tenants on the basis of race, color, religion, national origin, and sex. Discrimination on the basis of sex has been interpreted to also prohibit sexual harassment.

5. Most states have strict protections for tenant security deposits.

*Personal communication from Catherine M. Bishop of the National Housing Law Project, Berkeley, California.

Jerry Howard/Positive Images

share your concerns. It's an important time to add your voice to these issues! (See Resources for a list of ways and places to add your voice.)

Getting Help from the Government— for Tenants and Prospective Owners

Federal subsidies for housing come in three major forms: rent supplements, which enable renters to live in private housing; housing projects in which construction and operating costs are publicly subsidized; and fuel subsidies. Commonly called "Section 8 subsidies," rent supplements are administered by the U.S. Department of Housing and Urban Development (HUD). Only one fourth of households eligible for subsidies obtain them, however, and in urban areas there can be a three- to five-year wait. Nevertheless, they are still worth applying for. If you do get one you can continue to live in your present apartment, paying no more than 30 percent of your income for rent— HUD pays the rest. Landlords *must* agree to accept government reimbursement and to comply with Federal building codes for health and safety. The programs are complex; some offer the subsidy directly to income-eligible tenants and others offer it to owners or developers. To find out if you are eligible, how to apply, and how long the waiting lists are in your community, contact your local housing authority or state office on aging. Ask them about other programs in your area.

Another source of possible assistance is the voucher program. With limited appropriations to ten states, it provides funds directly to low-income individuals to be used for private or public rental housing. Some housing advocates oppose this program out of concern that it will serve as justification for further cutbacks in publicly funded construction of new housing.

Federal subsidies are also available to help defray fuel costs for both renters and home-owners. On the average, persons over sixty-five spend 30 percent of their income on energy.[6] The Federal Low Income Energy Assistance Program provides subsidies for households that meet certain income requirements. The program is badly underfunded (serving only one third of the eligible households), but priority is given to the elderly. An average subsidy is enough to cover between 20 and 30 percent of energy expenses. In addition, many states and some private agencies and utility companies offer consumers free energy audits and low-cost weatherproofing assistance.

If your apartment house is being converted to condominiums or going co-op, it may be worthwhile to buy your apartment if you can afford to. It may prove cheaper and more appropriate for your needs. Although the purchasing and operating costs for an apartment are usually lower than for a house, the tax advantages are the same. Federally insured mortgage and loan programs with lower-than-market interest rates offer additional assistance. HUD offers low-interest loans for condos, co-op housing, mobile homes, and rehabilitation of existing homes. Section 202 loans, available to nonprofit sponsors for new construction, are the only loans targeted specifically for elders and the disabled. The Farmers Home Administration offers several programs for those in rural areas: grants, loans at very low interest rates, and a rental assistance program [FmHA 515] similar to HUD's.

IF YOU OWN YOUR OWN HOME

Home Equity Conversion

Home equity conversion is a method that allows homeowners to convert some of what their house is worth into cash by selling it in advance, while continuing to live there for a number of years or the rest of their lives. The term "home equity conversion" covers a number of variations on this arrangement; information about them is continually updated (see Resources for details). In one type of home equity conversion, the "reverse mortgage," the homeowner receives monthly payments from a lender (usually a bank) which must be repaid at the end of the term. A reverse mortgage is useful only for a person who wants to stay in her home for five to seven more years before moving to another situation. A "lifetime reverse mortgage" is more useful in most situations because it allows the homeowner to stay in her home, keep the title, receive monthly payments plus a subsidy for maintenance. At the homeowner's death, the house becomes the property of the lender. It is preferable to make this arrangement with a prospective heir rather than with a financial institution. In a "sale-leaseback," a public or private investor buys the house and agrees to lease it back to the original owner for that person's lifetime. If you enter into such an agreement, be sure that it provides for your right to stay in the house even in the event of a subsequent resale by the new owner. Some plans allow the original homeowner to retain occupancy for a specified time only, or to defer property taxes and the cost of basic repairs until the property is sold, either after the original owner's death or if she decides to move.

Homeowners interested in converting home equity into cash should seek professional advice regarding the tax and estate-planning issues involved in these complex transactions before proceeding. Such plans may also have an impact on eligibility for Medicaid, SSI, or other government benefits, since the regulations often allow for home ownership but limit the amount of cash or other assets a recipient may have (see Money Matters and Problems in the Medical Care System chapters).

Tax Relief

In many cities and towns homeowners over a certain age can obtain tax abatements, tax reductions, or tax deferrals, through which they postpone paying property taxes until the house is sold. Deferrals can also be obtained for repair costs. Some cities also offer tax work-off programs, through which older people work at minimum wage in temporary part-time jobs in city government until they have earned an amount equivalent to their property taxes.

Taking in Renters

Sharing the space in your home is another way to reduce housing costs. Along with the extra income, such an arrangement can offer companionship, help with chores, or other benefits. There are a number of creative ways to be a landlady with a minimum of aggravation. Tailor your arrangement to suit your needs for privacy and draw up a written agreement which includes a specific provision for evaluating and renegotiating it in the future. For example, a woman with three children still at home decided to rent rooms but keep the kitchen for her family's use.

There are always the mistakes (and the learning by them). It's important to have a contract so that everyone's expectations are understood. I've had numerous

successful, delightful, and profitable experiences with tenants in the past eight years, and will continue to share the house as long as the arrangement works and the space is there. As a side benefit, I have made some good friends with whom I keep in touch. I feel that the rhythm established in this house is to allow a leisurely and pleasant "passing through" for a number of people, giving them time to think of the next step in their lives without the threat of having to leave. Keeping a business relationship and a comfortable psychological and physical distance helps each of us maintain our own private space.

A seventy-six-year-old woman who retired and worried about how to maintain her 130-year-old house with Social Security as her only source of income began renting rooms on a short-term basis to families of hospitalized people.

The first year I did this, I used to get so upset. It's hard not to feel bad for them. I'd think, what if I was far away from home? I'd want someone to talk to. If they have a motel room they go back and it's cold and lonely. Here they can come in and talk awhile. Somebody asked me if I was afraid to have strangers in the house. I told them that once someone comes in the front door, they're not a stranger.[7]

The Bed and Breakfast concept is growing in popularity, with benefits for both traveler and host.

I had moved into this seacoast community because I wanted to return to my roots. I decided to capitalize on my location and take people in overnight on a limited basis. This would not only supplement my income but add some spice to my life. And of course, one of the good things about Bed and Breakfast is that you can say no if you don't feel like having guests. [a seventy-nine-year-old woman]

LIVING ALONE VERSUS LIVING WITH OTHERS

One important decision to make is whether you want to live alone or with others. For some of us, the thought of having to accommodate the timetables, moods, habits, and needs of others may be a deterrent to shared housing. This may be especially true if we have often done that in the past—for parents, partners, roommates, spouses, and children.

I like living alone. It's peaceful. There's nobody to boss me around. The hardest time for me was when my husband first went to the hospital. We were married thirty-

three years and did everything together. Work, too. He was a fine carpenter and we had an antiques business. His doctor told me I couldn't live alone "out there in the woods," but I told him since I was a little girl someone has always told me what to do. Then, after my husband died, I was almost crazy, but I got hold of myself, and I fixed a rocking chair that was in such bad condition that he had said he'd never fix it. Well, I did—and I sold it for $35.00! So I found out I could get along alone. And that was twenty years ago and I'm still at it. At seventy-six, I work as much as I want to, and I do get out and see people—but only when I feel like it. I even helped fix my own roof last summer!

I like quiet—I don't like silence, there is a difference— and depending on how I am feeling, I may have the radio or TV on even if I am not paying attention, because it is too silent otherwise. In talking with others, I gather that this is not at all unusual. I do miss sharing a home with someone and yet I must say that I also really like the fact that I have a wonderful home which I have put together by myself. I like being able to do what I want when I want. [a woman in her fifties]

People are always asking me why I don't have a telephone. Well, I don't need one! I have so many friends here, and I can always walk down the road and use my neighbor's phone if I have to. And besides—I still ride my bicycle whenever I want. One of my friends and I cook dinner together almost every night, either at her house or mine. And sometimes we go out to eat. We pick apples, strawberries, go fishing, arthritis or not. I'm a very lucky person! [a seventy-seven-year-old woman]

Still, many of us find that no matter how active we are, how full our social or professional lives, living alone can be painful.

In spite of supportive children and a large circle of friends, I really don't like the idea that I may be living alone for the rest of my life. I even tried having a dog, but the disadvantages and limits to my freedom outweighed the joy of having her there to greet me as I opened my door. She is now romping happily on a farm, while I am often lonely and wondering what's next for me. [a woman in her fifties]

One of the reasons I opt for shared living in some form is that it can provide a balance which most of us need: privacy along with an opportunity for informal companionship. I even like the adjustments I have to make when my pattern comes in conflict with others. There is great satisfaction in learning to agree and work together in running our joint enterprise. I've found that a sense of being at home is a realizable goal. It may be greatly different from the home we grew up in or that we had when we were on our own, but it can have as much validity as those other homes. [a woman in her seventies]

Selecting a Housemate

How we go about finding someone to live with can vary with our individual circumstances. Some of us are lucky enough to have a close friend with whom we can share a house. Or we may start out with a temporary arrangement and find it so successful that it becomes permanent.

I met a teacher at the institution where I did volunteer work who was urgently looking for an apartment. She moved in temporarily with my father and me. She was helpful in doing things for my father that I didn't have time for, such as watching the ball game with him or taking him for a ride. I in turn would get the meals. After my father died, we just kept living together. For twenty years my roommate and I have had very separate but compatible lives. Financially she is better off than I am. It would be difficult for me to live alone on my shrinking pension. We still split everything right down the middle, except that she always had a car and I had household furnishings. I eat at home and entertain more than she and we often don't have lunch or dinner together, but we split everything. I became a "member" of her family, an adopted sister. When I have been hesitant to spend my more limited money, she will say "I think you should do it" and will provide the funds.

Nick Lammers

151

Whatever happens, happens, but after twenty years of being roommates, I would expect us to stay together. In my will I leave everything to her. [a seventy-two-year-old woman]

If there is no one in your circle who is interested in shared living and if you have never advertised for a housemate before, you may want to get some help. In addition to informal or private arrangements, specific home-sharing programs may exist in your area. Check with women's centers, social-service agencies, senior centers, Area Agencies on Aging, or your state department of elder affairs. Check also with your church, synagogue, YMCA, or other com-

---

Tips for Successful Home Sharing

by Fran Roberts

1. Spend some concentrated time together before you make a decision to share a home. Take a trip together, share a vacation house, spend a long weekend in each other's present homes.

2. Try to be clear, not only with a potential housemate but also with yourself, about your real plans and hopes for the future. If they include the possibility of marriage, re-marriage, or a continuing relationship which may be uncomfortable for your housemate(s), or if for some other reason you have doubts about how permanently you'll stay in the house-sharing situation, discuss the matter honestly. If you're not sure about the permanence of your plan, it might be better to share a rental arrangement.

3. To protect each other, discuss every aspect of your arrangement in advance, especially what provisions you want to make in the event that one person dies or chooses to withdraw. For example, does the remaining partner have lifetime use of the home and its furnishings? Can the remaining partner buy out the other's share? What provisions do you want to make for heirs? After you have mutually determined what you want to accomplish, work with a lawyer to develop the documents necessary to achieve your goals. These might include a written contract, a trust agreement, and new wills.

4. If you're planning to share a house by owning it jointly, it often works out better not to share a house that one partner already owns. It's easiest to establish new ground rules and break old patterns in an environment that is new to everybody. This can be especially important if either woman has children living at home. If you must consolidate into one partner's house, bring some of the other partner's things in and buy some new things together as soon as your budget allows.

5. You will need to clarify which decisions you will make individually and which jointly. It usually works best when both partners have a reasonably equal amount of spendable income, because without financial equality, joint decision-making—the core of a successful relationship—is much more difficult. However, where there is a strong desire to live together and where all parties believe in the principle, it can also work for each to contribute according to her means, recognizing the value of non-monetary contributions to a household.

6. It's useful to set up a joint bank account for household expenses in addition to your personal accounts. Discuss recurring expenses such as utilities, fuel, and mortgage payments, and how they will be handled, as well as major demands such as property taxes, insurance premiums, and housing maintenance.

7. It's good to set up a "kitty," or petty-cash fund, for day-to-day expenses such as groceries, and contribute equal amounts at the same time.

8. Be prepared for a few raised eyebrows from people who are curious about whether there is a sexual basis to your relationship, and decide together how to deal with this. Don't be surprised or dismayed if some jealousy erupts from a child, sibling, or close friend who feels threatened by her or his displacement in your life. Consideration of the needs of family and friends—and time—will work wonders in reducing tensions caused by the novelty of your living arrangements.

munity agency or university or college housing offices to find a program that can help prospective home sharers clarify needs and get through the early period of adjustment to living together. If you think you will have difficulty choosing, checking references, or saying no to someone, a social worker or some other neutral third party can serve as a mediator. This will give you time and support as you decide upon this important step.

What Makes Shared Living Work

The most important factor in the success of shared living arrangements is the willingness of all parties to change and compromise.

Living involves changes. Shared living is no exception. I have seen many changes both in situations and in the people who have shared them. I like it that way. Static living can be a bore. [a seventy-eight-year-old woman]

Another factor is respect and consideration of the desires, responsibilities, and needs of each person involved. Does one housemate have a child who is away at school but still living at home during part of the year? Or does one invite grandchildren for school vacations? Do any of you have frail or elderly relatives who may need temporary care? How will your prospective housemate(s) react to a short visit from a friend or lover (old or new), or an extended visit by an adult daughter or son who returns to the nest after a broken relationship or a lost job? Though no one can foresee the future, such issues should be clarified as much as possible before, not after, people decide to share a home.

Once housemates are living together, periodic house meetings or discussions are useful for evaluating how things are working out, airing differences, and negotiating changes.

Two women in their fifties, each having raised two children, decided to combine their resources and share their lives. One is divorced, the other widowed. On the opposite page the latter offers some suggestions that have worked well for them.

Communal or Group Living

This is an alternative that is usually associated with younger people but can work well with any age group or with persons representing a range of ages. It is usually an informal arrangement planned and carried out by the residents them-

selves without the help of agencies or professionals.

At midlife and newly divorced, Betty Dexter moved to Maine, where she took a course in house building and with her children built a fine house in the woods. As her children began leaving home, she realized that limited job and social opportunities began to outweigh the value of the rural tranquillity she had earlier sought. Ever a woman of action, she investigated housing opportunities in a nearby large city, and was courageous enough to risk another new beginning. Her story is on the next page.

Intergenerational Living

While many older people enjoy the company of their own generation, others have a strong preference for mixed-age housing. Young adults with no family members nearby can turn to older housemates for counsel, inspiration, and wisdom, while older women who either have never had children, live far away from their children and grandchildren, or have outlived all their family members can enjoy the companionship of younger housemates. The energy of the young can be channeled toward repairs and maintenance, snow shoveling, spring cleaning, heavy shopping, while elder housemates contribute time and skills to less physically demanding jobs.

Many old people prefer not to uproot themselves from long-established ties to friends, neighborhoods, churches or synagogues, clubs, health-care practitioners, or the comfort of familiar places. Having learned to cope with public transportation, social-service systems, medical resources, and other benefits or aggravations of a particular environment, they'd rather accommodate to new housemates than move to a new community.

The most familiar form of intergenerational living is the tradition of members of the same family sharing a house: either younger persons moving in with parents or older relatives, or an older parent coming to live with adult offspring and their children.

I am so fortunate that I still live in the house and in the town where I grew up and had my [medical] practice. Although I never married, I felt as close to my sisters' children as if they were my own, and now it's their children who live with me and help keep this place

153

Cheaper by the Dozen

by Betty Dexter

When people hear that I live with eleven other people, they raise their eyebrows and ask, "You're fifty-eight, why do you want to live like a hippie?" "How do you stand the noise?" "Don't you want privacy?" "Do you have a lock on your bedroom door?"

I really don't know where to begin—the image of group living, in so many minds, is one of chaos, dirt, nightly orgies, and deafening stereos. Our house has none of these. We are a multigenerational group of adults who want to save money and who believe that community is healthier than aloneness. Otherwise, we are the same as the rest of the world: we like our home clean; we want love, not one-night stands; and we enjoy solitude as well as festivity.

Where my life greatly differs from that of most single women my age is in the area of responsibility. I do not want to pay for, insure, repair, polish, paint, tend, display, or worry about a house and its furnishings. But I want to live well. To me that means not only comfort and good food but stimulation and fun. Group living provides all of these and much more. I'm not living barricaded behind multiple locks because I fear unfamiliar steps outside my door. My social life is based on a bunch of people doing things together. In our house there are joggers, music and art lovers, and sports fans. Some people love board games while others retire to their rooms with a new book. I and two others are theater buffs. But most important, all of these pursuits are guilt-free because the time for them is not stolen from our duties.

How do we run a sixteen-room house and still have lots of leisure? Organization. It's not a perfect world and sometimes people slack off, but on the whole this is the grand plan:

Decision-making:	Everybody attends house meetings twice a month.
Food shopping:	Rotation (two persons every six weeks).
Cooking:	Everyone makes her or his own breakfast and lunch. Twice a month each member cooks dinner for the group and cleans up afterward.
Kitchen cleaning:	Rotation (one person every twelve weeks; the job takes three hours).
Painting:	Everyone paints her or his own room.

going. I do all the cooking and some of the cleaning, and it works out just fine for all of us. [a woman in her eighties]

Though it is common today to look back with nostalgia at extended-family living arrangements, not all of these were idyllic. Many families lived together under the pressures of tradition or economic necessity, while chafing at the limitations on their freedom. Today, families who share a house are more likely to *want* to live together and to have compatible values and life-styles.

I've often wondered what my son and his family get out of living with me. My son and daughter-in-law both work and make good money, but they've never said anything about wanting to buy a house. I think I give my grandchildren a certain amount of security, especially because their parents aren't always there. If they want anything or need anything they come and ask me.

What do I get out of it? Respect and being comfortable in my own home. I feel safe and I enjoy the contact. They clean the house. My grandsons take care of the yard, though I wish I didn't always have to tell them to. But when I do they are very polite and say, "Yes, Grandma," and it's done. [an eighty-five-year-old woman]

If you are thinking of sharing a home with your parents or adult children, you should ask yourself some hard questions. Can you coexist

We have a once-a-year painting party at which everybody paints the common areas.

Other jobs, such as figuring and paying bills, cleaning bathrooms and living/dining/guest rooms, and performing minor repairs, are done by those who choose them. If a person gets sick of some job, he or she asks for a change and somebody swaps. When people leave, jobs are rearranged so nobody ends up, as the average housewife does, doing the same old jobs for a lifetime. If you have a bad back, you never have to lift a storm window. If you're hopeless at math, forget it, the bill payer will struggle with the bank statements.

At present my jobs are cleaning the living and dining rooms and washing the house linens. I usually devote Saturday morning to these chores. Besides that, I cook two big dinners monthly and in exchange I get twenty-two free evenings in which I come home, put my feet up, and wait for the dinner gong. I make two trips to the grocery store every sixth week. About four times a year I do kitchen cleanup.

There! The drudgery's finished; now let's talk about other aspects of group living.

1. *One's mindset:* If you're a woman who is upset if the house does not reflect *your* taste, then you'll have to decide whether that's important in the great scheme of things. If it is, then don't move into a group house where the common rooms belong to everybody and are dioramas of diversity. This was a stumbling block for me. I now confine my decorating efforts to my own bedroom. If you haven't missed an issue of *Better Homes and Gardens* in years, think about this, because you don't want to be apologizing for your home.

2. *One's role:* In my first group experiment, I took in to live with me two young men who had been orphaned early in life. (I had lost custody of my own ten-year-old son just three months earlier.) Of course at the time I didn't see any connection, but shortly thereafter I found I couldn't say the things that needed to be said to make the house run well. I was too sorry for motherless boys during that period.

3. *One's openness to change:* I think you have to let go. Admit there is more than one way to wash lettuce; try exotic dishes you'd never make for yourself; go along with the gang to a "far-out" film. (I'll bet next year you won't even call it far-out.)

But finally, best of all, if a middle-aged woman stays alert and tuned in, she can become a star in *Group Living*, the only soap opera I know that runs seven days a week all year round without reruns or commercial interruption!

as adults, or are there still unresolved power struggles between you? Are you—or they—flexible enough to adapt to new dynamics, new roles?[8] As with any other group living situation, mutually agreed upon ground rules and periodic reevaluation will help establish an equitable distribution of responsibilities and resources.

After my mother died, my dad took early retirement and came to live with us in the country. I don't even know who asked who. It just sort of happened. Things worked out really well for a while and then he began to seem depressed. He was still "young" in many ways—had kept up with old friends in the city and talked a lot about working again. In the beginning he enjoyed baby-sitting for our boys, but as they grew older, my husband and I realized his attitude about discipline was different from ours and we often felt we wanted more control over our kids' lives. It began to be tense all the time—the boys felt torn in their loyalties and my dad felt unappreciated. It was really hard to begin, but we finally talked it out. We did this at the urging of a friend who had correctly guessed that Dad wanted "out." He just didn't know how to tell us. We all had to acknowledge that the arrangement wasn't working any more. He's now on his own, happily back in the city, working part time. He spends holidays with us and we're friends again. [a woman in her forties]

A new variation on the familial pattern of intergenerational living is that of unrelated persons of different generations sharing a home. A

Sarah Putnam

Accessory Apartments and ECHO (Elder Cottage Housing Opportunity) Housing

One variation on intergenerational living is for an older person to live in a separate apartment, perhaps created specially for that purpose, in a single-family house occupied by her children or grandchildren (or other younger relatives or friends). This concept, called accessory apartments, is becoming increasingly popular in suburban communities across the country. It has a number of advantages, providing independent living for both generations with the opportunity for easier visiting and the reassurance of help and support when needed.

After I became a widow, I lived alone for twenty years and traveled all over the world until I was ninety-one, when I broke my hip. While I was recuperating, my only daughter and her husband fixed up an apartment for me within their house. I ate most of my meals with them, and we got along splendidly.

In ECHO housing, an older person lives in a small, separate unit built on the same lot as the home of a relative. With this arrangement, maximum independence can be maintained while assistance is close by if needed. This arrangement is more common in other countries. In the U.S., zoning regulations often forbid a second building on a single lot, or a second dwelling unit in a "single family" home. However, such regulations can sometimes be modified or changed. Or you can apply for an exception, variance, or special-use permit; since these apply to only one dwelling, neighbors are less likely to object, particularly if the new unit is for a family member.

Manufactured and Mobile Homes

The Office of Technology Assessment, a Congressional agency, reported recently that the U.S. is lagging behind other nations, particularly Sweden and Japan, in developing high-tech, factory-produced housing components which could make home-building significantly less expensive. Antiquated housing-industry regulations and local zoning ordinances continue to retard progress in this promising approach to providing well-designed housing at lower cost.[11]

Some women have found "mobile" homes[12] a low-cost energy-efficient alternative to conventional housing, either on their own land or in a trailer park. Zoning may be a problem, but re-

university program that was among the first to match people who had extra space with those who needed housing found that some of its most successful matches were between young adults and elders.

Mrs. D. is a woman in her early sixties who was widowed two years ago. She owns her own three-bedroom home in a suburb of Boston where she works daily as an accountant. She has a large circle of friends, mostly other widows. Because she is used to caring for someone and having someone there in the evenings, Mrs. D. requested a housemate from a local home-sharing program. Her first match was a young woman in the area for a six-month education program. That worked out so well that Mrs. D. has applied for her second match.[9]

After years of taking students into her home, one woman was cared for through a long and lingering illness by these same young people. Although they no longer lived with her, they took turns coming in and seeing to her needs. A lovely circle of caring![10]

cent technological and esthetic improvements in pre-fabricated houses or components (i.e. pre-assembled walls, windows) have inspired a new look at such restrictions. Recognizing the necessity for moderately-priced housing, a growing number of communities have mandated that some land be set aside for such homes.

After my husband died my house was just too big, but I knew I could take care of a mobile home. So when I sold the house, I kept an acre to put this on. I added a base and two porches, so I could sit out in the summer, and I can walk to my job at the library—I've never driven, you know. I've lived in this village since I was thirteen. I know a lot about the history and I want to be a part of it. Lonesome? I'm seventy-six and I can't stop long enough to be lonesome! Besides, I have an extra bedroom and my divan opens up, so I have plenty of room whenever my grandchildren visit. I like being independent. It's been the perfect solution.

We have heard reports of women's communities developing in trailer parks, as women who moved there with their husbands upon retirement elect to stay after widowhood. The women establish firm friendships and help one another with routine and emergency situations.

WHEN WE BEGIN TO NEED HELP

As the average life span lengthens, and as more of us grow older, the connection between housing and health becomes increasingly crucial. It is particularly critical to have housing that maximizes our independence while providing a range of supportive services to be used as needed: community-based health and therapeutic-care programs; household services; home-delivered meals; respite care; friendly visitors; and a variety of emergency response systems, from a telephone reassurance program to devices worn around the neck at all times. One or more of these can enable us to maintain a greater degree of independence than is possible in a supported residence or a nursing home.

Adapted Housing

Before we make a hasty move because of a sudden or gradually worsening disability or illness, an important alternative to consider is adapting the housing we already live in. Western culture

Norma Holt

is oriented to the individual and teaches us to look within ourselves for the causes and solutions to problems, but sometimes the problem is in our environment. We may panic and assume that because of changes in our physical condition, we can no longer live on our own, or in a familiar and loved home. Yet it may take only minor and inexpensive changes, such as grab bars, railings, or ramps, to make a place safer and more livable.

Changing the environment to meet our changing needs can be a liberating and expressive act that can give us a great feeling of personal power. Many people who could benefit from adapting or modifying their homes resist doing so because they feel such features as ramps and guardrails are stigmatizing, identifying them as "elderly" or "disabled." Yet both elders and disabled people are proudly claiming their rights to full citizenship and pushing for greater accessibility to public buildings. Universal design elements can make all housing better adapted to its residents. For example, if kitchen counters and shelves were easily movable and thus were *always* placed at the right height for new residents, then placing them conveniently for people in wheelchairs would not be such a big deal. Lever-type door handles could be routinely installed instead of doorknobs. They are easier to use for someone with a weak arm or hand.

On an individual level, another way we can overcome our resistance to making changes in our homes is to begin the process of adaptation when we are experiencing only minor problems, or to make our home more accessible to friends or family members who are frail or who use a walker or wheelchair. Then the adaptation does not become a major statement about ourselves.[13]

Typical Cost of Housing Adaptations, 1985 Estimates[14]

Exterior wheelchair lift	$7000
Interior stair lift	$2000 (and up)
Widening of interior doorway	$1000
Single lever faucet	$150
Lever door-handle set	$150
Electronic appliance control units	$150
Bathroom grab bar (if no major carpentry needed)	$100
Handrails (per running foot)	$40
Clamp-on levers	$20

Small accommodations for comfort or safety can sometimes be made at little or no cost—for example, a simple change in placement of furnishings. A first-floor bedroom can be provided when you need to limit stair climbing by moving a day bed or lounge into an infrequently used downstairs room. Moving chairs and getting rid of scatter rugs can help prevent falls.

Home Care and Social Services for Independent Living

Home-care services are a central part of independent living. Though such programs are cost-effective, misguided penny-wise budget cutters have reduced or eliminated them in many areas, prematurely forcing formerly independent people into institutional living. Housing activists must be aware of the importance of home-care services and work toward strengthening and expanding them and coordinating them with other community resources. Such services should be available to all who need them on a sliding-fee-scale basis, thus expanding the availability of beds for those who really need to be in a health-care facility. (See Home Care Services, page 211, for description of types of services available in many communities.)

Senior Apartments or Senior Housing

Senior housing usually refers to low-cost apartments built for elders and subsidized by Federal, state, or local agencies, or by private nonprofit sponsors. For those who find comfort and security by living primarily with others whose values, history, and culture are similar to theirs, religious, cultural, professional, and labor organizations often sponsor low- or moderately priced housing. When such housing is subsidized by Federal funds from HUD, it is more likely to be mixed-income housing, as applicants with housing subsidies must be accepted. A specified package of health and social services may be included.

For many older women, a subsidized apartment means being able to live within their means in adequate rather than substandard housing.

I live alone in the elderly apartments. They're ideal. After all, when you're getting along on Social Security, you can't do any better, because you've only got to pay the rent and the telephone. And they shovel out the snow! [a seventy-five-year-old woman]

Though most senior apartments are designed for living alone or in couples, many single and widowed women enjoy having so many potential friends and companions right in the building.

I live alone, but I'm never alone. I'm bouncing out all the time and knocking on the door here and there. We're all back and forth all the time. And at Christmastime, I do the tree trimming in the lounge. We have a big Christmas tree in the upper hall and it's real dressed up and nice. [a woman in her sixties]

For women who want to keep busy and active despite limitations on their mobility, having a variety of activities available where they live may be the ideal solution.

At the time of my involuntary retirement I was eligible to apply for senior housing, which I did. This opened up a new way of life. I am living among my peers, with whom I have much in common. This is a wonderful housing complex with so much to do. I have joined the art group, and the choral group, a discussion group, a nutrition group, and the tenants' group. I am also board secretary of a Jewish women's organization and do volunteer work sending out cards. People tell me I'm hard to reach at home. Gee, I wonder why?

I can just about navigate around the building, but I am very limited with walking any distance. I've had two unsuccessful knee replacements. I wonder what I'd do if I had a good pair of legs. [a woman in her seventies]

Many communities have adopted innovative solutions to the shortage of housing for elders. In Hallowell, Maine, an industrial building overlooking the river has been remodeled into apartments. It's within walking distance of town activities. In Virginia, a large building, rehabilitated and funded by church groups, now contains efficiency apartments and serves communal meals. If a resident has exhausted her funds, contributions from the church are used. A ninety-nine-unit cooperative built in 1984 in Chicago, sponsored by the Illinois Association of the Deaf, is specifically designed for older hearing-impaired people. In New York City, a seventy-one-year-old blind newsdealer and activist designed a two-hundred-unit apartment building for other blind adults. At Western Washington State College in Bellingham, Washington, a program called The Bridgers made on-campus apartments available on a permanent basis to anyone over sixty who can take a single course or study for a degree. Both generations benefit, and the accumulated wisdom revealed in class discussions (and out-of-class bull sessions) does more to destroy some of the myths of aging for *both* generations than a semester of human-development or gerontological studies.

Congregate Housing

Congregate housing is specially planned, designed, and managed multiunit senior housing. Each self-contained unit typically includes a bedroom and bath, possibly other rooms, and in some instances a small kitchen. Common space for shared cooking, dining, and group activities is centrally located, to be shared by several residents. Supportive services such as housekeeping, transportation, social and recreational activities, and sometimes meals, are often provided if desired. The staff is trained to respond to health changes or other needs. Home care, such as help with bathing, or physical therapy, can also be delivered here, if needed.

Congregate housing is an excellent concept but little is being built because there is so little funding available for the social services that were to be an integral part of the package. And the renovation of older buildings (large homes, phased-out schools, etc.) is often thwarted by obsolete regulations or building codes.

Sometimes congregate housing is described as independent living. I feel this is unfortunate. With this understanding, a new resident might come in feeling no need to change her way of living in the common spaces of the apartment. If she always cooks for a whole hour at 6 P.M., or doesn't like to work with other people, there will be trouble if another resident has the same feeling. The way I feel congregate living should be described is interdependent living. This conjures up a give-and-take, an accent on cooperation with others rather than insistence on one's own way. It puts the emphasis on mutual support. And it provides the opportunity for little successes. We can learn to live together by trying out procedures, discarding some, and working out more effective measures. [a seventy-eight-year-old woman]

Scattered Site Housing

Another concept is to have a network of social services available to elders who live in separate apartments dispersed over a designated geographical area. For example, the Jewish Council for the Aging in Washington, D.C. started a Group Homes program in 1973 for those who are mobile and able to do most things for themselves. For a basic fee, in addition to their housing, residents receive food, a daily newspaper, local phone service, and the services of a homemaker and a social worker. The residents enjoy the warmth and companionship of shared housing and the knowledge that their basic needs will be met.

A similar model is being developed in Philadelphia by the Quaker community. The plan encourages residents to live in twos and threes in apartments where health and social services can be delivered to them with efficiency and economy.

Supported Group Living

Rest homes and board-and-care homes are subject to less regulation than nursing homes, although most states have tightened their restrictions in the last few years. These homes provide shelter, food, and a twenty-four-hour resident staff person. Such residences should be located near sources for in-home services. If a nurse or personal-care attendant is needed, the care is usually only part time and for an addi-

Norma Holt

mer, and returned there in the fall. It's privately run and open to all ages, but has attracted mostly older people from right around here. Because it was an inn at one time, each room has its own bath—that would be important to me even if I had to give up other areas of privacy. The location is ideal—within sight of the church, town library, community center, firehouse, and —even more important—it's next to the post office, which is the social center of town. There's a boarding school right up the road, which provides some cultural activities as well as a chance for some interaction with teenagers far from home. People from the community come for lunch or craft workshops. My friends and I feel comfortable knowing the house will be there for our parents or for us if we can't be as independent as we are now, or don't want to be. [a woman in her fifties]

I went shopping for a place to live near my daughter and her husband and I found an ideal place. It's a small group residence and there's another woman there in her nineties too. I moved in for a trial month and then permanently. I have a first-floor room and can use my walker when I need to. An old beau of mine lives nearby so I called him and now he takes me for a weekly drive and dinner out. My daughter and granddaughter come over often, too. [a ninety-three-year-old woman]

Retirement Communities

These communities range in size from a single building to whole "villages" or towns, and offer a variety of services and recreation. They may be built, sponsored, and managed by nonprofit organizations, profit-making companies, or a combination of both.

Life-Care or Continuing Care Communities offer independent apartment living for people who are in relatively good health, with medical and social services nearby. Most include a nursing home on the premises. A resident may move from a residential part of the community to another building or section which offers intermediate or skilled nursing care. In return for a sizable entrance fee, as well as monthly maintenance charges, residents are guaranteed a permanent place to live and a specified package of medical and nursing benefits, which can be increased or decreased according to the resident's changing needs.

The type and level of available care should be specified in a written agreement. The agreement should also clearly state your right to terminate the contract and receive a refund should the arrangement prove unsatisfactory for any reason. It should state the conditions under which you might be involuntarily discharged and what al-

tional fee. The greater independence of such residences as compared with nursing homes may be attractive to those who do not require daily health and social services; however, some elders who live in such settings may need more skilled care than they are receiving.

The line between independent group living for the elderly and assisted group living is easily blurred, and different states have different laws regulating various aspects of group residences. It is important to have enough regulation to weed out those homes that are unsafe, poorly run, or exploitive, while not discouraging innovation by and for those who are able to manage well by themselves.

A big old place which was vacant for ten years has come back to life down in the village. It's now a residence for nine people, and you can rent a room (which includes three meals and laundry) either on a monthly, seasonal, or yearly basis—even weekly for recuperation, respite, or just to try it out. The first person who signed up went back to her own house and garden in the sum-

ternative care provisions will be made in such a case. Another question which must be answered is what happens to your assets if you die shortly after entering. Can your investment be returned to your estate, or does it remain the exclusive property of the retirement community? In some situations, you can buy your unit under various conditions and limitations, and the equity in it passes to your heirs when you die. One small liberal arts college in Connecticut, which built a nonprofit life-care community on its campus, guarantees a refund of two-thirds of the entrance fee should you leave the community at any time.

Various financial and management problems, however, have closed some life-care communities in recent years. Whether nonprofit or for profit, such communities need regulation. Be a prudent, knowledgeable consumer: obtain information in writing, and have the community's financial statement reviewed by your accountant, estate planner, or lawyer.

THE TRANSITION

When we begin to consider a possible move for any reason, it's a good idea to look as far ahead as possible—to visualize future needs, not just those of the moment. Become informed about what's available *before* you need it. Try to arrange a short-term stay. Once your house is sold and furniture dispersed, it can be hard to go back to your former life-style.

When my husband died, I felt very much alone in a large house which had been built for us over fifty years ago. The chance to move into an apartment building (where over a dozen of my friends live) came along five months later, but I wasn't sure I would really feel "at home" there. Fortunately, my grandson and his wife were house-hunting in a nearby community, and I asked them to live in the house for a year, to give myself a "fallback." Within a few months I was sure I did not want to go back to that big, empty house. Meanwhile, they had grown to love it there and decided to stay. I

The Clovers Retirement Community

by Kathleen McGuire*

The Clovers are a group of seven women who met between 1976 and 1978 through a self-help, peer-counseling group called Changes. By 1978, individual members of the group began to move all over the United States and Canada. We decided that we did not want to lose these good friendships to distance and time, so even though we were only in our early thirties then, we had a great idea: Why not commit ourselves to be lifelong friends and to care for each other when we became elderly? The Clovers Retirement Community was born.

Although we're widely scattered now, we committed ourselves to a yearly reunion and a yearly contribution of one hundred dollars each to the retirement fund. Since then, we have had six reunions (expanded from three days to seven) and have $4,200 plus interest in our money-market account. We have Clovers T-shirts, a round-robin newsletter, a photo album, an archive, a Clovers Chorus and collection of affirming songs, and a phone chain and support network that is activated whenever a Clover is in need. We also have increasingly deepening friendships which we know will be

there whatever the vicissitudes of our individual lives.

Plans for the distant future are open-ended. The dream is for a piece of land, one or more houses on it, and a nursing and health staff to assist us. We imagine incorporating surviving spouses or other partners and friends into the group at later times. We do some financial and medical planning now (guiding each other through issues like health insurance, wills, breast exams, giving up addictions, etc.), but are letting the formal structures arise organically over time.

Basic to the group are skills of empathetic listening and experiential focusing, which we learned in the Changes self-help community. We call upon our listening/focusing skills as a way of deepening our intimacy when we gather at reunions. The skills also provide us with a method for resolving interpersonal conflicts and for making decisions consensually. These tools have been invaluable to us and are part of our confidence that our commitment can survive and deepen over the next thirty years.

* See Resources—Self-help and Support Groups for Kathleen McGuire's book on starting and maintaining a supportive group or community.

now enjoy being their guest for Thanksgiving and other family gatherings, without having the hassle or the work of feeding an ever-expanding clan. [an eighty-year-old woman]

A small group of pioneering feminists in the Appalachian area of Ohio have purchased a 150-acre hill farm and are trying to develop a collectively owned land trust with individual homes, cottage industries, meeting spaces, and a guesthouse. Their goal is to be self-sufficient and to have an active, worldwide network with other similar communities. They call themselves the Susan B. Anthony Memorial Unrest Home. They welcome correspondence, tapes, calls, or an extended visit. Another feminist community-building project is the Crone's Nest in St. Augustine, Florida, where a group of women are raising funds for a proposed intergenerational community to include long-lived women.

What these stories have in common is a spirit of innovation, commitment, and mutual support grounded in long-range planning. We hope more and more women will be inspired by these examples to explore new ways of living that will enhance their later years.

NOTES

1. "National Conference on Homelessness." *The New York Times*, February 16, 1986, p. 31.

2. National Council on the Aging, *Perspectives on Aging*. Vol XIV, No. 5, September–October 1985, p. 29; and Chester W. Hartman, *Displacement: How to Fight It*, National Housing Law Project, Berkeley, California, 1982.

3. "New York Shelters Meet Special Needs of Elderly." *The New York Times*, March 29, 1987, p. 38.

4. Mary Ellen Hombs and Mitch Snyder with foreword by Daniel Berrigan, *Homelessness in America*. Washington, D.C.: Community for Creative Non-Violence, December 1982.

5. Anthony Barnes, "Unfamiliarity with the Law Heightens Tenant Problems," *Boston Seniority*, January 1985, pp. 1–2.

6. Coalition on Women and the Budget, *Inequality of Sacrifice: Women and the Reagan Budget*, section on public housing. National Women's Law Project, Washington, D.C., March 1984.

7. John Ferland, "She Makes MMC Visitors at Home." Portland, Maine, *Press Herald*, October 2, 1984.

8. Barbara Silverstone and Helen Kardel Hyman, *You and Your Aging Parent*. New York: Pantheon, 1982, pp. 148–50.

9. Personal communication from a woman on the staff of a town-sponsored home-sharing agency.

10. "MG's Friends." *Boston College Magazine*, Fall 1984, pp. 26, 27.

11. Washington (AP), "Report finds U.S. housing held back by poor research." Portland, Maine, *Press Herald*, September 16, 1986.

12. Formaldehyde, used in the construction of mobile and some conventional homes, may cause cancer. If you are concerned, check current standards with HUD and the Environmental Protection Agency. Ann Mariano, "Cancer Risk Seen in Mobile Homes." *The Washington Post*, April 26, 1987.

13. Clair Cooper, "The House as Symbol of Self," in H. Proshansky, W. Ittleson, and L. Rivlin, eds., *Environmental Psychology* (2nd ed.). New York: Holt, Rinehart and Winston, 1976.

14. Used with permission of Adaptive Environments Center, Massachusetts College of Art, Boston.

13

WORK AND RETIREMENT

by Edith Stein, Paula Brown Doress, and Mary D. Fillmore

Special thanks to Tish Sommers

All human beings need the sense of achievement and accomplishment that comes from satisfying and socially valued work.* For middle-aged and older women, work outside the home provides a sense of mastery and increased self-esteem. Social scientists used to believe that jobs for women conflicted with the homemaking role, but contemporary research shows instead that multiple roles for women are more likely to bring multiple satisfactions rather than stress and conflict, especially when the jobs are good, pay well, and provide opportunities for achievement.[1] Having an external source of rewards and respect, earning our own money, and meeting new co-workers and friends bring us greater independence from our families[2] and provide a hedge against the isolation and feelings of obsolescence that can plague older women.

Dramatic demographic changes have taken place in the past twenty years; more jobs for women have opened up and more women are in the work force. Today over half of all women in the United States are employed for pay and only 35 percent are full-time homemakers. In the late 1960s, the reverse was true. Women continue to enter many fields traditionally closed to them,

and the percentage of women in professional and managerial positions has doubled over the past two decades. These developments present not only special opportunities for middle-aged and older women but special challenges and pitfalls as well.

Women often find new directions in work and education at a time in life when men worry about their time "running out." Perhaps women's less conventional career paths can provide a model of what is possible for all workers in the second half of life.[3] Yet it is also true that many women find themselves in dead-end or entry-level jobs, or frozen out of the work force altogether, at an age when men are at the peak of their earning power. By their fifties and sixties, choices narrow considerably and making a change becomes increasingly difficult. Many communities have agencies that provide help to women and men over fifty-five who are seeking employment. The road to the rewards and satisfactions we seek can be a rocky one.

DISCRIMINATION

As women, we face sex discrimination throughout our work lives, and some of us face other forms of discrimination as well. Well-documented government publications report these shocking facts:

- Women earn only 64 percent of what men earn, though women and men are, on average, equal in years of education completed.

---

*Women in our culture are socialized to overvalue relationships and to undervalue work, always putting the needs of others first instead of seeking the best balance for our own well-being. See Jean Baker Miller, *Toward a New Psychology of Women*. Rev. Ed., New York: Harper & Row, 1986. Sigmund Freud said it most succinctly: A healthy person must be able to love and to work. Yet women are forced to choose.

- Women college graduates earn, on average, less than male high school graduates.
- 49 percent of employed women are concentrated in ten low-paying, virtually sex-segregated occupations.

One explanation for the wage gap between women and men is that women's labor has traditionally been associated with housework, which is usually not paid for at all or performed at low wages, often by women of color. The same undervaluation that affects us at home extends straight into the female job ghetto.

Employer's Advice

You can't trust older women
they put philodendron
on the file cabinets
dump real coffee grinds
into wastebaskets
and even hang posters
in the washrooms.

Next thing you know
they will be asking
for a raise because
they made the place
feel like someplace
you might like to be
if they weren't there
looking down noses
when you cheat or lie
to the customers.

*Ruth Harriet Jacobs**

In addition to sex discrimination in employment, many women also face discrimination because of race, class, sexual orientation, or disability. Though Black women work more continuously than white women, their earnings do not reflect their commitment. Black women constitute 12 percent of all women workers in the U.S., but 28 percent of low-income women workers.[4]

When we reach our middle years, the discrimination we have faced throughout our lives is compounded by age discrimination, which continues to be common despite laws against it. Contrary to widespread employer prejudice, older women are reliable workers with low turnover and low absenteeism.[5] In fact, the offi-

*Excerpt from *Button, Button, Who Has the Button?*, a play by Ruth Harriet Jacobs, printed at Clark University, Worcester, Massachusetts, 1985, and copyrighted © by Ruth Harriet Jacobs.

cial unemployment rate for older women is low because they seldom change jobs. However, the official rate fails to account for the many discouraged workers who give up the job search because they can no longer face repeated experiences of rejection. Older unemployed workers are unemployed for longer periods, and account for 23 percent of discouraged workers though they constitute only 14 percent of the labor force. In 1983, about 60 percent of "officially" discouraged workers were women. Almost one in three women leaves the job market entirely by taking early retirement, despite the permanent reduction in Social Security benefits that results from retirement before age sixty-five.[6]

I walked smack into age discrimination in employment at the age of fifty-six. Perhaps I'd been experiencing it for many years before and didn't know it because I was content to be underemployed for twenty-five years on the minimum-pay scales of stereotypical female jobs such as typist, nurse's aide, and clerk. After my three older children had received their college degrees, and the youngest was about to start, I closed the house and went to college at the age of fifty-two. I worked as house-mother in a state university. Four years later, in 1972, I received a B.A. in social service and expected to be recognized as a professional. But I was fifty-six years of age, so I took what jobs I could get, and finally in 1980, at the age of sixty-four, resigned to subtle pressures of age discrimination in the work place, I applied for Social Security as a means of financial survival.

I had looked forward to growing and developing professionally in my sixties but the world doesn't let you keep going as a worker. I think it is because younger adults see older women as mother figures. If you've spent a decade or more getting your mother off your back, you don't want to hire someone who looks like your mother. [a sixty-four-year-old woman]

My age, sixty, doesn't influence how I feel. My experience does. I don't feel old but the doors close on you at some point. When I started making applications twelve years ago, I thought I could work full time for one of the companies I had contact with. I wanted to work full time to have more income and put some aside for the future. I fulfilled all the requirements and I had been a reliable part-time worker. Each company had a reason why they couldn't hire me full time. The truth was because of age. They wanted someone young. So I stopped looking because it was demoralizing.

It is difficult to maintain self-esteem while being refused employment. Getting support from others is very important to keeping your spirits up during the job search.

Nicole Hollander

The Compounding of Age and Sex Discrimination

Although a higher percentage of older women than younger women are in the paid work force, older women are even more underpaid, as a result of the compounding of age and sex discrimination. Consider the following statistics:

- Only 6.9 percent of women over thirty-five hold managerial jobs, and only 15.2 percent hold professional jobs.
- The gender gap in wages increases with age. While young women (aged twenty to twenty-four) earn 76 percent of young men's salaries, middle-aged women (aged forty-five to fifty-four) earn only 54 percent of middle-aged men's salaries. By midlife, men who are going to rise to higher income levels have begun their ascent, and women are left behind—often in traditional occupations where pay and benefits are low, and where there is little opportunity for advancement.
- Women over forty suffer a one-third-higher unemployment rate than men over forty, and a six-week-longer period of unemployment than younger women.[7]

In addition to age and sex discrimination, two other factors, the caregiver role and need for training, contribute to older women's dropping out of the work force.[8] Middle-aged and older women may need special training to get into, or return to, paid employment, and should be given priority in job-training programs as compensation for unpaid labor in the home and the community.

Another barrier to employment that some of us may have to face if we become disabled in our middle or older years is lack of accessible facilities.

I lost a professorship because I couldn't gain access to the library or even my own office after 6 P.M. weekdays or on weekends. There were services to assist the disabled students, but older disabled faculty went without. We tried to have meetings but we couldn't get older disabled women together because there was no transportation for the disabled! [a forty-one-year-old woman]

Fighting Back

It is very difficult, either as a job applicant or as an employee, to defend oneself against discriminatory practices and attitudes, but speaking up can go a long way. One woman describes a situation in which her lifelong feistiness got her hired.

When I was sixty-three I applied for a job in a hospital. The woman interviewing me asked me how old I was. I said, "I don't think numbers count. Why don't we race

165

around the block, and if I win then you hire me?" [a ninety-one-year-old woman]

When standing up for ourselves doesn't do the trick, we can exercise our legal rights by filing a complaint of discrimination and work with others to organize for effective change. Thanks to affirmative-action programs, which put pressure on institutions to advance women and other minorities, a few of the many women who had been underpaid and underemployed for decades have begun to reap long-delayed rewards.

I got hold of the figures from the American Association of University Professors (AAUP) and found out that after fifteen years I was being paid two-thirds of the very lowest entry-level salary for what was a part-time position in name only. I decided I simply didn't want to put up with this any more and the only way I could think of dealing with it was to say "I am going to retire." At that point there was consternation and "What do you want? We'll give you anything you want." And then I began to get a decent salary, so I stayed on for two more years. But I hope that in another generation women will not wait as long as I did without insisting on being paid for what they are contributing. [a sixty-seven-year-old woman]

Another woman rose to the rank of branch manager and then vice president in the last decade of a long career spent primarily as a teller.

I was doing all the work of an assistant manager without the title and—of course—without the salary. Oh, God, did I argue! And then one year when I came back from vacation I found they had given me a new position, that of Assistant Manager. The former head of the City Division had been a guy who believed that a woman's place was in the home, or if you worked you should be a secretary. When he left, the big boss called me into his office and showed me a note from the personnel department wanting to know why, with the excellent reviews I had and my educational qualifications, hadn't I been promoted? Well, of course I was then, but I was still fuming. [a sixty-six-year-old woman]

If you have reason to believe you have been discriminated against, be careful that you do not speak out *too soon.* "Employees with discrimination complaints often make oral or written complaints which are misconstrued and hurt them later," according to an invaluable booklet published by the Older Women's League. Your first move should be to inform yourself and to gather the evidence. The booklet, *Older Women and Job Discrimination: A Primer,* is a concise, complete, and inexpensive ($1.50

Cathy Cade

resource which takes you step-by-step through the process of discovering, proving, and fighting discrimination. An appendix lists field offices of the Equal Employment Opportunity Commission (EEOC) throughout the U.S.

Despite the Reagan Administration's efforts to disempower the agencies that enforce civil rights, these laws are still on the books. Every woman should be aware that:

- Title VII of the Civil Rights Act of 1964 prohibits discrimination based on race, color, religion, sex, or national origin.
- The Age Discrimination in Employment Act of 1967 (ADEA) prohibited discrimination based on age and protected persons aged forty to sixty-five. In 1978, ADEA was amended to extend its protection to those up to age seventy. As of 1986, with the abolition of mandatory retirement, there is no upper age limit on protection by ADEA.

To file a charge under Title VII or ADEA you must file with either the local EEOC field office or with your state or local Fair Employment Practices Agency. Check with both of these agencies because there may be a time limit starting from the date of the discriminatory act within which you may file your claim. If you have missed the time limit of one agency, you may still be able to file with the other.

Proving either age discrimination or sex discrimination alone can be difficult and the procedures complex; it is even more difficult to prove the *combination* of age and sex discrimination that often keeps older women out of jobs. An employer who has many young women and older men on the job may be able to conceal his prejudice against the *older woman*.[9]

Comparable Worth, or Pay Equity

The majority of middle-aged and older women remain trapped in low-paying, traditionally female jobs which offer little possibility for advancement. Pay equity, or equal pay for work of comparable worth, is a new tool women can use collectively to upgrade pay through collective bargaining or court action. While women and men often perform different jobs, the monetary value of the jobs they do can and should be compared, so that men's work is not automatically seen as more valuable than women's work.

In 1973, the American Federation of State, County and Municipal Employees (AFSCME) in the state of Washington conducted a job-evaluation study, assigning point values to each job based on four components: knowledge and skills, mental demands, accountability, and working conditions. Then those values were compared with the wages paid. The study revealed that overall, when jobs with the same valuation were compared, those held primarily by women were paid about 20 percent lower than those held primarily by men. An example is the comparison between Clerk-Typist and Warehouse Worker I. Both jobs scored 94 points, but the clerk-typist was paid a salary ten grades below that of the warehouse worker.

After that study, The National Committee on Pay Equity was established in Washington, D.C. (see Resources). Since 1973, unions representing state, county, and municipal workers in all but five states have begun some action on comparable worth. At the Women in the Workplace Conference in Boston in 1985, Gloria Wright of AFSCME told the audience, "Most states are ready and ripe to begin comparable pay via their state legislatures."

Some courts have ruled in favor of comparable worth and others have ruled against it. The concept of comparable worth remains highly controversial, challenging as it does the conventionally accepted idea that wages should be governed by the rules of supply and demand. It should encourage us to remember that the union movement survived and flourished even though in the earliest days of union organizing in America, courts ruled against labor organizing, arguing that it interfered with the free market.[10] Pay equity is not something you can achieve for or by yourself, but should be accomplished through women's organizations, unions, or other associations. Labor unions are increasingly active in the fight for comparable worth, incorporating it into their organizing drives and raising it as a demand in bargaining for new contracts. As John J. Sweeney, president of the Service Employees International Union, says, "A woman shouldn't have to work nine days to earn what a man earns in five days."

Comparable worth holds special promise for middle-aged and older women, most of whom work in traditionally female jobs and would thus benefit from back-pay settlements. Comparable worth can also brighten our future as retirees by raising the base on which Social Security and pensions are figured.[11]

Labor Unions

Historically, labor unions have played a significant role in improving working conditions and raising the standard of living for many groups of workers. Regrettably, however, some unions have, over time, developed an "establishment" mentality, catering exclusively to a white male constituency. Today a few progressive unions are moving to reclaim their leadership of the fight for workers' rights by recognizing the significant growth of women in the labor force and trying to meet their needs.

I was the first organizer of women workers for a clothing workers' union in Boston. When I began, in 1955, the entire leadership of the union was male while 90 percent of the workers in the shops were female. The union was like a Banana Republic—women were regarded as unclean, like in some religions, and treated as

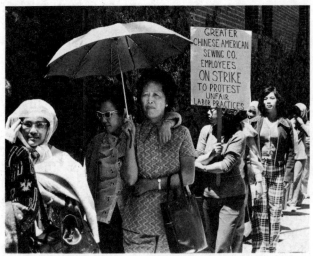

Cathy Cade

inferiors. But, finally, things are changing. Women are still 90 percent of the membership, but in 1985 three of the top fifteen people in the national leadership are women. [a sixty-three-year-old woman]

Women are the majority of workers in clerical and service jobs. Many service jobs are performed by older and minority women working in hospitals, hotels, and universities as part of the housekeeping or dietary departments. Yet only 13.2 percent of working women are members of a union.

Some unions are reaching beyond their traditional constituency to serve previously unorganized workers. For example, some service workers at colleges and universities are now represented by the United Auto Workers. Many unions now provide a "women's rights guidebook," which informs female employees of their rights in any position covered by that union. If you are not represented by a union, and would like to find out more about them, write to the Coalition of Labor Union Women (see Resources). Any inquiry is welcome.

Office workers, 99 percent of whom are women, are an important group of unorganized workers. Office workers have traditionally been cool to unions, but automation is changing the nature of office work, making it more like assembly-line or factory work.[12] In such a situation, being represented by a union becomes more appealing, even essential. In 1982, the first International Conference on Office Work and New Technology was convened by the Working Women Education Fund and 9to5 National Association of Working Women. Leaders in the field provided the latest information on the effects of office automation in such key areas as job loss, retraining, the quality of work life, health and safety, radiation dangers, and collective bargaining.[13] Such organizations lay the groundwork for bringing office workers together, which may lead to unionization.

Entering the World of Paid Work in the Middle or Later Years

Many women have worked for pay throughout their adult lives. For single women, women of color, and working-class women, earning money has been a necessity for survival. For a relatively small number of women, commitment to the world of paid work was an early and personal decision, a hard-won struggle against the forces that would deny women's aspirations.

However, many women enter and leave and reenter the work force at times and for reasons that do not fit into male-defined patterns. Rigid notions of a single career beginning at graduation and ending with retirement are breaking down as a growing number of workers exercise options to change careers, go back to school, or continue to work for pay or begin second careers after retirement.

Many women for whom home and family had been a primary focus redirect their energy toward jobs or careers, finding new work, getting more education, discovering new talents and interests, developing their capabilities. Work shifts to center stage in their lives. Those of us who have worked some twenty to thirty years raising children have managed a variety of challenging situations and have learned adaptability and skills which should give us confidence as we face the next step.

Entering or reentering the work force is a huge challenge. We choose to meet it either because we want a challenge equal to that of raising a family or because we must have employment to make money. But regardless of our individual situations, most of us approach reentry with some secret fears. Do my looks give away my age? Are my skills rusty?

The Displaced Homemaker movement—a phrase which graphically and accurately describes the predicament of those who must, in their middle or older years, support themselves for the first time—grew out of a support group for unemployed older women facing just this kind of dilemma (see Changing Society and Ourselves chapter). Today the Displaced Homemaker Network provides services to women reentering the job market in every state.

Many of us have used or developed our administrative skills in volunteer jobs in the community. Indeed, a volunteer position can sometimes lead to a paid position as you become known in a particular organization and make contacts, especially in nonprofit organizations that have a grant for only a year or two. It is important for women who have never worked for pay that volunteer experience be recognized by prospective employers. The Federal Government already does so. In Massachusetts, a 1986 bill requires employers to include on every application a statement that the applicant may include "any verified work performed on a volunteer basis" as part of her or his work history.

I hadn't worked [for pay] in seventeen years, but I wasn't scared of making the transition. I had done a lot of things in the community, so I felt competent. I went back to work a year after I was separated from my husband. I discovered that the personnel director at a hospital where I volunteered needed some help, so I offered my services and ended up staying nine years. In that situation, being a middle-aged suburban matron was a great plus because the hospital wanted its employees to project the image of being part of the community. So the fact that I lived in the community and was active in civic affairs meant to them that I was extending the hospital into the community.

My boss, a divorced woman who had raised two kids alone, was very sympathetic to my working flextime. If there was a school event, I could go and work on Saturday instead. Later I had a male boss who didn't like the arrangement but he said, "What you do, you do very well. I'd have a hard time getting rid of you." [a woman in her fifties]

I reentered the world of paid work at age fifty-five, having been at home for twenty-seven years. The manager of the Wall Street law firm who hired me was amazed at my capabilities. I told him I had been secretary of innumerable organizations and had therefore kept up my steno and typing. Also, while my husband was alive, we often discussed business matters together, so I was aware of what was happening in the business world. Women are constantly learning, even while at home raising a family. [a woman in her sixties]

Since many of us started working late in life and with fairly low career expectations, middle-aged and older women at all levels in the work force express surprise and pleasure in their accomplishments.

I am a reborn person. Widowed at age fifty-five, I had to fend for myself. Having been a homemaker for thirty-five years, I felt pretty inadequate so I went back to night high school for a refresher course in shorthand and typing. When I graduated, I was encouraged to take a clerical test at a bank. With much trepidation, I did. I passed with flying colors and was hired immediately. That was the start of my rebirth. I became a whole person who was appreciated for my labors and liked by my co-workers. The bank subsidized trips abroad for its employees at a very nominal cost and I visited London, Caracas, and Israel. I'm black and blue from pinching myself when I think that I did these wondrous things. The happiest years of my life ended with my forced retirement at age sixty-five. [a woman in her seventies]

When I was divorced at age thirty-seven I went looking for a teaching post. I could do math and general science but when I applied to the school where I wished to work I became a secretary because that was the only job available and I really wanted to be part of that school's community. Strangely, I had an enormous burst of energy—just full of good feeling—even though I was qualified to be a teacher and all I did was secretarial work. Soon they asked me to do some bookkeeping. Then I was asked if I could teach music so I started in the fall of my second year there inventing my own courses. I studied piano to continue to learn more about harmony and I continued to study as I taught. Later on I became the school treasurer. I knew I had managerial ability—I did my tasks well so that the school was never in the red—because I was using everything I had. [an eighty-year-old woman]

As a first step, if you are entering or reentering the work force, take a look at yourself and your own strengths and skills. Ask people who know you well for their opinions of what you are

Jerry Howard/Positive Images

Mikki Ansin

mornings to practice on the piano but I still went every afternoon. One day the social workers got after me. "You can't hang around here so much. This is an institution. You don't belong in an institution. You've got to get a job." And I thought, What can I do? I graduated from college and got married. I have a degree in music, specializing in public school music education, so I went into the music department of the public schools in the city and I asked the department head very timidly if he could find space for me in the fall. He asked me if I were available immediately and I said yes. The very next day I was teaching in a middle school, grades 6, 7, and 8, in an area of the city noted for its school discipline problems. Nobody told me what the kids knew, what their background was, nothing. But the best part was, I could do anything I wanted to. I had high aspirations for them! The place was bedlam. It was wild. My supervisor came in a couple of times and said, "You're doing very well. Just keep on smiling." I was running to all kinds of libraries getting material. And I prepared more than one lesson plan for each class in case one didn't work. I was terribly busy, but very happy. I had wonderful rapport

good at. The same qualities that serve you well in your personal life may be the very ones that can give you a sense of career direction. What is it that you like about painting a room or knitting a sweater? Think about what has made you feel most proud and successful in the past, and try to identify some common threads in what you achieved. Did you enjoy organizing the church bazaar because it brought people together in a new way, because it made a lot of money, or because it got you into managing money for the first time? All these are valuable clues as to what you might consider as a future direction.

Some employment counselors can help women reentering the work force put together a "skills resumé," which focuses on abilities and accomplishments rather than a chronological listing of paid employment.

I was sixty-one when my husband went into a nursing home. At first I stayed with him there every day until I was convinced that it was not like some of the terrible places we had tried before. Then I began to stay home

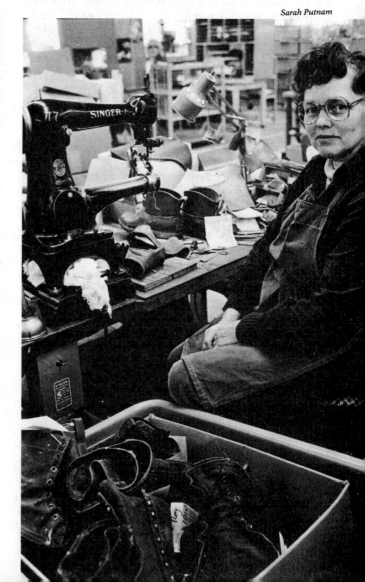

Sarah Putnam

music entirely because I wanted an inducement for preserving order in the classroom. If no time was wasted during the class, then they could play their records the last ten minutes of the period. The Black kids played one kind of rock and the white kids another and they learned to tolerate each other's music. I think the kids felt my vulnerability too and they were sort of protective of me.

I was probably the oldest teacher in the school. I'd be exhausted when I came home from teaching; I'd have to take a nap. And I didn't dare tell any of the younger teachers because they'd say, "Oh, she shouldn't be teaching. She's too old." Then I found out that all the younger teachers did the same thing! I taught on the third floor and I used to take the stairs two at a time to

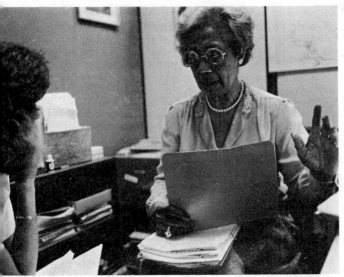

Marianne Gontarz

with the kids. I don't think they knew what hit them! I introduced the kids to opera. They had never heard of opera. They wanted only their own kind of music which was loud rock and roll, and each group liked only a certain kind of rock. I didn't eliminate their kind of

Ellen Shub

show that I could do it, that I had as much strength as the young people. I just had to prove to everybody that I could do it.

When I retired the school gave me a plaque. And I made a little speech. I told the parents that I started teaching there at a time of crisis in my life and that I blessed the kids every day just for being there so that I could infect them with even a little bit of my own enthusiasm for music. [a woman in her seventies]

Education and Retraining

Those of us who pioneered the movement of older women going back to school feared competing with younger, more up-to-date, and ener-

Joan K. Gordon

Norma Holt

Going Back to School—the Decision

by Norma Buchanan

Once the thought of returning to school occurs, the roller-coaster ride of your life begins. As you stand there waiting to enter, the questions and doubts begin to haunt you, "Can I afford to go to school? What will my family and friends think? How can I possibly fit into a classroom of youngsters?" Underlying all of these questions is the most fearful of them all, "At my age, can I possibly learn all that is required?" Your own insecurities and self-doubt begin to overwhelm you.

The best answer to all of these questions is YES YOU CAN—if you are willing to ride the roller coaster: the downward plunge into fear of failure, the bottomless pit of frustration; the soaring joy of success; the plateau of tiredness at the amount of work involved; and most of all, the acceptance of the challenge to grow and develop to your highest point as an individual.

You, the returning student, can be your own best friend or your own worst enemy. Don't be afraid to admit that you don't know the answer—seek out those who have been there already, ask for help. After all, you are not alone. Most universities and colleges are staffed with professionals eager and willing to help you through this roller-coaster ride of academia. Fellow students, both younger and older, can be a source of help and insight into this adventure. But most of all, give yourself credit for what you have accomplished and for what you are attempting. After all, you have survived childhood, adulthood, and in some cases marriage and/or employment outside the home—you bring to the academic world a wealth of understanding and knowledge that younger students cannot possibly have. You have the advantage of the experiences of life, organizational skills, and the discipline of reality on your side. The ride is not smooth or calm, but the highs far outweigh the lows.

getic students. By now, however, continuing education for women has changed the face of many college campuses. We are not as likely to be the only older woman in sight. Many college professors have commented on the determination and commitment of older women students, and on their ability to get good grades and complete demanding programs while still managing family responsibilities.

The statement in the box was sent to us by a forty-year-old woman who returned to school after dropping out at fourteen. Embarrassed to resume her education at the same level as her junior high school–aged son, she was advised to take a high school equivalency test, which she passed easily. Armed with her barely dry diploma, she conferred with advisers at the women's center of a nearby college and enrolled in a five-year master's degree program.

Obstacles are nothing new to Norma, who suffers from a degenerative spine disease. Together with others she spearheaded a campaign to make the campus and its buildings more accessible to students with disabilities. As a student, Norma had to advocate for herself to make special arrangements for exams, since she has a learning disability.

Because education is often proposed as a kind of "therapy," too many women, after completing an educational program, find themselves still unprepared for the job market. Education is not a luxury but a necessity. Remember that a woman needs a college degree in order to earn as much as a man with a high school diploma. According to sociologist Ruth Jacobs, women reentering the job market are often directed toward fields in which the wage is too low to support a household.[14] Some career counselors assume that older women are studying for personal growth only and do not really need a decent income.

When employment for pay is an important goal, be sure to inquire about the placement record of the school or department you are considering—with older women in particular. Talk to some recent graduates. Always compare the degree or diploma you will receive with the credentials of those working in the field. Sometimes alternative routes to a degree will not put you in the most competitive position. For example, if most social workers have an M.S.W. degree, will you be able to get the job you want with only a bachelor's degree in social work? If most college teachers hold a Ph.D., will you get a job with an Ed.D.? Also, check the market for the kind of work you plan to do. Government publications available from the Women's Bureau and the Bureau of Labor Statistics tell you about the availability of types of jobs by geographic area.

If you must start earning as soon as possible, consider a short training program, as this woman did:

I am writing to assure women of middle age or beyond that it is not too late to attend school and begin a career, or to switch careers.

All my life I had wanted to be a nurse, but instead was a secretary. Finally, at age fifty-seven, when the youngest of our children graduated from college, I took a year off from the workaday world to attend school and become a licensed practical nurse.

I made the highest grade in our class on the state board exam. I am not telling this to be boastful but to encourage others who might think they are too old to learn.

Seven years later, at age sixty-five, I am happily employed as an LPN—my lifelong dream.[15]

Many women who aspire to fulfillment and self-actualization through work are more willing to risk a longer period of schooling or a less certain future employment picture than are women who have an immediate need for in-

come. It helps if we have money saved or a supportive partner or family to help us.

I went back to school when I was forty-six; I had ten credits to my name, but I was determined to find a way to do something I liked. My partner was earning a good salary and was willing to help me to go to school. I had four splendid years, and when I graduated I got a job as a group worker with older people in a small agency. Later I began work on my master's degree in an evening program which took five years. It was great because I was able to pick my own courses. I majored in Women's Studies and when I finished I was invited to teach a course at the college. It was very exciting for me. [a sixty-five-year-old woman]

I wanted to be an artist when I was growing up but my father felt that wasn't a realistic aspiration for a Puerto Rican girl, so I became a social worker. I got my motivation for an education from my father but I had to delay my dream. Now my husband is doing very well in his business and the children are old enough that they are not a problem, so I feel now is the time for me to study art. Because I'm forty-three and not sixteen or eighteen, I feel this pressure to catch up...I don't know whether I will really become an artist or whether I will go back to social work, but right now I am going to art school full time and working very hard at it. It is the first time in my marriage that I haven't earned money, but my husband insisted we can afford it and he really encouraged me to go ahead.

In my fifties I earned an Ed.D. in Sociology, but I found out you need more than the degree to get an academic appointment. You need publications. I wasn't earning enough teaching part time at a state university, and I had no insurance or benefits, so I took a secretarial job where the pay is decent and the benefits are good. I can't get into the pension plan because I'm too old; nevertheless, I had to take a regular-paying job with benefits for my economic well-being. But it was painful after working so long and hard to give up the dream of an intellectually stimulating job. [a sixty-one-year-old woman]

I reached the point after nine years in personnel that I had no place to advance and the job had become too predictable. I found that about half my time was spent being somebody's listening ear or shoulder to cry on, and that was the part of my job that I got the most gratification from; so I decided to go off and do a social-work internship. But when I graduated, social-work jobs were hard to come by. After a long period of unemployment, during which I struggled with fears that I was not being hired because of my age, I finally got a job as an administrative assistant with a human-services agency. While it's not doing social work as I had planned, it pays more than anything I've seen of-

fered in social work recently, which is a sad commentary. What really lifted my morale is that they called the personnel director where I had been employed part time for a reference and she told them, "You'd better grab her while you have the chance because we would grab her if there were any way we could afford her and if we could make the job challenging enough for her." So I found out that I was not being rejected because of my age, and that at least two people thought I was not too old to be hired. [a fifty-nine-year-old woman]

Career Change

Those of us who have been in the work force fairly continuously may also want a change in our middle or later years. We may need to earn more money; we may be feeling "stuck" with no opportunity to advance; we may lose a job that we had thought was secure. We may have saved enough money to realize a long-delayed dream of more education or a more satisfying career. Or we may simply want a new challenge.

Here are two successful career-change experiences:

I had become an administrator and a large part of my job was juggling patient-care demands within the boundaries of a very rigid budget and insufficient nursing staff. I began to feel that I was contributing to the exploitation of the nurses. And so even though it was a "good job," it got to the point where it wasn't satisfying any more.

I sort of eased into studying gerontology, not really knowing that that was where I was going, because I had always had such a good time with my grandmother and I realized I wanted to work with healthy older people. I thought, "I'm getting older and maybe if I get in there and make some positive changes, then things would be generally better for older people and I'd benefit too." [a forty-five-year-old woman]

When the college folded, I lost a tenured teaching job as an assistant professor of art, and I needed to find something else to do to earn money. I decided that I wanted to explore the business world to see what my dollar value was and to save money so that I could later take some years off and paint full time. My artist friends said, "You can't do that. You won't be able to give up the money. You'll never be an artist again, and the work will change you, warping your artist's perspective."

I did it anyway, and was very successful. I made a really good salary for a couple of years managing (and later directing) a design department for a manufacturer, which entailed supervising people, traveling, and coordinating. The job was not valuable to me as an artist, but it did give me confidence and self-esteem as well as value in the eyes of others, which I greatly needed.

I left that job, having saved some money to travel and live abroad for a while, and to paint. When I left there, people were surprised, telling me I made a mistake in walking out on a career. I have learned that I am no longer in need of approval from others, nor am I identified with what I do; but rather, I am happy with who I am. My twenty-two-year-old daughter is very proud of me. I give her a role model of a woman who can take responsibility for her life. [a forty-six-year-old woman]

While there is nothing inherently wrong with staying in a job situation which offers little, it does waste a great deal of time and energy and deprives you of the possible satisfactions which come from meaningful and interesting work. If you are beginning to feel that you would like to move out into something new, but aren't sure what it is, take time to explore your options before resigning from a secure position. You don't have to settle for an unchallenging situation without making an effort to take stock and move in a new direction, but it is wise, particularly if you are over fifty-five, to assess what is available before burning your bridges.

Even women who have been in the work force continuously and with some degree of success find their opportunities narrowing in their fifties and sixties, especially if they want to change jobs. This is particularly true in fields like human services, where Federal cuts in programs have reduced opportunities for advancement. Some of these women are willing to begin again at a lower-level job, but employers are reluctant to hire them, saying that the job would be "demeaning" for them, that they would feel as if they were supervising their mother, and so on. All are variants of that great no-win dilemma, "overqualified."

Take a hard look at the job you have now. Even if you don't like it very much, there are aspects of it which are keeping you there. Perhaps you like the people you work with, the fact that you can leave it all behind at five o'clock, or the satisfaction of producing a few finished products every day. Think about what you would miss if you left that job, and how it would affect you. What would change in your life if you were working somewhere else instead? On the other hand, what would you be glad to leave behind? A thorough analysis of your likes and dislikes should help you decide what would and would not work for you in a new situation.

Next, start investigating the alternatives. Perhaps simply a change of setting rather than occupation would accomplish what you want. If you're working as a nurse in an inconvenient location miles from home, with a shifting schedule, you may be able to take the edge off your dissatisfaction merely by moving to another kind of institution, or one in another part of town.

For most women, further exploration will be needed. The technique of "informational interviewing" has become commonplace in the last fifteen years. Ask anyone whose work you are interested in whether they would be willing to talk with you to tell you about what they do, how they got into the field, and why.

In considering options, remember that you don't have to make drastic changes. Try the modest and attainable first. Don't push yourself toward inappropriate or unrealistic goals, but don't avoid an unorthodox path solely because of your age.

A few women have moved into blue-collar jobs.[16] Women in such jobs still face enormous prejudice, not only from employers but from their fellow workers. Yet women who have been able to break into such jobs have enjoyed the physical freedom from sitting at a desk and have dramatically increased their earning power.

Some women who are dissatisfied with their jobs have decided to stay put and concentrate on trying to make the job more rewarding.

I'm a little bored at work because I feel that I'm not working at the right level, but I would not leave unless someone tapped me on the shoulder and offered me a job, because the last time I made a change (from a university job back to industry) it took me nine months. Instead I am focusing on making some changes in my present job so that I can move up. [a fifty-five-year-old woman]

For women who want to advance within their present organization, a support system can be enormously helpful. Find at least one supportive person to help you feel less isolated. Start a "women and work" group in your community. Check out networks of women who work in your field.

We spoke with many women who felt stymied in their growth and creativity but were reluctant to risk accumulated benefits and pensions. For women at or near their sixties, this is a particularly prevalent problem. Some women who enjoyed part-time or freelance work in their younger years now want the security of a full-time salary and benefits. Some women want the daily structure and companionship of colleagues in the same office, rather than just occasional support and feedback.

Many companies are reluctant to hire someone whose experience requires a high salary and who will soon be of age to collect a pension. Some companies try to get older employees to retire early so they can replace them with younger workers at lower salaries. If you have always yearned to take time off—a sabbatical year to write, for example—do it as early as you can and have a plan for getting back into the work force.

If you are just a few years from retirement you may prefer not to "rock the boat" but instead to put your energy into exploring community activities and hobbies that may develop into satisfying retirement pursuits. We interviewed one woman in her sixties who turned a part-time avocation into a business, leading to a more satisfying work life after retirement than before it!

Starting a business of one's own may be a good option for older women whose accomplishments are less likely to be recognized in the conventional workplace. It can be an advantage to create one's own structure rather than trying to fit into someone else's. Yet this can be a particularly strenuous option. Consider carefully whether you have the health and energy to put in lots of extra hours, and the self-esteem to cope with the risk of failure.[17] Some women enjoy the convenience and economy of running a business out of their home, but may begin to feel isolated. For these women, networks of home-based entrepreneurs have been helpful in providing emotional support and exchanges of practical information.

Getting Help

Recently, some career-counseling agencies have come under fire for charging excessively high fees and/or not delivering on promised services. Unlike employment agencies, which arrange interviews with prospective employers, career counselors offer only counseling and support while the applicant pursues the job search on her own. It can be immensely helpful to talk with an experienced, objective outsider on a regular basis, but consider carefully: Are you unemployed or working in a low-paying job and not in a position to pay large fees? How will you feel if counseling does not lead to a better job? Frequently, the value of counseling is overstated and made to seem essential to the process of change. Can you go through the same decision-making process on your own, or by talking with friends and colleagues? Job seekers are advised to check a counseling firm's reputation with the Better Business Bureau.

Furthermore, many of the services offered by career-counseling firms are available free in the community. Books about job seeking and resumé writing are available in public libraries, as are reference books that list facts about corporations and names of personnel directors. You can take occupational-aptitude tests at colleges and other community centers and organizations.[18]

Talking with friends and acquaintances, especially those who have good jobs, can help you find what you are looking for. Don't let pride stand in the way of letting people know you are looking for a job. A good contact alone probably will not get you a job, but a recommendation can get your resumé noticed.

RETIREMENT

Resisting Retirement

As of 1986, new Federal legislation makes it illegal to force anyone to retire because of age.* Abolition of mandatory retirement provides us with the opportunity to make our own choices about whether or when to retire. Yet, given the weight of custom and ingrained prejudice against older workers, those of us who want to remain employed well into our later years had better be prepared to fight for our newly won right.

Mandatory retirement policies and laws were based on the ageist assumption that our abilities decline with age. In fact, most abilities stay the same or improve; only those involving speed or great physical strength or dexterity tend to

*In 1979, the official retirement age in Federal and privately run organizations and industries was raised to seventy. In 1986, new legislation made it illegal in the United States to force anyone out of work because of age.

decline. Older workers are contributing important skills in many organizations.

When we spoke earlier about a person's psychological need to find fulfillment through work, we did not say that this need ended at sixty-five or seventy or any other age. Many older people feel oppressed by the forced inactivity of retirement and enjoy the mental and social stimulation of working. Furthermore, few women have earned enough or accumulated enough pension credits to feel assured of an adequate retirement income. Some of us want to continue working full time or part time,[19] whether for activity or income or both.

Retirement is scary. I was getting to the age when people expect you to retire and [was] getting a lot of messages that younger workers were more valuable. It was not easy to cope with. Leaving was traumatic, but I was delighted once I got out. I would have left sooner had I realized how well my free-lance work would go. I left with a decent pension, but only half what men in my position would get, because I had been paid less all those years. It makes me mad! When I asked for raises, my boss would say, "But you have no family." It is scary to retire, and I wanted to get all the benefits I could get. [a sixty-six-year-old woman]

The word "retirement" has a final sound to it, as if it were the last and only option. This need not be the case. The Polaroid Company and the Travelers Insurance Company are pioneering programs of "retirement rehearsal," which offer the chance to try out retirement for a specified period of time while continuing to have the option of returning to work. You may want to suggest such a plan to your employer, or to work with advocacy organizations such as the Gray Panthers and the Older Women's League to promote such plans.

Other companies have begun to offer the option of part-time work to their retirees who wish to return. For the company this provides a pool of experienced workers on an as-needed basis, while for the retiree it provides an opportunity to continue contact with former co-workers and earn a partial income, meanwhile enjoying a less structured life and more freedom for recreation. However, this arrangement often does not include benefits, so be certain of what you are getting if you are asked to participate in such a plan.

Some of us who want to continue working face pressures from employers to cut back to part-time work or to retire simply because of age.

They encouraged me to retire and work part time running one of the elder programs I introduced, but part time means no benefits and half salary. Then they treat you like a flunky instead of a professional. They've just introduced an early-retirement benefit for workers who retire within the next three years and I plan to go for it even though it's not early for me. With that additional benefit I'll have a decent retirement income. [a seventy-eight-year-old woman]

Eight years ago I was forced under protest to retire because the state office I worked for said I was too old and too disabled to work anymore. Since then I have served three terms in the Silver-Haired Legislature,* and attended the White House Conference on Aging. I teach two classes a week at a community college, serve on two committees for a transportation system for the elderly and disabled, and work five afternoons at the Department of Elder Affairs. But I am too old to work!!! [a seventy-six-year-old woman]

We have good reason to fight against the forced inactivity of retirement. A recent study of 229 older members of a health-maintenance organization found that of those whose inductive reasoning and spatial orientation skills had declined since 1970, about 40 percent were able to recoup the losses after only five one-hour training sessions. The researchers recommend that older people "flex their mental as well as physical muscles for better health" and offer suggestions such as working crossword puzzles or playing word games to improve inductive reasoning, and doing woodworking, assembling objects, reading maps, or doing needlework to improve spatial orientation. Especially if you are no longer working at a job, it is important to have hobbies and activities that are mentally stimulating. Most important is to do something you really like and are interested in.[20]

Choosing Retirement

On the other hand, some of us *want* to retire. We may want more time to be with family and friends, or simply to enjoy freedom from the demands of a nine-to-five job.

---

*The Silver-Haired Legislature is a grass-roots nonpartisan body composed of elder citizens, elected at Councils on Aging by their peers (see General Resources).

The Tower

She struggled
heart pounding
inched up the tower
tested each rung
gay voices higher
mocked fear.

Halfway up,
a rung missing,
she froze.
Then—
    "Why am I climbing
      this tower?"

She danced down.

      Lois Harris

When the chairperson of my department asked me to reconsider and stay on, to my surprise I found myself saying, "I'm tired." The more I did, the more things would open up for me to do. I felt I was giving a lot more than I was getting paid for. Part-time jobs tend to be exploitive, and I felt that over the years I had been taken advantage of. [a sixty-seven-year-old woman]

One trivial reason I retired was that my work hours were changed. All of a sudden I had to be at work at 8:00 in the morning and I found that waking up a half hour earlier was a great burden. So today, eleven years later, I awaken in the morning and look at the ceiling and say I don't have to get up—and I get up! [a seventy-six-year-old woman]

My poor husband had this terrible back operation. I worked right through the whole time and then I thought, "We have to spend more time together. We have a place in Vermont which is a sheer delight, and our grandchildren live there. I want to see more of them, to really know them. We have a son in California. When do I get to see him?" [a sixty-seven-year-old woman]

I haven't regretted retiring. I didn't quit my job through any dissatisfaction with the job or the people, but I just felt that my life needed a change. I noticed that after working an eight-hour day I didn't have much steam left for social life and fun. It's been pleasant spending these years doing what I want to do because I spent so many years accommodating myself to other people's needs and plans. [a woman in her seventies]

When I retired and walked out of that place for the last time I felt so relaxed, so free. It took me about a year to finally believe I didn't have to hide. I had been so afraid that the people I worked for and those who worked for me might guess my secret. No matter where my lover and I went as a couple we held back. Only lately, now that she is sixty-two and I am retired, did we go to a

Ellen Shub

Marianne Gontarz

party where we knew there were others like us and we danced together for the first time publicly. I don't flaunt it anyway, so I never had any problems, but now I feel much better not having to worry about being found out. [a woman in her sixties]

After Retirement

Those of us who find a feeling of self-worth in work may be willing to retire if we can find an alternative way to make a meaningful contribution to society.

I had to begin a whole new life! I tried several different things. I worked for a U.S. Senator, not for money. I never worked for money after I retired, because I didn't need to earn money. But I could not live without work. I cannot live my life without a purpose, a humanitarian purpose. [a seventy-five-year-old woman]

I resented having to retire. Reorganization forced me out. For two years I did not know where to turn. I did small jobs; my years as an information and referral director had given me many contacts. As I got involved in community action—hearings on the Hill (i.e., Congress), work on many D.C. committees (Ambulatory Care, Nursing Homes, Health Advocacy), and national and local work with the Gray Panthers—I find myself almost busier than I was when I worked. I manage to keep time to spare for my great-grandsons; one is six months, the other is two. [an eighty-two-year-old woman]

After I retired at age sixty-nine, I tried to sign up for some classes I thought might be interesting. To my dismay I discovered they were all evening classes. The only daytime choice that interested me at all was a beginners' class in oil painting. I decided to sign up although I was sure I couldn't draw a straight line. My first attempt was a still life of a fruit basket flanked by colorful

straw-bottomed bottles of wine. Surprisingly, the fruit turned out lifelike and the whole painting was in good perspective, although very crude. I have now progressed to beautiful portraits with excellent likenesses. [a woman in her seventies]

All I could do when I worked was work. I always wanted to be involved in the community. Now that I am retired, I belong to a senior advocacy group, I work with kids in school, I live in subsidized housing that has a wonderful mixture of people of different ages, different races, various disabilities. I am one of their representatives on the neighborhood development association which is building more houses for sale and more rental apartments for low- and middle-income people. I also get paid for role-playing with students at a local college of optometry to help them learn to relate better with patients. My daughter asks me why I am so busy and I tell her that I am spending my time the way I want to. [a seventy-one-year-old woman]

Deborah Kahn

I do as I please with more freedom than when I was younger; I can decide how to occupy my time and what people I want to know. Sometimes I feel like a street-smart kid. I plan to continue to work on my memoirs, a book that is one-third completed. My book of poems is in the process of its second edition. My plans for more poetry are as varied as the issues that move me. [a ninety-one-year-old woman]

Retirement gives a growing number of older women the opportunity to pursue higher education through enrollment on campus or in a short-term adult education or Elderhostel program (see Resources). The large number of older people, mostly women, who go back to college testifies to their desire to remain mentally sharp. Evidence shows that older persons do just as well or better academically than their younger peers. Short-term memory may recede, but judgment is enhanced. "Use it or lose it" applies to both our bodies and our minds.

Volunteer Opportunities

Good volunteer opportunities are available in hospitals, schools, libraries, art museums, and numerous nonprofit organizations.

Before going to bed I plan my next day. The priority things I do first; then if I have time I do the rest. I find keeping busy keeps you alert and young. I belong to several organizations and always offer my services, such as being a corresponding secretary, getting ads for the calendar, helping arrange programs, etc. I have many friends who can rely on me for a ride to the doctor or shopping or just company. I taught remedial reading for several years and worked as a volunteer in the hospital. I'm enjoying my retirement. My grandson said to me he can't wait until he is a senior citizen so he can have as much fun as I do. [a seventy-eight-year-old woman]

Volunteer programs for older Americans, such as Elder Service Corps, Foster Grandparents, RSVP, and Vista are open to all women and men sixty and over who meet Government standards for low income (25 percent above the poverty line) and who wish to work with elders or children. Call your state house or city hall to find out which agency or department administers volunteer programs for elders. Most of these programs pay stipends, offering about $160 per month plus transportation and lunches. If you receive Supplemental Security Income (SSI) or a housing subsidy, such programs may be more advantageous for you than a minimum-wage

Marianne Gontarz

job, since they are not counted as income and thus will not affect your eligibility for such assistance.

If you are interested in part-time employment in human services, various senior aide and older worker programs under the Title V Older Americans Act provide jobs for workers who are fifty-five and older for twenty hours per week, paying at least minimum wage.

I don't worry. If I have no money, I'll go on welfare. I worked until I was sixty-nine at everything from factory work to the office at the shipyard. When I retired I stayed home and brooded. After I was home nearly a year I found the foster-grandparent program. It's been great. It's made a new life for me. [a seventy-two-year-old woman]

There is definitely a changing attitude toward older people. When I became director of the foster-grandparent program in 1976 I had to convince the directors of a day-care center that a foster grandparent could help the children. Now I have so many centers waiting for foster grandparents that I can't fill all the requests. The day-care teachers tell me that the mixing of the young and old creates a magic atmosphere, something they had never dreamed of. Now the foster grandparents also work (volunteer) in public schools, hospitals, and battered women's shelters. Everybody wants them. [a sixty-five-year-old woman]

The work I do now as a volunteer is very important. I feel that each of the three organizations I work for is important in a different way. One group does education, another does direct-action political work, and the third works for passing legislation. In each of these organizations work is saved for me, so I know that they rely on me for specific tasks. They used to have lots of women whose children were off at school, but now women are in paid jobs and so I am an important volunteer. [a ninety-year-old woman]

Work and retirement are two areas where we must expand choices for women of all ages. We must fight sex, age, and other types of discrimination and join together in women's organizations, labor unions, elder and other advocacy organizations to fight the gender gap in earnings and to enforce our right to decide when and whether we want to retire. We want retirement to mean that we have chosen to leave paid work for something else, and not survival on a pittance because we are no longer welcome at work. To accomplish all this we must keep informed and connected with movements for equal rights in the workplace. See Resources for names of organizations and publications that can help you fight for your rights and keep in touch with the struggle around the world.*

NOTES

1. Grace Baruch and Rosalind Barnett, *Lifeprints: New Patterns of Love and Work.* New York: McGraw-Hill, 1983.

2. Lillian B. Rubin, *Women of a Certain Age.* New York: Harper & Row, 1979.

3. David Karp, "Gender, Academic Careers, and the Social Psychology of Aging." *Qualitative Sociology,* Vol. 8, No. 1, Spring 1985, pp. 9–28.

4. Betty Woody, *Uncertainty and Risk of Low Income Black Working Women: Project Summary.* Wellesley College Center for Research on Women, Wellesley Massachusetts, December 1983.

5. Marilyn R. Block, et al., *Uncharted Territory: Issues and Concerns of Women over Forty.* College Park, MD: University of Maryland Center on Aging, 1978.

*Increasingly, as corporations become multinational, we need a global perspective to understand trends in work, employment practices, and unemployment. See Vilunya Diskin, "Developing an International Awareness," in Boston Women's Health Book Collective, *The New Our Bodies Ourselves.* New York, Simon and Schuster, 1984, pp. 611 ff.

6. Testimony of the Older Women's League (OWL) on "Older Women and the Labor Force" before the Joint Economic Committee, June 6, 1984.

7. *Vanished Dreams: Age Discrimination and the Older Woman Worker.* A 1980 report of 9to5 National Association of Working Women.

8. OWL testimony, June 6, 1984.

9. Ibid.

10. Eleanor Flexner, *Century of Struggle.* New York: Atheneum, 1973.

11. Francine K. Weiss, "Pay Equity Is Older Woman's Issue." *OWL Observer,* August-September 1985.

12. "Women Clericals Suffer Most When Offices Automate," in *Issues for Clerical Workers: Health and Safety.* District 925, Service Employees International Union, AFL-CIO, 2020 K St., NW, Washington, D.C. 20006.

13. *Office Automation: Jekyll or Hyde? Highlights of the First International Conference on Office Work and New Technology, 1982.* Cleveland, OH: 9 to 5 National Association of Working Women.

14. Ruth H. Jacobs, *Out of the Home to Where? Practical Advice for Counselors of Displaced Homemakers.* Working Paper No. 77, Wellesley College Center for Research on Women, Wellesley, MA 02181.

15. Paula Brown Doress et al., "Women Growing Older," in Boston Women's Health Book Collective, *The New Our Bodies, Ourselves.* New York: Simon and Schuster, 1984, p. 439.

16. Carroll Wetzel Wilkinson, "Work: Challengers to Occupational Segregation," in Mary McFeely, ed., *The Woman's Annual,* No. 5, Boston: G. K. Hall, 1985, pp. 149–67.

17. Mary D. Fillmore, *Women MBA's: A Foot in the Door.* Boston: G. K. Hall, 1987, p. 177.

18. Elizabeth M. Fowler, "Counseling Stirs Some Charges." *The New York Times,* August 6, 1985.

19. Hilda Kahne, *Reconceiving Part-Time Work: New Perspectives for Older Workers and Women.* Totowa, New Jersey: Rowman & Allanheld, 1985.

20. Sherry Willis and K. Warner Schaie, "Can Decline in Adult Intellectual Functioning Be Reversed?" *Developmental Psychology,* Vol. 22, No. 2, 1986, pp. 223–32.

14

MONEY MATTERS: THE ECONOMICS OF AGING FOR WOMEN

by Gillie Beram and Caroline T. Chauncey

Special thanks to Marilyn Rogers and Naomi B. Isler

The middle and older years are a time of many changes in our lives, some of which will be reflected in our financial situation. Some of us may have more money on hand as children leave home and household expenses diminish. Advancement in our work may bring us new resources to manage and to enjoy. Or we may receive an inheritance or insurance settlement and want to learn how best to manage it for our future security. For far too many of us, however, an illness—ours or our partner's—can create overwhelming medical bills; divorce, widowhood, or employment discrimination may leave us vulnerable financially. We may need to apply for public assistance for the first time. Whatever happens, we may find ourselves facing more complex financial decisions.

THE ROOTS OF POVERTY AND DOWNWARD MOBILITY

Economic discrimination based on sex and race affects us, as women, throughout our lives. As we get older, age discrimination compounds and deepens the inequality of resources. The poorest groups in the United States are older women over sixty-five living by themselves and women raising children alone. These two groups make up 70 percent of all poor people.[1] Consider these facts:

- 15.6 PERCENT OF OLDER WOMEN ARE POOR COMPARED TO 8.5 PERCENT OF OLDER MEN
- 26.8 PERCENT OF ALL OLDER WOMEN WHO LIVE ALONE ARE POOR
- 34.8 PERCENT OF OLDER BLACK WOMEN ARE POOR[2]
- 73 PERCENT OF BLACK WOMEN OVER EIGHTY-FIVE LIVING ALONE ARE POOR[3]

We who are in our forties and older are caught in the dilemma of meeting contradictory social expectations. Growing numbers of us need to support ourselves, to provide for children or dependent relatives, and to take responsibility for our own financial futures. Yet employers still perceive women as dependents of men. Because of low earnings and the pressure to interrupt paid jobs to care for families, women face a tremendous risk of poverty—especially when we do not accept or have access to financial support from men.

My situation has really changed. I was married to a professional in a high-paying field, but I worked with low-income people. It was as if I had one life by day and another by night. Now that we are separated, I'm poorer than I've ever been—more like the people I used to work with. [a woman in her forties with children still at home]

The risk of poverty for independent women is nothing new; what is new today is the rapid growth in the number of women who fall prey to this poverty.

- 47 PERCENT OF ALL POOR FAMILIES ARE HEADED BY WOMEN
- 46 PERCENT OF POOR HISPANIC FAMILIES ARE HEADED BY WOMEN
- 72 PERCENT OF POOR BLACK FAMILIES ARE HEADED BY WOMEN[4]

At midlife, many women experience a sudden loss of income, often precipitated by divorce or the death or disability of a partner. Women who have never worked outside the home may suddenly find themselves with no income and little or no experience to aid them in earning a living.

I have no home, no job, poor health, and no health insurance. I married at eighteen and spent thirty years raising six children. I graduated first in my class in high school and wanted to go to college, but I didn't have the money. My husband threatened to throw me down the stairs, and he hit me twice. There were no transition houses in those days, and when things were really bad I ran out in the woods and slept in the leaves. Today I realize that by staying I harmed my children. I shouldn't have tried to keep us together for financial reasons. It's incredible that I lived through it. [a woman in her fifties]

For a woman who performs unpaid work in the home, there are no benefits such as disability insurance, unemployment compensation, pension plans, or health coverage. Her financial security is tied to her husband's earnings.

When a marriage is dissolved, the woman who has been a housewife is like any other displaced worker—she needs a new source of income and new skills. But there are few sources of support to help her make this transition. Few widows can reinstate lapsed medical insurance, and those below the age of sixty cannot draw Social Security benefits. Only a small percentage of divorced women ever receive alimony or child-support payments. One study found that only 15 percent of divorced wives were awarded alimony, and of these, fewer than half received payment. Though about half the number of divorced mothers are granted child support by the courts, again, fewer than half of those receive their payments regularly.[5] Fathers must be forced to meet their child-support responsibilities; we hope that new laws will be applied to affluent and middle-income fathers, not just to families applying for welfare.

Changes in divorce laws have dramatically affected many older women. As Ellen Goodman observes, "Courts have treated husbands and wives, fathers and mothers...with an evenhandedness that is, in effect, unfair. Property has been divided both equally and inequitably."[6] For women who have devoted themselves to family and homemaking, who have put husbands through school, and whose own employment experience is either limited or paid at a much lower level, an equal division of assets is unfair. This is especially true when children are still at home or in school. And many women get even less than half the assets.

The overwhelming majority of states now permit "no-fault divorce," divorce which is granted without the necessity of finding that a spouse has been guilty of some marital misconduct. The most common no-fault ground is voluntary separation for a period of time. Prior to the enactment of no-fault divorce statutes, there had to be a specified fault, a wholly innocent plaintiff spouse, and a wholly guilty defendant spouse.[7]

No-fault divorce has made it easier to get a divorce, but it has reduced women's bargaining power toward winning a fair settlement. States vary, however, in the factors they take into account in determining alimony and assets settlements. In many states such factors as length of marriage, health of the parties, and ability to earn income and acquire assets in the future may be considered. In a very few states, conduct of the parties may be considered for purposes of the settlement, though not in granting the divorce. All states have laws concerning support of minor children.

One of the consequences of the spread of no-fault divorce has been a rapid rise in the number of lengthy marriages (fifteen years or more) that have dissolved.

Suddenly my (I thought so good) husband said, "You don't deserve this—I couldn't have a better wife, or a better mother on this earth, and certainly wouldn't be where I am without you—but I have to leave and think." I truly was my husband's buddy and helper. How I wish I could talk to the people who passed the [no-fault divorce] bill. Please forgive me for sounding bitter, but I got the bills today and where are the dollars for me to pay them? I do not deserve this kind of life, as hard as I worked. [an Indiana woman][8]

Divorce "reform" has been a financial disaster for women—especially older women—and for children. According to Lenore Weitzman's new study, the standard of living for a divorced women and her children declines by 73 percent in the first year after divorce, while her former husband's rises by 42 percent.[9]

New approaches are needed to strengthen women's chances of gaining an equitable settlement in divorce proceedings. The following factors should be taken into account. Many middle-aged and older women have not worked outside the home consistently enough to qualify for a job that pays enough to live on. Alimony should not be seen as a stopgap measure, since the gap between work in the home and paid work may be a difficult one to cross in the middle and later years. Spousal support (alimony) in such instances should be approached as compensation for past unpaid work in the home and for the cost of having dedicated oneself to a husband's career. Recent court decisions awarding a share of husbands' future earnings to wives who put them through school suggest a growing awareness on the part of the courts of women's contribution to husbands' earning capacity. Certainly midlife and older women should benefit from this trend. A substantial cash settlement instead of, or in addition to, monthly payments can protect women against the common practice of nonpayment and will provide funds for the divorced woman to manage and invest. Finally, the husband's pension—a product of his earning capacity—reflects our investment in his career, and so represents an asset that we have a legal right to share or to use as a bargaining chip in negotiations.

Some husbands, especially those who are self-employed, will intentionally limit, defer, or even deliberately misstate their income in order to appear less affluent during the divorce negotiations. Frequently, in the years following the divorce, a former husband's income may sharply increase, but his former wife, during the divorce negotiations may have bargained away her right to an increase in alimony. Even if she did not do so, it will require tremendous effort on her part and significant lawyers' fees to try to modify her divorce judgment in order to increase the alimony or child support to share in her ex-husband's increased income. Sometimes the high cost of getting a fair settlement forces women to drop their legitimate demands.

My husband is self-employed and has always had total control of the flow of income from the business, even though it was jointly owned by both of us. He has been consistently secretive about the amount and location of funds and property. In the settlement, my husband got the business and I got the house. My husband offered $10 per week in support to the child who is under eighteen and it cost me $10,000 in legal fees to get him to agree to $40 per week. The judge looked at me as if I were nuts to agree to so little, but I had to get it over with because the cost of the divorce process had gotten out of hand. [A fifty-two-year-old woman]

You have a right to sue for failure to pay court-ordered alimony or make child-support payments. You can also sometimes reopen divorce-settlement cases because of changed circumstances, though this can be very expensive and time-consuming. Check with your attorney or a Legal Aid office. (See Resources for helpful books on divorce.)

The Economics of Retirement

Traditional wisdom has it that sound retirement finances are like a stool with three legs. The three legs of the retirement stool are assets (such as savings or a house), pension payments, and Social Security benefits. However, because of economic discrimination, all three legs of the stool are rickety for older women.

Assets are the most obviously wobbly leg. Since women earn less than men, it's no surprise that we have little chance to accumulate savings. According to a 1981 survey, only one-third the number of people over sixty-five received any income from savings accounts, and less than one quarter had any investment income at all.[10] For many of us, our sole asset is our house. Not only is it difficult to cash in this asset but it costs money to keep it up. Reverse mortgages are one way for women to get out of this financial bind, but there are pitfalls in this arrangement (see Housing Alternatives chapter).

Women who are widowed are no better off economically than divorced or never-married women. One fourth the number of all widows have gone through the insurance benefits left by their husbands within two months; more than half have nothing left after eighteen months. Often the cost of a husband's final illness, or his funeral costs, will use up the money that a widowed woman expected to live on. Yet widows go on to live an average of eighteen and one-half years after their husbands' deaths.[11]

In 1984, only 20 percent of all women over sixty-five received any income from public or private pensions—the second leg of the stool—as a spouse or as a retired worker; 80 percent

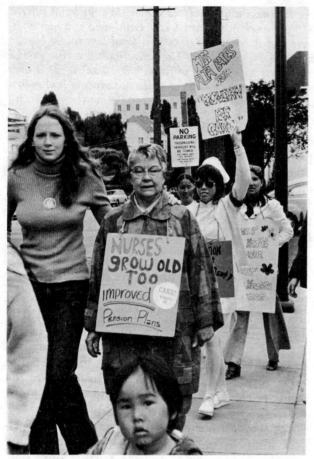

Cathy Cade

A statement about my pension came the other day. If I work until I'm sixty-five, I'll get $125 a month. My boss's came also—he'll get $900 a month. He has had the resources from his high salary to contribute to that fund over the years, but I have not. [a sixty-one-year-old woman recently employed]

Some of us who do not have pensions of our own qualify for benefits on the basis of our husband's earnings. Nonetheless, women are often left without these benefits through divorce or the death of their husbands before retirement. Until recently an employed husband could elect to receive benefits for his lifetime only. Though the pension checks received by the retired husband were larger under such an arrangement, the surviving wife was entitled to no benefits upon her husband's death. Many older women live in poverty today because this practice was allowed to go on in the past. Recent legislation requires the written consent of the wife before a married man can be permitted to receive benefits for his lifetime only.

In the absence of income from pensions or assets, most older women find themselves relying on Social Security—the third leg of the "retirement stool." Three-fifths of the number of women over the age of sixty-five have no other source of income.[14] In 1983, the average benefit paid to retired women was less than $4,500 a year, or $375 per month.[15] The poverty line for a single person over sixty-five living alone is currently $4,775.* Fifteen percent of all women over sixty-five are below the poverty line, and half receive less than $5,590.[16]

Like pensions, Social Security discriminates against women in a number of ways. Benefits are based on earnings averaged over a period of years, including years when we may have left the labor force and earned no income. Payment of benefits based on a low level of earnings extends the discrimination that kept them low in the first place. Most important, Social Security does not give recognition to the value of our unpaid work in the home. Those of us whose husbands' earnings exceeded our own may find that we receive more money if we draw benefits based on our husbands' earnings—as if we had never worked outside the home at all. In this case we forfeit all the money we paid into Social Security during our working years.

The association of poverty and old age for

received nothing.[12] Only 11 percent of Black women and 8 percent of Hispanic women received any public or private pension support.[13] Most employers require that workers stay in a job at least five continuous years in order to qualify for a pension. But middle-aged and older women have often interrupted employment to take care of children or others or to accompany their partners when careers of the latter demanded a move.

Even when we do earn pensions, our benefits are usually lower than men's. Those of us who stay home to raise children have fewer years in which to accrue pension benefits; special bonuses, such as those offered for more than twenty-five years of continuous service, are out of our reach. Sections 401(k) and 403(b) of the Federal tax code allow employees to shelter income from taxes and have it matched by their employer. But this primarily benefits those who work for corporations large enough to participate in these plans and those who earn enough to set some earnings aside for the future.

*See note on p. xxiv.

women seems inevitable if we look at the whole social structure and a woman's subordinate place in it. Yet, growing poorer as we age comes as a bitter shock to many of us. Some of us may feel ashamed, as if our economic problems reflect personal failure; others feel angry.

In fact, our poverty is the result of social pressures to be dependent on men, to put our families first and ourselves and our work second. Saving for our own retirement could not be a priority during the busy family years when resources were put into children's education or the immediate costs of living. Few of us envisioned our future selves alone and poor. Planning for ourselves alone would seem to undermine the sense of partnership we strove to encourage in marriage.

Legislation must be passed to provide benefits that recognize women's unpaid labor contributions, support during transition periods from homemaking to the labor force, and security for widowhood in old age. Employers must be encouraged to provide part-time work for all women, from young mothers and students to elders. Adequate retirement and disability benefits should be available to all, including women who have been homemakers all or most of their lives.

MANAGING OUR FINANCES WHATEVER OUR MEANS

Making Ends Meet

Despite our best efforts, few of us can expect to live without having to worry about making ends meet. The accumulated obstacles that women confront in working for financial self-reliance take their toll even among those who plan thoroughly and save diligently.

I'm on Social Security and SSI. I have no savings. I get two checks a month—one for $235 and one for $238. I have to pay $233 in rent. I get $10 in food stamps— that's gone in one minute. How am I supposed to survive on $250 a month? [a women in her seventies who lives alone in subsidized housing.]

Learning to cope with a lowered or inadequate income requires a creative outlook and a flexibility we may not have realized we possessed. Making a budget is one of the most im-

portant tools in knowing where money is going and altering or cutting expenses.

Here is one budget strategy. First, list monthly costs for survival expenses: food, rent or mortgage payments, utilities, taxes, loan repayments, transportation to work. Next, list flexible expenses: savings, clothes, entertainment, travel, and gifts. Flexible expenses can also be the ones we don't notice until after the money is gone, and a budget can serve to make us aware of these unconscious, sometimes expensive, spending patterns.

For most of us our largest expenditure is housing. Housing costs are difficult to reduce unless we are open to changing the way we live (see Housing Alternatives chapter.) Expenses can also be reduced through senior-citizen discounts in most communities. The AARP and other groups have obtained discounts for members from fast-food chains, hotels, car-rental agencies, and bus and train companies. Entertainment costs can be cut by joining community groups that may get discounts on group activities or provide free social events for elders. Some women barter skills and services with friends to conserve money. Each of us is the best judge of where we do or do not want to economize.

When I retired, I cut down a lot on my expenditures. I stopped going to the hairdresser every week—you'd be amazed how much that amounts to over the course of a year. I no longer bought expensive clothes, because I didn't need them for my job. I could dress any old way I wanted. I mowed my own lawn and shopped for food carefully so my money would last. But I kept my symphony tickets, even though they were expensive, because it gave me pleasure. [a woman in her seventies]

I am supporting myself and two children on $13,500, which is close to poverty level by Government standards. To make ends meet, I have yard sales when the weather is good, and I sell household items, used clothing, and plants. I never buy magazines or extras, to avoid anxiety about paying bills on time. [a fifty-two-year-old woman]

After I've paid the rent, I pay the phone bill. My burial plot is all paid for, and I have just a little insurance for my grown children. Then there's my health. My doctor refused Medicaid—after fifteen years—and now I have to pay him $27 out of every check. Then it takes $1.50 to do the laundry—you've got to keep your linens clean. I try to buy the cheapest things. I always make my own milk from powder. I only buy bread and chicken, and those no-name paper articles, but it still adds up. If I *need clothes, I go across the street to the thrift shop. I watch for yard sales—if you see something for half a buck, there's a Christmas present. If I have 80 cents I can go to the Council on Aging for a hot lunch. But the last two weeks of the month are always hard. You just can't make it. I'm down to my last $10, and I've got more than two weeks to go. [a woman in her seventies]*

"I'm finally old enough for Social Security. Now I can be a *subsidized* starving artist."

© *Maggy Krebs*

Applying for Benefits

Many older women do not sign up for Supplemental Security Income (SSI), food stamps, or Medicaid benefits because they don't want to take "welfare." Seventy-five percent of those eligible for SSI but not receiving it are women.[17] We need to realize that we earned those benefits through the taxes we paid on our earnings or by doing unpaid work while our husbands worked and paid taxes. We should not hesitate to apply for and receive whatever benefits we may qualify for. For many women, such benefits spell survival.

Supplemental Security Income is a cash-assistance program designed to meet the needs of the long-term disabled, the blind, and those elders whose income and assets fall below certain limits. Some states supplement the low SSI Federal payment. SSI eligibility may, in some states, also qualify you for Medicaid, food stamps, and other noncash assistance (see Problems in the Medical Care System chapter). The program is administered by the Social Security Administration and funded by the Federal and state governments.

We may find it difficult to apply for these programs and to persevere in spite of bureaucratic indifference or hostility. Often it is necessary to reapply or to appeal adverse decisions.

It's very difficult to make an application for all these kinds of things when one has been financially and personally independent, but if you get scared enough and hungry enough and desperate enough, you'll swallow your pride and go through it. The frustration of dealing with most of the agencies is indeed enough to deter most.

A piece of advice I have learned from people in the know: appeal absolutely everything. Don't ever accept no for an answer. In making applications and in making appeals, always smile and be gracious; be assertive without being aggressive. I have learned that little things help, like not blaming the person who must carry out a policy set by the Government. Most of us, when we apply, are naturally focused on ourselves, and I think it helps to acknowledge your interviewer as a human being, too. I say things like "Your job must be distasteful at times," "Gee, Susan, you seem rushed today," or "You're looking a little tired today, Linda. Has it been a rough day for you?" These kinds of things I think make a big difference. [a woman who applied for Social Security Disability Income (SSDI) when she became disabled at age forty-five]

I didn't have to work until after the divorce. My husband was a construction worker and made pretty good money—at least it seemed so at the time. We had a joint bank account, but he took it all and I worked for thirteen years as a practical nurse just to pay the bills. Then my health went. If I wasn't sick, I'd still be working. I didn't know where to go. I had to go on welfare in the beginning. Eighty-seven dollars a month—I don't know how I lived on it, but I did. It took me five years to get on SSI, but finally I did. Your forties and fifties can be a bad time. Once you're sixty-two and eligible for Social Security, you get a little more understanding. [a woman in her seventies]

Life was never easy. My husband was an alcoholic who worked when he felt like it. I wouldn't see a penny of his pay—he'd go down to the bar and cash his check there. I wasn't able to work—I have arthritis of the spine and diabetes. When we separated, I went on welfare. Now that I am on SSI, things have picked up a little. [a woman in her sixties]

For these women, one solution to their financial dead end has been to become politically active—pressing doctors to accept Medicaid, lobbying to protect Social Security, and fighting for fair treatment of women on welfare.

We're not sitting back and letting others walk all over us anymore; now we're fighting for the elderly. We've been on TV and in the papers and I've learned to chair meetings. It's encouraging to see things being accomplished. [a woman in her seventies]

Planning for the Future

It is not unreasonable for women in their middle years to prepare for living alone. It is no less necessary than preparing for illness by carrying a health-insurance policy. The massive obstacles we face as women make economic survival a difficult task. It would be a lie to pretend that, for the vast majority of women, saving for retirement on our low earnings is easy or even possible. But the key to a positive and self-reliant future is the ability to confront the financial issues of our own survival now.

I wish that from the age of eighteen I had had a really knowledgeable attitude about money. My God! It determines the quality of your life. Women should become aware of money as a power. If you are a middle-aged woman and you haven't got a pension plan, you'd better start thinking. So much of your future is going to depend on economic resources. [a fifty-six-year-old woman]

No matter what the circumstances, we must have effective control over our financial affairs. Money, after all, is not only essential to survival in our culture, it is a crucial part of our personal lives affecting our most significant relationships. To *expect* to understand it and use it effectively is the place to begin. This means educating yourself about your financial position, knowing exactly what would happen if your partner died or left, and setting priorities for the future. This can be done whether you are alone, in a marriage, or in another kind of partnership.

Many women, especially middle-class women, have grown up with some disabling assump-

tions about money: It's not nice to talk about it; I'll be cheated if I take a risk; men know more than I do; someone will show up to take care of me. Working-class women often grow up expecting to take care of themselves, but may have another set of disabling assumptions: Men are unreliable; I'll have to shoulder all the burdens myself; I'll cope with today—tomorrow will take care of itself; planning won't make any difference. All of these assumptions can have devastating results.

Looking back over my marriage now, I feel I set myself up for my present financial grief. I believed my husband when he said we didn't have money for recreation, vacation, or movies. This past year, in the process of working with my divorce lawyer, I learned that my husband had a great deal of money most of the time during our marriage, and had withheld that information from me. [a fifty-two-year-old woman]

My husband always wanted me to have a voice in our family's financial decisions. But my attitude was: I'm too busy doing my job. [a woman in her sixties.]

Some women take charge of the financial record-keeping for their household, paying the bills and balancing the checkbook. They may be more knowledgeable about the day-to-day financial picture than women who are less involved, yet they may still defer to a man to do the long-term planning, or they may rely on fate and hope for the best.

We *are* capable of understanding and managing our finances. Both self-supporting women and those supported by a partner are responsible for running a household at a given level of income. Much of our experience and expertise has been focused on knowing how to stretch a limited amount of money. We know how to "squeeze a dollar till the eagle screams," clipping coupons, buying at sales, and so forth. But when it comes to managing money and *making it grow*, many of us feel at a loss.

Until I was divorced at age forty-eight I never gave a thought to my old age, except to say that I didn't want to end up like my mother, who outlived my father by twenty-three years. But my marriage seemed solid and we were the same age, and my husband expected a sizable pension besides Social Security benefits. Who thinks that far ahead? The divorce was an awful shock and the lawyer (also my husband's) wasn't any help at all. I ended up with very little except my low-paying job and half of a house. No pension for me and not much Social Security. It took a while to get myself going again, but

Jerry Howard/Positive Images

thank God I did. I went back to school part time and decided to go into financial planning for women. I've not only done quite well for myself, but I've helped a lot of other women who were just as lost as I was. It was just like starting all over again, but worth it.

We should begin thinking of ourselves as independent financial entities, keeping some portion of our finances separate from our partner's if our budget allows—our own savings, checking, or investment account, or our own retirement plan. If we do not earn a salary of our own, we can look on this separate account as compensation for the unpaid work we do at home.

While having separate finances can contribute to a sense of self-respect, keeping our money totally separate can in some cases prevent a productive partnership from developing. A relationship deepens by considering both our independence and our interdependence.[18] Competence with money should support us, not isolate us, in all of our relationships.

Managing money effectively means paying attention to cash, credit, investments, benefits, taxes, insurance, and estate planning. Although these matters may seem unrelated, they fit together in a holistic pattern. We should come to view finances holistically, just as we do health and the body. Change in one area affects the other areas, and they must combine effectively in order to provide for overall financial security.

Information Roundup

A simple but essential step toward financial competence is to set aside one day a year for a financial roundup. The best time is usually at the beginning of the year, as you're getting your tax information together. Sit down, by yourself or with your partner, and go over all your sources of income and all your outstanding debts. Use this information to determine your household's net worth—that is, the sum of all your assets minus the sum of all your liabilities. Your assets include cash on hand, investments, real-estate holdings, life-insurance policies, personal property (such as automobiles and furniture), and money owed to you by others. Liabilities include outstanding debts, payments due on loans, bills, living expenses, and taxes. Once you have determined your net worth, you have a comprehensive picture of where you stand financially over the next year or so.

Cash and Credit

Budgeting is the most effective tool to help you handle cash and make decisions about credit. You can use the budgeting strategy described earlier to support you in using cash and credit appropriately.

Each of us should have a credit record in her own name. Department-store credit cards are usually easier to obtain than bank credit cards if you are a first-time cardholder. Another way to establish a good credit rating is to take out a small loan from a bank or credit union that you don't really need and deposit it in a savings account, paying it back month by month.

Credit can be an important part of financial health when used carefully. Keep safe limits in mind. One rule of thumb is that the total amount you owe excluding mortgage should not exceed 15 percent of your income. Can you pay off your debts in 18 to 24 months? If not, your debt-to-income ratio is too high.[19] Another rule of thumb is that one should borrow only to buy a major, permanent asset. Borrowing money at 18 percent annual interest and more for clothes, entertainment, or travel is not wise, even though it is tempting to use credit to cover everyday expenses when money is tight. The monthly payments for all you owe must not swamp your budget.

If your debts get too high to manage, you can get help. Most cities have branches of the non-profit National Federation for Consumer Credit (see Resources) whose advice is free. They can help you develop a workable budget and reschedule your payments so that you can reduce your debts.

Many women are afraid of any form of credit other than charge cards and mortgages, but we can all learn when and how to use credit *financing* to advance our own goals. Self-employed women and entrepreneurial women have to learn to deal successfully with lenders. Taking a financial risk requires us to look at ourselves as fiscally competent and capable of making commitments to meeting our own financial goals.

Insurance

Insurance should be carried to cover the financial cost of a major loss—earning power, health, property, or life. Without adequate insurance, assets we need for the future—savings, homes, investments—are very vulnerable.

Make sure you are insuring for the needs you actually still have. For example, if you no longer have dependents you don't need life insurance and may want only a small amount to cover final medical and burial expenses. However, life insurance is important when family members are dependent on your income, when business partners are dependent on your work contribution, or vice versa. The type of policy you buy should fit your circumstances:

- Is the size of the death benefit appropriate?
- Do the premiums fit your budget?
- Do you want to have a policy with a cash value to accumulate savings, or term insurance which is cheaper on an annual basis but accumulates no value?
- If there is a cash value with loan provisions, what investment and loan rates are guaranteed?
- Is the insurance company sound? (Choose only companies with "A" or better rating from the A. M. Best Company, which rates insurers based on an analysis of their financial statements.)

To calculate how much life insurance your partner should carry for your benefit or you should carry for your survivors, make a "survivors' budget." First, total the value of all liquid and convertible assets (savings, investments, other insurance). Then subtract all immediate expenses attendant to death (burial, estate tax, and settlement fees). If you have a deficit, you know you need to have at least that much insurance available immediately. Second, go on to add regular living expenses (including the costs

of new health insurance, long-term health care, and paying for caregiving, housework, repairs presently done by you or your partner.) Then add up any sources of income (survivor pension benefits, Social Security, wages). If your income is lower than your expenses, calculate what lump sum (i.e., insurance settlement) will yield that much in dividends annually, expecting (in 1987) an 8 percent return; $50,000, for example, will pay out $4,000 annually. Add the first and second figures to see how much your life-insurance policy should be worth. These figures should be revised as interest rates and your circumstances change.

Health costs are very high and usually increase as we get older. See Problems in the Medical Care System chapter for discussion of health insurance and related issues.

Many people don't think of taking out disability insurance, but it is a fact that between the ages of forty-five and sixty-five you have a three times greater risk of being disabled than of dying. Homemakers as well as employed women need disability coverage. Look for a policy that is guaranteed renewable and that pays if you are unable to work in *your current occupation*, rather than only if you are unable to do any work at all.

Your home and its contents can be insured against fire and theft through a homeowner's or renter's policy. According to insurance-company requirements, a homeowner's policy should insure your house at 80 percent of its replacement (not current market) value. You can then collect 100 percent of partial claims. Many agents are lax about this provision, and you may need to check to be sure your house is covered adequately and that you periodically raise the coverage to keep up with inflation.

Savings and Investments

After getting the day-to-day issues of cash and credit under control and *after* insuring against major losses, you can start building a nest egg for the future. Most financial advisers suggest saving about 5 to 10 percent of your gross income every month. This money should be put into a separate account for emergencies. You should build up that sum until it is equal to three to six months' income. It should be easily convertible into cash. You can keep it in a money-market fund or a conservative mutual fund, and/or consider cash values of life-insurance policies as part of your emergency fund. Once that emergency fund is built up, you can move on to other kinds of investments.

Getting in the savings habit takes some doing —especially when you are not earning much. Our culture is no help either. Every day we face pressures to buy, buy, buy. We're told that our identity depends on our possessions. Our jobs may demand that we wear expensive clothes; our children may pressure us for cars, stereos, trips, and luxuries that "everyone else" has. Often, the less money we have, the more we may feel that it's important not to let it show or to let our children feel "different." We are so quick to put money into everyone else's pocket—the grocer, the landlord, the store owners—yet we find it hard to put money into our own.

One way to approach saving is to think of it as paying yourself. Consider it a bill to be paid. Some people put a bank-deposit envelope in with their other bills—rent, utilities, phone— and "pay themselves" at the beginning of every month. Consider it a debt you owe to your own future.

Money saved should not sit around in a savings account. In fact, any time you have money on hand that you know you won't need for a month or more, put it in a money-market account or a certificate of deposit, where it will earn a higher rate of interest for you (most require a minimum balance of $1,000 or more). *Always* use a bank that is a member of the Federal Deposit Insurance Corporation (FDIC); your account will be insured up to $100,000.

The amount of interest and the frequency with which it is paid (or compounded) is the key to making savings grow. The more frequently interest is compounded, the faster your money will grow. Make sure you find out about all service fees and minimum-balance requirements, which may drastically reduce apparently high interest rates.

Shopping for the best interest rate is like comparative grocery shopping. Savings-and-loan companies and credit unions pay higher interest than commercial banks, and credit unions also give loans at lower rates to their members or depositors. A few percentage points, like a few pennies per item, can make a big difference. For instance, if you put $50 each month into an account earning only 4½ percent, the amount after ten years would come to $7,560, but an interest rate of 8 percent paid on the same deposit would generate $9,147 after ten years (compounded monthly, not counting effects of inflation and taxes).

To estimate how fast your money will grow at a certain rate of interest, use a handy trick called the "rule of 72." Divide 72 by the interest rate—the result is the number of years it will take your money to double. For instance, at 6 percent interest, a given deposit will double in twelve years.

Some women have developed considerable skill in investing, while others regard the process with dread and fear of failure. We need to develop a sense of taking the right risk. As women, we have often been trained not to take risks with money. The truth is that we are always taking risks with money, whether or not we are aware of it. Keeping money in a savings bank is a risk—the combination of inflation and low interest was not anticipated by many investors. We may think that by making conservative decisions we are protecting ourselves from loss, but that isn't always the case. It is important to inform ourselves about finances so that we can take the appropriate risks to meet our goals.

One way to begin learning about investments is to spend a few months tracking the stock market on paper. Pretend that you have bought some shares in stocks that you are interested in, then follow their performance in the newspaper. At the end of a period of time, you can see how well your choices worked out for you.

Some women have found it helpful to join or form investment clubs with a group of friends as a way of getting their feet wet without risking much money. Beware of those run by someone selling a particular stock or fund.

The Ethics of Investing

Owning a share or a bond in a company is a way of taking part in that company. A growing number of investors look at the products and practices of companies they invest in from an ethical point of view. They consider the companies' practices concerning environmental protection, occupational safety, and treatment of minorities and women. They shun companies that produce harmful products, from weapons to cigarettes.* The Social Investment Forum

*Institutional as well as individual investors are using these criteria, so we are seeing public and private pension funds, college endowments, and other large funds subjected to ethical investment standards. College stu-

Ellen Shub

(see Resources) is a nationwide network of financial advisers and institutions that supports ethical investing by both individuals and organizations.

Some women in relatively comfortable financial circumstances are putting their money to work for those who have less.

My parents left me a farm in Indiana. During their lifetime it wasn't worth much, but in the 1970s, when land values tripled, it became more valuable. If I hadn't had that farm, I would be in far more severe straits today. But what did I do to earn that money? I believe that land is a natural resource that ought to belong to all of us. Since I now have money that I didn't earn myself, I set some aside for my "sisters," women who through no fault of their own do not have enough money for old age.

————————

dents have taken the lead in pushing their schools to divest themselves of investments in companies doing business in South Africa. At any age investors concerned with fairness and justice may also want to avoid such investments and to find additional ways to use their financial power individually and collectively toward a more economically just society.

One woman who has inherited a considerable fortune chose to give away half her total income to what she terms "socially responsible community investments." Recognizing that women with wealth experience a sense of isolation, she started conducting seminars on "Managing Inherited Wealth," and organized a support group for women in this situation. The meetings are offered in conjunction with the Women's Foundation (see Resources) which provides grants to low-income women's groups. By bringing these women together, she also provided a role model for responsible management of economic good fortune.

I get calls from women all over the country. Women face unique problems with inherited wealth that have mostly to do with being left out of the decision-making process. The older men and brothers in the family have traditionally been given the responsibility. Men have tended to be much more involved in the family business than women. We're sort of kept in this "you needn't worry about this, dear" posture.

Income for Retirement

Those of us who want to retire or have retired must plan to earn enough money to live on and make it last. The assumption that "somehow it will work out" can have devastating consequences. Instead, we must look ahead to get a good sense of where we will stand financially at the time of retirement.

Pensions and Benefits

The first step is to review the financial benefits that we have coming to us, both public benefits, such as Social Security and Supplemental Security Income (SSI), and payroll benefits, such as savings and retirement plans and life, health, and disability insurance. Whatever the sources, we can take full advantage of them only if we know what they are. Often this takes aggressive pursuit of the facts—writing to government agencies, asking administrators for information, questioning their answers if necessary.

I checked my Social Security earnings record for the first time at age fifty-two and panicked when the report came back that no earnings were found under my Social Security number. Upon further investigation, I found that my deceased husband's number had been put on my earnings when I collected survivor's benefits. I was glad I had the opportunity to straighten my account then instead of facing a scary surprise at retirement.

In order to qualify for Social Security on your own (not as a spouse), you need to have worked for forty calendar-year quarterly periods (the equivalent of ten years) in employment that is covered by the Social Security system. You can find out what your current coverage is by sending in Form SSA-7004 to the Social Security Administration (get the form from your local office). Those who work part time or freelance for several employers must contribute voluntarily, and their employers are required to contribute too, yet many do not. This leaves many low-paid women, especially those who work as domestics, out of the Social Security system and out in the cold as far as medical coverage is concerned. *You need to be covered by Social Security in order to be covered by Medicare* (see Problems in the Medical Care System chapter).

While you are still employed, you should get an annual statement from your employer, telling you what your current pension and insurance benefits add up to. If you have questions, speak with the plan administrator. Always make written notes and keep them on file, especially if you are challenging a decision.

To know how much you need to save for retirement, calculate your yearly expenses and multiply them by the number of years you expect to be retired. Calculate your years of retirement by estimating your expected longevity and subtracting the age at which you expect to retire. If you are already sixty-five or over, it is wise to give yourself a generously long life expectancy, because you have already avoided or survived the health hazards of the middle years. While average life expectancy is seventy-eight years for women and seventy years for men, it is prudent to plan for your money to last until age eighty-six for women and age eighty for men. You may want to throw in a few more years if your parents were exceptionally long-lived for their time, or if you are in excellent health.

Suppose your expenses add up to $15,000 per year, you have a private pension that will provide $5,000 a year, and you expect to receive about $3,000 per year in Social Security benefits. If you expect to be retired for fifteen years, you can estimate that you need to save $7,000 for each year of retirement, or $105,000. If you have another ten years before retirement, you need to save $10,500 per year to meet your goal. Before you panic, remember that this rough estimate does not take into account the interest your savings will earn over this ten-year period. You can go to your local bank for help in calculating how much you need to save, given current interest and inflation rates. Also, remember to subtract whatever money you have already saved from the lump sum you need to accumulate. If you still do not have enough, you may want to postpone retirement, work part time after retirement, or consider ways of reducing your living expenses.

A good alternative to, or supplement for, a pension is either an IRA (Individual Retirement Account) or a Keogh Plan. Funds up to $2,000, plus $250 for a nonemployed spouse, are put in an account annually in your own name. You can put in less—don't miss doing it just because you don't have the full amount. You will pay a penalty—15 percent of the total fund—for withdrawing money before you reach fifty-nine-and-a-half. If you are self-employed and have an unincorporated business, you can open both a Keogh Plan and an IRA.

Under the 1986 Budget Reform Act, limitations have been placed on these accounts which have serious consequences for women who need to be saving in their own names for retirement. As of this writing, contributions to IRAs are fully deductible only as long as adjusted gross income does not exceed certain limits: $25,000 for a single person; $40,000 for a married couple. Deductibility is also limited if either the taxpayer or spouse is an active participant in a workplace pension plan. In place of these limitations, Congress should implement tax-deductible means for everyone, especially women, to save for their retirement years.

IRAs still offer some tax advantages. Even when you cannot deduct your contribution from your taxable income, you defer taxes on the interest and dividends your money earns until you withdraw it—when you will presumably be in a lower tax bracket. So, every year, you are accumulating interest on a larger and larger sum. By the time you retire, the savings from an IRA can be substantial. The sum of $2,000 invested at the beginning of every year, earning 7 percent interest compounded annually, would be worth $53,776 at the end of fifteen years. Like all tax advantages, these plans benefit the affluent disproportionately; however, middle-income women can also use them to advantage in planning for retirement. It is a good way for married women to accumulate assets in their own name. New legislation must be developed to assure economic security in old age for low-income women. SSI has helped, but it is not enough.

How Long Will Your Money Last?

PERCENTAGE OF SAVINGS YOU CAN WITHDRAW ANNUALLY AND FOR HOW MANY YEARS

Percentage of savings you can withdraw annually*	Number of Years Your Money Will Last				
	@5% Interest	@6% Interest	@7% Interest	@8% Interest	@9% Interest
5%	Forever				
6%	35 yrs	Forever			
7%	24 yrs	32 yrs	Forever		
8%	19 yrs	22 yrs	30 yrs	Forever	
9%	15 yrs	18 yrs	21 yrs	27 yrs	Forever
10%	13 yrs	14 yrs	16 yrs	20 yrs	25 yrs

Figures are approximate; annual compounding is assumed; inflation is not considered.

*For instance, if you are earning 5% on your capital, and you withdraw 7% annually, your money will last 24 years. If you withdraw the same, or a lesser, percent than you are earning, you will not use up your money.

Using Savings

Finally, it is important to know when it is time to stop saving and start spending. As we grow older, we become so concerned about the future and the need to maintain independence that we may find ourselves living marginally and denying ourselves pleasures and even necessities at a time when we can afford to be living off what we've saved. Some families assume that the principal is really there to be inherited by children and that parents are not entitled to it. This is fine for those who have ample funds. But with increasing life spans and major medical expenses facing us, this assumption must be reexamined. Just as we need to plan for accumulating savings, we need to plan for withdrawing money when we reach a certain age. The following chart shows a way to answer the question "How long will my money last?"

Getting Help

As we take more responsibility about finances, we may be working with brokers, bankers, agents, attorneys, accountants, and financial planners in a new capacity. Many of us have found our financial advisers in haphazard ways. "He was my husband's lawyer." "She was just getting started selling insurance and seemed so nice." You don't have to be afraid of hurting anyone's feelings by changing advisers. If you feel awkward at first, especially if you are not accustomed to acting on your own behalf, remember that *you* are employing this person to support *you* in taking care of *your* finances. You should come away from such meetings with an enhanced sense of your own competence and increasing sureness in the financial world. Keeping good records and knowing your actual income and expenses enable you to deal realistically with financial professionals.

Find advisers who respect you, are competent, and will help you educate yourself about money and finances. A good adviser will explain new concepts clearly, without hurry or condescension. You should be comfortable saying, "Would you explain that again? It's not making sense to me." Take your time, and take notes, or use a tape recorder if that makes you more comfortable. Our best learning takes place in a setting where it is safe to ask all the questions we have been afraid to ask and where we have classmates with whom to learn. Seminars and courses may be available at community colleges and adult-education centers.

Be wary of an adviser who pressures you to insure or invest in only one way or only through them. Financial planners are paid by fee, commission on sales, or both. They may charge a fee for their planning services, and also collect commissions on any investments or insurance you buy. Make sure the advice you get is at "arm's length"; that is, you should be able to implement financial recommendations through any qualified broker.

When you are starting out with a new adviser, ask for references such as former or current clients or other financial professionals. You want someone who's already done a good job with work similar to yours. We wouldn't ask a dermatologist to perform an appendectomy, yet we're often willing to let financial advisers do tasks for which they aren't qualified.

Taxes

It is important to consider your tax situation when you plan for retirement. Always base figures on your after-tax income when planning what you have to live on and invest.

You can take some of the mystery out of taxes by filling out your tax return yourself. You can get help by calling the local IRS office or your state tax bureau. Your call is anonymous, so you need not give your name. Senior centers and other community agencies sometimes bring in tax experts to offer help and answer questions.

If your financial situation is more complex, it is wise to get professional help in preparing tax returns, but you can learn a lot about your finances and save money by keeping careful records for the tax preparer.

If you file a joint return with your spouse, make sure you understand everything you sign your name to, since you are probably liable for your husband's errors, whether willful or accidental and whether or not you are still married when the return comes up for audit. There is an "innocent spouse" statute that can help some women in such situations. Ask your lawyer or accountant whether you qualify in the event that the Internal Revenue Service demands payment from you for taxes on a husband's or former husband's income.

Estate Planning: Wills and Trusts

For those of us with dependents, whether children, aging parents, disabled partners, or others, planning our estate and making a will to protect these dependents in the event of our death should be a top priority. Fortunately, this most important step costs very little.

If you're nervous about making a will, you're not alone. Seven out of ten Americans die without a will.[20] If a person dies without a valid will, the state's laws determine where that person's property goes and who the guardians and executors will be. This will happen even if the person's wishes and the needs of her or his dependents are well known. For couples in relationships with no legal standing, a will is especially important. The fact that you and another person have been lovers or friends or simply shared a house and lives for years does not establish a legally binding relationship. So it is especially important to have agreements or wishes for care and financial settlements in writing. If your finances are substantial and your relationships complex, it is risky to make a will without a lawyer, although many states may allow you to do so. If the wording is ambiguous or the will was executed under questionable circumstances, the will is useless and may lead to litigation. Many states are very particular about questions of duress, fraud, or incompetency of the testator (the person making the will). A will that accomplishes your purposes effectively is a loving gift to your heirs and community.

Before you make your will, you must choose someone to be its executor (to oversee distribution of your property and make sure taxes are paid properly). Banks, attorneys, and financially knowledgeable friends or relatives can be executors. The executor may charge a fee, and you should establish how the fee will be determined. Your executor should be given the power to hire legal, accounting, or financial services if necessary. It is wise to make sure that that person knows the provisions of the will, and also wise to tell her or him where all your financial records, the will itself, various insurance policies, tax records, bank statements, deeds, stocks, and so forth are kept.

When you choose an executor, you should also name guardians for any minors or developmentally disabled adult dependents, and trustees for any trusts that will be created. These precautions may sound depressing, but they can help your survivors avoid a great deal of confusion, worry, and trouble.

My cousin died five years ago, and nobody wanted to step in and settle her estate. I was the one who finally got stuck doing the job. We thought she died without a penny, so I had to pay for her funeral expenses. After we went through the mass of rubble in her apartment, we found this little black book where she had written down everything. It turned out she had three bank accounts stashed away and had two different kinds of pensions. If I had found that little black book right off the bat, things would have been a lot simpler. . . . She lived in an apartment, and when she died, they wouldn't let anyone in without the proper legal papers. I couldn't get the papers, so we had to keep paying the rent on the apartment for four months. [a woman in her seventies]

Some of the estate-planning methods described here are extremely simple. Some can be done without a will, such as opening a joint bank account. Wills and trusts and some powers of attorney should have competent legal advice behind them. Lawyers do cost money. However, money spent on a good lawyer can save untold grief and financial loss and can result in enormous savings. You can save some money by gathering all your records and writing out your wishes and intentions in your own words before meeting with an attorney. Local councils on aging or social-service agencies may be able to recommend agencies where low-cost legal assistance is available. Your state or county bar association can provide a list of lawyers with the kind of background you need (look for several years of estate-planning experience). Some banks do estate planning but they cannot draw up wills or trusts. Banks can, however, manage funds for a large estate or trust. If you are interested, ask about the minimum net worth requirement, and the type of accounting they will provide your heirs.

All estates go through a court process known as probate. Probate is the process used to make an orderly distribution and transfer of property from someone who has died to a group of beneficiaries. The probate procedure involves court supervision of property transfers, filing of claims against the estate by creditors, and public notice of a last will and testament when there is one.[21] It can never be totally avoided, but you can sometimes reduce the time and expense of the probate process by using some of the tools of effective estate planning. You should consult an attorney about how your property should be held to minimize financial loss.

Some people use joint ownership of property as a means of planning for its transfer immediately at their death. By holding property jointly, you can retain ownership of your asset(s) and be assured that when you die, the jointly owned property will pass directly to the joint owner or to heirs designated by you, depending on the type of joint ownership.

The cost of ill-advised probate-avoidance devices can be very high, however. For purposes of Medicaid eligibility for example, joint property may be construed to be the sole property of the applicant, leaving a spouse without funds for support. Joint property may also be attached or frozen by creditors of one owner, whether or not it was the other owner who contributed most of the assets in the account. Thus, a mother may lose her own savings in a son's or daughter's bankruptcy proceedings just because she put that child's name on her account.

There are three ways to hold property jointly with others:

· Joint Tenancy with Right of Survivorship (JTWROS).

This arrangement provides for two people to own property together. When one person dies, all the property goes to the other. The property can be real estate, securities, or bank accounts. This provision cannot be changed by a will, and property in such an account is not probated.

Bank accounts, securities accounts, or real estate held as JTWROS can require either one signature *or* the other, or one signature *and* the other to make a withdrawal or sell the property.

Be sure the person with whom you share the account is completely trustworthy, especially if you share an account which requires one signature *or* the other to make a withdrawal or sale. Many older people share ownership of their assets with a relative, thinking they will avoid probate or taxes and tacitly asking for emotional support, only to find that they have no assets left to live on.

I'm almost ninety years old...and I've been here between three and four months. How is it? Don't even ask. I can't go back to Florida because my son has tied me up here by taking all my money out of the bank and by making arrangements with the nursing home. I had all my money in joint accounts with my son. I've always kept my money in joint accounts, first with my husband and then with my son, because it avoids probate and inheritance taxes. But I wouldn't advise any older women to do that after my experience.

· Tenancy by the Entirety.

This works much like the above arrangement, except that it is available only to married couples. One tenant is not permitted to sell any of his or her interest in the property without the other's consent, and the arrangement automatically ends if there is a divorce. If one party dies, the survivor automatically inherits her or his spouse's share. The survivorship rights can be terminated only by mutual consent.

· Tenancy in Common.

Under this arrangement, ownership is measured in shares which do not necessarily have to be equal. These shares can be bequeathed to one's own heirs, not necessarily to the other tenants. If two or more people own property together, but want their *own* heirs to inherit it (as in a second marriage, for example), they should hold the property as tenants in common.

Do not assume that property held by husband and wife is automatically jointly owned. Except in "community property" states (Arizona, California, Idaho, Louisiana, Nevada, New Mexico, Texas, Washington, and Wisconsin), only property explicitly held by joint tenants with right of survivorship or tenants by the entirety is actually considered to be held jointly.

Other alternatives to joint ownership are available for sharing responsibility while continuing to direct the management of your property. Here are two examples:

Power of Attorney.

This is a useful tool for sharing responsibility for assets. It is a document in which you authorize someone to handle specific things for you, such as managing a piece of real estate or even all of your financial affairs. A power of attorney becomes invalid if the grantor should become mentally incompetent. Some states have a "durable power of attorney" which remains in force if the grantor becomes incompetent or a "springing power of attorney" for the purpose of having someone act in your name in the event that you *become* mentally incompetent. These are more thoroughly discussed in the chapters on Caregiving and Dying and Death.

Trust.

A *trust* is a legal entity, like a person or a corporation. It can provide a way to transfer ownership of assets while still making sure they are held according to your wishes. For example, a trust can own and manage property for someone who no longer has the energy to do so; it can allow an elderly mother to provide care and spending money for a disabled child after her death; it can provide income for the person establishing it while she is alive, and then give the money to a relative or a charity after her death. Putting assets in trust can also reduce estate taxes.

Depending on how it is created and what it provides, a trust can affect your Medicaid eligibility. If you think a nursing home could be in your own or your husband's future, you should do Medicaid planning with the help of a competent attorney familiar with your state's Medicaid requirements.

There is no such thing as a do-it-yourself trust. You will need a skilled, experienced attorney. This is a complicated area, and a person with good intentions but imperfect knowledge can make a complete mess of things.

My husband left close to half a million dollars in a trust fund—I was to get the income. Every time I asked for money I was sent a check, so I never questioned it. Then my son-in-law said I should get an accounting of it— and when we looked we found that there was only about $80,000 left—the trustee had been gambling in the stock market and losing; when I asked for money he didn't send it to me from the income but from the principal. So it's almost all gone now.

Whether you create a trust or are the beneficiary of one, you should watch it carefully to make sure that it functions as intended. A trustee should be required (in the terms of the trust) to give an annual accounting to the beneficiaries and to the court.

Passing On the Responsibility

A last step to protect our own financial health is to be prepared for the time when we will want to hand over our financial affairs to someone else. The plan doesn't have to be based on chronological age. Instead, it may be made effective at the point at which we no longer feel up to coping with balancing a monthly statement or making decisions on reinvesting money.

Those of us who have worked hard to learn about money matters find that giving responsibility for them to our children is a good way to pass on some of our financial acumen—especially to our daughters. We shouldn't assume that our sons will take care of our finances and our daughters will take care of our personal needs. It is a good idea to prepare for this time by keeping our affairs in order and by making sure that a responsible person understands our wishes.

Most of us were raised with the expectation that our work in the home would be rewarded in old age and that our financial security would come from a husband's income. Yet most women find that in their older years they must rely on their own ingenuity to supplement their often meager savings and pensions. Our learning, efforts and struggles should go beyond our own survival to teaching our daughters the skills we have so painfully acquired, and urging them to carry on the battle for a more secure economic future for older women.

NOTES

1. Martha Avery, "Prime Proposal." *New Directions for Women*, November-December 1984.

2. U.S. Department of Commerce, Bureau of the Census, *Money Income and Poverty Status of Families and Persons in the United States: 1985* (advance data from the March 1986 Current Population Survey), series P-60, No. 154, August 1986.

3. Alan L. Otten, "U.S. Agencies Awaken to the Need for More Data on Nation's Elderly." *Wall Street Journal*, December 9, 1986.

4. U.S. Department of Labor, Women's Bureau, *Twenty Facts on Women Workers*, 1984.

5. U.S. Department of Commerce, Bureau of the Census. "Child Support and Alimony: 1981," series P-23. *Current Population Reports*.

6. Ellen Goodman, "The Post-Modern Divorce—Another Way to Divvy Up the Assets." *The Boston Globe*, January 2, 1986.

7. Steven H. Gifis, *The Law Dictionary*, 2nd ed. Woodbury, New York: Barron's Educational Series, Inc., 1984.

8. "The Disillusionment of Divorce for Older Women," OWL Gray Paper. Available from Older Women's League. See Resources.

9. Lenore Weitzman, *The Divorce Revolution: The Unexpected Social and Economic Consequences for Women and Children in America*. New York: Free Press, 1985.

10. "Looking Forward to Retiring and Living a Life of Ease? Don't." *Washington Post*, September 14, 1984.

11. Sara E. Rix, *Older Women: The Economics of Aging* (second edition).Washington, DC. The Women's Research and Education Institute, October 1984.

12. Older Women's League, "Pension Equity for Women: A Fact Sheet," October 1985.

13. Ibid.

14. Frances Leonard, "The Three-Legged Stool: Women and Retirement (In)security." *Hastings Law Journal*, University of California, Vol. 32, May 1981, pp. 1195-238.

15. Jean Netherton, Testimony before the Joint Economic Committee, U.S. Congress, June 6, 1984.

16. "Money Income and Poverty Status of Families and Persons in the United States: 1984." Advance Data from the March 1985 Current Population Survey, *Current Population Reports: Consumer Income*, Series P-60, No. 149.

17. Lucy Freeman, "Anatomy of a Project: SSI Outreach." *OWL Observer*, March-April 1986, p. 9.

18. Tessa Warschaw, *Rich Is Better*. New York: Doubleday, 1985, p. 67.

19. Elizabeth Lewin, *Your Personal Financial Fitness Program*. New York: Facts on File Publications, 1984, p. 71ff.

20. *Consumer Reports*, February 1985.

21. Paul Cochray, *The Financial Planner's Guide to Estate Planning*. Englewood Cliffs, NJ: Prentice Hall, 1986, p. 265.

15

CAREGIVING*

by Louise Fradkin and Mirca Liberti

Material on finances by Naomi B. Isler

Special thanks to Tish Sommers

CAREGIVING IS A WOMAN'S ISSUE

Caregiving has traditionally been a woman's role. Women have always cared for dependent members of the family and community—infants, children, the infirm, the handicapped, and the frail elderly. Societal pressures and expectations have trained generation after generation of women to put others' needs before their own. Women constitute 71 percent of family caregivers;[1] they are "the invisible laborers without whom neither the health system nor the patient could survive."[2]

It is imperative for all of us to take a hard look at the unthinking way women are simply handed the job of taking care of whatever dependent person happens to be in their home or even outside their immediate home and family. I have a forty-five-year-old daughter who has been disabled by an obscure form of epilepsy since birth. When she is not institutionalized I take care of her and when she is, I am constantly doing errands to make her stay in the hospital more bearable. With a great deal of

*The word "caregiving" refers to caring for people; thus, we prefer it to "caretaking," which suggests caring for inanimate objects. Though we are focusing on the unpaid caregiver here, we do not wish to dismiss the work of paid caregivers in hospitals, nursing homes, and private homes. Paid caregivers also are predominantly women, and are underpaid and undervalued in society and in the institutions where they work. We feel that recognition of the importance of caregiving will contribute to better quality of life for all caregivers, paid and unpaid, and those they care for.

prodding from her professionals, my daughter is trying to be more independent at last. My mother lived to be ninety-eight, the last twenty-one years of her life as a

Marianne Gontarz

198

widow. I became her principal caregiver in my early forties. Now my husband suffers from memory loss and has been diagnosed as having Alzheimer's disease. Again I am the principal caregiver. I have given this kind of care without questioning it since the beginning of my marriage. [a sixty-six-year-old woman]

For the last four years of her life, I saw my grandmother every day on my way home from work. I did her shopping, her laundry, and anything else she needed. I now volunteer at Rosie's Place [a Boston shelter for homeless women], where I continue to give direct care to women. It's a way of acting on my need to be part of a community of older women who, in allowing me to be part of their lives, have given me immeasurable gifts—love, laughter, warmth, and occasionally tears. [a divorced woman in her fifties]

Caregiving Wives

Remember the poem that says, "Grow old along with me, the best is yet to be?" Unfortunately, many couples plan their retirement years with this in mind only to have their dreams end in a nightmare when one partner becomes disabled or chronically ill—a victim of Parkinson's disease, Alzheimer's disease, a stroke, or cancer.

I'm glad now that we did so much traveling before my husband became ill. I try to think of those times now and relive them. We had so many things planned for after the children had grown, but that's not the way it turned out for us. Because of my husband's illness, we never go anywhere. We're caged in, the two of us. [a woman in her seventies]

A familiar pattern is that when a man becomes ill or disabled, his doctor will send him home, commenting that he is lucky to have a wonderful wife to care for him. When the same thing happens to a woman, however, the doctor will recommend a nursing home. (In some cases, men *are* caregivers for their wives, and of course those who are certainly deserve the same relief and support argued here for women.) As medical science prolongs lives, women, who are frequently younger than their husbands, and also tend to live longer, will more and more often find themselves facing the difficult task of caring for their husbands.

I cry a lot because I never thought it would be this way. I didn't expect to be mopping up the bathroom, changing him, doing laundry all the time. I was taking care of babies at twenty; now I'm taking care of my husband.[3]

"Your husband is lucky to have you to take care of him at home, Mrs. Jacobs."   © *Maggy Krebs*

Wives usually have no special preparation for caregiving, and little choice about offering it. In many communities, when a husband needs constant care, the only alternative is a nursing home. Many women prefer to keep their husbands at home when faced with this alternative,[4] feeling that the separation would break the vow "Till death do us part." Also, both husband and wife may recoil from a nursing home because of horror stories heard from family, friends, and the media. Both partners may want to remain together without realizing what a physical and emotional strain will eventually be placed on the wife.

Caregiving wives carry a heavy emotional load. They often have no one to tell them how well they are doing or how to do the job better, and no one to help when a difficult situation arises. They usually put aside their own lives and aspirations to give their husbands' needs top priority. On top of all of this, they may have their own physical ailments, which may be aggravated by the work they have to do.

I'm seventy-three years old and use a walker. Last year I had a hip replacement. My husband is a paraplegic. When I'm helping him in the bathroom, I have to get into positions that hurt my hip. He doesn't want any-

one else to help him. [a seventy-three-year-old woman]

Caregivers often talk about being isolated, of losing companionship and social contacts. Friends and family who are upset by seeing changes in the husband tend to stay away. Sons and daughters—especially sons, who may see their own future in their father's illness and be unable to face it—may have difficulty coping with the new situation. Sons and daughters may also view their mother as the one who always holds things together, and may continue to expect her to hold this role in the family despite the change in circumstances.[5]

People tell me that he deserves all the care I can give him because he's such a nice person and was always so good to me. Well, I'm a nice person and have always been good to him—what do I deserve? [a seventy-three-year-old woman]

Wives feel isolated as caregivers because they have lost the support of their husbands—often the one with whom they had their closest relationship. This is especially the case when a husband is mentally impaired, since the wife has then essentially lost the man she married. He is still alive, but their relationship, with its shared memories, humor, hopes, and dreams, slips away as his illness progresses. Some caregivers in these circumstances experience apathy, nervousness, irritability, a decrease in vitality and mental energy, and a prevailing sense of depression. Many husbands are aware of the burden that their illness has created for their wives, saying, "This illness has been as much my wife's as it has been mine."[6]

Caregiving may mean taking over affairs that the husband took care of before. Such a change in roles may cause anger, pain, conflicts, and confusions for *both* husband and wife, adding even more stresses to an already stressful situation. In a marriage, spouses often act as loving fathers or mothers to one another during times of stress, uncertainty, or illness. When the husband becomes so ill that he cannot share in making decisions, the wife's sole responsibility becomes permanent.

He was such an intelligent man, an engineer, used to giving orders. Now he has no memory, I have to tell him what to wear and what to do, and he resents it. He doesn't really know who I am. For the first year or so he thought I was a housekeeper; now he must realize that I belong with him. If he had a moment of clarity and saw what has happened to him and to us, he would want to die. It would have been a blessing if he had died in the hospital. [a sixty-eight-year-old woman, with an eighty-one-year-old husband]

Wives may feel guilty if at times they wish for their husband's or a parent's death and resent the continuing need for care. For those women who have stayed married despite unhappy marriages, caregiving is even harder. To all the other stresses are added resentment over wasted years and dislike of their husbands.

Some wives caring for husbands are helping an elderly parent at the same time. The parent may not be able to understand the extent of care that the son-in-law requires and thus resent the time that the daughter gives to him, or the husband may resent time devoted to caring for the parent. Obviously the woman cannot divide herself in two to care for both equally, yet she may feel guilty over the conflicting demands. This situation places extraordinary stress on the caregiver.

Daughters as Caregivers

We live in a time when many of us are fortunate enough to see our parents live until they are quite old. The challenge of longevity is that older parents may need our help, not just occasionally, but on a continuing basis and at a time when we ourselves are getting older. It is not uncommon today to hear of a seventy-year-old

Marianne Gontarz

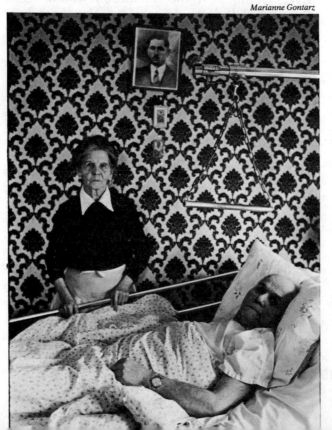

woman who is concerned about and responsible for her ninety-year-old mother.

Those of us who take on caring for parents often have to make major adjustments. Both caregiver and parents lose freedom and privacy and may have to give up or defer plans for the future. It is not easy for either the daughter or the parent; both feel resentment and frustration. Caregivers often feel caught between their parents' needs and their own. Women who still have children at home feel the additional squeeze of being "sandwiched" between generations.[7]

The Bath

My mother's eyes are tranquil.
She shreds bits of paper.
I give her more paper, more—
napkins, tissues, a forest.
She says, Yes, I'm grateful,
I'm so fortunate in my daughters.

I run the tub.
I bathe her.
I scrub the shadowed place beneath her breasts.
She says, Thank you my darling
you're so kind I love you.

In the moist, closed room
I see she is my grandmother,
the grandmother I never had:
a brand-new lady, dripping with gifts,
arrived in time for me to play with
like a baby

or a mother—
that unknown grandmother
who ripped the lining from her coat before she died
and gave this child who nursed her through the nights
all she had left to give:
a saved-up envelope of money.

I kneel on the mat.
The room dissolves me.
I become a pool of children, mothers, babies.
We pluck at coats.
We dip our hands in secret pockets.

The commandment floats, buoyant in water.
My daughter watches with her radar eyes.

*Kinereth Gensler**

*From *Threesome Poems*, Cambridge, Massachusetts: Alice James Books, 1976. Copyright © by Kinereth Gensler.

Jerry Howard/Positive Images

Most caregivers have very little understanding at first of what the job will entail. Many agree to take care of a parent when she or he is still somewhat self-sufficient, and are unprepared for what happens when the picture changes.

I decided I would take care of my father when he could still stay by himself and get snacks. But by the time he actually came to me (only a few weeks after I made the original decision) he was partially paralyzed and needed help doing everything. [a woman in her late thirties with two preschool children]

My father had a heart attack and my parents came to live with us when we still had children at home. Then my mother had a series of strokes. She died when my oldest was eighteen. I would really tell anyone in that situation not *to try to care for parents in your home— to make other arrangements, have your family life less conflicted and better balanced. It was a very difficult period. My father was very nervous from his illness. He was a helpless person who was taught that the woman did everything.* [a woman in her sixties]

Helping an older parent stay in his or her own home often requires extensive logistics and support systems.

I help my eighty-eight-year-old disoriented mother stay in her own apartment through a system of phone calls and hired help coming in four times a day. They give my mother her meals, bathe her, and dress her in the morning and help her get ready for bed at 10 P.M. I've accident-proofed the apartment and constantly modify the support system as my mother's condition changes. I drive fifty-eight miles round trip to do the laundry, the shopping, and pay the bills. In effect, I run two households and I also have a full-time job. This is a ten-year-old routine that is demanding but has worked for us both up to now. [a fifty-seven-year-old woman]

Despite the difficulties, however, keeping a parent in her or his own house may be preferable from the standpoint of preserving both the parent's and the daughter's independence.

Elderly parents often expect their daughters —rarely their sons—to care for them. Parents may not approve of their daughter's working (or of her involvement in outside activities if she does not have a paid job), as these take up time that parents may feel belongs to them.

My mother, a feisty, proud immigrant woman, always looked to me for her primary emotional support. My brothers were devoted to her but she rejected a good deal of what they offered because traditionally daughters are expected to be the primary caregiver. When I returned to college while my children were growing up, my mother was often hostile toward my pursuits, making my visits with her very uncomfortable. However, when I graduated, she insisted upon having her picture taken with me after the ceremony—a frail eighty-eight-year-old immigrant lady with a face full of pride posing with her daughter, the college graduate. It was a moment of pride for us both. [a woman in her forties]

Some parents believe that women belong in the home and that taking care of parents is a logical extension of that. Many daughters place themselves in the caregiving role in their own minds, subjecting themselves to internal as well as external pressures. Their brothers, husbands, and male friends do not feel the same pressures. Most men are able to separate themselves both physically and emotionally from their parents, and experience less guilt about doing so.[8]

I live near my parents and take care of them. I do the shopping, cooking, cleaning; you name it and I do it. My sainted brother lives in Florida. Once a year he flies up, takes them out for dinner and a show, then he's off again for another year. My parents think he's great and I get all the complaints. [a woman in her forties]

I am basically the only child for all practical purposes; my brother lives twelve hundred miles away and only comes home about once a year. My mother is in a nursing home and has had seven strokes as well as suffering from innumerable other cardiovascular problems. My dad has had one CVA [cerebral vascular accident—a stroke] and has other medical problems and is getting quite senile. He lives with me and basically I have very little family support. I am single, which makes it doubly hard. At times I think I'll be the third stroke victim. [a forty-five-year-old woman]

In traditional families, if the sons provide financial help, mend a broken door, visit, call, or send flowers at the appropriate times, then they are "good sons" and meet their parents' expectations. Although it is rare, some men do care for

parents; when they do they are usually not torn by the same conflicts as women. Most often, sons expect to hire help or delegate other people (fill in wife, sister, aunt, some female relation) to do the actual caregiving.[9]

My brother does most of the work of coordinating home care and medical appointments for my parents. We try to share the calling, errands, and visiting as much as possible, but I am a divorced parent with a full-time job, including some evening meetings, while he is married, without children at home. Though his job is also demanding, he has more time and energy to give at this point in our lives. When I hear some of the horror stories other women tell, I feel lucky that my brother is so responsible. [a forty-five-year-old woman]

Daughters may feel a nagging guilt over putting their own needs first. Some parents find it scary or difficult to make new friends and to be in new social situations, and thus rely heavily on their daughters to meet all of their needs.

My mother is eighty-two and needs assistance because she is partly deaf and has severe cataracts. She lives alone and spends most of her time by herself. She is nervous but very independent and I wouldn't consider a nursing home or an old age home for her. She is in fine health otherwise, but really needs a little more companionship. I don't have a lot of time to spend with her, since I work full time and have two children at home. She refused any help that I could get and will not go to a group in her church or join a senior citizens' center. She wants me to be there. [a forty-eight-year-old woman]

I usually call my mother every day to check on her. Sometimes I get busy and a day or two will go by and I forget to call. The calls are repetitious, we don't have much to say—she usually complains a lot. But what really riles me is that when I miss a day she calls me and starts out with "I thought your index finger was broken and you couldn't use a phone—how are you?" I can feel the hair on my body rise, but I ignore the moment and just say, "How are you?" [a fifty-five-year-old woman]

My grandmother lived to be almost one hundred and two years old, and my mother cared for her until she was ninety-seven and had to go into a nursing home. Now my mother obviously feels it is her turn, which it is. I am the real problem here, for I have led a very active life and cannot seem to adjust to this demanding and devastating situation. I do not know what to hope for and am almost overcome with the inevitable guilt at my resentment and anger. I have no one to talk to. [a seventy-two-year-old woman]

Some of us may have parents who were never happy or content with life. To maintain a sense of balance and sanity, we have to face the fact that we may not be able to make them happy and that their unhappiness is not our fault.

People who have lost eyesight, hearing, or mobility and are undergoing a lot of pain have legitimate reasons for being unhappy. Parents may also be angry about not being able to do things for themselves. It's important to recognize that they aren't angry at you, just as you aren't angry at them; it is what has happened to them that is the source of the anger.

If we have unhappy childhood memories of parents and believe that they wronged us, we may feel resentful and angry at having to care for them.

My mother left me when I was two and my father moved us into his parents' house. My grandmother actually raised me and I loved her. I rarely saw my father —he ran around and was not part of my life. After I had children, he and his new wife grew close to us because of the grandchildren. Now he's a widower and sick, so he moved in with us eight years ago. Our children are grown and we finally had the house to ourselves, but now he's here. We have no privacy. He expects me to wait on him. He was a lousy father, but I can't throw him out. He has no money and where would he go? Inside I'm angry at him and I resent him all the time. [a fifty-six-year-old woman]

Some of us may feel that we *want* to be the caregiver of a parent or close relative.

My aunt was still very active into her nineties. I felt as though she was almost like my mother. But she kept having these little "occlusions"—the blood wasn't getting through the arteries to the brain and she would pass out. Finally the doctor said she could never be left alone again. So I took care of her at home for five and a half years. I made the garden for her and cooked the best food in the world for her. She had taught me how to cook. She was a dear wonderful person. She gradually got worse. When she couldn't go down the stairs, I would carry huge pots of flowers to show her because she loved plants and flowers so much. She gradually got weaker and weaker until one day she said, "I'm just all tired out." She was just like a clock that had run down. And I was with her. So I felt that I had done all I could. I really loved her more by the time she died. It was a hard job but I'm glad I was able to do it. I feel very good about it. [a single woman in her fifties]

My mother never had any joy, only hard work and struggle. I tried to make it up to her, to do things for her and give her things, and felt guilty because I couldn't take away the old pains and troubles or make her into a happy person. But at least I was able to take care of her in her old age. I have no guilt about that. And she died

at home, in my house, where I could say goodbye to her in my own way and in my own space. That was five years ago, and as I get older I see more and more of my mother in myself, and that's okay because she was a wonderful woman and I love her. [a woman in her fifties]

Sometimes siblings rekindle old wounds and feelings when discussing how and who should help care for the parents. You hear statements like "You were always Mom's favorite," or "You always got what you wanted, so you take care of them now."

I have six brothers and I'm the only daughter. None of them wants to help out at all, they all feel it's a woman's job. So do my parents. After my parents die, I never want to see any of my brothers again. [a fifty-two-year-old woman]

We feel helpless as we watch elderly parents become more dependent and frailer. We may be afraid and sad, fearing our parents' death or our own old age. Deep inside we still think of our parents as dependable and strong, the way we saw them when we were children; and the child inside us still wants it that way. We may still want their approval and their wise, loving care.

I take care of my mother, who is physically well but has no memory and is disoriented. Several years ago my oldest daughter went into the hospital for a biopsy. I made arrangements for someone to care for my mother and I told her where I was going. For one moment she understood and said, "I hope everything goes well;" then she lapsed back into her usual state, and I wanted to cry. I realized that I wanted my mother; I wanted her to comfort me and tell me it would be all right like she did when I was a child. But she's like a child now and I'm her mother. [a fifty-eight-year-old woman]

Role reversal is one of the hardest aspects of being a caregiver. No one wants to think of her parents as incapable of making decisions. A healthier relationship will be maintained if you can take on caregiving responsibility without thinking of the parent as a child.

It is difficult for caregivers to find time for themselves. Most try to maintain their family obligations and perform well on their jobs, but may overlook their own personal needs, especially time for fun, exercise, and relaxation. The logistics of getting help for the dependent parent may seem so overwhelming that it doesn't feel worth it. It is not surprising that caregivers often develop physical manifestations of internalized emotional stress.

My father had a stroke in 1979 and has gotten continually worse since. I quit my job two years ago to take care of him and my mother at their house. But it became too much for me so I moved him to my house. The living room is set up like a hospital—the house is small so we had no other place for him. We have looked into nursing homes but my parents have so little savings that they can't even afford one year, and if all the money is used up and my mother gets sick there would be nothing for her. We are living day to day but I do not know how long I can do it. It's like having a 175-pound baby. He gets me up three to four times a night. He wants constant care. I pray for patience every day. But I am afraid that I am going to end up with an ulcer. We don't go out, and we've no place for friends to come visit. My husband is very helpful and understanding but our life isn't our own. [a forty-five-year-old woman]

No one should have to give up her own life or risk her health to the degree described by this and other women who care for family members at home. Family caregivers need a variety of support and respite services.[10] We must get together and fight for universal availability of such services, and for the funding to keep them going, so that we can keep going. The nursing-care system in this country depends on the in-home caregiver and threatens to move even further in this direction. More nursing-home beds are needed nationwide as well as a universal system of coverage for nursing-home care, but many family caregivers want to keep their family member at home, and they need help to do so.

Some of us have been able to turn to friends and relatives for help that should be forthcoming from the health-care system.

For many years after my mother's death, my father and I shared an apartment. The landlady lived upstairs with her elderly mother, who also needed someone to be around. So the landlady and I alternated taking weekends off. Both parents would leave the back door open so they could be in touch. I also had a "temporary" roommate, who was helpful in doing things with my father such as watching the ballgame or taking him for a ride. I in turn would get the meals.

After my father died, my roommate and I just kept living together. We each have had some illnesses and have recently developed a bond that has a different dimension. Now that we need each other, we do more things together, and our caring has grown. We still have our usual disagreements but we learned how to resolve them long ago.

The landlady and a friend who bought a share of the house are both older than we are. I heard one of them fall at 3 A.M. and we took her to the hospital. We shop for them often and they feed the cat for us, and vice

versa. I tell one of them when I will be coming in late and she keeps the spotlight on until I'm home. There's a reciprocal feeling of caring. [a seventy-two-year-old single woman who has lived with her roommate for twenty years]

Exchanging Caregiving

A retired librarian who works as a volunteer for the Gray Panthers and is connected with others in a "family of choice," as Maggie Kuhn has called it, reported:

Don't forget—the only way you achieve independence is through interdependence—when you do things for each other. I remember many years ago when I broke my arm and my neighbor had an eye operation. I had one arm and she had one eye, and I would go in and give her breakfast. Then she helped me with things I could not do.

A seventy-year-old woman, a leader in the Older Women's League, describes a mutual caregiving arrangement:

The maxim "the blind leading the blind" usually suggests poor leadership, but why shouldn't two people with disabilities help each other? We both have cancer, but of different degrees and with different ups and downs. We share a home and help each other in every way. To assure that the medical citadel doesn't try to take over beyond our wishes, we have "durable power of attorney for health care"* for each other so that our wishes will be respected even if we're not in a position to protest against "heroic measures."

Some women have figured out a way to make informal exchanges of help more available. The San Diego chapter of the Older Women's League found an enthusiastic response from members who were willing to respond to SOS calls from sister OWL members with help such as filling in for an in-home-care worker or lending a wheelchair.[11]

CAREGIVING IS STRESSFUL

Though each caregiver has her own set of problems and her own ways of coping—and sometimes falling apart—all caregivers experience emotional, physical, or economic stress, and sometimes all three. All experience feelings of frustration and isolation. To add to these stresses, many caregivers are the only bread-

*See p. 208, this chapter.

winners in the family. Some hold demanding jobs outside the home in addition to the demanding job of caregiving.

I've been caring for my father for over eight years. The first few years were good ones. He'd been a chef and contributed to the family by making all our meals. Now he is blind, confined to a wheelchair, and needs a lot of help. I am a special education teacher and love my work. I have hired a woman to stay with my father during the day, but from the moment I come into the house at 4 P.M. until he goes to bed around 8, I am the one who gives him all the care. I get up with him several times a night and I get up at 6 A.M. and get him ready for the day. One day my neighbor told me that if I really loved my father I'd quit my job and stay home to care for him. I was angry and hurt and asked her if she would have told me that if I were a man. My work is very important to me and it keeps me sane. [a fifty-seven-year-old woman]

No one can be a full-time caregiver without help. Think about friends or relatives who could sometimes fill in for you. One woman had a good idea:

I have often been at a loss when people offer to help, so I made a list of tasks I would like help with. Now, when friends offer, I say, "Would you like to come on Tuesday afternoon and help Mom write some notes while I go out to do some errands?" or "Would you help me take Mom to the shopping mall to buy some new clothes?"

"Woman's Work"—Balancing Our Jobs with Demands for Caregiving

by Paula Brown Doress

Most of us over forty can remember when women in traditionally "female" occupations—schoolteachers, nurses, airline stewardesses, telephone operators—were not allowed to keep their jobs once they married. Others, especially poor women and women of color, were expected to remain employed after marriage. Today, 50 percent of married women work in paid employment, compared with 4 percent at the turn of the century, and we think of such restrictions as archaic. Yet the demands of the women's movement for child care and maternity leave[1] have been ignored in this country, forcing women to give up their jobs in the early child-raising years. In countries where women have these options, their pay relative to men's is higher.[2] In our middle and later years, we may have to care for an older or infirm family member. When this happens, we fall even further behind men in our careers and retirement benefits.

Employed women who care for ill or older persons or a disabled child need day-care services and flexible working hours just as parents of young children do. These policies would cut down on absenteeism and be a strong selling point for attracting new employees. A 1982 survey found that 44 percent of women who cared for a parent were also employed, and many caregivers rearranged work schedules or reduced their hours. Some even had to quit their jobs.[3]

What can employers do? A survey conducted by The Travelers Insurance Companies found that 28 percent of their employees over thirty spent 10.2 hours per week caring for older relatives and friends and 8 percent devoted 35 hours per week! They found that many employed workers need a variety of support services, ranging from information and referral to flexible scheduling and adult-care programs. As a result, the company is exploring ways of providing information and support to those employees to prevent stress, exhaustion, and loss of productivity.[4] As women, we should not have to choose between family responsibilities and a satisfying work life.

1. Boston Women's Health Book Collective, *Ourselves and Our Children*. New York: Random House, 1978; and Margaret O'Brien Steinfels, *Who's Minding the Children? The History and Politics of Day Care in America*. New York: Simon and Schuster, 1973.
2. Sylvia Hewlett, *A Lesser Life: The Myth of Women's Liberation in America*. New York: Morrow, 1986.
3. National Center for Health Services Research, quoted in Older Women's League press release, "Family Caregivers—A Fact Sheet." November 1986.
4. Glenn Collins, "Many in Work Force Care for Elderly Kin." *The New York Times*, January 6, 1986, p. B5.

Sometimes, when I'm not sure what the person's preferences and scheduling are like, I just show them my list of "rescue coupons" and ask them to pick something they would like to do. [a woman in her fifties]

For the first time, only recently, after attending a self-help group, I was able to really hear my daughter when she offered to come home and stay with her father for a week or two so I could get away. [a sixty-six-year-old woman]

One third of caregivers are in fair to poor health themselves.[12] If you find yourself frequently feeling unwell, don't excuse it by saying, "Well, I had a bad night," or, "The weather is damp." Take time off to go for a complete physical exam. Explain to your health-care practitioner not only your symptoms but also your role as a caregiver so that she or he fully understands the stresses you are under. Beware of a doctor who dismisses your concerns or feels that the answer to all your aches and pains is a tranquilizer—which will make you feel groggy and only add to your problems. If your blood pressure is high—a common symptom among overworked caregivers—your body is sending you an important message. You have to learn how to reduce your stress level to help bring down your blood pressure. (See Hypertension, Heart Disease, and Stroke chapter and the section on stress management in Aging and Well-Being chapter.) Caregivers also often experience nausea, fatigue, and difficulty in sleeping. If your health care practitioner has determined that you don't have an underlying medical problem, you'll want to go beyond the medical community to get help and relief.

Self-Help and Support Groups

Those of us who are caregivers have found self-help and support groups a valuable source of comfort, advice, and understanding. Among other things, sharing experiences provides a safety valve for pent-up anger and frustration.

I need someone out there who will listen to me and not say, "But they're old, they need you." I already know that—boy, do I ever. I have eighty-two-year-old parents; my father is in a nursing home getting along pretty well, but my mother is another story which would take too long to tell. I feel sometimes as if I'm handling things pretty well, but some days I want to pack my suitcase and leave forever! [a woman in her fifties]

These groups offer a supportive and nonjudgmental atmosphere where members can openly express their innermost fears, discuss problems, and share coping skills. Joint problem solving is far better than what most of us can do on our own, especially because it's often difficult to keep a perspective on problems when you're alone. Members share their knowledge of community resources and services. New members often say, "It's great to learn I'm not alone. All of you understand what I'm going through." Members sometimes develop a buddy system, so each has someone to call in times of crisis. A member of Women Who Care, a support group in Marin County, California, composed of women who care full time for their severely disabled husbands, writes:

The best thing about it was that we found out we were not alone. I guess burdens are easier to bear if you know other people going through what you are, or even worse. We open up to each other more than we can to anyone else. We share our fears and our sorrows, our feelings of guilt and our occasional joys. Sometimes we cry, but it's amazing how much we laugh. We also trade ideas on how to make the job easier and we share resources that we've found useful. Some of us make pacts to call each other when things get too heavy. And knowing you can help someone else in the same spot you are in lightens the load.

Support groups can be self-run by members. They can decide on their own format, arrange for outside speakers such as social workers or pharmacologists, and organize fund-raising activities. Such groups require a lot of work from dedicated volunteers—they do not happen overnight.

Professionally led and organized support groups have been developing over the past several years as health, mental health, and social service agencies have begun to respond to the needs of caregivers. Some of these groups meet over a period of only six to eight weeks with a specific format and focus on a specified set of issues; others run continuously, with people joining and leaving according to their needs. Religious organizations are also starting professionally led and self-run support groups. Each caregiver can choose the kind of group that answers her needs and in which she feels comfortable.

PLANNING AHEAD

Ideally, families should plan ahead for various crises before they actually happen. Even though you can't anticipate everything, everyone in the family should have a turn to voice her or his feelings without the pressure of an imminent emergency. It is best to do this when your parents are still living active, independent lives, and are in relatively good health. Preplanning takes effort and thought on the part of everyone in the family, but can prevent irreversible or long-lasting errors of judgment, such as selling a house or furniture in the midst of a crisis and regretting it later. Though sisters and brothers who live far away can be part of the dialogue through phone calls or letters, it's best when a whole family can get together.

My brothers and I sat down one night with our mother and decided who would do what to care for her. My two brothers and I have been sharing the care of our mother for several years now. Mother is eighty-five and lives in a retirement apartment building that is convenient to all of us. I do her food and clothes shopping and the laundry, and sometimes my sisters-in-law help me. One brother handles the financial matters, pays the bills and so on, and the other brother takes her to the doctor, gets her medicines, and watches over her health. My brothers and I and our spouses meet for dinner once a week and then visit our mother. We all enjoy getting to-gether—it keeps us close as a family. Mother enjoys having us all as guests once a week. So far it's worked out well for us. [a fifty-eight-year-old woman]

Of course, preplanning doesn't mean making firm promises that can't be kept. Sometimes, out of love and with the best intentions, we say, "I'll never put you in a nursing home," or announce some other "never" regarding something we have no control over. These "nevers" may come back to haunt us. Since nobody has a crystal ball, none of us knows what the family situation will be in several years or even several

Marianne Gontarz

CARING AND CAREGIVING

by Lois Harris

This chapter devotes considerable attention to the problems faced by caregivers. However, *caring*, in the sense of loving concern, can be expressed by those receiving care as well as by those providing it. Examples abound of serenity despite pain, gallantry and thoughtfulness despite discomfort.

Several years ago in my late seventies I took up cross-country skiing. I remember an exercise that was scary. We took turns going down a hill. Only when we approached the instructor did we learn in which direction we were to turn. I thought of this recently as I was musing about aging and caregiving. I realized that most of us do not know whether later in life we will have to join the caregivers group or the care-receivers. We may experience both roles at different times. So all of us need to do some advance thinking about both.

months. Nevertheless, we can try to plan for a range of contingencies.

Planning discussions should be open and loving, with no secret pacts between family members. Unfortunately, even talking about caring for a parent can cause hard feelings and bitterness among brothers and sisters. If your family meetings deteriorate into fighting and recrimination, or if it has always been difficult for your family to communicate well, you may want to ask a third party, such as a social worker or member of the clergy, to join you. This person should be someone everyone respects and will listen to. It is ideal if she or he has had experience with the problems you are discussing. An understanding outsider can dispel family hostility, keep the discussion going in a productive way, and allow everyone to voice feelings and opinions.

Preplanning is easier to write and talk about than to put into practice because most people do not want to discuss growing old or getting sick. When parents are healthy and leading active lives, we may feel uncomfortable bringing up what we think of as a morbid subject. Try putting it this way: "Mom and Dad, we hope that you have many more healthy years. We'd like to talk together about what could happen in the future and ask what you would like us to do in the event of disability or illness. Do you have any plans that you'd like to discuss with us? We want to do what is best and what you think would be right for you." Parents may be thankful that you took the initiative.

Helping People We Care for to Manage Money

Whether or not any long-range planning has been done, there may come a time when an ill or confused person is managing financial affairs so poorly that it becomes necessary to intervene. Deciding when this should happen may not be easy. Some people live their entire lives missing appointments, losing keys, and paying bills only after they get threatening notices. Nearly everyone occasionally forgets a meeting, gets locked out, neglects a bill, or leaves the burner on under the teakettle. However, a developing pattern of such habits in someone who has not previously had them is a sign of trouble. People who suffer from disorientation, memory loss, or other conditions that make their handling of money erratic and unreliable may dissipate assets, become victim to frauds and swindles, or become poor credit risks subject to eviction and utility shut-offs. Families or other caregivers must step in to prevent such a person from harming himself or herself further.

My mother lived in Florida for years. She had started to slow down a little and was beginning to forget things, like when I was coming from Boston to visit, or the names of some relatives. The kitchen table always seemed to be piled up with stuff—papers she said she was sorting through, charitable appeals she couldn't throw out. She was always a saver, so even though this looked unusual, it didn't worry me too much until I found the overdue rent and Blue Cross notices. I took one of her checkbooks (she had my name on her checking account) and got the bills sent to me. It took her three months to notice this—and then she wasn't pleased about it. [a fifty-year-old woman]

Staying in contact with friends or neighbors who live near your parent(s) is useful. Case management services (see p. 210) have visiting services which, for a fee, will check on elderly people living at long distances from their families.

It is important not to do more than the situation really requires. A person who needs help with paying rent or utility bills may still be perfectly capable of shopping and paying for her or his own groceries and toiletries. Your help should be designed to recognize and support a person's abilities as well as compensate for weaknesses.

If the person being cared for should become mentally incompetent, the caregiver can act in her or his name if a "durable power of attorney" has been set up in advance.

Remember that in some cases confusion and memory problems may be reversible, so assistance may not have to be permanent.

If you are now entering into a caregiving relationship with someone who is mentally competent, it is important to talk over money matters at the beginning. This is especially important if you begin sharing living quarters with a parent. For example, a parent who moves in with an adult daughter or son may lose eligibility for subsidized home-care services she or he was previously receiving. This is because total household income, rather than just the parent's own, is considered for eligibility for home care and other services in many states.

If you are caring for a spouse, financial matters become much more complicated. If a husband's illness occurs before either partner reaches retirement age, for example, a couple may lose virtually all of their income. Early retirement due to illness may mean lower pension benefits. Wives often struggle to retain whatever savings the couple does have, knowing that they will probably outlive their husbands. See the Money Matters chapter for a fuller discussion of the financial and legal issues faced by older women.

Some couples have resorted to drastic measures, such as divorce, in order to preserve assets for the spouse who does not require long-term care.

Following are various legal devices available to caregivers. Others, such as joint bank accounts, trusts, and power of attorney, are described in the Money Matters chapter.

Durable Power of Attorney.

This is a form of power of attorney that continues to be valid despite the physical or mental incompetence of the grantor. It terminates only upon the death of the grantor or if revoked by a legally appointed guardian. The grantor, however, can revoke it at any time as long as she or he is competent. A *springing durable power of attorney* goes into effect only if the grantor becomes incompetent.

These arrangements can enable your wishes to be carried out even if you are no longer able to speak for yourself, owing to a coma or some other incapacitating condition. Most people would feel more secure knowing that, in the event of incapacity, a trusted person rather than the courts will be making decisions for them. Needless to say, if you decide to give someone a power of attorney, you should be sure that the person understands how you want things managed and agrees to it before you sign the document.

Simple and limited powers of attorney can in many cases be drawn up without the assistance of a lawyer. However, because of the far-reaching nature of the document, it is best to consult a lawyer before entering into such an agreement.

Social Security Representative Payee Status.

My dad is competent but blind, and with his arthritic hands he cannot handle a pen. When checks come in he can't even mark an "X" to endorse them. [a woman in her fifties]

In situations such as the one described above, it may be helpful for the caregiver to become a representative payee. In this arrangement, the Social Security office appoints a person, institution, or community association as representative payee. The name on the check is changed from the direct beneficiary's to the payee's. The payee is then responsible for distributing the money on behalf of the beneficiary. Periodic accounting statements must be filed by the payee with the Social Security office, so, if you are a payee, keep careful records of your expenditures. This is a relatively simple way of dealing with physical or financial incapacity that works when the beneficiary's income is basically limited to that one pension check.

Guardianships or Conservatorships.

These arrangements are useful when for whatever reason a person is not capable of managing financial and/or personal affairs, *and* does not know that she or he is managing poorly, *and* that incapability poses a major threat to her or his well-being. You must have an attorney arrange these.

My mother gives money away to anyone who comes into the house. She doesn't understand her own financial status. All she cares about is seeing the dollar bills and sharing them. I know she's incompetent, but how can I subject her to a courtroom? If only I had known, I would have planned something. [a woman in her forties]

All guardianships must be granted by a court. Actions taken by a guardian, who may be a relative, friend, or community agency or institution, are often subject to the court's prior approval. The strictness of supervision varies among courts.

In most states, guardianship can be of a parcel of property or of a person. The former is generally granted when financial management is a problem but other areas are not.

Guardianships and conservatorships, for all intents and purposes, prevent an individual from acting on her or his own behalf. The person placed under guardianship bears the stigma of having been judged incompetent. She or he may lose the right to vote, to decide where to live, to sign checks, to spend money, to make decisions about medical treatment, to enter into contracts, or even to get married. The court gives the guardian the ultimate responsibility for making decisions for another person.

It is important to remember that if an older person disagrees with her or his relatives about how to handle a situation, this is not in itself a sign of incompetency. People may knowingly refuse a medical procedure that will prolong life simply because they do not wish to live the way the procedure will require. A mother who decides to sell the family silver to take a trip to Paris before she dies is not necessarily incompetent. She may just want to go to Paris, and she has a right to do so even if her daughter wants to inherit the silver.

Some states are experimenting with limited guardianships for specific purposes, such as representation in the sale of property or in medical decision-making. In some states, the power of the guardian is limited to the areas in which the individual is incompetent to act, or to a specific period of time, after which the guardian must show that the incapacity continues in order for the guardianship to be extended.

SOCIAL SERVICES CAREGIVERS SHOULD KNOW ABOUT

Though a variety of social services are being developed in many places, too many communities still offer only two options when a parent or spouse needs constant care—a nursing home or a wife or daughter to provide full-time care. All communities should provide services that create a third option, one that allows people needing care to stay at home, while at the same time easing the burden of caregivers. All caregivers need help in the form of time off, emotional and social support, and financial assistance, including Federal and state aid for home care. Many communities have such services but face problems of funding programs and training workers.

Locating services and getting to the right contact person can be a major headache for the caregiver. The first place to look is the telephone book. Many communities have a separate section listing human services (sometimes in a contrasting color, usually at the beginning of the book or between the white and yellow pages), and some are adding "silver pages," listing services for the elderly. If your phone book does not have these, look under Home Care services, Visiting Nurse services, or under Aging, (State) Department of; or try Family Services, Jewish or Catholic Family Services, or Catholic Charities. Another place to call for help is the social-service department of a local hospital. Ask to speak with a social worker.

You may also want to call local churches and synagogues to find out if they offer any services you can use. The National Catholic Women have an excellent volunteer respite program, with several communities participating. Licensed practical nurse programs, in either community colleges or technical high schools, may have students who take part-time positions to help pay for their schooling. A youth employment service for high school students can be a reasonably priced source of chore services or companion sitting. Consider "piggy-backing" all these services—scheduling them back-to-back so that the infirm person is covered for the maximum number of hours. Organize family, friends, and services into a rotating schedule so that each person has a specific time slot and assignment. Caregivers have to learn to be creative and tap all the resources around them.

Case Management Services

A health-care professional or social worker evaluates, plans, locates, coordinates, and monitors services selected to meet the needs of a particular person. Fees vary; the agencies may be either private or public. This arrangement is particularly useful for long-distance caregivers, and especially helpful when you start planning for services you know nothing about. Elderly persons without family or friends nearby can engage a case management worker for themselves.

Adult Day Care Centers

These centers offer social, recreational, and therapeutic activities to older people who need supervision during the day. The centers are approved and staffed by professionals and may be subsidized by a government agency. They provide more personal attention and have a quieter atmosphere than a senior center. They are for individuals who are too dependent to manage alone and too independent for a nursing home. Some provide transportation.

Respite Care Service

Short-term institutional care is provided to give temporary relief to family caregivers who may need a vacation or medical care for themselves. Overnight, weekend, and longer respite care may be offered by some nursing homes. Expanded facilities for respite care could be developed using underutilized rooms, wings, or buildings in hospitals, live-in residential schools, and other medical facilities where round-the-clock staff and a physical plant already exist. Such programs have already been developed in some communities. Costs, hours, and availability vary.

See p. 211, on Home Care Services, for a description of other services we may want for someone we care for or for ourselves.

HOME CARE SERVICES

Home Health Services These services may include skilled nursing care, physical, occupational, and speech/language therapy, social work, and the provision of certain medical supplies. Agencies that provide such services usually operate under the direction of a social worker, nurse, or other health professional and may be licensed by the state. The quality, variety, and cost of service will vary with the community.

Home Health Aid Catalogs (see Resources)

Homemaker Services These agencies provide personal care for the invalid and perform household tasks related to maintaining individuals in their own homes. The quality, variety, and cost of services will vary with the geographical location.

Chore Services Community organizations sometimes offer the services of an individual who will perform minor repairs or housecleaning tasks for the infirm elderly. Their services are usually free if the resident pays the cost of materials.

Transportation Services (Dial-a-Car, Wheels, Dial-a-Bus) Reduced transit fare for "senior citizens" during off-peak hours is available in many states. Some states even operate private limousines and special vans for elders. Reservations are needed one day or more in advance; charges are minimal for people over sixty-five. Greater availability is needed especially in suburban and rural areas. School buses might be used after they finish their regular routes.

Friendly Visitors Paid or volunteer visitors offer to write letters, make phone calls, play cards, chat, and generally provide human companionship for homebound people.

In-Home Care Services Part-time nursing care, rehabilitation, nutrition, speech therapy, physical therapy, occupational therapy, and social services are available to homebound elderly people under a physician's care. In-home care nurses may work for a public or private health agency. There is a service fee, sometimes sliding or adjustable; some agencies take third-party payments, Medicare, and Medicaid.

Attendant Care Service This is a new service available in some states which is aimed at helping disabled adults live independently. It is for those who know exactly what services they need, who can interview helpers, and who can pay, supervise, and, if necessary, fire a helper.

Meals on Wheels This program delivers one hot meal each day to those homebound elderly who are unable to cook for themselves and who have no one to provide meals for them. It is usually funded and operated by local volunteer organizations or area agencies for the aging. Kosher Meals on Wheels are also available. The program may charge fees on a sliding scale or may be completely subsidized. This program also serves as a checking system in case of a fall or a sudden illness.

Emergency Alert/Emergency Screening This service is offered by many hospitals and private companies under various names. To use the service, a person wears a button that she or he can push when an emergency occurs. This button sends a signal to the hospital or "response station," which will then call the neighbor who has agreed to be the support person. If there is no answer, the hospital will send an ambulance with a medical team. Prices vary. Call your local hospital or your state hospital association for information.

Telephone Reassurance This is a volunteer program in which daily telephone calls are made as a "safety check" to homebound elders. Calls may be made on weekends and holidays as well, if requested.

American Red Cross In some areas the American Red Cross will lend medical equipment, such as wheelchairs, crutches, and walkers, to area residents free on a temporary basis.

Protective Services These services are designed to protect severely disabled elderly people who are subject to abuse, neglect, and exploitation. Protective service agencies optimally provide 24-hour coverage and are connected to a police radio.

ADVOCACY FOR THE SERVICES WE NEED

Caring for frail elders and others who need caregiving should be society's responsibility as well as the family's. More public support for caregiving will not weaken the family structure, but will instead strengthen it by making it easier for family members and friends to provide for each other.

A variety of legislation is needed at the state and national levels to meet the needs of caregivers for support services, respite care, and financial compensation. Grass-roots local action has been a way for many caregivers to begin to create institutions that respond to their needs. For example, Women Who Care, with the help of personnel from an adult-care center, devised and funded a program to give each woman some relief. Then they told their story on a national television network, which sparked other support groups and growing national interest in respite-care programs.

Another example of grass-roots action is Children of Aging Parents in Levittown, Pennsylvania, which began by offering support groups for caregivers and went on to found an organization that has collected and compiled information about caregiving services and legislation locally and nationally. The founders (co-authors of this chapter) have appeared on national television news shows, have been interviewed for national magazines, and have testified before state and Federal legislative committees regarding the need for support and respite for caregivers.

In several states, activists working with organizations such as the Older Women's League are introducing bills to provide for respite and support services for caregivers. As part of our own long-term planning, we must all get behind these and other efforts to improve the prospects for those in need of care and those providing it. As long as caregiving is viewed solely as a woman's concern, it risks being overlooked by legislators and policy makers—unless we be-

come advocates for change. When legislators, bent on balancing budgets, romanticize *family* care, we must remind them that *women* who care for family members need support services and compensation. Caregivers should not be forced to provide services by themselves that the Government has chosen to cut back on or totally ignore.

NOTES

1. National Center for Health Services Research, 1982 survey, quoted in the Older Women's League press release "Family Caregivers—A Fact Sheet," November 1986.

2. Elinor Polansky. "Take Him Home, Mrs. Smith." *Healthright*, Vol. II, No. 2, Winter 1975–76.

3. Alfred P. Fengler and Nancy Goodrich, "Wives of Elderly Disabled Men: The Hidden Patients." *Gerontologist*, Vol. 19, No. 2, 1979, p. 178.

4. Vanda Colman, et al. *Till Death Do Us Part: Caregiving Wives of Severely Disabled Husbands.* Older Women's League, Washington, DC. Grey Paper #7, 1982, p. 4.

5. Linda Crossman, et al. "Older Women Caring for Disabled Spouses: A Model for Supportive Services." *Gerontologist*, Vol. 5, 1981, p. 466.

6. Fengler, op. cit., p. 182.

7. B. Soldo, "The Dependency Squeeze on Middle-aged Women." Paper presented at the meeting of the Secretary's Advisory Committee on Rights and Responsibilities of Women, U.S. Department of HHS, 1980.

8. Sharon Johnson, "The Dilemma of the Dutiful Daughter." *Working Woman*, August 1982, p. 66.

9. Amy Horowitz, "Sons and Daughters as Caregivers to Older Parents: Differences of Role Performance and Consequences," pp. 12–6. Paper presented at the 34th annual scientific meeting of the Gerontological Society of America, Toronto, Canada, November 1981 (EDRS ED 216–52).

10. See pp. 210 and 211 for a brief description of services available in some communities.

11. "Owls Fly to Help." *OWL Observer*, May/June 1985.

12. National Center for Health Services Research, op. cit.

16

PROBLEMS IN THE MEDICAL CARE SYSTEM

by Diana Laskin Siegal

Special thanks to Norma Meras Swenson

Women are treated with less respect within the health care system and receive poorer medical care than men.[1] As we age we are in double jeopardy because the widespread bias and discrimination against older people that is so deeply ingrained in our culture exists even among the people and institutions we turn to for help and support.

I was knocked unconscious by a car and brought by ambulance to the hospital that has all my records. Though my head was badly swollen, my entire right side was bruised, and my right foot was swollen, I received minimal attention. They X-rayed my foot only because of my daughter's insistence. I was out of there within an hour even though all the bills would have been paid because I have Medicare and a good supplement. I couldn't walk for four weeks and my head is still swollen two months later. A friend told me that I probably would have been checked more carefully if I had been thirty-seven instead of seventy-three.

Ageism manifests itself first and foremost in the attitude that aging is a disease. Gerontology, meaning the study of the aging process from maturity into old age, as well as the study of older people as a special population, is often confused with geriatrics, meaning the medical treatment of old people. There is even a school of thought within gerontology which hopes to "cure and prevent the disease we now call old age or senescence."[2] The words "gerontology" and "geriatrics" were not even listed in a standard dictionary in 1940,[3] and one contemporary medical dictionary lists "gerontology" and "geriatrics" as synonyms, thus further confusing aging with disease.[4] Because of male domination in medicine, both researchers and study subjects in gerontology have emphasized general problems or male problems, without noticing that women experience aging and illness differently.

AGING IS NOT A DISEASE

There is a crucial difference between aging and disease. Both happen at all ages but health care providers and researchers don't always distinguish between the signs of aging and symptoms of disease. For example, the neurological literature reports that elderly people lack some knee and ankle tendon reflexes and experience weakening of the lower legs. These signs are assumed to be a part of natural aging. However, in the studies on which this information is based, these signs of the aging nervous system were largely restricted to people with diabetes, coronary heart disease, peripheral atherosclerosis and significant high blood pressure. People of the same age without these health problems did not lack knee and ankle reflexes or have weak legs.[5]

If we recognize that a particular problem is probably a symptom of disease rather than a normal part of aging, we will be more likely to seek solutions for it. Even if a cure for the disease is not available, specific interventions may help us live more comfortably. Disabling diseases such as senile dementia and chronic conditions such as arthritis may be preventable in the future if they are regarded as diseases deserving research, rather than considered "normal" aging problems.

Bulbul

Recognizing the distinction between aging and disease also helps us identify the effects of environmental and social factors on aging. Industrial laborers experience certain problems earlier than white-collar workers. Similarly, poor women are more susceptible to diseases associated with old age than middle-income women who have more opportunities to take advantage of preventive services and to deal with health problems before they interfere with daily life.

On television, treatment of injuries and acute illness is portrayed as a drama with heroic doctors winning a life-and-death battle. Western medicine emphasizes trauma and acute conditions, not care for chronic conditions. In reality, by age sixty-five most people have developed at least one chronic health problem; these rarely limit mobility or functioning but often require long-term management to prevent them from becoming worse. Our personal attention and much of the resources of society would be better

spent on prevention of disease, on the reduction of complications from disease, and on rehabilitation and continuing care. Only about six hundred physicians in the United States describe themselves as having particular expertise in geriatrics.[6] Many health care practitioners dismiss older people's complaints with the classic put-down: "What can you expect at your age?" Equating aging with illness and pain often causes physicians to overlook manageable complaints and problems.

Four years ago, after a coma from a virus, I couldn't walk. Neither my doctor nor the physical therapy department knew how to help me. The doctor wanted to put me in a nursing home. When I insisted on a referral to a rehabilitation hospital, the social service department helped me find the best one in the area. After five weeks of special physical therapy I could walk again— not as well as I used to, but I am walking. If I hadn't insisted on rehab I'd be immobile in a nursing home today. [a seventy-six-year-old woman]

214

Our Rights as Patients*

You have the right to control what happens to your body. This includes the right of *informed consent*, which means that before you permit anyone in a medical or mental health setting to do anything to you, they must first inform you fully as to:

1) what is being planned,

2) the risks and potential benefits of that treatment plan,

3) the alternative forms of treatment, including the option of no treatment at all.

For consent to be truly informed, you must also understand all that is being explained. It is not enough for a provider to simply catalogue the risks and benefits in a quick or complicated manner, to do so when you are under the effects of medication, or in English if it is not your first language. You should ask as many questions as you have and wait until they are answered to your satisfaction before proceeding. You might ask for a written statement of the treatment plan in order to monitor your care or in case you choose to seek a second opinion later. Where no medical emergency exists, take as much time as you need to think about your decision. You can make a decision and later change your mind, since informed consent includes the right to refuse *during* as well as before any treatment. And you must agree *voluntarily*, without coercion or pressure applied by physician, family members, or others.

It is essential to read any consent form very carefully and to inquire about any vague or technical terms before signing, since your signature suggests—often incorrectly—that you *were* informed. You may cross out, reword, or otherwise amend a prepared form before signing. Be sure to ask for a copy of any form you sign.

The laws in our country do not recognize an affirmative right *to* treatment, except in the case of medical emergencies seen in a hospital emergency room. *If either transfer or discharge will threaten or adversely affect a patient's condition, then emergency treatment must first be rendered, regardless of ability to pay.*

Ask to see the patients' bill of rights at your hospital. Many hospitals have patient advocates who will help you whenever you have questions or concerns about your rights and about your satisfactions and problems while you are in the hospital. In about a third of the states, patients have a legal right to see, obtain, or have access to their hospital records. Federally qualified HMOs must make records available. Physicians' records, on the other hand, are the doctors' property, though states vary in requiring physicians to make them available to patients. Your local branch of the American Civil Liberties Union can tell you of specific rulings in your state about all aspects of patients' rights.

*Adapted from the Boston Women's Health Book Collective, *The New Our Bodies, Ourselves.* New York: Simon and Schuster, 1984, p. 584.

GETTING AND PAYING FOR MEDICAL CARE

When we are sick, we want and deserve the best medical care available—and should be able to get it without regard to our age, sex, race, or financial situation. Medical care is now too expensive to pay for it ourselves without the help of some insurance. Just at the time when we need energy most for getting well, we may be frustrated by the difficulty of finding good care and paying for it. We are at the mercy of an inadequate system when we are least able to cope with it. The more we understand the medical care system, work to improve it, and— while we are well— arrange what we will need if we become ill, the more prepared we will be.

Many women today—too many—recognize themselves in the following situations:[7]

- I am a seventy-two-year-old widow. I was sent home from the hospital because they said my Medicare had run out. I am sick. Who will help me now?
- As a single mother, working part time, I can't get health insurance from my employer and I can't afford it on my own.
- Even though my husband and I both work, by the time we pay the rent we can't afford the HMO family premium of $2,700.
- My father's nursing home bill is over $1,200 a

month. My mother has to spend every cent they saved over the past twenty-two years before he can get assistance with the bills.

· I thought Medicare paid for everything, but when I went to get help with my teeth, they told me I had to pay for it myself.

· I just got my hospital bill—$2,300 for four days in the hospital.

Most Western industrialized nations have national health care systems, reflecting the belief that health care is a right for all people. Only the United States and South Africa do not support this right. Most people persist in believing that we have the best health care system in the world, despite statistics that prove that many other countries keep their people healthier longer[8] and spend less money per person than we do. The U.S. needs a new commitment to health as a right for all, and older women are among those most in need.

When we try to get the services we need in this country, we face a patchwork quilt of agencies and programs with confusing initials. Unlike the strong and warm patchwork quilts so beautifully designed and made by women, the patchwork quilt of medical services has many holes and does not cover us when we need it. Profit-making firms are taking over medical services, hospitals, and nursing homes, and prefer patients who can afford to pay and are

HOW TO BEGIN TO GET BETTER MEDICAL CARE *

Before Your Visit

Talk to many other women about individual doctors and clinics. In choosing a doctor consider also the hospital at which the doctor practices. Contact women's groups or consumer groups to get more information about costs, information, and medical competence of a number of practitioners and clinics. See *The Directory of Medical Specialists* in your local library or at your local medical society for the doctor's training history and qualifications. Check the medical society or the state board that licenses physicians for complaints against the doctor you are considering. Review your rights as a patient.

During Your Visit

Know your own and your family's medical history. If possible, bring a written record of your own. If you have a problem, write down when it began, symptoms, etc. Write down any questions that you want to ask.

Bring a friend with you.

Firmly ask the practitioner to explain your problem, tests, treatment, and drugs in a clear and understandable fashion.

Take notes or ask your friend to do so. (A tape recorder, if you have or can borrow one, will help in case of long, complicated

*Adapted from the Boston Women's Health Book Collective, *The New Our Bodies, Ourselves.* New York: Simon and Schuster, 1984, p. 579, based on material originally from HealthRight, Inc.

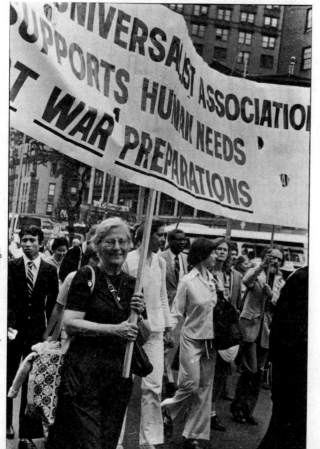

Jerry Howard/Positive Images

easy to care for. Housing, social, home-care, and medical-care services are run by separate agencies with different eligibility rules. These factors and more combine to produce unequal access to health care and poorly coordinated services.

Because our programs are so fragmented and are operated through separate bureaucracies, we have problems integrating them at the local level. It should not be so difficult, for example, to remodel a house for someone in a wheelchair, explanations.) Such record-keeping can be invaluable, so try to be assertive even if your doctor reacts defensively.

Ask the doctor to prescribe drugs by their generic rather than brand names (for example, aspirin, not Bayer's). This will save you money.

Talk to nurses and assistants. They are often sources of valuable information and support and may explain things better than the doctor.

Ask for a written summary of your visit and any lab tests and X-rays.

Remember, you have a right to a second opinion. If a series of expensive tests or surgery is recommended, you can tell the doctor to wait until you consult another doctor. This may prevent unnecessary procedures and treatment.

Don't forget—it's your body and your life. You have a right to make decisions about tests, drugs, and treatments. The questions on p. 335 can be modified to apply to other conditions and recommendations to help you make your decisions.

After Your Visit

After the visit, write down an accurate account of what happened. Be sure you know the name of the doctor and others involved, the date, the place, etc. Discuss your options with someone close to you.

"Shop" drugstores, too. Drugstores in poorer neighborhoods may charge more than those in middle-class neighborhoods. Ask to see the pharmacist's package inserts listing medical indications and contraindications. Some drugstores will keep track of all your prescriptions and will check for harmful drug interactions.

Have the name of the drug and clear instructions written on the label, because of the risk to others who may take it in error, and also because when traveling abroad you may be challenged for possession of pills.

If you get poor treatment, if you are given the wrong drugs, if you are not listened to, it is important for your own care and that of other women that you *protest*. Then write a letter describing the incident to one or several of the following:

- the doctor involved;
- the doctor who referred you;
- the administrator or director of the clinic or hospital;
- the director of community relations of the clinic or hospital;
- the local medical society;
- the state board that licenses physicians;
- the organization that will pay for your visit or treatment (for example, your union, your insurance plan, or Medicare);
- community agencies, councils, or boards;
- the local health department;
- local women's groups, women's centers, newspapers.

And about a hospital:

- Joint Commission on Accreditation of Hospitals, 875 N. Michigan Avenue, Chicago, IL 60611
- American Hospital Association, 840 N. Lake Shore Drive, Chicago, IL 60611

However, it is hard for one woman to keep working alone. Health care consumers can work together to get the treatment and services they need. So, to get changes made, work with a group (see Resources), or start one.

or to provide a woman with help in bathing and dressing when she needs it.

The housing for the elderly on my street should have full-time homemakers, whose time would be divided among residents who need help. Instead, many homemakers are arranged for separately by various agencies. They must travel long distances between clients with no pay for travel time, no health insurance, and low pay for the important care they give. [a fifty-six-year-old woman]

Medicare and Medicaid: What's the Difference?

Probably a majority of Americans are confused about these two programs which are both part of the Social Security Act. Because the details of these programs change so often, contact your Social Security and welfare offices for further information. Women have fewer opportunities for explanations of government programs and therefore tend to assume incorrectly that at age sixty-five all their medical costs will be covered by Medicare.

Medicare

Medicare is a Federal medical-insurance program for people over sixty-five who are eligible for Social Security or Railroad Retirement.*

Medicare is also available for people under sixty-five who have been entitled to Social Security disability payments for at least two years and to certain people who have kidney failure.

Medicare is set up to pay mostly for the care of acute conditions in a hospital, whereas most older people need preventive care and care of chronic conditions on an outpatient basis, or need supportive care. About 95 percent of people over age sixty-five are covered by Medicare, substantially more than the proportion with medical coverage before Medicare was started. However, Medicare actually pays for only about 40 percent of the medical care costs of the elderly. The poorer you are, the greater the percentage of income you spend on medical care.[9] Older people are now spending 18.5 percent of their income on health care—more than they were spending before the passage of the Medicare bill.[10]

The majority of ineligible people are women

---

*Retired Federal, state, and local government workers who are in pension plans separate from Social Security may remain in their group health plans after retirement. All government workers hired after 1985 are required to contribute to the Medicare Trust Fund through payroll deductions. Those hired before 1985 have the option of contributing.

Marianne Gontarz

and recent older immigrants. If you are over sixty-five but not eligible for Medicare, you may purchase it on your own for a monthly premium, just like buying any other private medical insurance. However, the premiums ($226 per month in 1987) are prohibitively expensive for many people, especially for many women.

The Medicare program is the same in every state and is available to every eligible person, regardless of income. However, not all health care providers accept Medicare patients, so the opportunity to use the Medicare coverage varies within states and cities. Payments are made from the Medicare Trust Fund (held separately from the Social Security Trust Fund), financed by the Social Security (FICA) tax paid by people presently working, and also by the premiums paid by people currently on Medicare. Before you reach sixty-five, you should determine whether or not you will be eligible and want to sign up. If you do not sign up for Medicare when you are first eligible, your subsequent enrollment can be delayed and your premiums can be 10 percent higher. **See your local Social Security Administration office for information and applications before your sixty-fifth birthday regardless of when you plan to retire.**

There are two parts to the Medicare insurance program. Part A is hospitalization insurance at no additional premium and is automatic when you sign up for Social Security benefits or for Medicare. This provides *limited* payment for:

- Inpatient hospital care
- Inpatient care in a skilled nursing facility after discharge from a hospital
- Home health care
- Hospice care

Services are also limited within time periods called "benefit periods." There is an extra sixty days of inpatient hospital care called "reserve days."

Part B is medical insurance for services other than hospitalization and it is optional. Part B provides *limited* payment for some doctors' services, outpatient hospital services, certain ambulance services, and some other medical services and supplies. If you choose Part B, you pay a monthly premium deducted from your Social Security benefits. In 1987, you will pay $17.90 per month for Part B. You can use your Parts A and B premiums to enroll in a Health Maintenance Organization (HMO).

Medicare will pay only for those facilities and agencies which it approves. They, in turn, must agree to accept Medicare payments and meet certain standards in addition to state licensing requirements. Always ask in advance of making an appointment whether a facility or agency is approved for and accepts Medicare payments. Always ask whether a physician will bill Medicare directly or whether you will have to pay the physician first and then file a claim for reimbursement with Medicare yourself. Also ask whether the physician will accept the Medicare rate or whether you will be responsible for paying any additional charges he or she asks over and above that. Some states require physicians to accept the Medicare rate.

Because of the lobbying efforts of the insurance industry, Medicare claims are not handled by the Federal Government but are processed in each state by private insurance organizations. Thus the claims-processing systems, forms, and responsiveness to beneficiaries' problems do vary in each state.

A few of the services Medicare **does not** pay for are:

- Routine physical examinations and tests
- Any care considered to be mainly custodial, such as most nursing-home care. It is payment for this intermediate or custodial nursing home care, rather than skilled care, that depletes many older people's assets. (See Medicaid, page 221.)
- Eyeglasses and hearing aids, and the examinations for prescribing or fitting them
- General dental work
- Routine foot care
- Drugs and medicines, prescription and nonprescription
- Meals, homemaker services, and more than part-time nursing care when those services are part of a home health care arrangement
- Services which are ruled *not* reasonable and necessary
- Care outside the United States, except for limited coverage in Canada and Mexico under special circumstances, *not* including tourist travel.

In addition, Medicare does not pay the entire cost of all the services it covers. You must pay for deductibles and copayments. A deductible is the initial dollar amount you pay before Medicare will begin making any payments; a copayment

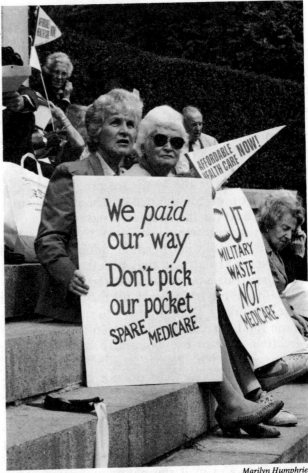

Marilyn Humphries

is your required or part share of the expenses above the deductible for these services which Medicare covers. The costs of the monthly premiums for Parts A and B, the deductibles, and the copayments have grown so great that many elderly people no longer can afford them. The costs will continue to increase each year unless we can stop the automatic increases which Congress has granted.

We recommend that every woman obtain a copy of *Your Medicare Handbook* and the *Guide to Health Insurance for People with Medicare* from her local Social Security Administration office. If you and/or your husband plan to work past the age of sixty-five, also get a copy of *Employed Medicare Beneficiaries Age 65 Through 69.*

Hospice Care Benefits Under Medicare

Hospice is a concept of care for the terminally ill which provides supportive rather than curative treatment (see Dying and Death chapter). Under Medicare, hospice is primarily a home-care program, including pain control, with some short-term inpatient care. Many expenses are covered when the services are received from a Medicare-certified hospice, but only 300 of the more than 1,500 hospice programs are certified because the Federal regulations exclude community-based programs. There is a 210-day lifetime limit within three benefit periods. (The pamphlet "Hospice Benefits Under Medicare" and the list of certified programs are available from your local Social Security office.)

Unfortunately, the Medicare program creates dilemmas both for the person choosing hospice services and for the hospice program providing them. A person who chooses to drop out of the hospice program and resume standard hospital and medical treatment may forfeit some hospice benefits. Thus a person is required to forego possibly lifesaving treatment and the sense of hope that can prolong life in order to qualify for humane final care. Critics have deplored these restrictive policies as potentially discriminating against older persons, since other ways of paying for hospice services do not have these restrictions.

The forced choice also assumes that doctors know more than they do about predicting life and death. The hospice provider institution, under these regulations, must care for patients as long as they live even if the payment benefits have been used up. When patients receive comfort and humane care, as they do in hospices, they tend to live longer. Yet when a patient lives beyond the specified time, Medicare withdraws the funding, leaving the provider institution with a terminally ill and potentially indigent patient. Congress agreed to provide payment for hospice care on the grounds that it would be cheaper than hospital care, but if the patients live longer, the per patient cost goes up. To get around such limitations and improve the quality of care, hospices that are affiliated with hospitals have been known to transfer hospital patients who are close to death onto their hospice rolls to get the total amount for that person. When that person dies, they then have the dollars beyond what the care actually cost to provide care for other patients. This is just another of the endless dilemmas created by the lack of a universal health care system that should pay for living as well as dying, for prevention as well as illness, for everyone regardless of age.

Purchasing Private Insurance to Supplement Federal Medicare Coverage

Medicare supplement insurance is sold by private insurance companies to pick up where Medicare leaves off. It is often referred to as "Medigap" insurance, because it is supposed to fill the gaps in Medicare. *There is no governmental agency which sells Medigap supplemental insurance.* It is difficult and confusing to purchase Medigap insurance because so many different kinds of policies are available, just as with other types of private insurance. Some general guidelines for buying this (or any other) insurance follow.

- Be especially cautious about policies sold to individuals by mail or on television.
- Coverage and premiums vary among states. Even states that regulate supplemental insurance do not regulate the premiums. Contact both the division of insurance and office of consumer affairs in your state for complete information.
- Policies with identical coverage often vary in price from one company to another, so shop carefully.
- Be careful to select insurance which *supplements*, but does not *duplicate*, what Medicare or another policy already covers. Many insurance companies will refuse to pay benefits covered by another policy.
- What is usually sold as nursing home (often called long-term care) insurance is coverage for a stay in a Medicare-approved, skilled nursing facility over and above the number of days provided for under Medicare Part A. These will **not** pay for admissions to most nursing homes. Private companies are beginning to offer insurance for the more often needed intermediate-level *custodial* care covered by Medicaid, but not by Medicare. Beware of pressure to buy expensive and risky private individual long-term-care insurance. Instead, lobby so that more people will be eligible for nursing-home coverage under Medicaid or some more uniform national program.*
- Special insurance policies which promise to insure against cancer and other specific dis-

*Watch for proposals before Congress and for reports of the long-term-care pilot insurance program the American Association of Retired Persons (AARP) is trying out in six states.

eases are not a good idea because they are expensive and rarely pay benefits. Many states have outlawed the sale of such policies.

• *Indemnity* policies, under which you receive a small amount of money for every day you are in a hospital, do not supplement Medicare. Any benefits paid by such a policy will be counted as income and could jeopardize your SSI and Medicaid eligibility. Indemnity policies, such as the one sold by the Older Women's League (OWL), are useful only for those who cannot obtain any other kind of hospitalization insurance.

• If you already have supplemental private insurance and then become eligible for Medicaid, you may want to keep the supplemental insurance, especially if it covers what Medicaid does not. You would be wise to keep your supplemental policy if you anticipate going off Medicaid.

I purchased medical insurance offered by a travel agency for a trip, because I knew Medicare wouldn't pay any hospital bills in the Middle East. I could have saved the money, however, because when I returned home I found out that my Medicare supplementary insurance does cover hospital expenses while traveling outside the country. [a seventy-six-year-old woman]

Medicaid

Medicaid is a joint Federal and state program which pays some medical bills for certain low-income people: those sixty-five and older, the blind, the disabled, members of families with dependent children, and some other children. Medicaid funds come from taxes. Each state designs its own Medicaid eligibility and services within Federal guidelines, so each state's program is different. Few states have any literature explaining their Medicaid eligibility or services, so you will have to inquire at your local social services or welfare office, your state Medicaid agency, or your regional office of the U.S. Department of Health and Human Services. Take someone with you and go prepared to take notes; otherwise you will have no record of what was said. The Federal Government contributes between 50 percent of the costs—to states with the highest average income levels—and 78 percent—to states with the lowest average income levels. State and sometimes local taxes provide the rest of the funding.

In some states, if your income is low enough

Marianne Gontarz

so that you are eligible for Supplemental Security Income (SSI), you are also eligible for Medicaid. Nearly 80 percent of persons eligible but not receiving SSI are women; most of them have never heard of the program.[11] Other states use their own, usually stricter, standards to determine who is "categorically needy" for financial and therefore Medicaid eligibility. Some states have programs for people who are "medically needy"; that is, for people who qualify for medical but not for other financial assistance. Even if you own a house and a car, you may still fall into the medically needy category, if your other assets and your income meet your state's guidelines for *income* and *assets*. Services for the categorically needy and the medically needy differ from state to state.

Because of the stigma of welfare and the lack of information about the programs available, fully a third of those eligible for Medicaid never apply. Of these, 79 percent are women.[12]

Many women now are homeless and have no medical care.[13] We have worked hard, paid taxes, and should receive what we are entitled to.

All through my marriage I supplemented my husband's low income by taking in boarders and sewing. As a widow my Social Security was so low that I gradually used my meager savings. Finally, reluctantly I went on SSI, which in my state means I am eligible for Medicaid. Now I can get the eyeglasses, hearing aids, and home care that Medicare never paid for. [an eighty-two-year-old woman]

If you are eligible, Medicaid *must* pay for:

• Inpatient hospital services
• Outpatient hospital services

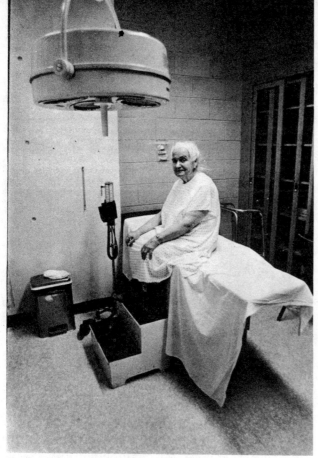
Marianne Gontarz

- Rural health clinic services
- Laboratory and X-ray services
- Skilled nursing facility and home health services for persons twenty-one and older
- Early and periodic screening, diagnosis, and treatment for persons under twenty-one
- Family-planning services and supplies
- Physician services
- Transportation to services covered

In most states, Medicaid will pay for prescription drugs. In some states, Medicaid will purchase Medicare Part B coverage; some states will pay for additional services such as dentures, eyeglasses, hearing aids, personal care services, foot care, preventive and screening services for adults, and other services.

Not all facilities, agencies, health practitioners, and other providers, such as ambulance companies, will accept Medicaid, so you should ask whether or not they do.

In all states (except Arizona) and the District of Columbia and the U.S. territories, Medicaid pays for intermediate-level nursing home care. This is the level of care most often needed by older people and it is *not* covered by Medicare.

Many people who have been struck with catastrophic medical and nursing home bills find that Medicaid is the only resource available, but it is available only after they have spent their assets. If they weren't truly poor before, they must become poor in order to qualify. In 1986, Congress allowed all states to include trust funds as assets in determining Medicaid eligibility, reasoning that such trusts were only used by wealthy persons to protect assets for an inheritance. The spouse, usually a woman, who needs to preserve half the couple's assets for her own future use, is left unprotected. The greatest threat to an older woman's financial security is that her husband may require nursing home care. Almost all of the couple's money will have to go toward that care—their savings, his pension and Social Security—before he becomes eligible for Medicaid. So even if Medicaid "allows" the wife to keep her home and car, she may not have enough money to maintain them, let alone buy groceries and gas. Even if household property is transferred from the prospective Medicaid recipient, or from joint ownership, to the wife enough in advance to meet the Medicaid guidelines,* she may still be held responsible for some bills or a lien may be placed on the house. Some women have had to sue their spouses in nursing homes for support or for divorce in order to be awarded some of his Social Security and assets. Federal legislation to correct this tragic situation was first introduced in Congress in 1986, and has gained support.

Many hospitals, nursing homes, and doctors refuse to treat people on Medicaid, claiming that the payments are too small and too slow in coming. Hospitals often refuse to treat those with no insurance in spite of the requirement that any hospital which ever received Federal construction funds must do so until the loans run out. (Most hospitals did receive these Hill-Burton construction loans.) In spite of their objections to the Medicaid program, it is the hospitals, nursing homes, and doctors who received the largest share of the $37.5 billion in Medicaid payments in 1985. In fact, Medicaid pay about half of all the nursing home costs in the U.S.[14]

Every hospital should be required to take care of a patient until her/his life-threatening condition is over and adequate continuing care is ar-

---

*State guidelines vary from the time one enters a nursing home to three years before entering a nursing home. Check your state's Medicaid regulations.

We're releasing you from the hospital early. You're cutting into our profit margin!

Bulbul

ranged. Only after a life-threatening condition has passed should a hospital transfer a patient to another hospital if it is more appropriate. To transfer, or "dump," patients because of lack of insurance or money should not be permitted. This practice is most common in states that have a large number of profit-making hospitals. A state law was passed in Texas in 1985 forbidding dumping because the situation had become so severe.[15]

Controlling Medical Care Costs

The Reagan Administration has systematically proposed cutbacks in social programs of all kinds, including Social Security and food stamps, in order to reduce Federal expenditures. In the early 1980s, the Medicare Trust Fund was reported to be on the verge of bankruptcy, so one method of controlling costs was quickly adopted.

How did the financial crisis develop? When Medicare was first set up in 1965, it did not control unnecessary hospitalization, procedures, and medications ordered by physicians. There was little incentive for hospitals to control costs

included in the daily charge (called per diem) since Medicare, Medicaid, and Blue Cross (called third-party payors) paid each hospital an amount based on the average costs in that hospital from the previous year for their subscribers. (Commercial insurance companies and patients who pay their own bills are charged whatever per diem the hospital sets.)

In the last decade, hospital costs rose two to three times faster than inflation in the economy as a whole. Hospitals, blaming increased labor costs, often resisted unionization and other efforts by hospital workers, who are mostly women, to improve their wages, but did little else to control costs. Some states, in an effort to control this upward spiral, instituted "prospective payment" systems, in which rates are set in advance of the year so that hospitals will have a clearer idea of expected income, can plan more securely, and will have an incentive to reduce costs. The states that adopted prospective payment systems showed a slower rate of increase in hospital costs than states without these programs.

The Social Security Amendment of 1983 (Public Law 98-21) set up one kind of prospective re-

223

Surviving Under DRGs*

- If you feel that hospital admission has been arbitrarily denied to you or to someone you know, send a protest to the peer review organization (PRO) covering your area. Your local medical society or hospital (try the medical records department if the chief executive officer's or director's office doesn't have the information) will know the name and address of the PRO. The PRO is supposed to respond promptly.

- If you do have to go into the hospital, find out from your doctor when you are to be admitted and when your discharge is anticipated. Find out what your medical condition and functional status are expected to be when you are discharged. Be sure the doctor or the nurse contacts the hospital's discharge-planning and social service offices *before* admission. If home-care or visiting nurse services might be needed after discharge, notify the appropriate agency *before* you are admitted.

- When you are in the hospital, ask the discharge-planning and the social service offices to help arrange the services you will need when you return home. If you are to be discharged over a weekend, it is important to have some services arranged before 5 P.M. on Friday. Some areas have seven-day-a-week services, but many do not.

- Beware if anyone says your hospital stay is over because "your Medicare or your DRG days are up." *There is no fixed number of days for each diagnosis-related group.* As long as the care you are getting is judged medically necessary and you have not used up your Medicare reserve days, you can remain in the hospital at no additional charge to you beyond the co-payment. In fact, the hospital receives a supplemental payment in addition to the regular reimbursement for a stay of unusual length or cost. The hospital receives an entirely new payment if you are discharged and then readmitted for a few more days—thus there are financial benefits to the hospital in having a "revolving door."

- The hospital may notify you that you no longer need inpatient care. If you feel you are being prematurely discharged, do not accept a verbal statement. Ask the hospital for a statement in writing that you no longer need to be there and note on it the date you receive it. Since your stay is covered by Medicare for only two days after receipt of the written notice, request a review by the PRO immediately if you disagree with the decision. The longer you delay the request, the larger your bill will be if the PRO doesn't rule in your favor. You have the right to be informed in writing of the PRO's decision within three working days of receipt of your request for a review. If the PRO doesn't approve a continued stay, you will be billed for the hospital costs beginning on the third calendar day after receipt of the hospital's notice of noncoverage. You can refuse discharge if the necessary home care cannot be provided at the time discharge is requested. Medicare will not pay for this extra time, but many patients have other forms of insurance coverage that will. Thus, your right of appeal also puts you in jeopardy for the cost of the extra days if you are turned down.

- If you are to be admitted to a nursing home from the hospital, try to enter during the week. Many homes have reduced staff during evenings, weekends, and holidays. Make certain the nursing home has received a medical summary from the hospital, especially if you have ongoing needs such as medication and bandage changes.

- Some states have set up advocacy units to help Medicare beneficiaries with questions or concerns about admissions and discharges under the DRG system. Find out which agency in your state is collecting this information and giving assistance. Get in touch if you are having problems.

*Adapted from suggestions by Mary Sullivan, president of the Boston Elder Communications Foundation, published in *Boston Seniority*, Vol. 9, No. 5 (April 1986), p. 15; Elliot Carlson and William Oriol, "DRGs. Surviving Medicare's New Obstacle Course." *Modern Maturity*, Vol. 28, No. 6 (December 1985-January 1986), p. 95; People's Medical Society, "Rights of Medicare Patients." *New Directions for Women*, Vol. 15, No. 2 (March/April 1986).

imbursement system based on diagnosis-related groups (DRGs).* In spite of the fact that the Medicare Trust Fund is no longer in immediate danger of insolvency, the amount of money budgeted for Medicare Part A was cut in 1986 and a further cut of $4.6 billion is proposed for 1987. This cut is equal to the amount proposed for the much-criticized "Star Wars" research.[16]

The DRG system assigns a rate for the treatment of 467 groups of illnesses. This rate is based on past audits of similar cases, including the range of days that a patient with a particular condition is expected to remain in the hospital and the services she or he will require. The DRG rate is the only payment any hospital gets from the Federal Government for its Medicare patients. If treatment actually costs less than the amount allowed, the hospital pockets the savings. If the treatment costs more than the set rate, the hospital takes the loss. If the cost of your hospital stay exceeds the expected rate for your DRG—because of the severity of your illness, its complications, or your frailty—your case may be considered on an individual basis. It is important to keep in mind that the DRG system limits *payments* only, not the length of a stay. *It is illegal for a hospital to tell a patient to leave because her or his "DRG or Medicare days are up."*

DRGs may result in special hardships for women, both as patients and as caregivers. Hospitals are already curtailing admissions or encouraging early discharge of frail elders. Since nursing home and home care supports are being cut rather than expanded, many older women are going without care. A woman may, for example, be discharged on a Friday but not have home-care services available until the following Monday, or not at all. Since sweeping surgery (like a hysterectomy-oophorectomy) may be cheaper than more delicate life-enhancing procedures (such as myomectomy, which removes a fibroid but leaves the uterus), the quality of medical care is affected.

The data generated by Medicare and Medicaid, including the DRG system, can make it possible to compile comparative statistics on hospitals. The first such data, released in 1986, for example, listed hospitals which had significantly lower success rates for coronary bypass

surgery performed on Medicare patients than on non-Medicare patients.

While patients are suffering from being denied admission, and from premature discharge, hospitals earned a 14 percent profit on Medicare patients in the first year of the system—more than double the average 6 percent profit on non-Medicare services.[17]

The public hospitals, which serve the sicker patients that others refuse, and rural hospitals, which are paid at lower rates than urban hospitals, are the ones in financial difficulty.

In addition, although the DRG system was supposed to be an incentive for hospitals to reduce unnecessary hospitalization and procedures and avoid duplicative testing, the evidence is that management costs are rising and savings are achieved by cutting corners on services.[18]

Since virtually every hospital in the country takes Medicare patients, the DRG system will be closely scrutinized and eventually extended to all areas of health care. DRGs are already used for the Medicaid system in California (Medi-Cal). New Jersey applies its system to all third-party payors. Coalitions of large businesses and industries were instrumental in the passage of these systems because of their concerns about the rising costs of providing health insurance to employees. Only massive lobbying by the American Medical association prevented the DRG principle from being applied to physicians' fees as well. The Kennedy-Gephardt bill, which was introduced in 1984 but not passed, would subject both private insurance companies and physician fees to the DRG principle nationwide.

To monitor hospital use and quality of care for Medicare patients, the Federal Government contracts with fifty-four physician-directed peer review organizations (PROs). Though they are supposed to reduce unnecessary admissions and procedures and avoid unnecessary deaths or complications, they are more likely to be interested in cutting costs than in improving the quality of patient care. Nevertheless, we should try to pressure the PROs to work on our behalf by filing complaints with them.

Private Medical Insurance

In the United States, medical insurance is so complicated, fragmented, and expensive that 38 million people (nearly 20 percent of the population) have no coverage at all.[19] More than 5 mil-

---

*Rehabilitation services in hospitals and specialty hospitals, such as those that treat alcoholic and psychiatric patients, are not included.

lion without insurance are middle-aged women.[20] Workers in large companies are usually covered by insurance plans offered through their employers; these plans can also cover the employee's family. Because individual plans are more expensive than group plans or plans in which the employer pays part of the costs, many women who are unemployed or are employed in part-time jobs or work for small firms (which frequently don't offer insurance) cannot afford medical insurance. Those who are neither working nor covered under the family benefits of working spouses must purchase their own individual health insurance plans. Medical insurance for the unemployed and uninsured has been proposed but not yet adopted at either the state or Federal level. Furthermore, nontraditional families, such as lesbian couples, are rarely recognized as families for health insurance purposes.

Women who have a preexisting condition such as asthma or breast cancer often cannot obtain health insurance at all, or can only obtain a policy that won't cover that condition for a specified period of time. Even women who have had benign breast lumps or cervical lesions have been excluded. Some states have designated groups of insurance companies to cover people with preexisting conditions who have no employee-based insurance but are not poor enough for welfare.

Before you purchase any medical insurance, examine the policy carefully to know what it covers and whether that coverage is worth the premium. Pay attention to the size of the deductible and the upper limit on total expenses figured annually, per family member, or per lifetime. Remember that advertisements can be misleading. Several states have passed legislation requiring insurance companies to "translate" the jargon found in most policies. Much of the information on purchasing insurance to supplement Medicare on page 220 applies to purchasing other health insurance as well.

Many women are working to patch some holes in our health care system immediately. Since its founding in 1980, the Older Women's League (OWL) has advocated increased access to health insurance. Partly as a result of those efforts, some states have permitted workers who divorce to keep their former spouse covered under the employer's family insurance or HMO until the worker or the spouse remarries. A Federal law passed in 1986 provides up to three years of continued membership in a worker's medical-insurance group for spouses and dependent children who would otherwise lose their membership because of widowhood, divorce, or retirement.[21] The law also helps unemployed workers and their families by offering coverage up to eighteen months after a layoff. However, the person remaining in the plan must pay the entire premium plus administrative costs and women with children will have to pay the higher family rates to cover their children. Thus, poorer women and those whose spouses had no insurance will still be excluded. Since the law is not retroactive, it does not help the millions of women who have already lost their health insurance. Also, because the continuation of group coverage is only temporary, women may still be without any coverage when the eighteen months to three years are up.

Health Maintenance Organizations

One innovation in health care delivery is the health maintenance organization (HMO). In this system, your monthly premium is paid to the HMO, which then provides you with all your health care, inpatient and outpatient. Some HMOs pay physicians a salary (closed-panel HMOs); others are composed of physicians in private practice (open-panel HMOs, also known as IPAs). Some HMOs have their own hospitals. The enrolled individual pays extra for any service obtained outside the HMO without approval.

In ancient China, healthy people paid physicians and stopped paying if they became sick. Today, we usually pay doctors when we're sick, so doctors have no incentive to keep us healthy. At the very time when we most need help, our care is dependent upon what we can pay. One advantage of an HMO is that we have paid a fixed amount in advance and don't have to pay for each service, so the doctor has an incentive to keep us well and we are covered in case of sickness.

One of the original fears about HMOs—that they would save money by undertreating enrollees—has not proved true over time. Though individual complaints should be monitored, in general HMOs provide less expensive treatment with fewer hospitalizations than conventional medical care. In one earlier survey of some HMOs, which served around 200,000 Medicare beneficiaries, the elderly appeared to do just as well, perhaps better, than in fee-for-service care, and with less hospitalization.[22]

Efforts have increased since 1984 to enroll as many people as possible who are on Medicare into HMOs. Currently, 3 percent of the Medicare population, nearly 870,000 people, are enrolled in 151 HMOs in 33 states. A recent study by the U.S. Senate Special Committee on Aging, based on reports from five states, reported that the Reagan Administration has been lax in following up complaints and reviewing the quality of care Medicare beneficiaries are receiving from HMOs.[23] Some HMOs have resorted to arbitrary exclusions and unscrupulous marketing tactics in their interest to increase enrollments and may be jeopardizing patient care.

We need to be aware that in HMOs some of our expected rights of informed consent and the right to sue may not apply in the same way. Find out about grievance procedures and get on the patients' boards that may be set up to make sure that you and everyone else in the plan are equitably treated.

Other Types of Medical Coverage[24]

Many large employers consider conventional insurance too expensive and are *self-insuring* their employees. The self-insured employer pays all employees' health costs directly, but just for a limited set of benefits. Some businesses get around paying for state-mandated benefits by self-insuring while other businesses have offered substantially better benefits than regular insurance.

Preferred provider organizations (PPOs) are physicians, hospitals, or clinics that agree to charge lower prices to the insurer in order to get more patients. Consumers are allowed to use any provider they choose (unlike HMOs) but have to pay higher copayments for using outside providers.

Four social health maintenance organizations (SHMOs), which combine social services with medical services on a prepaid basis, have been established. The SHMOs will enroll 20,000 persons who are on Medicare, including some who are also on Medicaid. Women's organizations should monitor these demonstration SHMOs in New York, Minnesota, Oregon, and California.

Health Insurance vs. Health Plan/Service

Many proposals have been made to fashion a whole new quilt. Some are for a national medical *insurance* system that would provide insurance coverage for everyone but continue the costs of retaining the present insurance industry. The Canadian system has controlled costs while insuring everyone by administering the insurance through the provinces rather than through the insurance industry. Administration costs in Canada are about 3 percent of health costs; in the U.S., administrative costs of private insurance approximate 15 percent of covered expenditures.[25] Other proposals are for some other kind of national health *service* or *plan* that not only pays for services but would also deliver them directly without the complications of a billing system. The President, members of Congress, Supreme Court Justices, members of the Armed Services and the Coast Guard, some veterans, and some Native Americans already receive health care under some type of national health plan. Why shouldn't the rest of us?

Evaluating New Proposals for Health Care Services and Financing

The best and most efficient way to repair the patchwork health care system is by providing tax-supported universal health care. Until we have the opportunity to support such a system, how can we evaluate the many new proposals expected at both the Federal and state levels? Among the important questions to ask are who will pay and who will benefit? A program that will benefit the greatest number of people, spread the costs among those most able to pay through taxes, and make certain that no industry profits unduly is a health care program that is worthy of our support. Programs should right inequities but not pit one segment of the population against the other. If a proposal falls short of a major overhaul of the health care system, and is simply intended to fill a gap in the present system, it should at least address a problem that affects a sizable number of people. The proposal should benefit women in proportion to their current or expected numbers in the population and redress past inequities.

Applying some of these criteria to the "catastrophic coverage" proposal of the Reagan Administration leads us to the conclusion that the proposal is inadequate and misleading. The plan proposes an additional Medicare premium to cover long-term hospital stays which will benefit less than 3 percent of the population on Medicare. It offers no protection to the approximately 37 million Americans of all ages who have no health insurance at all; and it ignores long-term care, which is the real catastrophic need of those on Medicare, especially women.[26] This proposal also reflects a bias toward institutional medical services and does not address the great need for home-care services, social services and out-patient mental health services for the elderly. In addition, it does nothing to support prevention and the need for chronic care.

NOTES

1. Public Health Service Task Force on Women's Health Issues, *Women's Health, Vol. II.* U.S. Dept. of Health and Human Services, No. (PHS) 85–50206, May 1985, pp. 1–26.

2. J. L. Gelein, "Aged Women and Health." Symposium on Women's Health Issues. *Nursing Clinics of North America.* Vol. 17, March 1982, pp. 179–85.

3. *Webster's Collegiate Dictionary,* 5th Edition. Springfield, MA: G. and C. Merriam Co., 1940.

4. *Taber's Cyclopedic Medical Dictionary.* 14th Edition. Philadelphia: F. A. Davis Co., 1981.

5. Adrian Ostfeld, "Summary: Five-Year Perspective on the Elkridge Conference." In *Proceedings of the Second Conference on the Epidemiology of Aging.* Bethesda, MD: U.S. Department of Health and Human Services, National Institutes of Health, 1980, pp. 349–57.

6. Elaine M. Brody, *Mental and Physical Health Practices of Older People.* New York: Springer Publishing Co., 1985, p. 45.

7. Excerpted from a leaflet published by the Gray Panthers of Greater Boston announcing its "Health Care Is a Right" National Health Program Referendum Campaign, April 1986.

8. United Nations, *1981 Demographic Yearbook.* New York, 1982.

9. "Growing Old in Reagan's America." *Staying Alive!* October 1984.

10. Older Women's League, "Give 'Em Health," *Fact Sheet,* April 1987.

11. Alice Quinlan, "Federal '87 Budget Hits Women, Poor." *The OWL Observer,* Vol. 5, No. 2 (March/April 1986), p. 1.

12. *On the Other Side of Easy Street: Myths and Facts About the Economics of Old Age.* Washington, D.C.: The Villers Foundation, 1987.

13. The situation is so bad that Boston has equipped three medical vans to provide care to homeless people.

14. Information from the Department of Health and Human Services.

15. Denise Grady, "The Cruel Price of Cutting Medical Expenses." *Discover.* May 1986, pp. 25–43.

16. Gray Panthers of Massachusetts, *Where Does Your Money Go?* 1986.

17. Statement of then Majority Leader Jim Wright before the House Select Committee on Aging, April 10, 1986, p. 3.

18. David U. Himmelstein and Steffie Woolhandler, "Cost Without Benefit: Administrative Waste in U.S. Health Care." *The New England Journal of Medicine,* Vol. 314, No. 7 (February 13, 1986), pp. 441–5.

19. Alexander Cockburn, "State of the Union Is Enough to Make You Ill." *The Wall Street Journal,* February 13, 1986, p. 63.

20. Older Women's League, "Give 'Em Health." *Fact Sheet,* April 1987.

21. Passed as part of the Consolidated Omnibus Budget Reconciliation Act (COBRA), Public Law 99-272. Continued Access to Group Health Insurance Act.

22. J. K. Inglehart, "Medicare Turns to HMOs. Health Policy Report." *The New England Journal of Medicine,* Vol. 312, No. 2 (January 10, 1985), pp. 132–6.

23. Associated Press, "Report Says US Should Probe, Not Promote, HMO Program." *The Boston Globe,* April 8, 1987.

24. "Playing the Market." *Staying Alive!* Issue No. 18, Summer 1986, p. 3.

25. Howard H. Hiatt, "Canada's Solution to Inequality in Health Care." *The Boston Globe,* February 23, 1987.

26. "Older Women's League Says White House Catastrophic Plan 'Inadequate, Misleading.'" Press release, March 2, 1987.

17

NURSING HOMES

by Susan Lanspery

This chapter assumes that dignity, quality health care, and control over one's own life are basic human rights. This chapter also assumes that a nursing home can be a good choice for some individuals and their caregivers. One's own or a family member's home can be more isolating than a nursing home.

That night I tossed and turned and I couldn't sleep. I felt so bad that my daughter couldn't go out with her husband because they didn't want to leave me alone. So I made up my mind that I would go into a home. And they tried to talk me out of it, but I said, "In a home I'll be with people my own age and we'll have things to talk about together." So, I've been here almost four years and I haven't been sorry. [a woman in her nineties]

My mother benefited from the mental stimulation of being surrounded by a lot of different people and activities which could never have been achieved in her own home. She was able to make new friends she never would have met had she lived alone in her apartment with a series of hired caregivers. I am sure the quality of her life during those years, although by no means ideal, was much better than it had been in those lonely and sick years before her collapse.[1]

After my husband had a devastating stroke, everything in my life other than that stopped. He was in hospitals, then in nursing homes, and then I took him home against everybody's advice. I felt like I was retired from life. It seemed as though the world deserted us. I used to say, "I'll never put my husband in an institution again. Home is the best place for him." But I was wrong. I really was wrong because there was very little contact with others and no diversions for him at home. [a woman in her sixties]

One reason so many of us react negatively to nursing homes is that serious problems *do* exist in some nursing homes. Even "better" nursing homes that provide a clean, safe environment

Norma Holt

and competent basic medical services may infantilize and dehumanize residents, ignoring their needs and desires for choice, control, privacy, and meaningful lives. All of these problems are part of our society's tendency to write off older people and people with disabilities, whether or not they reside in nursing homes.

The solution to these problems lies in action. Successful nursing home placement, care, and reform require information, planning, and maximum consumer/family involvement; in other words, a sense of control.

It's never too late—or too early—to start learning about nursing homes. Although only 5 percent of people over sixty-five are in institutions at a given time, 25 percent of people over sixty-five can expect to spend at least some time in one.[2] We must all recognize that alternatives to family-based care are essential. Negative attitudes only reinforce the imperfections of those alternatives and paralyze our ability to help ourselves.

It is particularly important for women to understand as much as possible about nursing homes. Women outnumber men as nursing home residents, as primary caregivers who may help others to make nursing home decisions and adjustments, and as workers in nursing homes. Most (71 percent) nursing home residents are women, and the percentages increase by age group: 6 percent of all residents are women under sixty-five; 10 percent are women sixty-five to seventy-four; 26 percent are women seventy-five to eighty-four; 29 percent are women over eighty-five.[3]

Furthermore, the number of poor older women is growing rapidly. Their poverty (often a lifetime's worth) increases their chances of poor health and of a need for long-term care. We must stretch the feminist ideals of empowerment, action, hope, cooperation, and respect to them—to us.

DIFFERENCES AMONG NURSING HOMES

One way that nursing homes vary is in type of ownership.

- *Proprietary nursing homes* are profit-making. Most nursing homes are proprietary. A relatively recent phenomenon is the proprietary chain, in which one corporation owns many individual homes.
- *Nonprofit nursing homes* are operated by such organizations as religious groups, service clubs, and labor unions. Some have endowments and receive private contributions. They may also provide volunteers from their membership.
- *Public nursing homes*, also not-for-profit, are generally supported by city, town, county, or state funds.

Nursing homes vary in quality, whatever their type of ownership. There are excellent proprietaries and inferior nonprofits, although proprietaries (perhaps unfairly) tend to have the lesser reputation.

Nursing homes also vary in level of care provided. They are licensed either as intermediate care facilities (ICFs) or as skilled nursing facilities (SNFs). Some facilities offer both levels of care. As the names imply, SNFs offer skilled nursing to a greater degree than ICFs; SNF residents receive more hours of nursing, more medical services, and more frequent physician visits. Your state may use other terms for ICFs and SNFs—in Massachusetts, for example, ICFs are called Level 3 institutions and SNFs are called Level 2 institutions.

The various levels of care were created primarily as a basis for Medicare and Medicaid reimbursement: the higher the level, the higher the reimbursement. Levels of care sound very precise, but in practice the differences between them can become muddled. A high-quality ICF may provide more intensive care than a problem-ridden SNF. Two "good" SNFs may provide quite different services. SNF residents whose conditions improve, or ICF residents whose conditions worsen, may be reluctant to move (or places may not be available for them). An SNF in a state where regulatory enforcement is weak may resemble an ICF in a state with strong enforcement. Quality depends on many factors, and knowing a home's level of care is only a first step in evaluating that home.

PAYMENT

Rates for nursing homes vary greatly around the country according to type of facility, location, services offered, size of room, number of roommates, etc. Like other medical costs, nursing home rates have risen faster than the overall rate of inflation. They are generally higher than people expect.

Almost all nursing home residents pay for their care with private funds, Medicaid, or Medicare. Though virtually all homes accept private funds, most homes also participate in the Medicaid program, and could not survive without it: well over half of nursing home income is derived from Medicaid funds. Medicaid is for people who cannot afford the health care they need. Most residents either are Medicaid-eligible upon admission or become eligible after they exhaust their assets by paying for care themselves. If your income is not enough to cover what you are charged, if your assets are below the limit for Medicaid set by your state, and if you need nursing home care, Medicaid will generally pick up the difference.[4] A home that does not accept Medicaid can legally evict residents when their funds run out. Thus you should make sure that the facility you choose accepts Medicaid. Protect yourself to some degree by getting assurances concerning Medicaid—and anything else related to finances—in writing. Don't be afraid to consult a lawyer before signing anything. Medicaid-eligible nursing home residents are permitted a personal needs allowance; that is, they can retain a portion of their income for personal expenses.

The following example shows roughly how Medicaid reimbursement works with respect to the personal needs allowance. Say Medicaid reimburses XYZ Nursing Home $40 per day for a bed in a three-bed room, or $1200 per month in a thirty-day month. Resident A, who receives Medicaid, lives in a 3-bed room. Her monthly income is $535—$335 from Social Security and $200 from a pension. The personal needs allowance in her state is $35 per month.[5] She or her designee pays the nursing home $500, keeps $35, and the nursing home then bills Medicaid for the remaining $700.

Many older people expect that Medicare will pay for nursing home care, but it rarely does. Medicare is *short-term* health insurance and pays only 2 percent nationally of costs for skilled nursing home care.

THE SYSTEM AND ITS PROBLEMS

Discrimination against Medicaid recipients in the admissions process is only one of many problems in the nursing home system. Because Medicaid generally pays nursing homes less than the homes would be able to charge private-pay residents, many are reluctant to admit Medicaid-eligible residents. In most communities it is widely accepted that only people with private funds are likely to find nursing home placement.

My mother was on Medicaid and languishing in a hospital, waiting to be more settled in a nursing home.

Every local facility had a one- to two-year waiting list for Medicaid or private pay. But we were sure these mainly applied to people on Medicaid. Finally my husband and I took out a second mortgage to pay for at least a few months of care. Shortly after we called around again, one facility notified us that a bed had "just" opened up. [a woman in her fifties]

Assistance from an advocate may expedite Medicaid admissions.

The home my father and I wanted for him kept telling us to wait. I contacted an agency to set up all the in-home services I could. The woman I spoke to felt that my father did need nursing home care, and she called the home we wanted. A place became available for him soon after. [a forty-eight-year-old woman]

Elder advocates argue that nursing home admission should be based on need, not ability to pay. Nursing home owners argue that they have to make enough money to run their businesses, and that no one is served when proprietary nursing homes close due to unprofitability.

Prospective residents and their families should be aware that, according to a 1977 amendment to the Social Security Act, nursing homes participating in Medicaid are not permitted to "charge, solicit, accept, or receive any gift, money, or donation as a condition of either admitting or keeping a Medicaid patient." You should seek assistance (see Resources) if such requests are made of you. Advocates argue that this provision applies to various common practices such as requiring, upon admission, a guarantee of funds sufficient to pay privately for a specified amount of time even if the prospective resident is Medicaid-eligible, or restricting admission to private payers.

The tension between private enterprise and public welfare accompanied by public financing raises complex issues. Some believe that a free-market approach would result in lower costs and care of a reasonable quality. Others believe that quality care will never be achieved through a private system. In the words of Elma Holder, Executive Director of the National Citizens' Coalition for Nursing Home Reform (NCCNHR): "Care that is driven solely by the profit motive is unconscionable. A system that largely puts Mammon first, and workers and residents last, is contrary to the maintenance of quality care." NCCNHR, a group of advocates, professionals, and residents, is the leading source of information, analysis, and advocacy at the federal level.

Founded in 1975, NCCNHR's goal was to present a united consumer voice to the nursing home industry and the government. This they have done, and they are stronger than ever (see Resources).

This continuing debate does not solve the admission problem faced by Medicaid recipients. Some states have attempted to address the problem through specific laws. For example, Ohio nursing homes participating in Medicaid cannot have more than a fixed percentage of private-pay residents; in Minnesota, participating facilities' private rates cannot be higher than Medicaid rates. Another proposed solution is higher Medicaid reimbursement rates.

A related type of discrimination concerns evictions and transfers that occur when a resident can no longer afford to pay privately. A facility that does not accept Medicaid *can* evict residents in this situation. Homes that do accept Medicaid *cannot* legally evict residents, but some have been known to find ways around the law. For example, a resident may be moved from, say, a two-bed room to a four-bed room when private funds run out. The facility contends it should be able to charge different rates for different rooms and that Medicaid won't pay the higher rate for the two-bed room. In other instances, residents are hospitalized, coincidentally, at just about the time they go on Medicaid. When they return to the home, they are placed in a cheaper room or are told that the home is full and they must find another facility. (There is a limit on the number of days beds must be held for Medicaid recipients.) In still other cases, residents newly eligible for Medicaid are suddenly accused of behavior problems and transferred—again to cheaper rooms—for the supposed safety of themselves and others.

Evidence suggests that the stress caused by transfers is harmful to residents, especially when the transfers occur without warning. Residents and their families have the right to receive ample notice of and an adequate explanation for any transfer. You should seek recourse if you feel that this right has been violated.

Discrimination also exists against "heavy-care" people, especially those on Medicaid. Because heavy care costs the facility more and is more troublesome, nursing homes sometimes narrowly interpret or limit the services they provide, or exaggerate the length of their waiting list.

The first nursing home said they couldn't handle a catheter—but we knew of a wealthy resident there who had one. The second place said they didn't take alcoholics—but my father's main problem was a stroke. His minor liver problem did result from alcohol abuse, but he hasn't had a drink in twenty years. The third home, after saying they had a long waiting list, said they'd like to "take the liberty of suggesting" that we should consider a chronic-care hospital instead of a nursing home. [a woman in her fifties]

People of color and people from various ethnic or religious backgrounds may also face discrimination. Admission may be denied outright; hostile insinuations may be made, such as, "We don't feel she'd be comfortable here—the other residents are prejudiced." Subtler problems arise in the lack of attention to traditional foods and customs, such as religious services, and language barriers. Nursing homes that offer alternatives to white middle-class food, language, and activities are usually sponsored by or affiliated with ethnic or religious organizations.

My mother was much better able to cope with Western food when she could look forward to occasional Eastern meals at the nursing home's new "international nights." Her health and attitude improved and she began talking to other residents and staff about her native Korean recipes.

In November 1985, the South Cove Manor Nursing Home opened to accommodate Chinese-speaking residents in Boston. The staff observed a dramatic improvement, noting in particular a 104-year-old woman who had been erroneously diagnosed as demented because no one understood her at the old nursing home.[6]

Deinstitutionalization of people with psychiatric illnesses presents a different kind of problem. It has resulted in the transfer of many to nursing homes, where other residents may fear or snub them. The nursing home staff often doesn't know how to deal with former psychiatric patients' special medication and communication needs. The result is a lower quality of care for all residents. Many of these individuals may fare better in noninstitutional settings; others continue to need residential psychiatric care.

Systemic problems also arise from government policies. For example, currently popular cost-containment measures encourage hospitals to discharge patients as soon as possible. Thus, people entering nursing homes or receiving home care upon a hospital discharge may need more services than if they had been kept in the hospital longer. In addition, if a person is Medicaid-eligible, the state can decide whether she needs nursing home care and, if so, at what level. This may not be good for that person, since the state can underestimate her need for care just to save money.

Other problems relate to the fact that all nursing homes that accept Medicaid and/or Medicare must meet stringent federal and state regulations, including regular inspections. Those few nursing homes that accept only private payment must meet only state regulations. The regulations—both state and federal—cover licensing, safety, cleanliness, staffing, food, programs, and medical care, among other things. Some are too vague; some are too weak. Some reinforce resident dependence. Others overemphasize details and foster compliance with the letter, not the spirit, of the law. In general, state regulations are weaker than federal regulations. As a result, residents on Medicaid and/or Medicare are vulnerable to attempts to shift all nursing home regulation to the states, as the Reagan Administration proposed in 1982. (The National Citizens' Coalition for Nursing Home Reform successfully fought that proposal.)

But perfect regulations perfectly enforced are only part of the story. A nursing home that is "in compliance" may not be homey, or loving, or fun.

At one facility, I saw residents who were very active despite numerous disabilities. Staff attitudes were excellent, and the atmosphere was cheery and warm. The stairwell walls boasted a brightly colored mural which residents had helped to paint. The mural extended to, but clearly outlined, the fire exit. The administrator said the home had received a deficiency on its last survey because this unorthodox mural supposedly obscured the exit.[7]

DIFFICULT CONDITIONS IN NURSING HOMES

"Medicalization" is an unfortunate fact of life in nursing homes. Set up to be like hospitals—although they are called "homes"—nursing homes' medical orientation encourages a narrow approach to residents' well-being. Loneliness, confusion, depression, and behavior problems resulting from a lack of freedom and meaningful activity are addressed medically (if at all). Drugs are too often the first choice, rather than the last resort, in dealing with what are often sane reactions to an impossible situation. Physicians have the final say in resident care, even as to whether or not a resident can receive visitors. The medical model requires efficiency and hierarchy. Because it cannot incorporate the chaos of individuality and assertiveness, it treats residents as patients or cases instead of as people and rewards those who conform.

Loss of Autonomy

The medical, institutional approach fosters regimentation and loss of privacy and autonomy. Most residents must share rooms, follow schedules, and accept a preplanned menu. Activities offered are often limited to the large-group, lowest-common-denominator type. Negative attitudes among staff and a lack of resources rarely allow for excitement, or choice. Also, because passivity is built into the medical approach, even kind and caring staff members tend to overprotect. Too much help takes away a resident's right to risk, experience, and learn.

Three groups from the same home were asked to complete a puzzle. One group was assisted by staff members. A second group was left to itself. A third received less help than the first group, more than the second. Result: those who received the most help thought the puzzle most difficult. The less help received, the easier the puzzle seemed.[8]

Lack of control over daily life has serious consequences for residents' well-being, in a vicious cycle of increasing dependence.[9] Residents themselves identified choice and control as key components of quality care in a national research project.[10]

I make my own bed. It's a small thing but it's important. I've seen those people who think they can't do anything. Sometimes their families or the staff don't take the time to encourage them or teach them. Soon they can't do anything for themselves. Any little thing you can do for yourself helps keep you going. [a seventy-year-old woman]

Sometimes, nursing homes can rise above their limitations and rescue residents from a medically dictated oblivion.

When [my mother] collapsed, her doctor advised me to find a nursing home "for her to die in." . . . As soon as she arrived at the nursing home, their doctor stopped all treatment: the tranquilizers, IVs, catheters. The dentist replaced her dentures.... The physical therapist had her up in a wheelchair and doing exercises, and the attendants and I started feeding her. Within two months, she was walking and talking. She lived for another four years as an active, loving, thinking, feeling individual, not the "vegetable" her doctor had predicted she would be.[11]

Abuse

An increasing problem inside and outside nursing homes is elder abuse and neglect. Within an institution, staff members are usually the guilty parties. Outside, family members are most often involved. The problem often stems from a history of abuse, including alcohol or drug abuse—for example, parents who abused their children may later find themselves victims; a nurse's aide who abuses alcohol or takes drugs may find it hard to maintain caring behavior.

In addition, both family caregivers and nursing home staff often feel frustrated, isolated, and under stress. In a home caregiving situation, a single caregiver may be responsible twenty-four hours a day. Nursing home staff are often underpaid, overworked, and inadequately trained and supervised. These conditions increase the likelihood of abuse.

A universally accepted definition of abuse and neglect has yet to be formulated. Most of us would agree that physical assault, from a pinch or slap to a severe beating, is abuse, as are physical carelessness and intentional cruelty, such as bathing someone in dangerously hot water. We could probably also agree on a definition of verbal abuse, and that treatment resulting in malnutrition, bedsores, infections, and other physical problems constitutes the worst kind of neglect. These are the more obvious problems, addressed to some extent by laws and regulations (which are very specific in some states).

Less Obvious Problems

Other common problems in nursing homes are less dramatic but no less damaging. They are difficult to detect, and prejudiced attitudes toward older people with disabilities may blind us to their seriousness. For example:

• *Overmedication,* or inappropriate medication, may be intentional, an attempt to control a resident's behavior. It may be the result of ignorance about the effects of medication on older people. Or it may occur because the nursing home's drug-monitoring systems are inadequate. In any case, this is very dangerous.

• *Physical restraints* may help some people to sit up and even participate safely in activities, but they should be used judiciously and removed or changed periodically. Improper use or overuse can cause pain, prevent needed exercise, and otherwise inhibit physical and mental rehabilitation. In addition, residents may not be able to express their discomfort.

• *Verbal indignities* can be harmful even when not extreme. A statement that doesn't sound threatening to a visitor may terrify a resident. A patronizing tone and low expectations may create or reinforce confusion, depression, and dependence.

I encouraged the residents to talk, but no one spoke. To get the discussion started, I asked one interested-looking resident to read a proclamation of independence written by another group of residents. The activities director quickly said, "Oh, she can't read." But the resident took the paper and read it to the group.[12]

• *Subtle, daily neglect* gradually wears residents down and may lead to withdrawal or apathy.

No one was cruel, but I just wasn't very happy. Then, after the new administrator started, little things started going right again and so did my spirit. Hot coffee, crisp toast, medication that comes at about the same time each day, and fewer clothes lost in the laundry—it made all the difference. [a woman in her eighties]

• *Financial exploitation* can take many forms. Family members, acquaintances, or nursing home staff or administrators may steal cash, property, or other assets outright. They may pressure the older person for gifts. Or they may deprive the older person of control over her or his resources.

• *Inadequate rewards and training* affect all staff, even the most caring and competent, and reflect the low status of nursing home residents. High turnover and unprofessional behavior are too often the result.

Another area of concern is the potential for easy spreading of infectious diseases, such as tuberculosis[13] or influenza. Some facilities don't take appropriate precautions. Others are so over-cautious that residents lose access to visitors and activities both inside and outside the home in return for only a marginal improvement in safety.

NURSING HOME PLACEMENT

This section mainly addresses long-term rather than short-term placements. However, it is worthwhile to resist the impulse to assume that a stay will be long-term and to try to keep your options open. (See Housing Alternatives chapter.)

The Decision

Many, if not most, nursing home decisions are made in the midst of a crisis. But prospective residents and caregivers who prepare in advance retain more control of the process and cope better with the strong feelings evoked by such a major transition. The likelihood of a waiting list adds to the importance of advance planning. All of us, even those who are healthy, should make our wishes known to loved ones in advance. Or, as caregivers, we can sensitively approach the subject before our loved one becomes incapacitated or we become exhausted.

My brother can't seem to handle what he calls the "sin" of abandoning Ma to strangers, but he lives 600 miles away. I'm the one who has to deal with the day-to-day problems, and I've run out of patience, energy, and understanding. My health, my job, and my other relationships have all been affected. I've just about lost my sense of humor, which always got me through the roughest days. [a woman in her sixties]

Decision-making should involve the prospective resident to the greatest degree possible. Even confused people can respond to caregivers' attempts to communicate lovingly the realities of a difficult situation. Avoiding the topic or misleading the prospective resident—even if intended as kindness—can have a devastating effect on morale.

How is it? Don't even ask. I was living by myself in Florida. My husband died many years ago. Four months ago my son came down to visit me and said, "Ma, I'm taking you home with me." He did take me to his home for one night, but the next day he brought me here and dropped me off. I've only seen him once since then. [a ninety-year-old woman]

Involvement in the decision, on the other hand, can have quite the opposite effect.

My mother was lonely and miserable, but would not even talk about moving. As her health deteriorated, my sister and I knew we had to look at facilities that would accept her. The dishonesty of a companion/aide finally shook her sufficiently, and I'm sure made her feel so helpless that she was willing to look at the places we had screened. Our preference was a small place, but she

---

Questions to keep in mind as you determine whether you—or a family member or friend—need a nursing home:

What kinds of services are needed and how many are available in your community? Home health care, homemaker assistance, personal care, visiting nurses, Meals on Wheels, congregate meals, shopping and chore services, and respite care are some of the services to look for. However, it is usually difficult to find quality in-home assistance, especially for evenings, nights, and weekends. Most workers do their best, but their salaries, benefits, professional prestige, training, and supervision are often inadequate. Consider what you would do if helpers quit, arrived late, got sick, or went on vacation.

What can you afford? Will Medicare, other insurance, or Medicaid pay for the home care you need? Are there other financial assistance programs in your community or are services available on a sliding fee scale?

What financial or other assistance can your family, friends, and neighbors realistically provide? The answer should be fair to both caregivers and the people they're helping. An exhausted caregiver helps no one.

What is your housing situation? If you are living in a high-crime area, or if your home needs numerous or extensive repairs, or if you simply feel isolated, a move of some sort may be wise. Again, a nursing home is only one option to consider if you decide you should change your living situation. It's hard to move from a home you love; but the further in advance you can plan for it, the better you will be able to cope.

chose a larger one, hoping to have a greater selection of bridge partners! She selected her clothes and those few belongings one is allowed to take. It seemed a pathetic end. Yet this was not the end. She is now in many respects more alert and interested and in constant contact with people. [a fifty-six-year-old woman]

Remember that a nursing home is only one of many options. Sometimes it is the right choice; sometimes it isn't. The more you plan for the *possibility* of living in a nursing home, the better you will be able to control the move if you need to make it.

The Search

In most communities, you can find nursing home directories, information on how to select a home, and information about residents' rights. Such information can come from the nursing home ombudsprogram,* a nursing home licensing agency, the area agency on aging or other elder service organizations, advocacy groups, or your state's nursing home association (see Resources). If you are in the hospital, the discharge planner or continuing-care coordinator should help you. Word of mouth is another good source of information, although opinions may be colored by emotion, stereotypical attitudes toward nursing homes and residents, and conclusions drawn from an unrepresentative incident.

The following general suggestions should be helpful in a search.

- *Be organized.* Make a checklist so that you can compare and contrast facilities. Make notes about items of importance.
- *Check into the track record of facilities you're interested in.* Your licensing agency (see Resources) conducts regular inspection surveys, the results of which are matters of public record. You should be able to call the agency with specific questions. Survey reports are supposed to be available from the agency and at your local Social Security office. Informa-

*The nursing home ombudsprogram is federally mandated to investigate and resolve or refer concerns related to resident care and residents' rights. It is officially known as the nursing home or long term care ombudsman program. "Ombudsman" is from a Swedish word for a government official who investigates citizens' grievances against the government. This chapter uses "ombudsprogram" and "ombudsperson."

tion on the home's financial status is also important. Financial troubles or negative survey reports can be precursors of a home's closing. (Homes close for other reasons, too, such as an owner's desire for high profits from a condominium conversion.) For some residents, especially for those who are very frail, the stress of having to move from a facility can be fatal.

- *Set your priorities.* Do you prefer a large or small home? Where should it be located? (The choice of location should take into account both your preferences and the distance from family and friends.) What services do you need? What level of care do you need? Do you want a facility where you can move from more to less dependence or vice versa? Do you prefer an ethnically and religiously homogeneous or diverse community? You'll probably have to compromise, but first set your priorities.
- *Visit homes that meet your criteria.* There is no substitute for a personal visit. This visit will not only help you evaluate the facility, it will help you adjust to it when and if you move in. It is worth some inconvenience. If the prospective resident definitely cannot make the trip, a trusted friend or relative should be dispatched instead. (In some communities, professionals will evaluate homes for you for a fee.) The person who visits should keep the prospective resident's needs and desires in mind. If any kind of visit is impossible, a phone conversation with residents and staff might be useful.

During your visit, ask questions, participate, and talk to as many people as possible—especially residents. Look for positive staff attitudes and resident independence. You should look for evidence of family and community involvement. As one resident put it, "If you know you're having lots of company, you'll keep your house clean."

If possible, visit more than once, and at varying times of the day, week, and month. Make one visit at a mealtime. Check the activities board. Use all your senses. Be critical, but be balanced: for example, a strong urine smell *probably* indicates a cleanliness problem and/or too little emphasis on progressive ways of managing incontinence. However, the odor may result from an unusual series of accidents or a temporary staff shortage, so a second visit may be warranted. Also, a slight odor may be tolerable

Nursing Home Residents: The Experts on Quality Care

In *A Consumer Perspective on Quality Care: The Residents' Point of View*, published by the National Citizens' Coalition for Nursing Home Reform (see Resources), nursing home residents around the United States were asked to discuss and define quality care. The 457 participating residents said that choices in and control over their lives were the most important factors. They also pointed out the need for:

- Positive staff attitudes and relationships with residents
- Adequate wages and other rewards for staff
- A wide variety of activities
- Food that is fresh, tasty, and varied to reflect ethnic differences and individual needs
- Explicit, workable channels for problem resolution (accompanied by love and understanding)
- Safety of the environment
- Maximum possible independence for residents
- Strong, enforced regulations
- Resident participation in policymaking and quality control, both in their own facilities and at state and federal levels
- An active, concerned, informed administrator
- Community involvement

if the facility suits you well in other ways. (Totally odor-free facilities sometimes achieve that status by discriminating against incontinent and other heavy-care people, or by emphasizing cleanliness to the exclusion of other important qualities such as resident activity.)

The Transition

A comfortable transition from a private residence into a nursing home is important to a resident's well-being. The decision-making process and the choice of a facility are only the beginning. You should also consider:

- *Planning for the disposition of personal belongings.* Most nursing homes allow you to bring a few possessions, and some will store a few valuables. What do you want to have with you? What do you want to leave behind? What would you like to give to loved ones? What can you sell? Do you want to keep anything in storage—especially in the event that your stay in the nursing home is short?
- *Thinking ahead about adjustments you will have to make.* You will probably have to get used to one or more roommates, a large group of people in close proximity, a loss of privacy, and having a daily schedule set for you. Many residents do make good adjustments; humor, a spirit of compromise, and self-confidence can help. Think about ways to retain as much independence as possible.

Once you're in the facility, you can do a few things right away to hasten your adjustment:

- *Get to know the staff and their procedures.* This applies to both residents and their families and friends. You will feel comfortable more quickly, retain more control, and get more satisfaction if you know who handles complaints. For example, do you tell the dietician, the nurse, the cook, the administrator, or the residents' council if you have a problem with the food?
- *Encourage family and friends' visits.* Having someone stay with you on your first day is especially helpful.

I stayed with my mother for most of her first day. Together we got to know the home, met the staff and learned their names, found out about schedules and procedures, and visited several residents. We set up her room and had lunch together. When I had to leave, we both felt sad, but we had both expected it to be much worse. [a forty-two-year-old woman]

Visits will keep your morale high, provide you with mental stimulation, and ensure better care for you and others. Do your best to make visits pleasant. If family and friends fail to visit, don't blame yourself. Some people feel so distressed by a hospital or nursing home, anticipating physical and emotional discomfort, that they are literally unable to visit.

Family and friends who don't know how to create an enjoyable visit, especially if their loved one finds communication difficult, should ask for help. Nursing home staff or other experi-

Marianne Gontarz

FIGHTING FOR RIGHTS AND CHANGES

The key to reform of the nursing home system is the concerted effort of residents and their allies —families, friends, community groups, and professionals. All must cooperate to improve both the present situation and the future of long-term care.

Numerous coalitions of such interested parties have developed since the early 1970s. Many of them work together through the National Citizens' Coalition for Nursing Home Reform, which can refer you to other groups in your area.

Resident involvement is an increasingly important part of reform. A major "discovery" resulting from this trend is that even frail residents are more able and willing to get involved than most people would expect. Their involvement lends legitimacy to reform movements—who knows more about nursing-home life than the people who live there? It also provides crucial opportunities for residents to exercise control and choice, and counter the negative effects of institutionalization.

We struggle against illness, and the tiredness of our age; against isolation from the larger community....But I am here to tell you that we have a lot to offer and to ask you to listen to us. We need a chance to share our ideas, to speak our mind with nursing home staff and administrators and with the government people who make the rules and make sure they're enforced. [a nursing home resident speaking at a press conference of NCCNHR]

As a resident, you can advocate for yourself through a number of channels. Residents do not lose their civil rights, such as the right to vote, when they enter a nursing home (unless they have been declared incompetent in court), and they also enjoy certain additional rights. These include the right to full disclosure concerning facility policies and medical treatment, to privacy, to access to the community, and to a maximum amount of independence. This "Bill of Rights" appears in the box on p. 240. It should be prominently posted in your facility. You can also obtain a copy from a nursing home ombudsperson.

Residents are also protected under their state's consumer-protection laws. Information on these laws should be available from the om-

enced people may have suggestions. Many people have solved difficult communication problems in spite of overwhelming odds against them.

Mama awakened, and I put her hand on my head, our code for showing her it was I. She is completely deaf and almost blind. "Oh, dear child!" she said with a delighted smile of recognition. "It's my youngest!" I took her hand and moved it up and down in a vertical signal to "nod" yes, and gave her a big hug and kiss. Her fragile warm hands took one of my big strong cold hands and rubbed it lovingly. I thought to myself, "How lucky I am to be receiving all this caring love!" [a sixty-three-year-old woman]

If you are a family member who feels guilty about placing your loved one in a nursing home —and most do—try not to withdraw from the situation. Keep visiting as often as you can. Nursing home staff who advise you to stay away because the resident "gets too upset" are looking for a short-term solution or trying to save themselves work. In the long run, visiting almost always pays off and makes both families and residents feel better.

Talking with others in similar situations can also help. Some nursing homes and communities sponsor family support groups. If none exists, consider starting one. Nursing home staff or self help groups may be able to make specific suggestions for dealing both with your emotions and with any anger a resident may feel. Above all, remember that you are a human being, too, with legitimate time, financial, and other constraints. Self-sacrifice almost always leads to resentment and that helps no one, least of all the person for whom the sacrifice is made.

budsprogram, a legal services agency, the state attorney general, or the state consumer affairs office.

Residents' councils, sometimes formally elected by the residents, meet regularly in an increasing number of nursing homes. They are important channels for resident involvement. Such councils range from the very effective to the purely symbolic (similar to company unions), which never do more than vote on which film to show next week. Some administrators and staff sabotage councils because they seem threatening (and indeed they can be). Others like the council idea but don't know how to help the residents get started. Still others provide support that empowers and enables residents to play a role in the facility's operation. Residents' councils should meet regularly and privately—ideally, staff and administration should attend by invitation only.

If your residents' council is inactive or ineffective, don't give up. Build from small achievements to larger ones. Choosing and planning activities helps build the confidence to discuss and decide bigger issues. Group projects, such as forming an orientation committee for new residents, can provide a real but nonthreatening service while strengthening the council. A group meeting with the administrator to discuss grievances might be a good next step.

If you do have a grievance, as an individual or a group, usually it's best to go to the staff member involved. If you're uncomfortable dealing with that staff member, try her or his immediate supervisor. Be polite, fair, and sensitive, but be firm: don't apologize for wanting a decent life within the limitations of a nursing home structure. Use your common sense in making suggestions for resolutions. Be as specific as you can in describing the problem and possible solutions. If your complaints are serious and you fear retribution, you should go immediately to the administrator or outside the facility, to families, the ombudsprogram, or the licensing and enforcement agency.

Community-wide residents' organizations are also increasing in number. There are now at least fourteen major residents' organizations nationwide, most of them coalitions of residents' councils. You can get information about them from the National Citizens' Coalition for Nursing Home Reform and the National Coalition of Resident Councils (see Resources). These organizations bring together residents from many facilities and support your involvement in your own facility while giving you opportunities to examine and act on broader policy issues. They can also help you to meet residents from other facilities and become more involved in your community.

One example of such an organization is L.I.F.E. (Living Is for the Elderly), founded in 1972. It has helped thousands of Massachusetts nursing home residents to become activists. In the words of some L.I.F.E. leaders:

The nursing home residents band together, go to the State House, and speak before the committees. We get there any way we can, in wheelchairs and using canes. We also write letters to the governor, representatives, and senators. We fight for things we know are right. [a seventy-eight-year-old woman]

I've become educated about the legal process. You have the feeling that you are contributing to the welfare of other people. When you advocate, it helps everyone! [a seventy-year-old woman]

You are not alone—you belong to a group with people you have never met and learn to help yourself and others. [a woman in her eighties]

We are a group of people working to make our lives in nursing homes as close as possible to what life in our own homes has been. [a woman in her seventies]

One of our nurses talked roughly to a patient. I knew that there was a law that said that people can't abuse us, even by yelling. They have the laws posted on the bulletin board, but a lot of residents don't understand them. I spoke to the head nurse and she spoke to the nurse on duty. A representative from L.I.F.E. had educated me to know I could go to someone. I think the solution to abuse is education. Teach us that we do have rights and that we can go to someone if we have a problem. [a woman in her middle seventies]

Family councils and other family groups are important adjuncts to residents' groups. Family (and friend) involvement encourages residents and keeps the nursing home on its toes, greatly improving the quality of care. Some nursing homes have even gone out of their way to encourage family groups—a "we're-all-in-this-together" approach.

Like residents' councils, family councils must work toward an effective, not a symbolic, voice in the facility, and may combine forces with the residents' council toward this end. Some family councils consist of only a couple of family

Patients' Bill of Rights—Skilled Nursing Facilities*

Federal regulations require that nursing homes have written policies covering the rights of residents posted where residents and visitors can see them. A Bill of Rights helps assure that residents and prospective residents will know their rights. Violations should be reported to state regulating authorities and ombudsprograms.

A nursing home resident:

(1) Is fully informed, as evidenced by the patient's written acknowledgment, prior to or at the time of admission and during stay, of these rights and of all rules and regulations governing patient conduct and responsibilities;

(2) Is fully informed, prior to or at the time of admission and during stay, of services available in the facility, and of related charges including any charges for services not covered under titles XVIII or XIX of the Social Security Act, or not covered by the facility's basic per diem rate;

(3) Is fully informed, by a physician, of his medical condition unless medically contraindicated (as documented, by a physician, in his medical record), and is afforded the opportunity to participate in the planning of his medical treatment and to refuse to participate in experimental research;

(4) Is transferred or discharged only for medical reasons, or for his welfare or that of other patients, or for non-payment of his stay (except as prohibited by titles XVIII or XIX of the Social Security Act), and is given reasonable advance notice to ensure orderly transfer or discharge, and such actions are documented in his medical record;

(5) Is encouraged and assisted, throughout his period of stay, to exercise his rights as a patient and as a citizen, and to this end may voice grievances and recommend changes in policies and services to facility staff and/or to outside representatives of his choice, free from restraint, interference, co-

*Model suggested by Health Care Financing Administration, Title 42, Chapter IV, Subpart K, Section 405. 1121 (k).

ercion, discrimination, or reprisal;

(6) May manage his personal financial affairs, or is given at least a quarterly accounting of financial transactions made on his behalf should the facility accept his written delegation of this responsibility to the facility for any period of time in conformance with State law;

(7) Is free from mental and physical abuse, and free from chemical and (except in emergencies) physical restraints except as authorized in writing by a physician for a specified and limited period of time, or when necessary to protect the patient from injury to himself or to others;

(8) Is assured confidential treatment of his personal and medical records, and may approve or refuse their release to any individual outside the facility, except in case of his transfer to another health care institution, or as required by law or third-party payment contract;

(9) Is treated with consideration, respect, and full recognition of his dignity and individuality, including privacy in treatment and in care for his personal needs;

(10) Is not required to perform services for the facility that are not included for therapeutic purposes in his plan of care;

(11) May associate and communicate privately with persons of his choice and send and receive his personal mail unopened, unless medically contraindicated (as documented by his physician in his medical record);

(12) May meet with, and participate in activities of social, religious, and community groups at his discretion, unless medically contraindicated (as documented by his physician in his medical record);

(13) May retain and use his personal clothing and possessions as space permits, unless to do so would infringe upon rights of other patients, and unless medically contraindicated (as documented by his physician in his medical record); and

(14) If married, is assured privacy for visits by his spouse; if both are inpatients in the facility, they are permitted to share a room, unless medically contraindicated (as documented by the attending physician in the medical record).

members; others are large. Effective ones usually meet regularly and keep in close communication with staff and administrators. Members should be aware of residents' rights and facility policies, and present their concerns and suggestions in the most organized and sensitive way they can. (To put it another way, they should be assertive but not aggressive.) Families must also recognize residents' need for independence. Sometimes family members are guilty (as staff can be) of overprotectiveness, which only encourages dependence and helplessness.

Community involvement can also be instrumental in improving the quality of life within nursing homes. For example, individuals and groups can volunteer at nursing homes, join with resident and family councils and other advocates to improve and reform nursing homes, and encourage nursing homes to make space available for community meetings and caregivers' support groups. Residents who have no family or friends benefit most from community involvement. For those of us who are not residents, volunteering or just visiting is the ideal way to learn about and confront our feelings about nursing homes.

Why do I devote time to this residents' group? That's simple. I want something like it around if I ever become a nursing home resident. [a fifty-year-old community volunteer]

Marianne Gontarz

The nursing home ombudsprogram investigates, resolves, or refers concerns related to resident care and residents' rights. The program exists in all states. Some states have only a small ombudsprogram staff, while others offer a large network of local staff and volunteers. Although the program has been criticized for being relatively powerless and overly bureaucratic, ombudspersons around the country have helped residents and families to organize and strengthen councils, intervened with staff and administrators when residents or others felt hesitant to complain, and helped to decertify administrators who have flagrantly violated the law. Ombudsprograms also educate residents and others about residents' rights and other long-term care issues.

Legal Aid can be a nursing home resident's best friend. Despite funding cutbacks, you can still find attorneys providing free nonroutine services to older people who meet low-income guidelines in most communities. If you can't find a listing for "legal services" or "legal aid" in your phone book, check with your local agency on aging or with your nursing home ombudsperson. Legal Aid lawyers have helped countless income-qualifying residents assert their rights; protect their personal funds from unscrupulous families, staff, administrators, and owners; and improve care. In addition, they have helped research and draft legislation beneficial to nursing home residents.

Nursing homes are part of our lives. The more we learn about them, the better we will understand them. Openness to new possibilities and a positive attitude will help residents, prospective residents, families, and friends face problems and influence the system, and provide residents with opportunities for choice, control, and more meaningful lives.

In the words of five hundred residents attending a L.I.F.E. conference in Massachusetts, "We have the power to make the changes!"

NOTES

1. Mickey Spencer, "Nursing Homes," *Broomstick: A Bimonthly National Magazine by, for, & About Women over Forty,* Vol. 8, No. 4 (July–August 1986). (See General Resources for subscription information.)

2. R. Kastenbaum and S. E. Candy, "The Four Percent Fallacy: A Methodological and Empirical Critique of Extended Care Facility Population Statistics." *Aging and Human Development,* Vol. 4, 1973, pp. 15–21.

3. National Center for Health Statistics, based on a 1982 survey.

4. Medicaid-eligible individuals must be officially screened to establish the level of nursing home care they need—if any—in some states.

5. The amount of the personal needs allowance is set by each state, but, by federal regulation, it must be at least $25.

6. Doris Sue Wong, "Nursing Home Ends a Language Barrier." *The Boston Globe*, January 27, 1986, p. 21.

7. Personal communication, staff member, L.I.F.E., Woburn, MA.

8. From *Investigative Newsletter Institutions/Alternatives*, Vol. 7, No. 9 (September 1984), p. 12.

9. This point is documented in various articles and books, notably Ellen Langer, *Psychology of Control*. Beverly Hills, CA: Sage Publications, 1983.

10. "A Consumer Perspective on Quality Care: The Residents' Point of View." National Citizens' Coalition for Nursing Home Reform (NCCNHR), a study of quality care with 457 resident participants.

11. Spencer, op. cit.

12. Personal communication, staff member, L.I.F.E., Woburn, MA.

13. W. W. Stead, et al., "Tuberculosis as an Endemic and Nosocomial Infection Among the Elderly in Nursing Homes. *The New England Journal of Medicine*, Vol. 312, No. 23 (June 6, 1985), pp. 1483–7.

18

JOINT AND MUSCLE PAIN, ARTHRITIS AND RHEUMATIC DISORDERS

by Robin H. Cohen

Material on TMJ by Martha Wood and Renée Glass

Special thanks to Jeanne L. Melvin

My left leg hurt all the time, down the outside, across the foot, behind the knee. My hip joint ached mightily. I thought, "What do you expect, over 60?" But it turned out a nerve in my spine was being pressed—and there were things I could do to hurt less. [a woman in her sixties]

As we grow older, we may experience aches in our joints and muscles. We may fear pain and immobility as a result of these conditions. It is important that neither we nor our health care providers dismiss pains and aches as inevitable signs of age. We should not assume discomfort is normal and so neglect preventable and correctable conditions.

As we age, our spines may change shape in response to stresses placed on them. Bony growths, called spurs, may limit joint motion. The soft tissues that stabilize the joints can become inflamed by overuse or strain. Arthritis can attack our joints. Muscles may weaken or become tight with disuse, tension, and postural habits, making it hard, for example, to look back when we drive or to hook a bra. What hurts and what shows up on X-rays don't always go together. As we understand the environmental and life-style factors that affect our joints, we can find ways to stay limber and comfortable.

A joint is formed where two bones meet. It is surrounded by a capsule of soft tissue lined with a synovial membrane that produces a rich fluid. This fluid lubricates the cartilage-covered bone ends as they move against each other. The cartilage absorbs shocks, protects the ends of the bones, and receives nourishment only through exercise. Ligaments, which attach bone to bone, and tendons, which attach muscle to bone, keep bones stable while permitting them to move. Bursae, small, pillowlike sacs lined with synovial membrane, cushion the movement of muscle over bone, or of one muscle over another.

Inflammation is an indication that the body is attempting to heal and repair injured tissue. Injury can result from many causes, including a blow, strain, overuse, or reactions to foreign substances or anything the body interprets as foreign. The symptoms of inflammation can be local pain, heat, redness, swelling, or general discomfort, including headaches and weakness.

Pain may arise from:

- *Overuse*—stressing joints or soft tissues by repetitive motions, such as hammering
- *Underuse*—not moving enough, resulting in stiffness and limiting mobility of the joint
- *Incorrect use*—habitually moving in ways inappropriate for the way the body is made,

such as holding the phone to one ear with a raised shoulder
- *Reactions to stress*—habitual tension in the muscles can create muscle spasm and pain
- *The pain-spasm-pain cycle*—pain causes further tightening or spasms in other muscles, creating still more pain
- *Inflammation*—in the joints (arthritis), tendons (tenosynovitis or tendonitis), bursae (bursitis), muscles, or blood vessels
- *Changes in bone shape*—pressing on nerves and causing other strains

PREVENTION OF JOINT PAIN

To prevent joint problems and to prevent re-injury or disability from them, you can:

1. Keep muscles strong with exercise and flexible with gentle stretching.
2. Reduce muscle tension. Regularly use relaxation techniques, such as systematically tensing and relaxing groups of muscles from head to toe, meditating, and getting massages.
3. Deal with difficulties in movement as soon as you notice them. Be alert to any difficulty you may have in performing daily activities, to pain where you never had it before, and to changes in the ease and range of your motion. For example, if you have trouble climbing stairs, your knees, hips, or front thigh muscles (quadriceps) may need attention.

I noticed in exercise class that I had pain when performing certain motions with my arms—my shoulders would not let me do things I had always done before. I wish I had paid attention to the slight signs earlier. Now I've lost quite a lot of shoulder motion. [a sixty-one-year-old woman]

4. Try to manage your weight. Being very heavy stresses the joints.
5. Use good body mechanics. This means using the body in ways that minimize joint stress. Use the largest and strongest joint for any given task—for example, push with your hips or thighs instead of with your hands.
6. Wear comfortable shoes. Foot problems can affect the whole body. Wobbling on high or thin heels creates strain on the knees, hips, and back as these joints try to stabilize the body when the feet can't do the job.

Home Care for Sprains, Mild Injuries and Inflammation, and Joint and Muscle Pain

Pain in joints and soft tissues often responds to home care and will heal in two to six weeks given rest, hot or cold compresses, and time. Rest gives the body a chance to make repairs and helps reduce inflammation, but too much bed rest for back pain caused by muscle or ligament strain may result in loss of muscle strength.[1] You may want to immobilize the joint with a sling, splint, or corset. Once or twice a day, move resting joints through their normal range of motion, because inflammation can make tissues stick together and become hard and tight ("frozen"). Heat relaxes muscles, while cold reduces swelling and inflammation, and can ease muscles in spasm.

When to Use Heat and When to Use Ice[2]

If there is swelling and warmth from inflammation in the joint or muscle, ice packs or ice massage (passing ice over the painful area, without pressure, for twenty minutes) is generally more beneficial for reducing swelling, inflammation, and pain.

When the main problem is stiffness and there is no swelling, moist heat—such as a shower or bath, wet compresses, or a wet washcloth placed between the skin and a plastic-covered heating pad—is more effective than dry heat. Guard against scalding or burning.

When an area is sore and painful and an application of heat does not bring relief, it is likely that an ice pack will.

For trauma to a joint, such as twisting an ankle or a knee, the best treatment is ice to decrease swelling and bruising.

If you "pull" your back muscles while exercising, the pain felt afterward is usually caused by a spasm in the muscle. It may be more comforting to apply heat at first. However, if you do not get good relief with heat, ice packs or ice massage can often be beneficial.

The treatment that gives the greatest relief is best for you.

Signs of Further Problems

The following symptoms require more complete investigation.[3] **Contact your health care practitioner if:**

- your temperature is over 100° F
- you feel numbness or tingling
- the pain runs down the back of your leg to your foot or down your arm to your finger
- the pain persists or is very bad
- you can't use the joint
- you have severe pain and swelling in one or more joints
- you have trouble in the same joint on both sides
- you have stiffness that lasts more than one hour after waking up
- you feel weak, fatigued, or generally unwell
- you have lumps under the skin, particularly near the elbow

MANAGING LONG-TERM PAIN

I've really learned to listen to my body. All my life I wasn't listening. My mind was too ambitious. But now, if I don't feel good one day and can't do anything, I say the hell with it and wait. If you say, "I'll do it tomorrow," somehow tomorrow comes. [a seventy-five-year-old woman]

Living with pain is physically and emotionally stressful. Work with a physical therapist may be essential to reduce pain but you may also have to use drugs before you can try the following important self-help program.

Exercise

When in pain we tend to tighten muscles and move less (the pain-spasm-pain cycle), so even a few gently performed small movements can have an astonishing effect and lead to larger pain-free movements. Even those confined to a wheelchair or bed will find exercise helpful. Mobility and strength do not develop in a straight line; remember that you will have bad days as well as good days.

Every morning and before I go to bed I do bicycling on my back, knee-chest stretches, leg lifts, and turn my head. When I rest I practice breathing from my diaphragm instead of my chest. I work on posture and thigh muscles by bending my knees and sliding my back up and down against the wall. [a seventy-five-year-old woman]

Listen to your body. Exercise gently and slowly, with relaxation between repetitions, only as much as is comfortable, up to but not beyond the point of pain. Increase exercise very slowly. One or two rest days a week may help. You may even need to begin exercising in the supportive environment of warmed water.

When my body seemed stiff beyond repair because of the pain-spasm-pain cycle, I used water to support me as I turned my head from side to side or slowly walked back and forth in the pool. Small changes gradually led to larger ones. Now I swim a half-mile. [a sixty-one-year-old woman]

I won a victory over arthritis in my fifties. I was acting in a mime troupe and walking got so painful I was crying as I was walking with the pain in my hip. A surgeon suggested surgery, but I refused. I started using a whirlpool and doing exercises in a swimming pool for a year, three times a day. I was so successful that at fifty-eight I learned to ski. [a fifty-nine-year-old woman]

I'm always stiff when I get up in the morning. Then I stand in a hot shower, and I'm okay for the rest of the day. [an eighty-five-year-old woman]

I don't like to use dishwashers. I like to do dishes by hand in hot water. The water feels so friendly to my hands. [a seventy-eight year-old woman]

The YWCA, YMCA, or the local chapter of the Arthritis Foundation in your area may offer exercise classes in water for people with joint problems.

The Feldenkrais method and Alexander technique (see Moving for Health chapter) realign our bodies and show people how to move with less effort. Yoga has helped many people with arthritis.[4] Like any other exercise, yoga must be modified to suit you.

I came to yoga in my fifties when my mother was dying. I couldn't sleep because I would see her dying face. All my pains got worse. When I read a book on yoga, I could feel that my body was full of tension. I got a record, took a course, and grew limber. When I saw my osteopath, he was astounded at how flexible I had become.

But my yoga teacher insisted that I could do a shoulder stand, which I knew was not right for me. Against my better judgment I tried it and injured my neck. I had to wear a collar until it healed. [a seventy-five-year-old woman]

Rest and Energy Conservation

Pain is exhausting, and feels worse when you are tired. You need to find the right balance between exercise and rest, and to avoid tiring yourself by learning to conserve energy.

Plan rest times into your day. Plan workspaces so you do not waste steps. Sit to work instead of standing, use gadgets that avoid straining your joints, and plan restful tasks between more energetic ones. Your body will tell you when you've done too much.

I thought I had done everything right in planning a small party. I bought most things, made others on three different days. The day of the party, I felt good and ran around a lot instead of resting. The next morning I could not get out of bed. Everything hurt. It took a week to get over it. [a sixty-one-year-old woman]

Only by trial and error can you discover the balance between rest and activity best for you.

I told my physician I had tickets for a show, but I was in such pain how could I go? He asked, "If you stay at home, will the pain go away? So why not go?" And that did a lot for me. I went. I had to stand against the wall from time to time, but I went, and I kept going. Once, when I felt like giving up, the same doctor said, "If you don't keep active, you'll end your days in a wheelchair." That shook me. I put a fancy scarf around my neck collar and I went out. [a seventy-five-year-old woman]

Dealing with Stress

Emotional or physical stress seems to increase pain, perhaps by suppressing endorphins, the body's natural painkillers. Try to limit the effects of the stress you cannot avoid. Exercise, relaxation techniques, and daily meditation are all useful methods for increasing endorphins.[5]

Sex

Sex can help to reduce pain. For helpful suggestions on sex when you or your partner has pain or limited mobility, see the Sexuality chapter.

Self-Help Groups

Self-help groups make it possible to exchange ideas for managing back and joint pains and rheumatic disorders, to share experiences, and to give and get support. The nearest chapter of the Arthritis Foundation (look in your phone book) or a local hospital may know of a group—

or you can start one yourself. Managing these disorders requires a lot of support. An important resource in coping with pain is the ability to *ask for help.*

My husband said to me, "Don't be a baby." I was terribly hurt. I was hysterical. He doesn't know how much pain I'm in. But my group knows. [a woman in her sixties]

Exploring What Is Available in Your Community

Massage, acupuncture, meditation and other relaxation techniques, visualization (making mental images of the way you want to be), and hypnosis have helped many people. Myotherapy (pressing on spots in the body that send pain to other parts) may relieve muscle spasms.[6] Acupressure, a form of massage that includes pressure on acupuncture points, has been a help to many.

During an acupressure massage, the masseuse found a very sore spot on my back. When she pressed it for a while, some of the pain on my right side went away. Now, if my right side pains me when I am walking, I just reach around and press the sore spot and the pain goes away. That's a wonderful trick to know. [a sixty-five-year-old woman]

Drugs

Drugs are often prescribed to break the pain-spasm-pain cycle and to reduce inflammation. Aspirin is useful because it relieves both pain and inflammation. Diazepam (Valium), however, is potentially addictive and is frequently misused and overused. See p. 256 for a summary of antiinflammatory and other drugs.

COMMON JOINT PROBLEMS

Foot Problems

It is important to take special care of our feet, since the entire body depends on them for mobility and stability. Much foot discomfort comes from the restrictive styles of women's shoes, which are rarely designed for comfort and health. High heels force our weight onto the metatarsal joints in the ball of the foot, distort our walking gait and posture, and strain other joints, including the back and neck. Pointed-toe shoes can push the big toe out of its normal position and place pressure on the joint, causing bunions. Instead of being a modern version of Chinese footbinding, women's shoes should provide the same level of comfort as good men's shoes. Try them sometime. You'll be amazed at the toe room.

A comfortable shoe should outline the shape of the foot—broad in front with rounded toes, heel wide enough to distribute weight, and with room enough for the top of the foot.[7] It should have plenty of room for the toes to wiggle, and thick crepe or soft rubber soles and heels. Sandals and properly shaped shoes give the foot room to spread.

I have found a style of flat sandals with built-in supports that keeps me pain-free. I wear them all the time. On the rare occasions, such as a wedding, when I feel I must wear another style of shoe, I change my shoes in the ladies' room so I wear the less comfortable shoes for the shortest time. [a fifty-four-year-old woman]

Check the bottoms of your shoes. If they are worn down unevenly, that can be an early sign of a problem. Repair your shoes frequently, because walking around in unevenly worn shoes can produce strain on your knees and back. If you have pain on top of your feet where laces tie, choose shoes with more than two shoelace holes on each side and loosen the laces over the painful area.

As we grow older, our toenails may be harder to cut. They may become horny, we may have difficulty reaching them, or our hands may not have sufficient strength to work the clippers. Try large clippers with long handles and a spring. Cut nails straight across a little at a time. Ask for help. You might want to exchange pedicures and foot rubs with a friend.

If you need molded shoe inserts (orthotics) but have flexible feet (feet with very loose joints), be sure the orthotics are molded without your weight on them but with your foot supported in the correct position.[8] People with flexible feet are often more comfortable in shoes with very flexible soles.

Flat feet may cause more pain as you get older. Exercise and well-fitting shoes, perhaps with arch supports, will make your feet and legs more comfortable.

If your second toe is longer than your big toe, you have a Venus de Milo foot. This sounds nice, but it may contribute to back pain because the long toe changes the way the foot rolls when walking. Padding under the ball of the foot may help.[9]

Bunions (swelling, tenderness, and redness of the big toe joint) do not usually cause pain if we wear comfortable shoes. A tendency to have them may be inherited, but the shoes we wear may also be at fault. If you see a bunion coming, visit a podiatrist or a physical therapist who specializes in foot problems. An orthotic, or new shoes, can reduce the stress that produces the bunion.

Morton's neuralgia, a condition in which a tender nerve at the base of the third and fourth toes causes tingling and numbness in the middle toes and pain in the ball of the foot, is common among middle-aged women. It can often be relieved by changing to shoes with wide toe room, support for the metatarsal arch, and low heels.

If your foot joints are affected by rheumatoid arthritis, ask your health care provider to monitor the circulation in your feet.

Back Problems

Almost everyone has a back problem at one time or another. Most back pain comes from muscle or ligament strain, muscle spasm, sacroiliac joint strain, disc problems, excessive curvature of the spine (kyphosis), or arthritis. Once injured, the back can take several weeks or months to heal.

The backbone, or spine, supports us and lets us twist, bend, and turn. It consists of bones (vertebrae) alternating with flexible units (discs) containing a gel-like center. The nerves of the spinal cord, which connects brain and body, pass through openings in the vertebrae. When viewed from the back, the spine should appear to divide the body into two equal parts. When viewed from the side, the spine has a characteristic S-curve that helps absorb shocks.

Avoiding Back and Neck Problems

Observe the basic rule: Don't do anything that causes pain. If something causes pain, stop doing it, and follow the suggestions for home care beginning on p. 244.

The suggestions above for preventing and managing pain apply especially to the two most common causes of back pain—back muscle sprains and sacroiliac joint inflammation. The

VERTEBRAE OF THE SPINE

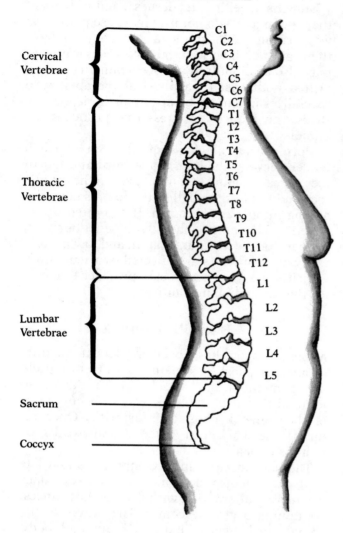

Cervical Vertebrae — C1 C2 C3 C4 C5 C6 C7

Thoracic Vertebrae — T1 T2 T3 T4 T5 T6 T7 T8 T9 T10 T11 T12

Lumbar Vertebrae — L1 L2 L3 L4 L5

Sacrum

Coccyx

following suggestions may prevent problems, ease the pain you have, and save you from reinjuring or aggravating a bad back or neck.* Suggestions marked with a bullet (•) are particularly useful for disc problems.

1. Strengthen your abdominal and back muscles. (See p. 74) Excessive back sway from weak muscles, a slack or protruding abdomen, and poor posture place severe stress on the mus-

*Some Ys, health centers, HMOs, and hospitals conduct back classes where they teach body mechanics, flexibility exercises, and pain management. They may also include group self-help discussions.

cles and joints of the lower back and can cause pain.

•2. When you sit or stand, try keeping your feet at different levels. Rest one foot on a stool, a book, a bar, or on the floor of the cabinet underneath the sink when washing dishes.

3. If your mattress sags, put a ¾-inch plywood board under it. The best mattress is soft on the top so it contours and supports weight evenly, but firm enough so it doesn't sag. However, you need to sleep well, and what is comfortably firm to one person may be a bed of nails to another.

•4. Don't sleep on your stomach. Sleeping on your stomach is especially bad for neck problems. If you can't sleep any other way, place a pillow under your waist to prevent the swayback position. If you sleep on your side, place pillows in front of you to support your top shoulder and top knee.

5. If your days are sedentary, get up often and walk around or lie down. While sitting, periodically round and straighten your back or, holding your elbows in opposite hands, twist gently to the right and left.[10] During car travel, stop and walk around every hour. Move around in a train and airplane as much as possible and exercise in your seat. Two examples of exercises to be done slowly and gently are stretching alternate arms upwards and lifting one knee at a time toward opposite elbows.

•6. Some positions put more pressure on lower back discs than others. Sitting exerts more pressure than standing, and both more than lying down. When you have to lift an object, don't twist. Lifting and twisting puts four hundred times more pressure on your lumbar spine than lying down.[11] Bending over and lifting can also harm your back. Don't bend at the waist, but instead bend your knees, keep your back straight while lifting, and hold the weight close. If you can't bend your knees that far or need help to get up, support your back by leaning a hand on a nearby solid object, or by resting a forearm on your own thigh. If you need to move furniture with someone, you should be the one in front with your hands behind your back.

7. Change a baby on furniture of comfortable height. Do not bend over. Carry an infant with her back resting on your forearm and her head cradled in your hand. Don't lift children. Let an older child climb on your lap. Some of us can kneel or sit to let an older child climb on our backs to be carried.

DO THIS　　　　　　　　　　　　　　　　　**NOT THIS**

8. Carry all objects close to your body *above* waist level. Use a backpack. If carrying shopping bags, divide the load in two so you are balanced. Lighten the load whenever possible.

•9. Don't reach for or lift an object over your head; stand on a stool so that you can keep your elbows bent.[12]

10. Since most chairs do not provide support for the lower back, supply it yourself by folding a towel or sweater 6 to 8 inches wide and about 1½ inches thick in the middle. Put it in the hollow of your back. You can do this at the movies or while riding in a car.

11. At work and at home, try to use chairs that are adjustable in height, so your feet can be flat on the floor with your knees bent at ninety degrees. Your chair should have an adjustable backrest placed where the back curves most inward. It should be upholstered in a nonslip material and be soft at the edge of the seat so that

circulation in the thighs is not cut off. It should have arms whenever possible.

•12. Get up from a chair by sliding to the edge so that your weight is directly above your feet. Don't lean forward, for this increases the pressure on your discs. Use the chair arms to help you, or push with your hands on your thighs to support your back as you straighten up.

13. Share helpful hints with others. You may find it easier to lie on your back in bed to put on shoes and socks. If pulling up the emergency brake in a car hurts, it may help to press against the dashboard with the other hand when you do it.[13]

14. If your back hurts, relax in the position that is most comfortable for you.

For me the most comfortable position is lying on my back, legs loosely together and raised at right angles at the hips and knees, with my calves and feet on a has-

sock or chair seat. Sometimes I even put the hassock in bed with me. [a fifty-five-year-old woman]

For most people, specific exercises are essential to help prevent back pain. Exercises that strengthen your back muscles, abdominals, and front thigh muscles (quadriceps) will help protect your spinal discs. Abdominal muscles provide the sole support for the lower lumbar vertebrae and help hold us erect. Women of middle age characteristically have weak abdominals. If your quadriceps are strong, you have less tendency to rely on back muscles to lift you up. If you have repeated bouts of back pain it is wise to invest in a consultation with a physical therapist who specializes in back problems for an individualized exercise program.

While exercise is important, choose sports with care. Warm up and gently stretch your back muscles before doing sports or heavy labor. Some sports are harder on your back than others.[14] Walking and swimming are good, but you may need to select and modify your strokes. The breast and back stroke, for example, arch the back and may cause pain.

Some Special Back Problems

A **herniated disc** occurs when the soft center inside the disc is forced through the outer casing. This may cause pain when it presses on a nerve. Most likely to herniate are the two lower lumbar discs, which can press on the sciatic nerve. When this happens, the lower back may hurt, followed by pain running down the back or side of the thigh, the outside of the calf, and possibly into the toes. You are most likely to have a herniated disc when you are between thirty and sixty. As we age, our discs dry out, becoming thinner, harder, and less likely to herniate. The majority of people with disc problems do not require surgery but respond partly or completely to conservative, nonsurgical treatment. The most common treatment is bed rest, which is very debilitating for older people. Ask for exercises you can do in bed to keep your muscles strong. A sudden severe pain in an older woman is more likely to be a fracture from osteoporosis than a disc problem.

Sometimes, to avoid surgery, chymopapain (the enzyme from papaya used in meat tenderizers) may be injected into the herniated disc. The injection is given only in hospitals, under anesthesia, and involves risks equal to those of

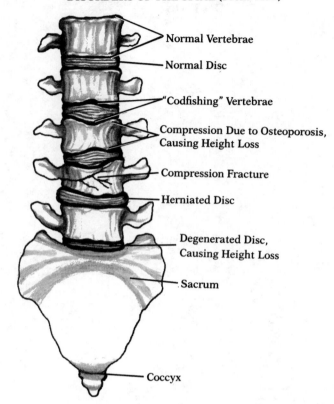

DISORDERS OF THE SPINE (Front View)

- Normal Vertebrae
- Normal Disc
- "Codfishing" Vertebrae
- Compression Due to Osteoporosis, Causing Height Loss
- Compression Fracture
- Herniated Disc
- Degenerated Disc, Causing Height Loss
- Sacrum
- Coccyx

surgery. It is important that the doctor first determine whether you are allergic to the injected material.[15] As with any surgery, always get a second opinion before undergoing the procedure. Long-term follow-up studies comparing surgery and chymopapain indicate that the end results from both procedures are the same.[16]

Vertebrae tend to develop rims of extra bone, called *spurs*, around their edges and on the projections at their rear. While spurs and/or narrowed spaces between vertebrae may combine to press on a nerve, not everyone who has rims and spurs experiences back pain. Stretching exercises, relaxation techniques, and traction may relieve discomfort.

Spinal stenosis is the name for a narrowing of either the spinal canal or the openings for nerve roots in the vertebrae. Appearing mainly in people over fifty, it is now diagnosed more often than before as a source of pain, because it can be seen with the CAT scan. The pain usually increases gradually over time. Treatment may involve appropriate exercise, antiinflammatory drugs, a corset or brace, and, as a last resort, surgery.[17]

Scoliosis is a condition in which the spine

curves to one side. Mild scoliosis is common in adolescent women and, as we age, can contribute to tight muscles or limited motion and strain on the back. If you have scoliosis, ask your health care practitioner about the role it may play in your back pain. Be sure to monitor the degree of curvature, especially after pregnancy, for any change. Chiropractic techniques cannot correct this condition.[18] Deep breathing and exercise can be helpful in counteracting the strain created by scoliosis.

Only 5 percent of back problems require surgery. A CAT scan may be used for diagnosis. Before surgery, most surgeons perform a myelogram, in which a flow of dye is injected into the space surrounding the spinal cord so that anything that blocks the flow will show up on an X-ray. Unfortunately, it is not a comfortable procedure and may result in severe headaches and backaches for weeks. The discomforts are lessened when water-soluble dyes are used.

I saw many doctors for my leg, back, and hip pain. I liked a woman neurologist best of all because she talked with me for forty-five minutes. She said either I had a disc problem or the openings in my spine might be closing down on my nerves. I had a CAT scan. It was spinal stenosis. The neurologist said that 80 percent of the people operated on for this problem felt better, but before surgery I would have to have a myelogram. I didn't want to have one. She said there was no hurry to decide. [a woman in her sixties]

Getting Help with Back Problems

What kind of specialist is most likely to help with back pain? An informal survey of former back patients indicates that they were most satisfied with sports medicine practitioners and physiatrists (physicians specializing in movement). They also had kind words for rheumatologists. The former back patients received temporary relief from both osteopaths (physicians who may prescribe medications) and chiropractors (who cannot prescribe medications), both of whom manipulate the spine; but manipulation is not advisable for herniated discs or sciatica. They found yoga teachers who understand back problems helpful. Physical therapists helped with massage and taught useful exercises, and occupational therapists showed how to perform daily tasks comfortably. The study indicates that the greatest long-term help came from life-style changes. A practitioner who, regardless of specialty, understands the interaction of bones and soft tissues in movement and encourages changes in daily habits gives the most help.[19]

Other Common Joint Problems

Knees

Many knee problems really originate in the foot. People who walk are less likely to develop knee problems than joggers or runners. Keep your quadricep muscles strong because they stabilize the knee. Arthritis and bursitis are also common causes of knee pain.

Hips

Finding the exact source of pain in the hip is often difficult because the joint is located deep in the body. The pain may come not from the hip but from arthritis of the spine. Pain caused by arthritis of the hip is usually felt in the groin, and may radiate to the area above the knee.

Stepping Out with a Cane

We hurt, we're stiff, we want to get around more in spite of the difficulties—but use a cane? Never! Everyone will think we're old!

But a cane can really help. Problems that severely limit our mobility can often be eased by the proper use of a cane. Like fans, which are so helpful for the hot flashes of menopause, canes used to be more fashionable than they are now. Let's make them so again. We can decorate them to match our outfits or save up for an elegant one with fancy carving. We can use a cane to get a seat on the bus, or stamp the floor with it when we want to emphasize a point. A cane can say, "Don't mess with me" if we choose.

Hold a cane in the hand opposite the sore leg. Your elbow will be at a 120 degree angle if the cane is the right height for you. Step out with the cane and the sore leg at the same time. The cane lessens pressure on the sore leg, resting it and giving it time to heal.

Be sure to have the height and your use of a cane (or crutches) checked by an experienced physical therapist or nurse. You can cause damage by incorrect use.

Pain felt on the outside of the hips (at the widest part) is usually caused by bursitis and is often most painful when we are climbing steps or rising to a standing position.

Shoulders

Pain in a shoulder most often comes from bursitis or tendonitis and is usually the result of repeated motions such as overhead work, throwing, or racquet sports. A progressive loss of motion with some stiffness and pain may be so gradual that we don't notice it until it has become quite serious.[20] "Frozen shoulder" occurs often in women over fifty. If not cared for, this condition can become permanent. Rest, hot packs, ice massage, and ultrasound treatments from a physical therapist can prepare the way for passive exercise (someone moves your arm for you) and regular exercise.[21]

Neck

When you sleep, your neck should be supported so that it is in a straight line with your spine. If you awaken with neck pain, the position you slept in may be the cause. For sleeping, fold a hand towel lengthwise to a width of four inches, wrap it around your neck, and pin it with a safety pin.[22] Or try a cervical pillow shaped to fit under and support the neck. Neck pain may also come from vertebrae or disc problems in the spine.

Jaw

I suddenly awoke about 4 A.M. with a severe earache. Aspirin kept the pain down, but it hurt to chew. A few days later it became painful to talk or even swallow. A friend who is a dental hygienist had told me about TMJ but I hadn't really paid much attention at the time. Then it dawned on me that this might be my problem. It was. My right jaw joint had slipped out of kilter.

The jaw joints—the temporomandibular joints (TMJ)—work twenty-four hours a day when we eat, talk, yawn, drink, and sleep. They must be synchronized to allow three-way movement: vertical, horizontal, and back-and-forth. When these joints get out of alignment, a wide range of symptoms may present themselves, among them headaches, earaches or ringing in the ears, eye pain or redness, dizziness, lower back pain, neck stiffness, numbness in the limbs, and a clicking sound in the jaw joint.

The causes of TMJ syndrome are diverse and some are not yet known. We do know that poor occlusion, or misalignment of the teeth, and grinding or clenching of teeth under stressful conditions are often causes, as are whiplash or other head injuries, arthritis, and injuries at birth caused by such practices as forceps delivery. Misalignment can be natural, caused by faulty dental work or orthodonties in youth, or caused by other problems such as ill-fitting dentures.

For years physicians and dentists dismissed those with TMJ symptoms, especially women, as complainers. It is now known that jaw joint disorders are very common and often overlooked, particularly among older people.

I'd had headaches for years that sometimes were so bad I really couldn't function. When the dentist did a lot of work, including realigning my teeth, my headaches stopped. When I remarked about my headaches stopping, my dentist said it might be TMJ syndrome—something I'd never heard of. He examined me closely and then made a mouthguard for me to wear at night. [a sixty-three-year-old woman]

TMJ problems should not be ignored. When diagnosed early, TMJ can usually be treated easily. When ignored, misdiagnosed, or mistreated, it can become intractable, forcing sufferers to stop working and socializing. The keys, therefore, are a careful diagnostic work-up done by a physician or dentist who is knowledgeable and sensitive to jaw joint problems, and treatment by an experienced practitioner.

The treatment of TMJ syndrome is controversial and is almost as varied as the symptoms and causes. Treatment can include a temporary switch to soft foods, stress management, corrective dental work, physical therapy, muscle relaxants, and, in rare cases, surgery. However, always get an independent second opinion—perhaps a third—before having surgery or any other irreversible treatment.

TMJ sufferers need to band together in self-help groups and as advocates to get better care from dental and medical groups. Insurance companies often define TMJ problems as dental problems and, therefore, deny payment under medical insurance policies that do not include dental payments. We must organize to make sure that reimbursement for needed treatment is included under both medical and dental policies.

Elbows

Much used and in a position to be bumped, our elbows are particularly subject to bursitis and tendonitis. Tennis elbow, which can come from any repeated strenuous movement (not just tennis), is a form of tendonitis. A wrist splint made by an occupational therapist to immobilize the wrist muscles that attach at the elbow is more useful than an elbow bandage.[23]

Wrists

Inflamed or swollen tissues in our wrists may squeeze a nerve as it passes through a tunnel on the underside of the wrist, causing pain in the wrist, prickling, numbness (usually in the thumb and first three fingers) and pains shooting up the arm. This syndrome, called *carpal tunnel syndrome*, is common in women who work in the garment and electronics industries, in food service workers, in cashiers and clerical workers,[24] and in some musicians. Discuss with your health care provider whether you would benefit from using a wrist splint, available from hospital supply stores.[25]

Hands and Fingers

Arthritis affects our fingers in many different ways. (The sign language alphabet is excellent exercise.) Osteoarthritis may enlarge just the joints nearest the fingernail (these enlargements are called Heberden's nodes). These swellings may be painful, but they do not usually interfere with activity and do not require medical consultation.[26] A tendency to have these seems to run in families. Rheumatoid arthritis can affect all of the joints in the hand and wrist, especially the knuckles and middle joints of the fingers, and warrants immediate medical attention. Splinting, cold or heat, and exercise are necessary to keep the fingers from becoming deformed.

Many women complain of pain and swelling in the lower part of the thumb, near the palm.[27] Ice packs are helpful for this. Pictured is one type of splint which rests the sore joint while still permitting movement in the rest of the thumb.

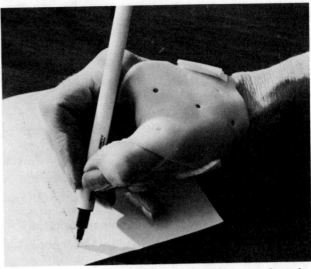

Pam White/Arthritis and Health Resources Centres, Inc.

The base of my thumbs hurt for two years. It got so bad that I couldn't write letters. Medications didn't help. An occupational therapist made a small lightweight plastic splint to support and immobilize the base of my thumb so the joint could rest. In two weeks the inflammation was gone. Now I use the splint during stressful activities such as writing and shopping to prevent pain and irritation. [a fifty-year-old woman]

A sixty-four-year-old woman who spends most of her working day typing ran tape from the back of her hand around the thumb joint to her palm to rest her sore joints in the evening.

ARTHRITIS AND RHEUMATIC DISORDERS

The word "arthritis" describes a condition in which a person has inflamed, painful, stiff, and sometimes swollen joints and muscles. "Rheumatism" is an older word for the same symptoms. There are many conditions that produce these discomforts, however, so if a health care provider uses these general terms, ask her or him to be more specific.

By age sixty-five to seventy, about 80 percent of all women have some arthritic complaint.[28] People who have arthritis and the health care providers who work with them are firm in stating: *All arthritis can be helped.* Although people with arthritic disorders require more rest than most others, millions of people with arthritis are living normal, rich, and fruitful lives. Ninety

Getting Help with Rheumatic Disorders

We can find appropriate people to help us when we have arthritis or another rheumatic disorder. We must not assume, as some physicians do, that pain, stiffness, and decreased mobility are inevitable. A thorough examination is essential. A physician specializing in internal medicine (an internist) can coordinate the evaluation and the care we may need. You may also want to consult a physician who specializes in joint and tissue diseases (a rheumatologist). A surgeon who specializes in bones (an orthopedist) is useful for an early consultation even if you do not intend to have surgery, but she or he should not be used exclusively. Nurse practitioners are skilled at helping you manage chronic conditions. Podiatrists fit orthotics and help with foot care; occupational therapists help adapt equipment for your use; physical therapists can teach body mechanics and evaluate which exercises are best for you. In addition, many women find relief through the services of acupuncturists and massage therapists.

percent of people with arthritis are employable,[29] although some may need help changing to more appropriate jobs.* Only 3 percent of those with arthritis are seriously disabled,[30] and prevention, self-help, early diagnosis, and new methods of treatment are reducing that percentage. Many react with disbelief at the pain and stiffness which may be the first indicator of arthritis.

I refused to consider that anything was wrong with me until I found myself going down the stairs one at a time holding the bannister with one hand and the wall with

---

*For help in making job changes, see your state vocational rehabilitation agency. Developmental disabilities agencies also exist in each state and will help protect your legal rights if you become disabled, and act as advocates with Social Security and in cases of job discrimination. Federal laws protect against discrimination by federal agencies and employers receiving federal funds. These laws cover most large organizations including defense contractors, hospitals, universities, and state agencies. Local and state statutes vary. Some states have comprehensive employment discrimination statutes that forbid discrimination because of disability.

the other. I was only forty-three. [a sixty-one-year-old woman]

Osteoarthritis

The most common form of arthritis is osteoarthritis, called "wear-and-tear arthritis" or degenerative joint disease (DJD) because of the gradual wearing away of joint cartilage. Although almost all adults past forty show signs of osteoarthritis on X-rays, only 10 percent of them have any symptoms.[31] So don't worry if an X-ray shows some osteoarthritis; just follow the suggestions for prevention of joint pain (p. 244).

Osteoarthritis is a localized, mechanical problem rather than an illness involving the whole body. It develops earlier in previously injured or stressed joints. Osteoarthritis of the spinal joints is called *spondylosis*. As with all osteoarthritis, pain or stiffness from spondylosis is worst after inactivity and improves as we move around.

Managing osteoarthritis involves combining rest, exercise, and pain relief (including, if necessary, drugs). Sometimes losing weight relieves the pain. Exercises involving gentle stretching of all muscles two or three times a week are helpful in reducing pain and maintaining mobility. Gently stretch frequently during the day to reduce stiffness. When you feel up to it, *slowly* begin an aerobic activity such as walking, swimming, or bicycle riding (if your knees can take it).

Keep warm—people with arthritis are often sensitive to cold, dampness, and changes in barometric pressure, which change the pressure inside the joint.

You may be tempted to move to a drier climate. This does not always help. Try a visit first. Moving can be one of life's most stressful experiences, and the loss of one's friends and familiar environment may be more painful than bad weather or aching joints.

Rheumatoid Arthritis

Rheumatoid arthritis (RA) is an inflammatory illness that affects the whole body. It feels, and is, systemic, like flu. While it may affect many organs, it usually causes most problems in the joints. In RA, the lining of the joint capsule (synovial membrane) becomes severely inflamed, producing enzymes that damage cartilage, bone, and soft tissue, in severe cases destroying the joint.[32]

RA affects three times as many women as men. While it first strikes most often between twenty-five and forty-five, half the women who have it are over fifty years of age. What causes the inflammation is not clear but may involve autoimmunity, in which the body attacks its own cells.

Joints, almost always the same ones on both sides of the body, become painful, stiff, swollen, warm, and tender. Early diagnosis and therapy can do much to prevent the disabling aspects of the disease: of those who start treatment *within twelve months* of the early signs of the disease, 75 percent will show substantial improvement.[33] Physical and occupational therapy should start early. Unfortunately, people sometimes wait years before seeking treatment, enduring needless suffering and sometimes irreversible damage.

A major U.S. study found some increase in RA at menopause, but found a particularly high instance of it in women who had had both ovaries removed (bilateral oophorectomy). Something other than estrogen may be involved, since neither oral contraceptives nor postmenopausal hormones are effective in preventing or treating RA.[34] For this and other reasons, removal of healthy ovaries should be avoided.

People with arthritis do best when they are active participants in managing their disease. Be sure you understand your illness, with its painful flare-ups alternating with good periods, and your consequent emotional ups and downs. You will be the best monitor of your condition.

The progress of this disease is so individual that it is entirely up to me to determine (by listening very hard to my body) what is appropriate, what is too much, when to rest, when to cut back on activities, when to call it quits. This entails constantly reassessing goals, resetting the "clock" back to zero when I overextend. It is very frustrating but even more so when friends and family pressure me, however subtly. A close friend said to me that the five-hour train trip to visit her is easy. "After all, you're sitting down all the way." It gets so hard to always have to explain. [a thirty-eight-year-old woman]

Lupus

Systemic lupus erythematosus (SLE), like rheumatoid arthritis, is considered an autoimmune disease. One mild form of lupus (called discoid lupus) affects only the skin. The inflammatory processes of lupus can attack connective tissue in any organ system, making the disease difficult to diagnose. It was not even recognized as a disease until 1946. Of the 500,000 to 1,000,000 people in the U.S. who have lupus today, 90 percent are women. About half of the people with lupus will have symptoms similar to the symptoms of rheumatoid arthritis.

Early diagnosis is important to protect the kidneys, and checking kidney function is part of living with the disease. Before the use of corticosteroids, lupus was often fatal within three years. Since corticosteroids tend to drain the body of calcium, people with lupus should pay particular attention to calcium intake. They require even more rest than those with other rheumatic disorders. Although lupus usually strikes during the childbearing years, more women with the disease now survive into middle and old age. One antihypertensive drug, hydralazine hydrochloride (Apresoline), may cause lupuslike symptoms, which cease when the drug is stopped.

Other Rheumatic Disorders

Inflammation that attacks the connective tissues of the body can cause other rheumatic disorders. Two of these disorders are relatively common:

Fibrositis is often called fibromyalgia or myofascial pain syndrome.[35] Symptoms, including aching, pain, stiffness which has persisted for at least three months, sore spots that radiate pain elsewhere when pressed, fatigue, and sleep disorders, may continue for months or years and then taper off. A long-lasting remission is possible. Antiinflammatory drugs, therapeutic exercise, relaxation techniques, stress management, and the attention of a physical therapist can make an enormous difference in the quality of life.

For some months I had been feeling sore, stiff, and tired. I found sore spots on my shoulders, neck, elbows, hips and knees. All my joints hurt. Then my cheekbones began to hurt (no joints there!) and pain in my shins kept me awake. My physician told me the sheaths of my muscles were inflamed and causing my pain. He prescribed an antiinflammatory drug and physical therapy. I was astonished at how limited my movements had become. I began a slow program of specific exercises, working up to walking and swimming. After ten months I feel much better. The main limitation is that I must avoid fatigue or choose to pay the price in pain. [a sixty-one-year-old woman]

Polymyalgia rheumatica, an inflammation of the small blood vessels that supply the muscles, has been recognized as a disease only since 1969. Appearing often in women over fifty, the average age of onset is seventy. One woman in several hundred experiences this increasingly recognized condition, which causes stiffness and aches. The symptoms of inflammation in the temporal arteries may include headaches on the side of the forehead and sudden severe stiffness in the shoulders and neck, on one side or both. **Inflammation in the temporal arteries must be treated immediately with corticosteroids to prevent blindness.**[36]

Drugs for Rheumatic Disorders

Control of inflammation and pain is essential for the management of rheumatic disorders. Inflammation can be so damaging to the body that even those who dislike taking medication may decide to do so. When necessary, medication can enable us to lead normal lives or even save our lives. (See OTC and Prescription Drugs, p. 30.) Several groups of antiinflammatory drugs are described below. All of them must be carefully monitored because people react to them in individual ways. What works for one person may not work for another. If one prescribed drug does not agree with or help you, talk with your physician about others. Patience is necessary to find the drug that works best for you.

Recent research indicates that very high levels of fish oils may have an antiinflammatory effect.[37] It is not clear, however, that the expensive omega-3 fatty acid supplements now sold by several drug companies contain the effective ingredient. Moreover, high doses, especially if combined with other drugs that retard clotting, such as aspirin, may result in excessive bleeding.[38] Instead of taking expensive unproven supplements, make fish a regular part of your diet. It is high in protein and vitamin D, low in fat and cholesterol, and may possibly have an antiinflammatory effect.

Antiinflammatory nonsteroidal drugs reduce inflammation and pain. Among these drugs are aspirin, ibuprofen, sulindac, and many others. Acetaminophen is a painkiller but has no antiinflammatory effect. All these drugs tend to irritate the stomach, so are best taken after food. Aspirin, the standard against which the other drugs are measured, is the cheapest. When pre-scribed to control inflammation, it is used in high doses over long periods of time. For some, the amount of aspirin necessary to control inflammation may cause ringing in the ears or other undesirable effects, or may not work at all.

One antiinflammatory drug, piroxicam (Feldene), which can cause gastrointestinal ulcers and bleeding, was in several countries labeled harmful to people over sixty but was marketed in the U.S. for several years before a warning label was finally added.[39]

Serious undesirable effects accompany two other nonsteroidal drugs, phenylbutazone (Butazolidin) and oxyphenbutazone (Tandearil). These two drugs are dangerous, because on rare occasions they can kill most of the white or red blood cells.[40] Older people cannot replenish these cells so quickly as young people. These drugs also cause fluid retention, which can lead to heart failure in older people.

Some people with rheumatoid arthritis respond well to antimalarial drugs: chloroquine (Aralen) and hydroxychloroquine (Plaquenil). Because these can cause damage to the retina, possibly resulting in blindness, eye examinations every six months are necessary.

For many of those who have severe rheumatoid arthritis, gold salts or penicillamine can bring dramatic relief. These drugs may actually halt the progression of the disease. However, both treatments also have rare but severe and sometimes fatal effects.

Corticosteroids (hormones obtained from the adrenal gland, most commonly cortisone and prednisone) are appropriate, even lifesaving, treatments for rheumatic disorders. They have severe effects, among them masking symptoms of acute infection, raised blood pressure, slowed healing of injuries, osteoporosis, cataracts, diabetes, water retention, and increased appetite. They can cause fat deposits on the face, shoulders, and abdomen. Never take corticosteroids without supervision; carry a warning card if you do take them. Don't decide on your own to stop or reduce the amount of corticosteroids you are taking even if you feel well.[41] Stopping steroids suddenly or failing to taper off slowly can cause serious problems, even death. Advise any new health care practitioner if you have been under corticosteroid treatment within the past two years.

Cortisone given by injection into a joint affects that joint but not the entire body. Its use should be limited to no more than three injections in the same joint in a year.

Surgery for Rheumatic Disorders

Long-endured pain makes us vulnerable to the hope that surgery may solve the problem. Since speed is rarely a factor in surgery for arthritis, you have time to get other opinions. When joints are so seriously affected that the results are disabling, surgery may be helpful. Arthritis surgery requires special skills and should not be performed by a surgeon who does such operations only occasionally.

For example, surgery can reposition tendons in the hands and feet moved by the bone changes of rheumatoid arthritis, thereby restoring some function in these joints. A synovectomy—removing the inflamed lining of a joint—can provide dramatic pain relief for some years, but the painful symptoms usually return.[42]

You may choose to have a hip or knee replacement if you have severe and worsening pain even when at rest, have great difficulty walking or performing movements such as putting on or removing shoes and stockings, and if other methods have not helped. Over 120,000 hips and knees are replaced each year and the number is rising. The main complications of these procedures are blood clots and infections (but a good facility for hip replacement will have an infection rate of only 0.5 percent to 1 percent—ask). Hip replacements are more successful than knee replacements, but both can improve the quality of life. Take time to consider; waiting will not affect the results. Be aware, though, that limping because of hip pain can increase pain and arthritis in the opposite hip.

A hip replacement is a *temporary* solution to a serious problem. The replacement will wear out in ten to fifteen years, but those years may be more mobile and pain-free than without the operation. *No one is too old for a hip replacement,* but those unable to take anesthesia or who are very heavy may not qualify. Replacements wear out faster under the impact of heavy weight.

A hip replacement has two parts. One, a polished metal ball and stem, attaches to the leg

Pelvis Before Surgery

Osteoarthritis of the Ball and Socket of the Hip Joint

Femur (Leg) Bone

Pelvis After Surgery

Total Hip Prosthesis

Stem of Prosthesis Inserted into Bone

HIP REPLACEMENT

bone nearest the hip (the femur—see illustration). The other attaches to the hipbone and is a socket into which the metal ball fits and moves. A glue or cement similar to Lucite holds these parts onto the bones.

Five years ago I had one hip replaced. I knew that before I left the hospital I would have to learn bed exercises from a physical therapist, what positions to avoid, how to use the toilet, get into the tub, and manage stairs. I knew I'd be on crutches for three months, then one crutch, then a cane. At first, I needed help getting dressed. I exercised on the floor, but now I swim and walk every day. The hips (I had the other replaced also) are not like my own when they were healthy, but they don't hold me back from anything like when my own were bad. If I knew someone who needed a hip replacement, I'd say, "Go ahead and do it!" [a seventy-two-year-old woman]

Knee joint replacements wear out faster, have more complications, and a slightly higher infection rate than hip joint replacements. Restriction on weight is important and regular physical therapy exercises are essential for a satisfactory outcome after the operation. Knee replacements have limited motion, but you should be able to get up from a chair, go up and down stairs, and walk without pain.

I had two hips replaced eight years ago because of osteoarthritis. They've been fine. But my knees also had osteoarthritis, and when I could no longer take walks with my husband, which I like to do, I had them both replaced. I worked very hard at exercising while I was in the hospital. I'm losing some weight now. I take exercise classes and swim. I have a little limitation of motion in my hips and I can't cross my legs any more, but that's not so bad. When I read in bed at night, I'd like to put my knees way up the way I used to, but I can't. But I can walk and do most of the things I want to do. [a sixty-year-old woman]

Two years ago after a very brief examination, an orthopedic surgeon advised a joint replacement for a knee problem I was having. I sought a second opinion from an arthritis clinic in a teaching hospital. They examined and questioned me for an hour and said I did not need an operation. One corticosteroid shot and their suggestions helped the problem and it hasn't returned. [a seventy-six-year-old woman]

Unproven Remedies

One characteristic of rheumatic disorders is that periods of pain alternate with periods of relief (spontaneous remission). People who experience this may be convinced that whatever they did just before the relief caused the relief, and therefore may easily adopt unproven remedies, thinking they are miracle cures. Many people make money promoting such cures. *Consumer Reports* estimated in 1979 that for every dollar spent for research in arthritis, $25 was spent on useless or, in some cases, dangerous treatments—nearly $1 billion a year of wasted money. Except for the value of eating fish for their fatty acids, research has not yet confirmed claims that vitamin therapy or dietary changes can help arthritis. Eating well will improve your general health whether or not it has a direct effect on your arthritis.

Some unproven cures may be relatively harmless, such as wearing copper bracelets or observing dietary restrictions that do not interfere with good nutrition. Some, like DMSO (a chemical that can carry medication through the skin), not only have no value for arthritis, but may cause other problems.[43] Many people take medications that indeed make them feel better, only to pay a terrible price in unhealthful effects later, if they have been unknowingly taking corticosteroids or hormones without supervision and necessary testing. Never take drugs if you don't know what they are, especially if they are provided by someone who does not oversee their use.

If you seek help from an arthritis center, look for one that has individually designed programs, including physical therapy, occupational therapy, counseling, nutritional advice, and exercise. The federal government funds fifteen arthritis centers at hospitals around the country (see Resources).

Protecting joints, exercising daily, balancing activity and rest, learning to ask for help, trying different techniques to relieve pain—these add up to changes (often modest, sometimes sweeping) that can help us enjoy life in spite of arthritis and joint pain.

I used to do ceramics, painting, leatherwork. The first time the doctor said "Stop before the pain starts," I said, "You must be crazy. I'm involved in creative work. I have to finish!" It took years before I learned. Later I discovered that flower arranging did not drain my strength and gave me pleasure. It became a new creative outlet for me. I joined a garden club and won several ribbons. [a seventy-five-year-old woman]

NOTES

1. Richard A. Deyo, et al., "How Many Days of Bed Rest for Acute Lower Back Pain? A Randomized Clinical Trial." *The New England Journal of Medicine*, Vol. 315, No. 17 (October 23, 1986), pp. 1064–70; and Nortin M. Hadler, "Editorial: Regional Back Pain." *The New England Journal of Medicine*, Vol. 315, No. 17 (October 23, 1986), pp. 1090–2.

2. Arthritis and Health Resource Center, *Newsletter*, Vol. 1, 1984, p. 2.

3. Adapted from James F. Fries, *Arthritis: A Comprehensive Guide to Understanding Your Arthritis*, rev. ed. Reading, MA: Addison-Wesley, 1986, p. 6.

4. Mary P. Schatz, "Yoga Relief for Arthritis." *Yoga Journal*, Issue 62, May/June 1985, pp. 29–34.

5. John Hoffman, et al., "Reduced Sympathetic Nervous System Responsivity Associated with the Relaxation Response." *Science*, Vol. 229, January 8, 1982, pp. 190–2.

6. Bonnie Prudden, *Myotherapy: Bonnie Prudden's Complete Guide to Pain-Free Living*. Garden City, NY: Doubleday, 1984.

7. René Cailliet, *Foot and Ankle Pain* 2d ed. Philadelphia, PA: F. A. Davis Co., 1983, p. 115.

8. Personal communication from Bruce Woods, M.D.

9. Prudden, op. cit., pp. 202–3.

10. Suggested by Connie Slater, physical therapist.

11. Personal communication from Alf Nachemson, M.D.

12. "Preventing Lower Back Pain." *Drug Therapy*, December 1982, pp. 97–102. Prepared with the assistance of Dr. Bernard Jacob.

13. Jack R. Tessman, *My Back Doesn't Hurt Anymore*. New York: Quick Fox, 1980, pp. 59–60.

14. Augustus A. White, III, *Your Aching Back*. New York: Bantam Books, 1983, pp. 193–219.

15. G. Timothy Johnson and Stephen E. Goldfinger, *The Harvard Medical School Health Letter Book*. Cambridge, MA: Harvard University Press, 1981, pp. 135–8.

16. J. Weinstein, et al., "Lumbar Disc Herniation." *The Journal of Bone and Joint Surgery*, Vol. 68-A, No. 1 (January 1986), pp. 43–54.

17. White, op. cit., pp. 43–5.

18. Arthur C. Klein and Dava Sobel, *Backache Relief*. New York: Times Books, 1985, p. 32.

19. Ibid.

20. Walter R. Sundstrom, "Painful Shoulders: Diagnosis and Management." *Geriatrics*, Vol. 38, No. 3 (March 1983), p. 91.

21. Ibid., p. 96. For exercise suggestions, see Kate Lorig and James F. Fries, *The Arthritis Helpbook: What You Can Do for Your Arthritis*, rev. ed. Reading, MA: Addison-Wesley, 1986, pp. 49–52.

22. Fries, op. cit., pp. 192–3.

23. Personal communication from Jeanne L. Melvin.

24. "Women's Health." Report of the PHS Task Force on Women's Health Issues, Vol. I. *Public Health Reports*, Vol. 100, No. 1 (January–February 1985), p. 92.

25. Fries, op. cit., p. 198.

26. Personal communication from William P. Docken, M.D.

27. Letters to *Broomstick*, Vol. IV, No. 4 (July–August 1982), p. 29, and Vol. VI, No. 6 (November–December 1984), p. 36.

28. Jane Porcino, *Growing Older, Getter Better: A Handbook for Women in the Second Half of Life*. Reading, MA: Addison-Wesley, 1983, p. 248.

29. Ephraim P. Engleman and Milton Silverman, *The Arthritis Book*. New York: Simon & Schuster, 1980, pp. 144–5.

30. Ibid., p. 144.

31. Patricia J. Cooper, ed., *Better Homes and Gardens Women's Health and Medical Guide*. Des Moines, Iowa: Meredith Corp., 1981, p. 639.

32. Fred G. Kantrowicz, "Rheumatoid Arthritis." *Medical Times*, Vol. 110, No. 2 (February 1982), p. 73.

33. Engleman and Silverman, op. cit., p. 20.

34. Preliminary Results from the Nurses' Health Study, Harvard School of Public Health. *Menopausal Status, Estrogen Use, and Incidence of Rheumatoid Arthritis*, abstract presented at the 110th Annual Meeting of the American Public Health Association, 1982.

35. Stephen M. Campbell, "Referred Shoulder Pain." *Postgraduate Medicine*, Vol. 73, No. 5 (May 1983), pp. 193–203.

36. Fries, op. cit., p. 63.

37. Tak H. Lee, et al., "Effect of Dietary Enrichment with Eicosapentaenoic and Docosahexaenoic Acids on In Vitro Neutrophil and Monocyte Leukotriene General and Neutrophil Function." *The New England Journal of Medicine*, Vol. 312, No. 19 (May 9, 1985), pp. 1217–24. "We conclude that diets enriched with fish-oil-derived fatty acids may have anti-inflammatory effects...." See also Summary in Jenny Dusheck, "Fish, Fatty Acids, and Physiology." *Science News*, October 19, 1985, pp. 252–4.

38. "Should You Begin Taking Fish Oil Supplements?" *University Diet & Nutrition Letter*, Vol. 4, No. 11 (January 1987), pp. 1–2.

39. "Feldene: Canada and Germany Protect Older People Better." *Health Letter*, Public Citizens Health Research Group, Vol. 2, No. 4 (September/October 1986), pp. 14–15; "Feldene." *Health Letter*, Vol. 3, No. 1 (January 1987), p. 18.

40. Fries, op. cit., pp. 106–7; and Cooper, op. cit., p. 636.

41. Lorig and Fries, op. cit., p. 218.

42. Engleman and Silverman, op. cit., p. 133.

43. Annabel Hecht, "Hocus Pocus as Applied to Arthritis." *FDA Consumer*, U.S. Dept. of Health and Human Services, September 1980, HHS Pub. No. (FDA) 81-1080.

19

OSTEOPOROSIS

by Kathleen I. MacPherson

Lately, osteoporosis is mentioned everywhere we turn—in newspapers, women's magazines, and television talk shows. Sunday newspapers have full-page advertisements for calcium supplements and for books on osteoporosis.[1] This strange term, which most of us had never heard until fairly recently, has suddenly become a household word.

An illustration of a woman with a "dowager's hump" is used repeatedly as the symbol for osteoporosis. The media blitz is raising our consciousness to the dangers of this "silent condition" that takes years to weaken our bones, making them vulnerable to breakage in old age. This sudden attention to a major health problem, which had been largely ignored in the past, can help us prepare for a healthy old age.

There is no denying the extent of the problem. Osteoporosis leads to more than one million bone fractures each year and touches the lives of twenty million older Americans, at a cost of $3.8 billion annually. One fourth of all white women are affected by the disorder. Osteoporosis is a

Norma Holt

vital women's health issue because we develop the condition more frequently than men. The condition leads to loss of teeth and wrist fractures, usually starting in our fifties, spinal crush fractures when we are between fifty-five and seventy-five, and hip fractures in our seventies and eighties.[2]

Still, there are some troubling aspects to all the new attention to osteoporosis. Why has this long-time public-health issue suddenly come to the forefront now? Why is osteoporosis being linked to menopause? Why are men who develop osteoporosis being ignored? How can we best cope with the conflicting advice we are given by various experts in medicine, nutrition, and exercise?

Understanding Osteoporosis

Our bones are made up of living cells in a state of constant breakdown and repair. Except for the skin, no other substance in the body has such excellent regenerative powers as bone. As new bone is produced, it is actually laid down on the solid outer shell (cortical bone). Old bone disappears from the softer, less dense substance inside (trabecular bone) where calcium can enter and leave. Normally, our body balances the two processes of building new bone and removing old bone so that our bones remain strong. This continuous building process is called remodeling. When new bone formation no longer keeps up with bone loss, bones begin to thin and weaken.

We lose a certain amount of lean muscle tissue and some bone cells as a natural result of the aging process, although most of us will not develop osteoporosis. Bone loss starts in women a few years after bone density peaks at about age thirty-five. The loss increases slightly in the four to five years following menopause.[3] There are large differences in the rate and amount of thinning among individuals.[4]

In addition, calcium can be leached out of the bones if the level of calcium in the blood drops below normal. Through an intricate process, the level of calcium in the blood is kept within a very precise, narrow range[5] necessary for muscle contractions, transmission of nerve impulses, and blood clotting. If the level of calcium in the blood is higher than necessary, the body excretes whatever cannot be absorbed.

A Glossary of Bone Conditions

Osteopenia: a general term for decreased bone density. Osteopenia refers to all forms of bone weakness, including osteoporosis and osteomalacia.

Osteoporosis: from "osteo," referring to bones, and "porosis," full of holes. In this condition, the actual bone is normal—there is just not enough of it. When osteoporosis exists, certain bones become so thin that they are likely to fracture or become compressed as a result of even a minor fall, or making a bed, or opening a door.

Osteomalacia: the adult form of rickets, a softening and weakening of bones due to vitamin D deficiency. It is caused by poor diet, lack of exposure to sunlight, or the inability of the body to absorb vitamin D. In this condition, bone cells are abnormal and the bones may actually change shape.

Osteoporosis is a complex condition that usually takes years to advance to the stage where it can be detected. Many interrelated factors affect the exchange of calcium between the blood and bones. These factors include the amount of calcium in the diet, how efficiently our bodies absorb it, hormonal balance, and our level of physical activity. Lowered estrogen level after menopause is only one factor—often overemphasized in the mass media and medical literature—that contributes to the development of osteoporosis. We can understand these factors and make changes that will slow bone loss and improve bone remodeling.

For example, when we are young, diet is our chief source of calcium. Vitamin D is added to milk because it helps the body absorb calcium from the small intestine and also promotes the transportation of calcium into bone. The level of calcium in the blood, in turn, controls the amount of hormone secreted by the parathyroid gland (parathyroid hormone, or PTH). If the level of calcium in the blood decreases, more PTH, which triggers leaching of calcium from the bones, will be produced to correct the deficit in the blood. Other hormones also play a role—normal estrogen levels protect women from producing too much PTH; cortisone-like products (corticosteroids) can increase PTH production, leading to excessive loss of calcium from the bones.

It is also important to understand how activity, or the lack of it, affects bone strength. Bone mass will increase or decrease according to the demand placed on it. The total amount of calcium in the body increases with exercise, but muscle strength, bone-mineral content, and specific bone mass will vary depending on activity patterns. For example, tennis players have thicker bones in their dominant arms. Demand in an active part of the body will pull bone mineral away from inactive parts. In one study, women aged thirty-five to sixty-five in an aerobic movement program showed loss of mineral in upper-body bone, which was regained when upper-body resistance exercises were added.[6] (See Moving for Health chapter for a balanced exercise regimen.)

All these factors—reduced activity, reduced calcium absorption in our intestines, and reduced levels of estrogen to counteract the effects of PTH—result in increased calcium loss as we age.

Symptoms

Seven years ago, I developed a pain up under my right breast and I couldn't imagine what it was. It hurt to move and it hurt to breathe and I ignored it for a little while. Finally it got so bad that I went to the doctor and he ordered X-rays of my back and rib cage. He said, "Oh, my, your bones are so thin I'm amazed you haven't broken everything you've got." The vertebrae had thinned and compressed—one was pressing on a nerve which caused the pain in my chest. [a fifty-nine-year-old woman]

MULTIPLE FACTORS AFFECTING THE CONDITION OF BONE

Adapted from an illustration by Nancy Lou Makris in Herta Spencer, "Osteoporosis: Goals of Therapy." Hospital Practice, Vol. 17, No. 3, March 1982, p. 133.

Early warning signs of osteoporosis include wrist fracture following a simple fall or blow, and muscle spasms or pain in the back while at rest or while doing routine daily work such as making a bed or picking up an object from the floor. This pain comes on suddenly; most women can recall the exact moment it began. It is often caused by the spontaneous collapsing (a spinal crush fracture) of small sections of the spine that have been severely thinned or weakened. These compression fractures can lead to "dowager's hump," which shortens the chest area and makes digesting food more difficult. Because compression fractures do not always cause prolonged, severe pain or disability, some women are not aware that they have this condition, although 20 percent of women do by age seventy.

Loss of height is another early sign of spinal crush fractures and osteoporosis. It would be wise to measure your height routinely. In extreme cases, women can lose as much as eight inches of height, all from the upper half of the body.[7]

Factors That Increase Your Risk of Osteoporosis

Biological Factors

- Being female
- Having a family history of osteoporosis
- Having Northern European ancestry
- Being thin and short
- Having fair skin and freckles
- Having blond or reddish-colored hair
- Early natural menopause
- Childlessness
- Lactose intolerance
- Teenage pregnancy
- Scoliosis

Medical Factors

- Oophorectomy (removal of ovaries)
- Anorexia
- Celiac disease
- Chronic diarrhea
- Diabetes
- Kidney or liver disease
- Use of certain prescription and over-the-counter drugs
- Extended bed rest or immobilization
- Surgical removal of part of the stomach or small intestine

Life-Style Factors

- Lack of exercise
- Smoking
- High alcohol intake
- Low-calcium diet
- Vitamin D deficiency
- Prolonged dieting or fasting
- High caffeine intake (over five cups a day)
- High salt intake

Environmental Factors

- Inadequate fluoride level in the water supply
- Living in a northern climate
- Being confined indoors

Risk Factors and Self-Help

Biological Risk Factors

Women are at greater risk of osteoporosis than men because men have 30 percent more bone mass at age thirty-five than women, and they lose bone more slowly as they age. If you are Black, the chances of your developing osteoporosis are rare. Black women have 10 percent more bone mass than white women, and may have more calcitonin, the hormone that strengthens bones.[8] If you are of Hispanic, Mediterranean, or Jewish ancestry, the risk seems to fall between the low risk for Blacks and the high risk for Northern European white women and Asian women. The fairer your complexion, the greater your risk.

A person's risk of hip fracture doubles approximately every six to seven years, regardless of sex or race. At any age, the risk for white women is approximately double that for men, regardless of race, and also double that for Black women. The unusual susceptibility of white women is, thus, not simply due either to sex or race, since there is no clear gender correlation among Blacks and no clear race correlation among men. This suggests that there is a similar underlying process which increases fracture risk in all groups as they age, but that this process either begins earlier or presents symptoms earlier in white women.[9] Therefore, if you are white, slender, short, and of Northern European descent, although you cannot change these biological factors, you can make a special effort to prevent osteoporosis by eating a calcium-rich diet and exercising.

In addition, talk to your mother, aunts, and grandmothers to find out whether any of your close relatives have had a dowager's hump, many fractures, or a diagnosis of osteoporosis. There appears to be a slight tendency to inherit the predisposition to osteoporosis, so you need to take special precautions if your relatives have had this condition.

Women who have never had a child or breastfed an infant have missed out on the temporary surges of estrogen that accompany pregnancy and follow breastfeeding and help protect us against osteoporosis in later life. Although estrogen levels temporarily drop during lactation and calcium leaves bones to go into milk formation, as soon as you stop breastfeeding your estrogen level rises again. This helps strengthen the bones in preparation for another pregnancy.[10]

A nutritious diet during pregnancy will help bones get stronger. If you are not on a nutritious diet, pregnancy and breastfeeding can actually draw calcium out of the bones—hence the adage about losing a tooth for each child. When the mother's own bones are not fully formed, adequate calcium is especially necessary. The adolescent mother can suffer as much as a 10 percent loss in bone content after four months of breastfeeding.[11] We can't change our own childbearing history, but we hope this information will influence young women to delay pregnancy until their own growth is complete, or, if they become pregnant and breastfeed, to eat wisely. Recommended dietary allowances for pregnant teenagers include a 2500-calorie diet daily, including 76 grams of protein and 1600 milligrams of calcium.[12] We believe a higher intake of calcium, closer to 2000 mg. during pregnancy and 2200 mg. while breastfeeding, is best for women of any age.

Medical research in this country reports that women experience increased bone loss four to five years following the onset of menopause.[13] If you have an early natural menopause, before age forty, you are at risk for osteoporosis because the cessation of menstruation causes estrogen levels to drop.

If you experience diarrhea, cramps, and gas after drinking milk or eating milk products you may be lactose intolerant—without enough lactase, the enzyme that helps us digest milk properly. If you are lactose intolerant, see page 59 in the Eating Well chapter for good alternative sources of calcium. About 70 percent of Blacks and Asians are lactose intolerant, compared with 15 percent of the general population. Sixty percent of women with osteoporosis are lactose intolerant, compared with 15 percent of the general population.[14] Note, however, that Blacks have a low rate of osteoporosis despite their high rate of lactose intolerance, which shows that other factors are involved.

Medical Risk Factors

In addition to biological factors, certain diseases or chronic conditions can make us vulnerable to excessive bone loss. Women with anorexia, for example, may develop osteoporosis as early as age twenty-five—even to the point of having spinal crush fractures, which are usually seen only in elderly women.[15] Extremely strenuous exercise, as a result of which the percentage of body fat drops so low that menstruation stops, can also lead to osteoporosis.

Celiac disease in childhood (malabsorption of food usually caused by sensitivity to the gluten in wheat) is never completely outgrown, and even if controlled may recur in adults when irritating food is eaten. Chronic diarrhea caused by ulcerative colitis or Crohn's disease (chronic inflammation or tuberculosis of the small intestine) also prevents the calcium in food from being absorbed.[16]

If you have diabetes, you have to contend with frequent urination, which causes excessive loss of calcium, and high blood acidity, which interferes with the absorption of vitamin D. If you have kidney or liver problems, the calcium in your food is not efficiently absorbed; kidney dialysis adds to calcium deficiency.

Certain surgery can also put you at risk for osteoporosis. Surgical removal of the ovaries, especially before, but even at the time of, menopause, reduces estrogen production more rapidly and for a longer period of time than a normal menopause. If you undergo this surgery, you need to take special care to maintain an adequate calcium intake and exercise program. Many researchers report a high rate of osteoporosis if hormone-replacement therapy isn't started soon after removal of premenopausal ovaries.[17] But we believe that each woman has to decide for herself if she wants hormone-replacement therapy, based on a careful evaluation of her individual situation.

Stomach surgery (a gastric bypass for weight reduction, ulcer removal) and intestinal surgery can also place you at risk for osteoporosis; stomach surgery can lead to insufficient hydrochloric acid, which is necessary for the proper digestion of food before it passes into the small intestine.[18] Calcium can get into the bloodstream only through the small intestines or bones. If there are problems with intestinal absorption, your bones pay the price.

It's also necessary to consider medications often taken for chronic health problems, such as cortisone for severe arthritis, thyroid for hypothyroidism, phenobarbitol or phenytoin (Dilantin) for seizures, aluminum-containing antacids for ulcers or heartburn. Exercise and a nutritious diet are a must if you take these drugs, because they all interfere with the body's ability to absorb calcium from food and calcium supplements.

Life-Style Risk Factors

Avoiding osteoporosis isn't as complicated as we are led to believe. Most of us can take immediate steps to improve bone strength by changing our daily habits.

Nutrition, for example, plays a major role in preventing and treating osteoporosis. (See the Eating Well chapter for a full discussion of the role of calcium in a balanced diet.) The amount of phosphorus (which aids in the development and maturation of bones)[19] we consume should be equal to the amount of calcium we consume. Most of us, however, probably take in too much phosphorus from eating red meat, processed cheese, baked goods that contain phosphate baking powder, cola and other soft drinks, instant soups and puddings, bread, and phosphate food additives. High amounts of phosphorus are absorbed very efficiently; high amounts of calcium, on the other hand, are absorbed less efficiently. Dried skim milk is very high in phosphorus—each 100 grams of milk contains 950 mg. of phosphorus[20]—so if you add powdered milk to soups or casseroles for extra cal-

cium, take care to cut out other unnecessary sources of phosphorus.

We also need magnesium for strong teeth and bones. The amount of magnesium we consume should be at least half the amount of calcium we consume—perhaps equal to it.[21] If magnesium intake is too low, the body is not able to utilize calcium or vitamin D, even if a sufficient amount of those substances is available. There is a rich supply of magnesium in nuts, whole grains, sprouts, beans, fresh vegetables, and fruit.

It's also important that we get enough zinc and manganese, because calcium added to the diet decreases their absorption. Zinc is found in whole-grain breads and cereals, nuts, and seeds. Manganese is found in sunflower seeds, nuts, rice, barley, oats, and blueberries.

Vitamin D is a vital factor in the body's use of calcium. In order for vitamin D to aid in calcium absorption, it has to be converted into a hormone in the liver and in the kidneys. Osteoporosis may occur when the conversion is not taking place, and hence may be a symptom of liver and/or kidney disease. In addition, vitamin D can't be converted to its active hormone form when the blood is too acid due to stress, diabetes, or fasting, or if you have a magnesium deficiency. Certain medications such as anticonvulsants, laxatives, cortisone, and mineral oil can also interfere with the absorption of vitamin D.

A summer holiday in the sun allows us to store vitamin D for prolonged periods of time. Half an hour in the sun with 30 percent of the body exposed several times a week is fine too. This is especially important if we live in the North, in overcast areas, or are confined indoors. But be sure to avoid excessive exposure to the sun.

Foods rich in vitamin D are egg yolk (if hens are allowed outside), certain fish, fish liver, and butter. Fortunately vitamin D is added to many milk products—eight ounces of milk contains 100 International Units (I.U.). We need 400 I.U. daily. Over the age of sixty-five we need 600 to 800 I.U. daily because our bodies have a decreased capacity to absorb and convert vitamin D as we get older, which may be a significant factor in osteoporosis. You can take a supplement if you dislike dairy products or are lactose intolerant. Supplementary amounts over 1000 I.U. a day interfere with calcium absorption and, because vitamin D is stored in the body for long periods of time, higher amounts can be toxic.

Prolonged dieting and fasting are common in our society because of its obsession with slenderness. If you habitually eat little, your daily requirements for calcium and related nutrients are not met, so that calcium has to be taken from your bones. Adequate weight and fat tissue offer protection from osteoporosis. The weight on the bones makes them work to produce new bone tissue, and the fat tissue helps to maintain some estrogen in the body after menopause. The ovaries continue after menopause to produce a little estrogen of the type seen in menstruating women and the adrenal glands continue to produce androgens, which are converted to another type of estrogen in fat tissue.

Other life-style factors, such as alcohol and caffeine abuse, can also contribute to bone loss. Both caffeine and alcohol act as diuretics that can cause loss of calcium and zinc in the urine. Alcohol damages the liver, interfering with vitamin D metabolism. However, one or two cups of coffee or tea, a beer or a glass of wine, or 1½ ounces of hard liquor daily probably do no harm.

Smoking is a known risk factor in osteoporosis. It is directly toxic to the ovaries. Women who smoke often experience menopause up to five years earlier than nonsmokers, and thus have lower estrogen levels for a longer period of time. Smoking may also interfere with the body's metabolism of estrogen, and may affect bone remodeling in other ways.[22] Smoking often accompanies high alcohol or caffeine use. If you smoke, try to stop or at least cut down.

Lack of exercise is another major risk factor that you can control. Part of the geographical and racial differences among women relative to the incidence of osteoporosis may be due to differences in physical activity.[23] In the past, women generally didn't exercise vigorously. To sweat was unfeminine, and our society equated femininity with a small frame, low weight, and a passive attitude toward life; certainly there was no approval of a female "jock" type. Fortunately it's never too late for us to start exercising. Weight-bearing exercises such as walking, jogging, jumping rope, and dancing all make our bones work harder and strengthen the muscles and ligaments supporting the skeleton. One researcher reported that weight-bearing exercise that excluded upper-body activity resulted in a 3.5 percent increase in spinal bone during an 18-month period, but a 3.6 percent decrease in wrist bone.[24] It is important to make our arms work also, by swimming, wearing weights on them as we walk, doing push-ups, or other arm exercises.

Environmental Risk Factors

Fluoridation of drinking water has been successful in the prevention of tooth decay—and it may also prevent bone fragility and osteoporosis.[25] New evidence supports research done twenty years ago (largely ignored at the time) that reported fewer bone fractures in communities with high-fluoride water than those with low-fluoride water.[26] In one study, the number of hip fractures during an eleven-year period was significantly lower in women over the age of seventy in a community with a water fluoride content of 1 mg. per liter than in a similar community with only 0–0.1 mg. per liter. Levels as low as one part fluoride to one million parts water are reported to reduce osteoporosis by up to 40 percent.[27] You may wish to check the fluoride level of your public or bottled water supply. Until your water supply is fluoridated you might consider individual fluoride supplementation.

When We Need Professional Help

If you have several of the above risk factors, or just feel you want further information, you can seek out a health provider who is knowledgeable about osteoporosis. Nutritionists can be extremely helpful in planning a preventive diet to your liking; exercise instructors can tailor a regimen that will strengthen the muscles and ligaments supporting your bones;[28] nurses and nurse practitioners can help you establish osteoporosis-prevention habits[29] and understand the politics of the current osteoporosis controversy;[30] physicians can order screening and medication for osteoporosis.

If you choose to visit a physician, ask other women to recommend one who treats each woman as an individual, who has an understanding of the complex factors that cause osteoporosis and doesn't give simplistic answers—for example, one who doesn't suggest hormone therapy for all postmenopausal women. If you live in an urban area, you may be near a metabolic bone disease or osteoporosis clinic that offers screening and treatment. If you have doubts about a medical recommendation, get a second opinion.

In the past, most physicians have concentrated on treatment of existing osteoporosis at the expense of early prevention.* They have often prescribed, after a fracture has occurred, the very procedures that might have prevented osteoporosis from developing in the first place —replacement calcium, vitamin D supplements, and weight-bearing exercise. Physicians are presently debating the value of certain drugs, such as hormones and sodium fluoride, in the prevention and treatment of osteoporosis.[31] Some physicians are very "pro-medication"[32]; others warn of its dangers and encourage exercise and dietary modifications instead.[33]

Screening and Diagnosis

Because the loss of bone cells leading to osteoporosis is so gradual, we need to be very alert to early signs. Screening and diagnosis of this condition can be difficult since low bone density alone does not necessarily indicate osteoporosis. There is substantial similarity in the bone densities of women with and without fractures.[34] Other factors, such as the strength of the muscles and ligaments supporting the bones, also affect susceptibility of bones to fractures.

Loss of teeth during midlife and thinning of the bones supporting the teeth are warning signals. This bone thinning may be detected by dental X-rays. A recent study reports that loss of teeth at midlife occurs more often in women than in men, and in white women much more often than in Black women. Women who lost their teeth early and smoked developed osteoporosis three times as frequently as women who did not smoke.[35] However, we women will have to question and convey information between our physicians and dentists, since they so rarely communicate with each other.

Ordinary X-rays don't clearly detect osteoporosis until at least 30 percent of bone density is lost, and are not suitable for screening purposes. One screening tool is a bone-density scanner, of which there are two types: single- and dual-photon absorptiometry.

Single-photon absorptiometry (SPA) scans are more common and less expensive—they take less than fifteen minutes and usually cost less than one hundred dollars. Radioactive iodine is directed at the patient's arm, which is submerged in water, and a detector counts how much radiation passes through the bone, thereby gauging bone density. The amount of radiation received from this procedure is less than 1 percent of that received from an X-ray.[36] This test can detect bone loss as slight as 1 to 3 percent. However, though SPA is a relatively simple and accurate measure of bone density in the hand and arm, it doesn't measure bone density at the other major fracture sites—the hip and the spine. One researcher found that the test erred an average of 14 percent of the time when predicting bone mass at the hip or spine based on a scan of the hand and arm, and so cautioned that no single method of bone scanning can definitively predict the risk of fracture before it happens.[37] Other researchers, however, have faith in SPA as a screening technique for detecting osteoporosis.

Dual-photon absorptiometry (DPA) can be used to scan the whole body, including the spine and hip. This method is also low in radiation, but is not generally available due to the high cost of the equipment ($30,000 to $70,000). The CAT scan, involving even more expensive equipment, is the most accurate method of detecting osteoporosis anywhere in the body. However, it involves exposure to more radiation than the SPA or the DPA.

In order to be certain that osteoporosis is the major problem, and not the result or symptom of another disease, other tests, possibly even a bone biopsy, are needed. A bone biopsy to test for osteoporosis is usually taken from a hip bone.

Most doctors outside of large research centers will probably continue, at least in the near future, to conclude that osteoporosis is the culprit whenever a female patient over fifty fractures a bone. The well-to-do can afford to be monitored and tested early if they wish, but poorer women generally do not have this option. If screening can predict osteoporosis before a fracture

---

*For the first time, a medical organization—the American Society for Bone and Mineral Research—has formally addressed the issue of osteoporosis prevention, announcing guidelines that stress adequate calcium intake, regular weight-bearing exercise, and avoidance of smoking.

occurs, then it should be available to all middle-aged women.

Such early detection is meaningless, however, unless it is accompanied by incentives for women to make the changes in diet and life-style that will strengthen bone mass or at least slow down its loss. Understanding the risk factors described in this chapter may go a long way toward achieving that end. The screening methods can then be used by those with high risk factors.

The Use of Hormones

Many physicians are likely to prescribe hormone therapy for osteoporosis even though low hormone levels have not been proven to be the direct cause of this condition. Until 1973, physicians in the U.S. who viewed menopause as a "deficiency disease" rather than as a natural event usually prescribed estrogen alone. Use declined after estrogen was linked to an increased rate of endometrial cancer. They then added progestogen. This combination "imitates" the hormones of our menstrual cycle. Estrogen (usually 0.625 mg. daily for 25 days) and progestogen (commonly medroxyprogesterone in a dose of 110 mg. daily on days 16 through 25 of a 28-day cycle), in combination, are supposed to prevent the lining of the uterus from building up to a dangerous precancerous level. Now the emphasis is on the use of these hormones for osteoporosis. Research is underway to determine if doses small enough not to cause periods are still effective in preventing osteoporosis. But some physicians don't prescribe this combination of hormones because:

- Research on the long-term effects is not yet available;
- Progestogens in the birth-control pill increase the risk of high blood pressure, strokes, and breast cancer;
- This combination of hormones causes menstrual-type bleeding;
- Extra medical examinations—such as regular Pap smears, pelvic and breast exams, blood-pressure monitoring, and endometrial biopsies—are necessary to monitor the effects of these drugs.

Prevention or Treatment?

There is a fundamental confusion in the medical literature and in the popular media between recommending hormone therapy to *treat* osteoporosis and recommending it to *prevent* osteoporosis. In April 1984, a National Institutes of Health Consensus Development Conference recommended the use of estrogen for white women to prevent osteoporosis, despite the known risks.[38] Now many physicians are indiscriminately prescribing hormone therapy for prevention.

To recommend widespread use of hormones to prevent osteoporosis without assessing the needs of each individual woman is the same as recommending that everyone take anti-hypertension drugs to prevent high blood pressure. For no other condition is anything as dangerous as hormones recommended for prevention.

One researcher recommends estrogen therapy both for what he calls Type I osteoporosis—which occurs in women within ten to fifteen years after menopause, resulting in spinal crush fractures and dowager's hump—and Type II osteoporosis—which affects elderly women and men and is caused by inefficient calcium absorption.[39] Estrogen therapy does appear to offer some protection against bone loss for three to five years.[40] We must remember, however, that both these types of osteoporosis can be affected by the life-style factors discussed previously, and that if we start hormone therapy and then stop we will lose just as much bone as if we never started.[41] We will just be postponing the bone loss. Some physicians recommend, therefore, that hormone therapy be continued virtually indefinitely if it is to offer any protection.[42] Others limit its use to high-risk women for a short period of time, while helping the women make dietary and exercise changes.

Physicians Disagree

Among physicians, we find a wide range of opinions on hormone therapy as a preventive measure. Some advocate it for all postmenopausal women,[43] some promote it for women "at high risk for osteoporosis,"[44] while others are against mass campaigns that recommend hormones for prevention.[45]

Generally, practicing physicians, in contrast to medical researchers, are more likely to use hormone therapy both to prevent and to treat osteoporosis. These physicians have direct contact with women and are thus forced to come to some decision regarding the prescribing of hormones. Women themselves may ask for hormones. The physician should explain the risks and possible benefits so that an informed decision can be made by the women themselves. Some physicians worry about the possibility of a lawsuit if they do not prescribe hormone therapy for a woman who later develops osteoporosis. The lawsuit could be based on the contention that the physician was unaware of "prevailing use" or "common medical practice"; after all, there has been a deluge of articles, advertisements, and public-relations campaigns on osteoporosis. But many medical researchers, on the other hand, are concerned with the possible dangers of hormone therapy (especially cancer, cardiovascular problems, and gallbladder conditions).[46]

Lowered estrogen levels after menopause are only one of several factors involved in osteoporosis. Almost all studies of bone loss in aging women show that the process begins before age forty in the bones of the hands, spine, hip, and wrist.[47] Furthermore, researchers have shown that while the age at which menopause occurs is relatively constant, enormous geographic and racial differences exist in the incidence of fractures related to osteoporosis.[48] Differences in fracture rates may be due to differences in nutrition and physical activity as well as to genetic factors.

Most of us who don't take hormones won't develop osteoporosis severely enough to cause fractures, and many women treated with hormones still experience fractures. There can be a similar amount of bone mass for women with and without osteoporosis, so that selecting appropriate subjects for preventive hormone therapy remains beyond the ability of medicine at this time.[49]

Hormones as Treatment

Doctors do not agree on the advisability of *treating* osteoporosis with hormones, either. Some believe that since hormones cannot reverse the course of osteoporosis, they only expose women to unnecessary cancer risks without any obvious benefit.[50]

Both doctors I consulted advised me that the history of cancer in my family was so strong—breast cancer particularly—that it was better not to take estrogen for my osteoporosis. They said it was better to leave it alone, so I did. [a fifty-three-year-old woman]

One woman with osteoporosis decided reluctantly to take hormones:

I've had a bad back for a long time—I walk stooped over and I can't stand up straight... it's gotten worse, especially the pain. After I was advised by three doctors to take hormones I started on estrogen and progesterone to prevent further development of osteoporosis. Does it help the pain in my back? No. The disadvantage is that I got my periods again and that feels just awful. It isn't natural for an older woman like me to be having periods. I was really against taking hormones, but when the three doctors told me to I didn't give up on my skepticism, but I did stop resisting. [a seventy-six-year-old woman]

Hormone Therapy: Estrogen and Progesterone

Advantages:

- Possible reduced risk of osteoporosis
- Elimination of hot flashes and sweating associated with menopause
- Reduction of vaginal dryness

Disadvantages:

- Increased risk of heart disease and stroke
- Increased risk of breast cancer
- Increased risk of gallbladder disease
- Accelerated growth of uterine fibroids
- More medical procedures at greater expense
- Dependency on hormones
- Continuation or resumption of periods in women who have not had a hysterectomy

The use of hormones may be appropriate for:

- a woman believed to be at high risk for osteoporosis, such as one who is taking corticosteroids for a life-threatening condition or who has definite multiple-risk factors that she is unable to change
- replacement therapy until the age of natural menopause for a woman who has had her ovaries removed at a young age. This is the only time when the word "replacement" is appropriate—the use of hormones *after* menopause is adding, not replacing, hormones
- a woman who has severe osteoporosis. Osteoporosis is treatable and further bone loss can be prevented.

Another woman decided to participate in an experiment:

I'm short, slim, and light-skinned and worried because my mother developed osteoporosis. I'm willing to be part of a research project in which I'm taking calcium plus estrogen and progestin in such low doses that I do not have periods. [a fifty-five-year-old woman]

One physician warns that the questions of whether, when, and how much of what hormone to prescribe should be based on individual evaluations after a diagnosis of osteoporosis has been confirmed.[51] Researchers who claim that hormones are effective commonly fail to have a control group to test for other factors, such as diet, efficiency of calcium absorption, and activity level. When we have osteoporosis, the most hormones can do is to help prevent further bone loss and keep our bones at the level they were when treatment started.

Women who should not take estrogens include those with a history of cancer, breast cysts, high blood pressure, blood clots, atherosclerosis, strokes, kidney, liver, gallbladder, or heart disease, sickle-cell anemia or trait, asthma, epilepsy, uterine fibroids, endometriosis, adenomyosis, and women who took DES during pregnancy. Though women who smoke are at high risk for osteoporosis, their use of estrogen further increases other risks.

Women who have not had a hysterectomy and who take estrogens are advised to take progesterones to reduce the risk of endometrial cancer. **Be aware that the effects of long-term use of progesterone are not known.** Progestin can cause changes similar to those of diabetes, can unfavorably alter blood fats and so may increase the risk of heart disease and strokes, and may stimulate the growth of breast cancer cells, which are more frequent in older women. Some brands of estrogens also include tranquilizers or testosterone. (See pp. 31 and 297.) Some women taking hormone therapy experience nausea, water retention, weight gain, breast enlargement and tenderness, or depression.

If you have been on hormone therapy and decide to stop, consult your health care provider on how to taper off. A sudden drop in hormones can cause hot flashes and other discomforts; a gradual drop may be more comfortable.

The Hormone Industry

When a condition has received as much public-

ity as osteoporosis has recently, there are enormous profits to be made by drug companies. Hormones are particularly profitable, and manufacturers are constantly seeking new markets. Ayerst Laboratories, manufacturer of the most commonly used estrogen (Premarin), aggressively advertises in medical journals and hired a public relations firm in 1982 to run a massive public education campaign on osteoporosis.[52] This campaign has been very successful in making osteoporosis a popular subject for TV talk shows and magazine articles and has culminated in the passage of Federal legislation for an annual Osteoporosis Awareness Week. A carefully orchestrated campaign by the pharmaceutical industry presents hormones as the best and sometimes the only defense against osteoporosis.[53] Pharmaceutical companies, with the endorsement of some physicians, are advocating a return to an "estrogen forever" approach. This idea, however, is not supported by all members of the medical community.

Given that by the year 2000 there will be 20 million of us over the age of sixty-five, we represent a potentially lucrative market for hormones if we and our physicians can be convinced of the simplistic point of view that hormones are the best means for preventing and treating osteoporosis. It seems advisable, in light of the lack of information about the long-term effects of progestogen and the DES tragedy,* to look at these claims with a healthy degree of skepticism. We must strengthen our resistance to the promotion of hormones as a universal way to avoid or treat

*DES (diethylstilbestrol), a synthetic form of estrogen, was prescribed for millions of women in the United States between 1941 and 1971 for many uses, including prevention of miscarriage. It was marketed under more than 200 brand names in pills, injections, and suppositories. Although studies as early as the 1930s showed estrogen to be carcinogenic in laboratory animals and as early as 1953 showed that DES was ineffective in preventing miscarriage, the FDA did not warn against its use in pregnancy until 1971, after its link to cancer was established. It is still prescribed for other uses.

Women who took DES thought they were taking a wonder drug but are now, many years later, showing an increased incidence of cancers of the breast, uterus, cervix, and ovaries, and noncancerous tumors of the uterus. The daughters and sons of women who were given DES during pregnancy have suffered abnormal structural development in their uteri and testes, abnormal and cancerous cells, and other problems, including fertility problems. By questioning the indiscriminate use of drugs and hormones, we can prevent similar medical mistakes from happening again. (See Cancer resources if you or your mother took or might have taken DES.)

osteoporosis, yet at the same time be able to recognize when their benefits outweigh their known dangers. We can always change our nutritional and exercise patterns first before opting for chemical solutions.

The present debate over whether to prescribe hormones to prevent or treat osteoporosis will continue. We believe that it is unethical and medically unsound to prescribe hormones for all menopausal women. Instead, we support a public health campaign to prevent osteoporosis by increasing women's knowledge of the risk factors and by encouraging exercise, good nutrition, fluoridation of the water supply, and avoiding or ending the habit of smoking.

Sodium Fluoride

Besides the small amounts of fluoride being added to the water supply, fluoride is also being used in higher doses experimentally to increase bone mass and lessen the chance of new fractures. One study showed that a fluoride-and-calcium regimen was associated with a 10 percent increase in spinal bone in women with vertebral osteoporosis, compared to a 3 percent increase in those on a placebo-and-calcium regimen.[54] Another study found that a fluoride-calcium-vitamin D regimen helped hip-fracture patients prevent future fractures.[55] But when fluoride is used therapeutically, the quality of the new bone cells is questionable.

Fluoride in high doses should only be used to treat severe osteoporosis under careful supervision and be accompanied by a good nutrition and exercise program. Sensitivity to fluorides varies; some people experience nausea and vomiting, inflamed joints, and gastric pain and should not take them.

New Research

Several new drugs are currently being studied for their effectiveness against osteoporosis. These include calcitriol (the body's working form of vitamin D), calcitonin (a thyroid hormone), a synthetic parathyroid hormone, androgenic anabolic steroids (steroids that increase bone mass but cause masculinization), thiazides (diuretics that reduce the amount of calcium lost in the urine), biphosphonates (used to reduce excessively high blood levels of calcium), "ADFR" (a complex system of several drugs), and various drug combinations.[56] If your doctor offers you these drugs, you should know that their efficacy and safety have not yet been established. We urge an emphasis on natural methods to prevent and treat osteoporosis. We also stress the need for adequate long-term testing for safety and efficacy of any drugs before they are marketed.

Living with Osteoporosis

After I was told that I had osteoporosis I slowly got my act together and began to realize that I, too, must help. I started reading about vitamins and calcium and had long talks with people who had gone the health food route. I changed my diet. This, with walking up to one hour per day, gradually brought my health up to par. [a sixty-seven-year-old woman]

Many of the same steps that help us live with osteoporosis can help us prevent it. An exercise program as short as six months can reduce the risk of bone fractures.[57] When we have osteoporosis, exercise must be vigorous enough to strengthen but not fracture the bones. Some exercise programs offer muscle-strengthening regimens and physical therapy in a swimming pool.[58]

In addition, look around your home to eliminate hazards likely to cause falls, such as slippery surfaces, loose rugs, and electric wires on the floor. Install rubber mats and handrails in showers and tubs, and lights and railings in all stairways. Wear shoes and slippers with low heels and nonslip soles. If you are unsteady on your feet, use a cane or a walker. If you need glasses, wear them, but never walk around with glasses that are meant just for reading.

Now the osteoporosis means little to me. My doctor told me not to worry about it. He said, "You're going to have aches and pains as this thing progresses. Be careful but don't let it ruin your life." So I didn't. When I asked him about cross-country skiing and the awful falls I take, he asked, "Do you enjoy it?" And I said, "Yes, I do!" He said, "Then do anything you enjoy, and when it hurts, stop." I believe that I shouldn't let it interfere with my life-style. The only concession I made was when I decided to wait to do cross-country skiing until after my daughter's wedding. I want to be on both feet for the ceremony. [a sixty-year-old woman]

When I was eighty-two I fell down a flight of stairs and injured a vertebra and my hip, and I have pain in one leg. The doctor told me I had osteoporosis, which I had never heard of before. He gave me a lot of information about it. I developed it after being on thyroid medication for ten years. My doctor said there was no cure but

271

we could arrest it. We had a long session about the alternatives. I decided to use exercise and nutrition. I walk at least three to four blocks a day. If the weather is bad I walk up and down the corridors of the apartment building. I use a set of exercises I learned at a course on aging and I do them every day. I have lost only a little height, am still very flexible and can touch my fingers to the floor. I drink four glasses of skim milk a day. I used to have a lot of salt but now I reduce it. I have red meat only one or two times a week. I'm a Southerner so I like to have collard greens and other vegetables. I'm still very active and belong to many organizations. [an eighty-six-year-old woman]

One of the best things you can do if you have osteoporosis is join an existing self-help group or start one with other middle-aged and older women. It is especially important to have a place to discuss what we read and hear about osteoporosis and the pros and cons of hormone therapy—outside the medical arena. As we tell each other about our experiences and feelings about living with osteoporosis, about ways to cope, treatments by physicians and/or self-help ideas, we start to feel less alone and we can help each other make desirable life-style changes.

NOTES

1. Morris Notelovitz and Marsha Ware, *Stand Tall! The Informed Woman's Guide to Preventing Osteoporosis.* Gainesville, FL: Triad Publishing Co., 1982.

2. National Institutes of Health, *Osteoporosis Consensus Development Conference Statement*, Vol. 5, No. 3. Washington, D.C.: U.S. Department of Health and Human Services, Office of Medical Applications of Research, 1984.

3. Diane M. Raab and Everett L. Smith, "Exercise and Aging Effects on Bone." *Topics in Geriatric Rehabilitation*, Vol. 1, No. 1 (October 1985), pp. 31–9.

4. A. Michael Parfit, "Definition of Osteoporosis: Age-Related Loss of Bone and Its Relationship to Increased Fracture Risk." Paper presented at the National Institutes of Health Consensus Development Conference on Osteoporosis, April 2–4, 1984. National Institutes of Health, Bethesda, MD.

5. Betty Kamen and Si Kamen, *Osteoporosis: What It Is, How to Prevent It, How to Stop It.* New York: Pinnacle Books, 1984.

6. Raab and Smith, op cit., p. 37.

7. Notelovitz and Ware, op. cit., p. 32.

8. Ibid., p. 53.

9. Mary E. Farmer, et al., "Race and Sex Differences in Hip Fracture Incidence." *American Journal of Public Health*, Vol. 74, December 1984, pp. 1374–9.

10. Sadja Greenwood, *Menopause Naturally.* San Francisco: Volcano Press, 1984, p. 55.

11. Gary M. Chan, et al., "Decreased Bone Mineral Status in Lactating Adolescent Mothers." *The Journal of Pediatrics*, Vol. 101, November 1982, pp. 767–70.

12. L. K. Mahan and J. M. Rees, *Nutrition in Adolescence.* St. Louis: Times Mirror/Mosby Co., 1984.

13. Robert Lindsay, et al., "Long-term Prevention of Post-menopausal Osteoporosis by Estrogen." *Lancet*, Vol. 1, No. 7968 (May 15, 1976), pp. 1038 +; and S. Meema et al., "Preventive Effect of Estrogen on Post-menopausal Bone Loss." *Annals of Internal Medicine*, Vol. 135, 1976, pp. 1436–40.

14. Joseph Lane, "Postmenopausal Osteoporosis: The Orthopedic Approach." *The Female Patient*, Vol. 6, November 1981, pp. 43–54.

15. Judy Foreman, "Study, Anorectic Women May Have Osteoporosis." *The Boston Globe*, December 20, 1984.

16. Kamen and Kamen, op. cit.

17. J. M. Aitken, et al., "Oestrogen Replacement Therapy for Prevention of Osteoporosis After Oophorectomy." *British Medical Journal*, Vol. 3, 1973, pp. 515 +; and Lindsay, et al., op. cit.

18. Notelovitz and Ware, op. cit., pp. 58, 73.

19. L. G. Raisy and B. E. Kream, "Regulation of Bone Formation, Part II." *The New England Journal of Medicine*, Vol. 309, 1983, pp. 83–9.

20. Kamen and Kamen, op. cit., p. 157.

21. Jane Porcino, *Growing Older, Getting Better: A Handbook for Women in the Second Half of Life.* Reading, MA: Addison-Wesley, 1983, p. 233.

22. John A. Baron, "Smoking and Estrogen-Related Disease." *American Journal of Epidemiology*, Vol. 119, No. 1 (1984), pp. 9–22.

23. J. Chalmers and K. C. Ho, "Geographical Variations in Senile Osteoporosis: The Association with Physical Activity." *Journal of Bone and Joint Surgery*, Vol. 52B, 1970, pp. 667–78.

24. Fran Pollner, "Osteoporosis: Looking at the Whole Picture." *Medical World News*, Vol. 14, January 1985, pp. 38–58.

25. D. S. Bernstein, N. Sadowsky, D. M. Hegsted, et al., "Prevalence of Osteoporosis in High and Low Fluoride Areas in North Dakota." *Journal of the American Medical Association*, Vol. 196, 1966, pp. 85–90.

26. O. Laitinen and O. Simonen, "Does Fluoridation of Drinking Water Prevent Bone Fragility and Osteoporosis?" *Lancet*, Vol. II, No. 8452 (August 24, 1985), pp. 432–4.

27. *Fluoridation, Nature's Tooth Protector.* Division of Dental Health, Massachusetts Department of Public Health, January 1986.

28. R. A. Yeater and Bruce R. Martin, "Senile Osteoporosis: The Effects of Exercise." *Postgraduate Medicine*, Vol. 75, February 1, 1984, pp. 147–58.

29. Jean Colls, "Osteoporosis Protocols." Developed for Inservice Education for the Nurses Association of

the American College of Obstetrics & Gynecology, 1983; Diane Palmason, "Osteoporosis: Catching the Silent Thief." *The Canadian Nurse*, Vol. 81, January 1985, pp. 42–4; and A. Mines, "Osteoporosis: A Detailed Look at the Clinical Manifestations and Goals for Nursing Care." *The Canadian Nurse*, Vol. 81, January 1985, pp. 45–8.

30. Kathleen I. MacPherson, "Osteoporosis and Menopause: A Feminist Analysis of the Social Construction of a Syndrome." *Advances in Nursing Science*, Vol. 7, July 1985, pp. 11–22.

31. Lombardo F. Palma, "Postmenopausal Osteoporosis and Estrogen Therapy: Who Should Be Treated?" *The Journal of Family Practice*, Vol. 14, 1982, pp. 355–9; Mack R. Harrell and Marc K. Dreyner, "Postmenopausal and Senile Osteoporosis: A Therapeutic Dilemma." *Drug Therapy*, April 1983, pp. 105–15; and Robert W. Cali, "Estrogen Replacement Therapy—Boon or Bane?" *Postgraduate Medicine*, Vol. 75, 1984, pp. 276–86.

32. Leon Speroff, "Menopause." Paper presented at the District I, American College of Obstetricians and Gynecologists, Copenhagen, Denmark, October 1983; and Robert B. Greenblatt, et al., *The Menopausal Syndrome*. New York: Medcom Press, 1984.

33. Sydney Wolfe, E. Borgmann, C. Lacheen, et al., Statement of Public Citizens Health Research Group. Read before the National Institutes of Health Consensus Development Conference on Osteoporosis, Bethesda, MD, April 2–4, 1984.

34. Pollner, op. cit.

35. Harry W. Daniel, "Post-menopausal Tooth Loss: Contributions to Edentulism by Osteoporosis and Cigarette Smoking." *Archives of Internal Medicine*, Vol. 143, September 1983, pp. 1678–82.

36. Product Reports, "Osteoporosis Diagnostic Centers Multiplying Rapidly." *Hospitals*, Vol. 59, May 1985, p. 126.

37. Pollner, op. cit.

38. National Institutes of Health, op. cit.

39. Pollner, op. cit.

40. Cali, op. cit., pp. 276–86; Speroff, op. cit.; Lindsay, op. cit.

41. Robert Lindsay, et al., "Bone Response to Termination of Oestrogen Treatment." *Lancet*, Vol. 1, 1978, pp. 1325+.

42. Speroff, op. cit.

43. One physician advises others not to "get bogged down with fancy tests, most of which aren't sensitive enough anyway," and just to increase the quality of life for midlife women by prescribing hormones. Pollner, op. cit.

44. C. Christiansen, "Estrogen/Progestogen as a Prophylactic Treatment of Postmenopausal Osteoporosis." Paper presented at the National Institutes of Health Consensus Development Conference on Osteoporosis, April 2–4, 1984. National Institutes of Health, Bethesda, MD., pp. 62–5.

45. Wolfe, et al., op. cit.

46. Patricia Kaufert and Sonja McKinlay, "Estrogen Replacement Therapy: The Production of Medical Knowledge and the Emergence of Policy." In Ellen Lewin and Virginia Olesen, eds., *Women, Health and Healing*. New York: Tavistock Publications, 1985, pp. 113–38.

47. Yeater and Martin, op. cit., pp. 147–58.

48. Chalmers and Ho, op. cit., pp. 667–75.

49. Harrell and Dreyner, op. cit., pp. 105–15.

50. Wolfe, et al., op. cit.

51. Herta Spencer, "Osteoporosis: Goals of Therapy." *Hospital Practice*, Vol. 17, No. 3 (March 1982), pp. 131–51.

52. Tacie Dejanikus, "Major Drug Manufacturer Funds Osteoporosis Public Education Campaign." *The Network News* (Publication of the National Women's Health Network), May/June 1985, p. 1.

53. MacPherson, op. cit., pp. 11–22; Kaufert and McKinlay, op. cit., pp. 113–38.

54. Pollner, op. cit., pp. 38–58.

55. Lane, op. cit., pp. 43–54.

56. National Institutes of Health, op. cit., section 5 and background working papers.

57. Yeater and Martin, op. cit., pp. 147–58.

58. Lane, op. cit., pp. 43–54.

20

DENTAL HEALTH

by Martha C. Wood

Dental health is important not only in itself but also for total health and well-being. Yet, although we are among the wealthiest nations in the world, 98 percent of American adults have caries (dental decay or cavities) and periodontal (gum and bone) disease,[1] and 42 percent of all Americans over the age of sixty-five are missing all their natural teeth.[2] Many people believe that tooth loss is a natural part of aging, but this is not the case.

Prevention of dental disease involves self-care and regular visits to a dentist or dental clinic. Having good dental health can help prevent a whole range of potentially debilitating and isolating conditions among older people. Continual tooth pain saps our energy and can distract us for days and weeks at a time. Tooth loss can prevent us from eating well if we don't learn to substitute nutritious soft foods for those we can no longer chew. If we are embarrassed about our appearance, we may avoid going out. We may avoid smiling and speaking, and we may feel awkward.

Four important rules for good oral health are:

- Brush your teeth after you eat anything and floss daily.
- Eat well and drink fluoridated water when possible.
- Schedule regular visits to a dental office for cleaning and checkups (even if you have dentures).
- Keep your natural teeth—avoid dentists who are quick to extract teeth (get a second opinion).

Many people, especially older people, never get the dental care they need because it is expensive. Despite the fact that chronic dental problems increase with age, more than half the U.S. population over sixty-five has not been to a dentist in at least five years or has never been to one.[3] Most of us expect that once we are over sixty-five, Medicare will cover all of our health care needs, but we learn that quite a number of things aren't covered, among them dental care problems.

Medical insurance should include dental coverage. We need a Medicare program and eventually a national health insurance program that recognizes the importance of and provides for dental care. Dental care should not be a commodity available only to those who can afford to pay for it. For some of us, raising the money to pay for needed dental care can be a major triumph.

Yesterday I got three brand new teeth—a permanent bridge; and I am as excited as when I awaited the tooth fairy at age five. They are crafted to match my original long, strong, yellow teeth, and since they hit my bottom teeth I can chew even better than with the originals.

They embody my new dedication to taking care of myself. I made the decision to save the surrounding teeth. And I alone paid for those three expensive additions to my upper right jaw.

What seems to make them most special is the fact that I am the only person who can see them. They are the three last teeth on the upper right; I can admire them in the mirror only when I pull my cheek back. They are my own special gift to me. [a fifty-seven-year-old woman][4]

SPECIAL DENTAL PROBLEMS OF OLDER WOMEN

The risk of losing teeth increases as we age, and women have higher rates of tooth loss than men.[5] Older white women have a higher rate of tooth loss than white men or Black women of the same age. Yet white women practice more careful dental hygiene than white men and have lower rates of periodontal disease than Black women. For these reasons, some researchers have begun to suspect that postmenopausal bone loss may be a factor in tooth loss for older white women.[6] Paying attention to prevention of osteoporosis, especially by not smoking and getting enough calcium and fluoride, may have the added benefit of protecting us against losing teeth in our older years.

HOME CARE FOR TEETH AND GUMS

Many of us were not taught as children to take proper care of our teeth and gums. The idea of preventive dental care dates back only to the 1950s in the United States. A seventy-eight-year-old woman remembered her father calling tooth brushing a thing "only sissies do."

Many dentists believe that an individual's careful attention to diet and self-care will do more to prevent tooth problems than the best professional care.[7] Proper tooth brushing and flossing are essential parts of this. Ideally, brushing and flossing should be done after every meal, but at least once a day. A machine that directs a stream of water to the gumline can be a helpful adjunct but does not replace brushing and flossing.

Tooth brushing guidelines have changed over the years. Now the preferred method is to use a brush with soft, rounded nylon bristles. (Natural bristles act as a bacteria reservoir because they take too long to dry.) Hold the brush alongside the teeth at about a forty-five-degree angle against the gumline, wiggle it in a circular motion and then brush away from the gum.[8] Move the brush back and forth several times using a gentle scrubbing motion. On the biting surfaces of the teeth, again use a back and forth motion. If you can't grasp a toothbrush easily, try wrapping it with adhesive tape or something like a sponge hair curler to enlarge the handle. If you have shoulder problems that make it hard to brush, try an electric toothbrush or extend the length of your toothbrush by gluing a strip of wood or plastic to the handle. Replace your toothbrush when it wears out (after about six months to one year of use) and after each time you have a cold or flu.

A mild, only slightly abrasive commercial toothpaste with fluoride is best for the teeth. Baking soda can be used, but don't brush with salt because salt damages the surface enamel of the teeth. Brush your tongue and the roof of your mouth, too. Bacteria collect on the tongue and then spread to the teeth. Plaque—the sticky, colorless layer of bacteria that forms around the teeth and along the gumline—often forms more quickly and in larger amounts because of reduced saliva flow as we age. (Saliva production is part of the mouth's cleaning process.) After brushing, rinse your mouth with warm water.

Floss between all teeth. Start with an eighteen-inch piece of floss. Wrap the ends of the floss around the third finger of each hand. Use your thumbs and forefingers to guide about one inch of floss at a time between the teeth. Holding the floss tightly, gently insert it to the gumline. Curve the floss against one tooth in a C-shape and gently rub up and down the whole height of the tooth side. Repeat on each adjacent tooth. In case you have trouble holding the floss, dental floss holders are available at most drugstores. Or you might try cutting a twelve-inch length and tying the ends together to form a circle. You can have someone prepare these for you if you have trouble tying the knots. If you haven't been flossing regularly, your gums will probably bleed when you start but will stop bleeding after a few days.

I hate to floss, but I've had a lot of gum problems and the dentist says I must floss. I've found it's more pleasant to do in the tub. [a fifty-four-year-old woman]

Dentures

If you have dentures, you should brush them with a soft brush. Soaking dentures, even in a denture cleanser, is never enough. Dentures must be brushed with a commercial denture powder or paste, hand soap, or baking soda. Never use scouring powders, as they damage the denture. Fill a sink about one-third full of water and place a washcloth on the bottom to prevent damage in case you drop the denture. Hold the denture over the water while brushing and brush thoroughly both inside and out. Rinse with cool water (never hot) before putting the dentures back in your mouth. Dentures should never become dry, because they may crack or warp. When they're not in your mouth, immerse them in water. To remove stains from full dentures, soak them overnight in a commercial denture cleanser or a combination of bleach and water (one teaspoon chlorine bleach to eight ounces of warm water). Never use bleach alone, as it can change the color of the pink base of the denture, and never use bleach at all on a partial denture, as it may harm the metal clasp. To remove stains from partial dentures, soak them in white vinegar or a commercial denture cleanser.

Denture adhesives are not very effective and should be used for a limited time only. The denture will still wiggle, and this cuts the inside of the mouth and interferes with chewing. Overusing adhesive powders can irritate the gums and soft tissue in the roof of the mouth. It is worth the investment to have your false teeth relined when they start to slip. The reason for the slippage can then be determined and the soft tissue checked for damage. Relining and other denture adjustments or repairs may be cheaper at a dental school than by your regular dentist.

It is important to wear dentures regularly. If you don't wear them for a few weeks, the shape of your mouth will start to change and the dentures won't fit. The tissues will then have a hard time readjusting to the old set of dentures. And if you don't wear your dentures, you are less likely to eat a nutritionally balanced diet, since you won't be able to chew properly. Make sure you massage and brush your gums and the roof of your mouth daily with a soft toothbrush or washcloth.

Denture problems may be caused by poorly made or poorly fitting dentures, not enough mouth tissue to cushion the fit, or even emotional upsets—or a combination of these factors.

I've had false teeth for over twenty years—a full upper plate and a partial on the bottom. I still see my dentist three times a year, since I have periodontal problems with my few remaining teeth and want to keep them at all costs. I have my dentures adjusted almost every time I see my dentist because my mouth tissue keeps changing. No one told me about bone reabsorption when I got my dentures. I've had three dentures made over time and both of the first two relined. Your jawbone just naturally gets narrower and shorter as you get older, though I think having your teeth pulled makes it happen more so. My current dentist is terrific and I can eat raw carrots, apples, and anything I want. But I expect to live another thirty-five years and I worry about whether I'll have enough bone left for my teeth.

My dentist says I should leave my dentures out at night to give my mouth tissue a rest. He may be right, but I don't feel self-confident—and certainly not sexy—without my teeth.

There are times I can't wear my partial for days due to soreness on my gums, not just from cuts but from when I have the flu or am under stress at work. My gums react and are extremely painful. [a fifty-one-year-old woman]

If you leave your dentures in while you sleep, be sure to remove them for some time each day to let the tissues in your mouth repair. Partial dentures increase plaque formation, so remove partial dentures each day and thoroughly clean the remaining teeth.

Mouthwashes

Mouthwashes, lozenges, and toothpaste can't cure bad breath. They only cover it up for a brief period of time. Warm, salty water is the best mouthwash. Persistent bad breath may be a sign of a medical or dental problem that needs attention, such as postnasal drip, digestive problems, diabetes, or badly decayed teeth. It may also be caused by medicines or smoking.

Dry Mouth

If your mouth feels dry, you should discuss the problem with a doctor. A slight decrease in saliva may occur as we grow older, but frequently dry mouth (xerostomia) is caused by prescription or over-the-counter drugs. More than 200 medications, including antihistamines, decongestants, diuretics, and some drugs used to treat Parkinson's disease, ulcers, and cancer, can cause dry mouth. In addition, smoking dries and irritates the mouth. Caffeine and alcohol both have dehydrating effects. Thus, the proper treatment of dry mouth depends on the cause. The treatment may be as simple as rinsing with a salt-water solution several times a day or avoiding very spicy foods. In some cases an artificial saliva may be prescribed. Because saliva is essential for a healthy mouth, not taking care of dry mouth can lead to tissue breakdown, tooth decay, gum disease, and ill-fitting dentures.

Nutrition

Good nutrition is an important factor in keeping teeth and gums healthy. Here are some pointers to keep in mind:

- Among the many good reasons to eat protein are the facts that it doesn't form plaque and it builds and repairs mouth tissue.
- Eating fiber helps to remove food particles trapped between teeth (chewing gum won't do this).
- Sugar plays a major role in causing cavities, and so keep the use of table sugar low, and watch for hidden sugars in such things as ketchup and lunch meats.
- If you do eat sweets, eat them with meals rather than in between. Acid produced from the bacteria formed by food particles eats into tooth enamel. The more often you eat decay-promoting foods, the more "acid attacks" the teeth suffer.
- The longer sugar is in the mouth the more chance the bacteria have to produce destructive acid, so avoid hard candy, cough drops, or anything else that is high in sugar and is sucked or chewed for a while. Foods like raisins and honey stick to the teeth and so remain in the mouth a long time.
- As we grow older we need more vitamins C, A, and B complex, as well as calcium. Vitamin C helps with healthy gums and tissue repair. Vitamin A keeps tissue soft. Vitamin B complex prevents tissues in the corner of the mouth from breaking down and also prevents sore tongue and other mouth sores.[9] Calcium strengthens the bones that support the structure of the mouth.

DENTAL CHECKUPS

It's important to have regular dental checkups that include a thorough cleaning. Someone with severe gum disease or diabetes should have a cleaning every three months. For most of us, twice a year is best. Only a dentist or hygienist, using special instruments, can remove hardened plaque, also called *calculus* or *tartar*, from the

teeth. It is also important to have your gums examined regularly. You need regular dental checkups even if you have full dentures.

If you don't have a dentist, ask a friend, call a dental school, or ask your physician for a referral. (Dental societies or associations merely recommend from a list with no reference to quality.) If you can't afford a private dentist, ask your community health department about dental clinics in your area. These may be affiliated with a dental school, a dental hygienist school, or a low-cost medical clinic.

A dentist should take a thorough medical and dental history. Make sure she or he offers emergency care. Avoid dentists who won't talk to you about fees, give estimates, itemize bills, or discuss a payment plan. (However, prompt payment keeps fees down, since billing costs money.) Beware of exceptionally low fees, as they may indicate a dentist who cuts corners on laboratory costs. Compare your dentist's fees with those of your friends' dentists. Interview a prospective dentist to make sure she or he is someone with whom you can feel comfortable.

Avoid dentists who want to extract teeth without discussing alternatives. There is almost always some way to save a tooth, and it is almost always to your advantage to do so. Saving a tooth or teeth is usually the healthiest and most economical thing to do in the long run. Six million teeth are removed unnecessarily each year. False teeth just can't do what natural teeth can. Some people are unable to wear dentures comfortably because of the shape of their mouths—a sad fact often not discovered until it is too late. Be sure to get a second opinion, not only about the need for extraction but about your ability to wear dentures. Sometimes pulling a tooth is necessary, but if that is the case a space saver must be fitted permanently into its place so the entire jaw structure doesn't shift.

Don't allow any dental work to be done without getting a full explanation of what it is, the amount of discomfort likely, other possible treatments, the consequences of postponing treatment a few weeks or months, and potential complications. Get a written cost estimate, and never be embarrassed to obtain a second opinion.

Because of a severe toothache I sought a dentist in the state where I spend half the year. He said an artificial tooth on a bridge had to be taken out, extensive gum surgery was needed, and then a replacement would have to be fitted. The estimated cost was very high. I took my X-rays with me to seek another opinion. Meanwhile, the tooth holding the artificial tooth broke and fell out with the bridge.

I went to the dentist I have used for many years in the state where I spend the other half a year. He explained how he would grind down the broken tooth and fit in two artificial teeth, and drew a picture for me. He recommended that I have my teeth cleaned twice a year instead of once a year and that I floss regularly. He did not think I needed gum surgery. He encouraged me to check his price, saying that I would find some prices higher than his and some lower. I checked with a dental school and another clinic for their prices for the way he was proposing to do the work. The estimated price was lower if students did the work or if other materials were used. I decided to have him do the work because he has treated me well through the years and explains everything clearly. The total cost will be much less than that quoted by the first dentist. Now I floss every night while I watch TV. [a seventy-six-year-old woman]

X-Rays

X-rays are used to detect abscesses or underlying decay, broken tooth roots, bone loss from periodontal disease, and ill-fitting dental restorations. Full-mouth X-rays as part of a regular checkup aren't necessary more often than every three to five years. Bite-wing X-rays, taken with the film holder held between the teeth, may be taken yearly—a clinical exam will not always find cavities between the back teeth and under fillings. X-rays are usually necessary when a problem is suspected. While X-rays are being done, your neck and body should be covered with a lead apron. Legally your X-rays belong to you, not to the dentist. Take them with you if you change dentists so you don't have to have them done again unnecessarily.

Dental Decay

Cavities (caries) can form at any age. Drinking fluoridated water reduces cavities in adults by 50 percent and contributes to stronger bones, thus reducing the possibility of fractures from osteoporosis.[10] Some evidence is emerging that very small cavities can actually be remineralized—that is, the tooth can rebuild itself—if we drink fluoridated water.[11]

Having work done on a root canal is one way to save a tooth when the nerve of the tooth is infected. In a root canal procedure, the nerve within the tooth is removed, and the nerve canal is cleaned and filled. The tooth can remain healthy and structurally sound. There is an alternative to root canal work, which can be used if decay has reached but not infected the tooth's nerve. In this option, a simple protective sedative is placed over the nerve and covered with a pulp cap.

A crown is a cap or jacket over the stump of a tooth. It is used to support a badly decayed tooth, for cosmetic purposes, or to anchor a fixed bridge. The dentist grinds the natural tooth to a stump, caps it with pure gold or gold mixed with other metals, and sometimes covers it with porcelain. (The all-gold is the most expensive.) If your dentist suggests crowning a decayed tooth and you can't afford it, ask about having a filling with reinforcing pins, which should cost much less.

Periodontal Disease

Periodontal disease is actually a group of diseases involving the gums and the supporting bones under the teeth in an infective process.

More teeth are lost because of untreated periodontal disease than from tooth decay. Studies of the periodontal health of persons fifty-five years old and older show that they have less gingivitis (surface inflammation of the gums caused by irritants) than younger people. However, the proportion of older persons with major periodontal problems has remained unchanged or increased slightly in the past twenty years.[12]

Plaque is the most common cause of periodontal disease. Other causes include grinding or clenching teeth, a bad bite (malocclusion), or bad jaw configuration. In addition, hereditary predisposition, hormonal imbalances, diabetes, and thyroid problems may worsen gum problems, since they impair the body's defense against disease.

The symptoms of periodontal disease include red gums, swollen gums, bleeding, loose teeth, and drifting teeth. It may be painless and often involves no bleeding. Only a dentist or hygienist can detect it in its early stages. Prevention of the disease begins with proper brushing and flossing. If it is caught early enough, treatment involves root planing or smoothing, scraping under the gum, and prescription antibacterial mouthwash. In more advanced cases, where the disease has caused deep pocketing, treatment becomes more complex. In some cases minor

278

surgical procedures are done in a dental office or, depending on the extent, in a hospital. A local anesthetic is used and a medical dressing is placed over the wounded area for a week or so while it heals.

Since the late 1970s a nonsurgical treatment, the Keyes technique, has been used by some periodontists. This technique combines deep scaling and antibacterial agents applied by the dentist plus a special paste treatment used at home daily. The technique is still controversial. (See Resources for information.)

SMOKING

Smoking and using snuff or chewing tobacco can damage the tissues in the mouth, increase the risk of oral or nasal cancer, stain the teeth, and cause bad breath. Anyone who uses a tobacco product should see a dentist or hygienist frequently—at the very least once a year. Smoking can also cause dryness in the mouth, resulting in chewing and swallowing problems as well as tissue damage and tooth decay.

DENTAL CARE IN NURSING HOMES AND HOSPITALS

People in nursing homes have special dental-care concerns. Although they need regular dental exams, their dental care is often neglected. Even in states that require nursing homes to have a dental consultant, the homes may have difficulty finding dentists who accept Medicaid, who have portable equipment, and who have offices accessible to people who can't climb stairs.

A frequent problem in hospitals and nursing homes is loss of dentures. A few states have passed legislation requiring that all false teeth be marked with the owner's name when they are made or relined. There are also other ways of marking dentures, even in a nursing home, ranging from etching to simply writing the name in ink and covering it with a clear acrylic finish. Dentures should be identified with the wearer's name (not a number or code) so they can be returned to the correct person quickly.

NOTES

1. "Teeth." *Health Facts*, Vol. II, No. 10 (July–August 1978).

2. "National Survey of Adult Dental Health...." *Dental Section Newsletter*, American Public Health Association, Washington, DC, May 1987, pp. 2–4.

3. Jane Porcino, *Growing Older, Getting Better*. Reading, MA: Addison-Wesley, 1983, p. 312.

4. Excerpted from an unpublished manuscript by Carolyn Ruth Swift.

5. Ronald J. Hunt, et al., "Edentulism and Oral Health Problems Among Elderly Rural Iowans: The Iowa 65+ Rural Health Study." *American Journal of Public Health*, Vol. 75, No. 10 (1985), pp. 1177-82.

6. Harry W. Daniell, "Postmenopausal Tooth Loss: Contributions to Edentulism by Osteoporosis and Cigarette Smoking." *Archives of General Medicine*, Vol. 143, September 1983, pp. 1678-82.

7. *Health Facts*, p. 4.

8. Ibid.

9. Maury Massler, "Oral Aspects of Aging." *Postgraduate Medicine*, Vol. 49, January 1971, pp. 179–83.

10. O. Simonen and O. Laitinen, "Does Fluoridation of Drinking Water Prevent Bone Fragility and Osteoporosis?" *Lancet*, Vol. II, No. 8452 (August 24, 1985), pp. 432–4.

11. National Institutes of Health, *Challenges for the Eighties*. National Institute of Dental Research Long-Range Research Plan 1985-89, U.S. Department of Health and Human Services, Public Health Service, December 1983, NIH Publication No. 85-860, pp. 2, 19.

12. Chester Douglas, "The Potential for Increases in the Periodontal Disease of the Aged Population." *Journal of Periodontology*, Vol. 54, No. 12 (December 1983), pp. 721–30.

21

URINARY INCONTINENCE

by Norma Meras Swenson and
Diana Laskin Siegal

Special thanks to Grace Q. Vicary and Mary D. Fillmore

Urinary incontinence, the involuntary loss of urine, is a very common problem among women, and yet we are ashamed to talk about it. The barrier to discussion is only one of the obstacles to finding satisfactory solutions. We also have to deal with how little is known scientifically, poor professional help, and treatments that are of dubious value. Many of us have arrived at adulthood and even old age without ever receiving adequate, accurate information about our bodies and how they work.

Bladder-control problems should not be looked upon either as an inevitable part of aging or as a disease, but rather as a problem that can be managed and possibly corrected if you are determined to do so. Shame, guilt, anxiety, fear, embarrassment, loss of self-esteem, and depression are common, legitimate accompaniments to this problem. Unfortunately, these feelings are harmful and can only make it worse. Finding the courage to take action is an important step in regaining self-confidence. Realize that you are not alone, and that many other women are finding ways to escape the prison which incontinence problems impose. Be aware that about 30 percent of incontinence is temporary.

Current figures show that over 50 percent of all those in long-term care institutions, mainly nursing homes, have urinary incontinence problems.[1] These problems may have contributed to the reasons for their admission or may have developed after they entered the nursing home. Cost estimates for dealing with this problem in nursing homes exceed a billion dollars annually, accounting for 3 percent to 8 percent of the costs of nursing home care in this country, more than half of which comes from public funds.[2] The cost for the care of the incontinent elderly in all institutions is estimated at over $8 billion per year.[3] Many of these people might be helped through timely evaluations and care if more staff were hired, through behavior modification, medication, surgical treatment, or some combination of these techniques. Since women comprise the overwhelming majority of the nursing home population, bladder-control problems are a major public health issue for women.

Only about 15 percent of all the incontinent elderly are institutionalized.[4] More elderly incontinent men are cared for outside of institutions, with the direct, unpaid burden of caring for them falling, in the majority of cases, on female caregivers in the home. In other words, whether we have the problem or whether we care for those who have it, incontinence is overwhelmingly a women's problem. The good news is that increasing attention, more accurate diagnosis, and more appropriate treatment are resulting in complete cure or great improvement in about two thirds of those with the problem.[5]

Women apparently suffer from bladder-control difficulties far more than men, both in number (approximately two to one) and in degree of severity, and the difficulties increase with each decade of age. These facts tend to reinforce the belief that incontinence is an inevitable accompaniment of female aging, yet fail to explain why some elderly women have the problem and others don't. Since many doctors believe that nearly 50 percent[6] of young, normal women have some degree of urinary-control problem, it is easy to conclude that existing figures indicating that 15 percent of non-institutionalized elderly women are incontinent are too low. It seems as though the problem is underreported. Many women are too embarrassed to speak about this problem, especially to a male physician; others don't speak about it because they believe nothing can be done. Sadly, many of those who have had the courage to bring it up have found their doctors uninformed, unsympathetic, and often embarrassed themselves.[7]

We women will have to chart our own course to deal with this problem. We hope this chapter will help you know more about how your body functions, what the different types of incontinence are, what you can do about bladder-control problems for yourself or for others, and how to find competent help.

Control of Our Social Lives

One of the very first ways we learn as little girls that we are different from boys is that if we can't "go" in some places, we can't "go" at all. Girls may be restricted from certain places or events because there are no toilets. It's usually okay for little boys to simply turn around, discreetly or otherwise, and pee if there isn't a toilet nearby, but it isn't always okay for little girls.

At a festival by the river in Cambridge, the nearest public toilets are several blocks away. I overheard a little girl about five years old say she needed to "go." She was then scolded by the man who appeared to be her grandfather. "Didn't you go before you left the house?" and all that. Because I have incontinence problems, I stepped in and asked whether he would just take a little boy over to the bushes. When he responded, "Yes, of course," I suggested he take the little girl there also. He was embarrassed but then the girl's grandmother, who had been sitting nearby, offered to take her. [a woman in her sixties]

Bladder control can be difficult for young girls to learn, and for women to maintain, because while we are being taught to control our bladders and anal sphincters we are also being taught that "nice" girls do *not* feel or experiment with anything "down there," especially with the

nearby sensations coming from our vaginas and clitorises.

When we are aware of our bladder sensations, we are often required to ignore them. Many of us remember when times to go to the bathroom were strictly regulated in schools. Adult women are also restricted in where they can urinate. There are usually no public toilets in shopping malls, grocery stores, and subways, and not enough in sports arenas and theaters, forcing women to brave bars and other places they don't want to enter just to find a toilet. Public toilets are often so filthy and unsafe that women can't use them.

At the Montreal Olympics I passed the time while waiting in the long lines for the ladies' room by counting the number of men and women leaving the toilets. I observed that the men's line moved four *times faster than the women's line. Architects should take that into consideration when designing rest rooms. [a woman in her fifties]*

Many workplaces still have inadequate toilet facilities for female employees. In rural areas where migrant workers are employed, often there are no toilet facilities whatsoever, and women sometimes feel they have to wait until dark to pee, trying to "hold it" hour after hour.

Even where toilets are available, women may have to sit hour after hour doing clerical work, with little chance to walk around or get other exercise. When there is a chance to take a break, that, too, is often spent sitting. Sitting is very destructive to the lower abdominal muscles, the pelvic floor, and the entire muscle system of the pelvic girdle. All of these situations can contribute to bladder problems by forcing women to hold urine, which overstretches the bladder, and by weakening muscles. These conditions may in turn lead to chronic infections, cystitis, and bladder control problems.

Our ability to manage our urine actually controls our social life far more than we realize. Finding a bathroom is a constant worry for many women, young and old. To lose urine, to wet one's pants visibly, or to smell of urine is simply unacceptable. Not only would we give offense, but we might be thought of as not fully adult—childish, regressed, or even "senile." We all try to learn how to "hold it," often longer than we should, without realizing that doing so may contribute to infections from urine retention. If the anxiety about making it to a toilet in time is too distracting, we may decide not to attempt certain trips, or only do so after we know exactly where the bathroom is and are sure we can be near it. We may resort to pads, or "adult diapers," now widely advertised, rather than tell anybody. In many cases of incontinence, women feel obliged to withdraw from social life altogether, not going out and often not having people in, either.[8] Use pads and other aids, if necessary, rather than avoiding people and activities, but do not assume that nothing can be done about incontinence.

An older person's inability to control urine is often the last straw for an overstressed caregiver, and institutionalization often becomes the solution. Pads are often used in place of adequate evaluation and treatment, especially in nursing homes with overworked and untrained staff. What is labeled incontinence is often ignoring a patient's request for a bedpan or toilet until she has no choice except to wet herself.

HOW BLADDER CONTROL WORKS

As shocking as it is, even experts know little about the basic anatomy and physiology of the female genitourinary system, as the female genitals and urinary tract together are called. The classic text, *Gray's Anatomy*, devotes several pages to the male genitals and urinary tract but only one sketch to the female urinary system. Most doctors see the female urinary system as an inadequate or defective variation on the male system, rather than as a complex system in its own right. Following is a summary of what experts believe about how the female genitourinary system works.

Urine comes down two tubes called ureters (one from each kidney) to fill the bladder. The bladder and the urethra (the tube opening from the bladder to the outside) constitute a unit for the purpose of storing and emptying urine. Normally, the bladder relaxes while it is filling with urine and the urethra tightens along its whole length from where it joins the bladder neck down to the outside opening, in order to hold urine in. When it is time to pee, the urethra opens along its entire length, and the top of the bladder (the fundus) contracts and drops, expelling the urine. The urethra then closes along its entire length and the whole bladder rises

again to its original position to fill with urine again and to expand automatically against the pressure of the closed urethra.

The anus has a true sphincter musculature which is capable of closing off completely in response to a conscious act of will. The vagina never closes off completely. The neck of the bladder and the area near the opening of the urethra have some additional muscle tissue, but we cannot contract it voluntarily the way we contract the anal sphincter. The urinary structure is capable of perfect control, but by the following mechanisms. Normally, the urethra will not open until we decide it should. At a certain point we become aware of the sensation that the bladder needs emptying, but we postpone it rather than wetting ourselves. This is the first stage of control. Though it feels automatic, this postponement until we can get to the right place is a discipline we learned years ago during toilet training.

As the pressure builds up, we deliberately control the muscle surrounding both the urinary and vaginal openings, called the pubococcygeal or levator ani muscle. This muscle is part of a group of muscles woven like a large sling or hammock under the bladder and uterus and around the delicate tubes of the vagina, urethra, and anus. The entire area controlled by this muscle, from the clitoris at the front to the anus at the back, is called the pelvic floor (see diagrams, p. 73 and p. 284). Using this muscle is the second stage of control.

Anxiety about getting in time to a place where they are comfortable urinating plays a role in incontinence for many women, especially if they know from experience that they may not make it. But even for a woman without special anxieties, after postponement has gone beyond a certain point, pain may set in and it will take squeezing her legs together and even holding her hands against her labia to keep urine from escaping before she gets somewhere to pee. This is the third stage of control.

Once at an acceptable place, we have to deliberately decide to release the urine, another act of will, which may be quick or take some time, depending on how distracted we are, how anxious we feel, and how long we have been postponing release. Sometimes sexual arousal may either stimulate or delay the release of urine.

It is also not clear how we know when we are really finished urinating, because we can voluntarily stop and start again. We think we're finished when no more urine comes out and the initial sensation of pressure is gone. Yet some women retain small or large amounts of urine in their bladders even after the sensations cease and the urethra recloses, which makes it clear that it is not just the complete emptying of the bladder that signals the urethra to close.

In fact, bladder functioning is one of the most complicated, sophisticated mechanisms of the female body. As many as thirty different reflexes may be involved in the retention and voiding of urine, and twelve have been shown to play direct, specific roles in incontinence. Incontinence in women involves a complex interaction of anatomical, neurological, social, and psychological factors.[9] Be sure your practitioner considers all these factors in your evaluation for treatment.

TYPES OF INCONTINENCE

Experts do not agree on how to describe the various types of incontinence. Since many women have a combination of types, individualized assessment and treatment are needed. We are naming the categories we will discuss as follows:

1. Stress incontinence
2. Urge incontinence
3. Overflow incontinence
4. Irritable bladder

Stress incontinence is a condition in which there is a loss of urine at times when sudden activity increases the pressure in the abdomen and bladder, such as when you cough, sneeze, laugh, or run. This type of incontinence is by far the most common, though experts disagree about whether it is the most common in older women. Often stress incontinence is combined with one or more other types of incontinence. Current theory suggests that urine loss results when the urethra is increasingly unable to maintain control along its entire length against the ever-filling bladder, changing the balance of pressure between the two systems. The bladder neck has probably widened, often in response to relaxation of muscles (against pressure of the bladder); the urethra may be stretched wider and wider at the top, and shortened, much the way a nylon stocking is when you take it off,

compared with how it was when you took it out of the package. The only remaining control mechanisms then are a very short area of the urethra near the outlet and the pubococcygeal muscle. Even when weak, the pubococcygeal muscle can usually permit normal functioning, but is unable to handle the "stress" of the laugh, cough, sneeze, or bearing-down pressure.*

Urge incontinence refers to a sudden, sometimes painful, urge to urinate, which is unexpected and so powerful that it is not always possible to make it to the bathroom. Most gerontologists and urologists believe that urge incontinence is most common among elderly women.

What gets me is that often I'll be fine all day out shopping—no trouble at all. Then just as I get home and start to put the key in the door, I'll suddenly have to go so bad that I can hardly stand it. Sometimes I just make it to the bathroom, but sometimes I lose it right there at the front door.

Overflow incontinence is the problem in a smaller percentage of cases. Usually, it comes on with no warning—no sensation or signal at all—and urine unexpectedly "overflows" after a woman changes position, such as standing up after sitting, or sitting up after lying down. We may lose a relatively small amount—a few drops—or enough to require a pad. Often there is a desire to urinate again a few minutes later, but very little urine emerges, a sign that the bladder is not emptying completely. The risk of bladder infection is high with this problem, which often happens because we have been sedentary or have learned to hold our urine too long.

"Irritable" or "spastic" or "unstable" bladders seem to behave erratically, causing the feeling that we need to urinate even though we may not—often just after the bladder has been emptied.† Irritable bladder may be confused with both urge and stress incontinence, or combined with them, and is often aggravated by anxiety.

---

*A few women who have this type of relaxation of the pelvic floor are apparently perfectly continent, and others with stress problems do not seem to have any noticeable relaxation of the pelvic floor, but this is not the general rule.

†Rarely, a fistula may have occurred as a result of a difficult childbirth, radiation treatments, or surgery, and not be detected. This often results in a more or less continuous drip from a break between the vaginal wall and the bladder or urethra. Most fistulas can be repaired surgically.

Because the condition is irregular rather than constant, experts believe it may be more psychological than physical.

CAUSES OF BLADDER-CONTROL PROBLEMS

Aging

Aging does not by itself cause female incontinence, even if the chances of being incontinent do tend to increase as women age. This is probably the single most difficult fact to get across to the medical profession and to the general public.

Weak Muscles

Our whole way of life in this culture has traditionally worked against women's maintaining good muscle tone. Many generations of women were brought up to think of exercise as something for men only. In these generations it was poor women who often had adequate muscle tone because of the physical work they did. A general fitness campaign directed at adult women as well as men, and also including the elderly, has only recently been started, and this is too often directed only to the affluent.

After midlife, the muscle tone that we tended to take for granted as younger women slowly decreases. Keeping in shape may take much more effort than previously. This partly depends

Normal

Cystocele: Bladder protrudes into vaginal canal

Prolapse of the uterus: Uterus descends into vaginal canal

Rectocele: Rectal wall protrudes into vaginal canal

on how active you have been throughout life. Without a fairly systematic and vigorous program, already weak muscles may deteriorate more rapidly. Even women who were active previously, however, will lose muscle tone and may gain weight through inactivity. "Use it or lose it" is as true for the pelvic muscles as it is for any others.

There is solid evidence that weak muscles of the pelvic floor and abdomen contribute to stress incontinence, and perhaps to other incontinence problems. Severe and prolonged immobility can contribute to incontinence problems such as "overflow." For incontinent women, exercise such as running, aerobic dancing, even walking may actually aggravate bladder problems because of the jarring and gravitational pull on the genital and urinary organs, so exercise is avoided. Breaking the cycle may well begin with Kegel exercises for getting control of that key set of muscles in the pelvic floor.

The Kegel exercises can be done conveniently and invisibly, whether sitting, standing, lying down, or during sex, and can partly counteract the negative effects of prolonged sitting and passive sex. Women frequently report a noticeable improvement in sexual response as well as urinary control when Kegel exercises are practiced regularly (see Moving for Health, p. 73).

Reproductive Events and Hormonal Changes

Reproductive events may contribute to a woman's bladder-control problems, or create problems where none existed before. For example, slight bladder-control problems, which may be temporary or permanent, are often associated with childbirth. While childbirth itself is often blamed for these problems, the actual cause may be damage caused by obstetric practices such as the use of forceps, episiotomy, the lying-down position in which most women have been required to labor, and pushing uphill to give birth, often with a partially full bladder.[10]

The reduction of ovarian estrogen production around the time of menopause, which may bring some degree of thinning and temporary drying or shrinking of vaginal tissues, often affects the nearby urethra as well. Some women may for the first time experience some type of incontinence, which may be temporary and disappear once the body has adjusted to its different production of estrogen (less from the ovaries but some from the adrenal glands and fat tissue), or may persist.

Inadequate Nutrition and Water

The role of nutrition in incontinence is somewhat controversial, but it is clear that poor diet can contribute to repeated bladder infections and poor muscle tone. Certainly one major factor in certain types of incontinence associated with bladder infections is dehydration due to inadequate water intake.

Magnesium deficiencies have been reported to contribute to bladder instability, but there is no solid evidence for this. However, magnesium (available in fruits and vegetables) is an important mineral for bone strength in elderly women, and should accompany calcium, which is also important for muscle fitness.

Infections and Inflammation

One cause of some urinary-control problems is a long-term pattern of chronic bladder and urethral infections. A vicious cycle is often involved in incomplete emptying of the bladder. Infection builds up in the stagnant urine, which may inflame the lining of the bladder and infect the urethra itself. One result may be intermittent, temporary, or permanent urge incontinence. Many women have low-grade infections of this type almost constantly, without even being aware of them until they flare up and overwhelm the system.

Interstitial cystitis also causes frequent urination and pain similar to the symptoms of bladder infection. Urine tests are negative, however, because the symptoms are caused by chronic inflammation and scarring of the bladder lining, which may bleed, rather than by bacterial infection.[11]

Medications and Drugs

Several specific prescription drugs for hypertension, heart disease, and fluid buildup (diuretics), as well as some sedatives, hypnotics, and tranquilizers, may provoke temporary incontinence. Many types of drugs (including many over-the-counter antihistamines) can cause the bladder to retain urine and lead to overflow incontinence.

Trauma and Medical Treatment

Violent sexual penetration, gynecological surgery—especially hysterectomy and other procedures carried out via the vagina—as well as radiation treatments for cancer all may contribute to problems with urinary control. In the case of hysterectomy, the cause may be physical —the loss of support that the uterus provides for the bladder and urethra,[12] or damage to the urinary structures or nerves during surgery—or it may be hormonal. For many women, hysterectomy causes a drop in estrogen levels, even when the ovaries have been retained. This drop can, in turn, affect the urinary structures. In some cases, repair of a uterine prolapse or cystocele may remove the blockage which was actually helping to control the urinary flow.[13]

Specific Diseases

Other causes of urinary-control problems include diabetes and progressive degenerative diseases involving the brain or spinal cord such as Alzheimer's disease, multiple sclerosis, brain or spinal cord tumors, and Parkinson's disease. Other specific physical causes include spinal cord injuries, stones in the urinary system, obstructive tumors, bladder cancer, strokes, or TIAs (transient ischemic attacks). Before diagnosing incontinence, a competent physician should try to rule out each of these conditions, and, if any are present, plan a treatment program which includes treating the incontinence as well.

Emotional Problems

Finally, there are bladder problems which result primarily from stress, anxiety, and depression. Since emotional factors are rarely the sole cause of the problem, it is vital to rule out physical causes first, while recognizing that the state of our emotions may aggravate any bladder-control problem we may have.

I started to wake up at night to urinate—sometimes once or twice, but sometimes every two hours. A gynecologist put me on estrogen cream that caused bleeding, so then he wanted to do a D&C. I said goodbye to the cream and to him and also to the leading urologist, who wanted to put me on antidepressants. He had said after observing me—and I was tearful—"The sorrow that has no tears to cry makes the body weep." I realized I had this dependency on "Doctor, doctor, make it better!" The only initiative I was showing was going to doctors. Then I decided to do as much as I could for myself. So I changed my whole pattern of eating to vegetarian (macrobiotic) foods, started swimming and doing Kegels regularly. I try to understand what is happening. Now I see that my waking up is related to stress and anxiety. I still expect to wake up once most nights, but when I have had a massage, I usually sleep through the whole night. [a fifty-five-year-old woman]

GENERAL SELF-HELP

Before seeking any type of medical solution to an incontinence problem in the absence of other symptoms, we encourage you to observe and record your problems and take some simple steps to try to help yourself. The first step is to review your diet, hygiene, and exercise habits.

Are you drinking enough water and other liquids? Many women avoid drinking in order to avoid accidents. The result is more likely to be urinary-tract infections and dehydration, which can actually trigger accidents and may even become life-threatening. Try cutting down drastically on caffeine, alcohol, and soft drinks (including "diet" sodas) and substitute water and clear unsweetened fruit juices such as apple juice. Drink six glasses of water throughout the day, most of them before your last meal.

Toilet hygiene tends to become more important as we age. Some women were never taught that it is important to wipe from front to back to avoid fecal contamination. Some may find that moist wipes do a better job now than conventional dry toilet paper. If you can get access to a bidet or a "telephone" shower (shower head extension with a flexible hose) for post-toilet cleansing, or switch from tub baths to showers, you may have fewer urinary infections.

A diet high in whole grains, fruits and vegetables, including some fish, and low in white flour, sugar, fats, and meats, can help keep the acid balanced in the urinary and vaginal systems to discourage infections and also improve overall digestion, muscle tone, and urinary output. Vitamin C, including bioflavenoids, is sometimes helpful. Many women find that unsweetened cranberry juice prevents or fights infections. How do citrus fruit juices affect you? Some women find they irritate the bladder, others that they help control the tendency to infec-

Keeping Records

While you are taking the initial steps in the self-help process, you may also want to keep a careful watch on your symptoms, both for your own use and to help any professional you decide to consult. A competent doctor will ask you many specific questions as one part of a thorough history and evaluation. Keeping this record will help you to be ready with answers. For example, many doctors ask, "How many pads do you use in a day?"

Begin by making a note of *every* time you have any type of urine loss or "accident"—exactly when it happened, what you were doing, where you were, how much urine you lost in ounces (approximately), and what you did about the loss. Try to remember when you first began to have a problem. How did it begin? Does it seem to be getting worse? Did it begin suddenly? Did it start for the first time after an operation or childbirth, after you started taking some new prescription drug, after an accident, after a time of stress, or after some episode of illness? Is it worse during the day or during the night? How long can you hold your urine after you sense a need to go? Do you feel your bladder completely empty? Do you strain to empty? Do you regularly wear pads to catch escaping urine? In some cases, simply keeping a record like this can improve bladder control by helping you pay attention to your patterns.

One of the things you need to establish is whether your condition is temporary or chronic. Try to distinguish between different types of episodes. Do you ever experience pain with an accident? What kind of pain (sharp, dull)? Is there itching, burning, or a feeling of pressure? Is it something that happens only when you laugh, sneeze, cough, run, jump, or lift something? Does it happen when you stand up quickly from a sitting position, turn suddenly, or stoop down? All the time or only sometimes? Have you gained weight recently? Do you (or did you) ever wet the bed at night while you are asleep? Do you drink caffeine or alcohol regularly? What does your usual diet consist of (include all liquids and snacks between meals, as well as meals)? Do you sometimes lose urine without any urge or warning? Do you experience sudden, overwhelming urges to urinate that you cannot control? Does the sound of running water cause you to start urinating? Do you have a history of chronic infections of the bladder or urinary tract? What is your menopausal status?

If you answer these questions carefully and keep records for several weeks or a few months, you should be able to get a rough idea of whether or not you fall into one of the major categories of urinary incontinence or whether you seem to have signs of more than one type. Mixed problems will call for several types of treatment, but many women will discover that they fall mainly into one category or another, which clearly calls for a specific set of medical or surgical options, and for which other approaches will probably not be as useful. When you have assembled this information, you will need to learn how doctors use it to make a diagnosis.

tions. Some women find that spicy foods aggravate their problems.

Are you getting enough general exercise, at least walking regularly every day? Decide now that you are not going to stay home or avoid exercise for fear of having an accident, but will find whatever kinds of protective devices and clothing you need in order to have brief walking trips, preferably every day (see Resources). Wear comfortable shoes when walking, and pay attention to posture to correct the alignment of the entire pelvis.

Next, check your overall weight and health. Many women find that losing weight through exercise improves their continence noticeably, though it isn't always clear why. It may be a combination of improved diet and increased exercise, removal of the drag of heavy fat across the abdomen, plus the improvement in self-esteem.

If you hold your urine for several hours and then have overflow problems, make an effort to identify earlier the feeling of needing to urinate, which you may be ignoring. Go to the toilet regularly, either at the very earliest sign of fullness, or at scheduled intervals regardless of sensation. If feelings of urgency are *very* frequent, allowing the bladder to fill up more may help.

If you have never done Kegel exercises, start today. While exercising this important set of muscles may not prevent or solve all problems of urinary control, it does keep the whole pelvic floor in good condition and almost always brings some improvement in urinary control. Add abdominal toning exercises if you can, slowly, until you can feel the improvement (see Moving for Health chapter, p. 73).

In my early forties I had some stress incontinence which I stopped by doing Kegel exercises. In my early fifties I started waking several times a night and, once awake, needed to urinate. When I went on a camping trip for several months I didn't like getting out of the sleeping bag and tent so many times at night. At first I kept a plastic container in the tent to pee in but then I decided to ignore the feeling and go back to sleep. By the end of the trip I was sleeping through the night. For a few years after that I was awakened several times at night because of hot flashes but never had to urinate more than once a night. Now that my hot flashes have subsided I am again sleeping through the night. [a fifty-five-year-old woman]

Next, review all your prescription and over-the-counter drugs (see pp. 30–32). Your pharmacist can tell you whether any of these drugs or combination of drugs actually aggravate bladder-control problems, as well as whether certain foods or drinks taken at the same time may make a drug's effects even stronger.

As you try all of these approaches, a self-help group can be extremely useful.[14] Composed of other women like you, groups offer an invaluable opportunity to realize that you are not alone, and to hear what others with the same problems have found helpful. Other women are the major source of information on this subject. You may learn from one another who and where the really helpful professional people are and how to avoid inappropriate care. If you attend a group sponsored by "experts," be sure you evaluate their biases. You may have to start your own group.

SEEKING COMPETENT MEDICAL CARE

One of the most serious barriers to a better understanding of the connections between the reproductive and the urinary system is their traditional separation into two different areas of specialization: gynecology and urology. The two physical systems, in fact, are subject to the same hormonal influences and are separated only by a thin layer of tissue. The whole unit is anchored together on the bladder side to the abdominal cavity.

Obstetrician-gynecologists generally have little training in urology—the study and treatment of the urinary system.[15] Some gynecologists are so eager to treat any incontinence with standard surgery that they may fail to ask even the most basic questions before proceeding. This often results either in failure to notice an underlying disease or in misdiagnosis of the specific type of incontinence. The urologists, meanwhile, know little more than the basics about female reproductive organs. Few doctors in either specialty are trained to treat middle-aged and older women. Despite repeated attempts to do so, the doctors have yet to get together on a commonly agreed-upon terminology.[16]

Whom should you see? As women, we tend to refer ourselves to gynecologists for most problems, without always realizing that they are surgeons, trained primarily to offer a surgical solution to many problems that might be better treated in other ways. Sometimes a medical or surgical approach (or combination thereof) is warranted. However, many women continue to suffer from bladder-control problems as a direct *result* of surgical or medical treatment (a phenomenon known as iatrogenesis, or illness caused by medical treatment). In some cases, the doctor did not diagnose the bladder problem correctly, or prescribed treatment such as gynecological surgery or certain drugs that caused bladder-control problems for the first time. Yet if surgery is appropriate, all of us want to be sure we are in the hands of the most skilled and knowledgeable people. Since so few surgeons have adequate training for successful treatment of female urinary-control problems, you may have to make considerable effort to locate satisfactory care.

A new medical specialty is developing called

"gynecologic urologist" or "urologic urologist." These doctors specialize in female urinary problems. They practice in Europe and even in a few places here in the U.S., but they are rare and very much in demand.

Since you may be unable to afford such specialists or might have to travel very far to find one, your next choice might be a competent internist or general practitioner. If that physician refers you to a surgeon (gynecologist or urologist) after a thorough medical evaluation, request that the internist continue to work together with you and the surgeon to help define the right approach to treatment. You should decide about surgery in the context of your total health and life situation.

Medical Diagnosis

A diagnosis involves many different processes, and you are an important part of all of them. How you feel and what you experience and remember definitely help the health care practitioner identify the cause of your problem. If you feel you are not being listened to, or are contradicted, or if a detailed history and questionnaire about your bladder functioning are not taken before tests are done, you may want to consult another practitioner.[17] The one you choose should make a diagnosis based on an extensive history, your observation of your own symptoms, clinical examination, and, where appropriate, diagnostic tests. A combination of different diagnostic tests and treatment options may be indicated for women who have an overlap between stress and urge incontinence, for example.

Diagnostic Tests

Tests alone, as important as they can be, cannot substitute for clinical judgment, and vice versa. *Most experts now agree that a test for stress incontinence performed with the surgeon's fingers alone, while the patient is lying down or standing, is an inadequate basis for planning surgery.*

Standard Tests

A urinalysis and a urine culture should be done first, in order to rule out infection as a temporary or chronic cause of bladder or kidney problems. Some doctors say only a clean specimen taken by catheter is adequate. Part of the urinalysis should also include screening for excess sugar, since some bladder problems (like too frequent urination) may actually be an early sign of diabetic or prediabetic conditions. The physical examination should include two pelvic (internal gynecological) exams, one while the woman is standing and the other while she is lying down to check that the position of the internal organs is not a problem. Basic neurological testing should rule out damage to the brain, spinal cord, or peripheral nerves. If physical causes are ruled out, a thorough practitioner usually looks for depression or other psychological causes of the symptoms.

Trial Use of a Pessary

One intermediate approach to testing whether or not you are an appropriate candidate for stress-incontinence surgery is the use of a pessary. A pessary is a stiff, doughnut-shaped rubber device varying in size that fits into the top of the vagina, somewhat like a diaphragm, except that it is a little larger and less flexible. Many women used pessaries for uterine prolapse in the days when surgery was not as safe or available (or insured) as it is today. One effect of the pessary is to raise the neck of the bladder to a position more nearly normal, thus reducing the tendency to stress incontinence. Today the pessary is becoming more popular as a noninvasive diagnostic test (in the sense that no body cavity or body system is being "invaded" as with X-rays or cystograms).

If there is significant reduction of stress incontinence when the pessary is in place, then the chances are improved that surgery (properly performed, of course) will be successful.[18] For some elderly women who are not good candidates for surgery because of other physical problems (heart conditions, etc.) or for any woman who wishes to avoid surgery, the pessary may also prove to be a valuable permanent alternative to surgery, as it sometimes was in the days of our grandmothers. It requires considerable manual dexterity (the kind necessary to use cervical caps, for example) for a woman to remove and clean the pessary herself, but many do. Otherwise, a health care practitioner will have to do this regularly for you.

I've had the pessary for about a year and a half. Before that everything was sliding down—there was a big "thing" [the prolapsed uterus] in my body and I had to pee every half hour or so. Once in a while the urine would leak out but mostly I got to the bathroom in time. Now I don't leak urine.

I think in the beginning the pessary was too small and it came out. Then they put in a bigger one. It was uncomfortable for about a month but then it was all right. About every two or three months they take it out and wash it and put it back again. It hurts when they are putting it in but once in it stops hurting. [a ninety-one-year-old woman in a nursing home]

Neurological Tests

Clinicians should test to see whether incontinence could be caused by damage to the nervous system itself. If this type of testing is to be done, however, consider having a separate examination by a neurologist/psychologist team experienced in identifying TIAs (small strokes), Alzheimer's disease, or other neurological problems. Distinguishing among these conditions is difficult but crucial for planning treatment.

Urodynamic Studies

These tests, also called urodynamic pressure profiles, evaluate how well the bladder, urethra, and anal sphincter hold and release urine. A catheter is inserted in the bladder, filled to capacity, and various measurements are taken while the patient is lying down, standing, and urinating.[19] While they provide a more complete picture than more orthodox methods, they may be stressful and unnecessary for elderly women.[20] Training programs often bring improvement without such detailed testing.

Tests in Preparation for Surgery

Today there are multiple diagnostic tests available to surgeons planning specific types of surgery, usually for stress incontinence.

Other common tests include cystoscopy and urethroscopy, a direct look inside to check the condition of the bladder and urethra. Bladder and kidney X-rays, using fluorescent dyes, also help visualize the shape and position of both the urethra and bladder. Some tests have the purpose of determining the precise angle of the urethra, so that the doctor will know how to correct it. Some doctors rely on physical examination for this, while others insert a beaded chain into the urethra, take an X-ray, and then remove the chain.

I went to a urologist who insisted on doing a cystoscopy in his office. He was aware of my great reluctance because an earlier cystoscopy was very painful, even under anesthesia, but he said he could not determine what he wanted to know when the patient was asleep. He was very reassuring and so was the nurse. He was so gentle and the procedure was so painless that I would not hesitate to recommend having this done in a doctor's office, if done by a doctor of this caliber. After doing the cystoscopy the doctor said he did not find anything wrong except a prolapsed bladder. He said he did not recommend an operation. This doctor said that stretching the urethra, which other doctors recommended, is a very outdated urological technique and he does not do it. [a woman in her sixties]

If your surgeon recommends a test, ask exactly which test it is, how it will be done, what it will show, and how that information will be used in planning the surgery, if necessary. If you do have the test(s) done, ask to see the results yourself and have them explained to you. Together with diagrams of the surgery being proposed, this should enable you to participate more meaningfully in the final treatment decisions.

Medical and Surgical Treatments

Treatments of Mild Stress Incontinence and/or Vaginal Dryness

Many doctors routinely recommend synthetic estrogen drugs either for complaints of vaginal dryness or urinary-control difficulties around the time of menopause. A condition mild enough to respond to estrogen treatment might respond to less risky dietary and exercise changes as well. On the other hand, if these other approaches have been tried and a thorough medical history and evaluation do not reveal any significant anatomical problems with the bladder or urethra (and estrogen is not contraindicated), estrogen is an option some women have found helpful. It may be that a low-dose estrogen cream for a short time is all that is needed for some mild problems (see p. 88). Be sure to check all drugs with your doctor and pharmacist for the availability of newer formulations, and possible undesirable effects.

Treatments for Severe Stress Incontinence

Surgery

After the less drastic approaches mentioned above have been tried, you and your surgeon may conclude that surgery is the only way to correct the overstretched muscles and/or ligaments in the pelvic area which contribute to stress incontinence.

For example, a woman with fairly severe stress incontinence may feel that the exercise/weight-loss approach, including Kegel exercises, is too slow (sometimes it takes several months), or she may have already tried it and found it unsatisfactory. Sometimes she has already had surgery that failed and wants to try again.

The major goal of most surgery for stress incontinence is to restore the bladder neck to its (normal) high position slightly above and behind the major bones that come together at the front of the pelvis (beneath the mons). Ideally, the dynamics of the normal pressure between bladder and urethra will thus be restored. Once raised, the bladder neck is "tacked" into its new position by attaching it to the bones or ligaments of the pelvis.

We do not have space here to describe all the possible surgical procedures for stress incontinence. Techniques for repositioning the bladder —specifically, the bladder neck—vary from tacks inside the vagina alongside both sides of the urethra (much like creating a short tunnel for a drawstring) to tacking the bladder neck to an abdominal ligament, to more complex sling devices, some made from a woman's own muscle tissue, others made from a synthetic substance like Dacron.

While all of these surgical procedures for stress incontinence *may* result in improvement, all of them do so by permanently altering the relationship of the internal organs to one another—actually cutting the bladder away from its natural attachment to the vagina or anterior abdominal wall. None actually alters the primary cause of the dislocation of the bladder, the stretched or weak levator ani or pubococcygeal muscles of the pelvic floor. Every woman considering surgery should obtain full information on the risks, benefits, complications, and alternatives before giving her consent.

After many years of bladder problems and avoiding a gynecological examination or evaluation, my mother finally had to submit to a vaginal hysterectomy because of a seriously prolapsed uterus. She was seventy-nine. At the same time, her doctor performed urethrovesical suspension surgery (she called it "tucking her up"), which has been totally successful. My mother has been liberated from the constant anxiety of having to be near a bathroom at all times. She only regrets not having done it much sooner.

Suspension

Many surgeons believe women with stress incontinence need some type of sling that can help support the bladder in a new position. However, this operation may offer only limited benefit if the urethra has become shortened, scarred, and rigid due to repeated infections or surgeries.

Dilation

Some doctors, including respected urologists, still practice a surgical procedure called dilation or dilatation, the insertion of a tube or a scalpel-like coring mechanism into the urethra to break up scar tissue. Today most specialists say this only further damages tissue already scarred from repeated infections, almost never yields permanent results, and frequently makes the condition worse.

Treatments for Urge Incontinence and Irritable Bladder

In prescribing treatment for urge incontinence or irritable bladder, it is vital to distinguish clearly between physical and emotional/psychological factors, but the average physician is largely unable to do so. Women need to be wary of snap diagnoses offered without thorough evaluations.

Newer approaches to bladder-control problems of either the urge or irritability type are emerging that involve combinations of nonsurgical techniques such as biofeedback, exercise, drugs, and even sessions of "bladder retraining," that is, going to the toilet at timed intervals.[21] These techniques do require competent and committed supervision. Such programs may use catheters or other devices to measure how much bladder control a woman is able to exert, and how that control is improving over time.

Women who experience irritable bladder syndrome may also be helped by certain antispasmodic drugs. Whenever a doctor recommends drug treatment, however, it is crucial to investigate exactly what is being recommended and why, as well as to make sure that other drugs already prescribed for you are being taken into account. In most cases, all these approaches involve long-term monitoring and follow-up.

Most experts believe that urge incontinence must result from some type of neurological impairment. Unfortunately, the classification "neurological" means different things to different doctors. Some perceive it as damage or a defect in the central nervous system's ability to transmit messages, perhaps because of a stroke or because of some other disease. Other doctors interpret "neurological" to mean "psychiatric," concluding that the problem behind urge incontinence is somehow "emotional" or "psychological" in origin, or represents evidence of senility. As a result, they conclude that nothing can be done about it. Most doctors are taught in medical school that complaints without any verifiable anatomical cause are "functional," implying, in psychiatric language, that, although the symptoms may be real enough, the patient's complaint probably serves some other purpose in the patient's life or relationship with her doctor, such as attracting attention.

However sure a woman is that an anatomical condition is the cause of her urge incontinence, she will usually be met with disbelief. Many older women with urge incontinence have actually suffered unknowingly from some type of neurological problem. Testing for various neurological abnormalities can't hurt and may yield benefits. If, for example, a small stroke is discovered, it is possible to commence both rehabilitation therapy and preventive therapy for future strokes at the same time that the incontinence is being treated.

However, it is entirely possible that no neurological cause will be found, even on the most searching examination. A few practitioners concede that there may be such a thing as an "unstable bladder" (detrusor dyssynergia), for which no neurological cause can be found—but most doctors secretly or openly doubt it.[22] As a result, the term "unstable bladder" has become a wastebasket category for many, often unrelated, conditions. The medical imagination is uncomfortable with highly individualized diagnoses and often accepts as one of its primary tasks the assigning of each case to some previously existing diagnostic category.

This prejudice can be devastating for many women. In some cases of incontinence, women are given tranquilizers, which can make the problem worse, or are referred to psychiatrists instead of receiving the neurological examinations they need. Many psychiatrists are also unaware that the complaint of incontinence may require physical and neurological evaluation.

Nevertheless, there may be some psychological aspects to the origin of urge incontinence. Also, the loss of bladder control in and of itself is capable of *causing* depression. This reaction is well within the range of normal, given our culture and given the social loss which this crucial malfunction represents. In fact, most incontinent people report their first reaction to this problem was one of depression. Many women have experienced noticeable improvement when antidepressant drugs are given for incontinence, even in the absence of a diagnosis of depression.[23] It may also be that some forms of depression actually bring on incontinence difficulties.

Drugs are used to help regulate the bladder or urethra during the filling or the emptying phases. Certain drugs reduce the tendency for the "irritable" bladder to contract. Others may improve the tone of muscles at the bladder opening. However, most drugs to treat incontinence also produce unpleasant effects, such as dry mouth or irritability, and should not be used without consideration of your total health condition and the other medications you take.

Treatments for Overflow Incontinence

In cases of overflow incontinence, specific drugs may help when combined with a program of regular, frequent, timed trips to the toilet. Such a program helps reestablish normal signals to prevent overflow and infection. For urine retention, self-administered catheterization or clean intermittent catheterization (CIC) may be desirable. Indwelling catheters are more controversial, and are rejected for overflow incontinence by many doctors because of the high risk of infection, even though they offer improved control. For certain conditions they may be necessary temporarily.

Issues to Consider Regarding Surgery

What factors should you consider in evaluating surgery as an option? First, there is a high failure rate—around 50 percent. Many surgeons dismiss that figure, saying that of the patients who come to them as "failures" from previous surgery, a significant percentage show that the original diagnosis was wrong or that the correct procedure was not performed in the first place.[24] However, it is also true that even many successful procedures become failures after several months or a year or two. Most procedures require general anesthesia, with its known risks. There are also risks of damage to nearby organs. Such damage may not be classified as a failure by the surgeon, but for the woman it most certainly is one.

If something goes wrong after surgery, we need to ask not only "Was the correct diagnosis made?" but also "Was the appropriate procedure performed?" The best approach is to take our post-surgery symptoms and complaints seriously and seek a second opinion for verification.

You might consult one of the major centers for the evaluation and treatment of incontinence that exist in the U.S. and Canada, usually in teaching hospitals or geriatric centers (see Resources), especially if you have already undergone unsuccessful surgery. You might also call the nearest center for a referral to someone knowledgeable in your community. While we do not have many firsthand accounts of women's experiences with such centers, we believe that, because of their interdisciplinary approach, you should receive a more thorough evaluation and a wider range of options for treatment of incontinence. This way you will be more likely to avoid unnecessary surgery than when you seek care directly from a gynecologist or urologist. However, you must always keep your critical awareness active in any medical setting.

A major issue when considering surgery for incontinence problems is whether to have a procedure done "from below"—that is, entirely through the vagina—or whether to undergo an abdominal, or "supra-pubic," procedure. As with hysterectomy, there are advantages and disadvantages to both, and disagreement among experts. Many gynecologists have preferred vaginal techniques in order to avoid two major problems with abdominal surgery: 1) the scar, which even with the so-called "bikini cut" (near the top line of the pubic hair) may show, especially on older women with less pubic hair; and 2) the invasion of the body cavity, which is always risky and may lead later to adhesions (scar tissue) on the surrounding organs. Nevertheless, the complication/infection rate in the case of hysterectomy, for example, is significantly higher with vaginal surgery than with abdominal surgery. There is also the risk of damage by gynecologists to the urethra and ureters during vaginal surgery (and during both abdominal and vaginal hysterectomy), which may actually cause incontinence. Many expert urological surgeons do perform corrective procedures through the vagina.[25] A painful bone condition called osteitis pubis, a slow disintegration of the pubic bone, is another complication frequently resulting from surgery that attaches stitches to the bony structure rather than to one of the ligaments. You will have to discuss the choices of techniques, consider your surgeon's experience, and compare your preference with your surgeon's preference.

When we realize how little scientific knowledge is available on this subject, and how poorly prepared most medical professionals are to help us, it is easy to feel depressed about incontinence. On the other hand, the more we learn about prevention and treatment, the more we can break through the barrier of silence surrounding this condition.

NOTES

1. Neil M. Resnick and Subbarao V. Yalla, "Current Concepts: Management of Urinary Incontinence in the Elderly." *The New England Journal of Medicine*, Vol. 313, No. 13 (September 26, 1985), pp. 800–5.

2. Joseph G. Ouslander and Robert L. Kane, "The Costs of Urinary Incontinence in Nursing Homes." *Medical Care*, Vol. 22, No. 1 (January 1984), pp. 69–79.

3. Resnick and Yalla, op. cit., p. 800.

4. Ibid.

5. Ibid., p. 803.

6. Estimate from Neil M. Resnick, M.D.

7. Jane E. Brody, "Personal Health." *The New York Times*, June 5, 1985; Pamela Jones and Marian Emr, "Studies Focus on Treatment and Prevention of Urinary Incontinence." *News and Features from NIH*, Vol. 85, No. 4 (1985), pp. 11–2; and Joseph G. Ouslander, et al., "Urinary Incontinence in Elderly Nursing Home Patients." *Journal of the American Medical Association*, Vol. 248, 1982, pp. 1194–8.

8. Jones and Emr, op. cit.

9. "Structural, Neurological, Psychological Factors in Female Incontinence." *Ob. Gyn. News*, Vol. 17, No. 12 (June 15–30, 1982).

10. Sally Inch, *Birthrights*. New York: Pantheon Books, 1984.

11. Betsy A. Lehman, "Health Sense: Interstitial Cystitis Pain Is Real." *The Boston Globe*, September 22, 1986, pp. 41–2; and Adriane Fugh-Berman, "Standard Bladder Infection Treatment May Bring on Interstitial Cystitis." *The Network News*, Vol. 10, No. 3 (May/June 1985), pp. 4–5.

12. Joanne West, "Urinary Problems Resulting from Hysterectomy." *HERS Newsletter*, April 1983, pp. 3–4.

13. David A. Richardson, et al., "The Effect of Utero-vaginal Prolapse on Urethrovesical Pressure Dynamics." *American Journal of Obstetrics and Gynecology*, Vol. 146, No. 8 (August 15, 1983), pp. 901–5; and Emil A. Tanagho, "The Effect of Hysterectomy and Periurethral Surgery on Urethrovesical Function." In Donald R. Ostergard, *Gynecologic Urology and Urodynamics*. Baltimore, MD: Williams & Wilkins Co., 1980, pp. 293–300.

14. Ann Landers, "Incontinence Is Treatable." *The Boston Globe*, February 28, 1985.

15. "Women Need Same Services That Urologists Provide for Men." *Ob. Gyn. News*, Vol. 18, No. 21 (November 1–15, 1983), pp. 1–14.

16. Patrick Bates, et al., "First Report on the Standardisation of Terminology of Lower Urinary Tract Function." *British Journal of Urology*, Vol. 48, 1976, pp. 39–42.

17. "Chart for Urodynamics and Gynecological Urology History." In Ostergard, op. cit. (Chart is copyright 1978 by Donald R. Ostergard.)

18. N. N. Bahtia and A. Gergman, "Urinary Incontinence: Pessary Test Predicts Surgical Outcome." *Modern Medicine*, September 1985. Taken from article in *Obstetrics & Gynecology*, Vol. 65, February 1985, pp. 220–6.

19. Kathleen Poole, "A Useful Way to Diagnose Bladder Disorders." *RN*, Vol. 47, No. 8 (August 1984), pp. 51–2.

20. Mark E. Williams, "A Critical Evaluation of Assessment Technology Regarding Urinary Continence in the Elderly." Presented at a 1984 conference sponsored by the National Institute of Aging.

21. William Frewen, "Role of Bladder Training in the Treatment of Unstable Bladder in the Female." *Urologic Clinics of North America*, Vol. 6, No. 1 (February 1979), pp. 273–7; Evan C. Hadley, "Bladder Training and Related Therapies for Urinary Incontinence in Older People." *Journal of the American Medical Association*, Vol. 256, No. 3 (July 18, 1986), pp. 372–9; and Kathleen A. McCormick and Kathryn L. Burgio, "Incontinence: An Update on Nursing Care Measures." *Journal of Gerontological Nursing*, Vol. 10, No. 10 (1984), pp. 16–23.

22. "Detrusor Dyssynergia: A Rare Cause of Urinary Incompetence in Women. Questions and Answers." *Journal of the American Medical Association*, Vol. 241, No. 12 (June 1985), pp. 15–30.

23. Alan J. Wein, "Pharmacology of the Bladder and Urethra." In Stuart L. Stanton and Emil A. Tanagho, eds., *Surgery of Female Incontinence*. New York: Springer-Verlag, 1980, pp. 195–6.

24. Stanton and Tanagho, ibid.

25. Shlomo Raz, ed., "Vaginal Surgery." *Seminars in Urology*, Vol. 4, No. 1 (February 1986), pp. 1–61.

22

HYSTERECTOMY
AND OOPHORECTOMY

by Dorothy Krasnoff Reider

Special thanks to Genevieve Carminati

Our reproductive organs, like most other parts of our bodies, have multiple functions. We are only beginning to identify and do not yet fully understand the many ways these organs affect our health and our sexuality. Therefore, our bodily integrity should never be tampered with unless absolutely necessary. Yet for well over a century in the United States, women's uteri and ovaries have been subjected to routine medical abuse. Only recently has the extent of unnecessary removal of the uterus and ovaries been exposed, and the rates are still too high. Anyone considering either of these procedures needs to be aware of *all* the possible consequences. Hysterectomy (removal of the uterus) and oophorectomy or ovariectomy (removal of the ovaries) can be lifesaving procedures, but before undergoing them every woman must be sure that they are truly necessary.

UNNECESSARY HYSTERECTOMIES AND OOPHORECTOMIES

Hysterectomy and oophorectomy will always have their place in sound medical practice, mainly as a treatment for confirmed cancer. As women get older the risks of uterine and ovarian cancer increase, so regular gynecological checkups including Pap smears are advisable.

In 1985, 670,000 hysterectomies and 525,000 oophorectomies were performed on women in the United States.[1] Only a small proportion of hysterectomies—8 percent to 12 percent—are performed to treat cancer and other life-threatening diseases.[2] Most hysterectomies are elective, that is, not clearly necessary. Almost every woman needs to believe that her hysterectomy was necessary. However, studies challenge her belief. The number of hysterectomies thought to be unnecessary is estimated at 33 percent to 72 percent, depending on the source.[3] And many surgeons unnecessarily remove healthy ovaries while performing a hysterectomy.

The percentage of women in the U.S. who have had hysterectomies has risen since 1962. In 1978, the chance that a woman would have a hysterectomy sometime in her life was estimated to be greater than 50 percent.[4] Ironically, a large percentage of hysterectomies are performed on women just before menopause, even though menopause itself often resolves some of the problems.

Some of the reasons for the high rates of hysterectomy may be economic. Obstetricians-gynecologists can make money faster by performing a hysterectomy than they can earn with "watch and wait" approaches, office treatments, checkups, and follow-up visits, or other surgery. Doctors have done them for training in teaching hospitals and made the decision to perform them for population control on poor and minority women who were not fully informed about what was being done.[5] Hysterectomies have been done for birth control in place of simpler tubal ligations. Hysterectomies also provide income to compensate for the declining birth rate and resulting loss of hospital and obstetrical fees. The tendency to recommend unnecessary surgery, including hysterectomies, is greater where there is an overabundance of surgeons and hospital beds.

In the U.S., hysterectomies are far more frequent among women who have "fee-for-service" medical care, covered by insurance, than among women who belong to health maintenance organizations; insured women, both rich and poor, have much higher rates of surgery than the uninsured. In England, Wales, and Sweden, where there is socialized medicine, the rate of hysterectomies is half that in the U.S., without any evidence that women are suffering poorer health.[6]

Hysterectomy rates vary dramatically from one region of the country to another. One study shows, for example, that 70 percent of women in one Maine city had had hysterectomies by the age of seventy, while in another Maine city the figure was 20 percent.[7] These wide variations among similar groups of women indicate that the practices of physicians should be closely examined.

Although most hospitals have committees to monitor surgeons' performances and ethics, they examine cases after surgery has been performed, and the findings are kept confidential. Presumably, surgeons who perform too many questionable hysterectomies are sometimes told to restrain themselves, but surgical review committees are not designed to protect patients.[8] The time for us to review a recommendation for surgery is *before*, rather than after, the surgery occurs. Part of the problem is that: (1) physicians believe that hysterectomies are good for women who are having problems and are past childbearing age (even women gynecologists may urge hysterectomy too casually); (2) women are uninformed about less drastic alternatives to hysterectomy; and (3) the permanent adverse effects of a hysterectomy have not been well publicized.

The good news is that there has been a slight decline in the number of hysterectomies since 1975.[9] This may be because of the rise of consumer advocate groups and other critics of excessive hysterectomies and oophorectomies, more openness among women about the negative aftereffects, the policy of Medicaid and some other insurance plans requiring a second opinion before a hysterectomy is performed, and the recent appearance of informative literature written by enlightened, concerned gynecologists.

PRESSURES TO HAVE A HYSTERECTOMY AND OOPHORECTOMY

Women in their forties and fifties who have gynecological problems face pressure to have hysterectomies and oophorectomies. They are encouraged to do so by medical authorities, many of whom believe older women have little to lose, since in their view the uterus and ovaries have by then outlived their usefulness and merely provide a potential site for cancer. They also believe, incorrectly, that artificial hormones can safely make up for whatever may be lost in surgery. Alternatives to hysterectomy are usually suggested only if the woman still wants children or if she is under forty.[10]

Most books and articles over the last few decades, even those written by women, stressed the benefits of hysterectomies, rarely mentioned the drawbacks, or else blamed women themselves for any adverse results. Though out of date, these misleading books are still in libraries. For example:

Far too many women remain convinced that the removal of the uterus will result in (1) a change in physical appearance, (2) a radical shift in weight, (3) a deterioration of sexual performance. Although these possibilities are at best remote, and have no medical basis at all, any woman can bring them about merely by believing strongly enough that they are inevitable.[11]

Another book states:

The uterus has nothing whatsoever to do with a woman's libido or capacity to enjoy sex. It is simply an organ for childbearing.[12]

Most books disregard reports from women who have had hysterectomies or discredit them as "old wives' tales."

No expert is more dogmatic than the woman who has had a hysterectomy and is suddenly the center of attention at bridge parties and coffee breaks, who determinedly hangs on to this attention by reciting all the horrible "changes" in her life that she attributes to a hysterectomy.[13]

Some psychoanalysts have suggested that women's problems after hysterectomy are caused by emotional problems rather than by surgery. Women have been told over and over that removing the uterus and ovaries only improves the quality of life, as long as we have the "proper" attitude. Being "too attached" to the uterus is considered "infantile," a sign that a woman's sexuality is inappropriately confused with her ability to reproduce. Most gynecologists and some psychiatrists still believe this. The few studies that did document problems were generally ignored.[14]

Women are not generally raised to love and appreciate their bodies and their bodies' functions, such as menstruation and sexuality. Some may view menstruation as a "curse" rather than as a part of nature's ingenious design. Many of us grew up in a time when the public's awareness of cancer increased and when surgery was the primary method used to treat cancer. Fearing cancer, we may be vulnerable to the medical profession's cavalier attitude—take it out! To compound the problem, most of us have been brought up to follow physicians' recommendations without question.

Moreover, as we approach menopause, our bodies are changing. The unpredictable nature of menstrual periods before menopause can be nerve-racking if we do not understand what to expect. Women who do not realize that gushes and clots of blood are common at this time of life may be terrified and look for quick solutions. Fear of accidental pregnancy later in life, coupled with fewer safe contraceptives available for older women, may make the idea of removing the uterus seem appealing. In addition, the vast number of women who have had hysterectomies gives us a false sense of confidence in the procedure. Is it any wonder that so many women accept, and some even request, a hysterectomy?

POSSIBLE AFTEREFFECTS OF HYSTERECTOMY AND OOPHORECTOMY*

Each woman is different, and it is impossible to tell in advance how a hysterectomy will affect her. Neither age, marital status, work, sexual preference, severity of symptoms before surgery, nor the number of children she has had will indicate how a woman will feel after a hysterectomy. Many women report a variety of adverse physical and emotional effects of hysterectomy, many of which are permanent and irreversible.

Both the ovaries and the uterus have important functions in the body long after the reproductive years are over. A study that tested ovarian function in 2,132 women whose uteri were removed found that many ovaries continued to function for up to twenty-five years after the operation.[15] In fact, hot flashes can appear when a woman's ovaries are removed years after her menopause occurred.[16]

Healthy ovaries should not be removed. Removal of the ovaries from premenopausal women creates an immediate "surgical menopause" that is often more severe than normal menopause. Today many doctors recommend hormone replacement therapy (estrogen in combination with progestin) for premenopausal women who have a surgical menopause. If the uterus has been removed, the major risk associated with estrogen—cancer of the uterine lining (endometrial cancer)—has also been removed. If the uterus has not been removed, the risk of endometrial cancer is minimized by adding progestin to the regimen. However, the long-term effects of progestin are not yet known, and the suspected risks of that hormone include a higher likelihood of heart attack or stroke. Long-term estrogen replacement may increase the risk of breast cancer, gallbladder disease, and phlebitis. A small percentage of women are allergic to hormones. For some women, such as those who have had endometriosis or breast cancer, estrogen replacement therapy (ERT) is contraindicated. On the other hand, *not* taking estrogen after *premature* menopause (whether surgical or natural) can result in premature osteoporosis, bone and joint pain, vaginal dryness or shrinkage, or atherosclerosis.

The relationship between hormones and osteoporosis is discussed in the osteoporosis chapter on p. 268. In addition to knowing what is stated there, women should be aware that hormone therapy, either estrogen or the estrogen-progestin combination, does *not* replace the androgens secreted by functioning ovaries. Androgens contribute to the libido (sexual desire).*

---

*We wish to be clear throughout this chapter about whether we are discussing hysterectomy, oophorectomy, or both. We will try to avoid the inaccurate, but common, error of referring to the removal of any part of the uterus or ovaries as a hysterectomy.

*Testosterone (one of the androgens) has been used to enhance libido but also results in "masculinizing" effects such as facial hair, acne, and permanently lowered voice. (See the Boston Women's Health Book Collective, *The New Our Bodies, Ourselves*, New York: Simon and Schuster, 1984, p. 516.)

And the hormonelike substances called *prostacyclins* that circulate in the uterus and help keep arteries open, keep blood platelets from excessive clotting, and help to prevent heart attacks are not replaced through hormone therapy.[17]

Even when the ovaries are left in place, a hysterectomy can cause a significant drop in hormone levels. The uterus is a living, functioning organ that secretes hormones and responds to ovarian hormones for many years after menopause. It is more than just a "baby carriage." When the uterus is amputated, a delicately balanced system (which includes ovaries, fallopian tubes, cervix, vagina, and clitoris and their blood and nerve supplies) is disrupted. Major blood vessels, nerves, and connective tissues are cut, leaving raw edges to heal and scar.

More than a hundred women who contacted a support group in New York reported varying degrees of fatigue, memory loss, and loss of sexual feeling following a hysterectomy. *None of the women had been forewarned by their doctors about any possible aftereffects.* Those who retained their ovaries had hot flashes for several weeks after surgery, but then the flashes disappeared if the women were premenopausal. Also reported were breast pain, breast enlargement and engorgement, cystic breasts, and feelings of lactation and oily skin. Those who had their ovaries removed reported severe hot flashes, bone and joint pain, and dry skin. Many of the women did not realize that their problems might be linked to their surgery until they talked with other women who had suffered similar problems following hysterectomy.[18]

Other consequences reported by women after hysterectomy with or without oophorectomy are: depression, loss of sexual sensation in the breasts and other parts of the body, lessened sexual desire, weaker orgasms, insomnia, vaginal dryness and shrinkage, loss of firm body tone, hair loss, premature graying, weight gain (despite dieting and exercise), unpleasant vaginal odor, protruding abdomen, bloating, recurrent vaginal yeast infections, urine leakage when coughing or sneezing from loss of the uterus as a support for the bladder, dry eye syndrome, lower resistance to colds, and less intense emotions.

Hysterectomy means the loss of uterine contractions during orgasm, which for many women reduces sexual pleasure. Many women report the loss of pleasure from penetration, fewer sexual fantasies, slower arousal, lack of interest in seeking lovers or a mate, loss of desire to masturbate, and sometimes even an aversion to being touched.

My hysterectomy had a result that I was most unprepared for. With breast stimulation, intercourse, and orgasm, there was a definite loss of a sensation which I can only describe as uterine. Having had a number of losses and having helped others through the losses that seem to come to us throughout life, I felt prepared for anything that life had to offer...meaning anything that I could conceive of. This was one thing that I had never conceived of. My greatest need at the time was simply to talk with someone who knew what I was talking about. I received a lot of unhelpful responses. The most insensitive came from female sex therapists. [a forty-one-year-old nurse]

One study reports that 33 percent to 46 percent of women experience varying degrees of diminished libido and diminished physical sexual responses after hysterectomy.[19] Estrogen therapy is of no benefit in this regard.[20]

The worst thing since my hysterectomy is the lack of desire. No more delicious cravings and wonderful radiating feelings of exciting anticipation. I always felt that my desire and enjoyment of sex was a special gift, my own private joy that could never be taken away from me even if I lost material things in life. If something turned me on, whether it was a love scene in a movie, a touch, or a thought, my body would feel all tingly and flushed. Even if I didn't get sex right away, I could luxuriate in thinking about it—how I would do it, where, and when.

Now there is just emptiness inside. I feel I could go one hundred years without sex and I'm aware of the enormous void. To me it is tantamount to death. I was so overcome by the loss that I cried to everyone about it. [a fifty-year-old woman]

For other women, loss of the cervix may prevent orgasm if they were dependent upon cervical stimulation. Some women also report loss of nipple and clitoral sensation; this may be the result of severed nerves and ligaments and loss of blood flow to the pelvic area. Changes in vaginal structure, loss of cervical mucus, and the loss of the copious discharge resulting from monthly ovulation and hormonal changes also contribute to the sexual deficits created by this surgery.

Depression is a common aftermath of hysterectomy. One physician who had a hysterectomy described her feeling as that of "chronic sorrow." One study found that 70 percent of women suffered depression after hysterectomy, which was double the rate of other postoperative depressions.[21] Depressions usually occur within three to six months after surgery and can be severe. The causes of posthysterectomy depression have not been researched thoroughly enough. One theory is that removal of the uterus lowers the estrogen level by altering the blood supply to the ovaries, and lowered estrogen level is associated with a lowered blood level of *tryptophan*, an amino acid that may prevent depression.[22] Other possible reasons for posthysterectomy depression may be the rage resulting from loss of sexual feeling or from concluding that one's surgery was unnecessary.

The removal of the uterus sometimes results in a surprising feeling of devastation over the loss of fertility.

After my hysterectomy, I grieved over the end of my childbearing potential, although I was fifty-five. Before I left the hospital, my concentration on babies became pronounced. I watched a TV program on adoption and fantasized about a foster child or about becoming a Big Sister or a Foster Grandparent. The woman across the hall told me that she found she could not look at new babies because she was grieving over having had her hysterectomy and never having had children. She was surprised at her grief at being childless because she had, she thought, long ago chosen to be a lesbian and to have no children. Now, she was once again having to reinforce that choice. [a fifty-seven-year-old woman][23]

Some women also regret other changes in their bodies.

I miss my periods so much. I think there's something barbaric about cutting off a woman's periods before her time. Two months after my hysterectomy I developed a raw spot in my internal scar that had to be cauterized. The procedure made me stain for a few days. I tried to pretend that the blood on my pad was a period. But I knew it wasn't and I felt sad. [a fifty-year-old woman]

Not everyone reacts negatively to having a hysterectomy. Some women are pleased with the outcome.

From the moment I woke up from the surgery I was optimistic. The recovery was smooth and swift. About three months later I began having hot flashes. (My ovaries had also been removed, at my wish.) I began a regimen of estrogen and later a progestin was added. From the recovery on, I have not had a bad day. It is a joy not to be bleeding either regularly or irregularly and to be interested in sexual activity any day of the month. The sense of security and comfort of not having periods is great. If I knew it would be so easy after the operation

I would have had it at thirty-nine, when my heavy bleeding started. My youngest child was then seven and I knew that I wanted no more. [a fifty-three-year-old woman]

The important point is that women should be made aware of all possible reactions to and consequences of hysterectomy before surgery is undertaken.

When the doctor recommended a hysterectomy for a fibroid, I tried desperately to get information from at least ten women who had the operation. Each one willingly told me about her hospital, her doctor, and the anesthesia she had. Not one of these women told me how she really felt afterwards, or mentioned a single word about aftereffects. Some of them encouraged me to have the surgery. From all this I naively concluded that a hysterectomy is not too bad.

When the shock of the sudden, unwelcome changes from my hysterectomy hit me with its full impact, I became overwhelmed with anger and hurt at these women for not telling me anything. I felt betrayed. Why didn't anyone warn me? Could they have all been so satisfied with their results? Could they have been too embarrassed to talk about sexual changes? If I had known more truths I would have tried harder to avoid the surgery!

Could they have simply not wanted to scare me or to assume too much responsibility in case my operation was really necessary? Or is there a baser emotion, a certain reluctance in some people to spare another person from making the same mistake they made—something like "misery loves company"? When anyone comes to me asking, "What is a hysterectomy like?" I tell them everything I've experienced and let them take it from there. [a forty-nine-year-old woman]

WHEN HYSTERECTOMY IS NECESSARY

There are times when a hysterectomy is lifesaving; each case must be evaluated individually. Some conditions that may require surgery are:

1. Invasive cancer of the uterus (endometrium), ovaries, cervix, or fallopian tubes. This operation should be planned in consultation with both a gynecologist and an oncologist (cancer specialist) to review all the treatment options.

2. Hemorrhaging (severe uncontrollable bleeding) combined with anemia that has not responded to medical treatments—such as a D&C (dilation and curettage, or scraping, of the uterus), hormone therapy, or laser technology—or to nonmedical treatments.

3. Fibroid tumors (common, noncancerous growths) that obstruct bowel or urinary function (a rare occurrence) and that are too large to remove by myomectomy (removal of the tumor alone). Frequent urination is usually not a sufficient reason for a hysterectomy.

4. Advanced pelvic inflammatory disease (PID), in which infection spreads to the peritoneal cavity (membrane that lines the walls of the abdomen). Sometimes a bad infection can be fought successfully with massive combinations of antibiotics (administered intravenously) and complete bed rest.

5. Severe uterine prolapse, in which the uterus descends completely through the vagina.

6. Severe endometriosis (the presence of tissue of the uterine lining elsewhere in the abdominal cavity), if it is untreatable by hormones or other drugs, or if it recurs with severe pain and bleeding after minor surgery.

7. Certain other obstetrical catastrophes and very rare cases of tuberculosis of the uterus.

SOME COMMON PROBLEMS AND ALTERNATIVES TO HYSTERECTOMY

The following conditions will often correct themselves with the coming of menopause. They rarely require hysterectomies and never require oophorectomies.

Fibroid Tumors

Fibroid tumors (myomas or leiomyomas) are the most common reason for hysterectomy in women between thirty-five and fifty. Fibroids are knobs of muscle tissue in or attached to the uterus. Do not automatically think of cancer when you hear the word "tumors"; 99.7 percent of all fibroids are benign (noncancerous).[24] Nearly 40 percent of white women over thirty-five have fibroids, and the incidence is even greater in Black women. The growth of fibroids is stimulated by estrogen, so if you know you have fibroids you should avoid birth control pills and estrogen therapy. Fibroids may stay the same size or grow in spurts, plateau, and shrink many times during a woman's reproductive years, often peaking just before menopause.

Usually they recede slowly after menopause as estrogen levels drop. A uterus can accommodate a surprisingly large number of sizable fibroids without showing any symptoms. The presence of large fibroids, and even feelings of heaviness and mild pressure, are not necessarily a reason for a hysterectomy.

The three most common types of fibroids, named according to their location in the uterus, are:

Subserous—Located outside the uterus. These usually do not interfere with uterine function, even if they are large (though very large ones may eventually disturb other organs).
Intramural—Located inside the muscle wall of the uterus. May cause pain and bleeding (not true hemorrhaging) at menstruation.
Submucous—Located just under the surface of the uterine lining and jutting out into the uterine cavity, this type of fibroid sometimes causes serious bleeding. Fortunately, this is the least common of the three.

The location of fibroids is determined by uterine X-ray, ultrasound test (sonogram), and D&C. Sometimes a fibroid is attached to the uterus with a *pedicle* or *peduncle*, a narrow-based stalk, which may twist and cause pain. The pedunculated fibroid is the easiest to remove regardless of its size.

We may be alarmed when doctors tell us we have "large" fibroids. How large is a "large" fibroid? Hospitals approve surgical removal of a fibroid that grows beyond a twelve-week pregnancy size, or is larger than four to five inches (the size of a grapefruit) when palpable from the abdomen. Some gynecologists consider a uterus massively enlarged if it is the size of a fourteen- to eighteen-week pregnancy. Unfortunately, many surgeons perform hysterectomies for much smaller fibroids. Sometimes nothing more than a surgeon's clinical judgment is used to measure these growths. A slight increase in size can make a fibroid seem enormous to the touch, and a gynecologist might rush a woman into a hysterectomy, telling her that fibroids are overtaking her uterus. In the operating room these "enormous" tumors often turn out to be much smaller than originally perceived.

Some women become alarmed because they think the rapid growth of a fibroid may be a sign of malignancy, although this is extremely rare. How does a woman know how rapid is

FIBROIDS (MYOMAS) OF THE UTERUS

"rapid"? Ultrasound tests can be repeated at three-month intervals, in order to compare sizes. A fibroid that increases by one-third its size in three months might be considered rapid growth, although most fibroids that grow rapidly are benign.

Fibroids may have to be removed if they cause extreme bleeding or pain, if they degenerate because they have outgrown their blood supply, or if they become infected. But in such cases the operation of choice is usually a myomectomy, *not* a hysterectomy.

If you are approaching menopause and have bothersome fibroids, you may choose to wait until menopause, when fibroids usually recede, before making a decision about surgery. Try the following suggestions in the meantime. Patience is advisable in this situation, because fibroid shrinkage may be very gradual, over a period of months or even years after the last menstrual period.

Self-Help for Fibroids

1. Do not take estrogen.
2. Do not take steroids, unless needed for a life-threatening illness. (Steroids stimulate the adrenal glands, which also produce estrogen and so may enlarge fibroids.)
3. Try to keep your percentage of body fat down by exercising. Estrogen is produced in the fat cells of the body.
4. Reduce the total percentage of fat in the diet. Cut out or cut down on sugar. Increase vegetables and whole grains. Cut out alcohol.
5. Try to manage and reduce stress. Many women recall that their fibroids enlarged after a particularly stressful time. Reactions to stress can stimulate the adrenal glands to produce hormones.
6. Try alternative healing techniques. Some women report help from acupuncture and from visualizing a uterus free of fibroids.

Myomectomy for Fibroids

Myomectomy, or surgical removal of fibroids without removing the uterus, was rarely done in the past and was reserved for younger women who wished to have children. However, with new awareness of the value of retaining organs, an increasing number of skilled surgeons are performing myomectomies on older women who do not intend to have children but who wish to preserve their uteri. In 1985, 35,000 myomectomies were performed in the U.S.[25]

During a myomectomy the surgeon will make an incision into the abdomen and examine the uterus. Fibroids on the outside of the uterus (subserous) can be removed. If the fibroids are inside the uterus, the surgeon will cut into the uterine cavity and remove the fibroids, which peel out like oranges peel from their skins. She or he will then repair and close the uterus. Uterine tissue heals easily.

Ironically, many insurance companies that will pay for hysterectomies do not offer full coverage for myomectomies.

I just had my second myomectomy in sixteen years because of extensive fibroids. Before the myomectomy, I had periods that were two weeks long, I looked five or six months pregnant, had to pee frequently because the fibroids were pressing on the bladder, and experienced discomfort during sex because of the fibroid in the cervix. The surgeon compared the sizes of the fibroids to fruits. He said he removed one grapefruit, one orange, several lemons, and a bunch of grapes. I had problems with my insurance policy because the bill was much higher than the usual allowance for a myomectomy. This was because of the time and the two units of blood needed to do such extensive surgery. [a forty-one-year-old woman]

Though not necessarily more difficult to perform than a hysterectomy, myomectomy does require a surgeon experienced in that technique. Such surgeons are more apt to be found in teaching hospitals and fertility clinics.

Every effort must be made to remove even the smallest fibroid during a myomectomy, since regrowth can occur in 10 percent to 25 percent of cases. An older woman is less likely than a younger woman to have fibroids regrow to a size that requires a second myomectomy. Fifteen, thirty, and even more fibroids have been successfully removed without damaging the uterus.

New methods of myomectomy with laser beams now exist, which cause less bleeding and require a much shorter recuperation time than conventional surgery.[26] Laser surgery through a hysteroscope (a device that allows the surgeon to see into the cavity of the uterus) can destroy submucous fibroids.[27] Long-term advantages of this technique over a standard myomectomy are being studied.

Unfortunately, gynecologists who are unfamiliar with or unskilled in performing myomecto-mies may discourage a woman from having one by telling her that it is dangerous, that it might require a second operation, that it is silly at her age, or that she should accept a hysterectomy instead.

My periods had increased in length to two weeks or more, and were accompanied by cramps, extreme weakness, and sometimes fever. Most of the rest of the month I suffered from PMS [premenstrual syndrome] and back pain. A doctor told me I had to have a hysterectomy. He said my uterus was the size of a four- to five-month pregnancy due to fibroids. While he mentioned myomectomy, he said it was a much more dangerous operation and I shouldn't think about it unless I felt strongly about having a child. I was not planning to have a child. He called the uterus a "baby-carrying sac" with no other purpose. A second doctor had the same opinion. A third doctor, more thorough, gave me a sonogram which showed my enlarged uterus pressuring my kidneys and rectum. While he did not push hysterectomy over myomectomy, he also felt that the basis of my decision should be whether I wanted a child.

A diagnostic D&C reduced the length of my periods but the other problems remained. I wanted more information. At a hysterectomy support group I learned of a wide range of side effects of a hysterectomy which none of the doctors had told me about. I arranged for a myomectomy with the third doctor, who had solid experience doing them and was up on the latest methods. I felt compelled to tell him, however, that the basis for my decision was that I wanted a child. I had six fibroids removed. One was the size of a small grapefruit, and three others were the size of tennis balls.

Now, a year later, my period is two and a half days long with little pain. I have PMS just two or three days before my period. For me, myomectomy was the best choice. [a forty-year-old woman]

Neither progestogens nor the hormone danazol (Danocrine or Cyclomen) shrink fibroids successfully. Since the growth of fibroids is stimulated by estrogen (fibroids are never found before puberty and only rarely after menopause in women who are not taking estrogens), research on drugs such as buserelin which suppress estrogen is underway. The drugs (called LHRH agonists) induce a state of pseudomenopause, shrinking fibroids, and also causing hot flashes and vaginal dryness. LHRH agonists may also reduce the beneficial HDL levels and may induce osteoporosis. Though the fibroids will grow back when the medication is stopped, the treatment may be used by itself as a way to "buy time" until menopause, or may be used to shrink fibroids before a surgical myomectomy is performed.[28]

302

Pain During or Between Periods

Do not have a hysterectomy just because you have pain in the lower abdomen during or between periods. Pain can come from many sources. A thorough diagnostic work-up should be done to discover whether the cause of the pain might be from the digestive system, the urinary tract, the bones or the joints. Do not automatically assume that the pain is gynecological.

Visualization, relaxation training, and hypnosis for pain control are often helpful. Pain can sometimes be caused by *premenstrual syndrome,* which sometimes increases in duration and severity in women nearing menopause[29] and then subsides after menopause. (See Menopause chapter, p. 118, for an explanation and suggestions.)

If self-help techniques are not effective, prescription drugs may be necessary. A group of antiarthritic drugs (generic names: ibuprofen, naproxen, and mefenomic acid; trade names: Motrin, Anaprox, Ponstel) may relieve menstrual cramps and pain from fibroids. These drugs contain prostaglandin-blocking substances that often lessen excessive menstrual flow as well.[30] However, such antiinflammatory drugs can also raise blood pressure, trigger asthma attacks in asthmatics, and cause fluid retention and depression. One drug may work better for one woman than another. (Take these drugs with milk.)

To relieve the pain caused by a fibroid in a tipped-back uterus that is pressing on the rectum, try the knee-chest position several times a day. This position will help straighten the uterus, thus lessening pressure on the rectum.

Knee-chest position   *Pam White*

Heavy or Prolonged Menstrual Bleeding (Menorrhagia)

Even though women are used to menstrual bleeding on a regular basis, unexpected and unpredictable bleeding can be frightening. We need to know that irregular or heavy menstrual flow is very common in women approaching menopause (see chart, p. 120). Discuss prolonged heavy bleeding with your health care provider. Also, any bleeding in a woman well past menopause should be checked.

A hysterectomy should not be done merely to stop heavy bleeding, at least until the reason for the bleeding is determined and all other efforts to control it have failed. Many hysterectomies performed because of bleeding are done without a preliminary D&C, hysteroscopy and suction curettage, or endometrial biopsy. In a letter to a medical journal, an indignant physician wrote, "Generally, menorrhagia seems to be diagnosed on the basis of a woman's description of her menstrual loss and is rarely confirmed by the methods available. I am unaware of any other important organ that is electively removed without first assessing its degree of malfunction."[31]

Be sure that you do not overestimate the amount of blood lost during a period. We suggest women keep menstrual charts, recording the number of days from the beginning of one period to the beginning of the next period, the number of days bleeding lasts, how many napkins or tampons are used, whether there are clots (red or brown), and any other details that seem relevant. You may be able to establish some pattern to the bleeding to discuss with your physician.

In addition, heavy loss of blood may lead to anemia, which causes fatigue, paleness, and heart palpitations. A blood test for anemia should always be given to a woman who is bleeding heavily. Normal hemoglobin values range from twelve to sixteen grams per 100 milliliters; normal hematocrit values (the ratio of red blood cells to the volume of whole blood) range from 33 percent to 46 percent. A mild anemia can often be improved by eating more iron-rich foods and taking iron supplements after you eat. Foods rich in vitamin C eaten at the same meal as iron-rich foods help increase the absorption of iron.

I'm forty-two years old and walking around with a twenty-weeks-pregnant-size uterus from fibroids. Several years ago, my uterus was eight- to ten-weeks size. I was told then to have a hysterectomy. My periods were heavy, on and off. Once I was so frightened that I took a cab to a hospital emergency room, but the bleeding subsided by the time I got there. I was told I was anemic. Two years ago I started taking iron pills. My red blood cells [hematocrit] went from twenty-nine in February to thirty-five in June and thirty-eight in October. It upset my system only slightly and cost $2 per 100 tablets. For the first five months my bleeding decreased significantly. But two months ago the doctor said my uterus is still twenty-weeks size, and he seems thoroughly disgusted with me that I haven't had a hysterectomy. I'm really in a quandary, with probably another six years to go before menopause.

In the absence of any diagnosed pathology, you can try these self-care and alternative treatments for heavy bleeding:

1. Try to remain calm. Anxiety can increase blood flow by raising your blood pressure and making the heart pump faster.

2. Stay off your feet, with your legs elevated, if "flooding" occurs. An ice pack applied to the abdomen for an hour or two (fifteen minutes on, fifteen minutes off) can stop or reduce bleeding. Also, try applying cold to the lower back with a towel that has been dampened and chilled in the freezer.

3. Avoid heating pads, hot showers, or baths on heavy-flow days. Heat increases blood flow.

4. Avoid aspirin products. They increase bleeding. Garlic and mint may also increase bleeding.

5. Try taking vitamin C with bioflavinoids. In amounts under one to two grams per day, these help to strengthen the walls of blood vessels and may reduce bleeding. Above this amount, vitamin C is sometimes toxic, and may actually increase bleeding.

6. Try taking 10,000 international units (I.U.s) of vitamin A twice a day (five times the recommended daily allowance for women).[32] Higher doses may be more helpful but should only be taken under the supervision of a physician or nutritionist familiar with the treatment who will monitor your symptoms and test your blood for toxicity. Amounts in excess of 25,000 I.U.s per day can be toxic.

7. Calcium, vitamin D, and magnesium encourage blood clotting and blood vessel contractions.

8. Acupuncture and other alternative healing methods have helped some women.

Acupuncture treatment for heavy bleeding. *Betsy Shapiro*

If self-help approaches do not work, some doctors may prescribe progestins. Use only the smallest effective dosage for the shortest time possible. You and your physician may have to experiment to find the proper dosage and type for you. Some doctors are suggesting intrauterine devices (IUDs) containing progestin for the older woman who has heavy or extended menstrual flow.[33] However, IUDs can cause pelvic inflammatory disease, a major reason for hysterectomies; in addition, IUDs are not recommended at all for women approaching menopause. (See Birth Control for Women in Midlife chapter, p. 99.)

A D&C is a diagnostic procedure that can also remove polyps (strawberrylike benign growths) and hyperplasia (the overgrowth of normal uterine tissue) that may be causing bleeding. For routine diagnosis, an aspiration-suction curettage done in the doctor's office costs less and is safer than a D&C. It involves neither the risk of damaging the delicate lining of the uterus nor the risk of anesthesia.

Developing from its successful use in eye surgery, an experimental technique, laser surgery, is now used for uterine conditions, especially to treat heavy bleeding. The surgeon needs special training to use a flexible glass rod with a laser beam tip to cauterize the uterine lining. The resulting scar tissue will not bleed. The surgeon is able to view the inside of the uterus through a hysteroscope inserted through the vagina and cervix. Being able to see the lining this way may have advantages over a D&C, which is performed blindly. The newer Nd:YAG laser beam can be focused more precisely than a CO_2 laser. The hormone danazol (Danocrine) is given for three weeks before the surgery to thin the endometrium. This procedure is not recommended for women with any signs of cancer or active pelvic inflammatory disease. *This procedure causes sterilization* but seems to preserve other uterine functions. It carries risks of anesthesia and perforation but the heat created and lack of incision minimize infection. Moreover, it can be done with a one- or two-day hospital stay or on an outpatient basis with immediate resumption of normal activities. The procedure has not been in use long enough to evaluate long-term effects.[34]

Uterine Prolapse (Dropped Womb)

About 35 percent of hysterectomies are done for uterine prolapse, or dropped womb. In general, prolapse results from stretching of the ligaments that support the uterus and/or weakness of the pubococcygeal muscle, which supports the pelvic floor. There are three stages of uterine prolapse:

First degree—The uterus has descended into the vaginal canal, but not yet into the vaginal opening.
Second degree—The cervix actually appears outside the vaginal opening, in whole or in part.
Third degree (called complete prolapse)—The entire uterus descends to the point that it shows outside the vagina entirely. This type is most common in women over seventy.

To prevent uterine prolapse and to improve your pelvic muscle support system, no matter how slight or severe your prolapse, do Kegel exercises regularly (see Moving for Health chapter, p. 73). Symptoms usually do not occur with first-degree prolapse, except for occasional bearing-down discomfort. *If you cannot tell you have a prolapse, then surgery is not necessary.*

Some women can avoid surgery by use of a pessary, a rubber doughnut-shaped device that helps hold the uterus in place. Pessaries come in various sizes and must be fitted and inserted by a physician. They must be removed periodically for cleaning. Any woman who is a poor risk for surgery because of age or vulnerability to anesthesia might find this her best choice.

A less drastic surgery to correct prolapse is uterine suspension surgery (sometimes called by women a "plastic"). This is abdominal surgery that lifts the uterus into its correct position by shortening the ligaments that hold the uterus in place. Unfortunately, however, some surgeons prefer to remove the uterus rather than repair it, based on their own value judgment that losing her uterus does not matter to a woman beyond a certain age.

Endometriosis

Endometriosis is a condition in which tissue of the uterine lining is found outside the uterus. This tissue thickens and bleeds with the menstrual cycle each month, forming cysts. The main symptoms of endometriosis are pain during menstruation or intercourse and heavy bleeding. The symptoms tend to get worse as the endometriosis spreads and grows. Endometriosis is often a cause of infertility.

Doctors sometimes diagnose endometriosis when they find tender, nodular growths behind the uterus during a manual pelvic exam, but a laparoscopy (examination of the pelvic organs with a lighted, periscope-type instrument through a half-inch incision in the navel) provides the most definite diagnosis.

Endometriosis is often treated with birth control pills or other hormones that bring on a state of pseudopregnancy. This can dry up the growths completely and is effective in about 50 percent of cases. However, relief is temporary, since the tissue can regrow, and the hormones have certain unpleasant and/or dangerous effects. Birth control pills are very dangerous for women over the age of thirty-five (see p. 100). Danazol (Danocrine or Cyclomen), a derivative of the male hormone testosterone, is reported to be very effective in the treatment of endometriosis, but it is not without its own potential additional effects, namely, depression, liver damage, and masculinizing reactions such as growth of facial hair, weight gain, loss of libido, and deepening of the voice. It is also extremely expensive. Danazol should only be taken under careful medical supervision. Instead of, or in addition to, danazol, you may choose to undergo conservative surgery, in which an abdominal incision is made and the endometrial implants removed, either by laser beams or by electric cauterization.

Hysterectomy is usually a last resort for endometriosis, especially in near-menopausal women whose symptoms will probably recede after menopause. Since endometriosis, like fibroids, is estrogen dependent, you can follow some of the same self-help tips for it as you do for fibroids (see p. 301).

Adenomyosis

Adenomyosis is a condition in which endometrial tissue that lines the inside of the uterus (and which is shed each month during the period) is embedded into the walls of the uterus. Previously the condition was called internal endometriosis, since both involved endometrial tissue in unusual places. Adenomyosis, however, is usually found in women in their forties and fifties who have borne children, while endometriosis is most commonly found in younger women who have not borne children. One theory is that the tissue becomes trapped as the uterus shrinks to normal size after pregnancy. Some degree of adenomyosis is so common that it is found in up to 60 percent of women whose uteri are removed and examined for some other reason. With adenomyosis, the examining physician may find that the uterus is firm and diffusely enlarged, but only 20 percent of women may experience heavy or prolonged periods and menstrual pain. A D&C will not help adenomyosis because the tissue is embedded in the wall of the uterus. Since the tissue swells with the increase of estrogen each month but is trapped in the uterine wall, use of estrogen or progesterone will only make it worse. See cautions (above) on the use of danazol. Try the self-help suggestions for heavy bleeding, pain, and fibroids. Menopause, with its drop in estrogen, brings relief.[35]

Precancerous Conditions

Many women have hysterectomies because of supposed "precancerous" conditions. Always question a doctor's suggestion that an area of tissue is precancerous. It is not clear whether precancerous means the tissue will almost certainly become cancerous or whether it means the condition can revert to normal, become cancerous, or stay the same. Sometimes what is called a precancerous condition may disappear

without treatment or can be treated with medication, self-help techniques, or less drastic surgery. If your doctor tells you that you have a precancerous condition, ask for a copy of your pathology report and get another pathologist to review your slides.

Be sure to have a second, or even third, Pap test several weeks or even a month after the earlier one before agreeing to surgery or any other treatment to destroy questionable cells. If the results of the Pap tests warrant further investigation, the physician should view the cervix with a colposcope. Areas of the cervix can be removed for study by a *punch biopsy* (removal of a small plug of cells for examination). Suspicious cervical cells have sometimes returned to normal when women had their male sexual partners use condoms to keep sperm from contact with the cervix. Then cauterization (with heat, electricity, or chemicals), cryosurgery (freezing the cells), or laser surgery can destroy small patches of malignant cells. *Cone biopsy*, or *conization* (removal of a ring of the cervix around the opening to the uterus), may also be recommended. These procedures can remove small amounts of tissue, reduce the spread of cervical cancer, and prevent hysterectomies.

The cells of the lining of the uterus (endometrium) can also undergo changes, many of which are not serious enough to justify hysterectomy. One such change, *hyperplasia* (an increase in the number of normal cells), is not cancer, rarely becomes cancer, and can be treated with medication or a D&C.[36] A hysterectomy or even a D&C is not necessary to diagnose uterine or ovarian cancer. An endometrial biopsy performed in a physician's office can diagnose cancer of the uterus with reasonable accuracy. A laparoscopy (described earlier in this chapter) can provide a view of the ovaries and even take samples of tissue or fluid for examination. This procedure requires general anesthesia.

TYPES OF HYSTERECTOMY

There are three different types of hysterectomy:

Total hysterectomy, sometimes referred to as *simple hysterectomy*—Removal of the uterus and cervix (mouth of the womb) but not the ovaries and fallopian tubes. A woman continues to produce hormones from her ovaries, but not at her

HYSTERECTOMY AND OOPHORECTOMY

FEMALE PELVIC ORGANS

Fallopian Tubes
Ovaries
Bladder
Urethra
Clitoris

Rectum
Uterus
Cervix
Vagina
Anus

TYPES OF HYSTERECTOMY

Supracervical:
Removal of uterus leaving cervix,
fallopian tubes, and ovaries

Total or Complete:
Removal of uterus and cervix,
leaving ovaries and fallopian tubes

Total with Bilateral
Salpingo-Oophorectomy:
Removal of uterus, ovaries,
and fallopian tubes

Radical:
Removal of uterus, ovaries,
fallopian tubes and top of vagina

optimum output, and the regular cyclical pattern of ovulation may be interrupted. Sometimes the ovaries are irreparably "shocked" and never resume functioning after the uterus is cut away.[37]

Total hysterectomy with bilateral salpingo oophorectomy—Removal of the uterus and cervix as well as both tubes and ovaries. Ovarian hormone production ceases abruptly.

Subtotal hysterectomy—Only the body of the uterus is removed. The cervix is left in, with the surrounding stump of uterus. The tubes and ovaries remain.

A subtotal hysterectomy is rarely done today, on the theory that the cervix may develop cancer later. But the rate of cervical cancer is no higher if the cervix is left than if all the organs are intact.[38] Researchers do not yet know whether the remaining cervix and piece of uterus will provide the body with beneficial hormones as a piece of ovary will. But leaving the cervix in when a hysterectomy is performed avoids the necessity of cutting the bladder completely away from the uterus, as the surgeon does in a total hysterectomy. The advantage of letting the bladder remain with the cervix is that it may prevent the prolapse of the vault of the vagina, as sometimes occurs after a total hysterectomy.[39] Leaving the cervix in may prevent the loss of sexual response among women who depend on cervical stimulation for orgasm.

If the cervix is left, then be sure to continue to have regular Pap tests.

Hysterectomy: The Operation

As with all surgery, hysterectomy presents hazards. The death rate is one to two per 1,000 women—approximately 800 women die each year from a hysterectomy. Most of these deaths are anesthesia-related. As many as half of all patients experience some operative complications, including adverse reactions to anesthesia, hemorrhaging that requires transfusion (one in ten women),[40] abdominal or urinary tract infections, abdominal adhesions, injury to the bladder, bowel, or rectum, and postoperative blood clots.

The surgery commonly involves five to seven days in the hospital and four to six weeks of recovery at home. As with any surgical procedure

requiring general anesthesia and involving opening the abdominal cavity, strenuous activity is usually curtailed for several months. Some women experience prolonged fatigue and loss of energy for six months to a year after surgery.

The operation may be done from inside the vagina (leaving no visible scar) or through an abdominal incision. Vaginal hysterectomy patients show a higher incidence of postoperative fever, bladder and other infections, and urinary tract problems. They also experience greater postoperative blood loss.[41] The number of vaginal hysterectomies has declined since 1975.[42] Since vaginal hysterectomies are performed less frequently and require greater skill, if you do have one it is important to use a surgeon who is experienced in this type of approach. Vaginal hysterectomies seem to involve a shorter recovery period and faster healing. However, many urologists and gynecologists specializing in the treatment of incontinence believe that the vaginal approach carries too much risk of damage to the urinary system, and that the abdominal approach is preferable for that reason. (See Urinary Incontinence chapter.)

Ovaries In or Out Over Forty?

The threat of ovarian cancer does not justify routine removal of healthy ovaries. Ovarian cancer, while a serious disease, is relatively rare, occurring in less than 1 percent of all women. While the risk increases in postmenopausal women, it should be noted that the average age of diagnosis of ovarian cancer is sixty-one, and this does not justify routine removal of healthy ovaries from women in their forties or fifties. In the United States a woman has a 1.3 percent chance of developing ovarian cancer by her seventy-fourth year.[43] One source estimated that 7,500 healthy ovaries would have to be removed to prevent a single cancer death.[44] The risk of ovarian cancer is no higher in hysterectomized women who keep their ovaries than in women who do not undergo a hysterectomy. Furthermore, because ovarian tissue can occur elsewhere in the abdominal cavity, removal of the ovaries does not absolutely guarantee that ovarian cancer will never occur.[45]

Removal of the ovaries in a woman with estrogen-dependent breast cancer, in order to

308

reduce the amount of estrogen that stimulates the growth of the cancer, is now virtually obsolete, since hormone treatments achieve the same effect.

During a hysterectomy, the ovaries should be examined for abnormalities. In *advance* of surgery, a woman should discuss with her doctor the conditions under which she consents to the removal of her ovaries. Often a gynecologist will say, "If the ovaries are unhealthy we'll take them out," without specifying what is meant by "unhealthy." A cyst, for example, can be cut out from an ovary without removal of the entire ovary. Experts disagree about cysts. Most ovarian cysts in menstruating women are harmless and disappear after several cycles. There is no evidence to date showing that the presence of cysts means an increased risk of ovarian cancer at any age.

If the ovaries are retained after a hysterectomy, regular ovarian checkups are advised. The ovaries are actually easier to examine once the bulky uterus is out of the way,[46] and any question as to their size or consistency can be checked by an ultrasound or laparoscopy.

Do's and Don'ts for Women Contemplating Elective Hysterectomy

A woman who has been advised to have a hysterectomy is often not at her best physically and emotionally. She may feel weak or sick and be under too much stress to be an assertive, active information-seeker. The pressures are often strong to "get it over with." But it is important to persist, for a thorough knowledge of your condition is your best assurance of making the right decision.

- *Do* have someone with you when you see your health care provider. Bring a person who will help you ask questions, assess the answers, and support you so you will not feel intimidated into making a quick decision.
- *Do* seek other opinions if surgery is recommended. In a medical system as geared to hysterectomy as ours, a second opinion may not be enough. Many insurance programs today will pay for second or even third opinions. *Don't* feel it is a *fait accompli* if the second doctor also recommends hysterectomy.

- *Do* talk with other women. *Do* try to find a hysterectomy support group in your community and attend a meeting. The women there cannot make your decision for you, but they will give you information unavailable elsewhere and, possibly, a physician-referral list. Some groups have a twenty-four-hour hotline. Other women's honest assessments are one of your best tools.
- *Do not* have a hysterectomy solely for sterilization purposes. (See Birth Control for Women at Midlife chapter.)
- *Do not* have a hysterectomy because that was the medical practice popular in your mother's and aunts' era.
- *Do* search out the most current information. Check copyright dates: books written even five or six years ago do not have the newest information about alternatives to and aftereffects of hysterectomy. Women's health centers and hospital medical libraries may help you find the newest information. Technical language may be difficult at first, but conquering the jargon is well worth the effort. *Do* check the source of all information read. A pamphlet produced by a drug company, for example, may subtly encourage surgery that would necessitate taking their drug.
- *Do* use an internist, family practitioner, or general practitioner as your primary physician. She or he is more apt to see you as a total person, rather than just a set of gynecological organs. This primary physician can recommend nonsurgical treatments and can refer you to a gynecologist or an endocrinologist (a specialist in glands and hormones) if necessary. CAUTION: many physicians were trained to regard hysterectomies as routine procedures.
- *Do* try to find a physician who is treating someone else's gynecological problem conservatively without a hysterectomy.
- *Do* try to be optimistic. This is very difficult when physicians take a somber, pessimistic approach to your condition. In an effort to manipulate you into a hysterectomy, some doctors may accentuate the negative.
- *Do* try to reduce stress by every means possible. Stress exacerbates all gynecological problems.
- *Don't* automatically reject proposed treatments because you do not want to take drugs regularly. Some drugs may be far less risky

than a hysterectomy, which involves anesthesia, prophylactic antibiotics, and possibly long-term hormone replacement therapy, not to mention the potential irreversible after-effects of the surgery.

- *Do* realize that you have a right to refuse or withdraw from any treatment or surgery at any time, even *after* you have entered the hospital.

If You Have Already Had a Hysterectomy

- Make sure you know exactly what was removed during the procedure. Many women do not know that they have had one or both ovaries removed.
- If you want to be sexually active, make extra efforts to promote sexual desire. This may be difficult if your interest in sex is low, but just thinking about sex as well as engaging in it increases hormone production in the ovaries and/or adrenal glands and contributes to health and well-being.
- Pay special attention to your diet. Avoid caffeine, sugars, salt, alcohol, and red meats. Hysterectomies often produce hormone imbalances that can lead to low blood sugar (hypoglycemia). Try to eat small meals high in protein or complex carbohydrates (see Eating Well chapter) every two to three hours. Vitamin supplements, especially the B-complex and vitamin E, may help deficiencies caused by hormone loss.
- Exercise helps to lessen depression and builds stronger bones, helping to prevent osteoporosis. Some women find that yoga, swimming, dancing, and walking are especially helpful after a hysterectomy. Exercise helps firm muscles and increase muscle and tendon strength, which is helpful in preventing urinary problems and osteoporosis.
- If you undergo an oophorectomy before menopause, you may wish to consider estrogen or estrogen-progestin replacement therapy only until the time when menopause would be expected, tapering down gradually to imitate a natural menopause. If you are undergoing menopausal changes or if you are postmenopausal already, you may prefer not to add hormones when your system has already decreased its production.

Seeking Legal Recourse for Hysterectomy Abuse

If you feel you have been wronged by your surgeon, you should not delay too long before contacting a lawyer, since the statute of limitations (the definite time within which you may initiate a lawsuit) varies from state to state (Pennsylvania's is only two years). Some women's health groups keep a list of health-law specialists. In several recent court cases, women have successfully used the right of informed consent to fight hysterectomy abuse. *Informed consent* (see p. 215) means that a woman must have the opportunity to refuse a diagnostic procedure treatment, or any type of medical care if she decides the contemplated procedure involves unacceptable consequences. Women have won court cases because of doctors' failure to inform patients of possible consequences before getting their consent.[47]

The "good patient" attitudes that were held in high esteem in our growing-up years cause us to be all-brave, all-accepting in the face of medical adversity. Sometimes being a "good patient" attitude works to our disadvantage and makes the older woman an easy target for medical abuse. As we learn more about pelvic cancer, we can become more courageous about questioning or refusing treatments that may risk our good health as a price of saving us from a disease we are not likely to contract.

NOTES

1. Estimated figures from the National Center for Health Statistics.
2. The Boston Women's Health Book Collective, *The New Our Bodies, Ourselves.* New York: Simon and Schuster, 1984, p. 512.
3. The 33 percent figure is quoted in Niels Lauersen and Eileen Stukane, *Listen to Your Body.* New York: Simon and Schuster, 1982, p. 455. The 72 percent figure is in Penny Wise Budoff, *No More Menstrual Cramps and Other Good News.* New York: G. P. Putnam & Sons, 1980, p. 181.
4. Winnifred Berg Cutler, et al., *Menopause, A Guide for Women and the Men Who Love Them.* New York: W. W. Norton & Co., 1983, p. 156.

5. Claudia Dreifus, ed., *Seizing Our Bodies*. New York: Vintage Books, 1978.

6. The Boston Women's Health Book Collective, op. cit., p. 511.

7. John E. Wennberg, "Dealing with Medical Practice Variations: A Proposal for Action." *Health Affairs*, Vol. 3, No. 2 (Summer 1984), pp. 6–32.

8. See Marcia Millman, *The Unkindest Cut: Life in the Backrooms of Medicine*. New York: William Morrow and Co., 1977.

9. Richard Sattin and Joyce Hughes, "Hysterectomy Among Women of Reproductive Age, United States, Update for 1979–1980." *Urban Health*, Vol. 13, No. 1 (January 1984), pp. 44–8.

10. Statistics for hysterectomies performed in short-stay, non-Federal hospitals in 1982 showed that 65 percent of patients were ages fifteen to forty-four (with the bulk of them from thirty-five to forty-four), 27 percent were ages forty-five to sixty-four, and 8 percent were sixty-five or older. National Center for Health Statistics, "Surgical Operations in Short Stay Hospitals." *Vital and Health Statistics*, 1983; and Sattin and Hughes, op. cit., pp. 44–8.

11. Nancy Nugent, *Hysterectomy*. New York: Doubleday & Co., 1976, p. 85.

12. Harry Huneycutt and Judith L. Davis, *All About Hysterectomy*. New York: Reader's Digest Press, 1977, p. 257.

13. Ibid., p. xi.

14. Katherine Dalton, "Discussion on the Aftermath of Hysterectomy and Oophorectomy." *Proceedings of the Royal Society of Medicine*, Vol. 50, 1957, pp. 415–8. Surveyed women for ten years after surgery.

15. Brooks Ranney and S. Abu-Ghazaleh, "The Future Function and Fortune of Ovarian Tissue Which Is Retained In Vivo During Hysterectomy." *American Journal of Obstetrics and Gynecology*. Vol. 128, No. 6 (July 15, 1977), pp. 626–34.

16. Sherwin A. Kaufman, *The Ageless Woman*. New York: Prentice-Hall, 1967, p. 127.

17. James D. Shelton, "Prostacyclin from the Uterus and Woman's Cardiovascular Advantage." *Prostaglandins Leukotrienes and Medicine*, Vol. 8, No. 5 (May 1982), pp. 459–66.

18. Personal communication from a member of the group, which has been in existence since 1982.

19. L. Zussman, Shirley Zussman, R. Sunley, and Edith Bjorson, "Sexual Responses After Hysterectomy/Oophorectomy: Recent Studies and Reconsideration of Psychogenesis." *American Journal of Obstetrics and Gynecology*, Vol. 140, No. 7 (August 1, 1981), pp. 725–9.

20. Wulf H. Utian, "Effect of Hysterectomy, Oophorectomy and Estrogen Therapy on Libido." *International Journal of Gynaecology and Obstetrics*, Vol. 13, No. 3 (1975), pp. 97–100.

21. J. Anath, "Hysterectomy and Depression." *Obstetrics and Gynecology*, Vol. 52, No. 6 (December 1978), p. 729.

22. D. H. Richards, "A Post-Hysterectomy Syndrome." *Lancet*, October 26, 1974, pp. 983–5.

23. From an unpublished manuscript by Carolyn Ruth Swift. The writer has since become a substitute grandmother for a lesbian couple raising a child.

24. Sandra Beaman Jordan, "The Facts About Fibroid Tumors." *McCall's*, July 1985, p. 62.

25. Estimated figures from the National Center for Health Statistics.

26. Peggy Eastman, "Hysterectomy—No Longer the Only Way." *Self*, September 1984, pp. 183–5.

27. Robert S. Neuwirth, "Hysteroscopic Management of Symptomatic Submucous Fibroids." *Obstetrics and Gynecology*, Vol. 62, No. 4 (October 1983), pp. 509–11.

28. Charles C. Coddington, et al., "Long-Acting Gonadotropin Hormone-Releasing Hormone Analog Used to Treat Uteri." *Fertility and Sterility*, Vol. 45, No. 5 (May 1986), pp. 624–9; and Rodolphe Maheux and André Lemay, "Uterine Leiomyoma Treatment with LHRH Agonist." *Progress in Clinical and Biological Research*, Vol. 225, 1986, pp. 297-311.

29. Niels Lauersen, *PMS: Premenstrual Syndrome and You*. New York: Pinnacle Books, 1984, p. 88.

30. Lauersen and Stukane, op. cit., p. 61.

31. M. Greenberg, "Hysterectomy, Hormones and Behavior: Letter to the Editor." *Lancet*, Vol. 1, No. 8217 (February 21, 1981), p. 449.

32. "Hysterectomy," in *The Prevention Guide to Surgery and Its Alternatives*. Emmaus, PA.: Rodale Press, 1980, pp. 287–328.

33. Jonathan Parmer, "Long-Term Suppression of Hypermenorrhea by Progesterone Intrauterine Contraception." *American Journal of Obstetrics and Gynecology*, Vol. 149, No. 5 (July 1, 1984), pp. 578–9.

34. Maryann Napoli, "Medical Breakthrough: Laser Hysterectomy." *Ms.* March 1986, p. 30; and Jane Brody, "Laser Lessens the Trauma of Surgery in the Uterus." *The New York Times*, April 13, 1987.

35. Lynda Madras and Jane Patterson, with Peter Schick, *Womancare: A Gynecological Guide to Your Body*. New York: Avon, 1981, pp. 386–9.

36. Budoff, op. cit.

37. Ranney and Abu-Ghazaleh, op. cit.

38. Richard Mattingly and John D. Thompson, *Te Linde's Operative Gynecology*. Philadelphia: Lippincott, 1985.

39. Niles Newton and Enid Baron, "Reactions to Hysterectomy." *Primary Care*, Vol. 3, December 1976, p. 793.

40. The Boston Women's Health Book Collective, op. cit., p. 513.

41. Cutler, et al., op. cit., pp. 154–76.

42. Sattin and Hughes, op. cit.

43. J. L. Young, Jr., et al., "Surveillance, Epidemiol-

ogy, and End Results: Incidence and Mortality Data 1973–77." National Cancer Institute Monograph, 1981, p. 57.

44. Lauersen and Stukane, op. cit.

45. Joanne Tobachman, et al., "Intra-Abdominal Carcinomatosis After Prophylactic Oophorectomy in Ovarian-Cancer-Prone Families." *Lancet*, Vol. 3 October 9, 1982, p. 795.

46. Budoff, op. cit., pp. 178–99.

47. Sybil Shainwald, "A Legal Response to Hysterectomy Abuse." *The Network News*, Vol. 10, No. 3 (May/June 1985), p. 6. For a hysterectomy consent form send a stamped, self-addressed envelope to the National Women's Health Network, 1325 G. St., N.W., Lower Level B, Washington, DC 20005.

23

HYPERTENSION, HEART DISEASE, AND STROKE

by Ellen Dorsch

Many of us have had someone close to us become ill or suddenly die from cardiovascular disease, the leading cause of death in the United States. Cardiovascular disease, or disease of the heart and blood vessels, can damage every other part of the body. Some of us have experienced a heart attack or a stroke. Many of us fear being well at one minute and seemingly at death's door the next.

Although healthy habits are no guarantee that we can prevent cardiovascular disease, we do know that high blood pressure, smoking, eating foods rich in saturated fats and cholesterol, and inactivity all increase our chances of developing it. We can decrease the probability of serious illness or premature death by reducing these risk factors, regularly checking our blood pressure, and knowing the early warning signs of heart attack and stroke.

HEART DISEASE *IS* A WOMAN'S DISEASE

In the past, heart disease was considered a man's disease. Most research until recently did not include women, so much of the information we have about heart disease is based on studies of men, assuming that they are the norm. In fact, heart disease is the leading cause of death in women over sixty today, and women who have heart attacks are more likely to die from them than men. Women are also more likely than men to have strokes. We can no longer afford to ignore the impact of heart disease on women's health—more research is needed on women and heart disease.

Because heart disease is often regarded as a man's disease, many physicians pay less attention to symptoms in women than in men, and don't emphasize preventive steps, such as lowering cholesterol levels. Women often suffer needless discomfort because they or their physicians ignore or minimize early symptoms.

I was lying in bed at about 2:00 in the morning. I felt a pain in my chest, which I thought might be indigestion. Then the pain went into my arm and up to my neck and head. That really hurt. I jumped up and it seemed to get better, so I didn't tell my daughter. The next night it started again. I knew there was a problem, but it went away again when I jumped up. The next morning I told my daughter but I refused to go to the doctor. I knew what had happened. But after the pain stopped, I thought maybe nothing happened. I'm stubborn and we fought for two days. Then I went and the doctor put me in the hospital for fourteen days. [a seventy-two-year old woman]

How the Heart Works

The heart, a four-chambered muscular organ, is divided into a left and right side. The right side receives blood through the veins that is low in oxygen and high in carbon dioxide and passes it to the lungs, where oxygen is added and carbon dioxide eliminated. The oxygen-rich blood from the lungs then goes to the left side of the heart where it is pumped to all parts of the body through the arteries of the circulatory system. Valves in each chamber of the heart regulate this flow of blood. The circulating blood supplies nutrients and oxygen to all organs and tissues of the body. It picks up waste products from the cells and carries the waste to the kidneys or lungs to be eliminated. The pumping action of the heart is controlled by a bundle of nerves that acts as a natural pacemaker.

313

HIGH BLOOD PRESSURE (HYPERTENSION)

Hypertension, or high blood pressure, increases the risk of strokes and often contributes to heart attacks and other diseases. Most people who have hypertension experience no signs or symptoms; some may experience headaches, dizziness, fainting spells, ringing in the ears, or nosebleeds.

Blood pressure is the force of blood against the walls of the arteries and veins. The force is created by the heart as it pumps blood to every part of the body. Blood pressure is recorded with two numbers, for example, $\frac{120}{70}$, read as "120 over 70."

- *Systolic*, the first or upper number, represents the blood pressure in the arteries when the heart is pumping blood;
- *Diastolic*, the second or lower number, is the pressure in the arteries when the heart is filling with blood for the next beat.

The American Heart Association (AHA) considers any systolic pressure over 140 to be abnormal. (Other researchers arbitrarily have defined hypertension as blood pressure over $\frac{160}{90}$.)[1] For people over sixty-five, systolic pressures of 150 to 155 are not uncommon, but the AHA suggests that they be lowered, if possible. If your diastolic pressure remains above 90 to 95, you are considered hypertensive.

A painless and simple test measures blood pressure. Taking blood pressure is an easy skill to learn. Since many women are under stress in a doctor's office, it may be preferable to check your blood pressure at home or at work. A family or a group could share the cost of the equipment. If you are a large woman, be sure that the cuff you use is big enough to fit around your arm, as one that is too small may cause a false reading. Don't rely on coin-operated machines that are available in drugstores and supermarkets; they are not always adjusted properly and can give false readings.

A diagnosis of high blood pressure should not be based on only one reading, because blood pressure varies with the time of day, activity, and stress, including the stress of having your blood pressure taken. At least three elevated readings, taken days or weeks apart while both sitting and standing, should be found before hypertension is diagnosed.

Norma Holt

Blood pressure tends to rise with age and after menopause. About 50 percent of people over sixty-five have hypertension.[2] Women of color are more susceptible to hypertension than white women.

More Black women than white women develop hypertension, and they develop it earlier in life, more severely, and suffer hypertension-related deaths more frequently. Death rates from strokes, in particular, are much higher among Blacks than whites. Some researchers attribute these high hypertension rates to a genetic adaptation useful for survival in the African climate but not needed at colder temperatures. Others criticize this theory and state that these high hypertension rates are related to high-stress lives caused by poverty, diets high in salt and fats, and limited accessibility to health care.

I am a sixty-one-year-old Black lady who has been diagnosed as having severe hypertension. For thirty-odd years I have tried hard to accept and cope with this problem: no salt, no fat, weight control, etc. It is very hard but if you want to live a fairly normal life, you have to try to do what's best. After having all kinds of tests and medication I have learned one of the best remedies for me is to try and not let things bug me. I try not to get upset over things which I have no control over. Sometimes it doesn't work, but I still keep on trying. My doctor has tried different medications and when something new comes along she will suggest it to me, tell me the side effects, and then leave the decision up to me. Usually I try these medications because maybe something will come along that will help me, or someone else.

What Can Be Done for High Blood Pressure?

If you have mild hypertension you may be able to lower your blood pressure without medication, or with less medication, if you adopt the following good health habits.

· Eat well for weight management.
· Exercise. If you are not accustomed to exercise, start by taking a walk each day. If you are not able to get around see the section When Movement Is Limited, pp. 70–72. Exercising also helps weight management. (See Weighty Issues chapter.)
· Reduce salt intake.
· Reduce stress and use relaxation exercises. (Read Aging Well chapter for a more complete discussion of these suggestions.)

Medication/Drugs for High Blood Pressure

If your hypertension is severe, or if the above suggestions do not lower your blood pressure enough or soon enough, you may need medication to lower it. However, good health habits will contribute to your well-being and should be continued even if you take medication.

If medication is necessary, the first type of drug tried is usually a diuretic (often called a "water pill," because it reduces the amount of fluid in the body). Possible effects include a low potassium level and elevated uric acid and blood glucose levels, which can cause fatigue, muscle weakness, leg cramps, and other prob-

lems. Do not take over-the-counter diuretics without consulting a health care provider. Anyone taking diuretics should be carefully monitored for signs of dehydration and urinary problems. If you are taking a potassium-depleting diuretic, you should eat four servings a day of potassium-rich foods.* If you cannot eat enough of these foods, you may have to take a prescribed potassium preparation.

If diuretic therapy alone is not effective, you may be given additional medications. *Beta-blockers*, such as propranolol (Inderal), metoprolol (Lopressor), nadolol (Corgard), and atenolol (Tenormin), lower the heart's demand for blood. Beta-blockers are not considered a good choice for treating hypertension in Black people, some older people, or people with asthma or heart failure. For others, in low doses, beta-blockers effectively treat heart pain (angina pectoris) and irregular heartbeats (arrhythmias). Some women may experience other effects from beta-blockers, such as nausea, cold feet, insomnia, tiredness, depression, a slow heartbeat, or wheezing asthma. Sometimes, though not often, these medications may cause lowered sexual desire. Too high a dose can cause dizziness and fainting spells. If you are taking insulin for diabetes, you should carefully review any possible reactions with your health care practitioner. ***Never stop taking beta-blockers abruptly; you must taper off gradually.***

Calcium-channel blockers are still being tested but are increasingly used as the second step, rather than beta-blockers, in medically treating hypertension. Because calcium-channel blockers prevent spasms of the coronary arteries, they keep the supply of blood flowing into the heart and are useful when spasms play a role in causing angina pain. They also slow a racing heart rate.

Vasodilators are another kind of drug commonly taken for high blood pressure. These relax the blood vessel wall, allowing more blood to flow through. Some women who take them complain of headaches, swelling around the eyes, heart palpitations, shortness of breath, dizziness, or aches and pains in the joints. If these

---

*Apricots, avocados, bananas, broccoli, cabbage, cantaloupe, dates, figs, raisins, grapefruit, molasses, mushrooms, oranges, peanuts, pineapple, plums, potatoes, prunes, pumpkin, radishes, rhubarb, tomatoes, watermelon, wheat germ, whole grains, cooked dried beans.

symptoms continue after the first few weeks, talk to your doctor about changing medications.

A combination of small doses of various hypertensive drugs is often more effective for older persons than a single form of medication. Attempting to lower blood pressure over a period of weeks or months, rather than suddenly, produces better results with fewer side effects.

Some General Suggestions for Reducing High Blood Pressure with Drugs

- Your pharmacist is a valuable resource. Ask her or him about generic or less expensive substitutes for your prescription; food and drinks to avoid; and best times to take medication.
- Don't mix drugs. Tell your physician and pharmacist about all drugs (prescription and over-the-counter), including vitamins and birth control pills, you are taking and any drug reaction you have had in the past.
- Keep to your schedule for taking drugs. Your blood pressure is only lowered while the drugs are working, so you must keep a continuous supply in your body. Some people need medication for the rest of their lives; others may be able to reduce or stop medication if changes in life-style lower their pressure sufficiently over a significant period of time.
- Do not stop medication because your blood pressure is normal or because you feel okay. Remember, you have to *keep* your blood pressure normal.
- Drink little or no alcohol.
- Know your blood pressure. Keep a record of it. You can only know your blood pressure by measuring it, not by how you feel.

ATHEROSCLEROSIS

Atherosclerosis, often called "hardening of the arteries," is a condition that underlies cardiovascular diseases. With this condition, over time the walls of the arteries become thickened with deposits of a combination of fat (cholesterol) and calcium, called plaque, which can narrow or block the arteries leading to any part of the body, including the heart and brain. The deposits are likely to form where damage has occurred because of high blood pressure. The

deposits can cause intense pain in the heart (angina pectoris) if there is partial blockage; heart attack, if total blockage occurs in a coronary artery; or a stroke, if the blockage occurs in arteries in the brain.

Angina can occur whenever less oxygen reaches the heart than is needed. Exercise, extremes of temperature, reactions to stress or strong emotions, or other causes, such as anemia, may cause angina. Some of us experience pain but can live full lives with it for many years, even when the cause is not clear.

In school and the early years of marriage and childrearing, I was always hurrying from one activity to another. I developed chest pains that the doctors diagnosed as angina. At the suggestion of my doctor I took vitamin B-complex for some years and seemed to get better. My blood pressure was never high. Now at age seventy-four the old problem is back and I live with it. My current doctor also prescribes B-complex. I drive, work, clean, mow lawns, go to meetings. I do get tired but I sleep well. My hands and feet get cold easily and I wear sweaters much of the year. My mother also had the same problem. She lived to be eighty-four and died of what the doctor called a tired heart.

Cholesterol is one of several blood fats (lipids) in the blood. Lipids must be combined with proteins, forming lipoproteins, to transport fat in the blood. High-density lipoprotein (HDL) contains the highest proportion of protein and is important in transporting fat away from body cells, preventing the accumulation of cholesterol and other fats within the artery walls. Women tend to have higher levels of HDL than men. Athletes also have high levels, especially long-distance runners. Smokers have lower levels of HDL.

Low-density lipoprotein (LDL) contains the largest proportion of cholesterol of any of the lipoproteins. LDL is a factor in the accumulation of fatty materials in the artery walls and is significantly related to risk of heart attack and stroke.

Lowering the cholesterol level in the bloodstream reduces heart attacks and heart attack deaths. Every 1 percent drop in the cholesterol level means a 2 percent decrease in the likelihood of a heart attack.[3] Although women have not been included in most past studies, a recent study shows that women benefit more than men from low cholesterol diets.[4]

In addition to food sources, the body also produces cholesterol. Blood cholesterol levels generally increase with age. An estimated 15 million American women have blood cholesterol levels of 260 milligrams per 100 milliliters (260 mg/100ml) or above, placing them at high risk of developing heart disease. Recommended levels of blood cholesterol vary among medical professionals—some set the desirable level under 200mg/100ml for adults,[5] while others suggest 100-plus-your-age (up to a maximum of 160) mg/100ml.[6] The average American adult consumes between 400 and 700 milligrams of cholesterol each day.[7] The American Heart Association recommends that Americans limit cholesterol intake from food to no more than 300 milligrams a day (a medium-sized egg yolk contains about 275).

PREVENTING CARDIOVASCULAR DISEASES

We can do a lot to reduce the factors that affect our chances of having a heart attack or stroke. The first step is understanding the role of hypertension and other risk factors. Then we can make changes to improve our health and reduce the risks. Understanding these factors is the first step.

Smoking and Heart Disease

Cigarette smoking definitely increases the risk of heart disease.[8] Women who give up smoking can lower that risk. Studies show that smokers who quit return to nonsmoker risk levels for heart disease within approximately ten years.[9] Some studies suggest that after age sixty-five the influence of cigarette smoking on heart disease declines,[10] though all the other negative effects of smoking continue.

Smoking affects the circulatory system in a number of ways. It damages the linings of the arteries, making it easier for plaque to build up in them. Nicotine from cigarettes overstimulates the heart. Smoking causes the oxygen in the blood to be displaced by carbon monoxide, causing the heart to work harder to remove the carbon monoxide. Finally, smoking harms the respiratory system. (See pp. 23–25 for help in stopping smoking.)

Exercise and Weight

Regular aerobic exercise helps regulate weight, raises beneficial HDL levels, and increases overall cardiovascular fitness by improving blood circulation throughout your body. Exercise is especially important for those whose bodies produce high levels of cholesterol. If you have cardiovascular disease, check with your health care practitioner before starting an exercise program, to make sure you know the level of exercise suitable for you. (See the exercise cautions on p. 72.)

Research shows that those of us who are very overweight are at greater risk for developing hypertension. Some studies show that increasing exercise to lose weight can be as effective as diet and drugs in controlling hypertension; others suggest that regular exercise is more important than weight loss.[11]

As we age, the eating patterns of our younger years tend to stay with us, but we often exercise less, causing an increase in fat in our bodies. Women who accumulate fat around the waist and abdomen are at higher risk of heart attack, stroke, hypertension, and diabetes than others who accumulate fat around the hips and lower extremities.[12]

Diet

Diet influences HDL and LDL levels in the blood and therefore influences the likelihood of developing heart disease. We can reduce this risk by: (1) replacing saturated fats with unsaturated fats, (2) eating less food high in cholesterol, (3) eliminating "empty calorie" foods with little nutritive value, and (4) increasing exercise to reduce the ratio of fat on the body.

Salt contributes to fluid retention, increasing the amount of energy the heart must exert. It also counters the effect of diuretics, which are often prescribed for hypertension. Take the salt shaker off the table and avoid most canned foods, baking soda, ketchup, relishes, and cold cuts, all of which contain high amounts of salt.

Eat poultry and fish rather than meat. Limit meat to lean cuts, trimming all visible fat. Replace butter and shortenings with vegetable oils. Eliminate coffee.[13] Try reducing egg yolks to no more than three a week. Eat more garlic, onions, whole grains, fruits, and vegetables. Choose low-fat milk and cheeses, but take care not to eliminate calcium (which is found in dairy products) from your diet, since calcium is a factor in the prevention of both hypertension and osteoporosis.

Reports indicate that eating fish two or three times per week reduces risk of atherosclerosis. Not only does eating fish reduce the number of high-cholesterol, red-meat meals you consume, but fish oil contains omega-3 polyunsaturated fats, which appear to have beneficial effects on blood cholesterol.[14]

Stress Factors

Although reactions to stress vary, most health practitioners agree that reducing emotional stress benefits general health and particularly heart disease. The Framingham Study, a long-term project that looked at various aspects of heart disease, found that women who work outside of the home have fewer heart attacks than women who do not. However, women who have children, work in stressful clerical jobs, and have unsupportive bosses and husbands, are the most frequent victims of heart disease.[15] Some employers offer employees stress reduction programs to reduce lost time on the job and prevent stress-related disease. Many community recreation departments, clinics, or hospital outpatient departments offer stress management programs. (See Disarming Stress, p. 12.) Many of us, as we get older, need to balance rest and activity. Take a rest in the afternoon if you feel tired and can fit it into your routine.

Heredity

Some health practitioners believe there is a link between family history and likelihood of developing cardiovascular diseases. Others think this link reflects family behavior more than inherited traits. We not only pass on genetic traits to our children but often also eating, smoking, and exercising habits, which may have greater effects than hereditary factors. Nonetheless, if several members of your family have died of heart attacks or strokes at a young age, you should pay particular attention to preventive measures.

Age and Gender

Although heart disease is not directly related to aging, it does occur with greater frequency after the age of forty. On the average, it occurs in women ten years later than in men. Up to age fifty-five, men have higher death rates from heart attacks and stroke. After that, women catch up.

Hormones and Heart Disease

The relationship between hormones and heart disease is not fully understood. Oral contraceptives, which contain hormones, cause a twofold or greater increase in risk of heart attacks and strokes—an increase well beyond their blood-pressure-raising effect.[16] Smoking has an additional harmful interaction with hormone use. Women who use oral contraceptives and smoke are ten times as likely to suffer from coronary heart disease as nonsmoking women who take oral contraceptives.[17] Among a group of heavy smokers (twenty-five or more cigarettes per day), aged forty to forty-nine and currently using oral contraceptives, the risk of a heart attack was thirty-nine times greater than that of women who neither smoked nor used oral contraceptives.[18]

Because heart disease among women increases at about the same age that menopause occurs, the assumption was made that the hormone estrogen offers some protection. Menopause, especially caused by the early surgical removal of the ovaries, reduces estrogen and seems to remove some of our protection from heart disease. Estrogen use in women seems to reduce LDL cholesterol and increase HDL cholesterol, both effects which should protect against cardiovascular disease. However, the research results in women have been mixed and have not shown a significant association, either positive or negative. In fact, estrogen use among men increased heart disease.[19] The hormone progesterone (progestogens or progestin) may increase LDL cholesterol and lower HDL cholesterol, and it has been linked to an increased risk of heart attack and stroke.[20]

While one study that took cigarette smoking into consideration supported the hypothesis that the postmenopausal use of estrogen therapy reduces the risk of coronary heart disease,[21] another study published at the same time found no benefits from estrogen use but rather an increased stroke rate among nonsmoking estrogen users and an increased heart attack rate among smoking estrogen users.[22]

More research is needed on the effects of postmenopausal hormones (both estrogens and progestogens) on cardiovascular diseases. Unfortunately, the 2 million to 3 million women in the United States who are taking these hormones before all the long-term effects are known are themselves the unwitting subjects of this research.

HEART ATTACK

When the supply of blood to the heart is interrupted, because of narrowed arteries or a blood clot, part of the heart muscle dies from lack of oxygen and nutrients. This is called a heart attack, or myocardial infarction (MI).

How to Know You Are Having a Heart Attack

You will be the first one to suspect you are having a heart attack. Look for these signals:

- Uncomfortable pressure, fullness, tightness, squeezing, or pain in the center of your chest, lasting two minutes or more. The pain may fade away and then return. Unlike the pain of angina, the pain of a heart attack does not go away after physical or emotional stress ceases.
- Pain that spreads to your arms, shoulders, neck, jaw or stomach.
- Severe pain, dizziness, fainting, sweating, nausea, or shortness of breath.

Everyone does not experience all these symptoms. If you experience any of these conditions, try to stay calm. Do not panic, but do not wait. Get help immediately. The sooner you begin treatment, the greater your chances of surviving. Call your local emergency rescue number or go to the emergency room at a nearby hospital. In the emergency room, a health care practitioner will take your history, give you a complete physical exam, take an electrocardiogram (EKG), and draw blood for lab tests.

Diagnosis of Heart Disease

A wide variety of tests exists to determine whether someone has heart disease or has had a heart attack. All tests are not necessary for everyone who suspects heart disease—some are expensive and should only be performed when necessary. Ask your doctor why a particular test is being ordered and what you will learn from it.

An *electrocardiogram (EKG)* to identify abnormal heart rhythms is usually the first test performed when heart disease is suspected. This can be done in a medical office or hospital.

Exercise testing, or *stress testing*, primarily determines the nature and cause of any chest pain and is useful in the early detection of coronary heart disease. Through graded exercise, the stress test determines whether the coronary circulation is capable of increasing the oxygen supply to the heart muscle. Unfortunately, the results for women often show damage when none exists (called a false positive result). Some physicians, therefore, always order thallium scanning (radionuclear imaging) along with stress testing for women. Other physicians, to avoid unnecessary testing and save expenses, order thallium scanning only if the stress test is positive.

Radionuclear imaging, sometimes called a *thallium test* or *thallium scanning*, is a technique in which a small amount of thallium, a short-lived radioactive substance, is injected into an arm vein. The thallium circulates with the blood and concentrates in the heart. There it gives off gamma rays that are translated by computer into a picture. The physician can tell if any areas of heart muscle have been damaged by heart attack, or if any part of the heart is not getting enough blood and oxygen, the cause of angina. This test may also be done while exercising.

Echocardiography uses sound waves to study the heart's structure and function. It is noninvasive (does not penetrate the body and therefore does not cause pain or discomfort). It can be helpful in identifying patients with disease of the heart valves, an often overlooked problem with the elderly.

A *Holter monitor exam* is a twenty-four-hour EKG. You wear a portable EKG machine for twenty-four hours. This gives the doctor a longer record of your heart's activity than she or he can get in the examining room.

Coronary arteriography, sometimes called *cardiac catheterization*, is a procedure in which a long tube, or catheter, is inserted in an artery and dye is passed through it. The dye allows X-rays to show whether any arteries to the brain or heart are blocked. Catheterization is not recommended for everyone, especially not for the elderly. If your heart disease can be managed with medication, or if you are considered a high-risk candidate for bypass surgery, little useful information will be gained from performing a catheterization.[23]

Treatment for Heart Attack

Most people who have suffered a heart attack are admitted to a hospital coronary care unit (CCU) or intensive care unit (ICU). Here their heart is monitored, and life-saving services are available in case they are needed. For some people, however, the atmosphere in the ICU or CCU is itself tension-producing and may slow recovery.

Two kinds of drugs are prescribed for people who have suffered a heart attack: those that increase the flow of blood, bringing extra oxygen to the heart; and those that reduce the need for oxygen.

After a heart attack, the blocked artery that was responsible for the heart attack may need to be opened, allowing the heart to get adequate oxygen. New treatments to open blocked arteries have been developed. These use the same process as cardiac catheterization. One method involves injecting streptokinase, a clot-dissolving drug, through a catheter or directly into the artery. If used within a few hours after a heart attack, streptokinase will dissolve the clot within twenty minutes. It is not recommended for anyone who has a bleeding disorder or who has recently had surgery. Although streptokinase is no longer considered experimental by most physicians, it is not widely used, especially not in small hospitals. Tissue plasminogen activator (TPA) is a newer drug with fewer adverse effects that is beginning to replace streptokinase. The sooner you get treatment after you suspect you have had a heart attack, the more likely it will be effective.

Another method used to clear a blocked artery is balloon angioplasty. In this treatment, a small balloon is inserted and is inflated at the site of the obstruction to clear a partially blocked artery. For some patients, this procedure is a less expensive alternative to coronary bypass surgery. It does not require the chest to be opened and involves shorter hospitalization, lower cost—$4,000 to $5,000, compared to $20,000 for a bypass—and shorter recovery time. Laser procedures combined with angioplasty are more effective than angioplasty alone.[24]

Cardiac bypass surgery is sometimes performed when an artery is blocked and cannot be cleared with medication or balloon angioplasty. Surgeons use a vein, usually taken from the leg, or an artery from the chest[25] and construct a detour, or bypass, around the blocked artery. In bypass surgery, the chest is opened and a heart/lung machine keeps blood circulating while the new segment is attached to the heart.

I had a history of heart condition. You can imagine what it's like going someplace and never knowing what's going to happen. I was so tired and depressed all the time that I wasn't enjoying my retirement. After the second heart attack they suggested a bypass operation but I wasn't ready for it then. They tried all the medicines and nothing worked. After my third heart attack I decided that was enough, I would have the surgery.

I did quite well and had as much physical therapy as Medicare would pay for—the limit was $500 for one year. At $49 a session, three times a week, I didn't have as much as I should have had.

I do what I can to keep fit. I bought a stationary bike and ride it a half hour, five days a week. I walk a mile several times a week. I cut down on meat and stay away from cold cuts. I haven't had any bacon for two years. At the hospital where I had the surgery they said, "Be careful, but have it, don't crave it," so I have a hot dog once a year at a Labor Day cookout. I'm a good vegetable eater and since my operation I planted a garden. Today I'm making eggplant parmegiana with low-fat mozzarella cheese. My cholesterol level was high for years but is better now. My blood pressure is fine.

I get tired and have my limitations but I can do so much more than I could before. I have entered a three-mile walk this month for persons over the age of forty. [a sixty-nine-year-old woman]

Some women who have bypass surgery experience dramatic relief from pain and lead physically active lives again. However, bypass surgery primarily relieves pain; there is no proof that surgery increases life expectancy for most people. For only one group, those with obstruction of the left main coronary artery, does surgery improve chances of survival. Yet over 100,000 operations are performed each year at a total cost of over $1.5 billion.

Several studies have shown that a more conservative approach is as effective as bypass surgery for most people.[26] These studies suggest that bypass surgery could be avoided through the use of medication, exercise, diet, stress reduction, and smoking cessation. These changes must be made even with surgery or the bypass may clog.

Before having bypass surgery, you may want

to consult with a cardiologist who specializes in the *medical* rather than surgical treatment of heart disease. This will ensure that you get opinions from two different perspectives. Finally, death rates for bypass surgery vary from hospital to hospital. Generally, medical centers with specialized surgical teams have the best records. The more often a team operates, the better their record. *Never consider undergoing bypass surgery at a hospital where fewer than 200 procedures a year are performed.*

Many women are concerned about how their scars will look after surgery, and they should ask.

My scar starts above my ankle and goes almost up to my throat. I love to swim, but the scar turns blue when I get it wet. This summer I didn't swim or wear shorts. I don't care too much about my chest scar. They sewed it on the inside and it doesn't show as much as the scar on my leg. The men at rehab all bragged about their scars, whose was longer and meaner looking. We didn't do that. Some women in the rehab program only wear turtlenecks or high-neck blouses, because they don't want anyone to see their scar. [a sixty-eight-year-old woman]

Some Other Surgical Procedures

Modern heart surgery may extend life and improve its quality. Unfortunately, it can also hold out false promises and be performed unnecessarily, at great cost to the individual and to society.

Pacemakers

A bundle of nerves in the upper-right chamber of the heart—our natural pacemaker—transmits electrical impulses that control our heartbeat. When these impulses slow down or become irregular or blocked, we may not experience any symptoms or we may experience weakness, breathlessness, slow pulse beat, lack of increased pulse beat when exercising, or even loss of consciousness.

No treatment is needed in many instances. In some instances, a battery-powered artificial pacemaker is used externally for a time or implanted permanently under the skin of the chest wall. The artificial pacemaker controls the heart rate by sending out rhythmic electrical impulses to activate the contractions of the heart. The implantation carries a risk, as does any surgery. The Food and Drug Administration reviews the safety and effectiveness of new models of pacemakers developed since 1976, but does not review so thoroughly those pacemakers which are similar to models developed before passage of the 1976 medical-device amendments to the Food, Drug and Cosmetic Act.[27]

As useful and necessary as pacemakers are in many instances, estimates of their overuse range as high as 75 percent. Controversy also continues about whether unnecessary or no-longer-necessary pacemakers should be removed.[28]

An artificial pacemaker's batteries usually last an average of four years, despite claims made by some manufacturers that theirs will last longer. Monitor your pacemaker by telephone with a pacemaker monitoring company to detect problems before they are serious. A recent study of pacemakers led to the suggestion that they be checked more often and earlier than some manufacturers recommend.[29] Medical insurance policies do not but should be required to cover the costs of monitoring pacemakers.

Valve Replacement

Some procedures, such as replacement of the valves in the heart, can affect positively both the length of life and its quality.

For at least two years I had progressively less strength and was feeling more and more tired. I couldn't do physical activity like gardening, which I loved. I also felt psychologically under a cloud, that my life was draining out. I wasn't feeling pain in my chest but I was feeling spasms, quivering, palpitations, and butterflies that I thought would go away. I kept attributing these symptoms to getting older, but when I had headaches, which I never had before, and couldn't do a lot of walking, I knew something was the matter.

I went to the doctor where they did all the tests and said that I needed a valve replacement within a month. I read up on it a bit first and then went into the hospital for twelve days, five of them in intensive care. After I came home the stairs were difficult for a while and there were some days when I couldn't walk very far. I gradually went back to work. I started feeling really great after about six months. [a fifty-four-year-old woman]

Transplants and Artificial Hearts

Research in cardiology today often emphasizes sophisticated treatment of existing disease conditions at the expense of prevention and early intervention. Newspapers are filled with stories about patients receiving procedures costing

$200,000 or more, while prevention programs go unreported and often unfunded. Insurance plans pay for heart transplants yet do not pay for us to attend a cardiopulmonary resuscitation (CPR)* course to learn how to save lives or support group meetings to help us change habits in order to lower our risk of developing heart disease.

STROKE

A stroke, sometimes called a "shock," occurs when the blood vessels that supply oxygen to the brain are blocked. One of the most common forms of stroke, cerebral thrombosis, occurs when a clot develops in an artery damaged by atherosclerosis. In cerebral embolism, a wandering clot, or embolism, lodges in one of the arteries, blocking blood to the brain. In a cerebral hemorrhage, a burst artery floods the brain tissue with blood, causing blood loss to the brain and pressure on the brain tissue. This bleeding can be caused by a head injury or an aneurysm—a blood-filled pouch that balloons out from a weak spot in the artery wall.

Long-standing hypertension is a major cause of strokes. Diabetic women, especially those with hypertension, are at greater-than-average risk of stroke and should especially take action to keep their blood pressure normal.

How to Know You Are Having a Stroke

The following symptoms may be warnings that you are about to have a stroke or are having little strokes already. Even if they are temporary, you should not ignore them.

* Temporary weakness or numbness in the face, arm, or leg on one side of the body.
* A severe, persistent headache.
* Temporary loss of speech or difficulty speaking or understanding speech.
* Temporary dimness or loss of vision.
* Dizziness or unsteadiness, possibly causing you to fall.
* Memory loss.

*CPR is an emergency procedure combining mouth-to-mouth resuscitation and closed-chest heart massage that can be performed by a lay person while waiting for trained help to arrive. In Seattle, Washington, the extensive training of the population in CPR is credited with saving 200 lives annually.

I was frightened to realize that there were parts of three days I couldn't reconstruct. I usually have a fabulous memory; people call me for details from a meeting held seven years ago. And now I couldn't recall last week's appointments, phone calls, or letters. I was in a real panic by the time I got to my doctor's office.

A thorough examination turned up things I hadn't even noticed—a generalized weakness on my left side, the inability to make a fist, a little problem with my speech, and bruises on my left leg that suggested I'd been bumping into things. My blood pressure was very high. The doctor had me see a neurologist that same day. After many tests the final diagnosis was made—I'd had several strokes. [a sixty-year-old woman]

Little strokes, or transient ischemic attacks (TIAs), sometimes precede a major stroke by days, weeks, or months. These are generally warning signs of a major stroke to come. If you experience any of the symptoms listed above, *see your health care practitioner right away.*

Treatment for Strokes

Treatment for strokes starts with treatment of those very conditions that are also risk factors for strokes: hypertension, cardiac disease, TIAs, high hematocrit (percentage of red cells in the blood), and diabetes. TIAs are treated with

Elizabeth Layton

322

aspirin or other anticlotting medication to reduce the possibility of forming new clots.

None of what followed my stroke was easy. Getting my hypertension under control proved to be difficult. I found it hard to let my children and my friends do things for me. Most of all, I had to face my own feelings. I felt older. I was depressed and scared. Would I have another, more crippling, stroke? Just how much would my life have to change?

I continued to work and now, three years later, I'm about to take a new job. I don't forget anything important. I walk and use a stationary bike and have cut down on fats and sugar, so I feel great and thinner. My blood pressure was 130 over 70 yesterday. The amount of medication has been reduced over time. Taking it has become just one more thing I do regularly each day— like brushing my teeth. [the same sixty-year-old woman]

RECOVERY AND REHABILITATION*

After heart attacks and surgery, people often reevaluate their lives and find new directions.

I now celebrate two birthdays—the day I was born and the day I had the surgery! [a sixty-nine-year-old woman after bypass surgery]

After surgery I took a trip to Europe. I felt well physically and I was beginning to think of alternative things I might do. Seeing people dress and think differently had an effect on me. New possibilities presented themselves. I felt a physical and emotional connection between my heart and my experience that I hadn't completely grasped before.

When I came home I started seeing a therapist. She said, "Now you have a new life and you want to figure out what to do with it." One of my goals is to make more connections and to get involved in organizational and political work. I'd like to change my job to one where I can meet more people. I realize I'd be better off if I had more friends and more associations with other women. [a fifty-four-year-old woman]

Formerly, a person who had a heart attack was told to rest in bed for three weeks. Recent

*Not all insurance plans cover rehabilitation, but Medicare covers some of the costs. In some states, Medicaid does not cover rehab programs, making it impossible for Medicaid recipients to get vocational services, which would in some cases lead to paid employment and help them get off Medicaid.

evidence shows that this can be harmful. Rehabilitation, or rehab, programs help people who have had a heart attack or cardiac surgery return to health. Many rehab programs begin in the ICU or CCU, where you can begin doing ankle circles and limited-range exercises while your heart is monitored. By the time you leave the hospital, you will be walking and climbing stairs. In a good rehab program you will learn exercises to continue at home and diet changes to follow. You should be fully informed about any medications you will be taking.

What About Sex?

A common myth about heart disease is that having sex will cause heart attack or even death. This is not true. Nor does a heart attack or heart surgery or stroke mean an end to a satisfying sex life. Most women find that after their initial recovery, lovemaking is as pleasurable as before. (See Sexuality chapter.)

The second phase of rehabilitation is usually an outpatient program lasting about twelve sessions. This combines monitored exercise, discussion groups, and education. Here you have a chance to increase your physical capacity and talk about your concerns with people who have experienced a similar trauma.

After my heart attack, my morale was very low. In rehab, I was with people who had already gone through what I was going through. I felt encouraged. [a seventy-two-year-old woman]

Most rehab involves counseling, along with occupational/vocational therapy for patients who aren't able to return to their previous jobs.

A third phase of rehab programs continues the exercise component (often in groups and sometimes at a rehab facility) without monitoring. Some women choose to exercise at home and walk on their own, instead of participating in this part of the program. Other women stay in rehab for the support and motivation of exercising in groups.

Physical, speech, and occupational therapy help people who have had strokes regain all the skills possible. A stroke can affect speech, behavior, thought patterns, memory, and ability to understand, and sometimes can cause paralysis.

Mikki Ansin/The Picture Cube

In the past, rehabilitation stressed compensation for the disabled parts of the body, so the stroke victim depended more on the unaffected side of the body. Today's approach to rehabilitation emphasizes relearning control over the affected side.

She heard the doctor say as he left her hospital room, "There can be no hope of recovery from this." She could see everything; words were exploding in her mind but none escaped into sound. She couldn't believe the doctor's words. Would she be helpless for years to come? She was a photographer. Would she never take another picture?

"It isn't so!" The voice of the nurse reached her. She was leaning over the bed, her face very angry. "He shouldn't have said that!" The nurse was whispering furiously. Recovery was possible. She had seen it often in people who put their will into it. A tremendous sense of confidence welled up in her. Of course, she knew the nurse was right. Relief flooded her, and she became possessed of a single thought: recovery. The nurse stayed with her for an hour, talked with her, encouraged her.

That night, she slept soundly, dreamlessly. The next morning she glanced down at her hand on the white sheet. Two fingers on her right hand flickered. Watching

her hand, she willed it to happen again. Slowly her forefinger lifted, then her second finger. The little movements occurred slowly, bit by bit.

On the third day her speech returned. By the tenth day she was able to lift her right hand up to her chest. The next day she lifted both hands, a few inches below her heart. A deep sigh went through her. It would be all right, just a matter of time and effort. She wanted to tell her family, the nurse, everyone, just what it meant to her to lift her hands in that gesture with just enough space to hold her camera. That was how she knew she wasn't finished. She could go back to work again. [a seventy-year-old woman]*

Families and friends should be included in the rehabilitation of persons who have had strokes. Not only must they be kept up-to-date about expectations for the patient, but they can help in the process by encouraging her or him to reach the highest level of independence possible.

*Adapted with permission from the section about Eleanor Milder Lawrence in *Gifts of Age: Portraits and Essays of 32 Remarkable Women* by Charlotte Painter and Pamela Valois. San Francisco: Chronicle Books, 1985, pp. 126–9.

A massive stroke impaired my ability to function independently and seriously damaged my physical and emotional stability. Facing life was difficult. Learning to swim was one of my most effective coping techniques. Two swimming sessions weekly (forty-five minutes each) increased my strength and endurance. The constant verbal encouragement by the therapist and members of the group for even a tiny accomplishment provided enormous support and was a tremendous morale booster. We adopted the motto "Press on regardless." I discovered that working in a group was the most effective technique for helping me and my family cope with a long-term disability. [a thirty-eight-year-old woman]

NOTES

1. Franz H. Messerli, ed., *Cardiovascular Diseases in the Elderly.* Boston: Martinus Nijhoff, 1984, p. 65.

2. Ibid., p. 77.

3. John Langone, "Heart Attack and Cholesterol." *Discover*, Vol. 5, March 1984, pp. 20–3.

4. "Study Says a Low Cholesterol Diet Does Little to Increase Longevity." *The Boston Globe*, April 1, 1987, p. 11. Note that the headline states the finding for men at low risk for heart disease, not the different finding for women.

5. National Institutes of Health, *Lowering Blood Cholesterol to Prevent Heart Disease.* Consensus Development Conference Statement, Vol. 5, No. 7 (December 10–2, 1984), p. 5.

6. Nathan Pritikin with Patrick McGrady, Jr., *The Pritikin Program for Diet and Exercise.* New York: Grosset & Dunlap, 1979, p. 16.

7. American Heart Association, *An Older Person's Guide to Cardiovascular Health.* National Center of the AHA, 7320 Greenville Ave., Dallas, TX 75231, 1983.

8. Walter C. Willett, "Cigarette Smoking and Non-fatal Myocardial Infarction in Women." *American Journal of Epidemiology*, Vol. 113, No. 5 (May 1981), pp. 575–82.

9. R. Paffenburger, "Physical Activity and Fatal Attack." In E. Amsterdam, ed., *Exercise in Cardiovascular Health and Disease.* New York: York Medical Books, 1977.

10. Francis D. Dunn, "Coronary Heart Disease and Acute Myocardial Infarction." In Messerli, op. cit., p. 156.

11. Ulf Smith, Report at the American Heart Association Seminar, Monterey, CA, 1985. Cited by Richard A. Knox, *The Boston Globe*, January 18, 1985, p. 8.

12. Per Bjorntorp, "Regional Patterns of Fat Distribution: Health Implications," in *Health Implications of Obesity*, program and abstracts. National Institutes of Health Consensus Development Conference, February 11–3, 1985, p. 35.

13. Dag S. Thelle, et al., "The Troms Heart Study: Does Coffee Raise Serum Cholesterol?" *The New England Journal of Medicine*, Vol. 308, No. 24 (June 16, 1983), pp. 1454–7.

14. Daan Kromhout, et al., "The Inverse Relation Between Fish Consumption and 20-Year Mortality from Coronary Heart Disease." *The New England Journal of Medicine*, Vol. 312, No. 19 (May 9, 1985), pp. 1205–9; and Beverly E. Phillipson, et al., "Reduction of Plasma Lipids, Lipoproteins, and Apoproteins by Dietary Fish Oils in Patients with Hypertriglyceridemia." *The New England Journal of Medicine*, Vol. 312, No. 9 (May 9, 1985), pp. 1210–6.

15. Suzanne Haynes and Manning Feinleib, "Women, Work, and Coronary Heart Disease: Prospective Finding from the Framingham Heart Study." *American Journal of Public Health*, Vol. 70, No. 2 (February 1980), pp. 113–41.

16. Nancy R. Cook, et al., "Regression Analysis of Changes in Blood Pressure with Oral Contraceptive Use." *American Journal of Epidemiology*, Vol. 121, No. 4 (April 1985), pp. 530–40.

17. Boston Women's Health Book Collective, *The New Our Bodies, Ourselves*, New York: Simon and Schuster, 1984, p. 37.

18. Charles H. Hennekens, et al., "Oral Contraceptive Use, Cigarette Smoking and Myocardial Infarction." *British Journal of Family Planning*, Vol. 5, 1979, pp. 66–7.

19. Patricia A. Kaufert and Sonja M. McKinlay, "Estrogen-Replacement Therapy: The Production of Medical Knowledge and the Emergence of Policy." In Ellen Lewin and Virginia Oleson, eds., *Women, Health, & Healing: Toward a New Perspective.* New York: Tavistock Publications, 1985, p. 116.

20. Erkki Hirvonen, et al., "Effects of Different Progestogens on Lipoproteins During Postmenopausal Replacement Therapy." *The New England Journal of Medicine*, Vol. 304, No. 10 (March 5, 1981), pp. 560–3.

21. Meir J. Stampfer, et al., "A Prospective Study of Postmenopausal Estrogen Therapy and Coronary Heart Disease." The Nurses' Health Study. *The New England Journal of Medicine*, Vol. 313, No. 17 (October 24, 1985), pp. 1044–9. See also Graham A. Colditz, et al. "Menopause and the Risk of Coronary Heart Disease in Women." *The New England Journal of Medicine*, Vol. 316, No. 18 (April 30, 1987), pp. 1105–10.

22. Peter W. F. Wilson, et al., "Postmenopausal Estrogen Use, Cigarette Smoking, and Cardiovascular Morbidity in Women over 50." The Framingham Study. *The New England Journal of Medicine*, Vol. 313, No. 17 (October 24, 1985), pp. 1038–43.

23. Messerli, op. cit., p. 155.

24. Larry Tye, "Lasers Show Promise for Heart Patients." *The Boston Globe*, January 20, 1987, p. 6. Report of the American Heart Association held in Monterey, California, January 19, 1987.

25. Floyd D. Loop, et al., "Influence of the Internal-

Mammary-Artery Graft on 10-Year Survival and Other Cardiac Events." *The New England Journal of Medicine*, Vol. 314, No. 1 (January 2, 1986), pp. 1–6.

26. Marcia Millman, *The Unkindest Cut: Life in the Backrooms of Medicine*. New York: William Morrow and Co., 1978; and Office of Technology Assessment, U.S. Congress, *Assessing the Efficacy and Safety of Medical Technologies*, GPO Stock No. 052-003-00593-0, 1978; and Kenneth M. Kent, "Coronary Angioplasty: A Decade of Experience." *The New England Journal of Medicine*, Vol. 316, No. 18, April 30, 1987, pp. 1148–50.

27. Esther R. Rome and Jill Wolhandler, "F.D.A. Is Lax in Enforcing Medical Regulations." Letter to the Editor, *The New York Times*, November 30, 1985, p.

22. Information on pacemaker models can be obtained from the medical devices section of the Food and Drug Administration, tel. (202) 427-7594.

28. "Correspondence: Complications of Permanent Cardiac Pacemakers." *The New England Journal of Medicine*, Vol. 313, No. 17 (October 24, 1985), pp. 1085–8, in response to B. Phibbs and H. J. L. Marriott, "Complications of Permanent Transvenous Pacing." *The New England Journal of Medicine*, Vol. 312, No. 22 (May 30, 1985), pp. 1428–32.

29. Leonard Dreifus and Douglas Zipes, report at the American College of Cardiology Meeting, March 1985. Associated Press report in *The Boston Globe*, March 12, 1985, p. 3.

24

CANCER

by Sharon Bray and Diana Laskin Siegal

Breast Cancer by Jane Hyman

Colorectal Cancer by Edith Lenneberg

Special thanks to Norma Meras Swenson and Jane Jewell

Forty-nine years ago when I had my first surgery and radiation for ovarian cancer, people were so afraid of cancer that they couldn't use the word. They would say, "She has C." They lied to me but I knew they were lying when they gave me radiation. I'd read enough to know I had cancer. Today things are better, more open, people talk more. Now I visit other cancer patients and they mostly know. They can talk about it more now. [a seventy-five-year-old woman]

The diagnosis of cancer is not a death sentence; many live long lives with the disease and eventually die of other causes at a ripe age. Most of us know at least one person who has lived many productive years after a diagnosis of cancer. The same woman continues:

Eight years ago, at age sixty-seven, I developed colorectal cancer and had a colostomy. I went back to work afterwards and I wear a bag all the time. I do everything I did before. I'm in a relationship with a man and it doesn't make any difference to him. I walk a lot. I like to keep my shape. I tell my doctors, "I feel good, I just get cancer once in a while."

While it is true that most of us will never get cancer, three out of ten of us will; so we need to know more about it for ourselves and for those close to us. We have heard stories of painful, lingering death and of treatments that sound more miserable than the disease itself. We may worry that we will lose a breast or go bald and be less attractive, less womanly. Cancer is still one of the most feared diseases, even though women's risk of death from heart and circulatory diseases is much higher.

I Have Held Hands with Fear

I have held hands
with fear;
We have gone steady
together.

Sorrow has been
my mate;
We have been bed-
companions.

The days of my night
have been long.
They have stretched
to eternity.

Yet have I outlived
them.
And so shall you.

Mitzi Kornetz

What Is Cancer?

We call it by one name, but cancer takes many forms, alike only on a basic biological level. The cancerous patch of skin removed from a forehead bears little resemblance to breast cancer or to leukemia until we understand how cancerous cells develop, grow, and spread through a living body.

Most cells in our bodies reproduce themselves and grow in order to repair or replace damaged organs and tissues. But sometimes the cells change so that they lose their ability to function properly, and they begin an abnormal process of uncontrolled growth. Cancerous lung cells, for example, lose the ability of normal lung cells to transfer oxygen into blood cells. Scientists think this change begins as a result of contact with carcinogens (cancer-causing agents). While the process of normal cells evolving into cancer cells is not fully understood, it appears that the abnormal change happens in steps. Some carcinogens *initiate* the change and others *promote* the process. Some carcinogens may be both initiators and promoters. Others work as a destructive team, as when alcohol promotes mouth and throat cancers started by tobacco.[1]

Some inborn genetic factors may predispose a woman to developing a cancer, making her more vulnerable to carcinogens. Many experts now believe it is likely that everyone has some cancerous cells at one time or another, but our immune systems eliminate them before they develop sufficiently to cause problems. Virtually all experts agree that 85 to 95 percent of all cancers are *environmentally* caused, that is, from substances in cigarettes, air, water, food, cosmetics, or from workplace hazards or medical treatment. Increasingly, women are banding together with neighbors and colleagues to fight for a safer environment.

How Cancer Grows

At its earliest stage, a cancer is limited to one location, one organ, perhaps one cell. The number of cancer cells may increase rapidly or very slowly. (Some cancers are not discovered until up to twenty years after the first cells change.) A cancer may totally destroy the ability of that one organ to function without ever spreading to other parts of the body—or it may spread.

One kind of spread occurs when the mass of cancerous cells in one organ (a "primary" cancer) touches another organ and begins to grow in it, also. This regional growth (sometimes called a "secondary" cancer) should not be confused with a new cancer (called a second "primary") that grows in another place.

Another kind of growth occurs when cancer cells are carried to other parts of the body from the primary site by the blood or lymph system and begin to replace normal cells in other organs; the cancer has then become "systemic" or "metastatic." This may never occur, or may not occur until many years after cancer is first discovered. It also may happen simultaneously with the first growth of cells in the primary site. Many cancers are slow-growing, produce no symptoms, and are not discovered until many years after the cancer begins. Both regional spread and systemic distribution of cancer may be referred to as metastasis.

A number system (I–IV, from localized to metastasized) is used to describe the stages of cancer according to where it appears to have spread. When evaluating research and other people's experiences with various treatments, always take the type and stage of the cancer into consideration.

RISK AND PREVENTION

Lists of cancer-risk factors are based on statistics and on scientific studies. Many risk factors are identified by the fact that, since so many people with a particular cancer have them, it seems unlikely to be mere coincidence. Some risks, such as exposure to asbestos, have also been studied in laboratory tests on cultured cells in dishes (in vitro) or in animals, where scientists have been able to observe the cancer-causing process.

If you know about some risk factors, you may decide to change your habits to reduce the risk. Those risks you cannot control—things that happened at work years ago, your family health record, where you live—may alert you to watch for symptoms and to be conscientious about regular checkups. Even though early cancer detection does not guarantee cure, it does help in many cases.

Some risk factors may involve things you do not want to give up. If you are eighty years old and love pickles and bacon, giving them up is not likely to make much difference in whether you will ever have cancer (though there are other reasons to avoid the salt and the fat they contain). On the other hand, research has shown that giving up smoking, even for people who have smoked for fifty years, very quickly improves health.[2] **Smoking is the number one controllable cause of cancer.**

Anyone who has a history of cancer is at risk of developing another one. Reducing the risk factors, especially stopping smoking, may help prevent further cancers. Regular checkups with a health practitioner can help discover new cancers early.

Sometimes we make important choices for our bodies in spite of known future risks. For example, the immune system has to be suppressed in anyone receiving an organ transplant so that the organ from the donor will not be rejected. People who have had a kidney transplant have a higher risk of cancer years after the transplant than people who did not undergo such treatment.

Things You Can Do to Reduce Your Risk of Cancer[3]

(In the list below, factors which minimize the risk of breast cancer specifically as well as other cancers in general are marked with an asterisk.)

*1. Don't smoke. Avoid smoke-filled places. Smoking also markedly increases the risks from other carcinogens such as alcohol, asbestos, and industrial agents. Don't use smokeless tobacco products such as snuff and chewing tobacco, which also cause cancer.

2. Know the risks and follow the health and safety rules of your workplace. Where needed, wear protective clothing and use safety equipment. If your employer does not enforce safety rules, ask for help from your state's Department of Health or Attorney General.

*3. Avoid unnecessary X-rays whenever possible. Don't hesitate to ask your doctor if an X-ray is necessary, but do not refuse an X-ray needed for a diagnosis because you fear cancer. If you need an X-ray, be sure shields are used to protect other parts of your body, especially the trunk.

*4. Avoid taking estrogen except for severe symptoms that have not responded to other treatments. If you do take estrogen, ask about combining it with progestin, which reduces the risk of endometrial cancer. (Progestin does not reduce the other risks of using estrogens, such as gallbladder disease, and progestin may even increase the risk of breast cancer and heart disease. See Osteoporosis chapter.)

5. Eat a well-balanced diet with a variety of foods (see Eating Well chapter).

- Eat a variety of whole grains, vegetables and fruits rich in bran and fiber—grown without pesticides (if available and affordable).
- Eat foods high in beta carotene and vitamin A: carrots, pumpkin, sweet potatoes, cantaloupe, spinach, winter squash, greens, apricots, broccoli. Eat cruciferous vegetables such as kale, broccoli, cauliflower, cabbage, Brussels sprouts, greens, bok choy, kohlrabi, turnips, and rutabagas. Vitamin A pills are *not* a substitute for beta carotene, and high doses can be toxic.
- Eat foods high in vitamin C: citrus fruits, sweet peppers, leafy greens, broccoli, cauliflower, tomatoes, fresh potatoes, berries, melons, bean sprouts. Eating the whole fruit gives you more nutrients than just drinking the juice.
- Eat foods high in selenium: brewer's yeast, garlic, onions, asparagus, tuna, shrimp, mushrooms, whole grains, brown rice. Eggs, liver, and kidneys contain selenium but are also high in saturated fat. Selenium can be toxic in high doses, so it is best to get it in foods instead of pills.

*6. Reduce the fat in your diet (see Eating Well chapter). Adding fish may be beneficial.

7. Minimize consumption of smoked, salted, or pickled foods, and avoid chemical additives, including food coloring.

*8. Limit or eliminate alcohol.

*9. If you are substantially overweight, try to take off weight by increasing exercise and by reducing fat and sugar in your food. There is evidence that people who weigh more than 40 percent over recent recommendations have higher rates of cancer.

10. Maintain frequent and regular bowel movements by exercising, drinking water, and including fiber in your diet.

11. Avoid sunburn and excessive tanning, especially if your have light skin. You do need some sun for vitamin D, or foods or supplements with vitamin D such as cod liver oil, if you live in the North during the winter.

*12. Avoid hair dyes made from petroleum bases.

Most of the above are really basic cancer preventive care measures that also promote general good health. Doing as many of them as your willpower, interest, and life-style allow should make your body all the stronger to prevent cancer or to help you fight it. While quitting smoking, eating better, or making other changes will not guarantee you a cancer-free life, they will influence your statistical chances and should make you generally healthier. Some choices seem to be contradictory. Cancer experts may warn you against alcohol, while heart experts may advise that a couple of ounces a day is good for you. Fat women have higher cancer risk but lower risk of osteoporosis. Given the incomplete knowledge of these diseases today, the best you can do is emphasize moderation in lifestyle and understand your own body and health history.

Environmental and Occupational Risk Factors

It can be upsetting to read cancer statistics for your state or town if you happen to live in an area with higher than average rates of specific cancers. The fact that most places vary considerably from one year to another indicates that higher rates may be only chance variations. Contaminated water supplies, toxic-waste dumps, nuclear radiation, and other environmental factors, however, may contribute to higher than expected cancer rates. So does living or working in buildings without adequate ventilation. Individuals can be effective through organized community action to prevent, publicize, regulate, and clean up some of these problems. Actions in several states against companies that pollute the air or water supply have been started by women who noticed something unusual.

Some higher rates of cancer may also be caused by natural environmental factors. If you have light skin, for example, the closer you live to the equator, the higher your risk of skin cancer related to sunshine.

There are clear links between certain occupational hazards and diseases. Many common household products contain carcinogens, and some studies show that housewives have higher than average rates of cancer. Artists, craftswomen, laboratory and medical workers, and others should seek information about the proper handling and ventilation of the materials they use. There is increasing evidence that chemicals used in the microchip industry can cause immune system problems.[4] Always investigate the risks of any chemicals or equipment used at your work site.

Other Risk Factors You Cannot Control

Age. The longer you live, the greater your chances of discovering some kind of cancer. Half of all cancers are diagnosed in people over sixty-five. The cancer incidence begins to rise at about age thirty-five for women (and a little later for men). Cancer is the leading cause of death of women thirty-five to fifty-four, second for ages fifty-five to seventy-four, and third for ages seventy-five and older.[5]

Gender and Race. A higher percentage of men than women, and Blacks than whites, die from cancer. Controllable factors such as variations in smoking rates, access to health care, eating habits, and exposure to occupational hazards can account for some of the differences in these cancer statistics.

Family. Some cancers are found more often in people whose parents or close family members have had them. Be sure to inform your health care providers if anyone in your family has had or has died from cancer. Some cancers can be stopped early when family members are alert to a familial disposition or a common environmental hazard.

Let's Not Blame the Victim

Cancer patients face stigmas that have yet to be obliterated. Some people still think cancer is "catching," despite research that proves otherwise. Others believe that all cancers are inevitably fatal. These stigmas can lead to personal isolation and to discrimination in employment. Only three states have laws against such discrimination. Federal legislation was proposed in 1985 that would include people with a "cancer history" in the Federal employment anti-discrimination statute.[6] We need to continue to push lawmakers until this proposal is passed. We should also fight for state definitions of "disabled" to include people with cancer who require regular treatments over an extended period or who are unable to carry out major activities.

People with cancer often feel shame or guilt, wondering what they have done to be so punished. Sometimes they blame themselves, and others blame them also, for exposures to the risk factors that might have predisposed them to the disease. Many people still try to hide the fact that they have cancer—even from close family and friends. But the stigma will never go away until we all learn as much as possible, as well as talk much more to each other, about our cancer experiences. We should not accept isolation when we most need support.

Right after the surgery, a lot of my friends came to cheer me up. But I had to put them at ease first. They didn't know what to say. The cancer was like a wall between us. So I just took a deep breath and started talking about it. Then it was all right. [a forty-year-old woman with breast cancer]

Much of what has been written about cancer ends up "blaming the victim." Particular personality traits have been attributed to persons with cancer, just as they were attributed in the last century to persons with tuberculosis.[7] Doctors themselves tend to hold patients responsible for their progress, giving great credit to "gallantry and grace in the face of hardship," and therefore by extension blaming those who do not get well for "not trying hard enough."[8]

There are two dangers in believing that your state of mind is the major influence on the course of your cancer: (1) You may suffer guilt and feelings of failure if your cancer advances to more destructive stages in spite of your own efforts. (2) You might abandon medical therapies that might actually help you. It is very important to get the best treatment you possibly can. Periods of anger, fear, grumpiness, depression, hopelessness, and passivity are common, as you can discover by talking with others who have experiences with cancer. The success or failure of any treatment is not caused by the strength or weakness of your faith in it, by living right, or being a happy person. One study found no relationship between "psychosocial" factors such as marital status, other companionship, work and life satisfaction, and hopefulness and how people with advanced cancers responded to treatment or how long they lived.[9] People who are at all times full of courage, grace, faith, and endless, cheerful endurance are rare. On the other hand, we should not abandon all sense of control. We have many decisions to make about how we will live and what treatments we will choose. Sometimes both the person with cancer (or other chronic disease) and those in relationships with her or him take more control over their lives and are stronger than before.

Cancer Research

Money and institutional support for cancer research come from private organizations, individuals, and government agencies. Scientists as individuals and in groups ask for more funding than is given out each year. Decisions may speed up one researcher's projects while forcing another to delay or abandon research. Many factors go into deciding who gets how much money for which kind of research: assessments of how many people could be helped; how close the investigator is to a breakthrough or to being able to put a discovery to a practical use; what other experts think of the excellence of the project; the applicant's past record; the reputation of the research institution (university, hospital, etc.); and a number of even more subjective criteria. Political considerations such as the state the applicant works in, the power of that state's Senators and Representatives, and the research institution's connections with decision-makers controlling funds do influence funding for cancer and other health research.

The special interests of politically powerful groups also influence funding of cancer research. Labor unions, for example, have demanded answers when their members have occupation-related cancers. The "right-to-breathe" anti-smoking movement has spurred research on links between smoking and various kinds of cancer. At the same time business and industry have used their economic and political power to block legislative action on substances and practices that seem to cause cancer or to limit the funding of relevant research.

Physician, Do No Harm!

Too often drugs or other methods for treating medical conditions are adopted without sufficient research; and too often they prove useless, and even harmful, only after many people have been exposed to them. Examples include radiation to pregnant women, resulting in leukemia in the child; radiation to the neck in childhood that leads to an increase in thyroid cancer in adulthood; DES (diethylstilbestrol) prescribed during pregnancy, leading to a rare cancer in female offspring and an increased risk of breast cancer in the mother many years later. Inform your physician if you had radiation to the upper body as a child to increase the chance that any possible cancers can be diagnosed and treated early.

Use of DES (a synthetic form of estrogen) was approved by the Food and Drug Administration in 1942 to stop milk flow in mothers and to treat menopausal symptoms and vaginal inflammation (vaginitis) despite studies as early as the 1930s showing estrogens to be carcinogenic in laboratory animals. In 1947, the FDA extended approval of DES in even higher doses for use during pregnancy, even though there had been no studies to examine potential effects on the fetus or on the mother. Doctors commonly prescribed DES if a woman had a history of miscarriage, diabetes, high blood pressure, or slight bleeding during pregnancy. Some researchers and drug companies recommended DES as a routine preventive measure to avoid miscarriage even before there were signs of trouble.

Although studies showed conclusively as early as 1953 that DES was ineffective in preventing miscarriage, the FDA did not warn against using it in pregnancy until 1971, after its link to cancer was established. Even now, doctors still prescribe it for nonpregnant women who may be infertile or suffering some other gynecological problem.

If your mother or you were among the group of pregnant women for whom DES was prescribed, be sure you and your daughter are checked as needed. Some DES sons also show abnormalities. (See DES Action in Resources, page 468.)

Some studies suggest that women who took DES when pregnant have a moderately increased incidence of breast cancer[10] and cancer of the uterus, cervix, or ovaries, and noncancerous tumors of the uterus. Most studies agree that there is a time lag of ten to twenty years between taking DES and developing a related disease. If you are a DES mother, get a professional breast exam every year in addition to performing monthly breast self-examination. Be sure your health care provider is informed of your DES history.

DIAGNOSIS

Why find out early? With some cancers, early detection offers the possibility of cure or substantial remission with years—even decades—of symptom-free life. Many cancers are more easily treated and controlled when discovered early. Certain skin cancers, cervical, and colo-

rectal cancer are common and can be detected early and cured.

- Basal- and squamous-cell skin cancers are visible, grow very slowly, and cure rates approach 100 percent following removal.
- Cervical cancer, which grows unnoticed, can be stopped before it leaves the cervix. A Pap smear every one to three years will catch cervical cancer at its earliest stages. Discuss the appropriate interval with your health care practitioner. Heterosexual women who are sexually active and whose partners do not use condoms should have regular tests. Not all abnormal Pap smears mean that cervical cancer will develop, however, and it is crucial to try to reverse changes in the cervical cells (dysplasia) before agreeing to surgery (see Hysterectomy and Oophorectomy chapter).

Other, less common cancers may also be treated effectively if discovered early. Sometimes, however, early detection does not prolong life. It only bolsters statistics on survival rates because, while the person survives only as long as most others who have the same disease, the counting starts sooner. Improved survival rates for lung cancer and breast cancer, for example, seem to be a direct result of earlier diagnosis and better recordkeeping rather than of improvement in actual survival rates. Many cancers cannot be detected earlier than the time when they produce symptoms.

Some women would rather not know they have cancer at all, especially if the symptoms are not likely to disturb their lives until a late stage shortly before death.

By the time my mother had cancer in her early forties, she had already had two close women friends about ten years older than her die of cancer. She was terrified of the disease and of the idea of death itself. So when her lung cancer was diagnosed, we didn't want anyone to tell her. But an X-ray therapist did anyway. She died about two months later, and it was as awful for all of us in the family as it was for her to die so young. [a forty-year-old woman]

Others take steps immediately:

My second husband had cancer, but I remember so many good times in our all-too-short marriage when his treatments led to remission. So when my mammogram showed a suspicious shadow, I was very motivated to do something about it. Yes, I was scared, but I knew I could get some help. As it turned out, my internist urged me to wait a couple of months before having a surgical biopsy, and the second mammogram was clear. [a sixty-year-old woman]

If you have one of the following warning signals publicized by the American Cancer Society, tell your nurse practitioner or physician:

- *C*hange in bowel or bladder habits
- *A* sore that does not heal
- *U*nusual bleeding or discharge
- *T*hickening or lump in breast or elsewhere
- *I*ndigestion or difficulty in swallowing
- *O*bvious change in a wart or mole
- *N*agging cough or hoarseness

None of these is a sure sign of any disease, and all have other possible causes besides cancer. But you should at least talk it over with a practitioner you can trust.

Diagnostic Methods

You may want to make choices about diagnostic methods in cases where several approaches are possible. Breast cancer is the most widely publicized disease where you can make these choices (see p. 342). Ask your practitioner to explain exactly the methods she or he uses, whether there are others, and why those others are not suggested for your specific condition.

X-rays, including mammograms, can suggest but not definitively diagnose cancer. Often cells are taken from a suspicious mass (the procedure is called a biopsy) to make a more certain diagnosis. A few cells can be removed and sent to a pathologist for examination. Needle biopsies can be done for breast, lung, or pancreatic tumors. A corkscrew-shaped needle (trucut needle biopsy) may be used to draw tissue out of a solid lump. A D&C (dilation and curettage) or an endometrial biopsy of the inside of the uterus yields cells to examine for endometrial cancer. Biopsies can be done through a small incision using an endoscope (a device consisting of a tube and an optical system) to reach polyps in the colon and stomach, and lung tumors.

Depending on the size and location of a lump, and whether there is more than one, the surgeon will recommend *incisional* or *excisional* biopsy. Incisional means taking a small slice, usually of a larger mass. Excisional means removing the entire lump (lumpectomy). The tissue removed is divided and prepared into permanent sections and sometimes frozen sections on glass slides for the pathologist to examine. Results from the frozen section are known quickly, while the permanent section, which is more accurate, takes at least twenty-four hours. Sometimes, as in abdominal surgery, the decision for additional surgery during the operation is made on the basis of the frozen section in order to avoid another operation. In other sites, such as breast cancer, there are good reasons to wait for the results of a permanent section before deciding on further treatment, so a frozen section is not needed.[11]

The slides prepared from the sections become part of your medical record. Slides and X-rays should be available if you want the opinion of another pathologist or radiologist.

Some women report complications of the diagnostic surgery itself; so make sure your surgeon is experienced in dealing with your specific condition and preferably has a reputation for conservative, but adequate, surgery.

LIVING WITH CANCER

"How long will I live?" is a frequently asked question. We fear death, and the statistics, showing little improvement in survival rates for many cancers, only compound the fear.

Every time a friend of mine dies of cancer, it's not necessarily the same kind of cancer as mine. It's not the same stage or in the same place, etc. But knowing that doesn't keep me from getting frightened. I wonder if I will keel over this afternoon or tomorrow. It's not intellectually sound, but I do feel that way. [a fifty-seven-year-old woman now being treated for cancer]

How many stories have you heard about people who were only supposed to live two years... or one year...or six months...five years ago? We marvel to see them "still going strong at seventy-five." Stories like these, mostly true, are one reason why doctors hesitate to set time limits for survival with cancer diagnoses, even for very advanced cases. You might want to know how long you will remain active or will live because you have things to get done, relationships to mend or a book to finish, but what will you do as you approach that time limit?

Time limits for living with cancer come from two basic sources: statistics that count hundreds of thousands of people, and the individual physician's own experience with the specific disease. Remember that half the people live longer than the often quoted "median" figure for survival of any given cancer. Those who live longer can live anywhere from just a little longer to very much longer—maybe even decades longer.[12]

Doctors often use the word "cure" for what should be more correctly five- to ten-year survival rates. Statistics for remission (a temporary stopping of growth and of related symptoms and shrinkage of the cancer) and for cure (disappearance of all detectable signs of cancer) should never rule the outlook of an individual with cancer. Hope is essential, and many of us find that knowledge makes the reality of cancer easier to live with.

I feel very positive about recovery—wrong word—how about remission? My playful platelets are good and high, blood tests terrific and blood pressure down. I feel better than ever. [an active seventy-year-old woman with breast cancer]

American Cancer Society/Massachusetts Division/Allen Smith

Take Along a Friend

Whether you suspect that you have cancer or a diagnosis of cancer has been confirmed, you should consider taking someone with you whenever you go for diagnostic work, checkups or treatment, particularly when decisions have to be made. You can probably use the moral support of someone who cares about you, and you may need help getting home after some procedures. It is useful to have a second person to ask questions and to listen to the answers, even to take notes, and to talk things over with afterward. The person you take could be your mate, your sister, a friend, or a volunteer from a

American Cancer Society/Massachusetts Division

women's group, the local Cancer Society, or other helping organization.

Everyone asks if you have any questions, but you just don't know what to ask when it's your first consultation. My doctor and the surgical nurse kept asking if I had any more questions and I really didn't just then. [a fifty-seven-year-old woman with cancer]

I had been to enough programs on women's health issues to know I should take someone with me when I went to hear the results of my mammogram. I took a woman I hired to clean my house and she turned out to be just the support I needed. [a sixty-year-old woman]

Support and Mutual-Help Groups

It has taken many years to break down the barriers keeping people with cancer from talking to each other. Only recently could a woman, rather than her physician, request the limited contact provided by the Cancer Society's Reach to Recovery Program. Groups dealing with specific problems such as ostomy and laryngectomy have a longer history. Many communities now have support groups. Because of the fears, silence, and misinformation about cancer, we especially need help when we face the diagnosis of cancer and the challenge of learning to live with it. Often, those close to us need support and information just as much as we do and can benefit from support groups. If none exists in your area, you can start one.

Questions to Which You Need Answers*

Select from this list the questions that pertain to you. *Similar questions will apply to other diseases.* Ask your health practitioners to give, or help you find, the answers. Use the resources listed at the end of this book and any others you hear of to give you this vital information for making decisions.

1. Exactly what kind of cancer do I have? Can you tell if it is slow- or fast-growing?

2. What therapies are available? Where?

3. How effective is each therapy? What is the probability of cure? What definition of "cure" is being used?

4. What benefits can I expect? Prolonged life by months? Years? Reduced symptoms? Reduced pain?

5. What percentage of people treated benefit from the therapy? How is that benefit measured?

6. Will I be able to continue my regular activities during therapy? What about sex? Working? Exercise?

7. Will the therapy require overnight stays in the hospital or can it be done on an outpatient basis?

8. What are the potential negative effects of the treatment? How serious are they? What percentage of people get them? Are they permanent? Are there any drugs that will help alleviate these effects? Do these drugs themselves cause any negative effects? How soon after treatment are symptoms likely to begin and how long do they usually last? (For example, does nausea generally start immediately, within twenty minutes, or several hours later? How long does it last?)

9. How long will the therapy last? Each session? How many sessions?

10. How many people get recurrences after this treatment? How soon?

11. Are there statistics on survival, cure, mortality, and remission rates for this therapy for my type of cancer, considering such factors as stage of cancer, age, sex, race, socioeconomic status, occupation, geographical location?

12. Who is my health care provider while I am undergoing therapy? Whom do I contact, and how, if I have new symptoms while I am in therapy? After I finish the therapy?

13. What are the costs involved? Will my insurance cover all the costs? What part of the costs? Where can I get help to pay the costs?

14. May I speak with some of your other patients? Do you know of any local groups for people with cancer? Any groups for family members and friends?

15. Whom do I call, and when, if I have further questions?

You should take a written list of these questions with you to your practitioner's office and make notes, take a tape recorder, and have someone with you. This is a lot of information to assimilate at one time; it may take more than one question-asking session. But having these answers will make you a well-informed patient, and your physician will know it. Most health care providers will respect you for asking such questions and try to keep you informed of your progress.

*Adapted from the Boston Women's Health Book Collective, *The New Our Bodies, Ourselves.* New York: Simon and Schuster, 1984, p. 527.

TREATMENTS

Each of us must be able to trust the decisions we make when cancer is found in our bodies or in our loved ones, in spite of the contradictory recommendations in the media and even within conventional medical circles. Gather all the information, advice, and support you feel you can use—but ultimately you will have to make the choices about which treatments to accept or reject.

I am their pet patient at the moment though they learned to treat me rather gingerly after I refused to start chemotherapy until my incision stopped draining. Blew the young oncologist out of his chair when I remained firm, especially after he said he'd talk it over with my surgeon. To which I replied, "You can talk to her till hell freezes over—this is not a medical decision; it is my personal decision since it is my personal body." The surgeon, a great woman, agreed. [a seventy-year-old woman]

One consideration in selecting a doctor is that you will also be expected to use the hospital in which the doctor practices. If possible, choose a hospital where there is a tumor board—an interdisciplinary committee that meets to review cases and treatments. This gives you access to other specialists instead of relying on one physician alone. In the past, surgeons controlled the treatment of cancer, but now treatments are more complicated, and it is important to have a team approach, the team including a surgeon or surgical oncologist, radiation therapists, and medical oncologists. (An oncologist is a specialist in the diagnosis and treatment of cancer.) Request a tumor board review at the time of the initial diagnosis before you agree to any treatment and at all future decision points, such as the time of a recurrence.

I read everything I could find on cancer; so I could have rushed right in and told my doctor, "You're not doing the latest thing." I still read a lot on it. I'd be very disappointed if I found the treatments I've had aren't the best procedures. [a fifty-seven-year-old woman who had a mastectomy in 1977 and is now being treated for metastases from the breast cancer to the bone]

Treatments for cancer range from high-technology radiation and chemical therapies to home remedies found in family herb gardens. All treatments for any disease are experimental to the extent that no one knows for sure exactly how *you* will respond to any given treatment or combination of treatments.

The three most common treatments for cancer are surgery, radiation, and chemotherapy (including hormone therapy and immunotherapy). These may cure the disease, slow it down, or relieve symptoms and make your life easier.

Surgery removes cancerous tumors, tissues, or areas where cancer cells have invaded normal tissue; or it can open up a blocked system or ease painful pressure on other body parts. You should try to find out as much as you can about your surgeon's and your hospital's experience and qualifications for doing the kind of surgery proposed.

After I had the tumor removed from my neck, I discovered that the doctor who did it had almost never done that kind of operation before. Had I known, I would have done what a friend at church did and gone to the medical center in a nearby city where they do similar surgery all the time and really know what they are seeing. [a sixty-year-old woman living in a small town]

Ask how the surgery will help your specific condition. Get second or third opinions, especially if a doctor suggests removing some healthy part of your body to prevent it from becoming cancerous. Breasts, ovaries, and uteri have too often been removed just in case they might develop cancer someday; medical literature has no accounts of men having anything removed "just in case."

While your surgeon may urge you to decide immediately whether to have surgery and tell you a delay will allow the disease to spread, you always have time to get those additional opinions unless you have an emergency condition such as intestinal or bladder blockage. A cancer will rarely cause sudden life-threatening symptoms, but even if it does, you can get a second opinion within the hospital or from the tumor board.

Radiation therapy uses X-rays or radioactive substances to destroy cancerous cells instead of cutting them out. Sometimes the radiation is used instead of surgery; often it is used before surgery to shrink a mass, or after surgery to destroy remaining traces of the cancer.

Radiation is also used for palliative reasons without curing, for example, to ease bone pain.

Radiation may cause nausea, diarrhea, fatigue, and burns, depending on the part of the body treated. But radiation therapy may also prolong active, meaningful life when used for some cancers, especially for Hodgkin's disease and some stages and forms of cervical, lung, nose, and throat cancers.

I just had modest side effects. I had a rash that developed after about the second or third week, a very itchy rash. I couldn't put anything on it because cream affects the way the beams go through. And I had a rash on the front that went all the way through so I had a sunburn on my back as well as on my front. The rash went away in a relatively short time. [a woman in her fifties]

336

In general, the more radiation, whether larger doses (more units of radiation—rads) or over a larger area, the more complications arise. Some of these do not show up for many years. Complications are minimized by dividing the therapy into several treatments.[13] You might be willing to put up with more adverse effects if the radiation holds the possibility of cure than if it is only intended to make you more comfortable.

Radiation therapy often causes nitrogen and other nutrient deficiencies. You can prepare yourself by eating a high-protein diet with a good balance of vitamins and minerals before you start radiation therapy; and you can try to put on a little weight in case you become nauseous and can't eat.

Both radiation and chemotherapy aim to destroy the abnormal, cancerous cells. The aim is to do so without harming too many normal cells nearby or elsewhere in the body. Techniques are being refined to make cancer cells more vulnerable than normal cells to treatment or to restore damaged normal cells more quickly. One technique is to apply heat, especially to tumors near the body surface, as an adjunct to both chemo- and radiation therapy. Implanted heat sources may work on deeper tumors. A number of drugs are being investigated either to make the cancer cells more vulnerable or to reinforce normal cells, protecting them against radiation. Techniques to salvage and restore bone marrow are being tried.

Cancer cells tend to have less oxygen than normal cells (to be hypoxic) and tend to block the effects of radiation. So researchers are trying to find ways to oxygenate cancer tumors before irradiating them.[14]

Large university or research hospitals are likely to have the most modern equipment and technology, plus well-trained personnel. You should always ask about the age of radiation equipment, when it was last inspected, and how often the therapists' training is updated. If the equipment is more than ten years old or you have doubts about the staff, contact the Cancer Information Service (1-800-4-CANCER) for the name and number of the nearest university or research hospital with radiation therapy and oncology departments.

Chemotherapy—treating cancer with chemicals or drugs—is the only method which has the potential to reach cancer cells in every part of the body. It is called a systemic therapy. It is the basic treatment in cancers such as leukemia (cancer of the white blood cells) and a supplemental (or adjuvant) therapy to destroy cancer cells that are beyond the reach of primary surgical or radiation therapy. Chemotherapy sometimes has other effects, because anything strong enough to kill cancer cells damages other cells as well. Possible temporary adverse effects of chemotherapy are hair loss, nausea, diarrhea, and cessation of menstrual periods. Possible long-term and serious effects include permanent cessation of periods in premenopausal women over forty, kidney damage, heart disease, a weakened immune system, and leukemia. But many drugs and many combinations of drugs are used. Not everyone gets sick from them, and many people have been helped.

Have had two and about to have a third chemo treatment (injection of combined drugs) and NO side effects! Absolutely none. [a seventy-year-old woman]

When my hair grew back, it was all gray, and soft like a baby's hair. And curly! I had straight dark hair before. [a sixty-eight-year-old woman]

When a woman in my cancer support group said she was going to have chemotherapy, I told her I had had the same exact thing. No problems at all. But she turned out to be as sick as a dog. Now we both laugh about it, and we both know how different each person is. [a fifty-seven-year-old woman]

Your health practitioners should have enough experience with the chemicals they propose for your treatment to be able to explain exactly how they work, what could go wrong, and how well the treatment works on your specific cancer at the stage you are in. You should not have to carry a pharmacy textbook to the office or hospital to understand what they tell you. If they cannot be clear about the therapy, talk to another physician; get another opinion or two. You should also be aware that some therapies can actually *shorten* your life if given inappropriately.

Hormone therapy is slower-acting and generally less toxic than most chemotherapy. Hormones are substances which originate in one gland or organ of the body and are carried through the blood to stimulate another part of the body. Hormone therapy changes the hormonal environment in which the cancer is growing by removing the source of the hormone (surgically or medically), adding hormones, or using substances which block the action of hormones (antihormones), such as tamoxifen. Hormone therapy is used to treat breast, uterine, ovarian, and thyroid cancers as well as leukemia (cancer of the white blood cells), lymphomas (cancers of the lymph system), and other cancers. Corticosteroids (hormones from the adrenal glands) are also used to control nausea and vomiting caused by some chemotherapy and for treatment of tumors in the central nervous system.

Immunotherapy is an attempt to stimulate the body's immune defenses to recognize and attack cancer cells. Many substances are under study for their possible effectiveness.

Experimental/Investigational Therapies

New drugs or combinations of drugs are constantly being studied. You may choose to take part in an experimental or investigational cancer treatment program. Before you give your consent, you should understand all the potential risks as well as benefits, and the investigators should take all the time needed to answer your questions. They should explain how you were selected for the study, who is funding it, what outcomes they expect, what risks are known, and how the study could benefit you as well as others. They should tell you how the experimental treatments differ from the standard protocol (treatment plan) for someone with your diagnosis. In addition, they should tell you what any health practitioner should tell you about any treatment recommendation: how it works, what effects to expect, what your possibilities are for relief, remission, and/or cure.

Alternative Treatments

The things you can do to reduce your risk of cancer can also help the body fight existing cancer. Most alternative treatments have little or no statistical data to help you decide how well they have worked for large numbers of people like you with your specific cancer. You will have to judge them according to the kind of cancer you have, the experiences of people who have tried them, what you know about the prac-

titioners who offer them, and by your own feelings about trying something outside the mainstream of current medical practice.

Some alternative treatments may be combined with conventional treatments. But promoters of many alternative methods claim their treatments will not work if you have had radiation or chemotherapy because of the damage these therapies may have done to the body. If so, you might have to choose between an established therapy with only fair outcomes and a treatment that is severely questioned or totally rejected by your physician. However, some hospitals now offer alternative treatments along with radiation or chemotherapy.

Many alternative approaches were originally developed by physicians, but are either ignored or considered invalid by the medical establishment. Often these alternatives seem logical in their approach, and a great many people credit them with curing or controlling their cancers. The preventive diets now being tested by several medical research centers are based on the same principles as some alternative cancer therapies.

Some alternative therapies receive so much publicity that public demand forces the medical establishment to evaluate the treatment's safety and efficacy. One such case is that of Laetrile. Laetrile was finally tested and considered useless after thousands of people with potentially controllable cancers spent their energy and considerable money traveling to foreign countries where the unapproved drug was available. Yet some people still place their faith in it.

Many alternative therapies are simply another kind of chemotherapy, using natural or synthetic substances in different forms or amounts than in ordinary use. *Consumer Reports* recounts its investigation of "Drugs in Disguise"—mostly disguised as "nutritional supplements."[15] Marketers of these supplements claim they cure ills ranging from herpes virus to many forms of cancer. The contents of these food/drugs range from herbs and citrus extracts to ground-up animal glands to industrial solvent. Congress has been making some attempts to reduce, or at least regulate, this "quackery," as Consumers Union labels it, but the FDA has done very little to protect us from false, even dangerous, products like these.

We do not know yet how to mobilize fully the body's self-healing capabilities and the mind's ability to influence the body's recovery. Many methods, such as the Simonton technique, whereby the body's strength and the treatments chosen are imagined (or visualized) to fight the cancer, are used both to treat symptoms of cancer and to enhance the effectiveness of the treatment (see Resources). They have reportedly induced remission. Prayer, meditation, and religious rituals are especially useful as supplements to other treatment choices; sometimes they are credited with cure, and sometimes not with cure, but an enriched life.

The risk of relying solely on faith healers and psychics is that a person whose cancer has a chance of responding to medical treatment may forgo that treatment and rely only on this method until her cancer has progressed to a stage that is much more difficult to treat.

Scientific Breakthroughs

The media frequently report new wonders of science that may help cure cancer. The sad reality for most people with cancer is that these reported discoveries are in the laboratory stage, at most being tested on animals. Even those that have had successful human trials are usually many years away from being available outside a few teaching and research institutions.

When you read or hear about something new that you think may help you or a friend, you can call your doctor, your local hospital, the closest medical school, the Cancer Information Service or even the school or hospital mentioned in the report. You might also write to your legislators urging their support of the research if it sounds worthwhile to you.

As we move into the late 1980s, some of our most respected cancer scientists are coming to a different conclusion. Because cures for most cancers are not likely in the near future, focusing so much money and energy on treatment research may be actually robbing us of the motivation and resources to try to prevent cancer.[16] Also, by focusing more on the quality of life than the quantity of life, we could better help those people who already have cancer to live with the disease constructively.

LUNG CANCER

There are several types of lung cancer, caused by different environmental conditions or carcinogens, but the most common one is bronchial carcinoma, caused by smoking. It is possible to get lung cancer if you never smoked or lived with a smoker, but more women now die of lung cancer caused by smoking than from breast or any other cancer. The chances of getting bronchial carcinoma depend directly on how much you have smoked and for how long. Quitting pays off—after only ten years your chances of bronchial cancer are the same as a non-smoker's, though passive smoking (breathing the smoke from other people's cigarettes) probably continues your risks.

Lung cancer is the best example of why prevention is superior to cure, because the disease is so difficult to detect until its advanced stages. A persistent cough is usually the only warning. Lung cancer is usually treated with a combination of surgery, radiation therapy, and chemotherapy. Only 13 percent of people with lung cancer live five or more years after diagnosis.[17]

I didn't feel well for a long time but a year ago nothing showed up on my physical. Six months ago I was down to 101 pounds and didn't care about eating. It was a blow to find out I had lung cancer. I had smoked since I started college—everyone did. Have you noticed how much smoking there was in the old movies? Katharine Hepburn, all the stars I admired, smoked in the movies. After the diagnosis I just stopped smoking even though I still have the urge. I got a lot of lectures from everyone. I get chemotherapy every three weeks. I lost my hair but I'm feeling better. My appetite has returned and I'm up to 115 pounds. I'm doing pretty well now but I wish no one else had to go through this. I've been to two funerals for women who have died of lung cancer in less than a month, and now my dental hygienist has lung cancer also. My faith and my friends are helping me. [a seventy-five-year-old woman]

What is diagnosed as lung cancer may also be a metastasis from a malignancy elsewhere in your body, even one which was apparently cured years ago. Many of these have a better prognosis if detected early.

CANCER OF THE OVARY

Ovarian cancer is rare, and while it did increase for a brief period, it now appears to be declining again. Because this disease has been so difficult to detect until considerably advanced, it is often fatal, with five-year survival rates of 38 percent for all stages combined.[18] Newer diagnostic technology may improve earlier detection but it remains to be seen whether earlier treatment will actually improve survival. Early warning signs are usually intestinal upsets of different kinds and often pain in the shoulder. Ovaries feel swollen to the examining practitioner.

For a long time a lot of things I ate would make me gassy, but I thought, "I'm just getting old, I can't eat the things I used to." I went to the doctor and he gave me fluid pills [diuretics] for the swelling I had, but he never examined me "down there." It wasn't until I started bleeding down there that I found out what I had. I nearly died in surgery, they couldn't get it all, and though the radiation made me sick, I'm a little better now. [an eighty-four-year-old woman, during remission, who later died of ovarian cancer]

Even though the risks of removing healthy ovaries clearly outweigh any benefit, many doctors believe the poor prognosis for ovarian cancer justifies the removal of healthy ovaries during other abdominal surgery. But ovarian cancer tissue can and does grow in the abdomens of some women after the ovaries are removed. (See Hysterectomy and Oophorectomy chapter.)

While researchers don't completely understand the causes of this cancer, some factors are becoming clearer. The fewer children you have, the greater the risk, childless women being at greatest risk. Women who already have cancer of the breast, intestines, or rectum appear to be at increased risk, as are women whose jobs involve electrical, rubber, or textile manufacture. The use of talcum powder, especially in the genital area, may increase the risk as much as three times. Cornstarch is a safe substitute for bath powders containing talc.

Most recent studies are beginning to suggest that some of the same preventive changes in diet which could reduce breast cancer may also reduce ovarian cancer, specifically fat in the diet. This may help to explain why women who are significantly fat, who have taken menopausal estrogens, or who have a family history of ovarian cancer also appear to be at increased risk. Estrogen overproduction is the central factor here. Treatment of ovarian cancer usually involves surgery, radiation, and chemotherapy, with surgery and chemotherapy currently showing the most favorable results.

COLORECTAL CANCER

Colorectal cancer (cancer of the large intestine) is the third most common cancer among women in the U.S. Almost half of all people with this disease are cured, usually by surgery. Many experts say survival rates could be improved if the cancer were discovered earlier. Early detection not only improves the chance of survival but often makes it possible to save greater portions of the large bowel because the cancer has not yet spread so far.

Women should be examined for colorectal cancer, particularly if they are, for one reason or another, considered to be at higher than usual risk of developing this kind of cancer. Colorectal cancer grows slowly; it may take months or years before it causes symptoms. Bleeding or changes in bowel habits such as constipation, more frequent movements, or diarrhea may be the first symptoms.

You should see a physician as soon as possible if you notice that any of the symptoms described above persist or if you have abdominal pain that doesn't go away. In doing an evaluation, your physician or nurse will take a complete personal and family history, give you a physical examination (including a rectal exam) and perform laboratory tests; special attention will be paid to your large bowel, including tests for blood in the stool and looking into the bowel with an instrument (colonoscope or sigmoidoscope). X-rays of the bowel are often taken; they require a barium retention enema. Your regular health care provider may refer you to a specialist (surgeon or gastroenterologist) for more tests or treatment.

Since at this time we know very little about the prevention of colorectal cancer (a well-balanced diet rich in fiber and low in fat is the only recommendation available),[19] the only other thing that can be done is to promote early detection.

Who Is at Higher Than Usual Risk?

1. *All people when they get older.* Up to age forty, this risk is very low unless special circumstances are present (see 2 and 3 below). From then on, the risk doubles every ten years. Thus, a person at age seventy-five has an eight times higher risk of developing colorectal cancer than one at age forty-five. This is why the American Cancer Society recommends that people, *even if they feel completely healthy,* should routinely have certain tests beginning at age forty or fifty. Such tests are: an examination of the rectum with a gloved finger (digital rectal); a test for blood in the stool (guaiac test); a "procto," which means inspection of the inside of the bowel with an instrument called a proctosigmoidoscope or with a flexible colonoscope (which allows examination of more of your bowel). New flexible instruments cause less discomfort than the rigid instruments used in the past. These tests can be carried out by the family or primary-care physician, who would refer you to a specialist if any of the results suggest cancer, or if other kinds of problems are found.

2. *People with a personal or family history of colorectal cancer, breast cancer, or cancer of the endometrium* (lining of the uterus). Since such individuals have colorectal cancer more often than others—sometimes also at a younger age—doctors should take careful family histories and may do periodic examinations for colorectal cancer regardless of age. It is only recently that researchers have noticed this family tendency. They also recommend such examinations for blood relatives of these patients, beginning at age twenty or thirty. In this situation, the whole bowel may be inspected by colonoscopy. Make sure that your health care provider is aware of your family history.

3. *People with bowel diseases which are not cancer in themselves but often lead to cancer.*

(a) Inflammatory bowel disease (ulcerative colitis or Crohn's disease—sometimes called regional ileitis or enteritis). If one of these conditions exists for eight or ten years, the chance of developing colorectal cancer is greatly increased.

(b) Familial polyposis. In this condition, the bowel is studded with polyps and examinations should begin much earlier, even in adolescence. The disease is inherited and leads to cancer in 50 percent of the cases. Close blood relatives of anyone who has this condition should be examined early and periodically, for they might develop the same life-threatening disease.

(c) Single polyps, especially of the cell type called "adenomatous," are also associated with cancer of the bowel. These should be removed surgically (not a major operation), and the surgery followed by regular examinations.

Living with an Ostomy

When a part of the intestine must be removed, the two cut ends are sewn together to maintain a passageway for food. When this is not feasible, an opening (a "stoma") is made in the abdominal wall, through which the undigested matter can pass into a pouch (appliance). The operation is called a colostomy when the stoma is made in the colon, and an ileostomy when the stoma is made in the portion of the small intestine called the ileum. People with colostomies may or may not return to a predictable time of bowel evacuation, depending on the location of the colostomy in the large intestine, on prior bowel habits, on the presence of other medical conditions, on use of medicines, or other cancer treatments. Some people with a colostomy flush or irrigate the stoma with water to promote a bowel movement at a certain time of day, others prefer to wear an appliance most of the time. Those with ileostomies must keep the bag in place all the time.

People often fear that a diagnosis of colorectal cancer leads automatically to a colostomy. This was never the case, and is even less true today because of new surgical techniques that reconnect parts of the large intestine after removing the cancerous section. Furthermore, living with an ostomy today is significantly easier than it was in the past. Women who have an ostomy can lead completely normal lives that include sexual relations. (See the pamphlet "Sex and the Female Ostomate" listed in Resources. See also the Sexuality chapter.)

COLOSTOMY

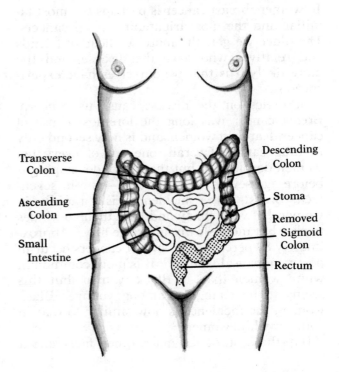

Transverse Colon

Ascending Colon

Small Intestine

Descending Colon

Stoma

Removed Sigmoid Colon

Rectum

I've always loved clothes and fashion. My lifelong ambition was to become a model. Two years ago I went to a modeling school to learn to be one—me and my colostomy with all the twenty-year-olds. Recently I went to the restaurant where I do informal modeling. I donned a dress which tied low on my right side and slipped into the bathroom to check it out in the mirror. One woman commented to another about my dress being the type she could wear because it had a tie to hide her right side. Then she said to me, "I wear a pouch, you know." To which I replied, "You do? Well, so do I!" I told her that if she was going to be in the restaurant a while longer, my next outfit was going to be a very brief bathing suit. The only kind of clothing I can't wear is a bikini. She only had the ostomy for three months and was wearing a tent dress so I thought it was very important that she see me in a bathing suit. That encounter really made my day as I'm sure it did hers. [a fifty-year-old woman]

To find help from those who have gone through the experience, contact a chapter of the United Ostomy Association (see your local phone book) or your local chapter of the American Cancer Society (see also Resources).

I've been an ostomy hospital visitor for about nine years. I feel it is important for people to talk to others who have "walked the same road." [a fifty-year-old woman]

BREAST CANCER

To women, breast cancer is perhaps the most familiar and the most frightening of all cancers. The older we get, the more we hear of friends and relatives who have the disease, and the more likely it is that we ourselves have experienced it.

Statistics on the disease cause us concern. Breast cancer was long the foremost cause of cancer deaths in women, and is now second only to lung cancer. Overall, one out of every ten women develops it, but the risk of developing it before age seventy is much less—one in seventeen. Breast-cancer incidence rises rapidly in women between thirty and fifty, then continues to rise, but more slowly, after age fifty.[20] Approximately 80 percent of all breast cancers occur in postmenopausal women.[21] It is more common in white women than in Black women, but this seems to be changing; among younger Black women, the incidence is now similar to that in younger white women.[22]

But these statistics mask other facts about breast cancer, facts that are both reassuring and complex. Breast cancer is actually many different diseases, some aggressive and rapidly fatal, some so indolent and slow that they may not kill, and many between these two extremes. The rate at which breast tumors grow varies enormously, as does our immune systems' ability to fight them. Although many women with breast cancer die within a few years of diagnosis, others live as long as thirty or forty years before dying either of breast cancer or of other causes in old age.[23] **Sixty percent of women with breast cancer live as long as their peers without the disease.[24]**

Nonetheless, some researchers think that some or all breast cancers spread immediately, and as cancerous cells leave the breast through the lymph nodes or bloodstream, others remain in the breast to form a lump. But when breast cancer spreads, it does not necessarily kill. Whether or not a spreading breast cancer is fatal seems to depend on the same vital factors: How fast or slow is the cancer? Can the immune system keep it under control?

Detection

The Breast Self-Exam

Although most breast lumps are benign (noncancerous), a lump is the most frequent first sign of breast cancer, far more frequent than pain or nipple discharge. Unlike cancerous lumps in other parts of the body, a sizable lump in the breast is relatively easy to feel. For this reason, doctors usually encourage us to examine our breasts regularly for lumps in order to detect cancer "early" if it is there. But is the breast self-exam actually beneficial?

Researchers now know that breast cancer is in the body not months, but years, before it is detected through a lump in the breast. In most cases, by the time a lump is large enough to be felt, it has been in the body at least three to five years, more likely five to fifteen years, depending on its rate of growth.[25] If it is going to spread at all, it has probably spread long before we can feel its presence.

But even if breast cancer has already spread, there are arguments for early detection: (1) removing the lump as early as possible leaves the immune system free to fight cancer cells that have spread rather than having to fight the cells in the lump as well; (2) the longer a cancerous lump remains in the body, the more time it has to populate the body with additional cancer cells, making it harder for the immune system or cancer treatments to fight them.

However, many women question the emphasis on breast self-exam and feel blamed if a cancerous lump is found and they didn't find it "early enough." A Federal panel recently supported women's doubts by deciding that there is not enough evidence in favor of the breast self-exam to advocate it as a detection test.[26] It is unlikely, but still not definitely known, whether the practice of monthly breast self-exams can lengthen a woman's life. Statistics show that in fact most women do not examine their breasts regularly, partly out of fear of finding a lump and partly because, as healthy women, they don't want to look for disease. Other women like the idea of becoming familiar with their bodies by monitoring normal, cyclic changes in their breasts. They see regular or occasional breast exams as a way of taking care of themselves, and they examine their breasts when the time feels right for them.

Mammogram Screening

A mammogram, an X-ray picture of the breast, is now the most widely publicized method of regularly checking or screening healthy women for breast changes. Its purpose is to locate a suspicious lump in the breast so it can be removed and examined under a microscope to see if it is cancerous. A mammogram itself cannot diagnose cancer and it is not a treatment.

Theoretically, the arguments in favor of breast self-exam hold true for the mammogram, with the advantage that, in some women, a mammogram can indicate the possibility of a small cancerous lump years before it is large enough to be felt. Large-scale studies in Sweden and in the United States show that women over fifty benefit from regular mammogram screening with 30 percent lower breast-cancer death rates.[27] The same advantage has not been shown for younger women. Some researchers believe that mammograms are equally effective for women in their forties. However, there are no reliable statistics yet to prove or disprove the value of this practice. In the meantime, these studies contradict the American Cancer Society's recommendation that women in their forties be screened every one or two years.

Mammogram screening has its dangers. One is that radiation from an X-ray can cause breast cancer. Radiation is cumulative: many small doses over time equal one large dose. No one knows how large a radiation dose has to be to cause breast cancer, and the amount probably varies from woman to woman.* But the breast seems to become less vulnerable with age, the adolescent breast possibly being the most vulnerable to radiation. Since it takes ten to twenty years or more for radiation-induced cancer to appear, the older you are, the less risk.

Make sure that the radiologist uses the lowest feasible dose of radiation, if possible as low as 0.1 or 0.2 rads per examination. Also, it appears that screening only every two or three years, using a single X-ray exposure for each breast, may be just as beneficial as yearly screening with double exposure.[28] The practice in this country is to take at least two views of each breast, and some radiologists argue that this provides better accuracy.

Mammograms do not distinguish a cancerous lump from a benign one. Since some breast lumpiness is normal in women, many mammograms interpreted as "suspicious" lead to needless worry and to countless unnecessary breast biopsies. The breast biopsy rate is increased by physicians who are afraid of malpractice suits and who protect themselves by recommending biopsies "just to make sure."

Perhaps the most disturbing aspect of mammogram screening is that of overtreatment. A mammogram can find lumps so small they are difficult to diagnose correctly under a microscope. Some of these lumps are cancers that may not spread, called *in situ* cancers. Women

*Estimates for mammograms indicate that one rad (radiation absorbed dose) to the breast per examination can result in six cancers per one million women beginning ten years after exposure. Another estimate shows that approximately 788 cases of breast cancer per year are caused by X-rays. However, this figure includes all X-rays in which the breast was exposed to the rays, such as X-rays of the chest and back, and CAT scans, as well as mammograms. I. Craig Henderson, "Breast Cancer," in John A. Spittell, Jr., ed., *Clinical Medicine*. Philadelphia: Harper & Row, 1986, p. 4; and John S. Evans, John E. Wennberg, and Barbara J. McNeil, "The Influence of Diagnostic Radiography on the Incidence of Breast Cancer and Leukemia." *The New England Journal of Medicine*, Vol. 315, No. 13 (September 25, 1986), pp. 810–5.

The "High Risk" Controversy

You may have read or heard a long list of factors that supposedly make a woman a high risk for breast cancer. The list includes having fibrocystic disease (see below), early menarche and late menopause, Jewish ancestry, and many more. More recent studies show that most of those factors do not actually increase a woman's risk.

Women who are more likely than others to develop breast cancer are those who:

- Have already had breast cancer;
- Have a mother or sister who had breast cancer before age forty, especially if she had it in both breasts;
- Have taken estrogens after the age of fifty,* or the synthetic estrogen diethylstilbestrol (DES) during pregnancy.†
- Have had frequent high-dose X-rays that exposed the breast.

No risk factor warrants removal of the breast to *prevent* breast cancer, a procedure called a prophylactic mastectomy. Some physicians urge women to undergo this operation. These physicians overrate the significance of risk factors and of microcalcifications and do not know that *removal of a healthy breast is no guarantee against breast cancer.* A cancerous lump can grow in any remaining breast tissue or on the chest wall, and there is always a chance that breast cancer is already somewhere in the body. Breast reconstruction after a mastectomy makes detection of a later cancer even more difficult.

*Women without ovaries who took 1.25 mg. of estrogen for three years after the age of fifty had double the risk of breast cancer compared with women who did not take estrogens. The risk of breast cancer was 2.5 times higher among women whose ovaries were intact. Ronald K. Ross, et al., "A Case-Control Study of Menopausal Estrogen Therapy and Breast Cancer." *Journal of the American Medical Association*, Vol. 243, No. 16 (April 20, 1980), pp. 1635–9; and P. A. Wingo, et al., "The Risk of Breast Cancer in Menopausal Women Who Have Used Estrogen Replacement Therapy." *Journal of the American Medical Association*, Vol. 257, No. 2 (January 9, 1987), pp. 209–15.

†E. R. Greenberg, et al., cited in note 10, page 349.

with such cancers may be misdiagnosed and treated as though they have rapidly spreading disease. Also, these women will be called "cured," thus distorting figures on the supposed benefits of the mammograms and the treatment.

Mammograms also find fields of what are called microcalcifications, tiny spots of calcium deposits that show up almost like grains of sand in the mammogram. While it is true that calcium deposits are often present in cancer cells and are one of the signs radiologists look for in the screening process, it is also true that 75 percent of microcalcifications are normal and do not indicate cancer.[29]

To date, mammography is the only imaging method of screening which can show benefit to women. Other forms of breast pictures, such as thermography, diaphanography, and ultrasound, are not yet reliable enough to be beneficial. Further study of effective screening methods that do not involve radiation is needed.

If You Have a High Risk of Breast Cancer

If you have already had breast cancer it is worth having regular mammogram checkups no matter what your age, since cancerous lumps often recur in the same or the other breast. Also, the benefits of mammogram screening probably outweigh the risks if you are over fifty and have a higher than average risk of breast cancer. If you are at high risk for breast cancer, but under fifty, have a mammogram every one or two years if it helps put your mind at ease, but remember that benefits for women your age are not yet proven.

If You Find a Lump

If you or your partner or health care practitioner find a lump in your breast, keep in mind that 80 to 90 percent of lumps are benign (noncancerous). Breast lumps are common and normal in women, and most conditions causing change, lumps, or pain in the breast are not cancer. Probably the majority of older women have found one or more isolated lumps in their breasts through the years, and a general lumpiness of the breasts is common in half of all women. Many physicians call lumpiness or even one isolated lump "fibrocystic disease." But lumpy breasts are not a disease and do not increase our risk of breast cancer. For this reason, some physicians more appropriately refer to breast lumpiness as a fibrocystic condition.[30] Most benign lumps are related to the hormonal fluctuations of menstruation, however, so a new lump after menopause should be checked. There is no sure way of reducing noncancerous breast lumps, but some women find that reducing fat, salt, caffeine, chocolate, and cigarettes, while adding dietary supplements of vitamin E and evening primrose oil (available in health food stores), has helped.

There is no harm in monitoring a lump yourself for a few weeks. If a lump fluctuates with your period, this is an indication that it is a harmless cyst, or fluid-filled sac. If you are past menopause, check the lump on the same date each month, since women continue to have cyclical changes in their breasts even after periods cease.

If your lump does not fluctuate and/or worries you, have an experienced physician examine your breast. Many women find that their own general practitioners or gynecologists do not know how to examine the breast properly, nor are they knowledgeable about how to distinguish a benign lump from a cancerous one. If possible, see a practitioner experienced in benign breast problems and breast cancer. A surgeon would be a likely choice for a first or second opinion. You can see a surgeon simply for a diagnosis of your lump. You do not have to plan on surgery or agree to it. Your physician should give you a thorough breast exam in both seated and supine (lying down) positions, palpate your underarms for swelling and your abdomen for suspicious masses, listen to your lungs, and take a complete blood count. These examinations are a precaution to check for cancer in the body. If your lump is large and feels like a cyst, your physician may omit these examinations and try an immediate needle aspiration.

Diagnosis

If both you and your physician think your lump is harmless, you may choose to forgo any further procedures. However, even if the lump feels harmless, you should consider a biopsy if you are considered in a higher-risk category of breast cancer or if there are other symptoms of possible cancer present, such as hard, swollen glands in the armpit, a skin rash on the breast, nipple discharge, or dimpling or puckering of skin around the nipple. There are two basic diagnostic procedures to determine whether a lump is cancerous, both of them office procedures.

1. *Needle aspiration:* your physician inserts a needle into the lump. If the lump is a cyst, fluid is withdrawn and the lump collapses. If the lump proves solid, or if it is too small to insert the needle accurately into it, the next step would be a surgical biopsy.

2. *Surgical biopsy:* the removal of the lump in order to examine it under a microscope. The surgery can usually be done under local anesthesia—unless you prefer general anesthesia, which entails risks and requires longer recovery time. Do *not* agree to a biopsy under general anesthesia so that the surgeon can remove the entire breast immediately should your lump prove cancerous. This "one-step procedure" is unnecessary and detrimental.

It is best to remove an entire solid lump (excisional biopsy), since some lumps are made up of both benign and cancerous cells. If only part of the lump is removed and proves benign, the part left in the breast could still be cancerous. The excised lump should be analyzed by permanent section, which will take a few days, but is more reliable than the quick frozen section. There is no need of a bone scan or any further tests unless your lump is diagnosed as cancerous.

If you have a biopsy make sure your physician plans to order an immediate estrogen-receptor test on the lump if it turns out to be malignant. This test will show whether or not your tumor cells contain a certain protein called an estrogen receptor. This test is vital to planning future treatment and must be done upon the diagnosis of cancer, without delay.

Fine needle aspiration of a solid lump and *trucut needle biopsy* are less common and are not definitive. If the needle shows only noncancerous cells, the cells remaining in the lump could still be cancerous. But if your lump is so large that removing it would greatly distort the breast, these procedures can help you decide whether or not to have surgery.

Wire localization biopsy may be used if a mammogram shows a suspicious area such as microcalcifications which can't be felt but which your physician thinks should be removed.

While an X-ray shows a picture of your breast, the radiologist inserts a fine wire into the breast under local anesthesia, and points the wire to the area in question. The surgeon then follows the wire and removes the tissue at the end. Further examination is done to confirm that the correct area was removed.

A mammogram is not appropriate for diagnosing a lump which can be felt. However, some physicians recommend a mammogram before a biopsy to see if there are other suspicious masses in the same or the other breast.

If Your Lump Is Cancerous

If your lump proves cancerous, there is no need to rush into action. Give yourself time to adjust to the powerful feelings you will have and to find out which treatment, if any, might be most beneficial for your special case. There is no harm in taking up to six weeks before making any decisions.

Making a Decision About Treatments

Since breast-cancer treatments are so controversial among physicians, and new studies are constantly clarifying treatment options, it is especially important to get second or even third opinions about the right treatment for you. Be sure to find out the results or trends of current studies, especially larger "randomized clinical trials."

You and your physician need to know as much as possible about your cancer in order to make a sound judgment on possible treatments. The first step is the estrogen-receptor test. Your tumor cells may contain an estrogen and/or progesterone receptor (called an estrogen/progesterone-positive cancer, or ER+ and PgR+). This indicates a hormone-sensitive cancer, which is often a slower-growing one. It is most prevalent in postmenopausal women. The absence of this receptor is called an estrogen/progesterone-negative cancer, or ER− and PgR−. Estrogen/progesterone-negative cancers tend to be more aggressive than estrogen/progesterone-positive cancers.

As a second step, your physician may suggest removing a few lymph nodes from your armpit. The presence of cancerous cells in the nodes (called "positive nodes") is a sign that cancer may be elsewhere in the body and that your immune system, in which lymph nodes play an active role, is not successfully fighting the spreading disease. Conversely, cancer-free lymph nodes (called "negative nodes") indicate that your immune system is more successful in fighting the disease elsewhere in your body than if the nodes are positive.[31] Lymph-node sampling is for diagnosis only, to help decide which treatment might be beneficial. Removing them does not help eliminate cancer from the body. Removing more than about ten nodes may cause arm problems later.

Your physician should also do an abdominal exam and order blood tests, a chest X-ray, and possibly a bone scan. If any of these tests show that cancer has already reached a detectable stage in a distant part of your body such as the bone or liver, available treatments can only relieve uncomfortable or painful symptoms. They are not likely to lengthen life more than a few months, and this small advantage must be weighed against the negative effects of the treatments.

Treatment Options

1. Local Therapies.

The purpose of local therapies is to remove (surgery) and/or kill (radiation) cancerous cells at the site of the lump and in the surrounding area.

Lumpectomy. Lumpectomy is the surgical removal of the lump with varying amounts of surrounding tissue. If your biopsy included the entire lump and some surrounding tissue, this is considered a lumpectomy and you probably need no further surgery.

A recent study shows that women with tumors up to one and a half inches in diameter live as long with lumpectomy alone as with lumpectomy and radiation, or with mastectomy.[32] Although this U.S. study is relatively new, it is supported by Canadian and European research with up to twenty-five year results. This study included women with positive and negative nodes but with no evidence of distant spread. However, it probably also applies to women with obvious distant spread. It is what happens in the rest of the body that counts.

The possible adverse effects of a lumpectomy are some scarring and disfiguring of the breast.

346

Lumpectomy with Radiation. In this procedure, after the lump and surrounding tissue have been removed, the area surrounding the site of the lump is irradiated by X-ray beams and sometimes by temporary implants of radioactive materials (radiation implants). Radiation can evidently help prevent a cancerous lump from growing back again in the same breast, but it does not prolong life. Although radiation can have adverse effects, some women choose it to reduce the risk of a repeated lump and surgery in the same breast. However, this is a matter of choice. If you have a lumpectomy you do not have to agree to radiation also.

Adverse effects can include fatigue, dry, red, itchy skin, extreme sun sensitivity, muscle pain, and occasional cracked ribs or a temporary lung ailment similar to bronchitis. Theoretically, radiation therapy can also cause breast cancer, but this appears to be rare.

2. Systemic Therapies.

Chemotherapy. Drugs in the form of pills or injections attempt to kill cancer cells nesting or circulating in distant parts of the body. Two major studies showed that 14 to 24 percent of premenopausal women with positive nodes live longer as a result of chemotherapy.[33] Women in this category who have one to three positive nodes or whose tumors contain poorly differentiated cells (cells in an undeveloped, embryonic state) seem more likely to be helped by chemotherapy than women who have four or more positive nodes or whose tumors have well-differentiated cells.[34]

A combination of drugs called CMF (cyclophosphamide, methotrexate, and 5-fluorouracil) may work better than single drugs used separately, and a six-month regimen seems just as beneficial as longer use. But the optimal drug dosage, timing, combination, and duration of treatment are still being debated. Studies are underway to see if chemotherapy can help premenopausal women with aggressive cancers but no node involvement, but there are no clear answers yet.

Physicians now tend to overuse chemotherapy for breast cancer, routinely giving it to women with no sign of cancer in the lymph nodes and regardless of their menopausal status. This is a dangerous trend, since the drugs used can take a serious emotional and physical toll. Further research is needed to pinpoint which women are most likely to benefit from chemotherapy.

Hormone Therapy. Some hormones in the form of pills or injections, aim to repress or eliminate estrogen in the body, thus curbing the spread of cancer. The hormones most commonly used are tamoxifen and male hormones.

There are no definite answers yet on the effectiveness of hormone therapy, but current estimates indicate that tamoxifen can prolong life in some postmenopausal women, especially those whose lumps have been diagnosed as estrogen-positive and whose nodes show signs of cancer.[35] Long-term use (two years or perhaps longer) seems to be more effective than shorter use. The drug evidently has few adverse effects on women past menopause except hot flashes and vaginal dryness. Therefore, many feel it is worth trying without awaiting more definite study results, although it is fairly expensive.

Physicians sometimes include tamoxifen in chemotherapy regimens. Premenopausal women should not take tamoxifen until test results of such mixed treatments are more conclusive. Ask your physician which drugs will be included in your regimen and why.

Current studies show that postmenopausal women with estrogen-receptor-negative cancers and those with no node involvement may also benefit from hormone therapy. Further studies on tamoxifen are underway for these women.

3. Outmoded and Rarely Necessary Treatments.

Surgical Techniques to Limit Estrogen Production. These techniques include adrenalectomy (removal of the adrenals) and hypophysectomy (removal of the pituitary gland). The drugs discussed under hormone therapy can generally produce the same effects with fewer problems. There are still open questions about oophorectomy (removal of the ovaries), and studies are underway.

Mastectomy. Mastectomy is surgical removal of the entire breast. This procedure, long thought the only way to treat breast cancer, is no more effective than removal of the lump alone. A mastectomy is probably only necessary if:

a. Your breast is small and the lump so large

1985 over one and a half million women had mastectomies of some kind, including the Halsted radical.[36] In the belief that time was essential, surgeons often performed the operation while the patient was under general anesthesia given for the biopsy. A woman awoke to find that she had cancer and had lost one or both breasts.

Most one-breasted women wear a prosthesis, a breast form made of foam rubber or silicone. Some have had surgical reconstruction to take the place of the amputated breast. If, on a warm summer day when light clothing would normally be worn, all women who had mastectomies decided not to wear a prosthesis, or could temporarily discard their reconstructed breasts, we would see in the streets, the shops, and beaches many one-breasted women.

Women who have lost one or both breasts face the emotional trauma of losing a part of their body so strongly associated with sexuality and a sense of womanhood.

It's been a long process coming to terms with the loss of my breast. The mastectomy seemed unreal for a long time. I would look in the mirror and not believe it! I think it takes a lot of courage to say goodbye to a part of your body no matter what your age. But I was very young, and it seemed especially sad to lose my breast before I had lived with it and enjoyed it fully. I hadn't seen it get full of milk and breastfed with it; hadn't watched it age. Only long after the operation was I able to really say goodbye to my breast. [a thirty-nine-year-old woman]

American Cancer Society/Massachusetts Division/Allen Smith

that a lumpectomy would be more disfiguring than removing the entire breast or

b. The cancerous cells have not formed a lump but are diffuse in tiny clusters throughout the breast. In this case, many women and doctors want to "get it all out" by removing the entire breast, although there is no proof, even then, that a mastectomy prolongs life.

A radical mastectomy, also called the Halsted radical (removal of the breast, underlying muscles of the chest wall, and lymph nodes), is *never* necessary. However, some surgeons still recommend and perform it.

If You Have Had a Mastectomy

The mastectomy has been standard practice for over one hundred years. From 1970 through

For some women, the physical discomfort and pain resulting from a radical mastectomy are also a lasting concern. When the lymph nodes have been removed and the lymph and blood vessels cut during surgery, the lymph fluid in the arm cannot drain off and sometimes accumulates, causing swelling in the arm and even pain. At times, women who have had less extensive mastectomies or only a lymph-node sampling experience a similar, but milder, discomfort. There is no cure for this condition, called *lymphedema,** but there are ways of making it easier to live with. Wearing an elastic custom-fitted sleeve, and treatment with an inflatable sleeve (pneumo-massage) can allevi-

*Lymphedema can occur in the leg after lymph nodes are removed from the groin. Try the same methods mentioned above for the arm to alleviate discomfort in the leg.

ate discomfort. Some women find that exercise, especially under the instruction of a physical therapist, reduces the discomfort of lymphedema as well as any stiffness and numbness in the shoulder and arm (see Maggie Lettvin's book listed under Resources). Talk with your physician or contact "Reach for Recovery" at your local American Cancer Society chapter or the Encore program at your local YWCA for more information.

NOTES

1. National Cancer Institute, *Cancer Prevention*. National Institutes of Health Publication No. 84–2671, February 1984.

2. Robert L. Rogers, et al., "Abstention from Smoking Improves Cerebral Perfusion Among Elderly Smokers." *Journal of the American Medical Association*, Vol. 253, No. 20 (May 24/31, 1985), pp. 2970–4.

3. Adapted from the Boston Women's Health Book Collective, *The New Our Bodies, Ourselves*. New York: Simon and Schuster, 1984, p. 524.

4. Amanda Spake, "A New American Nightmare." *Ms.*, March 1986, pp. 35–42ff.

5. William Mann, "Reproductive Cancer." *Women and Health*, Vol. 10, No. 2/3 (Summer/Fall 1985), p. 63.

6. United Press International, "Cancer Survivors Said to Face Jobs Bias." *The Boston Globe*, September 17, 1985, p. 10.

7. Susan Sontag, *Illness as Metaphor*. New York: Random House, 1979.

8. Marcia Angell, "Disease as a Reflection of the Psyche?" *The New England Journal of Medicine*, Vol. 312, No. 24 (June 13, 1985), pp. 1570–2.

9. Barrie R. Cassileth, et al., "Psychosocial Correlates of Survival in Advanced Malignant Disease." *The New England Journal of Medicine*, Vol. 312, No. 24 (June 13, 1985), pp. 1551–5.

10. E. R. Greenberg, et al., "Breast Cancer in Mothers Given Diethylstilbestrol in Pregnancy." *The New England Journal of Medicine*, Vol. 311, No. 22 (November 29, 1984), pp. 1393–8.

11. Office of Cancer Communications, National Cancer Institute, *The Breast Cancer Digest*. U.S. Department of Health and Human Services, Public Health Service, NIH Publication No. 84–1691, 2nd edition, April 1984.

12. Stephen Jay Gould, "The Median Isn't the Message." *Discover*, Vol. 6, No. 6 (June 1985), pp. 40–2.

13. Martin B. Levene, "Radiation Therapy." In Blake Cady, ed., *Cancer: A Manual for Practitioners*. Boston: American Cancer Society, Massachusetts Division, 6th edition, 1982, pp. 49–51.

14. "Overcoming Tumor Resistance in Therapy. Dr. Coleman Cites Efforts to Enhance Response to Cancer Treatment." *Focus*, Harvard Medical Area News Office, October 19, 1985.

15. "Drugs in Disguise." *Consumer Reports*, May 1985, pp. 275–83.

16. John C. Bailar III and Elaine M. Smith, "Progress Against Cancer." *The New England Journal of Medicine*, Vol. 314, No. 19 (May 8, 1986), pp. 1226–32.

17. American Cancer Society, *1985 Cancer Facts & Figures*, p. 9.

18. Ibid., p. 14.

19. Peter Greenwald and Elaine Lanza, "Dietary Fiber and Colon Cancer." *Contemporary Nutrition*, Vol. XI, No. 1 (1986).

20. John L. Young, Jr., Constance L. Percy, and Ardyce J. Cesire, eds., *Surveillance, Epidemiology, and End Results: Incidence and Mortality Data, 1973–77*. U.S. Department of Health and Human Services, June 1981, pp. 2081–2330.

21. *Health Facts*, April 1985. Center for Medical Consumers, Inc., 237 Thompson Street, New York, NY 10012.

22. H. Austin, Philip Cole, and Ernest Wynder, "Breast Cancer in Black American Women." *International Journal of Cancer*, Vol. 24, 1979, pp. 541–4.

23. I. Craig Henderson, *Breast Cancer Management: Progress and Prospects*. Wayne, NJ: Lederle Laboratories, 1982, p. 5.

24. M. S. Fox, "On the Diagnosis and Treatment of Breast Cancer." *Journal of the American Medical Association*, Vol. 241, 1979, pp. 489–94. The National Cancer Institute reported a rise of 7 percent in the breast-cancer death rate among white women under fifty between 1983 and 1984. It is not yet known whether this figure will hold or drop again.

25. P. M. Gullino, "Natural History of Breast Cancer." *Cancer*, Vol. 39, 1977, pp. 2697–2703.

26. Michael S. O'Malley and Suzanne W. Fletcher, "Screening for Breast Cancer with Breast Self-Examination." *Journal of the American Medical Association*, Vol. 257, No. 16 (April 24, 1987), pp. 2197–2203.

27. S. Shapiro, et al., "Periodic Breast Cancer Screening in Reducing Mortality from Breast Cancer." *Journal of the American Medical Association*, Vol. 215, No. 11 (March 15, 1971), pp. 1777–85; and L. Tabar, et al., "Reduction in Mortality from Breast Cancer After Mass Screening with Mammography." *Lancet*, April 13, 1985, pp. 829–32.

28. Tabar, et al., op. cit.

29. "Differentiating Benign Breast Conditions, Breast Ca[ncer]." *Ob. Gyn. News*, Vol. 20, No. 20 (October 15–31, 1985), p. 41.

30. Susan Love, et al., "Fibrocystic 'Disease' of the Breast—A Non-disease." *The New England Journal of Medicine*, Vol. 307, No. 16 (October 14, 1982), pp. 1010–4.

31. Loren J. Humphrey, et al., "Immunologic Re-

sponsiveness of the Breast Cancer Patient." *Cancer*, Vol. 46, 1980, pp. 893–989.

32. Bernard Fisher, et al., "Five-Year Results of a Randomized Clinical Trial Comparing Total Mastectomy and Segmental Mastectomy With or Without Radiation in the Treatment of Breast Cancer." *The New England Journal of Medicine*, Vol. 312, No. 11 (March 14, 1985), pp. 665–73.

33. Gianni Bonadonna, "Results of the Milan Adjuvant Chemotherapy Trials." In *Adjuvant Chemotherapy for Breast Cancer*. National Institutes of Health Consensus Development Conference, 1985, pp. 31–4; and I. Craig Henderson, "'Adjuvant Systemic' Therapy of Early Breast Cancer." In J. R. Harris, et al., *Breast Diseases*. Philadelphia: J. B. Lippincott Co., 1987, pp. 324–53.

34. Edwin R. Fisher, "Pathologic Features as Prognostic Variables." *Adjuvant Chemotherapy for Breast Cancer*. National Institutes of Health Consensus Development Conference, 1985, pp. 26–7; and I. Craig Henderson, "Adjuvant Chemotherapy of Breast Cancer." *Journal of Clinical Oncology*, Vol. 3, No. 2 (February 1985), pp. 140–3.

35. "Consensus Report: Adjuvant Chemotherapy for Breast Cancer." National Institutes of Health Consensus Development Conference, September 1985. In *Clinical Insights*. Meniscus Ltd., Health Care Communications, Philadelphia.

36. Figures from the National Center for Health Statistics.

25

DIABETES

by Dorothea F. Sims

Diabetes is a major health challenge today. Statistics show it to be the third leading cause of death in our country because it is the underlying cause of much heart and kidney disease.[1] In recent years, however, we have learned measures to prevent some diabetes and to allow those who have it to live fairly healthy lives. These measures include the same practices that also keep all of us active and healthy during and after midlife.

Diabetes is of special concern to women over forty. Women are more likely to develop diabetes than men.[2] Black and Hispanic women are even more at risk.[3] The disease is not only dangerous in and of itself, but also because people with diabetes often develop complications that result in severe disability and even death.[4] Because it involves our eating habits, those of us with diabetes may suffer from guilt as well as anxiety in connection with the disease.

For a long time I felt really guilty about being diabetic because doctors told me that what I ate was causing some difficulty in my body and that if I would take care of myself I would be in better shape. I think a lot of diabetics stay in the closet about their diabetes because of the guilt. [a fifty-three-year-old woman]

Anything to do with food and eating touches issues of "ideal body weight," dieting and body image, and our own needs in relation to our role as nurturer in our homes and in society.

What Is Diabetes?

In diabetes the pancreas does not produce enough insulin. The pancreas is the part of the communication system in the body that directs the use and storage of energy from foods. This system is an awesome network of biochemical signals that maintains the body's energy balance whether we are at rest or running, hot or cold, old or young, sick or well. Appreciating this balance (called homeostasis) helps us to collaborate with our bodies, even when we are not healthy, instead of viewing our bodies as enemies.

Insulin is a vital link in this communication system. A slow trickle of insulin is normally produced in the body at all times, with larger amounts secreted when eating. Insulin facilitates the movement of fuels from the food we eat into our cells so that these fuels can be used for energy, growth, and healing. The main such fuels are glucose from carbohydrates, amino acids from proteins, and fats from the fat in our diet. When insulin is lacking, glucose builds up in the bloodstream because it is unable to enter cells, and we are short of energy. Some proteins then combine with the abnormally high level of glucose in the blood, blood fats are increased, and blood-vessel walls are damaged. This sequence of events causes further injury throughout the body's tissues and nervous system.

Insulin performs another important task. When we eat more than we can use right away, it promotes the storage of those extra calories for future use. The extra calories are stored in the liver and muscles as glycogen, and in fat cells as fat. That trait helped prehistoric people survive times when food was not available. However, today in our country, where most of us are able to eat every day, this trait is no longer so useful.

Two Types of Diabetes

Diabetes really should be thought of as a plural noun. There are at least two types and possibly more. The two main types differ in cause, inheritability, and treatment. They are now called

Type I, insulin-dependent, and Type II, non-insulin-dependent. Type I usually occurs in young people and used to be called "juvenile-onset." People who have Type I are usually thin, no matter what age they are when it develops. Type II usually appears after the age of forty and used to be called "adult-onset." Eighty to 90 percent of people with Type II diabetes are fat.[5] It is now known that each type can occur at any age.

Diabetes, especially Type II, is on the increase in industrialized countries like ours, where the natural balance between physical work and eating has been disturbed.[6] Our society is food-oriented and sedentary.

More than 6 million people in the United States have diabetes. It is estimated that there are another 6 million who have it and don't know it yet.[7] Most of those who are undiagnosed have Type II diabetes. Unlike those with Type I, they still have some of their own insulin available and so may not have any dramatic symptoms. The warning signs for *both* types of diabetes include fatigue, thirst, frequent urination, slow healing of cuts and bruises, vaginal infection and itching, steady weight gain or recent weight loss, dental disease, and difficulty with eyesight. In Type II, these come on gradually and can easily be mistaken for "just getting older." Some people have undiagnosed Type II diabetes for many years.

In both types of diabetes, not enough insulin is secreted by the pancreas to regulate the blood sugar within the narrow range (60–140 milligrams per deciliter) needed for normal health. However, there the similarity between the two types stops. In Type I diabetes, the cells in the pancreas that produce insulin have been destroyed. The pancreas fails to produce any insulin and the body is quickly starved. The person becomes rapidly and acutely ill and diabetes is easily diagnosed. Recovery is also rapid when insulin is given. Type I has been the most publicized kind of diabetes, but only 10 percent of the people with diabetes in this country have Type I.

Though some people do develop Type I diabetes as they grow older, middle-aged and older women are at more risk for Type II diabetes. The most important thing to keep in mind about Type II diabetes is that people who have it still produce generous amounts of their own insulin. However, their bodies have become resistant to insulin, and they are not able to

make enough insulin to compensate for this resistance. Though why this happens is not yet completely understood, it is clear that becoming overweight and relatively inactive has a lot to do with insulin resistance.[8] So our sedentary and food habits have a lot to do with the increase in Type II diabetes.

Type II diabetes is inherited much more often than is Type I. Knowing your family history is useful. People who are overweight often feel guilty because they have long been indirectly and unfairly blamed for their condition. Now science tells us that some people have genetic traits that give them a tendency to store excess calories as fat. They may also have another genetic factor in the way insulin influences the energy balance inside the cells of their body.

We develop diabetes because it is hereditary and it isn't because we have been "bad." It took me a long time to understand that I was OK. Actually it was when I went into the hospital for an eye operation and was talking to a doctor there about the cause of my blindness and some of the things I wish I had done differently. He said, "You really sound very guilty." I said that I do feel guilty about the way I have taken care of myself and particularly the way I have eaten. And he said, "If you really think that diabetes is caused just by the way you eat, then practically every American should be diabetic because look at the diet of the average American—it is full of sugar." And it wasn't until that time that it occurred to me that, of course, there was something more to it than that. I certainly had been off sugar for quite a while at that point. [a fifty-four-year-old woman who lost her vision at age fifty]

Those who have inherited the likelihood of getting diabetes if they get fat are at an unfair disadvantage in our overfed society, especially if they were brought up in families where heavy eating was encouraged. In addition, people often use food as a comforting substitute when they are scared, lonely, or angry, and this can make it hard to change eating habits. Understanding how these environmental and cultural elements interact with inherited tendencies can relieve feelings of guilt and helplessness about diabetes. We should not be blamed for genetic defects, but we don't have to remain at their mercy. We should offer the same respect and support to those struggling to change eating habits as we do to those who have to inject insulin every day.

Type II Is NOT a "Mild" Form of Diabetes

Because people with Type II don't usually need to take insulin, it has been called a "mild" form of diabetes. However, it is now known that this is not the case. Type II diabetes can cause such long-term complications as large-blood-vessel disease and loss of vision and kidney function, just as Type I can.[9]

When my doctor discovered I had diabetes, he said, "But it is only mild." So I assumed it was not necessary to be careful and ate sweets anyway. Then I remembered my brother who had recently died of kidney and liver failure and was totally blind. His urine never showed any sugar. The first symptom he had was when he awakened one morning, blind. The eye doctor said he had had diabetes for fifteen years to have such severe hemorrhage in his eyes. I hope these types of accidents can be prevented more now with the new light on Type II diabetes. [a sixty-eight-year-old woman from a family of ten, five of whom have diabetes]

There is a brighter side to this picture. When people with Type II diabetes lose weight and increase their physical activity to maintain a steady weight, their own insulin often comes back into healthy play. If so, they may be able to avoid the expense, inconvenience, and possible reactions of taking insulin or pills.

I have had Type II diabetes for several years. When I was fifty-six years old, I was on 34 units of insulin, my blood sugar was 180 and I weighed 210 pounds. Then I cut down on my calories but kept the healthy foods such as ½ cup servings of vegetables. In three weeks I had to stop taking insulin because of reactions. My doctor knew I was doing this and has records on it. I had lost 20 pounds. I did some bike riding. I had had a heart attack a year before, but now my heart seems okay. One year later, my weight is 148, my blood sugar 125, and I'm walking five to ten miles a day, am insulin-free and feeling wonderful! [a fifty-seven-year-old woman]

People with Type II diabetes who have a great deal of difficulty in keeping to a treatment plan of diet and exercise may need insulin injections or the pills for diabetes called oral agents, either separately or in combination. However, neither of these interventions works without the diet and exercise aspects too. Diet and exercise are necessary to restore the body cells' sensitivity to insulin. Insulin cannot be taken by mouth because it is a protein and would be digested in the stomach. In addition, there are some disadvantages to taking insulin without implementing a diet and exercise program as well. Insulin makes you hungry, so it's harder to keep calories down. This may lead to a cycle of weight gain which, in turn, increases insulin resistance and calls for higher doses of insulin. Oral agents can be used in Type II diabetes, in which people still produce their own insulin. The oral agents help to increase the release of the body's insulin. Although the oral agents are now considered to be very useful for many people, they must be prescribed and utilized appropriately for each individual and be very carefully monitored.

The sixty-eight-year-old woman who had five family members with diabetes now reports:

I recently lost 10 pounds. For exercise, I never use the elevator, sometimes walk up five flights. I work as a Foster Grandmother at a school for the retarded. I push wheelchairs there. For a while, I was taking one of the pills for diabetes, but it made me confused and gave me a low blood sugar, so I stopped. I am doing quite well.

Heed Early Warning Signs

If you have a strong family history of obesity, gave birth to a baby with a high birth weight, or developed temporary diabetes during pregnancy, you may be able to prevent Type II diabetes both for yourself and your children by following the life-style recommendations in this chapter. You will have a good influence on your family's diet and exercise habits at the same time.

Gestational diabetes is the "temporary diabetes" which sometimes surfaces during pregnancy. Even if we don't plan to have more children, or are past menopause, we can alert our daughters, granddaughters, and other younger women to the dangers of developing sugar in their urine during pregnancy. Sixty-five percent of women who have gestational diabetes and who *also* are overweight during pregnancy eventually develop full-blown diabetes.[10] If they can be persuaded to change their habits while they are still young, to keep their weight down, and to increase their activity, they may improve their chances of avoiding diabetes.

I was one of those women who had gestational diabetes. My blood sugar went high during a pregnancy and then was fine again. I was told that I might be a borderline diabetic. "Be careful but you don't have to worry about it." Because no one ever told me what might really happen to me if I developed diabetes, I had absolutely no inkling of what would happen. Even though I had seen at least two doctors, they never gave me much information. So for years my weight went up and down with my age, with emotional stuff, with whatever. I was not really very careful until eight to ten years ago. I would eat sugar and just was not very good about my diet.

Basically it wasn't until I became a vegetarian that I began to be a little more clear about diet. [the fifty-four-year-old woman who lost her vision at fifty]

My granddaughter just had a nine-pound baby and she showed some sugar while she was pregnant. She goes on gaining weight. I worry about it because I don't know if her doctor takes it seriously. He says that lots of people have sugar when they carry a child, but that it goes away later. My father had diabetes and so have I. I'm going to ask my diabetes doctor to visit with her. [a sixty-eight-year-old woman who developed diabetes in her fifties]

Complications of Diabetes

The worst aspect of diabetes is that people who have undiagnosed or poorly managed diabetes are more likely to develop complications than those who keep control of their blood glucose. The most common of these are heart disease, stroke, kidney failure, visual impairment, sexual problems, and amputation of legs and feet. All of these problems are caused by inadequate circulation of the blood in both the large and small blood vessels. For example, diabetes causes one-half of the 80,000 leg and foot amputations performed annually because the blood flow in the arteries has been damaged.[11]

I didn't take care of myself when I was told I had diabetes at age eighty. My husband was sick and I had to pay more attention to him. I didn't go on a diet, I would drink too much orange juice and have no exercise at all. After my husband passed away my diabetes came right down on me. It was then that I went to the hospital and was told I had no circulation in my leg at all so that's why I had to have my leg taken off. [an eighty-four-year-old Black woman]

Women with diabetes and hypertension should take special care to keep their blood pressure normal (see p. 314) as well as their blood glucose level. When blood glucose is normal, the quality of all aspects of life improves. If your blood glucose is high, so is your urine glucose. Sugary urine turns the vaginal area into a perfect environment for infections and breakdown of the tissues. The resulting discomfort is a major barrier to sexual satisfaction for women with diabetes. However, there is now evidence that working hard at keeping your blood-glucose level as close to normal as possible may minimize, postpone, or prevent these complications.

Diabetes is the leading cause of blindness in adults in the U.S. Too many physicians super-vising diabetes control fail to refer their patients for an annual eye exam. Many fail to do even a rudimentary eye exam themselves. Every person with diabetes should have an annual eye exam by an ophthalmologist.

Self-Care

Diabetes is the supreme example of the value of self-care. Since it is a disorder of the body's use of the fuel we get from food, we always have to think about energy-in (eating) and energy-out (work and exercise) in relation to each other. Recently there has been a real revolution in the treatment of diabetes, with new tools for self-care and some techniques for treating complications if they do develop.

One of these tools is a blood test that can be self-administered at any time of day or night to find out how well your treatment plan is working. A drop of blood is obtained with an automatic spring-loaded finger lancet and the blood-glucose level is read from a test strip. The finger prick is practically painless with good equipment, and if the sides of the fingertips (rather than the central pads) are used. This self-blood-glucose-monitoring (SBGM) allows you to read your body signals with regard to food and exercise. It rewards you with immediate feedback. Self-blood-testing takes the mystery out of the daily chores of living with diabetes and puts the power of management of diabetes squarely in your hands. You can share your record with your supervising health professionals, who will help you stay up to date on new advances and make suggestions that fit your particular needs.

What are other daily tasks of self-care for the person with diabetes? They differ according to the type of diabetes. People with Type I have to take insulin injections two to four times a day, and they have to learn to match their food intake with their energy output and the dosage of insulin. There are many alternatives to choose from in accomplishing this difficult routine, including the use of insulin pumps, which are worn outside the body and can be programmed to give insulin automatically. The greatest daily hazard faced by people taking insulin is an unpredictable lowering of blood sugar (hypoglycemia) called "insulin reaction," which requires immediate ingestion of sugar. **People who have diabetes should carry medical identification at all times.**

David Whittier/Greater Boston Diabetes Society

Many people with Type II diabetes don't need to take oral agents or insulin unless their supply of insulin is so reduced that there isn't enough to overcome insulin resistance. However, those with Type II may need to take insulin temporarily during times of physical or emotional stress, such as before, during or after surgery, or during a personal crisis. They are faced with the demanding task of losing weight and becoming physically active, sometimes after having been sedentary for years, and the lifelong task of remaining active and keeping their weight down.

Conquering these challenges is well worth the effort. People with either type of diabetes who succeed in effective self-care feel well most of the time and lead productive lives of normal length.

Support Groups

A support group of people with diabetes can be very comforting in keeping up courage, and a practical help, too. The American Diabetes Association and many hospitals offer such groups.

See page 20 for how to start a support group if one does not exist in your area.

You don't always have to have a professional person there. We learn more from each other than any other way—like don't drink a diet soda between meals because the sweet taste starts up the hunger reflexes even if there aren't any calories in it. Salty snacks will do the same thing. Chew a carrot instead! We help each other to shop sensibly too. We read the labels and consider the costs. Many of the so-called dietetic foods cost more than ordinary brands and are no more healthy. But in general, the supermarkets are offering better food today

than even a few years ago. [a woman in her forties with diabetes]

Exercise

Exercise plays an important part in the self-care of people with diabetes. We are all familiar with the many reasons for remaining as active as possible throughout life (see Moving for Health chapter). In addition, persons with diabetes are at high risk for osteoporosis and must exercise in order to utilize the calcium in food to strengthen bones (see Osteoporosis chapter). For those of us with diabetes, exercise brings the added benefit of increased sensitivity of the body's cells to the actions of insulin.[12]

The management of exercise as a vital part of self-care differs for the two types of diabetes. For Type I diabetes, this means that in order to avoid having too much insulin when exercising, each individual has to learn how much to reduce insulin dosage and increase food intake in order to exercise safely. For Type II diabetes, exercise not only burns unwanted calories but also helps to overcome the inherited resistance to insulin. In fact, there are many people with Type II diabetes who have normalized their blood sugar by exercise, even though they do not lose all the weight they had gained over the years.

If I forget my exercise for two weeks, I am depressed and tired. When I exercise, I feel fine because my blood glucose is within normal range. So it's worth it to keep at it, though I've had to accept the fact that my body will never be really slim again. [a fifty-two-year-old woman]

In addition, those who make the switch to a more active life find it has lasting psychological benefits, although the routine may not have been easy to establish.

For me, running has made a tremendous difference in this regard. This is not to say that I don't have to watch my diet. It does mean that I don't have to count every calorie. I no longer gain three pounds after one decent meal. My weight is at a fairly reasonable level and isn't constantly fluctuating five to ten pounds as under the starve/stuff routine. You soon disprove the old exercise-produces-increased-appetite myth. Right after and during exercise, food is the last thing on my mind, since the blood has been diverted away from the digestive system to the muscles. One of the primary fringe benefits is the psychological one. I can start out feeling anxious, depressed, fatigued and/or angry, and as I push myself it all dissipates. [a woman in her forties]

Diet

Everyone says that diet restrictions are the most irritating part of living with diabetes. Today, however, dieticians are taking a new and more flexible approach to food for people with diabetes.[13] Most dieticians now recognize that social, cultural, and emotional habits of eating have to be taken into consideration, and that when people eat food, they are not necessarily thinking about nutrients. You can adjust your diet to include your preferences as well as your caloric needs, but you will need to know about the components of foods to do so. Your diet will vary depending on your age and general level of activity as well as general health and type of diabetes. For this reason, the services of a dietician can be of great value.

Most people who monitor their blood carefully and are willing and able to exercise vigorously can eat at least a little of almost everything, but some diabetics must restrict their food choices and may feel severely deprived.

I was greatly surprised to find that I had Type II diabetes six years ago. I'm supersensitive to food and if I break my diet in the smallest way, it makes a difference in weight gain and blood sugar. I do get sick of it. It seems that everything that makes food attractive is what I can't have. After trimming the pork chop, cutting it up in pieces and weighing it, who wants to eat it, all by itself in the middle of the plate? Sometimes I feel that people who have Type I diabetes are lucky. They really need to eat to stay even with their insulin. [a fifty-two-year-old woman]

No Smoking

As well as adopting new diet and exercise habits, there is another vital self-care decision to be made. That is the decision not to smoke. Smoking does a great deal of damage to the body's circulatory system. Nicotine acts to constrict the smaller blood vessels and thus increases the risk of hypertension. Combining that hazard with the risk of damage to blood vessels from the high blood glucose and blood fats of diabetes is virtually inviting heart attacks, strokes, and other serious complications.[14] Therefore, although it may be difficult to quit smoking, doing so is a crucial investment in a longer, healthier life for those of us with diabetes.

Use the Health Care System to the Best Advantage

People who have diabetes themselves or in their families need to make the best use of the entire health care system. Find a doctor who is up to date on diabetes and interested in working with you as an individual in coordinating your health care. Nurse practitioners are also skilled at helping with management of diabetes. Since diabetes can affect all the body systems, you may also need the support and advice of specialists such as a dietician, a podiatrist for foot care, and an eye doctor. Fortunately, health insurance providers and health maintenance organizations are beginning to pay for these services to prevent costly complications requiring hospitalization and lost work days. Coverage varies from state to state, so ask.

Since diabetes can complicate and slow down recovery from other illnesses, those of us with diabetes have to insist that our caregivers collaborate on their treatment suggestions. Inform any other doctor you use that you have diabetes and make sure that she or he is in touch with the doctor who manages your diabetes.

Diabetes and Stress Management

The way our bodies respond to stress goes back to prehistoric times when the threats were to life and limb, calling for quick energy for flight or fight. Chemical signals mobilize fuels stored in the liver and muscle and raise the heartbeat and breathing rates for rapid circulation of energy. This outpouring of glucose was fine when we had to run away from a lion, but it is not useful or healthy for a person who is caught in a traffic jam or mad at her boss. The rise in blood sugar, with no way to compensate for it through physical action, is not good for those of us who have diabetes. We need the support of people who are coping successfully in order to learn how to avoid stress and to minimize it when it develops.

Diabetes causes stress both for those of us who have it and for our families and friends. Maintaining the balance of food, activity, and insulin takes time and money and requires planning that limits freedom of choice and spontaneity. Diabetes is yet another challenge to test our native adaptability and lifelong experience. Others may not understand why we have to eat right on time or why we have to avoid certain foods. We need to let them know what we need and why. We must respect our personal needs and learn to meet them even when they differ from the needs of those who share our lives.

NOTES

1. National Diabetes Data Group, *Diabetes in America 1985.* NIH Publication 85-1468, National Institutes of Health, Rockville Pike, Bethesda, MD 20014, Chapter 1, pp. 3–4; and J. K. Davidson, *Clinical Diabetes.* New York: Thieme-Stratton, Inc., 1986.

2. P. H. Bennett, "The Epidemiology of Diabetes Mellitus," in *Diabetes Mellitus*, Vol. 5, H. Rifkin and P. Raskin, eds. A Diabetes Association Publication. Bowie, MD: R. J. Brady Co., 1981, p. 87.

3. National Diabetes Data Group, op. cit., Chapter 8, p. 1, and Chapter 9, p. 1; and American Diabetes Association, *1985 Fact Sheet on Diabetes.*

4. National Diabetes Data Group, op. cit., Chapter 1, pp. 1–4.

5. Bennett, op. cit., p. 92.

6. E. A. H. Sims, "Effects of Overnutrition and Underexertion on the Development of Diabetes and Hypertension: A Growing Epidemic?" in *Malnutrition: Determinants and Consequences.* New York: Alan R. Liss, Inc., 1984, pp. 151–63; and E. S. Horton, "Role of Environmental Factors in the Development of Non-Insulin-Dependent Diabetes Mellitus." *American Journal of Medicine*, Vol. 75, 1983, pp. 32–40.

7. National Diabetes Data Group, op. cit., Chapter 1, p. 1.

8. M. Rosenthal, et al., "Demonstration of a Relationship Between Level of Physical Training and Insulin-Stimulated Glucose Utilization in Normal Humans." *Diabetes*, Vol. 32, 1983, pp. 408–11.

9. National Diabetes Data Group, op. cit., Chapter 1, pp. 1–4.

10. J. B. O'Sullivan, "Body Weight and Subsequent Diabetes Mellitus." *Journal of the American Medical Association*, Vol. 248, 1982, p. 979; and J. B. O'Sullivan, "Gestational Diabetes: Factors Influencing the Rates of Subsequent Diabetes." In, Sutherland and Stowers, eds., *Carbohydrate Metabolism in Pregnancy and the Newborn.* New York: Springer-Verlag, 1979, pp. 425–535.

11. American Diabetes Association, *1985 Diabetes Facts.*

12. C. Bogardus, et al., "Effects of Physical Training and Diet Therapy on Carbohydrate Metabolism in Patients with Glucose Intolerance and Non-Insulin-Dependent Diabetes Mellitus." *Diabetes*, Vol. 33, 1984, pp. 311–8.

13. F. Q. Nuthall, "Diet and the Diabetic Patient." *Diabetes Care*, Vol. 6, 1983, pp. 197–207.

14. U.S. Office of the Assistant Secretary for Health and Surgeon General, *The Health Consequences of Smoking for Women.* Rockville, MD: U.S. Department of Health and Human Services, Public Health Service, 1983. U.S. Government Printing Office, No. 410-889/1284.

26

GALLSTONES AND GALLBLADDER DISEASE

by Glorianne Wittes

Gallstones are a common problem faced by many women in midlife. Women have a higher incidence of gallbladder disease than men. It has been estimated that twelve million women, compared to four million men, have gallstones. Gallstones can be detected in almost 90 percent of Native Americans and others with Indian heritage (mostly women), such as Mexican-Americans, and at a much earlier age than in whites. In one study, 35 percent of Mexican-American women had symptoms of gallstones by age sixty-five.[1] Such high rates in certain groups warrant special study and care.

Gallstones have been disparagingly labeled by some specialists as an affliction of women who are "fat, forty, and flatulent."[2] Some add "fertile" to the list. This label discloses a bias against aging women in general and fat women in particular. Because of these prejudiced attitudes, we must be certain that any recommendations for treatment are carefully considered and truly helpful, and not made just on the basis of stereotypes. We must be able to recognize this bias when it surfaces so that we can look for more enlightened care.

Symptoms of Gallbladder Disease

The gallbladder is a small sac located on the right side of the abdomen under the liver. It serves as a reservoir for bile, which is produced in the liver. Following a meal, the gallbladder contracts to release bile into the duodenum (the beginning of the small intestine), where it assists in the digestion of food.

Bile is made up of cholesterol, lecithin, bile salts, and bilirubin (yellowish pigment). When this balance is disturbed and there is too much cholesterol in the bile, the excess separates out in the form of hardened matter called stones, or very fine material called sludge or sand. One type of stone contains mostly cholesterol; another type contains mostly bilirubin (often called pigment stones). Some stones are a mixture of these two types.

Many common signs of indigestion (dyspepsia), such as belching, bloating, and heartburn, are rarely symptoms of gallbladder disease as well. But such signs should be investigated early on, especially if accompanied by nausea, acute pain, fever, chills, vomiting, or jaundice, which are the most common indicators of gallstones, and possible infection.

Once formed, if a gallstone stays in your gallbladder, you usually suffer no pain or only mild pain, belching, bloating, or nausea. Any pain would probably be caused by the stones rubbing against the lining of the gallbladder, producing irritation and inflammation. However, if the stone lodges in the cystic duct, the bile duct, or the pancreatic duct (see illustration), you will suffer severe pain in the upper abdomen (often more pronounced on the right side) which travels through to the back and under the right shoulder blade. This pain, known as biliary colic, comes on suddenly, frequently after a meal, and usually remains very intense for several hours.

In addition, when a stone is lodged in the cystic duct, the gallbladder becomes inflamed (a condition known as cholecystitis), and fever, nausea, and vomiting may develop. When the stone lodges in the common bile duct, jaundice and infection of the liver may develop. In either duct, the stone can block the draining of bile from the gallbladder into the small intestine. If

DIGESTIVE ORGANS

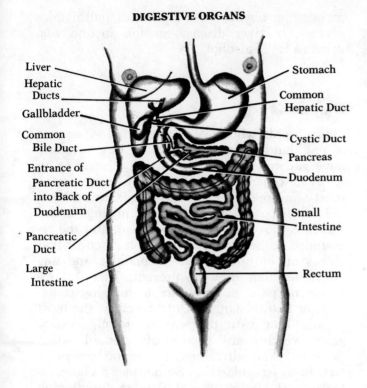

Liver
Hepatic Ducts
Gallbladder
Common Bile Duct
Entrance of Pancreatic Duct into Back of Duodenum
Pancreatic Duct
Large Intestine

Stomach
Common Hepatic Duct
Cystic Duct
Pancreas
Duodenum
Small Intestine
Rectum

a stone obstructs the pancreatic duct, it may cause severe inflammation and the destruction of the pancreas. Pancreatitis, as this complication is known, is a potentially fatal condition.

If the gallstone can enter the duodenum, it passes out in the feces and causes no further problem. If an attack of biliary colic subsides spontaneously, a stone that was temporarily lodged in a duct may have passed into the duodenum or passed back into the gallbladder.

What Causes Gallbladder Disease?

Dietary Factors

While many gallstones are caused by an over-abundance of cholesterol in the bile, there is no direct relationship between the amount of cholesterol in the diet or blood and the cholesterol content of the bile. Cholesterol not only comes from the food we eat, but also is manufactured within the body. Some studies claim that a high-cholesterol diet has not been firmly linked to gallstone formation—but a correlation has been found between gallstones and a diet high in calories and sweets. Yet high-calorie diets are high-calorie often because they contain high

amounts of fat, which in turn contains high amounts of cholesterol. Still, cutting down on cholesterol (though that kind of modification is recommended for prevention of coronary artery disease) does not seem to prevent gallstones altogether.[3]

There is conflicting evidence as to the connection between a diet high in *saturated* fat and gallstone formation.[4] Some studies find a significant correlation and others do not. However, saturated fats do bring about gallbladder attacks, as follows: Fats stimulate the pancreas to produce certain hormones, which in turn cause the gallbladder to contract. The contracting gallbladder may force stones out into the ducts, where they create the symptoms of a gallbladder attack. *Thus, a low-fat diet is crucial for the treatment of an already diseased gallbladder.* It should be noted here that the most common symptoms of fatty food upsets, such as indigestion, belching, and bloating, are seldom caused by gallbladder disease. Indeed, the simultaneous presence of gallstones and indigestion is usually a matter of chance. For example, in one study, only twenty-four of 142 women who complained of "chronic indigestion" had gallbladder disease.[5] It is therefore critical to establish that gallstones are indeed the culprit before surgery is considered.

Many fat women are warned to follow a strict weight-reduction program once they suffer a gallbladder attack in order to prevent further attacks. The amount of cholesterol in the bile is greater in fat people than in thin people. The cholesterol level in the bile may increase further during weight loss and then stabilize at a lower concentration when a lower weight level is maintained. Therefore, alternately losing and gaining weight increases the risk of gallstone formation.[6]

In addition, it is likely that the high fat and sugar content of a high-calorie diet sets off gallbladder attacks in fat women, rather than excess weight itself.[7] Thin or average-weight people who ingest a lot of fat are also vulnerable to gallbladder attacks. It is cruel and unfortunate that in our "thin society" the fat woman with gallbladder disease is made to feel that her weight caused her medical problem, and that therefore she is her own worst enemy.

Studies show contradictory results regarding the effect of wheat fiber on cholesterol metabolism. Oat bran has been shown to have some effect on lowering cholesterol. Foods high in sulfur, such as cabbage, asparagus, Brussels sprouts, celery, cauliflower, onions, and radishes, stimulate the flow of bile and may be included in both prevention and management programs. Some experts recommend adding supplements of lecithin, taurine and methionine (amino acids), copper, vitamin B_{12}, folic acid, vitamin C, and magnesium to a low-fat diet to increase the solubility of bile.

Some holistic nutritionists believe that gallbladder disease may be related to food allergies, especially to eggs. Some suggest that the gallbladder can be stimulated to flush and clean out sludge, although this is not effective with large stones. Others say they will not supervise such a program because of the danger that a piece of stone will get lodged in a duct and require emergency surgery.

Unfortunately, an improved diet, though promoting health in many ways, does not seem to dissolve gallstones that have already formed. Thus, changing your diet does not reduce the risk that a stone will block a duct and cause serious complications. However, avoiding fatty foods does help *prevent symptoms* when stones are present.

Hormonal Factors

Estrogen appears to raise the fat content of bile, which in turn contributes to the formation of gallstones. A 1974 study showed that women taking estrogen after menopause were *two and a half times* more likely to develop gallstones than women not taking estrogens.[8] This study was virtually ignored in the wake of controversy over estrogen as a carcinogen and in the promotion of estrogen as a prevention for osteoporosis. The 1979 National Institutes of Health Consensus Conference on Estrogen Replacement Therapy did list gallbladder disease as a risk of taking estrogen, but said more study was needed.

The incidence of gallbladder disease is high in women who use oral contraceptives, in pregnant women and in women who have had several pregnancies because estrogen level is high during pregnancy. The incidence of gallbladder disease among women was even higher between 1961 and 1971, before the amounts of estrogen in the oral contraceptives were reduced.[9] Oral contraceptives and estrogen are not recom-

mended for anyone with gallstones, gallbladder disease, or liver disease, or for anyone who drinks a lot of alcohol.

Diagnosis

Many people who have not reported symptoms of gallbladder disease are often discovered to have gallstones when they undergo tests or an X-ray for other, unrelated reasons. Currently the most widespread diagnostic test is an abdominal ultrasound. A machine emitting sound waves is moved over the abdomen, and the rebounded echoes are recorded on a machine that shows an outline of the gallbladder and any gallstones that may be present. This test involves no pain, no exposure to ionizing radiation, or known danger. Until recently, the most popular diagnostic test was an oral cholecystogram, which is still used in questionable situations after an ultrasound shows no stones or structural irregularities. Sometimes a cholecystogram shows poor gallbladder functioning when the dosage of dye given for the test is too low. If the test is repeated with more dye, and the gallbladder is still not clearly outlined, then poor functioning of the gallbladder is assumed.

Treatment Methods

In many cases, gallstones may never cause any problems at all—or any severe enough to warrant removal of the gallbladder. Studies of autopsies show that 20 percent of women who never had their gallbladder removed had gallstones at the time of death.[10] This raises several questions: Will "silent" gallstones that are not producing symptoms cause problems later? What, if anything, should be done about them and when?

In 1985, of 475,000 people who had their gallbladders surgically removed, 69 percent of them were women.[11] Removal of the gallbladder (cholecystectomy) and hysterectomy are the most frequently performed unnecessary operations. While the removal of the gallbladder is sometimes necessary, in other instances the decision of whether and when to operate is not so clear. Is removal of the gallbladder, like hysterectomy and oophorectomy, recommended frequently because it is a good learning experience for surgeons-in-training, and a financial staple for those in medical practice? Do some physicians recommend the operation as a good way to silence the complaints of a woman who is "just a menopausal whiner"? Are physicians assuming that every complaint by a middle-aged woman is related to menopause and ignoring signs of gallbladder disease until the last minute, when surgery is necessary?

What is clear in any case is that when a gallstone is lodged in a duct, immediate hospitalization and (usually) prompt surgery are required. This condition is potentially life-threatening. But when you have a "silent" gallstone—one that is causing no symptoms, or only mild, painless symptoms—the gallstone does not necessarily have to be treated with medication or removed surgically. Many women with a silent or painless gallstone simply follow a prudent low-fat diet and undergo no further treatment.

Many surgeons advise the removal of a gallbladder with silent gallstones because they may cause life-threatening complications in the future by lodging in a duct. Every individual must weigh the risk and pain of surgery against the risk of developing these complications.

Two and a half years ago, an X-ray for a slipped disk showed a number of stones the size of chick-peas. An ultrasound confirmed the stones and a lot of sludge, and I was strongly advised to have surgery right away. In retrospect, I had been having symptoms of fatty food intolerance for a long time. I did not want to have major surgery since I would be moving across the country to start a new job in a month. When I moved I found a family-practice doctor and told her that I knew I might face an emergency situation if a stone lodged in the duct and became infected. She encouraged me to wait until the balance of problems outweighed my not wanting to have surgery, and encouraged diet changes. So I waited. At the end of the second year, I became sick with a fever and weakness and pain. That was the signal that the time had come. I had the surgery six weeks ago. I believe the surgery was then necessary and I am also glad I waited. [a forty-year-old woman]

Some experts consider cancer of the gallbladder a threat if gallstones are left untreated, though others do not.[12] A study was done at the University of Michigan on 123 faculty members with silent gallstones. It was found that over fifteen years none of them died of gallstone complications or developed cancer of the gallbladder. Only sixteen of the 123 developed symptoms of biliary colic. The researchers concluded that very few people with untreated si-

lent gallstones will die from gallbladder disease and that an elective cholecystectomy need not be considered unless attacks of biliary colic occur.[13]

A person with gallstones who also experiences abdominal discomfort or mild pain, especially after a fatty meal, should be considered in the category of people with "symptomatic" gallstones. Someone who has had one or more attacks of biliary colic that have subsided spontaneously (which means that a gallstone was temporarily lodged in a duct and then either passed back into the gallbladder or passed out to the duodenum) also faces a dilemma about whether or not to have surgery.

I had two attacks while away on holiday. The symptoms were excruciating. Pain in the upper abdomen and across the back made me wonder if I was having a heart attack. During the second attack I went to the hospital. They called my symptoms biliary colic and said they were due to fine sand [a form of stones] in my gallbladder, which I should have surgically removed. They described the complications that could occur if I didn't do so, that is, that sand could slip out of my gallbladder into the ducts and cause infection, requiring emergency surgery. This presented me with a terrible dilemma. Since my condition was not life-threatening at the moment I decided to go back home for further opinions there. The second opinion I received concurred with the need for surgery. The third opinion argued that the presence of sand did not require immediate surgery. This physician did not want to operate on me, since I was very fat, and recommended weight loss and a fat-restricted diet. I went along with the third opinion and have been well now for five years. [a fifty-five-year-old woman]

For two years I suffered with flatulence, belching, and stomachaches that were mild but annoying. Tests did not reveal gallstones, but my internist suspected them from my symptoms. He wanted them surgically removed. The surgeon refused to operate on stones that didn't visualize. I initially decided that a low-fat diet was preferable to the pain of surgery and the time I would need for recuperation. However, I found that maintaining such a strict diet was enormously stressful and ultimately decided in favor of surgery. Was I ever glad I did! The surgery revealed multiple stones that might have caused me complications. [a forty-nine-year-old woman]

For years I was uncomfortable after eating the least amount of fat and had to watch myself like a hawk. Gallstones were never diagnosed. Finally, after a severe attack of biliary colic, my doctor suggested gallbladder surgery, though no stones visualized at all in my tests. The surgery revealed that sludge [fine sand] had lodged in the common duct and that the pancreas duct and gallbladder were also infected. I was furious that the diagnosis of gallbladder disease hadn't been made earlier, for if surgery had been done earlier I might have been spared all this infection and post-operative discomfort. [a fifty-six-year-old woman]

I could not face the possibility of ever again having an attack like this one. I dreaded the presence of little demons inside me threatening to strike again at the least expected moment. So I insisted on surgery, and do you know, I sailed through it with no complications, despite my age? They found thirty-two small stones in my gallbladder! Now I guess it took me longer to recuperate than a younger person with this same surgery, but that's to be expected at my age and with my medical problems. [an eighty-two-year-old woman]

Alternative Holistic Treatments

Some people who have gallstones find that alternative holistic treatments, such as acupuncture and imagery, have helped them (though not in emergency situations, when a stone is lodged in a duct).

An acupuncturist stimulates specific points on the body by inserting needles, applying heat, pressure massage (acupressure), or a combination of these methods.

During my acute gallbladder attacks my friend massaged my back to give me some relief from the agony I was experiencing. As she touched a certain point in my back I asked her to dig in deeply to reach the pain inside. She did so and the pain suddenly disappeared, totally and completely, in these few seconds of deep pressure. I embarked on a series of acupuncture sessions. This felt similar to the experience when pressure relieved my pain. The acupuncturist I chose said that acupuncture was unlikely to dissolve the stones, but could possibly rectify the bile imbalance and other physical dynamics that were forming them. I haven't been troubled by any gallbladder attacks since that series and I attribute it, in part, to this treatment, along with careful diet and imagery work. [a fifty-five-year-old woman]

Imagery is a technique that encourages the body to fight disease by visualizing the body as a strong heroine overpowering the disease. The same woman continues:

I was familiar with the use of imagery to fight cancer, and use imagery regularly myself to relax or envision how a design project will look when completed. It comes easily to me and I believe in it. So I imagined my bile salts armed with spikes shattering the stones that were plaguing me and excreting them effortlessly out of my body. I did this imagery work daily during the six weeks I was undergoing acupuncture. It made me feel less anxious about my condition because I felt I was doing something that could potentially cure me.

Surgery

A cholecystectomy is considered by physicians to be a simple operation. An incision is made below the right rib cage; the gallbladder is removed, and the abdomen is explored for any problems not related to the gallbladder. Your surgeon should not remove your appendix unless you give your consent in advance. If the presence of a stone in the common bile duct is suspected, or if there has been an infection, a small plastic drain that protrudes through the surgical wound to the outside of the body is left in place for several days. As with any abdominal surgery, you may have several days of pain and discomfort.

Most people are able to return to work and normal activity two to four weeks after the operation. Some people complain of difficulties with digestion after a cholecystectomy, because bile will be entering directly into the duodenum without the gallbladder to time its entry. On rare occasions, a stone may form in the common bile duct, necessitating another operation.

The likelihood of complications from gallbladder surgery depends on your age, your general physical health before surgery, your surgeon's skill, and the length of time it takes to perform the operation. The older you are, the more likely you are to experience complications. If you are jaundiced and infected at the time of surgery, the likelihood of complications also increases. The most common among these are infection (which can usually be controlled with antibiotics), pneumonia and other lung problems, phlebitis, clots in the lung, and operative errors. A hernia may develop at the site of the incision.

Several new experimental methods of treatment are currently being studied. Percutaneous ultrasonic lithotripsy (PUL) involves inserting a catheter through the skin, which traverses the liver into the cystic duct and from there into the gallbladder. A collapsible basket attached to the catheter snags the gallstone and removes it. The gallbladder is left intact. The advantage of this procedure is that only a local anesthesia is required, and you can return home the same day and get back to work and normal activity immediately. It thus costs considerably less than surgery and inflicts minimal discomfort.

Drugs to Dissolve Stones

No drug has been found yet that dissolves all gallstones without other injurious effects, though many are being tried singly or in combination. Synthetic bile acids include chenodeoxycholic acid (chenodiol or CDCA) and ursodeoxycholic acid (UDCA). In one study of CDCA,[14] gallstones were completely dissolved in only 13.5 percent of those who received 750 milligrams daily and in 5.2 percent of those who received 375 milligrams daily. When the drug worked, it usually did so within nine months. Drug-induced diarrhea was common but responded to treatment. A more serious problem was that the drug altered liver function and caused liver inflammation in many patients, more severely in those on the higher dose of CDCA.

UDCA is more effective but is expensive, since large daily doses are required for six to twelve months. In 85 percent of patients taking 600 milligrams per day, cholesterol stones smaller than 15 millimeters in diameter were completely or partially dissolved.[15] The drug caused very little diarrhea and appeared to carry no risk of liver damage.

The currently preferred drug, mono-octanoin, usually requires three to twenty-one days to dissolve cholesterol duct stones but is successful only one-third of the time, irritates the gastrointestinal and biliary tracts, and may cause pain, nausea, and vomiting.[16]

Another experimental procedure involves placing a catheter through which methyl tert-butyl ether (MTBE) is infused into the gallbladder to dissolve the stones in place, without removing the gallbladder.[17] Careful studies are needed to confirm the safety over time of the use of this toxic substance.

Another experimental method for treating gallstones uses a combination of bile-acid drugs and very loud shock waves from a machine called a lithotriptor already used to smash kidney stones. The procedure is administered under anesthesia because it is potentially painful. This method was not successful for everyone in the first small study, but only for those with choles-

terol stones no larger than 25 mm. and a functioning gallbladder. Damage to nearby organs is possible, but did not occur in this study.[18]

To date, drugs are not being seen as a general panacea for dissolving gallstones, but as an alternative for the sufferers who cannot or will not undergo cholecystectomy.[19] If you are taking any of these drugs, it is imperative that you have blood tests of the liver at regular intervals to detect any possible damage. You should also bear in mind that even if gallstones are completely dissolved, they may recur once you've stopped taking the medication. Having to take the drugs for a long time may be a serious drawback since they are expensive and their long-term effects are not known.

NOTES

1. Kenneth M. Weiss and Craig L. Hanis, "All 'Silent' Gallstones Are Not Silent." *The New England Journal of Medicine*, Vol. 310, No. 10 (March 8, 1986), pp. 657–8.

2. Quoted in "The Gold Bladder (Gallbladder)," Chapter 1 in Siegfried Krat and Robert Boltax, *Is Surgery Necessary?* New York: Macmillan, 1981. Now available in paperback from New American Library.

3. "The Gallbladder and Gallstones, Part 1." *Harvard Medical School Health Letter*, Vol. II, No. 9 (July 1977).

4. L. J. Bennion and S. M. Grundy, "Risk Factors for the Development of Cholelithiasis in Man, Part 2." *The New England Journal of Medicine*, Vol. 299, 1978, pp. 1221–7; R. K. R. Scragg, L. J. McMichael and P. A. Baghurst, "Diet, Alcohol, and Relative Weight in Gall Stone Disease: A Case Control Study." *British Medical Journal*, Vol. 288, 1984, pp. 1112–9.

5. "The Gallbladder and Gallstones, Part 1," op. cit.

6. L. J. Bennion and S. M. Grundy, "Effects of Obesity and Calorie Intake on Biliary Lipid Metabolism in Man." *Journal of Clinical Investigation*, Vol. 59, 1975, pp. 996–1001.

7. Bennion and Grundy, op. cit; Scragg, McMichael and Baghurst, op. cit.

8. Boston Collaborative Drug Surveillance Program, "Surgically Confirmed Gallbladder Disease, Venous Thromboembolism, and Breast Tumors in Relation to Postmenopausal Estrogen Therapy." *The New England Journal of Medicine*, Vol. 290, 1974, pp. 15–9.

9. Ann Jarnfelt-Samsioe, et al., "Gallbladder Disease Related to Use of Oral Contraceptives and Nausea in Pregnancy." *Southern Medical Journal*, Vol. 78, No. 9 (September 1985), pp. 1040–3.

10. American Medical Association, *Family Medical Guide*. New York: Random House, 1982, p. 489.

11. Statistics from the National Center for Health Statistics.

12. P. Goulin and L. M. Preshow, "Silent Gallstones." *Medicine North America*, Vol. 20, 1985, pp. 2676–80.

13. W. A. Garcie and D. F. Ransonhoff, "The Natural History of Silent Gallstones." *The New England Journal of Medicine*, Vol. 307, 1982, pp. 798–800.

14. L. J. Schoenfield, et al., "Chenodiol (Chenodeoxycholic Acid) for Dissolution of Gallstones. The National Cooperative Gallstone Study. A Controlled Trial of Efficacy and Safety." *Annals of Internal Medicine*, Vol. 95, 1981, pp. 257–82.

15. Tokyo Cooperative Gallstone Study Group, "Efficacy and Indications of Ursodeoxycholic Acid Treatment for Dissolving Gallstones." *Gastroenterology*, Vol. 78, 1980, pp. 542–8.

16. Erwin K. Kastrup, et al., eds., *Facts and Comparisons*. St. Louis: J. B. Lippincott Co., 1986, p. 315e.

17. M. J. Allen, et al., "Rapid Dissolution of Gallstones by Methyl Tert-Butyl Ether." *The New England Journal of Medicine*, Vol. 312, No. 4 (January 24, 1985), pp. 217–20.

18. Tilman Sauerbruch, et al., "Fragmentation of Gallstones by Extracorporeal Shock Waves." *The New England Journal of Medicine*, Vol. 314, No. 13 (March 27, 1986), pp. 818–22.

19. M. C. Bateson, "Dissolving Gallstones." *British Medical Journal*, Vol. 284, 1982, pp. 1–2.

27

VISION, HEARING, AND OTHER SENSORY LOSS ASSOCIATED WITH AGING

Vision Changes by Ellen Barlow, Diana Laskin Siegal,
Faire Edwards, and Paula Brown Doress
Special thanks to Penny Gay and Jane Bailey-Blood Strete

Hearing Impairment in the Older Years by Ellen Barlow,
Paula Brown Doress, and Diana Laskin Siegal
Special thanks to Judith Chasin, Jessie Buck, and Lois Harris

Our senses—sight, hearing, smell, taste, and touch—connect us to the world outside ourselves. There are substantial differences from one person to the next, but most of us can expect the acuity of our senses to dim somewhat as the years pass. Usually changes occur so slowly that we adapt without being aware of the differences in perception.

Someone else may be the first to point out to us that we don't seem to be hearing or seeing as well as we once did. We might lose our appetite before we notice that our sense of taste or smell has diminished. Our sense of touch may become less dependable for such formerly rote tasks as fixing the clasp on a necklace, separating bills in a wallet, or turning pages.

While all of the above may seriously interfere with our efficiency and enjoyment, the most serious effects of sensory losses have to do with health and safety. Changes in our sense of touch may result in burns due to failure to withdraw from a hot surface in time. Older persons are actually less sensitive to changes in temperature. As a result their body temperature may drop to a dangerous level (hypothermia) before they are aware of it. (See Resources for more about hypothermia.) Changes in the sense of balance increase the risk of falling and injury.[1]

Some changes are genetically determined; some are influenced by injuries or environmental factors, such as exposure to noise; some are caused by illness or disease. Some change is in-

evitable with aging, but no one should settle for a medical dismissal of her concerns as "simply aging" without a careful diagnosis of the cause of any changes in vision, hearing, or other senses. There *are* things we can do when we recognize changes in our senses.

VISION CHANGES

At this very moment, your eyes and your brain together are producing the images you are now perceiving on this page. The eye has the ability to adjust to see near and far objects, shading and colors, and variations in lighting from almost complete darkness to sudden emergence into light.

Most people retain good vision into their older years and don't need to worry about losing their sight. For some of us, though, changes in vision, whether minor or quite serious, can bring troubling changes in our lives. Age-related changes in vision occur in two primary areas of the eye: the lens and the retina.

Presbyopia is the term used to describe slowness in changing the focus from far to near, stemming partly from the loss of elasticity in the lens.[2] The eye's ability to accommodate for near distances starts diminishing at age ten, but not enough for us to take notice of it until about age forty or so. According to medical textbooks, the loss in flexibility of focus is usually fixed by age fifty-five to sixty, though there are ways to promote flexibility. With proper correction (reading glasses, bifocals, contact lenses) and/or self-help eye exercises, sight can be restored to normal.

I now wear bifocals—originally an embarrassment— and find reading increasingly tiring, a big problem for someone who has been a compulsive reader since childhood. [a fifty-year-old woman]

I really thought they had changed the size of newsprint. I complained that they were making the type size of phone books and the eyes of needles smaller to save money. I'd never had any problems with vision before, so it was a slow realization that it was really me that was changing. [a woman in her seventies]

If you need simple magnification in both eyes and have no other conditions that require correction, you may want to try over-the-counter reading glasses, which are now available in some states. Always begin with the weakest glasses with which you can read. This will reduce strain. Start with the highest number (32, the weakest magnification). Take something to read to test the strength you need. These glasses do not correct for any other visual problems, nor do they allow for differences in each eye.

Do not neglect regular eye exams: a complete eye examination is important to check for glaucoma and other serious eye diseases and may detect other undiagnosed systemic conditions such as diabetes and hypertension. Everyone over forty should have her eyes checked every two years by an ophthalmologist or an optometrist, and a test for glaucoma should be performed at every eye examination of persons over twenty-five. The intra-ocular-pressure reading test takes only a few seconds, but good diagnostic procedure requires, in addition, taking a family history, checking for structural abnormalities, and viewing the optic nerve with an ophthalmoscope, a flashlight-like instrument that allows the eye-care practitioner to see the optic nerve at the back of the eye. If you have a family history of glaucoma, or have had test results which are borderline or glaucoma-suspect, you should have your eyes tested at more frequent intervals.

Minor problems, such as excess tearing and dry eye, can become annoying as we age. Eyelid skin becomes thinner with age. Because the lid skin does not hug the eyeball as tightly as it once did, drainage function may be affected. Increased sensitivity to wind, light, and/or temperature can cause tearing. If you tear easily, you can help yourself by more frequent blinking and other exercises to relax your eyes;[3] and for dry eyes, by using artificial tear or lubricating drops. Do not use drops that "get the red out" (called vasoconstrictors). These are not helpful for dry eyes and can even lead to some types of glaucoma in predisposed individuals.

Self-Help Alternative for Healthy Eyes

Vision Therapy

A number of women have used vision therapy, that is, various eye exercises, as a form of self-help, and to improve their mental, as well as physical, focus and ability to relax. Vision therapy relaxes and focuses the mind and eye while keeping the muscles flexible. Though it cannot cure serious eye diseases and conditions such as those described below, it is a self-help technique for putting to full use the vision one has. It can alleviate eye strain and improve the ability of the eye to focus, in some cases making it possible to continue reading without glasses.

Advocates of vision therapy believe that by continuing to keep the muscles and other parts of our eyes relaxed and flexible as we age, we may even avoid cataracts. A young lens rarely develops cataracts. It is flexible and easily changes focus between distant and near objects. By regaining most of this flexibility, the lens is less likely to stiffen and deteriorate.[4] The eye, like every other part of the body, needs nutrients; relaxed, mobile muscles assist the flow of nutrient-rich blood to reach the lens through the aqueous humor—the fluid inside the eyeball.

To rest and focus your eyes, try:

Blinking: Blink about once per line when reading, and always when a change of focus is needed, as when looking up from reading or if you experience any momentary blur.

When Reading or Doing Close Work: Look off and focus on something at a distance for about five seconds, at least every five minutes to keep your eye muscles from stiffening.

Palming: Lean your elbows on something to support them, then close your eyes and cover them with your palms. Breathe and relax. With your mind, either observe your breath, counting in-out cycles of ten, or visualize as clearly as possible pleasant memories and/or fantasies. Include as many of your senses as you can. Do this whenever your eyes feel tired, including once before you sleep.[5]

Nutrition for Healthy Eyes

Growing interest in the role of nutrition as a factor in preventing eye disease has prompted some new research which is still in a fairly preliminary stage. For example, one study found a lower incidence of cataracts in people who ate a diet high in antioxidants, that is, vitamin E, vitamin C, and beta-carotene.[6]

Eye-Care Practitioners

An *ophthalmologist* is a doctor of medicine (M.D.) who diagnoses and treats eye diseases and performs eye surgery; an *optometrist* is a doctor of optometry (O.D.) who is trained to examine, diagnose, and treat conditions of the visual system. Both can prescribe corrective lenses, but if you require surgical or medical treatment beyond what an optometrist is licensed to provide, the optometrist will refer you to an ophthalmologist. The role of the optometrist as primary eye-care provider is regulated by the states, and the scope of practice varies from state to state. An *orthoptist* specializes in diagnosis and treatment for problems of binocular vision (problems coordinating the use of both eyes). An *optician* fits and makes eyeglasses and in some states fits contact lenses from a doctor's prescription.

If you think you have a vision problem and are over sixty-five, and haven't seen an ophthalmologist for three years, you can call a hotline set up by the American Academy of Ophthalmology. Call toll-free 1-800-222-3937 weekdays, 8 A.M. to 5 P.M. (in Hawaii 8 A.M. to 3 P.M.). Services are free to those who qualify as "economically disadvantaged" but cost of glasses, drugs, and hospitalization is not included.

Diseases of the Eye

Four diseases are the principal causes of visual impairment and blindness in older persons: cataracts, glaucoma, macular degeneration, and diabetic retinopathy.[7]

Cataracts involve no pain or discomfort, just less clarity. Gradually the lens of the eye becomes cloudy until there is no longer enough light passing through to the retina to focus a clear image. Vision becomes hazy or blurred and sensitivity to light and glare increases. Sometimes cataracts are caused by injury, radiation exposure, infections, or inflammation within the eye, but by far the most common type is associated with aging. More than 90 percent of Americans over sixty-five have some evidence of cataracts.

Not all cataracts develop to the point where removal is necessary. Some people can live with considerable loss of vision; others may have their livelihood or hobbies threatened by even mild vision loss. There is no need to have surgery unless you experience vision loss that seriously limits your activities.[8] As with any surgery, you should seek a second opinion. Medicare and some private insurance plans require you to do so. Before agreeing to cataract surgery, be sure to ask whether other eye problems exist which could seriously interfere with vision. Cataract surgery should not be performed unless vision will be significantly improved.[9] Given a long life span, a person is more likely to undergo a cataract operation than almost any other surgery. And according to one report, no other operation in medical practice is as dramatically successful so much of the time.[10] Sight is restored after removal of the lens by implantation of an artificial plastic lens (during the same surgical procedure as the removal), or by wearing eyeglasses or extended-wear contact lenses. The contacts or implanted lenses restore a full field of vision; there may be some distortion with glasses.

Glaucoma is one of the more common and potentially severe eye disorders in people over forty.[11] Glaucoma occurs when there is too much fluid pressure in the eye, causing internal eye damage and gradually destroying vision. It is a myth that glaucoma inevitably leads to blindness. With *early detection* and *prompt treatment*, it can usually be controlled and blindness prevented.

Chronic Wide-Angle or Open-Angle Glaucoma (75 percent of glaucoma cases) seldom produces early signs, and usually there is no pain from increased pressure. Symptoms can include blurred vision that comes and goes, difficulty in adjusting to dark rooms, and reduced side vision. Testing for glaucoma should be part of every routine eye examination.

Chronic glaucoma is more common among Blacks.

STRUCTURE OF THE EYE

Sclera
Choroid
Retina
Vitreous Body
Fovea
Hyaloid Canal
Optic Nerve

Cornea
Posterior Chamber
Iris
Anterior Chamber
Lens
Ciliary Ligament
Ciliary Muscle

Muscles

Normal Vision

CATARACTS

Progressive Clouding of the Lens

Blurred Vision

GLAUCOMA

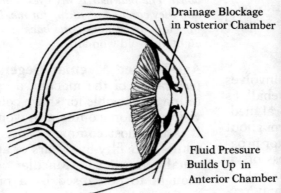

Drainage Blockage
in Posterior Chamber

Fluid Pressure
Builds Up in
Anterior Chamber

Blurred Peripheral Vision
and Possible Blindness

MACULAR DEGENERATION

Gradual
Degeneration of
the Macular
Cones and
Possibly the
Pigment
of the Retina

Blurred Central Vision

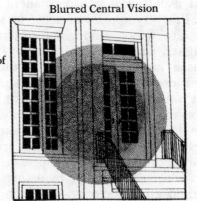

369

I first noticed a spot six years ago. I thought it was a spot on my glasses but it was still there after I cleaned my glasses several times. I believe that eyes are precious and have always taken care of mine so I went right into an eye doctor's office that very day. He examined me and referred me to a special eye clinic where I went the very next day. They said I had glaucoma in one eye and started me on medication, but it did not bring the pressure down enough. Laser therapy was new then but I was willing to try it. Then two years later the pressure started in the other eye so I had laser therapy in that eye also. The pressure is down now but I will have to stay on medication for the rest of my life. It's expensive but I don't want to lose my sight. [a seventy-one-year-old Black woman]

Treatment for chronic glaucoma involves bringing down the pressure in the eyeball as quickly as possible with eyedrops and oral medication. This treatment continues throughout life and, with regular checkups to monitor progress, usually insures that no further loss of vision will take place. If the drugs fail to reduce the pressure, the eye-care practitioner may recommend surgery (usually done with a laser beam) to create an artificial drainage channel.[12]

In *Acute Glaucoma* (about 25 percent of glaucoma cases), a sudden blockage occurs in the network of tissue between the iris and the cornea that is called the drainage angle. In far-sighted people, the distance between the cornea and the iris is shorter than normal and the drainage angle narrower, thus making it more likely for pressure to build up.

Sometimes preliminary (subacute) attacks occur, but usually with no permanent damage to vision. Early symptoms of acute or subacute glaucoma are foggy vision, colored rainbows around lights, sudden pain in the eyes, headache, nausea, and vomiting. In an acute attack, permanent loss of vision can occur, especially if treatment is neglected. Early treatment is essential. If you experience such symptoms, go **immediately** to your eye-care practitioner or a hospital emergency room. Emergency treatment consists of eyedrops to bring the pressure down, followed within a day or two by a surgical procedure called an iridectomy, in which a small piece of the iris is removed to relieve the pressure. This is usually done with a laser beam.[13] Laser therapy is sometimes done preventively in persons who may be predisposed to acute glaucoma because of an especially narrow drainage angle in the eye. There is time to get a second opinion if preventive laser therapy is recommended.

Retinal Disorders.
The retina is a thin lining on the back of the eye made up of receptors that receive visual images and pass them on to the brain. Retinal disorders include macular degeneration, diabetic retinopathy, and retinal detachment. These are the leading causes of blindness in the United States.

The thing I fear most about getting older is being disabled. The real fear is my eyes. I have retina problems and they can't do anything for me. But I got a magnifying glass and I have gone back to reading. [an eighty-eight-year-old woman]

Age-Related Macular Degeneration.
The deterioration of the macula, a center spot in the retina responsible for sharp color and fine-detail vision, is more common in women than in men. It is the most common cause of vision loss in adults over fifty-five years of age. Side vision is usually retained. Macular degeneration is thought to be caused by a breakdown in the supply of blood to the retina. An early sign of macular degeneration is wavy distortion of horizontal or vertical lines. Check yourself periodically by looking for a few seconds at a line of print, a door, or a stairway to see if this occurs. Use an object with strong contrast such as light color against black. Sometimes laser therapy can help with one form of macular degeneration, but it must be done promptly. A variety of low-vision aids (magnifying glasses, telescopic glasses, light-filtering lenses, and electronic devices) can in many cases compensate for visual difficulties.

Diabetic Retinopathy
was uncommon a few decades ago. Improved survival rates for diabetes means that many diabetics live to suffer complications of the disease. Diabetic retinopathy is at present the leading cause of new blindness in the United States for adults ages forty-one to sixty. Early diagnosis increases the chances of controlling this disease of the retina's blood vessels and eye fluid.

It never occurred to me that I would ever become blind. Even knowing I had diabetes and knowing it was a possibility, I still never believed that it would happen to me. [a fifty-three-year-old woman]

Many physicians specializing in diabetes control still fail to refer persons with diabetes to an eye-care practitioner for an annual eye exam, and many fail to do even a rudimentary eye exam themselves. Every person with diabetes should consult an eye-care practitioner regularly.

Detached Retina. Frequent eye complaints include spots that seem to swim in front of the eye; these so-called "floaters" are common and usually insignificant, caused by changes in the eye's vitreous fluid. **Warning:** Sudden, new, or unusual floaters that do not move or flashes of light or loss of side vision may indicate a torn or detached retina. Get emergency medical attention at once, and have an eye-care practitioner make the determination.

I developed floaters in my eyes and was told I'm at high risk for detached retina. My father lost his sight in one eye. I'm a visual person, I love color and nature and beauty, and blindness terrifies me. I don't want to go crazy if it happens, so to compensate I'm learning touch typing, flute, and drums. [a fifty-four-year-old woman]

Degrees of Vision Loss

Very few people actually lose all their vision to the point of not seeing light or dark. Three primary degrees of vision loss are:

Low Vision: Imperfect vision that cannot be improved with conventional eyeglasses or other medical or surgical means. Low-vision aids, such as telescopic lenses, can help the wearer use her remaining vision, but do not restore vision to near 20/20. Forty-eight percent of the almost two million Americans with low vision are over the age of sixty-five.

Severe Visual Impairment: Inability to read ordinary newspaper print, even using glasses. Four percent of older people in the community and 26 percent of those in nursing homes have severe visual impairment.

Legal Blindness: Defined as 20/200 vision (or less) in the better eye as corrected by glasses, or as having peripheral fields (side vision) of no more than 20 degrees diameter or 10 degrees radius.[14] Of the 1 to 2 million legally blind Americans, 70 percent are over the age of sixty.[15] Many resist being labeled "legally blind," yet it is a status that makes one eligible for tax exemptions, tax abatements, and certain services. Legally blind people may also be eligible for special financial benefits depending on their income level, such as Supplemental Security Income (SSI) or Social Security Disability Income

Anne Chapman Tremearne

(SSDI). SSDI has no financial need requirement. The local Social Security office will have this information. (See Money Matters chapter for more information.)

Getting Help

There are many skills in getting around and managing on one's own with a loss of vision. These can be learned with help from others. The ability of eyes to adjust to changing amounts of light diminishes somewhat with age. Dark glasses reduce visibility; yellow shades cut glare without reducing visibility. Night driving can be a problem, but glancing at the right side of the road instead of at oncoming headlights, installing halogen headlamps, wearing yellow shades and keeping the windshield clean can help. Having to give up night driving can be isolating if our community doesn't have public transportation or if we are reluctant to ask for help.

I had to learn patience. I used to wait until the last minute to jump into the car to do an errand or to meet someone. Now I have to make a lot of time for whatever I am doing because I either go on a bus or by cab or I have to ask someone to pick me up. These all take some

time and some waiting. [a fifty-three-year-old woman whose vision loss started at age fifty]

Each state has a Commission for the Blind, which is a good resource, as it provides catalogues of low-vision aids and referrals to eye-care practitioners. However, in most communities, organizations that serve the legally blind cannot provide services to those with low vision or visual impairment who have not yet been declared legally blind. Even if the diagnosis clearly points to a future loss of vision, services are not available until the person qualifies as legally blind.

VISION Foundation is an organization founded by three women who were coping with the oncoming loss of their sight. Frustrated by their inability to get help from established organizations in learning how to manage the expected changes in their lives, they reached out for help by writing to the "Confidential Chat" (a readers' letter exchange of *The Boston Globe*), then banded together for mutual help.

Today, VISION Foundation is an information and referral organization for Massachusetts residents which provides telephone support and self-help groups. It is staffed primarily by persons with sight loss. Your local information and referral center or the National Self-Help Clearinghouse can refer you to a self-help group in your area. (See Resources—Self-Help Groups for further information.)

Doctors often fail to refer people who are losing their sight to self-help organizations. Medical emphasis is on surgical solutions, which, unlike other areas of medicine, have had great success for elders. However, physicians may feel a sense of frustration and failure when surgery cannot succeed in saving sight. They may continue to have a patient come back every six months but do little to help the person learn to adapt to low vision, to find the resources she needs to learn new skills, and to find adaptive products, appliances, and other aids. Doctors in many states are not required to report loss of vision to the State Commission for the Blind, except when the patient is "legally blind," and even then they frequently fail to do so. Yet many older people can be helped to live with low vision (see Resources).

Several states have radio stations which broadcast special programming such as reading daily newspapers. These can be heard on special radios. Inquire at your State Commission for the Blind. In 1987 large-print telephone directories of businesses and organizations of special interest to elders will be available free in 110 cities.

Magnifying devices, self-threading needles, and other gadgets are available to aid near vision. Some sewing-machine stores or notions departments sell magnifiers to attach to your sewing machine. For people who are losing their vision, there is a wide variety of articles available, including talking watches, talking clocks, and other electronic items.

Our Association for the Blind sells aids to clients at cost. I bought a lamp which I can adjust to give me better lighting on my work table. The library loaned me a wonderful magnifier which included a light and lets me see work I do with my hands.

One lady's vision became so bad that it seemed as though she must go into a nursing home. The peer counselor from the Association came and taught her a lot of ways she might use to stay in her own home, including a dot of adhesive tape at the 350-degree mark on her oven control. Now she's still independent, with just a little help from her friends in the building. [an eighty-year-old woman]

Help in learning to manage household tasks, some of it free of charge, may be available from state services for the visually impaired or from your local Association for the Blind. Some associations also offer activities.

For people who are totally blind, and still have a good sense of touch, braille has a lot to offer. Others become very skilled at taking notes on tape recorders.

Large-print books are available from your public library or its regional lending service. Books and magazines on records and cassettes and the special equipment needed to play them are available to order by catalogue through the Libraries for the Blind and Handicapped; if you do not have one near you, your local public library can make the contacts for you. Don't give up on your library because of vision loss. Local libraries can be a wonderful resource for the visually impaired. If your librarian is not aware of these services, you can inform her of their existence and learn together.

Since I have become partially blind my life has become one of learning and study. Recordings for the Blind has all the best dissertations, scientific publications, all the classics, all the best poetry—so I can get anything. And the joy! What difference does the body make when you've got the joy of learning inside you? [an eighty-five-year-old woman]

HEARING IMPAIRMENT IN THE OLDER YEARS

As we reach our fifties and sixties it is increasingly likely that we will experience some degree of hearing loss. Hearing loss is the number one chronic health problem of older Americans. Twenty-five percent of people over sixty-five and 40 percent of those over seventy-five have some degree of hearing impairment.[16] Severity of loss tends to be greater for men than for women.

Hearing loss is invisible; thus it is often overlooked by others, who would be more helpful if they were aware of the problem. Because hearing loss begins so gradually, we ourselves may not be aware of it for some time. We may gradually begin avoiding situations with groups and/or with a lot of background conversation or noise. We may appear to go on with our lives as usual but become progressively more isolated. Even a mild-to-moderate hearing loss can be isolating. We may go through a grieving process in stages similar to mourning a death before we can accept ourselves as having a hearing impairment.[17]

At first I stayed home by myself, until a friend came to talk with me. She said I didn't have to do that to myself. I decided to make myself come to groups—like this exercise group. I have to be willing to hear less. I can't hear half of what the other women say. I can hear R. [male leader] because he has a low voice. [an eighty-eight-year-old woman]

I have hearing loss and cannot hear speech when there is competing loud noise. That means I cannot talk to anyone in the clubs, a primary social gathering place for gay women. It has become an impossibility for me to carry on conversation in any public place (restaurant or club) where there is competing music in the background. The louder sounds mask or distort the voices of my companions. I am reluctant to go to these social gathering places and am becoming more of a stay-at-home. I feel increasing stress in wanting and needing social contact with other women and at the same time having to consciously avoid the very places where I am most likely to meet people. [a fifty-year-old woman]

For those of us who have not experienced any hearing loss, it is difficult to comprehend the isolation and frustration experienced by someone who is losing one of her major sensory connections to society, and along with it, the consequent loss of access to information and social cues.

My two hearing aids help in communication, at least sometimes they do. Often the light, particularly enjoyable part of the conversation doesn't get through. The punch line of the joke gets lost. The resulting smile, if I produce one, is artificial. I may use the occasion to educate my hearing friends. Other times I don't. At least my judgment of others is tempered as I remember how often I was thoughtless about hearing problems before I had one of my own.

And I think of various ways by which I can experience lightness, relaxation. Since my sight is adequate, foreign movies with English subtitles are a godsend for me. There we are, all of us, whether we can hear well or not, using those subtitles together. It makes me feel more part of the group.

Perhaps most important of all are small mutual support groups. In the intimate, caring atmosphere of such groups, communication between hearing and hearing-impaired persons can flourish. Each can truly be at ease. [an eighty-two-year-old woman]

Sensitivity on the part of others is crucial. Those of us who have hearing loss, and others of us who have close friends or family members with hearing loss, have learned a variety of skills to improve communication. It should be accepted practice for all cultural and political events to be signed for the hearing-impaired. Regrettably, this is still the exception and still requires strong advocacy on the part of every one of us.

Ellen Shub

The Structure of the Ear and How It Works

The ear is an intricate structure that can process and distinguish over 350,000 different sounds. Sound is funneled into the ear canal and transmitted by vibrations to the eardrum where it is pushed along through the middle ear by bones known, because of their shapes, as the hammer (malleus), anvil (incus), and stirrup (stapes). It is the stirrup that starts the fluid in the cochlea of the inner ear vibrating. The hair cells then convert sound energy to electrical impulses which telegraph sound interpretations through the nervous system to the brain.

The cochlea looks like a spiral seashell and has approximately 25,000 sensitive hair cells lined up on its membrane. The mechanism by which pitch is discriminated can only be theorized at this time, but it seems to depend on which hair cells are stimulated. Those cells near the base of the cochlea are the high-note cells and those farther along are the lower-frequency ones. Changes in the inner ear, particularly the loss of hair cells associated with high-frequency hearing, have been shown to accompany the aging process. Loss of hair cells is irreversible and occurs throughout our lives from exposure to jet takeoffs, loud music, machinery, and a myriad of other recreational and occupational noises we encounter.

The loud sound systems at rock concerts and in clubs really impair hearing, and should be a health concern for everyone. Tests of hearing in the population at large show that the hearing of people in their twenties and thirties has already begun to deteriorate, and is often as impaired as that of older people. Unless young people take steps to protect their hearing, hearing impairment in old age will increase even more in the decades to come.

Recognizing and Acknowledging the Signs of Hearing Loss

As a slight hearing loss progresses to the point where we become aware of missing much of what is going on, we may react to the first signs of hearing loss with disbelief and denial. Before we can act to help ourselves we must come to terms with our feelings of loss and the consequent change in our image of ourselves.

I can't say exactly when it started. Hearing and understanding telephone conversations is the first difficulty I recall. I found myself asking people to speak up: "This is a poor connection." Sometimes an abrupt silence followed my comment, indicating it had not been entirely appropriate. "I must be more attentive. It's not considerate of the other person for me to let my mind wander while talking." The next clue was that I could hear when someone spoke to me from another room but I could not understand what was said, and it made no difference how loud the person was speaking. A year or two or three passed and these two problems became worse before I took action. [a woman in her fifties]

Signs of hearing problems to look out for in ourselves and others:

- Consistent difficulty in hearing over the telephone or hearing the telephone ring;
- Saying "What?" or "Please repeat" frequently;
- Leaning forward or tilting head to hear better;
- Preferring the television louder than others do;
- Complaining that others are mumbling;
- A ringing in the ears or feeling a blockage.

If our hearing loss develops slowly, we may be the last to become aware of it. Family members and close friends are usually the first to notice the problem because they find themselves raising their voices when speaking. The advance of the loss is almost imperceptible to the one experiencing it. But even a mild loss is well worth checking out. There are hearing aids geared to all kinds of losses, and hearing specialists who can instruct us on ways to improve overall communications.

The degrees of hearing loss are:

Mild	Difficulty hearing faint speech
Moderate	Frequent difficulty hearing normal speech
Severe	Can understand only very loud or amplified speech
Profound	Cannot hear very loud or amplified speech

A common misperception is that hearing loss is a simple reduction in the volume level of sound. This is true for a conductive loss—but not for the type of loss caused by very gradual but irreversible changes in the inner ear.

The main types of hearing loss are:

Conductive Hearing Loss, which involves blockage or impairment of the structures of the outer or middle ear so that sound waves are not able to travel properly. Packed ear wax, extra fluid, abnormal bone growth, or infection can cause this condition. The symptom: Your own voice sounds abnormally loud and other voices sound muffled. Flushing the ear, medication, or surgery may correct the condition.

I started going deaf at about age thirty-six. I was examined by an ear, nose, and throat specialist and by an audiologist and both thought it was nerve deafness, which my mother also had. I didn't know to question the diagnosis at that age. I tried several kinds of hearing aids, which helped only a little. I had four or five really tough years until another audiologist told me she didn't think it was nerve deafness and suggested that I go to another physician. What I had was otosclerosis—a tiny growth which prevents the stirrup from vibrating and so causes conductive deafness. I had an operation called a stapedectomy in one ear when I was forty-two. At that time they used an artificial material to replace the stirrup. When they did my other ear last year they actually used a bit of my own ear lobe. I had a little dizziness for a week or two each time and then it went away. I can hear normally now. [a fifty-eight-year-old woman]

Sensorineural Hearing Loss, caused by damage to the inner ear and/or the nerve pathways to the brain. A high fever or severe infection, head injury, use of certain drugs, vascular problems, and lengthy exposure to loud noises are among the causes. This condition cannot usually be treated medically or surgically. A hearing aid can improve hearing of those with sensorineural loss but won't restore hearing to normal. For some, speech reading and aural rehabilitation can be beneficial.[19] Aural rehabilitation classes teach how to use one's remaining hearing to best advantage by positioning oneself with the better ear toward the speaker, using light and vision effectively, etc. This can be done with or without a hearing aid.

Some hearing loss is temporary and may just go away. Aspirin in large doses (20 to 30 per day), sometimes prescribed for arthritis, may cause a temporary hearing loss. Switching to a non-aspirin product will often remedy the problem. Discuss this with your physician.

Age-Related Hearing Loss (Presbycusis), a sensorineural hearing loss, and the most common type among older persons. As we grow older, many of the hair cells of the inner ear disappear or wither, causing words to sound mumbled. In most cases there is an increasing loss of sensitivity to high-pitched sounds.

I went to a violin and piano concert and I only heard the piano! [a woman in her eighties]

The symptoms vary, but often people with presbycusis have a problem with "speech discrimination," or the ability to understand words when spoken loud enough to be easily heard. For example, the words "sail," "fail" and "tail" all begin with high-pitched consonants; with this type of hearing loss, it would be difficult to tell them apart.

Manipulating the Environment

Once we get used to the idea of having a hearing loss, we can learn to help ourselves by arranging the environment to enhance the hearing we still have.

For many of us hearing is not a problem in an ideal quiet environment with well-articulated face-to-face conversation. At home we can sit facing others and can use soundproofing materials such as carpets and drapes to improve the acoustics. Also, there are many sound-amplifying devices that can be attached to the telephone, television, radio, alarms, doorbell, etc. In addition, visual signaling can be used when you can't depend on hearing. Devices such as a "moonbeam alarm clock" or smoke alarms that light up your bedroom may be ordered by mail. A special device costing about two hundred dollars can be installed to enable you to receive closed-captioned television programs. Ask your audiologist or hearing-aid dispenser how to order such devices.

Manipulating the outside environment is more difficult. What we can do is to physically position ourselves to maximize lighting and acoustics.

At home or away, we can ask people we are conversing with to repeat sentences more clearly and slowly, and to emphasize consonants. We can learn to deal with impatient people, be persistent in our requests for clear speech, and learn to listen better ourselves.

I began confronting the reality that my hearing acuity was less than normal. I quietly but firmly informed friends, relatives, peers, supervisors, and clients that I had a partial hearing loss and needed them to face me, *to speak more slowly and distinctly and in lower tone ranges.*

Prevention

As part of a regular physical checkup, insist on a routine hearing check. The primary-care physician should routinely screen everyone over age fifty for pure-tone sensitivity as part of the general physical examination.[20] Too often, people with remediable ear disease fail to get proper attention until the condition is beyond medical help. If you already have some hearing loss it is still important to have your hearing checked regularly and to act on changes in your hearing.

Where and How to Seek Help

If you suspect that you may have some hearing loss, have a medical evaluation by a licensed physician, preferably an otologist (one who specializes in diseases of the ear), or if none is available in your community, an otolaryntologist (ENT), specializing in ear, nose, and throat. Ear specialists can diagnose the different types of hearing impairments and can tell you whether the problem can be treated with surgery, medicine, or by use of a hearing aid or rehabilitation. The importance of establishing the cause and type of loss, and thus the treatment, cannot be overstated. In some cases, particularly where surgery is recommended, you may want to seek a second opinion. Once medical or surgical treatment is ruled out or completed, the ear specialist can refer you to an audiologist for tests and recommendations.

Audiologists are professionally trained and in some states must satisfy specific requirements for a license. They are certified by the American Speech-Language-Hearing Association, and the initials CCC-A after their name indicates a Certificate of Clinical Competence in Audiology.

The principal testing instrument is an audiometer, which emits carefully calibrated pure tones as well as recorded or live voice speech. It precisely measures and records a patient's hearing threshold, the quietest level at which a person can hear a specific sound stimulus 50 percent of the time. Physicians may use audiological test results to diagnose specific hearing problems. This testing is particularly significant because it can be repeated over time to detect changes in hearing.

Norma Holt

The audiologist may help the physician evaluate test data to determine whether you would benefit from a hearing aid and in some cases may recommend a particular type. For example, some hearing devices amplify only those frequencies which you need to have amplified. If you tried a hearing aid in the past and were not able to use it, you may want to try again, as they have been improved a great deal in recent years, especially in their capacity to screen out background noise.

Role and Responsibilities of the Dispenser

A dispenser sells or rents hearing aids. The dispenser may or may not be a medical doctor or an audiologist. A dispenser's functions include giving the patient hearing tests for selection and fitting of hearing aids, encouraging prospective users to try amplification, making impressions for ear molds, counseling hearing-impaired people on adapting to a hearing aid, and repairing damaged hearing aids.

In most states hearing-aid dispensers are licensed under standards of competence and a strict code of ethics. The National Hearing Aid Society has a voluntary certification program for qualified dispensers.

An FDA regulation effective August 25, 1977, imposes conditions for the sale of hearing aids to help prevent misrepresentation and to assure adherence to proper medical standards. Hearing aid dispensers must obtain a written statement from the patient signed by a licensed physician and stating that the patient's hearing has been medically evaluated and that the patient is considered a candidate for a hearing aid. This medical evaluation must have taken place no longer than six months before the date of sale. The dispenser must give you written instructions for using the hearing aid selected and make sure you understand them.

Dispensers must also advise patients to consult a physician or ear specialist promptly if the dispenser finds any of several conditions, such as conductive hearing loss, dizziness, or sudden fluctuating loss of hearing, which may indicate a medical problem.

Patients eighteen or older may waive the medical evaluation requirement, but the dispenser is required to warn them beforehand that it is not in their best health interests. The dispenser must avoid encouraging patients to waive the medical examination. Whenever a patient chooses to waive, the dispenser is required to obtain her or his signature on a waiver statement. The dispenser must keep a copy of each patient's medical evaluation or a signed waiver on file for three years.[21]

Adapting to a hearing aid can be trying because, in most cases, all sounds are amplified—not just the sounds you want to hear. It takes time and practice to learn when and where and how to use your hearing aid.

The first few weeks almost convinced me that I wanted only to retreat into "my silent world" and manage as best I could. It was like living in a noisy factory. It was a constant bombardment of sound, and all of it too loud! Finally all the fine adjustments were made and now I can enjoy movies and concerts and theater again. I can hear my grandchildren as they learn to make sounds and form words and conversation.

All is not as before though. Large gatherings of people are simply noisy confusion. Driving my car with the window down is very tiring emotionally because of the assault of noise, and I must regularly visit the audiologist to adjust the aid. [a fifty-eight-year-old woman]

An ethical hearing-aid dispenser will allow you thirty days to try out a hearing aid, charging you only for the ear mold and/or a fee for her or his time if you are unable to adapt to it and must return it. You may have to try out several hearing aids before finding the one that works for you.

Many hearing-aid dispensers offer trial rentals or a money-back guarantee if you are not satisfied with the hearing aid. This is a good indication that they will take the time to serve you properly. Be sure to ask this in advance. Other questions to ask include: Does the cost include an ear-mold fitting, if needed? How long will the dispenser provide free service? How long do the batteries last and what do they cost? This can vary greatly and can become an expensive item.[22] Will the dispenser provide you with a loaner hearing aid if your aid needs repair?

Rehabilitation

Rehabilitation includes a broad range of services such as occupational services—finding alternative employment and/or adaptations to enable you to continue in your present occupation.

I became aware that if my hearing loss continued I'd not be able to function in the same way, especially at work. I am a registered nurse and just a year or two earlier had completed the education and certification to qualify me as a nurse practitioner. Bedside nursing or ambulatory care—it really didn't matter which: I had to be able to accurately hear the patient's complaints, history of illness, breath sounds, abdominal sounds, heart sounds, doctors' instructions and orders—I had to hear! Having also been recently divorced, I was supporting myself entirely. I struggled to not hit the panic button.

I decided the time had come to plan the necessary changes before complete hearing loss inflicted change in my life—perhaps at a time when I would be at a disadvantage.

I consulted the local office of the State Rehabilitation Commission for guidance. First a complete medical exam of my ears and a full audiological evaluation. Then conferences with my nursing director and the administrator of the health care facility where I am employed. Amplifier headsets were added to telephones I had to use, and an electronic stethoscope (extremely sensitive to even the slightest sound) was purchased for my use. [a fifty-seven-year-old woman]

Rehabilitation also includes help in discriminating sounds and speech reading, sometimes called lip reading. Classes may be available at low cost in your community. See Resources for referral sources, or call your local Council on Aging.

"Why a lip-reading class?" my friends ask. The reason is a gradually increasing hearing loss I have had for sev-

Marianne Gontarz

eral years. Unless I'm in a room with good acoustics and with people who speak clearly, I have trouble following the conversation.

In the meantime, here I am in the lip-reading class of our community education program, learning a lot about how to face up to hearing difficulties. The mutual support of the group is reassuring.

While there is no magic cure, hearing aids, signing, and lip reading can help. Lip reading is hard work. Many sounds can't be seen, so we are learning to be aware of other body clues and are improving our visual skills in general.

We are also planning strategies for better community understanding: distributing a leaflet titled, "Tips for Talking to the Hard of Hearing" and doing a skit demonstrating some of the problem issues. [an eighty-year-old woman][23]

Policy Issues

Hearing loss is one of the most common conditions of the older years, one which can lead to social isolation and withdrawal, yet little is done about it. Most services are medical and surgical, yet these are not helpful for the kind of hearing loss that affects most older people. Fragmentation of services seriously limits the ability of older persons to get help for hearing impairment—medical doctor for checkups, audiologist for hearing-aid evaluation, and in some cases a hearing-aid dispenser to get the hearing aid. Many accept the dispenser as the primary provider of hearing-related services and never go back to the physician for regular care of the ears. Some of us cannot afford hearing aids because neither Medicare nor Medicare supplementary insurance will cover the costs. Charitable organizations, such as the Lions Club, sometimes help purchase hearing aids for those who cannot afford them. Our patchwork system of health care delivery must be changed so that all who need hearing aids and rehabilitation services can have them as a matter of right. You can join with advocacy organizations such as the Gray Panthers and the AARP (see General Resources) to fight for a comprehensive and integrated national health care program.

NOTES

1. Jeffrey R. M. Kunz, *The American Medical Association Family Medical Guide.* New York: Random House, 1982, pp. 720–1.

2. Gay Becker, et al., *Vision Impairment in Older Persons,* Policy Paper No. 9, 1984. Aging Health Policy Center, University of California, San Francisco.

3. Personal communication, Ro G. Gordon, D.B.O. (Diploma of British Orthoptists), vision therapist.

4. Ibid.

5. Ibid.

6. Personal communication, Allen Taylor, Ph.D. Laboratory for Nutrition and Cataract Research at the USDA Human Nutrition Research Center on Aging. Tufts University, Boston, MA 02111.

7. Becker, op. cit., p. 10.

8. "Cataracts," *Health Letter.* The Public Citizen Health Research Group (see Resources—General Health), Vol. 3, No. 3 (March 1987), pp. 1–6.

9. Ibid.

10. T. J. Liesegang, "Cataracts: What They Are, What to Do About Them." *Mayo Clinic Proceedings,* Vol. 59, August 1984, pp. 556–622.

11. Kunz, op. cit.

12. Ibid., p. 322.

13. Ibid., pp. 320–1.

14. Fran A. Weisse and Mimi Winer, *Coping with Sight Loss. The VISION Resource Book.* Watertown, MA: Vision Foundation, p. 3; and Jane Porcino, "Vision Capacity of Women Over Forty," in *Growing Older, Growing Better.* Reading, MA: Addison-Wesley, 1983, pp. 301–2.

15. Personal Communication, Annette Maleson, Massachusetts Commission for the Blind.

16. Gay Becker, et al., *Management of Hearing Impairment in Older Adults,* Policy Paper No. 13, 1984. Aging Health Policy Center, Room N631, University of California, San Francisco, CA 94143.

17. Beatrice A. Wright, *Physical Disability: A Psychological Approach.* New York: Harper, 1960. Quoted in Maurice H. Miller, "Restoring Hearing to the Older Patient: The Physician's Role." *Geriatrics,* Vol. 41, No. 12 (December 1986).

18. Reprinted with permission from the Boston Women's Health Book Collective, *The New Our Bodies, Ourselves.* New York: Simon and Schuster, 1984, p. 459.

19. *Aging Notes,* U.S. Senate Special Committee on Aging January 8, 1985, p. 2.

20. Maurice H. Miller, "Restoring Hearing to the Older Patient: The Physician's Role." *Geriatrics,* Vol. 41, No. 12 (December 1986).

21. *FDA Consumer,* HHS Publication No. (FDA) 80-4024. U.S. Government Printing Office, May 1980.

22. *Boston Seniority,* August 1983, p. 6.

23. Reprinted with permission from the Boston Women's Health Book Collective, op. cit., p. 459.

28

MEMORY LAPSE AND MEMORY LOSS

by Jane Hyman

Special thanks to Guila Glosser

As we grow older, some of us find ourselves becoming more forgetful. We notice that we cannot remember names as easily, forget errands, or often misplace keys or household items. Frequently what we notice is not a memory loss but a memory lapse. It simply takes us longer to retrieve names, addresses, and dates from our memories than it used to. When this happens in our older years we may see it as a sign of age and become flustered, frustrated, embarrassed, or angry with ourselves. We may even think this forgetfulness could be a sign of senility.

When I'm with friends my age and I forget a name of something—we laugh. That makes it easy. Not so when I'm with younger people. For example, when I'm giving information to a salesperson—I know where I live but occasionally I have to think a minute to remember my address. And I always feel as though they're looking at me thinking, "Oh, this senile old thing." I'm not senile! Now I just say to myself, someday they'll be my age and they'll know what this is like. [a seventy-three-year-old woman]

The dictionary definition of *senility* is "a loss, associated with old age, of mental faculties." But the word has no real meaning, because it has become a catch-all term for any forgetfulness or mental disorder experienced by an older person. Until recently physicians assumed that senility was an inevitable part of old age. This assumption kept them from identifying and treating true memory disorders.

Alzheimer's disease is gradually replacing senility as a specific focus of our concerns. Media coverage of Alzheimer's can lead to unnecessary fears over signs of forgetfulness. This emphasis

on the negative—on potential losses as we get older—can make us feel that forgetting names or misplacing objects is more significant than our interests, our knowledge, and our wisdom gained over the years. It also obscures research that shows that some intellectual abilities often increase with age.[1] It is important to put memory changes into perspective and to understand the differences between normal forgetfulness and memory disorders. We want to stop feeling uneasy about forgetfulness—but we also want to know when to seek help.

There are three categories of memory lapse or memory loss associated with age.

1. Normal forgetfulness, *benign senescent forgetfulness,* is part of the normal aging process. But it does not necessarily worsen with the years and does not interfere with our lives in any significant way or endanger our health.

2. Memory loss related to disorders or conditions such as depression or malnutrition. These conditions and the resulting memory loss are reversible and can and should be diagnosed and treated.

3. A disease of the brain, *late-life dementia* or *senile dementia,* not normally part of the aging process. It is irreversible and progressive, preventing the individual from carrying out even simple responsibilities. Late-life dementia needs medical diagnosis and special care. The most common form of late-life dementia is Alzheimer's disease.

The difference between normal forgetfulness and the early stage of Alzheimer's disease is not always clear-cut. But in Alzheimer's disease memory loss becomes progressively worse and is accompanied by a general decline in intellectual abilities and changes in behavior.

BENIGN SENESCENT FORGETFULNESS

Throughout our entire lives, beginning at birth, the brain loses nerve cells that are not replaced through regeneration. From around age fifty and on, parts of the brain can show other signs of change, such as cell tangles (abnormal protein substances in nerve cells, also known as neurofibrillary tangles) and senile plaques (degenerated nerve cells that form scars). These changes can be accompanied by a decline in memory, but for many of us such a decline never occurs, and we can continue to live well into our eighties and beyond experiencing little or no change in our mental vigor.[2]

It is not known why some of us experience a decline in memory and others do not. But our brains, like other parts of our bodies, differ from person to person because of genetic factors and in response to emotions and to physical and environmental changes.

Throughout our lives, including our older years, fatigue, anxiety, inattention, stress, and depression can cause moments of memory lapse or periods of memory decline. As we grow older we also become particularly vulnerable to changes in our social situations. Deaths of loved ones, relocation to an unfamiliar place, or increased social isolation can bring about emotional changes that trigger forgetfulness, confusion, and disorientation. Diseases and physical disorders can be accompanied by emotional distress that can lead to increased forgetfulness, especially when treatment in an unfamiliar place, such as a hospital or nursing home, is required. A loss of sight or hearing contributes to mental confusion by restricting a person's knowledge of the world around her and by putting additional stress on already weakened learning abilities and memory. Eye and ear impairments can also worsen a sense of social isolation or actually cause us to avoid social contact, possibly bringing about depression and a decline in mental functioning. These causes of forgetfulness, confusion, and disorientation are reversible, and mental capacities can return to normal after an adjustment period with proper medical treatment or sometimes with the help of friends and family.

Helping Ourselves Remember

Often we notice ourselves being forgetful for no apparent reason. Our memory changes can become bothersome to the point that some of us develop strategies for remembering. We avoid interruptions when concentrating on a task, knowing that distracted attention can be detrimental to our work. We write lists and notes to ourselves instead of relying on our memories. We adjust our surroundings to help us find objects (including our lists) more easily.

In the morning when I wake up I go through what I call a name exercise. I have various friends whose faces come before me, and then I go through that exercise of recalling the names I need for the day, up to ten or twelve at a session. I find that very useful. Sundays before going to church, I try to recall many names of church members who may be present so that they're fresh in the front of my memory. I do this same exercise before I go to meetings or social gatherings. In my bedroom I have my closets organized so I can find things. I even organize my refrigerator! [an eighty-six-year-old woman]

An orientation area can also be helpful: a room or corner with a calendar and bulletin board for written reminders, and a place to keep essential items such as glasses, keys, umbrella, and writing accessories. Such a special area can save energy we would otherwise waste in being upset over forgetting, losing, or misplacing something.

Some of us may want to seek outside help offered in the form of memory clinics, which are often affiliated with hospitals. Such clinics offer memory skill training and individual and group counseling concerning emotional issues related to memory. They can also help to reduce stress and fear concerning memory changes.

DISORDERS AND DRUGS THAT CAN LEAD TO MEMORY LOSS

A number of specific disorders and drugs can lead to memory loss and mental confusion. These effects are not limited to the elderly, but the older brain is more vulnerable to them. *Most of them are reversible and should be identified and*

Organize, Don't Memorize[3]

What to buy and tasks:
Make a list rather than relying on your memory. Keep a pad available to jot down items as needed.

Taking medication:
Place medication in a special receptacle each night for the following day. When you see the receptacle is empty, you know the medication you have taken.

or

Use containers (paper cups, saucers, an empty egg carton, or boxes sold for this purpose), each marked for the day of the week. This is especially helpful if you take different medications on different days. (Caution: Do not leave medications within the reach of children.)

Turning off the stove, removing the laundry, leaving on time for an appointment:
Use a timer with a bell, or wear a watch with a timer. Set it for the appropriate time, and take it with you around the apartment or house so you will be sure to hear it.

Names and ages of grandchildren, names of friends and acquaintances:
Write the grandchild's name and date of birth under each photo in a photo album or frame. Write names under pictures of friends. Periodically look through your address book to refresh your memory or to recognize a name you are trying to think of.

Paying bills:
Place all bills to be paid in one place. Mark on your calendar the date on which to pay the bills. Cross off the reminder after you pay the bills.

Ask your local librarian for books on techniques for remembering. And remember: *You don't have to remember everything.*

Depression. Some of the symptoms of depression include a slowing of movement and speech, slowing of thought, changes in sleep and eating habits, decreased pleasure in activities, underestimation of one's true capacities, and low self-esteem. Depression is probably the disorder most commonly misdiagnosed as Alzheimer's disease, particularly when low self-esteem causes poor results on mental status tests. The profound changes in thinking and memory sometimes associated with depression have been called *pseudodementia*. However, thorough neurological and neuropsychological examinations usually differentiate depression from dementia. The two are different in both onset and behavior. The onset, or beginning, of depression is usually more sudden than the slow and gradual process of Alzheimer's disease. And a depressed person is more likely to exaggerate her or his difficulties, while a demented person will try to hide, deny, or minimize them and usually will not be aware of her declining mental abilities. In many cases of pseudodementia there is a previous history of depression. There are currently a number of very effective treatments for depression, and a mental health clinic or provider with experience in treating older persons should be consulted if this is suspected.

Elizabeth Layton

treated. Correct diagnosis is extremely important, since the mental symptoms of these disorders often resemble those of Alzheimer's disease and can be misdiagnosed as Alzheimer's or as "senility" and left untreated.

MEMORY LAPSE AND MEMORY LOSS

Drugs and Alcohol. As we grow older our tolerance for drugs (including prescription medicines and over-the-counter preparations) and alcohol decreases and our reactions to drugs may differ greatly from those of younger people. Certain drugs alone, as well as alcohol alone, can affect mood, memory, and speed of reactions. Alcohol can worsen depression, and drugs or alcohol can worsen the symptoms of Alzheimer's disease. Chronic, long-term alcohol abuse may lead to serious decline in memory and other cognitive functions. Recent studies have also shown that drugs that diminish or inhibit acetylcholine, a chemical in the brain, can produce significant memory loss in the elderly.[4] Such anticholinergic drugs include several prescription medications and over-the-counter remedies for diarrhea, nausea, and coughs. The older we get the more likely we are to be taking numerous drugs simultaneously to treat medical conditions or chronic diseases. Estimates show that in the United States most people over seventy-five take up to eight prescription drugs at the same time.[5] The brain is very vulnerable to drug interactions that can produce symptoms similar to those of dementia. Drugs are often necessary and valuable, but we need to be aware of the possible negative effects of any drug, *including over-the-counter remedies*, and of what the effect may be when we take two or more drugs at the same time, or combine a drug with alcohol.

Nutritional Deficiency and Anemia. As we age we may develop health problems that can cause malnutrition and anemia. Also, some of us develop poor nutritional habits because of physical infirmity or loneliness. A restricted budget can limit our choice of fresh and wholesome food, and weakness, frailty, or infirmity can make us reliant on others for transportation, food shopping, and food preparation. One or a combination of these factors can lead to malnutrition. Malnutrition (especially a vitamin B_{12} and folic acid deficiency) or anemia (a shortage of red blood cells and/or low hemoglobin content of these cells) can cause a person to appear disoriented and confused, to have severe memory lapses, and even to appear delusional. These deficiencies can be ruled out by blood tests and corrected by an adequate diet and supplements and by treating any underlying health problem.

Diseases and Other Health Problems. Some diseases and physical conditions can cause memory loss and mental confusion. These include thyroid disease, diabetes, kidney or liver problems, lung disease, gallstones, and syphilis. Other health problems such as heart and lung ailments, feverish conditions, and even constipation can cause mental confusion. Generally speaking, as we grow older we are less likely than before to develop specific symptoms when we become ill. We may become confused or withdrawn instead.

Brain Disorders. Disorders of the brain or central nervous system that can lead to memory loss include Parkinson's disease, a single stroke, brain tumor, trauma to the brain, subdural hematoma (bleeding in the brain because of trauma), and hydrocephalus (abnormal increase in the fluid surrounding the brain). Often these disorders can be treated, and timely treatment can prevent further damage.

LATE-LIFE DEMENTIA

Late-life dementia refers to a group of diseases of the brain that most frequently afflict those over sixty-five. The dementia influences all aspects of behavior, not only memory but also judgment, temperament, and social interaction. Late-life dementia is a neurological disorder (a disorder of the nervous system), not a psychological disorder, and it has nothing to do with a person's previous intelligence, education, or mental health. An estimated 90 percent of all late-life dementias are primarily caused by two irreversible conditions: multi-infarct dementia and Alzheimer's disease.[6]

Multi-infarct Dementia

Multi-infarct dementia is a condition of the brain caused by many small strokes. A stroke is a rupture or blockage of a blood vessel in the brain, which stops the flow of blood and destroys an area of brain tissue by depriving that area of oxygen and other necessary nutrients. The accumulated damage of many small strokes leads to an inability to function in various ways, depending on which parts of the brain are damaged. The mental and behavioral symptoms of multi-infarct dementia can be identical to those of Alzheimer's disease. However, multi-infarct dementia may also involve early signs of physical dysfunction, such as impairment of vision or sensation and muscle weakness or paralysis. The condition may begin abruptly and can be episodic, with short-term improvements and exacerbations. (This contrasts with Alzheimer's disease, which is hardly noticeable at first and progresses gradually.) Risk factors for multi-infarct dementia include atherosclerosis, previous strokes, heart attacks, severe chest pains (angina pectoris), high blood pressure, and diabetes. High blood pressure should be treated in order to prevent further small strokes (see Hypertension chapter).

Multi-infarct dementia is preventable to the extent that we can prevent heart disease, strokes, and diabetes by not smoking and by drinking alcohol only in moderation, exercising regularly, eating well, and getting early treatment for high blood pressure.

Multi-infarct dementia alone makes up an estimated 15 percent to 20 percent of late-life dementias. It can also occur in conjunction with Alzheimer's disease.[7]

Alzheimer's Disease

I'm going to fight it. Now what I do is write down everything I want to do. As I get them done I mark them off. Also I read a lot. This is the way I'm fighting it. It makes me so mad that every day I pound the table with my fist, because I don't want to be like this. I'm going to fight it every way I can. I'm stubborn. [a seventy-two-year-old woman in an early stage of Alzheimer's disease]

Since Alzheimer's disease, alone or in conjunction with multi-infarct dementia, makes up an estimated 75 percent of cases of late-life dementia, the term *Alzheimer's disease* has come to be the term most frequently used for late-life dementia. It is often abbreviated as SDAT (Senile Dementia of the Alzheimer Type). It afflicts an estimated 5 percent of those over sixty-five, rising with age to approximately 20 percent of those over eighty.[8] The incidence is expected to triple as the number of elderly people increases within the next three generations. It is more common in women than in men (two to one), although this seems to be a result of women's longer life span. Alzheimer's disease ranks as the fourth or fifth leading cause of death in the United States.[9] Currently dementia, of which Alzheimer's is the major cause, afflicts an estimated 4 million people.[10]

Abnormalities in the chemistry of the brain and changes in the structure of brain cells prevent nerve cells from functioning. The cell tangles and senile plaques that occur in normal aging (see p. 381) are more frequent and widespread in Alzheimer's disease. As more and more cells degenerate and parts of the brain die, the person's functioning deteriorates.

Stages of Alzheimer's Disease

At the beginning of the disease relatively few brain cells are affected, and the symptoms of memory loss may be noticed only by the victim herself* or, more typically, by a partner or employer. The victim may begin to forget once-familiar names or where she has put things, have difficulty finding words, become withdrawn, lose energy, anger easily, or avoid the unfamiliar. These can be signs of the first stage of Alzheimer's disease. But since an increase in forgetfulness can also be a part of the normal aging process, it should not cause concern unless it grows progressively worse and is accompanied by other symptoms which noticeably reduce the person's ability to carry out everyday activities.

I first began to suspect my mom might have Alzheimer's when I noticed a marked change in her personality. I was getting all kinds of nasty notes and telephone calls from her. She would call me thirteen times a day asking the same question. She couldn't remember what day it was and couldn't remember to take her medication. She was getting angry, frustrated, and more and more forgetful. [a thirty-eight-year-old woman]

When forgetfulness *is* a sign of Alzheimer's it will eventually be accompanied by rambling and repetition in conversation, lack of concentration, difficulty with orientation and travel, and spatial disorientation. These symptoms signal a more advanced stage of the disease. At this stage most people will no longer consciously recognize the symptoms and may deny them, since their reasoning and judgment become impaired. However, some people may have periodic insight into their deficiencies and become depressed or frustrated by them. The depression, frustration, or anxiety can, in turn, complicate the symptoms.

As the disease progresses the person may forget the names and faces of intimate family members; become disoriented in the home, or wander off and get lost; become unable to drive

*Since more women than men have Alzheimer's disease, the afflicted person is referred to as "she" throughout the text although the information applies to men also.

a car; become emotionally unstable and irritable; become incontinent; and eventually forget how to speak, eat, dress, and use a toilet. Some become agitated and occasionally abusive and assaultive while others may become increasingly withdrawn and apathetic. At this stage the person is completely dependent on others for basic human needs and can no longer survive without full-time care.

For unknown reasons, during the later stages of the disease the patient often loses weight. Muscle control diminishes, making any form of exercise difficult or impossible. The person may eventually become confined to a wheelchair or bedridden. The immobile or inactive person becomes more vulnerable to disease, infection, or heart attack. Pneumonia, viral infections, and heart attack are the most frequent secondary causes of death, the primary cause being Alzheimer's disease itself. The disease shortens life expectancy, but many people live for years in the final stages. Survival after the earliest symptoms varies anywhere from four to twenty years. The average survival is seven to ten years. In most cases the person will eventually require twenty-four-hour nursing home care unless the caregiver(s) can provide or hire private assistants around the clock.

Diagnosis

As larger numbers of the population become sixty-five and older, incidence of Alzheimer's disease will increase. Research on the disease has become more urgent and extensive, but to date there is no cure for Alzheimer's disease, nor any treatment to reduce its intensity or halt its progression. Nonetheless, careful diagnosis is extremely important in order to rule out treatable disorders that can cause mental confusion as well as other forms of dementia such as multi-infarct dementia, viral dementia (such as Creutzfeldt-Jakob disease or sometimes AIDS), and hereditary dementia (such as Huntington's disease). Diagnosis is also important in order to help the person who has the disease and to help future caregivers understand what they are dealing with and obtain the necessary social, psychological, and medical support. When the afflicted person and her family finally know she has Alzheimer's, the disease is recognized as the reason for bizarre behavior. This may alleviate the anger family members feel toward the afflicted relative and soften the blame they sometimes place on her for inappropriate behavior. It may also help to alleviate the victim's own embarrassment and self-blame.

My mother has Alzheimer's disease, but she was first diagnosed as having "geriatric depression." We went through years of her behavior getting worse and worse and driving me up the wall. If only we had had an earlier correct diagnosis, it would have saved us so much emotional pain and strain and turmoil. Now that the disease has been diagnosed it makes it easier for me to at least put a reason to her behavior. When you know what Alzheimer's disease is all about, the diagnosis is a relief—and not a relief. [a thirty-eight-year-old woman]

For diagnosis and future care, look for a physician who specializes in treating dementia or the elderly in general, such as an internist specializing in geriatrics, a neurologist, or a geriatric psychiatrist, and look for a gerontological nurse practitioner. The Alzheimer's Disease and Related Disorders Association (ADRDA) in your area, the American Association for Geriatric Psychiatry, the American Geriatrics Society, or the Gerontological Society may help you find a suitable physician (see Resources). If you cannot find a physician in your area who specializes in geriatrics, or if you do not feel comfortable with her or him, the ADRDA will be able to give you names of internists, neurologists, or psychiatrists interested and experienced in treating the elderly, or hospitals that have set up special clinics to treat diseases of the Alzheimer type.

To date, the only definitive diagnosis of Alzheimer's disease is a postmortem examination of the brain. The only direct means of diagnosing the disease during the person's lifetime is the surgical removal and examination of brain tissue, a procedure too dangerous to perform routinely. Therefore, diagnosis takes place through the careful elimination of all other possible causes of a person's mental confusion. Diagnostic tests should include a complete health history and physical examination, a neurological and a psychiatric examination, neuropsychological and neurodiagnostic tests, and a functional evaluation to discover how much the person can do for herself. The physical exam should include diagnostic tests for endocrine, hormonal, liver, kidney, and heart problems. The physician should also ask about family history and any history of mental disturbances, as well as the patient's social and occupational background, including education and exposure to toxic chemicals. The possiblity of a fall or accident within the last six months should be explored. The neuropsychological examination tests functions such as a person's ability to remember, to concentrate, to do abstract reasoning, to do calculations, and to copy designs.

Neurodiagnostic tests are procedures to evaluate brain function and include a brain wave recording (electroencephalogram, or EEG) and a CAT or CT scan (computerized axial tomography), which forms a picture of the brain from X-ray images. The CAT scan can also locate possible brain cell loss, and can rule out the possibility of a stroke or brain tumor. Nuclear magnetic resonance (NMR) may be used to assess structural changes in the brain, and the PET scan (positron emission tomography) is sometimes used to evaluate the metabolic activity of the brain. NMR and PET scans are valuable in research on Alzheimer's disease but are as yet too experimental to be useful in routine diagnosis.

Extensive diagnostic testing can be an exhausting trial. It is important to find health care personnel who understand the condition, and who will not upset or exhaust the person by forcing too much testing at one stretch.

Treatment of Alzheimer's Disease

There is currently no treatment that cures, halts the progress of, or has a predictably and reliably helpful effect on Alzheimer's disease. However, many studies are underway. There is much false information in the media concerning possible cures. This misinformation takes advantage of our understandable need for encouraging, hopeful news. It is important to get reliable information on the results of new research.* Your physician, nurse, social worker, and the Alzheimer's Disease and Related Disorders Association nearest you can be of help. There are now ten major federally funded research centers in the United States. Some large hospitals and research centers are conducting studies of drugs

*If you wish to aid future research on Alzheimer's disease, you can plan ahead for an autopsy of the afflicted person by contacting the National Autopsy Assistance Network. (Call the national headquarters of the ADRDA, listed in Resources, p. 475.) The purpose of the network is to provide families with a posthumous, definitive diagnosis of Alzheimer's and to provide brain tissue for research.

that may help treat Alzheimer's disease and related disorders. You may want to consider entering the affected person in such a study if one is being conducted near you. (Contact the national headquarters of ADRDA, listed under Resources, for information on these studies.)

Some symptoms of Alzheimer's disease, such as uncontrollable agitation, sleeplessness, night-wandering, and hallucinations, are extremely hard on the caregiver; drugs to control these behaviors without harming the stricken person are urgently needed. Sometimes sedatives will make the stricken person's behavior more tolerable. However, all drugs, especially those that alter mental function, can have negative effects. It is important that drugs be administered under the care of a knowledgeable physician. In general, it is advisable to be cautious with all tranquilizers and to begin with the lowest possible doses, advancing slowly. Caregiver and physician should closely watch the stricken person for positive as well as adverse effects of all prescribed drugs, and they should frequently reevaluate the need for continued doses.

Cause and Prevention

There is probably no single cause of Alzheimer's disease but instead many contributing factors that work together to lead to the development of the disease. Since the cause or causes are not known, prevention is also a matter of speculation. The aging of the brain may in itself be a main contributing factor, accelerated and augmented by other factors such as smoking, environmental toxins, hormonal changes, nutritional deficiencies, stress, a slow virus, hereditary and familial predisposition, or malfunction of the immune system. Research showing concentrated forms of aluminum in the brains of Alzheimer's victims has led to speculation that exposure to aluminum contributes to Alzheimer's disease. However, there is no higher incidence among aluminum workers than among the general population; and exposure to aluminum in daily life, for example through cookware, does not lead to higher aluminum concentration in the body.[11] It is equally likely that higher brain levels of aluminum are a consequence rather than a cause of the disease.

A small group of people develop Alzheimer's disease earlier—between the ages of thirty-five and sixty-five—and experience a more rapid progression of the disease and an early death. For this subgroup, hereditary factors seem to be stronger, and their children, brothers, and sisters have a higher risk of getting the disease than the rest of the population. Researchers have found a defective gene which may be a cause of this familial form of the disease. However, it appears that the relatives of those with late-life Alzheimer's (onset after age sixty-five) have no higher risk of the disease.[12] People with Down's syndrome develop Alzheimer's disease if they live long enough. A gene that produces the amyloid protein found in the plaques in the brains of people with both early and late-life forms of Alzheimer's disease has been located in the same chromosome that is involved in Down's syndrome and in the familial form of Alzheimer's. However, it is not yet known whether this will prove to link the diseases genetically.[13]

Counseling for Caregivers and Persons with Alzheimer's

Group or individual counseling sessions can be important for the caregiver. They also are sometimes offered for the afflicted person, but only people in the early stages of the disease do well in counseling sessions. To find out about counseling programs, consult your physician or get in touch with local hospital and mental health centers that might offer such sessions. The ADRDA chapter nearest you will also know about types and locations of help available.

- *Respite:* In adult day health centers, people with Alzheimer's take part in activities according to their own abilities within a supervised, structured program. These provide the ill person with attention and social interaction, and provide caregivers with much-needed intervals of rest and relief. Respite in-home services, weekend assistance programs, and long-term (one to two weeks) respite care programs are also starting to develop in some hospitals and nursing homes.
- *Family Treatment:* In group sessions, partners, relatives, children, or close friends who are involved in caring for a person with Alzheimer's come together with a therapist to discuss fears and frustrations, deal with family crises that arise when a family member is diagnosed with dementia, ask questions, and exchange ideas for solving practical management problems.

Anne Chapman Tremearne

- *Caregivers' Support Groups:* Caregivers meet regularly to talk about their situation and exchange information informally or with a group leader. Such groups offer the caregiver practical information and ideas, emotional support, and social contact.
- *Support Groups for Persons with Alzheimer's Disease:* Persons in earlier phases of the disease meet without family members but under the guidance of a therapist to discuss the fears, embarrassments, and needs of their daily lives; to talk about what may happen in the future; and to exchange ideas for coping and support.
- *Reality Orientation or Cognitive Training:* Memory training sessions are offered in which an impaired person practices using association to remember information such as important names and addresses, and is repeatedly reoriented as to date, time, and place. It does not appear that such methods actually help the memory of the person with Alzheimer's, but in the early stages of the disease the sessions pro-

387

vide human contact and a supportive, structured environment. For people in the later stages, such sessions may be confusing, frustrating, and even detrimental.

The caregivers' support group certainly has been one thing that has kept my sanity together. Some group members are up to date on all of the resources for care and support agencies and are tremendously helpful. Also, I think just the feeling that you're not the only one in the circumstances is helpful. We're there to support each other with whatever knowledge and information we have or to hand out tissues to those who are in tears. [a fifty-seven-year-old woman]

Personal Impact of Alzheimer's Disease

Alzheimer's disease and other progressive dementias perhaps cause more stress and change in the stricken person and within the home than any other conditions. This is because of the devastating personality change and loss of control that the stricken person experiences.

Impact on the Stricken Person

I feel like half a person. Where's the rest of me? I really hate this and I'm frightened. Maybe listening to me will open a world that's closed to a lot of people. Nobody knows what it's like. They just don't understand. [a seventy-two-year-old woman in the early stage of Alzheimer's disease]

With the disease, both recent and remote memory are eventually lost. Losing recent memory means forgetting what happened an hour or even a minute ago and being unable to learn new information or lay down new memories. For the person with Alzheimer's, life is like continually walking into the middle of a movie, with no idea of what happened before, and no understanding of what is happening now.[14] She may forget the names and faces of recently met friends and acquaintances, forget recent births and deaths in the family, and forget that she has just eaten and ask when dinner will be ready.

Losing remote memory means forgetting the past, including what we learned as children. This includes activities we take for granted— brushing our teeth, taking a bath, getting dressed, holding a conversation, using the toilet. As the disease progresses the victim regresses. She may forget how to use eating utensils, forget how to dress, forget the sensations of hot and cold, forget how to control bowel and urine, forget what food is, and how to chew and swallow. She may forget inhibitions learned in childhood and may expose or touch her sexual parts in public. The person with Alzheimer's loses a sense of time and can no longer look forward or back, or turn to the collected knowledge of her life for help. With such helplessness, partnerships between adults slowly change to parent/child-type relationships, or an adult child may have to become responsible for a stricken mother or father.

I miss having a partner. Max used to go to the office and stay all day five days a week. Now he doesn't go anywhere at all without me, and that makes a difference in my home life, because I'm very conscious of this individual who is solely dependent on me. And going to parties—well, anywhere—Max used to go to church with me some, and he always did the driving—he was an excellent driver. I find that I've lost the independent mind and gained a dependent one. [a seventy-six-year-old woman]

The stricken person's response to dementia is complex, changes as the disease progresses, and varies greatly from person to person. During the early stages the person may notice the changes within herself and be frightened and depressed by them. She may lose her job because she is progressively incompetent or because of personality changes unacceptable to those around her. She may be aware of her changed role within the household, as more and more responsibilities are taken from her.

It's like being in a ship by yourself. I can't function as I did before and I feel as if I'm odd. I'm so different from everybody else and I wonder if they like me. I'm so forgetful that I'm afraid when I'm with other people I'm going to sound stupid. But when friends ask me out, I go. And I find I'm much more relaxed once I'm with them. They're very kind to me. [a seventy-two-year-old woman in the early stage of Alzheimer's disease]

Throughout the course of the disease, but especially in the early stages, the stricken person may notice changes in the way others treat her and react with anxiety and embarrassment at her own behavior. But usually she is unaware of her declining capacities and may blame the caregiver for hiding things she cannot find or for keeping dates and names a secret. She may become angry with the caregiver who prevents her from driving or managing her bank account.

Impact on the Caregiver

I think Alzheimer's disease is probably harder on the caregiver than it is on the victim. But I wouldn't change places for anything. [a seventy-eight-year-old caregiver]

Mourning to Do

The new year and a fresh fall of snow,
The new year and mourning to do
Alone in the lovely silent house,
Alone as the inner eye opens at last—
Not as the shutter of a camera with a click,
But like a gentle-waking in a dark room
Before dawn when familiar objects take on
Substances out of their shadowy corners
And come to life. So with my lost love,
For years lost in the darkness of her mind,
Tied to a wheelchair, not knowing where she was
Or who she had been when we lived together
In amity, peaceful as turtledoves.

Judy is dead. Judy is gone forever.

I cannot fathom that darkness, nor know
Whether the true spirit is alive again.
But what I do know is the peace of it,
And in the darkened room before dawn, I lie
Awake and let the good tears flow at last,
And as light touches the chest of drawers
And the windows grow transparent, rest,
Happy to be mourning what was singular
And comforting as the paintings on the wall,
All that can now come to life in my mind,
Good memories fresh and sweet as the dawn—
Judy drinking her tea with a cat on her lap,
And our many little walks before suppertime.
So it is now the gentle waking to what was,
And what is and will be as long as I am alive.
"Happy grieving," someone said who knew—
Happy the dawn of memory and the sunrise.

*May Sarton**

Caring for someone with Alzheimer's disease takes a tremendous physical and emotional toll on the caregiver. In addition to the usual strains of caring for anyone with a long-term illness, unlimited patience and self-control are needed to cope with repetitive or unintelligible conversation, with complete silence, with extreme agitation, sudden aggression, or assault, or with any other of the possible changes in a stricken person's character. Along with this comes anger at the stricken person and inevitable feelings of guilt for becoming impatient, angry and resentful, and showing it.

If I'm a little tired and Bob pursues a subject until— you have no idea how people like that can pursue a subject—I can feel myself getting tense and angry. Occasionally, only when I get really angry, does he stop. But I don't like to get angry like that. It's hard on me, and I feel that I've got to work something out to help. I've thought about biofeedback that lets you know how tense you are so I can learn to relax. That might help me, relieve me. [a seventy-seven-year-old woman]

We literally had to watch Mother minute by minute because she was active enough then to put an empty pot on the stove and turn it on. She wasn't sleeping at night so at midnight she thought it was morning, would dress herself in several layers of clothing, and walk down the stairs and out the door. We were chasing her all night long. I didn't have the emotional energy to think out some of the solutions like having a bell on the door which would buzz when she went out. All those things you figure out when you have enough leisure to think them through, but when you're in the middle of it you're so exhausted, so overwhelmed, that you're just sort of getting through the next second. We were all just grimly going step by step, putting one foot in front of the other. [a woman in her forties]

The caregiver may feel deserted as she takes on more and more responsibilities in the home and perhaps becomes the sole means of financial support. Unlike people with diseases that mainly affect the body, a person with Alzheimer's disease often gives little or no thanks or recognition. The caregiver may feel resentful at the lack of reward for constant care. This resentment can be fed by a feeling that she is caring for a stranger—for someone whose behavior has become odd and embarrassing and who no longer knows or loves her. Added to this may come further feelings of guilt, as the caregiver feels love dying under the strain, and perhaps wishes for the death of the stricken person.

Caregivers of sexual partners experience a loss

Marianne Gontarz

Caring for the Caregiver

Public discussion of the need for care, information, and financial aid is increasing. Several states have established commissions or task forces on dementias related to aging, and some have authorized further, but still inadequate, state funding for long-term care. But state funding cannot compensate for the lack of a national funding policy. Many of us who are caregivers have become vocal in demanding more help and are working with others through local ADRDA associations.

We need:

- Health professionals who are trained in the diagnosis and care of Alzheimer's disease and related disorders, and who will take the time to listen and talk to us.
- Current, reliable information about research on the cause, prevention, and cure of Alzheimer's disease.
- A supportive community of persons sharing their caregiving experiences.
- Regular periods of relief from daily caregiving—relief in the form of adult day care or aides in the home.
- Regular one- to two-week periods of respite from caregiving in order to maintain our own physical and mental health. Government-funded respite centers and home nursing are needed to make this possible.
- Nurse practitioners who can make home visits to prevent unnecessary disease complications.
- Medicare and private insurance coverage for long-term care within the home, in day-care centers, and in nursing homes.
- Hospital and nursing-home staff trained in caring for the demented who will treat our loved ones with dignity and with respect for their humanity.
- Help of lawyers trained to advise us when a victim becomes legally incompetent.
- Financial guidelines to protect assets from being completely depleted by the cost of full-time care.
- Police and Fire Department personnel who are informed about Alzheimer's disease and related disorders to help lost and wandering afflicted persons and to intervene in serious crises.
- Support of family and friends.

---

of companionship and intimacy and often turn to others for close friendship. They have to decide whether such relationships will include sex. Painful conflicts between loyalty to an ailing partner and one's own needs often result.

The strain of caring for a demented person leads to a high rate of stress-related disorders. Over 50 percent of caregivers show symptoms of anxiety and depression including insomnia, headaches, irritability, and increased blood pressure.[15] The caregiver can become increasingly forgetful under stress, and fear that she or he too is developing the disease. In addition, when whole families are involved in the caregiving process, family life may virtually cease under the burden.

When we took my stricken dad in to live with us, supper table conversation became nonexistent. When you've got relationships within a family, you've got to have time to get together as a family, go away together—just have a meal together and talk together. I have two college-age daughters. One is saying, "I can't wait to get away from this place." The other is saying, "Home's the most awful place in the world." I feel terribly guilty and also frightened that they will never want to come home; that they won't remember home with enough pleasure to want to spend time with me. [a woman in her forties]

In addition to the burden of caring comes the insult of a medical insurance system which ignores the victim's and the caregiver's urgent needs. At present neither Medicare nor supplementary insurance covers the cost of long-term care at home, in respite programs or nursing homes. Only those eligible for Medicaid receive long-term care benefits. An estimated 80 percent of the cost of all long-term care both at home and in a nursing home is provided by the caregivers and by informal community support, not by public funds.[16] The financial burden can be ruinous for family members, especially elderly partners.

The Special Role of Family and Friends

In such a difficult time, the support of friends and relatives becomes more important than ever. With Alzheimer's disease such support is difficult to sustain, since the stricken person loses the social traits that drew others to her: a sense of humor, kindness, special interests and talents. She also loses control over language as a means of communication. The stricken person becomes a stranger to relatives and friends, who may react with withdrawal and avoidance, appalled at the loved one's condition. In addition, visits can be difficult to manage since the victim is often confused by any changes in the daily routine and embarrassed by her inability to remember who the visitors are. The resulting isolation of the victim may also lead to isolation of the caregiver.

As relatives or friends of Alzheimer's disease victims, it is important for us to remind ourselves that the stricken person still needs and recognizes affection even if she may neither remember nor return it. Often just quietly holding the stricken person's hand will help. We should also keep in mind the caregiver's needs for social contact, a change of scene, and an understanding ear. However, our instinct to withdraw is understandable, since many of us fear becoming demented more than we fear any other illness or infirmity that may come with age. Understanding as much as we can about the disease may help alleviate our anxiety, especially when we know that in most cases the increased forgetfulness that many of us experience is not a sign of disease. For those of us who do not have friends or relatives with Alzheimer's, understanding the disease will help us give support to those who do. It will keep us from isolating stricken people and their caregivers out of fear.

NOTES

1. K. Warner Schaie and James Geiwitz, *Adult Development and Aging*. Boston: Little, Brown, 1982, pp. 217–39.

2. Some studies show that approximately 33 percent of those between eighty and eighty-five show no decline on neuropsychological tests, including tests of memory, compared with younger age groups. A. L. Benton, et al., "Normative Observations on Neuropsychological Test Performances in Old Age." *Journal of Clinical Neuropsychology*, Vol. 3, No. 1 (May 1981), pp. 33–42.

3. Adapted from Florence Garfunkel and Gertrude Landau, *A Memory Retention Course for the Aged: Guide for Leaders*. Washington, D.C.: National Council on the Aging, December 1981.

4. "Memory Loss May Follow Use of Anticholinergics," *Medical World News*, August 12, 1985, p. 51.

5. Robert N. Butler, "Clinical Needs Assessment Studies Can Benefit Research on Aging." *Hospitals*, Vol. 55, No. 8 (April 16, 1981), pp. 94–8.

6. Barry Reisberg, *A Guide to Alzheimer's Disease: For Families, Spouses, and Friends*. New York: The Free Press, 1981, p. 14.

7. Incidence of concurrent multi-infarct dementia and Alzheimer's disease is unknown. One estimate is 25 percent of late-life dementia. See ibid.

8. This estimate is from the *Report of the Secretary's Task Force on Alzheimer's Disease*, U.S. Department of Health and Human Services, September 1984. However, accurate statistics on Alzheimer's are relatively new and in the process of revision. Some researchers consider 20 percent a conservative estimate, and say that prevalence may rise to 30 to 40 percent in those over eighty and 50 percent in those over eighty-five years of age.

9. U.S. Department of Health and Human Services, *Alzheimer's Disease Handbook, Vol. I*. San Francisco: Aging Health Policy Center, University of California, April 1984, p. 2.

10. Donald B. Tower, "Alzheimer's Disease—Senile Dementia and Related Disorders: Neurobiological Status." In Robert Katzman, R. D. Terry, and K. L. Bick, eds., *Alzheimer's Disease: Senile Dementia and Related Disorders*, Vol. 7, *Aging*. New York: Raven Press, 1978, p. 1.

11. Conversation with Dr. Lon White, Chief, Epidemiology Office, National Institute on Aging; and "Smokers Risk Alzheimer's Disease." *ASH Review*, August 1986, p. 10.

12. L. L. Heston and J. A. White, *Dementia: A Practical Guide to Alzheimer's Disease and Related Illnesses*. New York: W. H. Freeman & Co., 1983, p. 57.

13. Harold M. Schmeck, Jr., "A Form of Alzheimer's Is Linked to Defective Gene." *The New York Times*, February 20, 1987, p. 1. This article mentions four recent research reports.

14. Nancy L. Mace and Peter V. Rabins, *The 36-Hour Day: A Family Guide to Caring for Persons with Alzheimer's Disease, Related Dementing Illnesses, and Memory Loss in Later Life*. Baltimore: John Hopkins University Press, 1981, p. 24.

15. J. R. A. Sanford, "Tolerance of Debility in Elderly Dependents by Supporters at Home: Its Significance for Hospital Practice." *British Medical Journal*, Vol. 3, No. 5981 (August 23, 1975), pp. 471–3.

16. Lisa Gwyther, "A Statewide Family Support Program Mobilizes Mutual Support." *Center Reports on Advances in Research*, Vol. 6, No. 4 (December 1982), p. 2. Duke University Center for the Study of Aging and Human Development.

29

DYING AND DEATH

By Mary C. Howell, Mary C. Allen,
and Paula Brown Doress

Special thanks to Jane Bailey-Blood Strete

In many cultures, preparing for and making sense of death is the work of women, especially of old women. Whether or not it's fair or best, women in most societies, including our own, still act as the nurturers, caregivers, and custodians of those near death. Even with the removal of death to the institutional sphere, dying remains the province of women who work in those institutions.

The last person most of us see on earth is a woman—the nurse's aide (significantly one of the least paid and least valued workers in our society)....These are, in a sense, the midwives of death.[1]

Thus, it is most often women who meet the emotional and pragmatic needs surrounding death.

By the age of fifty-seven I had nursed my husband through terminal cancer, lived through widowhood, and been close to two dear friends who died. I assisted one friend and supported her family through the process of her committing suicide. I feel that my middle years have been significant in bringing me into close and familiar contact with dying and death.

BEREAVEMENT AND GRIEF

On a rational level, we know that any fully lived life inevitably contains the experience of death. But observers like psychiatrist Elisabeth Kübler-Ross have remarked that almost everyone who goes through the process of mourning her own impending death or that of a loved one

Sarah Putnam

does it in stages: first, denial ("This can't be happening"), then anger ("It's not fair"), followed by bargaining ("Maybe if I do exactly as the doctor says, I'll beat this"), depression ("I can't bear this sadness"), and finally, often with great sorrow and regret, a time of acceptance.[2] Although these different facets of the process of mourning are sometimes referred to as stages—implying that each one is fully experienced and comes to an end before the next begins—it is more likely that these different emotions and thoughts come and go, mingling with each other over a period of years.

The following is excerpted from a woman's journal recording her feelings about her lover's death over a period of years:

In what later seemed to be extraordinary word usage, the doctor called me to say the operation on Karen was "successful." They resectioned her colon and took out the tumor; she would not need a colostomy. But the tumor has metastasized and she will die; six months to two years is all they give her. No real hope.

It is 2:30 A.M. and I can't sleep because of rage at God, and then because of guilt. And because of fear for myself. How will I live without Karen to tell me I am brilliant and beautiful?

Images run through my head. Her hand warming my asthma-congested chest. Her step—quick, strong, fast up the stairs. As I remember that sound, I smile; the pain recedes. But if I shut my journal, the pain will return.

Does everyone who is dying look bewildered? Her head in my lap; her body spooned in pain. Dying means dependency. Pain. Listlessness. Fever. Exhaustion. Dying is frightening.

Death is final, but dying can drag on and on and on, destroying everyone. It saps the strength of the healthy and makes them sick.

My first birthday without her. Our anniversary. Her first birthday dead. My first Christmas and first New Year without her. One year it was the greatest New Year of my life, and the next year the woman who gave it to me was dead.

Each marker brings Karen to me and takes her. Soon my first spring without her. My first summer. Then a year since I last saw her will pass. A year since her death; a year since her funeral. And I will put a headstone in my heart: Karen, my dearest.[3]

Any one loss can remind us of all the other losses we have known—especially the earliest ones, which might not have been fully understood or explored.

When my lover died I was fifty-six. Over the next two years I relived, in a way, all of the other great sadnesses of my life—when my father left us when I was little, my mother's death, the endings of other love affairs. I don't think I had realized how much there was for me to mourn! [a sixty-two-year-old woman]

Acceptance of death can come only after a full experience of mourning that may last many months or even years.

My daughter died almost forty years ago, when she was ten. I'm still angry, and I still miss her. But for years after she died I couldn't quite believe that it had really happened—I kept thinking I heard her in the house. Now I can accept what happened, even if I don't like it. [a seventy-eight-year-old woman]

My husband died eighteen years ago and even though today I have a happy, full life, I still miss him. I am often reminded of what he is missing, especially at happy moments, such as the children's high school and college graduations, which are tinged with the wish that he were alive to share the joy. [a fifty-four-year-old woman]

Mental health experts have observed that "troubled mourning" can be a principal reason for unhappiness and problems later in life. Mourning can go wrong in a variety of ways. We may be unable to grieve at the time of loss, feeling too numb to cry or to express our feelings in any way at all. We may begin to grieve but cut the process short, because of pressure to appear self-possessed for a job or family or friends. Or we may suppress our grief, drive it underground, in which case it is likely to erupt again, perhaps with surprising intensity, at the time of some later loss.

In these cases, we may try to protect ourselves from the pain of grief by adopting a self-protecting mask of composure which allows us to carry on with life as usual. Sometimes a physical illness may appear, or self-destructive behavior such as drug or alcohol addiction, an eating disorder, or repeated involvements in unsatisfactory relationships. One or more aspects of mourning can become exaggerated. We may dwell on guilt, self-blame, anger, anxiety, or sadness until we become completely incapacitated and such feelings take the place of grieving.

In each of the above cases, the underlying problem is that the person who mourns has in some way not completed the mourning process. Sometimes, friends or relatives, in a misguided desire to be helpful, urge us to "get on with it," when in fact what we need is to honor the urgency and depth of our feelings for as long as we need to do so. Paying attention to our feelings and talking about them with friends or relatives is extremely important.

When my husband was dying people helped us so much. They came to visit and brought food so that I could spend more time with him. They gave flowers and hugs, gave the children extra attention. Some people were too frightened to visit and I understood. But the friend who came fifteen hundred miles to see him before he died, the friend who came five hundred miles to hold my hand during the funeral, and the friend who stayed at the cemetery to cover his grave after the service will forever have my gratitude.

I was comforted by the notes and cards people sent me. I read them over and over again for many months, nurtured by the care, sympathy, and support they provided. Best of all were the handwritten notes that in-

cluded something about the writer's relationship with my husband or memories of times together—sometimes things that were new to me. I received notes from people I had not known and was strengthened by their consideration. Even the printed cards and the simplest notes indicating that someone was thinking of me comforted me. Nineteen years later, I still have all the messages in a box so our now-grown children can share with their children how the grandfather they will never know touched the lives of so many others. [a fifty-four-year-old woman]

When my husband died it was like I was paralyzed socially for months after. My two good friends did me a great service just by sitting with me. Sometimes I would cry and sometimes I'd just be angry. Sometimes I was so sad I could hardly talk. They'd come over to visit me at least twice a week, and they stayed with it for more than a year. When I felt better I could be a good friend to them again. [a sixty-four-year-old woman]

I learned a lot about anger after my mother died. Somehow, when I was mourning, lots of anger came out that I didn't know was in me. My daughter suggested beating a pillow with a stick to get the anger out, and finally I got so I could talk with my husband and also with my daughter about some of the reasons why I felt so much anger at my poor mother. [a forty-three-year-old woman]

Observing religious and/or cultural traditions, writing about our feelings in a journal, talking to family and friends, meditating, reading poetry, watching emotion-evoking movies or plays, and singing or listening to familiar songs can all help us feel our grief as deeply and fully as we need. Joining a self-help group of people who are grieving, such as a widow-to-widow group or a hospice group, can be a great comfort. Such groups help us realize that what we are feeling is "normal" and is shared by others.

How to Help a Dying or Recently Bereaved Person

- Give them the time and quiet listening to express their feelings. Express your own sadness and regret, but do not presume to tell a bereaved or dying person that a death is "for the best," even if after a long illness. We don't really know how someone feels unless they tell us.
- Offer distractions, other topics of mutual interest, but be comfortable with silence and resist the need to fill every minute with words. Your very presence will help.
- Offer help, and be specific in your suggestions. Say, "I have two hours free on Saturday. Do you want me to shop for you, or is there something else I can do that would be helpful?"
- Take care of a dying or bereaved person: do not expect her or him to take care of you. Bring food if you visit someone's home.
- Do send cards or notes if you can't visit.

For some of us it is useful to get professional help—from a clergyman, for example, or perhaps from a bereavement counselor—to deal with the process of mourning.

I functioned extremely well most of the time (everyone always said how well), but I felt like I was just going through the motions, waiting for my husband to come home. Three times in the past four years I've arrived at the point where I felt a need for counseling. Each time I've learned more about myself. The counseling has helped me grow and find new meaning in my life. [a woman in her fifties]

The loss of a child or grandchild can be particularly painful. If death is caused by a sudden, unexpected accident that allows little or no time beforehand for preparation, as is often the case when someone we love dies young, the loss may be even more difficult to come to terms with. We

Deborah Kahn

Deborah Kahn

My father died of a heart attack and my mother died of cancer. My father's death was a surprise and a shock, and my mother's death was a long ordeal. I know that people sometimes think that a sudden and quick death is easier, but for me it was important to talk with my mother and even just to sit and hold her hand, and though those last weeks and months were hard I'm grateful we had them. With my father there was no time to say good-bye. I wish there had been. [a forty-nine-year-old woman]

When we are faced with the shock of a sudden, unexpected death, we often console ourselves with the knowledge that the person we loved did not suffer. While having time to prepare for a death may be easier on our survivors, many of us would choose an unanticipated and painless death for ourselves.

For myself, I want my death to be sudden, quick and easy for me, even if it is harder on those who survive me. [a woman in her fifties]

When death comes at the end of a prolonged and chronic illness, our feelings may take longer to sort out. We may have already grieved, years ago, for the loss of the whole, well person we used to know.

My sister developed the first symptoms of Alzheimer's when she was sixty-two. I took care of her, moved into her apartment for five years so she could stay in familiar surroundings. Then I had to put her into a nursing home, where I visited her twice a week. I never missed a week for nine more years until she died. There was very little that anybody could do for her. It was very hard to see her become just a thin little curled-up ball in her bed. For the last seven years she didn't recognize me or even talk at all. She was my only sister, and it was terribly sad for me. [a sixty-two-year-old woman]

We may feel a sense of release for ourselves and for the person who died after prolonged suffering. But later, intense, renewed feelings of loss may surface.

Even though I thought I had prepared myself mentally for the inevitable, I found I was terribly shocked, even surprised, when my mother finally did die. I understand now that shock after a death is common among those close to a person, even when the death was expected.[4]

cannot comfort ourselves by saying, "Well, she's lived a long and full life and it was her time to die." Even if we lose a child in her or his middle or late years, we may feel a sense of unfairness, as if the natural order of things has been violated. This was not a loss we expected to sustain.

When my husband died at age thirty-nine, his mother cried out how against nature his death was. She said, "I was supposed to die first."

We may feel this way even if our child has lived a full life span.

It's no good to live so long if you have to see your children die. [a ninety-five-year-old woman at the funeral of her seventy-five-year-old son]

When death is expected, not only the person who is dying but also those who expect to be survivors have time to make some preparations, get relationships and business affairs in order, and to reminisce and say good-bye.

Coming to Terms with Our Own Deaths

One of the important developmental tasks of the second half of life is coming to a personal understanding, perhaps even an acceptance, of death.

Some of us continue to feel ambivalent and scared about acknowledging death.

A few of my friends have died young. We all knew each other for so long. (We had a card-playing group.) Three of them were my age. One of them I met recently and recognized her name from elementary school, and so we were the same age. Another one was a few months older, so we were all in the same age bracket. Now my sister-in-law just died and she was only sixty-three. This has been on my mind so much lately, you know, reaching this point that people my age are starting to go. I never used to think of these things before. Like if an aunt or an uncle died that's one thing, but now it's cousins! One cousin my age died this summer, so I start to think "It's our turn" and in what order are we going? [a sixty-seven-year-old woman]

Intellectually, I'm very glib about it, but in my gut I can't accept that one day I won't be here. [a seventy-four-year-old woman]

Marianne Gontarz

Maybe no one can ever be fully "ready" for death in the sense of knowing about and fully accepting the experience in advance. But we can prepare ourselves in a variety of ways.[5]

I feel a greater awareness of a mystery and beauty in life since I have accepted death as a personal eventuality for me. I don't remember exactly when that awareness came. Before then, I had thought of death "out there," and now I know that one day it will be a reality for me. Eventually I am going to die. In a way, that has released me for more vivid living. [a seventy-eight-year-old woman]

I've dealt with losing loved ones many times in my life, and after seventy years of repetition of that experience of grief I find the thing that's so hard to deal with is that some person who has been a reality in your life no longer exists. When you're a kid, you learn how to separate fantasy from reality. But then, when you get older, you have to learn how to let go of a reality—that person no longer exists. I've got a handle on that from years of experience with it. So I no longer worry about my own personal death. [a seventy-three-year-old woman]

Some of us are comforted by religious, spiritual, or humanistic beliefs about life and death.

I believe that I am not just a body which is perishable but I am a spirit which is eternal. I believe that death is only an exit from this temporary life of unreality into a glorious new life of reality. I hope, therefore, that there will be only rejoicing, not grief, at the time of my release. I am trying to avoid being "earthbound" by releasing my attachments to material objects and persons before I enter this transition. [a ninety-two-year-old woman]

What I've been aware of lately because of a number of instances of my being thrown up against death is that I have a different perception of relationships. Death is not a termination of my life because my influence will continue until the last person who knew me has died. [a woman in her fifties]

Some Day This Flesh

Some day some atom of this flesh shall be
commingled with a tree,
Will taste the resinous sap spicing its veins;
Wrestle with tempests; dance with silver rains;
And stand a singing tower against the sky.

My lapping blood existence will partake
with some far, hill-girt lake,
will cherish water-lilies on its flood;
Will shadow winging bird and dreaming cloud;
And hold the evening star within its cup.

I have so joyed in campfire's comradeship;
Have felt such grip
of awed delight at dogwood's miracle;
Such rapture in the living slope of hill;
Surely I shall be fire and flower and grass!

Fear? Fear transfiguration glad as this?
Such loveliness?
With these I have so loved, to be enfurled,
inwoven in all the beauty of the world?
Perhaps—who knows?—My very heart shall be
for one mad hour of flaming ecstasy
a sunset!

Florence Luscomb

Living each moment as fully as possible is probably the most important way to help ourselves become less fearful of death.

Florence Luscomb, suffragist, labor organizer, civil rights and peace activist. Died in 1985 at age ninety-eight.

I do not look to the future with dread. It has to be shorter than my past but it does not have to be less rich. I'm more relaxed. I don't try to do everything.

That means I can take time for quiet, for meditation, alternate this with activity, and see how I can keep a moving, living balance between the two. [a seventy-eight-year-old woman]

Death, I am learning through my own experience, need not be frightening. After all, we are all born terminal cases, because we will all die, at one time or another. Death is part of life. I have lived life fully and enjoyed it greatly, which makes it easier to consider bowing out than if you feel that you have missed out on a lot.*

Providing support to others can also help us come to terms with death. We can serve as resources for one another and create supportive networks that give us the strength and companionship we need to get through hard times.

*Tish Sommers, age seventy, in a letter to members of the Older Women's League about her expected death. Tish founded and led the 23,000-member organization after her cancer was diagnosed.

On the day before her fifty-eighth birthday, my friend Maggy Krebs died in a Boston hospital. Maggy was a feminist artist.* Her humor, her drawings and paintings, and her music had filled many lives with joy. Because I believe that the final months of her life and her death were models for all independent women, I want to tell you part of the story.

For months, Maggy gathered around her a group of her friends, who tended to her at her home and at the hospital. In addition to caring for Maggy, we met each other regularly, often weekly, to share our grief and anger at the anticipated loss of a friend, to find ways to share the responsibility of taking care of her and to support one another. We became a family for Maggy and for each other.

One of Maggy's legacies to us is the pride we feel that we were able to give her the comfort and love she needed. But Maggy also left a legacy of hope to all women who feel themselves to be alone by teaching us that we can support each other through the depths of illness, exhaustion, fear and loss.[6]

Sharing the responsibility as this women's group did avoids the guilt women sometimes feel when they can't do everything by themselves. An illness support group allows each woman to participate to the extent she is able to do so.

In the last four years I have come from the depths of despair to feeling that life is good and that there still is a reason and a need for me to be in this world. Helping to train hospice volunteers continues to be therapeutic for me. With the death of my husband, things which I'd only read about in books or heard others talk about became very real and personal to me. Much of my own grief work was done with the volunteer training classes, where the volunteers gave me the opportunity to talk about my experiences and my life, and the aloneness I felt at the loss of my best friend and life's companion. [a woman in her fifties]

Most of my friends are gone. You just have to say to yourself that it's something that's going to happen. But it's not easy. It helps to do all you can for your friends while they're living. I do a lot of calling on the telephone. I have a friend I call every day. He's been in the hospital a long time. I have another friend who lives down in another town who's quite sick that I call at least once a week. Death used to be scary to me. Four or five years ago, if I thought of dying, I'd push it out of my mind. But now, I think, after all, I've lived out my days and I know I've got to go. [a woman in her eighties]

Another way to prepare ourselves for dying is to take care of any unfinished business in our

*See pp. 186 and 199 for cartoons by Maggy Krebs.

lives. Most of us have unresolved relationships —some that go back quite far—that we may want to work out or perhaps just make a final statement on. We can seek out people with whom we have unfinished business and see to it that some old unforgiven hurts are healed—and recognize that some can't ever be healed. Those who have made the effort to do this say it is very important.

Before her death my sister asked to see each of her five brothers and sisters. We talked about the ways we had been close and trusting with each other, and we also talked about some of our long-standing fights and grudges. I know that the hour that she and I spent going over our times together was very important to me. It was one way to say good-bye. And I think it was important and healing for her, as well. [a forty-seven-year-old woman]

The Medicalization of Death

Understanding death has become more difficult and complicated because, in our culture, death is often a medical event. Most people in the last stages of life are in hospitals and nursing homes, and are thus "out of sight." Life-threatening situations at any age often take place in a hospital. Institutional methods of caring for the sick and dying make it difficult for us to experience and understand death as a natural end to life.

I can remember the day my grandfather died, in a tractor accident on the farm. The men brought him in from the field to the house, and my grandmother, my mother, and my aunt bathed and dressed him. It was a loving act, and a ritual, and I was terribly impressed. I was eight at the time. My own father went from the hospital bed where he died to a funeral home, and I know my mother doesn't feel like she was a part of his dying. I'm trying to understand that difference, and what I myself want to do in that regard. [a sixty-seven-year-old woman]

In some cultures, death is understood to be a natural transition at the end of life. Among some Native American tribes, for instance, each life is seen as a road that is expected to come to an end. The healers in those societies see themselves as "keepers of the road," guardians of health for as long as the journey goes on—not as persons who work to prevent the journey from ending in its expected transition.

But in our contemporary culture, we invest heavily in science and want to believe that through it we can control all the events of our

lives. We have hope that the discoveries of science will allow us to prolong life and prevent death. These attitudes make it hard to look on death as the natural, expected end of life, and make it harder to accept the inevitability of death.

Physicians often use every possible means to prolong life without regard for its quality. The result can be feelings of anguish and helplessness on the part of the dying person, relatives and friends.

When my husband had his heart attack I thought I should rush him to the hospital. The ambulance came right away but by the time they resuscitated him he already had a lot of brain damage. He never recovered consciousness. Everyone in the ICU [Intensive Care Unit] worked very hard to save his life, and he did live for another two weeks, but as far as I'm concerned he wasn't really alive—just a body attached to a lot of tubes and machinery. I wish now that I had just held him, cradled his head, when he first fell. I could have said good-bye that way. [a sixty-five-year-old woman]

As some medical professionals are beginning to recognize, focus on the inappropriate pursuit of a cure when the situation is clearly beyond hope can lead medical personnel to make a person's last days more painful and difficult than necessary. Of course, there are situations of acute emergency in which one cannot be sure whether recovery is possible; it is very hard to know the right thing to do in such a case. But some medical treatments designed to cure, such as chemotherapy and radiotherapy, may increase the dying person's discomfort.

Many of us may feel more secure in a hospital when we are very ill. Or we may feel we want to try, or should continue to try, medical remedies on the chance that one may heal us.

My daughter died of breast cancer at age forty-two. We thought she wanted to die at home and we were ready to take care of her there. But in the end the doctors urged her to try one more round of treatment with chemotherapy and she went back into the hospital. She never came home again, and for the last week she was so sick and in such pain that she didn't even want her teenage children to visit her. [a sixty-eight-year-old woman]

Discomforts such as pain, shortness of breath, weakness, nausea, and vomiting often precede death. The last days of living can be eased by concentrating on comfort rather than cure. (See "Dealing with Pain" in the chapter Habits Worth Changing, p. 34.) Occasionally, treatments such as radiotherapy or even surgery may be used to bring relief of pain and discomfort, though it is more common to use high doses of pain-relieving drugs.

We were lucky enough to find a doctor who was willing to come to the house and could prescribe drugs for Grandma's pain and also for the nausea. We heard about the doctor because she had performed the same service for a neighbor down the street, and she made a hard time much easier than it might have been. [a thirty-six-year-old woman]

Taking Control of Our Own Deaths

Many of us would prefer not to be subjected to machines and tubes and complex technological procedures that may extend life a few extra days, weeks, or months at the expense of whatever quality it may be possible to achieve. Some of us who have such thoughts, however, will surely die in the very circumstances we deplore. How does this happen?

We tend to forget experiences that most of us have had as patients, like being moved from one treatment to another with little explanation of what is really thought to be wrong, how the treatment is supposed to work, and what to expect next, as if once we become patients we have given over the right or desire to make choices. The physician often doesn't present alternatives from which we can choose; the alternatives of *no* treatment or of treatments such as acupuncture or herbal remedies are rarely discussed. This failure to present alternatives makes it difficult for the ill person to make informed decisions. Being a patient can feel like being on a slippery slide you can't easily get off.

My daughter spent the last months of her life going to the hospital for outpatient treatments, and feeling terrible. I won't ever do that. I'm not saying it's any better to be sick from the cancer, but at least you'd feel like it's your body and your life. I'd want to have some time to myself to live a little if I thought I was going to die soon. [a fifty-nine-year-old woman]

Here are some things to remember about doctors and dying:

- Physicians cannot actually predict recovery, death, or future disability for any single patient; they can only make broad, educated guesses based on statistics for large populations. They deal in group probabilities.[7]
- Many people whose death was predicted with firm certainty by medical experts have recovered; this happens with sufficient regularity to

remind us that illness is not fully understood by science.

Each individual has a right to say how she or he will live out the last days of a soon-to-be-ended life. If living outside a hospital or without the discomfort of medical treatment is what you want, your right to do so ought to be honored.

Ten years ago, when I was forty-five, I was told I had breast cancer. For the next year I had chemotherapy and radiation—I was sick and worried the whole year. But now I feel that when the cancer comes back I just want to live with it, except for painkillers when I need them. I feel that if I'm going to live on, or die, I want to be able to experience each day as my day. I've written letters to each of my children to let them know how important this is to me.

Even when we try to stay in control, an illness can become overwhelming and may deplete our energy reserves, especially if we do not have a dependable support system. Though we may aspire to a serene death for ourselves or a loved one, surrounded by familiar faces, we must recognize that humans have never been able to control or predict death.

I felt like I was in a dream. I had promised my husband I wouldn't send him back to the hospital, but I was up for twenty hours each day taking care of him and I just couldn't go on. He agreed to go back because I promised him that I would live there with him. The last ten days he didn't talk but he seemed to be comfortable. They were giving him morphine intravenously. The doctor woke me at 3 A.M. to tell me he had died while I was sleeping. It bothered me that I was sleeping when he died because I had promised him that I would be with him. I don't know if he would have said anything if I had been awake. No matter how hard you try, it doesn't always work out the way you want. [a woman in her sixties]

The Living Will

If you decide that you want to die at home, or that in some circumstances you would prefer to have no treatment, or treatment for comfort only, you have a right to make that decision and to refuse treatment. It is a good idea to put your wishes in writing, in the event that you are unable to participate in decision-making yourself. In order to do so, you will have to think now about the possibility of your death. For some of us this can be very difficult. Nevertheless, it is important to leave some written statement of your wishes. The pressure for the ill and dying to become and remain "patients" is often so great that your spoken word alone may not be enough to give your family and friends the strength to carry out your wishes.

My mother at age ninety-seven was in a nursing home. By then she was hard of hearing and blind, so we communicated by touch. She had often told me that she wanted to die in the nursing home, not in an unfamiliar hospital. However, she became ill and was sent to the hospital, where she lapsed into a coma for three weeks. Then they wanted to put a feeding tube in. I threatened to sue unless they sent her back to the nursing home. The doctor and I stood over her bed arguing. He said, "You are murdering your mother." I said, "No, I want it to be her choice." My mother opened her eyes and looked at me and said, "Thank you." I got her back to the nursing home that night. Next day she was up, all over the home, and talking with everybody. Then the nurse called, telling me that my mother wanted roast duckling. I baked it and pureed it in a blender. She ate the whole thing. That night she threw her false teeth down the toilet and she died three days later. [a sixty-five-year-old woman]

My mother always said that she didn't want to die in a hospital and didn't want lengthy, complicated, and expensive care at the end of her life. But when she got weaker and weaker because of her failing heart, she was treated with one drug after another. When she got pneumonia, again she was treated and hospitalized because she seemed to be having trouble breathing. I said to my Dad, "Of course she's having trouble breathing, she's old and she's weak and she's dying." But he was too scared to let her stay at home. If she had made a legal record of her wishes we could have done as she asked. Weak as she was, I felt that I had betrayed her by letting her go into the hospital and die there. [a fifty-six-year-old woman]

One form of such a written statement is called a living will. Thirty-eight states plus the District of Columbia now have statutes that approve the use of living wills; often a suggested form is included in the statute. (A sample living will is available from Concern for Dying or the Society for the Right to Die—see Resources.) And in every state, constitutional and common law support the right of any competent adult to refuse medical treatment *in any situation*.[8]

The majority of states with living-will legislation require physicians to comply with the terms of a living will, or else transfer the patient to a physician who will. Even in states that do not yet have living-will laws, you can draw up such a document and inform the people close to

you and your physician of your wishes, because recent court decisions give more weight to individual choice.[9] A *written* document is helpful in protecting and supporting those who will be arranging final care.

Living wills which comply with statutory guidelines usually deal with instances in which there is medical certification that a person's condition is "incurable"—that is, the person is expected to die in the near future, usually within six months, as a direct consequence of injury or illness—and that the application of life-sustaining procedures will artificially prolong the process of death. In a living will, we can state that under these conditions we want any artificially life-extending procedures withdrawn or withheld, and require that the attending physicians, our family, or whomever we designate to make decisions for us honor these wishes if and when we ourselves are unable to participate in decision-making.

Living wills are valid only in cases of terminal illness. They are not honored in situations when a person has a slow, degenerative disease, or when a very old person has "multiple systems failure." In these situations, you may be able to use a durable power of attorney (see Caregiving chapter, p. 209).

One drawback of the living will is that it works only for treatment *refusal*. If you want all possible treatments tried in your case, a durable power of attorney is more useful,[10] and may help for treatment refusal as well. Assuring that you get adequate medical treatment if you are severely ill may take more than writing out your wishes. The new cost-containment emphasis in medical care has resulted in people being discharged from hospitals when they still hope for recovery and do want treatment. Older persons, especially those with limited funds, are at an especially high risk of being discharged prematurely, against their wishes.

Dying at Home

At one time, almost everybody could have expected to die in their own homes—even in their own beds. Now, death more often occurs in a hospital or nursing home. Recently, however, more people are insisting that they be allowed to die outside of these institutions.

I don't want anyone to tell me what to do. I lived all these years with my eight children, and made decisions,

Roxanne Cummings Potter

Marion Cunningham

right or wrong, about how we'd live. I want to decide for myself now. I've no need for medicine, drugs, or hospitals, never have, and I don't want to start now. I want to die with dignity. *I'm comfortable in my home among my own things and with my family around me. They'll care for me. They'll respect my wishes. I can see who I want in my own home. I can eat what I want to eat. I know my own body and what it needs or can handle. I'm a private person. There's no privacy in the hospital. I want my children around me. I need their touch, their love.* [a seventy-six-year-old woman]

Mom needed to be hostess and be in charge in her home even while dying. She continued to direct and guide her children about her care. While we held a cup to her mouth, she would urge, "Eat with me." When she needed more care, we hired hospice workers. When I introduced my mom to the new worker, Mom was already in her "withdrawal from the world stage." But she drew herself together from her fetal position under the blankets to peek at this new person, and, in her weak, raspy voice, said, "Welcome to my home." These were her final words to the world. What a magnificent, feisty, independent woman this mother of mine was. She showed us how to live and how to die. Mom passed on as peacefully as possible considering her pain and weakness. [a fifty-seven-year-old woman, the daughter of the woman quoted above]

A woman who is a midwife wrote the following account of her mother's death:

*This past year brought serious illness to my mother, Marion Cunningham. We sought conventional medical attention, plus an array of alternative healing practitioners. After months of misdiagnosis, Marion diag-*nosed herself as dying. We admitted her to the hospital and, alas, the diagnosis of lung cancer was finally acknowledged. My brother, my sister, and I stood in disbelief at her side. A pioneer in natural childbirth and in single parenting, she had always been our source of strength and inspiration. We all cried together that day. Then Marion spoke to me, words which would affect our caring of one another in the months to follow: "Why don't they have midwives for what I've got?" We decided to care for her at home.

One night at midnight I received a call from my brother... "Mom says she will die today and that you all should come."

And thus it was that we gathered round. My brother requested that I sing "The Goodbye Song," which I had written just a month before.

> *I'll see you in the babies' faces*
> *I'll feel you in the wind*
> *I'll hear you in the quietest places*
> *I'll hold you in my friend.*

I played on my guitar and sang to Marion, and in the midst of the song I could hear her breathing relax and I knew she would die. We watched one tear roll down her face and then she took her last breath.[11]

Hospices

A relatively new institution called the hospice has developed in response to the growing interest in dying at home. The hospice is modeled after medieval way stations that accommodated both travelers and those who were dying (death being, metaphorically, another form of travel).

Contemporary hospice agencies started out as coalitions of volunteers who were trained to visit and offer help to dying people in their own homes. Most hospice agencies now also have specially designed inpatient buildings where people can get short-term help managing uncomfortable symptoms and then go back home. The services of medical professionals are a relatively minor part of the care offered by hospices. They also provide trained volunteer visitors, visiting nurses, nurses' aides, homemakers, and bereavement counseling for family and friends.

One of the major goals of a hospice program is to maintain the quality of life through spiritual and emotional support, medication, and methods such as meditation and visualization for pain control. They will also provide temporary relief for caregivers.

Our son died of Hodgkin's disease two years ago.

401

Toward the end he said he didn't want to go back into the hospital, no matter what. We called the hospice and they sent a volunteer who came to visit John two days a week at first and then, at the end, every day. He was almost like a member of the family, and the help he gave made a big difference to all of us—especially to John. [a seventy-six-year-old woman]

Some of these services have always been available from visiting-nurse and home-care agencies, clergy, church-visitation committees, and other local sources. But a hospice program coordinates all these services. Medicare, Medicaid, and some other insurance plans may pay part of the bill. Not all communities have hospice agencies, however. If you want to locate the hospice nearest you, call a visiting-nurse agency or a local hospital's social service department. (See Resources for the two national hospice organizations.) A local Social Security office can also tell you which hospice programs are Medicare certified.

Choosing the Time of Our Death

Two years ago my mother, who was then eighty-three, told me that she planned to end her life by taking an overdose of pills. Her health was failing rapidly and she was going blind. She didn't want to become weak and dependent. She had always been a fierce and active woman. She wrote her intentions in a letter to me—I was her only close family member—and she told two friends and her doctor. We all told her that we would not help her accumulate enough pills to do the job. And I think we all worked very hard to help her find new reasons to be happy to be alive. But finally I understood that she really wanted to do what she had planned, and in the end, after she gathered together enough pills and took them, I sat with her for the last thirty-six hours as she slipped away. I can't tell you how many of her friends and acquaintances told me how graceful my mother was in her life to the very end. For my mother, given her personality, staying in control of her own life made her graceful. [a forty-one-year-old woman]

There is a great difference between someone, terminally ill and in pain, who says, "I've lived a full, long life and I think this is my time to die," and someone who is viewing life through the fog of depression and says, "I don't want to go on living." For a depressed person, a suicide attempt may be a call for help in finding resources to regain pleasure in living. You can get help for such a person through a suicide-prevention organization like the Samaritans (see Resources).

It is very difficult to know what to do when a loved one wants to end her or his life. Talking with this person can help us distinguish temporary feelings of discouragement from the conviction that a life of pain and deterioration would be unbearable.

Laws vary from state to state, but nearly everywhere, a person who helps a dying family member or friend commit suicide risks prosecution as an accessory to a crime. To protect their loved ones, some dying persons have chosen to go off by themselves and take a fatal substance. They have had to do without the loving support and the talking and planning that would have eased the transition for everybody.

Claiming the right to control the end of our lives in no way minimizes the seriousness or the finality of the decision, nor the pain and grief of those we leave behind. A number of organizations, such as the Society for the Right to Die and the Hemlock Society, now publicize these issues and can help us deal with them personally (see Resources).

Practical Matters

Before we die, some of us may want to arrange to donate vitally needed organs, such as kidneys and corneas, for transplant purposes. We can also plan the kind of funeral or memorial service we want. Helpful, practical information on these matters is available from the Older Women's League as part of their "Living Will Packet" (see Resources).

A growing number of people today want to keep matters relating to death under the control of their immediate circle of friends and family. Preparing the body for burial, the burial or cremation itself, and last rites and memorial services can all, within broad limits, be designed to suit the wishes of the person who has died and her or his survivors.

The person I talked to about renting a place for the memorial service told me sharply that I had no business planning a memorial while my mother was still alive. But I am very thankful that we did plan it when we did. First of all, I was amazed to find that I was in absolutely no condition to make sensible plans after she died....Planning the forms of the memorial beforehand helped me face the reality of my mother's death. Thinking about and writing what I would say brought the love we had shared back to me once more. Participating in the memorial gave me a kind of peace and acceptance I hardly dared hope for.[12]

If you have preferences about your burial, it will be much easier for your family and friends to carry out your wishes if you make them known in writing. This will also protect your loved ones from having feelings of guilt, because they will be assured they are following your wishes.

Remember that the funeral business is just that—a profitable business. There are some regulations, varying from state to state, that govern this industry. You can learn about them by calling your local consumer affairs office.

I found out later that the funeral director lied to me when he said state law required a cement lining for my husband's grave, contrary to our personal and religious beliefs. [a fifty-five-year-old woman]

Those of us who are struggling to come to a better understanding of the great, universal transition at the end of life have many opportunities to ponder the matter. Experiences such as watching persons we are close to approach death, becoming aware of symptoms that might signal the beginning of life-threatening illness, putting our affairs in order in a written will, working as a volunteer in a hospice agency, or being part of a supportive network for a dying friend or relative, all can help us come to a peaceful, personal understanding of death.

NOTES

1. Tish Sommers, *Death—A Feminist View.* Paper presented at Drake University Law School, Des Moines, Iowa, March 27, 1976.
2. Elisabeth Kübler-Ross, *On Death and Dying.* New York: Macmillan, 1969.
3. Carolyn Ruth Swift, unpublished manuscript.
4. Mickey Spencer, "Plan Ahead." *Broomstick*, Vol. 7, No. 6 (November–December 1985), pp. 40–2.
5. J. W. Worden and William Proctor, *Personal Death Awareness.* Englewood Cliffs, NJ: Prentice-Hall, 1976.
6. Swift, op. cit.
7. See Stephen Jay Gould, "The Median Isn't the Message." *Discover*, Vol. 6, No. 6 (June 1985), pp. 40–2.
8. George Annas and Joan Densberger, "Competence to Refuse Medical Treatment: Autonomy vs. Paternalism." *University of Toledo Law Review*, Vol. 15, 1984, pp. 561–96.
9. Joseph F. Sullivan, "Wishes of Patient in Refusing Care Backed in New Jersey: Right to Die is Extended. Rulings in Three Cases Give Interests of Individuals Priority Over State's." *The New York Times*, June 25, 1987, pp. 1, B12.
10. Barbara Mishkin, "Making Decisions for the Terminally Ill." *Business and Health*, June 1985, pp. 13–6.
11. Roxanne Cummings Potter, "To Life—To Death." *California Association of Midwives Newsletter*, Spring 1984, p. 7.
12. Spencer, op. cit.

30

CHANGING SOCIETY AND OURSELVES

by Tish Sommers

Special thanks to Laurie Shields and Fran Leonard

What kind of an older woman do I want to be? That's a good question to ask. Too often middle-aged and older women feel that it is too late to plan for the future, to make important changes in themselves, to have significant impact on the world around them. Not so. At forty we can expect half our adult life to be still before us. Sometimes the things that happen to us which we can do little about—like the death or desertion of a spouse—may trigger a whole new look at our priorities. Sometimes our way of life is curbed by a serious health condition, and this may also touch off a reordering of what is really important to us and spur us forward. Even the shadow of impending death can be a stimulus to helping us put our lives in order.

Growing old is not easy, especially if you are poor and alone, as is the case with the majority of aging women, many of whom slip into poverty in their later years. It takes a lot of internal strength to cope with increasing infirmities or chronic pain, and the loss of choices brought about by reduced finances and physical limitations. It also takes preparation well before the calamities strike, and deciding as early as possible what kind of older woman you want to be. Will you go into a shell or be able to push past obstacles to make the last half of life as rich as the first? And what impact will you have on the people around you and the world at large?

You may decide to become an advocate, as some of us have. Pushing the establishment to be more in tune with the needs of those who are hurting—including yourself—can be as rewarding in your seventies as in your thirties.

Contributing to something important beyond ourselves can keep us feeling that what we do still matters. And it can be a great impetus to personal growth.

I strongly believe that the advocacy work women do benefits the whole of society. It throws light on injustices and then eventually changes are made that help men too. [Annette Smail, advocate for ex-wives of military personnel]

Starting with Ourselves

The image of older women is changing. What we do today, both as role models and as forces for change in public policy, will greatly influence our daughters' futures. The present road to aging, especially for women, is a rocky one. But we, the old and the soon-to-be-old, can change that in our lifetimes. We can develop new ways of providing mutual help in our communities, and we can work together to assure that public policies do not neglect the needs of the aged. To achieve *interdependence* we need the wherewithal to be *independent*, which is why we must fight so hard to keep the entitlements and social programs that maintain dignity. The two—advocacy for rights and benefits, and working to create new forms of interdependency or mutual help—go hand in hand. As we improve the road to aging, we ourselves are changed in the process. We remain to the end of our lives contributing, caring, and creative members of society. As we change ourselves, we continue to make waves in the world around us.

After Sixty

The sixth decade is coming to an end
Doors have opened and shut
The great distractions are over—
passion...children...the long indenture of
marriage
I fold them into a chest
I will not take with me when I go

Everyone says the world is flat and finite
on the other side of sixty
That I will fall clear off the edge
into darkness
That no one will hear from me again
or want to

But I am ready for the knife slicing into the
future
for the quiet that explodes inside
to join forces with the strong old woman
to throw everything away and begin again

Now there is time to tell the story
—time to invent the new one
Time to chain myself to a fence outside the
missile base
To throw my body before a truck loaded with
phallic images
To write Thou Shalt Not Kill
on the hull of a Trident submarine
To pour my own blood on the walls of the
Pentagon
To walk a thousand miles with a begging bowl in
my hand

There are places on this planet
where women past the menopause
put on the tribal robes
smoke pipes of wisdom
—fly

Marilyn Zuckerman

Ageism is as much a part of the fabric of society as sexism and racism. Think of all the conscious and unconscious ways we disparage our aging. "You're sixty-two? You certainly don't *look* that old. You shouldn't tell anyone because you could easily pass for forty-five." Or, "That dress makes me feel *old*." Or, "All those old people together. I find it depressing."

Just telling your age forthrightly can be an act of defiance and a blow against ageism. Remember Gloria Steinem's rejoinder to a reporter who said she didn't look forty: "This is what forty looks like. How would you know? We've been hiding our age so long."

When Maggie Kuhn, founder of the Gray Panthers, was introduced by President Gerald Ford as a "young lady," she stood up and said, "Mr. President, I am not a young lady. I've lived a long time. I'm an old lady."

Age is part of our identity. To deny it is to say to the deepest layers of ourselves, as well as to the world, "I am unacceptable." Denial of age slowly erodes our self-esteem. The Older Women's League consciously selected its name —despite objections from many who said "mature" would be more acceptable—to help women take a conscious stand on the age question, to come out of the closet on age, so to speak.

Liberation from the shackles of ageism starts with learning to like ourselves and other older women. We must recognize the strength and beauty of our own age group. We have been separated from each other by our dependency on men, and many of us because of ageism and sexism have avoided the company of older women. Polls show that older people hold the same negative opinion of their peers as do the rest of the population. Yet older women like ourselves can provide us with great support in our later years when we are likely to be without a spouse. And if we are going to make changes on our own behalf and that of other older women, we must find each other. In the process we will discover our potential power.

Whatever our age or degree of disablement, feeling *connected*—being part of a family, either biological or a family of choice, or both; feeling part of a community of older women, but not isolated or alienated from other folks; having a sense of the continuity of generations—is essential. When we have this, growing older can be as rich and productive as any other time of life, especially if it is enjoyed in good company.

Advocacy organizations like the Older Women's League (OWL) and the Gray Panthers, women's support groups of all kinds, and local women's projects all provide opportunities for developing friendships and linkages. We need each other, especially as we grow old.

We also need to feel useful, productive, and self-realized. It's not enough to be part of a larger group if we don't feel we're contributing to it and to society as a whole. Because older people, if they are not careful, are relegated to the trash heap, this takes initiative. Determine early to "keep on keeping on." Then explore the many ways to do that in accordance with your own talents, desires, and opportunities. Paid and unpaid work, personal and group advocacy,

405

Jerry Howard/Positive Images

seems most fragile. The second half of life is different from the first. There are losses: physical limitations can curb one's life-style, and the specter of death is present. But even when all seems lost, we can find new incentives for making each day count.

Too many women *endure* old age rather than *enjoy* it. Preventive measures taken while we still have time to prepare for our old age could mitigate some of the problems of growing older as a woman. Many of us have been touched by the women's movement—positively, in that we are seeking new solutions and greater independence, and negatively, in that traditional homemaking roles of women to which so many of us have devoted years of our lives have lost status. We often feel caught in the middle.

We are all affected by role models, both positive and negative. Our mothers and grandmothers may or may not have been women of strength and courage. Strong role models decrease the fear of aging, so if we don't have them in our own families we should look for them elsewhere. Strong role models also help change the generally negative public image of older women. Think of Elizabeth Cady Stanton and Susan B. Anthony, both of whom were vigorous fighters to the end of their days. Susan B. Anthony continued to actively campaign into old age, making her final speech to a Woman's Rights Convention in 1904 when she was eighty-six years old. Mother Jones, the heroic fighter for unions and the oppressed, was ninety-three when she addressed the convention of the Farmer-Labor Party, telling them:

...not today perhaps, not tomorrow, but over the rim of the years my old eyes can see the coming of another day.[1]

And there are plenty of role models in today's society. Look around, choose one or more to draw substance from. Then decide to become a role model yourself. The changes we make in ourselves will not only warm our own lives but will have a ripple effect on the lives of others. Each of us in our own orbit influences others, combating the effects of ageism. Over the rim of the years we will see the coming of another day together.

Forms of Advocacy

Whatever our situation as we grow old, there is usually some way we can play an active role in

any project in which you feel passionate interest, whether it's a garden or the Government—can be rewarding. For example, there was never a better time of life to get on boards and commissions, which regulate a great deal of the way things function. If one-to-one helping makes you feel more connected and involved, by all means become involved in personal service.

I have been a volunteer for the last three years at Rosie's Place—a shelter for poor and homeless women in Boston. We provide meals for many women, beds for a few each night, clothing, and most importantly, respect, caring, concern, and love. I started doing this after the death of my grandmother, who took care of me while my mother worked. She and I were always very close. My volunteer work is a way for me to continue giving direct care to women on a regular basis. [a woman in her fifties]

Hope is the most important ingredient in a meaningful old age. Is the glass half full or half empty? In old age it may seem only a quarter full, but ah—how precious those few remaining drops can be! Hope is never out of season. It is the fuel that keeps the furnace going. We need to cultivate it, treasure it, and keep it alive when it

Ellen Shub

Rosa Parks, the woman who refused to move to the back of the bus, touching off the demonstrations that signaled the start of the civil rights movement of the 1960s.

making changes in ourselves and in society. Some things we can do for ourselves, some we accomplish as individual advocates for another person, some we accomplish best when we have support from a group with similar concerns, and some need sustained organizational effort. Each kind of advocacy is important and contributes to the others. Social change does not come quickly, but over time the glacier does move. Awareness of the plight of older women is much greater than it was ten years ago.

Here is an example of personal action, the first kind of advocacy. A woman experiences age discrimination on her job. She is consistently bypassed for promotions, works in a back room and notices that this is the pattern in the company. All newly hired persons are young people. Finally a manager lets slip that the company wants a "young image" and wants the employees to reflect this. That is a "smoking gun"—evidence of intentional discrimination!

I filed a complaint with the EEOC [Equal Employment Opportunity Commission]. I also filed one with the state agency which is responsible for employment discrimination. It was a long, hard battle and my employer did everything he could to make me quit. My workplace was pretty unbearable and I was expected to handle heavy boxes. But I knew he couldn't fire me without making a lot of trouble for himself so I stuck it out. After three long years I finally won my case. I was upgraded in my job and received $12,560 back pay. It finally was worth it!

Although many others will have to go through the same ordeal to make combined age and sex discrimination less pervasive in the job market, the woman who fights for her own rights makes a contribution to all of us.

In the second kind of advocacy one individual advocates for another.

Bonnie M. lived in an apartment house by herself and became acquainted with some of the other tenants, one of whom, Marianne, lived on disability benefits. One day Bonnie met her friend in tears.

Marianne showed me a letter which said her disability benefits would be cut off because she was not totally disabled and therefore presumed able to work. But she is sixty, she has no skills, and she has crippling arthritis.

Cathy Cade

407

The poor woman felt completely at a loss about how she would survive because she has practically no assets and no relatives close by. In fact she was seriously thinking of doing away with herself. I read that letter again and saw that she could request a hearing. I said, "What do you have to lose? I'll go with you. Let's fight it." I helped her collect all the necessary medical data and tried to calm her down, and I could see that just having someone help her meant a lot. Well, the administrative judge overruled the decision and she got her monthly payments back. I wasn't too surprised, because I knew that a very large proportion of such decisions are overruled if they are challenged. I haven't been a social worker for nothing. In this system, the squeaky wheel gets the grease.

Bonnie became an advocate who in effect saved a life; the woman with the disability learned that when an injustice is done, it can be challenged. Neither woman will ever be quite the same again.

Cooperative caring is a kind of advocacy that is not so dramatic but equally important in the overall plan of making things happen. Older women can take the lead in breaking down generation barriers to foster mutual understanding and support among women. For example, the Seattle chapter of the Older Women's League decided to hold a workshop to help women of all ages strengthen their relationships with each other. They also wanted to encourage women to discuss more deeply and honestly how they feel about aging and to help women of different generations see what they have in common. They called their workshop "What Kind of Older Woman Do I Want to Be?" To make sure that there was a good balance of young, middle-aged, and old who attended, the admission "ticket" was five dollars *and* a woman of another generation. The talk was lively and very revealing.

I brought my grandmother, who is seventy-nine. We've talked before but never quite like we did in the small group where we were discussing how we felt about the age we are now. She said she was afraid of dying but even more afraid of being a burden to me. Hearing other women also talk about their fears made it easier. We all seemed to help each other and by the end of the day there was a lot of hugging.

That workshop was so successful that it was copied by other chapters of OWL and has been incorporated into *Wingspan,* a curriculum for midlife planning used by OWL chapters and now being picked up by community colleges. That is how influence spreads and how intergenerational solidarity can be built.

This brings us to the fourth form of advocacy, organizational and legislative efforts. Midlife and older women can build bridges between the dynamic advocacy of the women's movement and the well-organized constituency of seniors. Conventionally, women are seen as joining a new category on reaching sixty or sixty-five. They are no longer seen as women but as "seniors" or "senior citizens," without gender distinctions. Government policies are devised without recognition of significant differences between aging women and men, and women's organizations, until quite recently, tended to avoid issues of aging. Consciousness has been raised to some extent in both arenas, but only the active voice of older women speaking about their own special concerns can catch the ear of either constituency.

I belong to a senior group—all men, mostly from the trade union movement. They're real sexist. But they are

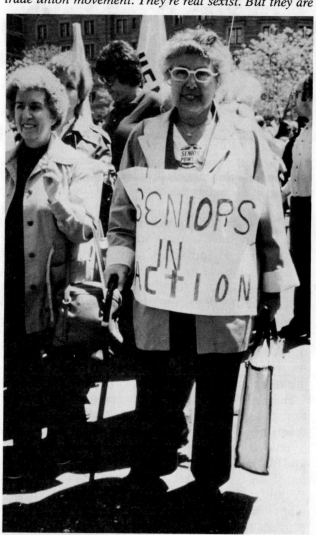

Ellen Shub

working on issues like Social Security and Medicare, and it's important for them to realize how women will be doubly hit by the proposed cuts. I talk about their wives as widows—something they don't like to think about, of course—and their sisters and mothers, and I give them all the facts and figures about how poor older women are. They are beginning to see the light. Now they want me to testify for the organization.

My NOW chapter is made up mostly of younger women. In fact I'm the only member over forty. They are real concerned about abortion and of course the ERA, and so am I, but I had a terrible time getting them interested enough to do something about the Retirement Equity Act. At first they just couldn't think that far ahead, but I kept saying that NOW was supposed to represent all women and that they were the ones who would benefit most from passage of this legislation when they themselves are ready to retire. They finally got the message and really got behind it.

Building a bridge between the women's and seniors' organizations has enormous potential for positive change in society. If women's organizations recognize the extent to which aging is a women's issue, and if organizations of the elderly come to the same recognition, we will make great strides in finding new solutions to the problems of growing old in a youth-oriented society.

Women of color have the additional task and opportunity of building bridges between their cultural group and the concerns of older women. Too many older Black women live on very low incomes and have not benefited proportionately from the programs that have generally improved the situation of the elderly. Women who worked in jobs that were not covered by Social Security, such as domestic work, or who raised their children as single parents, still suffer the effects of poverty.

Marching in a Martin Luther King Memorial demonstration in Washington, D.C., Dorothy Pitts of California carried a sign, "One Half of All Older Black Women Are Poor—Why?"

A year later, Dorothy Pitts organized a conference for Older Women of Color to which she invited representatives of twenty-four Black women's organizations, such as the National Council for Negro Women, Black sororities and churchwomen's groups, and women's counterparts of Black lodges, civic clubs and associations.

It was the first conference in the San Fran-

Faire Edwards

cisco area in which the problems of older Black women were addressed. Aileen Hernandez delivered the keynote address: "Our whole survival has depended on being strong Black women.... What we have done, we have done for our families. Now is the time to do for ourselves as older Black women."

Sometimes when women get together at a conference or meeting, an idea emerges that inspires continued involvement. Jane Porcino was involved in such a group and reports on its emergence:

Hot Flash, the quarterly newsletter of the National Action Forum for Midlife and Older Women, was conceived during a national conference on the health issues of women over forty. Following the three-day meeting, funded by the Administration on Aging, a group of twenty-five women remained to follow up on the enthusiasm generated by the conference. They envisioned a national newsletter to address the myriad health issues which affect all women in the second half of their lives. Traditionally, the physical and mental-health concerns of aging women have been shrouded in mystery, fear, and silence. This health newsletter would openly acknowledge the issue of aging and bring information to women which would help empower them in their lives. The name Hot Flash *was unanimously chosen, since hot flashes are experienced by most women, but rarely publicly acknowledged or celebrated. Four years later that project is still going strong, distributed nationwide and in fourteen other countries. (See Resources—General Health for subscription information.)*

Supports We Need to Overcome the Barriers We Face

Support groups (see p. 18) are especially useful to women facing a crisis. Many support groups have already been described in earlier chapters. Widowhood, serious illness, or any situation that requires a major life adjustment are times when we need all the help we can get from each other. Widow-to-widow groups, caregiver-support groups, cancer-support groups, and chapters of the Alzheimer's Disease and Related Disorders Association are all examples of mutual-help groups which have emerged to fill a very real need. Not all, but most of these, are women's groups. For women who are not in crisis but interested in getting connected with other women, consciousness-raising groups for older women can be a useful starting point, either organized independently or formed in conjunction with organizations such as the Older Women's League. Job hunting can be so difficult in later years that support groups are helpful for that too.

Support groups are also stepping-stones to advocacy, or can be, if a leader or member of the group moves the group forward in that direction. Organizations like OWL promote consciousness-raising groups for midlife and older women in which feelings are shared and participants feel renewed. When women begin to recognize that their problems are not just personal, but have societal implications, too, then they can move on to consider what can be done to tackle the causes, not only in their own lives but by taking action together with other women to change the social institutions and laws that penalize us for growing older.

Where your community doesn't have the kind of a support group you need, what do you do? You create one. Here is an example:

The doctor gave me the bad news—a recurrence of cancer, incurable, but perhaps controllable. There were so many decisions to make and I was so unprepared. But I had a friend who had cancer too, a very solid person. I called her and she was extremely helpful. She suggested a doctor for a second opinion, she gave me other resources to call, and she was an anchor when I felt most adrift. We talked several times and agreed we needed a support group. Our first meeting of four people was a picnic by the bay. We set the "rules": a women's group; we would help each other as much as we could, but [would] understand that at times we might not be up to it; we would meet monthly or more often to tell how we were doing, to share ideas and resources, and to talk freely about problems we are facing. The cancer-support group has been going now for over five years. We have lost some members, which has grieved us, but the group made their last days less painful. We had one wonderful retreat and are planning another. Our members, now twelve, have become resource persons who have appeared on television, spoken at conferences as cancer patients, and carried a message of hope wherever we go. Many cancer victims and their families call us for advice and support. We even sent a delegation to Kaiser Hospital to suggest changes in handling of cancer patients, which was well received. All those who are part of the group are grateful to it and to each other.

Any kind of support group has the potential for advocacy. The members of the cancer group above started out only helping each other, but as they became more knowledgeable and recognized that medical treatment of the disease left much to be desired, some of the members moved beyond the limits of personal support to become advocates for changes in the medical system. Some had all they could do just to cope with the illness. Others felt that fighting to improve the lot of others like themselves was a strong incentive to stay alive. The group accommodated both sentiments.

Another group that performs both functions—mutual help and social advocacy—is the Displaced Homemakers Network. Women, participating in support groups designed to help them become self-sufficient in the job market, find the small groups essential for gaining the confidence to begin a whole new life. In larger groups, members move to the bigger issues and begin to take part in social and political change, beginning with such immediate concerns as working for support of Displaced Homemakers programs. The extension, despite budget cuts, of such programs is largely the result of advocacy by those most directly affected, including those who have moved on to jobs. All of these women have taken steps outward from personal crisis to mutual help to advocacy.

Becoming Agents for Change

Our past experience can be very useful in bringing about social change. If you have experienced a problem, you may be the best advocate. When Annette Smail was divorced from her military husband she lost access to the medical care that had been available to her as a service dependent. In midlife, and not in the best of health, she found, as have many other women who are dependents on another's insurance coverage, that individual policies are both very expensive and grossly inadequate, with exclusions for "existing conditions." Feeling strongly the injustice of this unequal treatment, she convinced her Congressman to introduce a bill in Congress to continue medical benefits for ex-wives of military personnel. She says:

My own experience triggered my action. I had a background in community organization and I knew I could organize this community of women to accomplish something on this problem. I had looked for a job without success, so I appointed myself to this job and had to raise the money to do it. First I made the problem visible through the local newspaper, so that other women in the same straits would call me. And then I went national, urging other women to speak out as well. It's been the most marvelous experience in my life. I needed a challenge and here was a big one. And I met it. It required head work and homework—meeting people and learning how the system works. Most of all it required persistence. The Medical Rights bill was finally passed and triggered advocacy on other issues of ex-military wives. Now I'm working to establish a Federal Council on Women, because it wouldn't have taken eight long years to pass that bill if there had been such a Council.

How do you choose an issue and then begin to work on it? Chances are, if you have a problem, other women are likely to have it too, but first you must find them. Perhaps some of your friends share your problem and would be interested in a support group or study group. You can reach out to other women through community bulletin boards or organizations. A women's center may be willing to help you call a meeting to reach out to others who share your concern. Recognizing the common problem and talking about it together is the first step toward turning a problem into an issue. A group can begin by defining the problem very clearly and planning how to work together toward a solution. When the group comes up with a solution that it will support and work for, you are ready for the next step—broadening your constituency by publicizing your concerns.

The media offer the best opportunity for doing this. A little initiative can often lead to a radio or TV interview or a story in the local paper, which can provide a means for others to contact you. Then you can hold a public meeting to attract new participants and plan together how to deal with the problem.

If your group decides to work for passing legislation, be aware that timing is very important. When budgets are tight and lawmakers feeling stingy, a bill with a large price tag is not likely to pass. On the other hand, Congress passed the Retirement Equity Act even though at the time legislation on women's concerns was getting nowhere; this was because the bill required no appropriation and both Democrats and Republicans were vying for the favor of women voters. This important piece of legislation improves the women's chances of receiving a pension. For more information, contact the Older Women's League, listed under Resources.

Passing legislation can be difficult. It helps to take time to define your issue in a way that will appeal to the public and to get some experienced person's help in writing the bill. A group of women in California reported:

We had been meeting together for some time as Jobs for Older Women, trying to help each other and trying to alert the public to our difficulties in finding jobs. But we weren't making a great deal of progress. We decided we needed some legislative help. Fortunately there was a young lawyer working with us at the time so we asked her to write us a bill. But first we needed a name to describe our problem, something that would get their attention. We decided to call ourselves "displaced homemakers" and our model bill (into which we put everything but the kitchen sink) we called a Displaced

Norma Holt

Homemakers Bill. From that moment we had a handle with which to organize. We got a version of that bill passed through our state legislature in 100 working days, almost a record for that kind of lawmaking.

Laurie Shields, a widow in her mid-fifties, had never been involved in political action beyond driving people to the polls on election day. But she was energetic, a natural organizer, and ready to go when the first model displaced homemakers bill was written. She had experienced the problem of women long out of the work force and of the ageism in her field (advertising). She discovered and developed talents she was not aware of and made use of all her former work experience, paid and unpaid, when she became head of the Alliance for Displaced Homemakers.

Crisscrossing the country in my tennis shoes, I met thousands of women who, with disquieting unanimity,

greeted the message of the legislation with a teary "My God, I thought I was all alone." ... I built up a relationship with many of these women that transcended our shared problems. I came to know them as friends; I found myself deeply moved by their quiet courage in the face of real adversity. Sharing their lives, however briefly, and observing their battles against loneliness and despair gave new meaning to the importance of the legislation and the work we were collectively doing. ... I would never have believed I could do it or accomplish so much. For myself and for the others, there is a new awareness of the truth and hope spelled out in Doris Lessing's words: "Any human being anywhere will blossom into a hundred unexpected talents and capabilities simply by being given the opportunity to use them."[2]

The effects of becoming an agent for change can be very dramatic. For example, Rosemary Bizzell of Jeffersonville, Indiana, a widow with seven sons and eight grandchildren, had never been involved in community affairs. In 1981 she

Elizabeth Layton

"Her strength is in her principles."

412

joined OWL. Three years later, she had become an important figure in the statehouse and city council. She wrote:

My self-image as an older woman has improved tremendously, in spite of much rejection in job hunting. Apparently I was supposed to count my blessings and not expect to advance. Well, becoming involved in OWL has certainly challenged me....I cannot thank the OWLs enough for opening up a whole new world for older women. I am proud of the opportunity to be part of it.

The later years can indeed be a time to have an impact on the world instead of being put on the shelf. Working to build a movement or an organization that works for a better future for all of us and for those coming along behind puts excitement into the later years.

Building the Organizational Forms for Social Change

There is much we can do as individuals, both as advocates and as role models. We can work collectively in small groups and carry out significant projects on a local level or through court battles. But inevitably we come up against the "power structure" and the laws of the land. How can older women have a significant voice in the making of public policy? How can we be assured that we will be heard on matters that affect our lives? To accomplish that purpose we need organizations with large enough memberships to impress legislators, and the skills to use that voice effectively. See Resources for activist organizations that advocate for women, for older persons, and specifically for older women.

The women's movement has produced national organizations in the form of the National Organization for Women (NOW), National Women's Political Caucus (NWPC), the Women's Equity Action League (WEAL), the National Women's Health Network (NWHN), and many others. There are traditional women's organizations, such as the League of Women Voters and the National Council of Negro Women, which are often influential in policy-making circles.

Older people have developed organizations of impressive size, notably the twenty-four-million-member American Association of Retired Persons (AARP), the union-based National Council of Senior Citizens (NCSC), and the more professionally oriented National Council on the Aging (NCOA). A smaller but more activist organization, the Gray Panthers, is intergenerationally structured.

A "new kid on the block" of activist organizations is the Older Women's League, which focuses on the specific problems of midlife and older women and bridges the gap between organizations in the aging field and women's groups.

All of these organizations have representatives who testify at hearings on the national and state level and mobilize support for issues of concern, as well as working with administrative bodies. If it seems that despite all this the needs of women and the aged are given short shrift by government, consider how much worse the situation would be without their input.

Organizations work both singly and in concert. Coalitions are built in support of, or in opposition to, specific measures, or to speak for a whole spectrum of organizations. For example, the Coalition on Women and the Budget brought together fifty-five organizations two years in a row to critique Federal budget proposals and produce the report *Inequality of Sacrifice: The Impact of Reaganomics on Women*.

Specialized support organizations like the Pension Rights Center in Washington and the National Senior Citizens' Law Center (NSCLC) contribute to the cooperative advocacy efforts of the others. The newly formed Villers Foundation provides assistance and financial support for actions aimed at empowerment of older persons, including women.

Very important, however, is building harmonious working relationships between organizations so that they can join forces when necessary and move forward as a united front on an important issue. In the hostile political climate of the 1980s, this circling of the wagons is happening more frequently. The strong underlying current of desire for peace and for a national health care program, concern about the growing military budget and cuts in social services and entitlements designed to address human needs—all these offer common ground for collective action.

How can midlife and older women build alliances without losing our special goals? We can work as a "Concerns of Older Women Committee" raising issues within organizations with diverse membership, or we can work in our own independent organizations, and then in coalitions with others.

There are direct advantages to older women having their own established organization which can work as an equal in alliance with other organizations. This was a primary reason why the Older Women's League was formed as an independent entity. In a coalition of groups, a group with a proven constituency, such as OWL, is listened to quite differently from one with a good cause but no followers.

Working inside an established body with a broader base and forming an independent organization with our own specific focus are not mutually exclusive. In fact, both types of advocacy work best in unison. A close working relationship with the Older Women's League can make a "Concerns of Older Women Committee" more effective. For example, the "Women's Initiative" within the American Association of Retired Persons has been working toward increased recognition of the special issues of women after retirement. In their magazine they recommend OWL's handout *Women and Pensions* in addition to their own pamphlet, *A Woman's Guide to Pension Rights;* thus AARP members have access to the work of both organizations, and OWL has access to a wider audience for its own material.[3]

In advocacy work we need to judge where we fit in. We may have special skills that come from wide experience, and we may have our own style or styles of organizing. Sometimes an older woman feels out of place in a feminist organization with a primarily young membership. Some women work more effectively with their own peers while others prefer the company of a mixed age group. In trying to reach out to women older than ourselves, or to any women whose background and experience may be different from our own, it is important to respect "where they are coming from." Avoid downgrading the role of homemaker, when the real problem is the lack of recognition for homemakers, the inadequacy of Social Security, and the absence of other benefits. Rather than disparaging a traditional style, it may be better to adapt that style to new content. We all start on the road to liberation from a particular point, wherever that may be. The important thing is the direction that road is taking.

Often, as formerly excluded groups enter the mainstream, we all learn and benefit from their special insights and experiences. As older women we have benefited from the experience of the Black movement, the women's movement, and the elder advocates. We reject the demeaning images of older women and the exclusion of older women from policymaking for elders. We proudly claim our age and experience as demonstrating our right to define who we are and what we need to live lives of dignity, activity, and involvement in our communities: decent health care and housing; an income sufficient to enjoy, rather than simply endure, our later years; and the recognition that we are important members of society with much to contribute.

Epilogue

Our later years, when we have a lifetime's worth of experience, and possibly lighter work loads to carry, can be a time to bring things together and to find spiritual and ethical coherence. Maggie Kuhn is a beautiful role model of someone who has contributed greatly to a better future through social and political involvement. Only after she formally retired did Maggie convene the Gray Panthers, calling upon young and old to join forces to work for a better world. This "little old woman" with white hair and arthritic fingers is an articulate voice for right and justice, the epitome of an "elder of the tribe," as she calls old people. Social and political involvement can be a fine way of making life meaningful to the very end. In Maggie's words:

In this age of self-determination and liberation many groups are struggling for freedom. All these struggles are linked in the worldwide struggle for a new humanity. Together they have the potential of a new community-based social justice system of human compassion and selfhood. Old people have a large stake in this new community—in helping to create it and extend it. The winds of change are impelling and empowering. They can free us or destroy us.

And I, Tish Sommers, age seventy, concur with all my heart. This summer, as in the past, I plan to go on a white-water river-rafting trip in Idaho. For me, rivers are a symbol of an activist's life. Last year our little raft was dashing down this churning cauldron, the young boatpersons yelling directions, the river about to make a figure S, and right in the middle of it a great big rock. Would we wrap around it or pass on through? We did flash by, but another boat was not so lucky. Then all the people descended on it to get the boat peeled off that rock and the passengers out of danger. No one was hurt. But for those few days, when the only concerns were the next rocks up ahead, I realized how lucky we are to be testing our strength and skill against the raging river of this period we are living in. There are lots of rocks and plenty of danger and it's very difficult to row upstream. But we can all learn to read the river, scout out the rocks ahead, find the eddies where the water moves upstream, and we can throw out a line if things go wrong. How much better to be in there with all the excitement than moping on the bank!

NOTES

1. *Autobiography of Mother Jones*. Chicago: Kerr & Co., 1972.

2. Laurie Shields, *Displaced Homemakers: Organizing for a New Life*. New York: McGraw-Hill, 1981.

3. "Pension Information Free to Women." *Modern Maturity*, April-May 1986, p. 18.

Women gathered in Washington, D.C., carrying homemade banners, encircle the Pentagon demonstrating for peace. (For more about the "ribbon demonstration," see Marianne Philbier, ed., *The Ribbon: Celebration of Life: The Remarkable Ribbon Around the Pentagon, A Unique Worldwide Plea for Peace*. Love Books, 50 College Street, Asheville, NC 28801, 1985.)

Ellen Shub

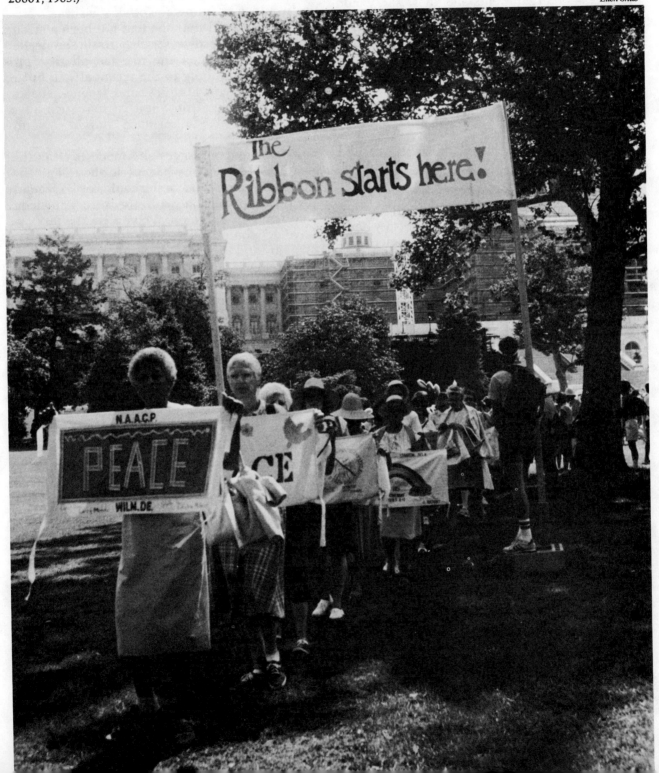

Afterword by Laurie Shields

Tish Sommers died at home, as she wished, on October 18, 1985. Her death was neither unexpected nor unplanned—for she had lived with stage four (meaning widespread) cancer for almost six years. During that time she practiced what she preached—she "kept on keeping on." She spent time with friends and colleagues, said her good-byes, but more to the point, gave each of them a "job to do for OWL." She taped two messages—for two events she knew she would not be attending—the December board meeting at which she would propose Lou Glasse to take over the presidency of OWL, and OWL's 1986 convention in September. She completed a proposal that would, she hoped, fund a project to develop model state legislation dealing with health care problems of older women. She even planned her own memorial service!

Tish consistently acted upon her belief that personal problems can be turned into public issues. She viewed her experience with cancer as affording an opportunity to help other women. Because *she* found it helpful, she advised other women to "question authority" and not accept, for example, a doctor's advice simply because it came from a doctor. She felt that patients, rather than doctors, were apt to be inventive about "make do" matters. A case in point: When she had a supra-pubic catheter inserted just before going on a river-rafting trip, the doctor insisted she not swim, indeed, not even take tub baths. In her journal she records wondering about this. "Why should I accept that dictum? Why couldn't I find a way to water-proof the area?" With the help of a public-health nurse, she did just that and won grudging approval from the doctor.

Tish strongly advocated staying in control of one's life to the very end. She pushed hard for national legislation which would give durable power of attorney to those entrusted to follow the wishes of a terminally ill patient. She and I had such documents in our medical files and, under the laws of California, felt reassured that we would each follow the other's wishes.

Tish regretted that she had not been a strong advocate for hospice services until she needed them herself. When she realized all that program gave, not only to the terminally ill but to their caregivers, families, and friends, she extracted a pledge from me that that such advocacy would be a primary target for my organizing efforts.

In her final messages she made it clear that death was a part of what life is about, and that because of her own life she could say, "I face my own last transition with the sure knowledge that you will all go on to complete the tasks we have set for ourselves. And that is why I feel such joy and love."

And now it is we who must "keep keeping on." Knowing that we have her assurance we can. "I bequeath to you," she said, "and to my fellow fighters for a better life, my faith in the future, even when things seem impossible and out of kilter." All it takes, as she knew, is caring, communication, and commitment.

RESOURCES

GENERAL RESOURCES

Following is a list of organizations and publications that pertain to women and aging in general, or that relate to more than one of the subjects covered in the book. When you look for the resources for a particular chapter, remember to review these general resources also.

Organizations

Area Agencies on Aging (sometimes called Triple A's) are good centralized sources of information about services and agencies in your area. Set up by the Older Americans Act to provide information and referral, advocacy, and planning, they are federally funded but often receive additional money from local or state governments and may be located in a state, county, or private agency. Senior centers, councils on aging, and other elder groups are other possible sources of information for elders.

Advocates Senior Alert Process
  1334 G St. NW
  Washington, DC 20005
  Tel. (202) 737-6340
Fourteen national senior organizations (many of which are listed below) have joined together to provide an information and action network for politically active advocates. Participants receive information on many issues at no charge. In return the participants agree to mobilize at least five other persons and to act on important issues affecting older persons by writing letters, making phone calls, and initiating other activities to influence the legislative process.

American Association of Retired Persons (AARP)
  1909 K St. NW
  Washington, DC 20049
  Tel. (202) 872-4700
Membership for age fifty and up. Provides information, services, and advocacy for issues concerning older and retired people. Publishes *Modern Maturity*, a bimonthly magazine, *AARP News Bulletin*, a monthly newspaper, and a list of excellent books and pamphlets. Has local chapters and a Women's Initiative Program.

Boston Women's Health Book Collective
  47 Nichols Ave.
  Watertown, MA 02172
  Tel. (617) 924-0271
Authors of all editions of *Our Bodies, Ourselves*, their Women's Health Information Center includes an extensive collection of books, periodicals, and clippings on such subjects as sexuality, birth control, abortion and reproductive rights, feminism, and women in Third World countries. This collection is available to the public by appointment. The files and books used to compile *Ourselves, Growing Older* have been donated to the Collective and form the basis of a new collection on women and aging. Information requests by mail or phone are answered for a nominal fee or donation to cover costs.

Gray Panthers
  311 S. Juniper St., Suite 601
  Philadelphia, PA 19107
  Tel. (215) 545-6555
An intergenerational organization of women and men opposed to ageism and active on behalf of world peace and a universal health care system. Write to the national organization (address

above) for information on how to join or start a local chapter. Members receive *Network,* a quarterly newsletter.

League of Women Voters
1730 M St. NW
Washington, DC 20036
Tel. (202) 429-1965

Encourages informed participation of citizens in government. Membership is open to all. The League was founded right after women won the vote by some of the most active suffragists who wanted to educate women on how to use their newly won clout effectively. They expected that in ten to fifteen years all the major social reforms would have been passed and they could disband the organization. The League has been around for over sixty years and does not appear to be running out of work.

Legal Services Corporation
400 Virginia Ave. SW
Washington, DC 20024
Tel. (202) 863-1820

Legal Services Corporation has affiliates in most major cities. Check your phone book under "Legal Assistance," or under "Elder Services—legal," or call your local bar association for the name of the organization in your community that provides free legal services for qualified low-income persons. For those over sixty, it is easier to qualify, and advocacy services are also available for dealing with Medicare, Medicaid, and the Social Security Administration. Or call or write to the national office listed above.

National Association for Lesbian and Gay Gerontology
1853 Market St.
San Francisco, CA 94103
Tel. (415) 626-7000

An organization of seniors and professionals in gerontology, promoting responsible research, education, advocacy, and the development of services for aging lesbians and gay men. Their local program, Operation Concern—Gay and Lesbian Outreach to Elders, is an example of the services they promote. Quarterly newsletter and resource guide.

National Caucus and Center on the Black Aged
1424 K St. NW
Washington, DC 20005
Tel. (202) 637-8400

Formed in 1971 to research and advocate for Black elders, especially those whose employment formerly had not been covered by Social Security and who have inadequate retirement income.

National Coalition on Older Women's Issues
2401 Virginia Ave. NW
Washington, DC 20037
Tel. (202) 466-7834

Midlife and Older Women: A Resource Directory (of 50 organizations working on issues of concern to aging women) is available from the coalition for $4.00.

National Council on the Aging (NCOA)
600 Maryland Ave. SW, West Wing 100
Washington, DC 20024
Tel. (202) 479-1200

A national advocacy organization for elders, with seven affiliated organizations working in areas such as senior housing, adult day care, rural elders, and older workers. Membership, at reduced rates for elders and students, includes subscription to *Perspective on Aging,* membership in one of the affiliates, and a variety of other discounts.

National Council of Jewish Women
15 E. 26 St.
New York, NY 10010
Tel. (212) 532-1740

A national volunteer women's organization working in the areas of education, community service, and advocacy in response to community needs. Two of their six priority areas are Women's Issues and Aging Issues. For information, including their program on "The Sandwich Generation," write to the Program Services Department at the above address; for information on local chapters, write to the Field Membership Department at the above address.

National Council of Negro Women
701 N. Fairfax St.
Alexandria, VA 22314
Tel. (703) 684-5733

A coalition of 31 organizations in 42 states dedicated to ameliorating the problems of Black women and their families and to promoting their participation in the political, cultural, social, economic, and civic life of the United States. Membership can be acquired either directly or through organizations, and student memberships are available.

National Council of Senior Citizens
925 15 St.
Washington, DC 20005
Tel. (202) 347-8800
This organization's assertively activist orientation may stem from its labor union connections. NCSC's 4,800 local clubs provide a network for grass-roots advocacy efforts on behalf of legislation at the national, state, and local levels. Persons of any age may join, but certain benefits have age requirements.

National Interfaith Coalition on Aging
P.O. Box 1924
298 S. Hull St.
Athens, GA 30603
Tel. (404) 353-1331
Advocates the inclusion of gerontology in religious education; seeks to expand the role of church and synagogue in improving the quality of life and the spiritual well-being of the aging.

National Organization for Women (NOW)
1401 New York Ave. NW, Suite 800
Washington, DC 20005
Tel. (202) 347-2279
A membership organization working to bring women into full participation in the mainstream of American society, exercising all the privileges and responsibilities thereof in truly equal partnership with men. Works in a variety of areas such as economic rights and pay equity, lesbian and gay rights, eliminating racism and violence against women. Their legislative task force sometimes works on issues affecting older women, such as divorce and Social Security.

NOW Legal Defense and Education Fund
99 Hudson St.
New York, NY 10013
Tel. (212) 925-6635
Studies and litigates on issues relating to women's rights. Work includes a family law project, ERA impact study, gender-neutral insurance, and legal cases, such as affirmative action.

National Pacific/Asian Resource Center on Aging
811 First Ave., Suite 210
Seattle, WA 98104
Tel. (206) 622-5124

Professionals concerned with improving and ensuring services to elders of Pacific/Asian ancestry.

National Senior Citizens' Law Center
1302 18 St. NW, Suite 701
Washington, DC 20036
Tel. (202) 887-5280
Operates a legal services support center and advocates for poor elder clients. Sponsors conferences and workshops on areas of law affecting elders. Maintains a library. Publishes weekly newsletter, monthly *Nursing Home Law Letter*, various handbooks, guides, and testimony.

National Women's Political Caucus (NWPC)
1275 K St. NW, Suite 750
Washington, DC 20005
Tel. (202) 898-1100
NWPC's goal is to get more women elected and appointed to political office.

Older Women's League (OWL)
730 11th St. NW, Suite 300
Washington, DC 20001
Tel. (202) 783-6686
National organization with chapters in nearly every state. Focuses on issues of concern to middle-aged and older women. The 1987 agenda includes employment discrimination, Social Security, pensions, health insurance, caregiving, the effect of budget cuts on older women, and staying in control of our death and dying. The bimonthly newsletter, *The Owl Observer*, contains excellent coverage of older women's issues. Issues special reports and publishes a series of "Gray Papers." Local chapters educate and advocate for a range of older women's issues.

Senior Action in a Gay Environment (SAGE)
208 W. 13 St.
New York, NY 10011
Tel. (212) 741-2247
Ask for their resource list of lesbian and gay aging groups.

The Silver-Haired Legislature is a grass-roots nonpartisan body composed of elder citizens, elected at Councils on Aging by their peers. Its purpose is to educate elder activists about the workings of a legislative body and to make recommendations to the legislature about issues of concern to elders and their communities.

Twenty-three states have some form of Silver-Haired Legislature. Inquire at your area Council on Aging or your state legislature.

Women's Equity Action League (WEAL)
    1250 I St. NW, Suite 305
    Washington, DC 20005
    Tel. (202) 898-1588
WEAL promotes economic equity for women through legislation, litigation, and public education.

The Villers Foundation
    1334 G St. NW
    Washington, DC 20005
    Tel. (202) 628-3030
Provides financial support and assistance for projects aimed at empowerment of older persons. Write for their list of publications.

Books

Alexander, Jo, Debi Barrow, Lisa Domitrovich, Margareta Donnelly, Cheryl McLean. *Women and Aging: An Anthology by Women.* Corvallis, Oregon: Calyx Books, 1986. Delightful collection of fiction, poetry, journal excerpts, photographs.

Anderson, Barbara G. *Aging Game: Success, Sanity and Sex After Sixty.* New York: McGraw-Hill, 1981.

Ascher, Carol, Louise DeSalvo, Sara Ruddick. *Between Women.* Boston: Beacon Press, 1984. Biographers, novelists, critics, teachers, and artists write about their work on women.

Baruch, Grace K., and Jeanne Brooks-Gunn, eds. *Women in Midlife.* London: Plenum Publishing, 1984. Informative collection of scholarly articles.

Block, Marilyn R., Janice L. Davidson, Jean D. Grambs. *Women Over Forty: Visions and Realities.* New York: Springer Publishing, 1981.

Brown, Judith K. *In Her Prime: A New View of Middle-Aged Women.* South Hadley, Massachusetts: Bergin & Garvey, 1985. Reports of women from widely divergent cultures.

Browne, Susan, Debra Connors, Nanci Stern. *With the Power of Each Breath: A Disabled Woman's Anthology.* Pittsburgh, Pennsylvania: Cleis Press, 1985.

Building Community: A Manual Exploring Issues of Women and Disability. Produced by the Women and Disability Awareness Project. A program of Educational Equity Concepts, Inc., 114 E. 32 St., New York, NY 10016.

Buss, Fran L. *Dignity: Lower Income Women Tell of Their Lives and Struggles.* Ann Arbor, Michigan: University of Michigan Press, 1985.

Butler, Robert N. *Why Survive? Being Old in America.* New York: Harper Colophon, 1973. A classic on aging and ageism.

Cohen, Leah. *Small Expectations. Society's Betrayal of Older Women.* Toronto: McClellan and Stewart, Ltd., 1984. Analysis of the discrimination against older women drawn from interviews of women in Canada, the United States, and Great Britain. Highly recommended.

de Beauvoir, Simone. *The Second Sex.* New York: Vintage, 1974. First published in 1952, this is an early classic of modern feminism.

Fonda, Jane. *Women Coming of Age.* New York: Simon and Schuster, 1984. Author's personal reminiscences are the most touching part of this book. Health and grooming advice suitable for middle-aged women.

Hemmings, Susan. *A Wealth of Experience. The Lives of Older Women.* London, Boston, Melbourne, and Henley: Pandora Press, 1985.

Jacobs, Ruth Harriet. *Life After Youth: Female 40, What Next?* Boston: Beacon Press, 1979.

Koppellman, Susan, ed. *Between Mothers and Daughters: Stories Across a Generation.* New York: Feminist Press at the City University of New York, 1985.

Lesnoff-Caravaglia, Gari, ed. *The World of the Older Women,* Vol. III, Frontiers in Aging Series. New York: Human Services Press, 1984.

Markson, Elizabeth W., ed. *Older Women.* Lexington, Massachusetts: D. C. Heath/Lexington Books, 1983. An excellent collection of articles which capture the social diversity of women growing older. Sections cover changes beginning at midlife, occupational and retirement patterns, variations in families and lifestyles, and selected health issues.

Matthews, Sarah H. *The Social World of Old Women*. Beverly Hills, California: Sage Publications, Inc., 1979.

Miller, Jean Baker. *Toward a New Psychology of Women*. Rev. ed. New York: Harper & Row, 1986. A critique of sex inequality with an appreciation of women's traditional strengths and their value for women and men today.

Myerhoff, Barbara. *Number Our Days*. New York: Touchstone/Simon & Schuster, 1978. A moving account of the lives of elderly Jews in Venice, California, and how they affected the author, a prominent anthropologist.

Painter, Charlotte, and Pamela Valois. *Gifts of Age: Portraits and Essays of 32 Remarkable Women*. San Francisco: Chronicle Books, 1985. A visually beautiful book.

Paull, Irene. Cartoons by Bulbul. *Everybody's Studying Us: The Ironies of Aging in the Pepsi Generation*. San Francisco: Volcano Press, 1976.

Porcino, Jane. *Growing Older, Getting Better: A Handbook for Women in the Second Half of Life*. Reading, Massachusetts: Addison-Wesley, 1983.

Salber, Eva J. *Don't Send Me Flowers When I'm Dead. Voices of Rural Elderly*. Durham, North Carolina: Duke University Press, 1983.

Secunda, Victoria. *By Youth Possessed: The Denial of Age in America*. Indianapolis: Bobbs-Merrill, 1984.

Seskin, Jane. *Alone—Not Lonely: Independent Living for Women Over 50*. 1985. Order from American Association for Retired Persons (see Organizations, above).

Simon, Barbara Levy. "C'est La Vie: Never Married Old Women and Disability, A Majority Experience." In Michelle Fine and Adrienne Asch, eds., *Voices from the Margins: Lives of Disabled Girls and Women*. Philadelphia: Temple University Press, 1987.

Walker, Barbara G. *The Crone: Woman of Age, Wisdom & Power*. San Francisco: Harper & Row, 1985. One woman's spirituality and the historic role of female elders. Offers a key to respect for older women today.

Wilson, Emily Herring. *Older Black Women of the South*. Philadelphia: Temple University Press, 1983.

Other Publications

Broomstick: A Bimonthly Feminist Periodical By, For and About Women Over Forty. Options for Women over Forty, 3543 18 St., San Francisco, CA 94110. Subscription: U.S. $15.00 per year. Sample copy $3.50. Highly recommended.

Hot Flash: A Newsletter for Midlife and Older Women. c/o National Action Forum for Midlife and Older Women, Box 816, Stony Brook, NY 11790-0609. Contains articles and news about health and social issues. Quarterly. $15 per year.

Prime Time Women: An Analysis of Older Women on Entertainment Television. This report profiles all female characters over the age of fifty on network television programming as to marital status, economic condition, occupation, race, appearance, and behavior, analyzing the social messages presented and their significance for older women and society. 25 pp., $5.00 per copy, from National Commission on Working Women, 1325 G St. NW, Washington, DC 20005.

Reinharz, Shulamit. "Friends or Foes: Gerontological and Feminist Theory." *Women's Studies International Forum*, Vol. 9, No. 5, 1986, pp. 503–14. An excellent article analyzing the relationship between feminist and gerontological concerns and what each can offer the other.

Sojourner: The Women's Forum. 143 Albany St., Cambridge, MA 02139. Feminist monthly newspaper. $15 per year.

Older Women's Presses

The number of women's presses is too long to publish here. They are listed in reference books such as Len Fulton and Ellen Ferber, eds., *International Directory of Little Magazines and Small*

Presses. Paradise, California: Dustbooks, 1986. Check your library.

Crones' Own Press
  310 Driver St.
  Durham, NC 27703
This press specializes in publishing and distributing writings of older women.

Audiovisual

Acting Our Age, produced by The Older Women's Film Project, 131 Concord St., San Francisco, CA 94112. Tel. (415) 496-7532. A new documentary film showing women in their sixties and seventies from diverse ethnic groups in the context of aging in America today. The project is endorsed by the Older Women's League, Gray Panthers, and others.

A few films are listed under specific chapters. The catalogs of the following libraries and distributors are good sources to rent or purchase films or videos of interest to older women. See your library for local and other sources.

Filmmakers Library, Inc.
  133 E. 58 St.
  New York, NY 10022
  Tel. (212) 355-6545
Films and videos can be viewed in their office by appointment.

New Day Films
  New Day Film Co-op, Inc.
  22 Riverview Drive
  Wayne, NJ 07470
  Tel. (201) 633-0212

The Pennsylvania State University
  Audio-Visual Services
  Special Services Building
  University Park, PA 16802
  Tel. (800) 826-0132 or (814) 865-6314
Request their catalog, *Films and Video about, for, and by Women.*

Women Make Movies
  225 Lafayette St., Suite 212
  New York, NY 10012
  Tel. (212) 925-0606

AGING WELL

AGING AND WELL-BEING

The General Health Resources starting on p. 456 include entries which are also relevant to aging and well-being.

Stress Management

Books

Benson, Herbert, and Miriam C. Klipper. *The Relaxation Response.* New York: Avon, 1976; and Benson, Herbert, and William Proctor. *Beyond the Relaxation Response.* New York: Berkley Publishing, 1985. Two excellent books for understanding and learning basic meditation techniques.

Borysenko, Joan. *Minding the Body, Mending the Mind.* Reading, Massachusetts: Addison-Wesley, 1987.

The Editors of *American Health* magazine with Daniel Goleman and Tara Bennet-Goleman. *The Relaxed Body Book: A High-Energy Anti-Tension Program.* Garden City, New York: Doubleday, 1986. Particularly useful sections on TMJ, self-massage, sleep, and exercises for people who work at a desk.

Green, Elmer, and Alyce Green. *Beyond Biofeedback.* New York: Delta, 1977.

Kravette, Steve. *Complete Relaxation.* Rockport, Massachusetts: Para Research, Inc., 1979.

LeShan, Lawrence. *How to Meditate: A Guide to Self-Discovery.* New York: Bantam Books, 1986.

Pelletier, Kenneth. *Mind as Healer, Mind as Slayer: A Holistic Approach to Preventing Stress Disorders.* New York: Dell, 1979.

Massage

Organizations

To locate massage therapists in your area, contact:

American Massage Therapists Association
1130 W. North Shore Ave.
Chicago, IL 60626
Tel. (312) 761-2682 (AMTA)
This professional organization certifies massage therapists and sets educational standards for training programs.

Or try massage therapy schools, physical therapists, massage collectives, women's centers, holistic health, fitness, and yoga centers, chiropractors, or acupuncturists in your area.

Books

Benjamin, Ben E., with Gale Borden. *Listen to Your Pain*. New York: Penguin, 1984. Self-help book for understanding injury. Anatomic drawings of body parts as well as photographs showing most common injury locations. Includes tests to help you diagnose your injury, and treatment choices (both self-help and medical).

Berkson, Devaki. *The Foot Book: Healing the Body Through Reflexology*. New York: Barnes & Noble, 1979. Includes work with older adults, and treatments for specific conditions such as lower backache, arthritis, high blood pressure, in addition to standard reflexology. Includes dietary suggestions and exercises.

Downing, George. *The Massage Book*. New York: Random House/Bookworks, 1972. Good basic handbook with instructions and illustrative drawings.

Lawrence, D. Baloti, and Lewis Harrison. *Massageworks: A Practical Encyclopedia of Massage Techniques*. New York: Phantom Publishing Group, 1983.

Ohashi, Wataru. *Do-It-Yourself Shiatsu*. New York: Dutton, 1976. Each of the fourteen meridians with the important points are shown separately. Gives Shiatsu exercises and specific points for common ailments.

Prudden, Bonnie. *Myotherapy*. New York: Doubleday, 1984. Divides trigger-point therapy into the "quick fix" and the "permanent fix," the latter involving satellite points in addition to primary ones. Section on the "Self Center" includes exercises built on stair-climbing.

Struik, Monika, with Connie Church. *Self-Massage: Touch Techniques to Relax, Soothe and Stimulate Your Body*. New York: Simon and Schuster, 1983.

Tappan, Frances M. *Healing Massage Techniques: A Study of Eastern and Western Methods*. Reston, Virginia: Reston Publishing Co., 1980.

West, Ouida. *The Magic of Massage*. New York: Putnam, 1983. A holistic approach that combines acupressure with Swedish strokes. A comprehensive book that includes tips on self-massage, nutrition, and exercise.

Self-Help and Support Groups

Organizations

National Self-Help Clearinghouse
33 W. 42 St.
New York, NY 10036
Tel. (212) 840-1259
An information and referral center to self-help regional clearinghouses and self-help groups around the country. Publishes a newsletter, runs research projects, and provides technical assistance.

Older Women's League (see General Resources for address) can provide materials for older women's consciousness-raising groups. Ask for their *Wingspan* curriculum for intergenerational workshops.

The Supportive Older Women's Network (S.O.W.N.)
2805 N. 47 St.
Philadelphia, PA 19131
Tel. (215) 477-6000
Helps older women in the Delaware Valley through support groups and other outreach services. Their lively, chatty newsletter may be helpful in starting a similar project in your area.

Books and Other Publications

Humm, Andy. *How to Organize a Self-Help Group*. 49 pp. $6.00. Available from the National Self-Help Clearinghouse (see above under Organizations).

Jackson, Maggie, and Zeb Harel. "Social Support Networks of the Elderly: Racial Differences and Health Care Implications." *Urban Health*, September 1983, pp. 35–38.

Jacobs, Ruth. *Older Women: Surviving and Thriving*, 1986. Order from Family Service America, 11700 W. Lake Park Drive, Milwaukee, WI 53224. $17.95 plus $2.00 for mailing. A manual to help older women build self-esteem and solve practical problems. Outlines twelve workshop sessions to be led by a peer or professional leader, with handouts for participants on subjects such as health care, housing, community involvement, and sexuality. It also offers exercises to help older women deal with the prejudice they face.

Jerrome, Dorothy. "The Significance of Friendship for Women in Later Life." *Aging and Society*, Vol. 1, No. 2, 1981.

Lidoff, Lorraine. "Sharing a Common Concern." *Perspective on Aging*, Vol. 8, No. 1, January/February 1984, pp. 26–27.

McGuire, Kathleen. *Building Supportive Community—Mutual Self-Help Through Peer Counseling*. Center For Supportive Community, 186 Hampshire St., Cambridge, MA 02139, Tel. (617) 864-5866. $9.95. Self-help for creating a support network. Includes such techniques as peer counseling, empathic listening, conflict resolution, and consensus decision-making.

Reissman, Frank, et al. *Self-Help and the Elderly. Considerations for Practice and Policy*. Washington, DC: National Council on the Aging, Inc., 1982.

The Self-Help Source Book. A nationwide directory of self-help groups. The New Jersey Self-Help Clearinghouse, Picono Rd., Denville, NJ 07834.

Silverman, Phyllis R. *Mutual Help Groups: Organization and Development*. Beverly Hills, California: Sage Publications, 1980. A guide to starting groups with emphasis on professional relationships and roles.

Other sources of information on existing self-help and support groups in your area include referral services (often operated by the United Way organization), community activity lists in the newspapers, and women's centers. The National Council on the Aging (see General Resources for address) also has a directory of self-help groups.

For books and articles on friendship, see Resources listed for the chapter Relationships in Middle and Later Life.

Self-Discovery and Life Review

Books

Houston, Jean. *A Course in Enhancing Your Physical, Mental, and Creative Abilities*. Los Angeles: J. P. Tarcher, 1982.

Maas, James. *Fifteen Past Seventy: Counsel from My Elders*. Berkeley, California: Shameless Hussy Press, 1986. Profiles of women and men who, regardless of their life situations, have some future event to anticipate.

Rainer, Tristine. *The New Diary: How to Use a Journal for Self-Guidance and Expanded Creativity*. Los Angeles: J. P. Tarcher, 1979.

Rainwater, Janette. *You're in Charge: A Guide to Becoming Your Own Therapist*. Marina del Rey, California: DeVorss and Co., 1979. Exercises in self-discovery and life review.

Robey, Harriet. *There's a Dance in the Old Dame Yet*. Boston: Atlantic/Little Brown, 1982. Author tells of her journey of self-healing and self-discovery in her later years.

Feminism, Religion, and Spirituality

Books and Other Publications

Broner, E. M. "Blessing the Ties That Bind." *Ms.*, Vol. 15, No. 6, December 1986, p. 50. Describes rituals developed by older women to celebrate their ages. On page 51 is "New Rites, New Rituals" by Hattie-Jo Pursglove-Mullins—an annotated list of books, cassettes, liturgies of pagan, Jewish, Christian, and ecumenical traditions.

Cady, Susan, Marian Ronan, and Hal Taussig. *Sophia: The Future of Feminist Spirituality*. New

York: Harper & Row, 1986. The biblical figure of Sophia (Wisdom) is explored as a link between Western religion and feminist consciousness.

Christ, Carol, and Judith Plaskow, eds. *Womanspirit Rising: A Feminist Reader in Religion*. San Francisco: Harper & Row, 1979. A comprehensive look at feminist theology in Christianity, Judaism, and goddess-centered religion.

Daly, Mary. *Pure Lust: Elemental Feminist Philosophy*. Boston: Beacon Press, 1984. Includes the visionary wisdom of older women.

Demetrakopoulous, Stephanie. *Listening to Our Bodies: The Rebirth of Feminine Wisdom*. Boston: Beacon Press, 1983. Starts with our physical body and moves to spiritual wisdom.

Feinman, Bonnie. *Midlife and Its Rite of Passage Ceremony*. Women's Institute for Continuing Jewish Education, 4079 54th St., San Diego, CA 92105. $4.95 plus $1.00 postage and handling. Jewish ritual which can be used by anyone.

Iglehart, Hallie. *Womanspirit: A Guide to Women's Wisdom*. San Francisco: Harper & Row, 1983. A guide for individuals or groups to learn meditation, dreamwork, mythmaking, and healing and to create new rituals.

Mariechild, Diane. *Mother Wit: A Feminist Guide to Psychic Development*. Trumansburg, New York: Crossing, 1981. Exercises for healing, growth, and spiritual development drawing on ancient and modern traditions.

Peters, Erskine. *African Openings to the Tree of Life*. Norwood, Pennsylvania: Norwood Editions, 1987. Describes life principles extracted from African philosophy and religion. These principles pertain to the person, the social group, and the community.

Spretnak, Charlene, ed. *The Politics of Women's Spirituality: Essays on the Rise of Spiritual Power Within the Feminist Movement*. New York: Anchor/Doubleday, 1982.

Starhawk. *The Spiral Dance: A Rebirth of the Ancient Religion of the Great Goddess*. New York: Harper & Row, 1979. Manual for the practice of a woman-centered, goddess-centered religion.

Rituals and exercises designed to aid women in reclaiming their power.

Woman of Power: A Magazine of Feminism, Spirituality and Politics. P.O. Box 827, Cambridge, MA 02238. Quarterly. $22 per year.

HABITS WORTH CHANGING

Fishel, Ruth. *Affirmations! A Tool to Turn Stumbling Blocks into Stepping Stones*. A 21-Day Workbook for Change. 1985 pamphlet. $3.00, from Serenity, Inc., P.O. Box 664, Natick, MA 01760.

Smoking

Organizations

Action on Smoking and Health (ASH)
2013 H St. NW
Washington, DC 20006
Tel. (202) 659-4310
A national organization concerned with policy issues and regulations about smoking.

The American Lung Association and the American Cancer Society have literature and groups to help you stop smoking. See your local or state chapters.

Group Against Smoking Pollution (GASP), 25 Deaconess Road, Boston, MA 02215, and Americans for Nonsmokers' Rights, P.O. Box 668, Berkeley, CA 94701 are two of the organizations that work to protect the rights of nonsmokers to clean air in public places and in the workplace through nonsmoking ordinances. Similar organizations in other states may be found through ASH (see above). *The Smoke-Free Workplace*, a directory of about 75 nonsmokers' rights groups in the United States and Canada, is published by Prometheus Books, 700 E. Amherst St., Buffalo, NY 14215.

Books and Other Publications

American Cancer Society. *1985 Cancer Facts and Figures*. 90 Park Avenue, New York, NY 10016. Contains statistics on smoking-related illnesses, treatment, and education.

Jacobson, Bobbie. *The Ladykillers: Why Smoking Is a Feminist Issue*. London: Pluto Press, 1981.

Smoke in the Workplace: An Action Manual for Non-Smokers (1985) is available for $9.45 (postpaid) from the Non-Smokers' Rights Association, Suite 308, 344 Bloor St. W., Toronto, Ontario M5S 1W9.

Taylor, Peter. *The Smoking Ring: Tobacco, Money and Multinational Politics*. New York: Pantheon Books, 1984.

Whelan, Elizabeth. *A Smoking Gun: How the Tobacco Industry Gets Away with Murder*. Philadelphia: George Stickey, 1984.

Audiovisual

The Feminine Mistake. Distributed by Pyramid Films, P.O. Box 1048, Santa Monica, CA 90406.

Alcohol

Organizations

Alcoholics Anonymous (AA)
General Service Office of AA
Box 459, Grand Central Station
New York, NY 10163
Tel. (212) 686-1100

AA is the most successful self-help group in the world and is listed in every phone book. Admission to AA is free, and a list of meeting times and locations in thousands of cities and towns can be obtained by calling any office. Though some meetings are open only to previously self-proclaimed alcoholics (the list of meetings indicates those for which this is the case), many others are open to anyone. Members of AA consider it part of their responsibility to offer newcomers transportation to and from meetings. A phone call to the closest office is all it takes to arrange a meeting. There are also lesbian and gay AA meetings.

Al-Anon and Alateen
Al-Anon Family Group Headquarters
P.O. Box 182, Madison Square Station
New York, NY 10159-0182
Tel. (212) 481-6565

Al-Anon is a self-help group that can be of great value to family and friends of alcoholics, and Alateen is for teenagers whose parents or friends drink. Both groups are listed in the phone book.

Alcoholics Together (AT)
Alcoholics Together Center
3596 Beverly Blvd.
Los Angeles, CA 90004

AT is sometimes also called Gay Alcoholics Anonymous (GAA). It follows the same program as AA but is exclusively for gay and lesbian persons. Write the AT Center if it is not in your phone book.

American Council on Alcoholism, Inc.
8501 LaSalle Road, Suite 301
Towson, MD 21204
Tel. (301) 296-5555

The council publishes educational materials and has a referral list to alcohol treatment centers. Members include individuals and treatment centers.

Mothers Against Drunk Driving
MADD National Headquarters
669 Airport Freeway, Suite 310
Hurst, TX 76053
Tel. (817) 268-6233 (MADD)

Funded by donations. No charge to victims. Literature and materials for adults and youth.

National Association of Gay Alcoholism Professionals (NAGAP)
P.O. Box 376
Oakland, NJ 07436

Write for a list of programs specializing in the treatment of gay and lesbian alcoholics.

National Council on Alcoholism, Inc. (NCA)
12 W. 21 St., 7th floor
New York, NY 10010
Tel. (212) 206-6770

A nonprofit organization with information and publications on alcohol. Consult your phone book or write to their national office for their 190 local and state affiliates.

National Council on Alcoholism, Inc.
1151 K St. NW, Suite 320
Washington, DC 20005
Tel. (202) 737-8122

The District of Columbia office of the NCA concentrates on public policy issues and is lobbying for warning labels on alcohol products.

Alcohol and Drug Agencies. Every state has an agency that can provide you with information on organizations and treatment programs. You can find them in your phone book, or write:

National Association of Alcohol and Drug Abuse Directors
918 F St. NW, Room 400
Washington, DC 20004
Tel. (202) 783-6868

Alcohol Helpline. A nationwide twenty-four-hour telephone referral service. Free of charge, run by Doctors' Hospital, Worcester, Massachusetts. Tel. (800) 252-6465.

Books and Other Publications

AA for the Woman. Alcoholics Anonymous World Services, Inc., Box 459, Grand Central Station, New York, NY 10163.

Alcoholics Anonymous (also known as *The Big Book*). 2nd ed. New York: Alcoholics Anonymous World Services, Inc., 1955. Box 459, Grand Central Station, New York, NY 10163. Highly recommended for everyone who wishes to learn more about alcoholism, the alcoholic and his friends, loved ones, and family.

Alcoholism, A Merry-Go-Round Named Denial. Al-Anon Family Group Headquarters, Inc. (see above under Organizations).

Black, Claudia. *It Will Never Happen to Me.* Denver: MAC Printing and Publications Division, 1982. About children of alcoholics and the effect alcohol has on their lives.

Fishel, Ruth. *From Mediation to Meditation. Gentle Meditation for Gentle Beginners on the Road to Recovery.* Useful for dealing with any kind of addiction. Available from Serenity, Inc., P.O. Box 664, Natick, MA 01760. 24pp. $3.00.

———. *The Journey Within: A Spiritual Path to Recovery.* Pompano Beach, Florida: Health Communications, Inc., 1987 forthcoming.

Greenleaf, Jael, ed. *Co-Alcoholic, Para-Alcoholic —Who's Who and What's the Difference?* Available from the author, P.O. Box 30036, Los Angeles, CA 90030.

Kirkpatrick, Jean. *Turnabout: Help for a New Life.* New York: Doubleday, 1978. Alternative self-help program for women.

Nellis, Muriel. *The Female Fix.* Boston: Houghton Mifflin, 1980.

Pinkham, Mary Ellen. *How to Stop the One You Love from Drinking.* New York: Putnam, 1986.

Sandmaier, Marian. *The Invisible Alcoholics: Women and Alcohol Abuse in America.* New York: McGraw-Hill, 1981.

Sober Days, Golden Years: Alcoholism and the Older Person. Minneapolis: Johnson Institute, Inc., 510 First Ave. N, Minneapolis, MN 55403, 1982. 42pp. $2.50. Excellent national resource guide.

Swallow, Jean, ed. *Out from Under: Sober Dykes and Our Friends.* San Francisco: Spinsters, Ink, 1983.

Wegscheider-Cruse, Sharon. *Choicemaking.* Health Communications, Inc., 1721 Blount Road, Suite 1, Pompano Beach, FL 33069, 1985.

Woititz, Janet G. *Adult Children of Alcoholics.* Pompano Beach, Florida: Health Communications, Inc. (address above), 1983.

———. *Struggle for Intimacy.* Pompano Beach, Florida: Health Communications, Inc. (address above), 1985.

Youcha, Geraldine. *Women and Alcohol. A Dangerous Pleasure.* New York: Hawthorne Books, 1986.

Youcha, Geraldine, and Judith S. Seixas. *Children of Alcoholism: A Survivor's Manual.* New York: Crown, 1985. A self-help book for adult children of alcoholics.

Over-the-Counter and Prescription Drugs

Organizations

Commission on Accreditation of Rehabilitation Facilities
2500 N. Pantano Rd.
Tucson, AZ 85715
Tel. (602) 886-8575
Accredits rehabilitation and pain-control facilities.

Narcotics Anonymous
World Service Office
16155 Wyandotte St.
Van Nuys, CA 91406
Tel. (818) 780-3951
Narcotics Anonymous has a program modeled after Alcoholics Anonymous for persons addicted to any kind of drug, including tranquilizers and other prescription drugs. See your phone book or contact the national office.

National Digestive Diseases Education and Information Clearinghouse
1255 23 St. NW, Suite 275
Washington, DC 20037
Tel. (202) 296-1138
This service of the National Institutes of Health answers questions, makes referrals, and provides publication lists and publications to promote understanding of digestive health and disease.

American Association of Retired Persons (AARP) operates the largest nonprofit mail-order pharmacy service in the world. The *AARP Pharmacy Service Catalog* contains over 800 generic and brand-name prescription drugs as well as vitamins and other health care products. For the address of the pharmacy that serves AARP members in your area, contact your local office or send your name and address with a request for the catalog to:
AARP Pharmacy Service
1 Prince St.
Alexandria, VA 22314

Books

Bresler, David E., with Richard Trubo. *Free Yourself from Pain.* New York: Fireside/Simon & Schuster, 1979.

Graedon, Joe. *The People's Pharmacy, Totally New and Revised.* New York: Avon, 1985.

Long, James W., ed. *The Essential Guide to Prescription Drugs.* New York: Harper & Row, 1985. Includes effects of drugs on sexuality.

Physicians' Desk Reference. 40th ed. Oradell, New Jersey: Medical Economics Co., 1986.

Physician's Desk Reference for Nonprescription Drugs. 7th ed. Oradell, New Jersey: Medical Economics Co., 1986.
These basic reference books describe the ingredients and effects of many medicines.

Using Your Medicines Wisely: A Guide for the Elderly. Elder-Ed, P.O. Box 416, Kensington, MD 20740.

Zimmerman, David. *The Essential Guide to Nonprescription Drugs.* New York: Harper Colophon, 1983.

If your local library does not have drug reference directories, request that they purchase them.

WHO NEEDS COSMETIC SURGERY?: REASSESSING OUR LOOKS AND OUR LIVES

Books and Other Publications

Baker, Nancy C. *The Beauty Trap: Exploring Woman's Greatest Obsession.* New York: Franklin Watts, 1984. Contains chapters on women's feelings about looking older, cosmetic surgery, and weight.

Brumberg, Elaine. *Save Your Money, Save Your Face: What Every Cosmetic Buyer Needs to Know.* New York: Facts-on-File, 1986. Contains a detailed list of hundreds of cosmetic products, their ingredients, and possible irritants.

Conry, Tom. *Consumer's Guide to Cosmetics.* New York: Anchor/Doubleday, 1980.

Freedman, Rita. *Beauty Bound: Why We Pursue the Myth in the Mirror.* Lexington, Massachusetts: D.C. Heath/Lexington Books, 1986.

Hansen, Joseph, and Evelyn Reed. *Cosmetics, Fashions, and the Exploitation of Women.* New York: Pathfinder Press, 1986. Includes reprints of classic articles from the 1950s on the relationship between the capitalistic system and the oppression of women, along with new material.

Hutchinson, Marsha Germaine. *Transforming Body Image: Learning to Love the Body You Have.* Trumansburg, New York: The Crossing Press, 1985. Exercises in learning to love our bodies.

Macdonald, Barbara, with Cynthia Rich. *Look Me in the Eye: Old Women, Aging, and Ageism.* San Francisco: Spinsters, Ink, n.d. Collection of essays and reviews on aging and ageism.

Melamed, Elissa. *Mirror, Mirror: The Terror of Not Being Young.* New York: Linden Press/Simon & Schuster, 1983.

Moss, Zoe. "It Hurts To Be Alive and Obsolete: The Aging Woman." In Robin Morgan, ed., *Sisterhood Is Powerful.* New York: Vintage, 1970.

Scheiner, Ann. "My Face-lift: A Cautionary Tale." *Ms.*, November 1986, pp. 58, 63, 81–83.

Sontag, Susan. "The Double Standard of Aging." *Saturday Review*, Vol. 95, No. 39, September 23, 1972. The ground-breaking article on this subject.

Troll, Lillian E., Joan Israel, and Kenneth Israel, eds. *Looking Ahead: A Women's Guide to the Problems and Joys of Growing Older.* Englewood Cliffs, New Jersey: Prentice-Hall, 1977. Several good chapters on body-image issues.

WEIGHTY ISSUES

Organizations

Bulimia, Anorexia Self-Help (BASH)
6125 Clayton Ave., Suite 215
St. Louis, MO 63139
Tel. (800) BASH-STL (toll-free) or (314) 991-BASH

Assistance and information, support and education for individuals suffering from eating problems (anorexia, bulimia, atypical eating habits) and mood disorders. Two state chapters. Monthly newsletter by subscription and publications by order.

National Anorexic Aid Society
5796 Karl Road
Columbus, OH 43229
Tel. (614) 436-1112

Provides information and education. Publishes an international referral directory for treatment and support groups. Quarterly newsletter for members. Annual conference for professionals.

American Anorexia/Bulimia Association, Inc.
133 Cedar Lane
Teaneck, NJ 07666
Tel. (201) 836-1800

General meetings led by professionals and recovered anorexics/bulimics are free to members and open to the public by donation. A reading list and a newsletter are mailed to all interested persons in the U.S. and elsewhere.

Anorexia Nervosa and Related Eating Disorders, Inc.
P.O. Box 5102
Eugene, OR 97405
Tel. (503) 344-1144

Collects and distributes information about eating disorders. Provides speakers, workshop and seminar leaders, trains professionals. Operates a treatment program in Eugene.

Books and Other Publications

Bennet, W., and J. Gurin. *The Dieter's Dilemma.* New York: Basic Books, 1982. Looks at scientific evidence that indicates dieting is not a form of weight control. Advances the theory of "setpoint" as determining weight, with exercise being one method of changing the setpoint. Accepting of different body shapes and sizes.

Boskind-White, Marlene, and William White. *Bulimarexia: The Binge-Purge Cycle.* New York: W. W. Norton, 1983.

Chernin, Kim. *Reflections on the Tyranny of Slenderness.* New York: Harper & Row, 1981.

Hall, Lindsey, and Leigh Cohn. *Eat Without Fear.* Santa Barbara, California: Gurze Books, 1980. True story of Hall's recovery from bulimia.

Haskell, William, James Scala, James Whittam, eds. *Nutrition and Athletic Performance.* Palo Alto, California: Bull Publishing Co., 1982. Proceedings of a 1981 conference including papers on consequences of rapid weight loss and advice for older athletes.

Kano, Susan. *Making Peace with Food. A Step-by-Step Guide to Freedom from Diet/Weight Conflict.* Amity Publishing, P.O. Box 2786, Danbury, CT 06813. Highly recommended.

Kaplan, Jane R. *A Woman's Conflict: The Special Relationship Between Women and Food.* Englewood Cliffs, New Jersey: Prentice-Hall, 1980. Hard-to-find but excellent collection of articles attentive to race and ethnic cultural differences that shape women's conflicts with food. Good section on fatness.

Millman, Marcia. *Such a Pretty Face: Being Fat in America.* New York: Berkley Publishing Corp., 1981. Excellent. Explores balance of cultural and personal factors in being fat for middle-class white women.

Orbach, Susie. *Fat Is a Feminist Issue. A Self-Help Guide for Compulsive Eaters.* New York: Berkley Publishing Corp., 1979. The anti-diet guide to permanent weight loss. Helps distinguish between "mouth hunger" and "stomach hunger" and teaches how to enjoy food. Contains section on self-starvation.

———. *Hunger Strike: The Anorectic's Struggle as a Metaphor of Our Age.* New York: W. W. Norton, 1986. An insightful, sensitive, and empathic book on anorexia nervosa as a "hunger strike in the cause of selfhood." Orbach analyzes the structural relationship of women to food and the culture's desire to control women's bodies. Addresses issues of self-help; offers therapeutic guidelines.

Radiance: A Publication for Large Women. Quarterly. P.O. Box 31703, Oakland, CA 94604. Tel. (415) 465-5246.

Schoenfielder, Lisa, and Barb Wieser, eds. *Shadow on a Tightrope: Writings by Women on Fat Oppression.* Aunt Lute Book Co., P.O. Box 2568, Iowa City, IA 52244, 1983. Anthology of articles about fat oppression and fat liberation.

Schwartz, Hillel. *Never Satisfied: A Cultural History of Diets, Fantasies and Fat.* New York: Free Press, 1986. Takes a detailed and political view of the pressures and contradictions facing women throughout history.

Audiovisual

Size 10 by Susan Lambert and Sara Gibson. Film, 20 minutes, color, 1978. Available from Women Make Movies (see under General Resources, Audiovisual). Australian film that shows how women's body image has been formed and deformed by advertising and sexism. Helps us reclaim our bodies.

Portraits of Anorexia by Wendy Zheuthin. Sixty-minute documentary, 16 mm., video. Available from Fat Chance Films, 390 Elizabeth St., San Francisco, CA 94114.

EATING WELL

Organizations

Food Not Bombs
  Room 306-335
  1430 Massachusetts Ave.
  Cambridge, MA 02138
  Tel. (617) 864-8786
Supplies vegetarian food at political rallies and events in New England. Activists for other political issues including the food needs of homeless people.

Society for Nutrition Education
  1700 Broadway, Suite 300
  Oakland, CA 94612
  Tel. (415) 444-7133
Has educational materials (some in Spanish) for lay and professional persons.

Books

Ballantine, Rudolph. *Diet and Nutrition. A Holistic Approach.* Honesdale, Pennsylvania: Himalayan International Institute, 1978. Overview of nutrition with recommendations based on scientific research and on the habits of traditional cultures.

Bland, Jeffrey. *Nutraerobics*. San Francisco: Harper & Row, 1985. How to assess how healthy your diet is and change it if necessary.

Brody, Jane. *Jane Brody's Nutrition Book*. New York: W.W. Norton, 1981. Basic nutrition book, good practical suggestions.

Consumer Reports Editors. *For Older People: Eating Right for Less: Consumer Union's Practical Guide to Food and Nutrition*. Mt. Vernon, New York: Consumers Union, 1975. Large type.

Lettvin, Maggie. *Maggie's Food Strategy Book: Taking Charge of Your Diet for Lifelong Health and Vitality*. Boston: Houghton Mifflin, 1987. Contains eight food plans which meet dietary requirements, lists of foods highest in each major nutrient, and techniques for balancing calories with various levels of activity.

Moyer, Ann. *Better Food for Public Places: A Guide for Improving Institutional Food*. Emmaus, Pennsylvania: Rodale Press, 1977. Discusses strategies and recipes.

Roe, Daphne A. *Geriatric Nutrition*. Englewood Cliffs, New Jersey: Prentice-Hall, 1983. Nutrition factors that affect people over sixty-five. Aimed at nutritionists rather than lay people, but understandable by the latter, and with good research.

Shapiro, Laura. *Perfection Salad: Women and Cooking at the Turn of the Century*. New York: Farrar, Straus & Giroux, 1986. Traces the history of domestic science and scientific cooking from its turn-of-the-century beginnings, focusing on the women who set out to modernize the American diet.

Thomas, Sherry. *We Didn't Have Much, But We Sure Had Plenty: Stories of Rural Women*. New York: Anchor/Doubleday, 1981. Contemporary stories of twelve midlife and older women farmers.

U.S. Dept. of Agriculture. *Handbook of the Nutritional Contents of Foods*. New York: Dover Publications, 1975. Vitamin, mineral, calorie, protein, carbohydrate, and fat content of common foods.

U.S. Dept. of Agriculture and U.S. Dept. of Health and Human Services. *Dietary Guidelines for Americans*. 2nd ed., 1985. Home and Garden Bulletin No. 232.

U.S. Senate Select Committee on Nutrition and Human Needs. *Eating in America: Dietary Goals for the U.S.* Cambridge, Massachusetts: MIT Press, 1977. Complete text of the dietary goals.

Watkin, D.M. *Handbook of Nutrition, Health and Aging*. Park Ridge, New Jersey: Noyes Publications, 1983. General information about nutrition and aging.

Cookbooks

Bagg, Elma. *Cooking Without a Grain of Salt*. New York: Doubleday, 1981.

Brown, Edward Espe. *Tassajara Cooking*. Boulder, Colorado: Shambhala Books, 1973. Vegetarian cooking made simple. Great "how to" book.

Ewald, Ellen. *Recipes for a Small Planet*. New York: Ballantine, 1975. Excellent vegetarian recipes.

Giobbi, Edward, and Richard Wolff. *Eat Right, Eat Well—The Italian Way*. New York: Knopf, 1985. Healthy Italian cooking with emphasis on low-fat, low-salt foods.

Goulart, Frances Sheridan. *The Vegetarian Weight Loss Cookbook*. New York: Simon and Schuster, 1982. Creative, simple recipes of interest to anyone. Disregard the concern with weight loss. Lots of nutritional information.

Harlow, Jan, et al. *The Good Age Cookbook: Recipes from the Institute for Creative Aging*. Boston: Houghton Mifflin, 1979. Low fat, low cholesterol, low salt and low calorie count.

Harsila, Janis, and Evie Hansen. *Seafood: A Collection of Heart-Healthy Recipes*. National Seafood Educators, P.O. Box 60006, Richmond Beach, WA 98160, 1986.

Lappé, Frances Moore. *Diet for a Small Planet.* New York: Ballantine, 1975. Rationale for vegetarian diet, good explanation of food combinations to increase protein content. Easy recipes.

Pritikin, Nathan. *The Pritikin Program for Diet and Exercise.* New York: Bantam, 1983. *Very* low-fat diet designed for people with diabetes and heart disease.

Robertson, Laurel, et al. *Laurel's Kitchen.* Petaluma, California: Nilgeri Press, 1976. Vegetarian cookbook with lots of nutritional information, such as charts of nutrients in food. Good for ideas when you are trying to change your diet.

Stillman, Joan P. *Fast and Low.* Boston: Little, Brown, 1985. Quick recipes for low-fat, low-salt cooking.

Wilson, J. Randy. *Non-Chew Cookbook.* Glenwood Springs, Colorado: Wilson Publishing Co., 1985. Tasty recipes for those who must be on a soft or liquid diet.

Other Publications

"Food and Fat," a series of annotated bibliographies, is available from the Women's Health Information Center, Boston Women's Health Book Collective. Write to:
47 Nichols Ave.
Watertown, MA 02172
Topics include agribusinesses/hunger, curriculum materials, eating problems, nutrition, self-help, vegetarianism, and women and fat. $2.00 each.

Food and Nutrition Information Center
National Agricultural Library
10301 Baltimore Blvd., Room 304
Beltsville, MD 20705
Tel. (301) 344-3719
Reference and lending service for materials on specific nutrition topics. Publishes *Pathfinder* series of resource lists for lay and professional persons.

Nutrition Action Newsletter. Center for Science in the Public Interest, 1501 16th St. NW, Washington, DC 20036. $19.95 for 10 issues per year. Offers a refreshing, critical view of the politics of nutrition.

Public Documents Distribution Center
Pueblo, CO 81009
Distributes Government pamphlets, including many on food and general nutrition. Write for list.

Tufts University Diet & Nutrition Letter. P.O. Box 10948, Des Moines, IA 50940. Monthly newsletter containing the latest research findings and food analysis. $18.00 per year.

U.S. Department of Agriculture. County Extension Services. These offices exist in urban areas also. Check your local telephone book under the name of your county. Provides general nutrition information, and information on preparing and preserving food.

MOVING FOR HEALTH

Organizations

Melpomene Institute for Women's Health Research
2125 Hennepin Ave.
Minneapolis, MN 55413
Tel. (612) 378-0545
Focuses on women, physical activity, and health through research, conferences, and a resource center. Annual membership of $25 includes *The Melpomene Report*, published three times a year.

Organizations for Outdoor Activities

Outdoor Vacations for Women Over 40
P.O. Box 200
Groton, MA 01450
Tel. (617) 448-3331
Provides opportunities for women over forty to learn new skills and add adventure to their lives by vacationing out-of-doors.

Outward Bound
384 Field Point Road
Greenwich, CT 06830
Tel. (800) 243-8520 or (203) 661-0797
Outward Bound teaches group and individual survival skills for all ages. Has courses for older women and will design them for individuals and groups with special needs or interests.

432

The Salvation Army
  799 Bloomfield Ave.
  Verona, NJ 07044
  Tel. (201) 239-0606
Inexpensive programs are available at about 55 rural camps throughout the country. Contact your local branch or the national headquarters above.

The Sierra Club
  730 Polk St.
  San Francisco, CA 94109
  Tel. (415) 776-2211
A national environmental protection organization, with publications and local group affiliations, that combines outdoor activity with exploration and preservation of beautiful natural sites.

Vacation and Senior Centers Association
  275 Seventh Ave.
  New York, NY 10001
  Tel. (212) 645-6590
Has general information about summer camps for the elderly. Applications must be made directly to each camp's sponsoring agency.

Women Outdoors, Inc.
  Curtis Hall
  474 Boston Ave.
  Medford, MA 02155
A clearinghouse for information on outdoor activities and skills. Lists local and regional programs. Encourages an ethic of environmental stewardship. Can refer women to existing programs and outings which will meet their needs. Annual membership is $15.00 ($8.00 for those over sixty-five) and includes quarterly publication, *Women Outdoors Magazine*.

Regional groups such as The Appalachian Mountain Club, 5 Joy St., Boston, MA 02108, Tel. (617) 523-0636, sponsor activities and hikes.

Books and Other Publications

Anderson, B. *Stretching*. Bolings, California: Shelter Publications, 1980.

Barker, Sarah. *The Alexander Technique*. New York: Bantam, 1981.

Bender, Ruth. Several books by this experienced teacher are still in print. Check your local library or bookstore.

Caplow-Lindner, Erna, Leah Harpaz, and Sonya Samberg. *Therapeutic Dance/Movement: Expressive Activities for Older Adults*. New York: Human Services Press, 1979.

Bernstein, Betherat. *The Body Has Its Resources*. New York: Avon, 1979.

Casper, Ursula Hodge. *Joy and Comfort Through Stretching and Relaxing for Those Who Are Unable to Exercise*. New York: Seabury Press, 1982.

deVries, Herbert A., with Diana Hales. *Fitness After Fifty*. New York: Scribner, 1974.

Feldenkrais, M. *Body and Mature Behavior*. New York: International Universities Press, 1979. An international list of Feldenkrais practitioners and information about books and tapes is available free from The Feldenkrais Guild, P.O. Box 11145, San Francisco, CA 94101. Tel. (415) 550-8708.

Godfrey, Charles, and Michael Feldman. *The Ageless Exercise Plan—A Complete Guide to Fitness After Fifty*. New York: McGraw-Hill, 1984. Includes tips on life-style habits and progress charts.

Hayden, Sandy, Daphne Hall, and Pat Stueck. *Women in Motion: The Basic Stuff to Get You Started and Keep You Going to Total Fitness*. Boston: Beacon Press, 1983.

Jamieson, Robert H. *Exercises for the Elderly*. Verplanck, New York: Emerson Books, Inc., 1982. Large type and easy-to-follow pictures. Includes exercises to be done in a chair or bed, and for those with special needs, such as people with partial paralysis.

Kuntzleman, Charles. *The Complete Book of Walking*. Paperback ed., Skokie, Illinois: Consumers Guide, 1982.

Lance, Kathryn. *Getting Stronger*. New York: Bantam, 1978. Includes exercises using household objects as weights.

Lederach, Naomi, Nona Kauffman, and Beth Lederach. *Exercise as You Grow Older*. Intercourse, Pennsylvania: Good Books, 1986. Highly recommended. Large print, good illustrations. Contains seated, standing, and moving exercises and nutritional guidance.

Leen, Edie. *Complete Women's Weight Training Guide*. Mountain View, California: Anderson World, Inc., 1959. Still an excellent book.

Lettvin, Maggie. *Maggie's Woman's Book*. Boston: Houghton Mifflin, 1981.

Long, Kate. "A Joint Venture." *Medical Self-Care*, No. 15, Winter 1984, p. 38. This issue also provides an overview of social, psychological, and health issues of aging.

Lowen, Alexander, and Leslie Lowen. *The Way to Vibrant Health*. New York: Harper & Row, 1977. Bioenergetic exercises.

Maisel, Edward. *Tai Chi for Health*. New York: Holt, Rinehart & Winston, 1972.

Olinekova, Gayle. *Go For It*. New York: Simon and Schuster, 1982. Good inspirational book for women.

Rush, Anne Kent. *Getting Clear: Body Work for Women*. New York: Random House/Bookworks, 1975. This book is recommended for its variety of physical-movement techniques that incorporate a mind-body approach. It's certainly a book for self-exploration that can teach us to value ourselves.

"Step Lively." A pamphlet about health- and race-walking available for $3.00 from Walkers Club of America, 445 East 86 St., New York, NY 10028.

Audiovisual

Light on Your Feet. Exercise Videotape, VHS, Beta. Designed by and for the large woman. It celebrates the larger body in a total workout of special exercises to music. Available from Rosezella Canty-Letsome, 54524, Atlanta, GA 30308-0524. $45.20 including postage.

LIVING WITH OURSELVES AND OTHERS AS WE AGE

SEXUALITY IN THE SECOND HALF OF LIFE

Organizations

American Association of Sex Educators, Counselors and Therapists (AASECT)
11 Dupont Circle NW, Suite 220
Washington, DC 20036

Impotence Anonymous
119 South Ruth St.
Maryville, TN 37801
Tel. (615) 983-6064
Helps impotent men and their partners through informational brochures and support groups. Referral to state and local chapters and appropriate professionals.

Senior Action in a Gay Environment (SAGE)
P.O. Box 115
New York, NY 10023
Network of social services for older lesbians and gay men.

Sex Information and Education Council of United States (SIECUS)
80 Fifth Ave., Suite 801
New York, NY 10011
Provides information about, and advocacy of, sexuality as a healthy part of life. Information service and Mary Calderone Library housed at New York University, Tel. (212) 673-3850.

Books and Other Publications

Bacon, Natalie, and Ralph Bacon. *Love Talk: A Model of Erotic Communication*. Shakti Press, P.O. Box 7581, Oakland, CA 94601, 1985. Autobiographical account of an older couple learning to communicate about sex.

Bahr, Robert. *The Virility Factor*. New York: Putnam, 1976. Well-written explanation of testosterone replacement therapy for men.

Barbach, Lonnie. *For Each Other*. New York: Anchor/Doubleday, 1982. A book for couples to practice sexual intimacy through communication exercises.

————. *For Yourself: The Fulfillment of Female Sexuality*. New York: Anchor/Doubleday, 1976. Relaxed approach teaches masturbation and self-pleasuring techniques leading to orgasm.

Barbach, Lonnie, and Linda Levine. *Shared Intimacies: Women's Sexual Experiences*. New York: Anchor/Doubleday, 1980.

Bellview, Fred, and Lin Richter. *Understanding Human Sexual Inadequacy*. New York: Bantam, 1970. This book explains Masters and Johnson's book in lay language.

Blumstein, Phillip, and Pepper Schwartz. *American Couples*. New York: Morrow, 1983. Compares heterosexual, gay, and lesbian couples.

Boston Women's Health Book Collective. *The New Our Bodies, Ourselves*. New York: Simon and Schuster, 1984. See especially chapters on Sexuality and Women Growing Older.

Brecher, Edward. *Love, Sex and Aging*. Boston: Little, Brown, 1984. Positive report on sex and aging. Sample is disproportionately middle class and male.

Butler, Robert, and Myrna Lewis. *Love and Sex After 40: A Guide for Men and Women for Their Mid and Later Years*. New York: Harper & Row, 1986. Revised and enlarged edition of *Sex After Sixty: A Guide for Men and Women in Their Later Years*. New York: Harper & Row, 1976. Knowledgeable and insightful. Available in large-print edition.

Comfort, Alex. *Joy of Sex*. New York: Crown, 1972. Compendium of sexual variations. Good for ideas.

Dodson, Betty. *Liberating Masturbation*. Published by Betty Dodson, Box 1933, Murray Hill Station, New York, NY 10156, 1983. Good for feeling positive about our bodies.

Friday, Nancy. *My Secret Garden*. New York: Pocket/Simon & Schuster, 1974.

————. *Forbidden Flowers*. New York: Pocket/Simon & Schuster, 1975. Women's sexual fantasies.

Hite, Shere. *The Hite Report*. New York: Dell, 1976. Women's sexual experiences.

Kaplan, Helen Singer. *The New Sex Therapy*. New York: Brunner/Mazel, 1974. Medically oriented. Contains excellent charts discussing effects of medications on sexual functioning.

Kehoe, Monika, ed. *Historical, Literary and Erotic Aspects of Lesbianism*. New York: Haworth Publications, Inc., 1986. Includes Kehoe's national survey, "Lesbians Over Sixty-five: A Triply Invisible Minority," and her article, "A Portrait of the Older Lesbian."

The Kensington Ladies Erotica Society. *Ladies' Own Erotica*. New York: Pocket/Simon & Schuster, 1984. Collection of erotic short stories written by a group of women.

Kinsey, Alfred, et al. *Sexual Behavior in the Human Female*. New York: Pocket/Simon & Schuster, 1953.

Kitzinger, Sheila. *Woman's Experience of Sex*. New York: Putnam, 1983.

Ladas, Alice, Beverly Whipple, and John Perry. *The G Spot*. New York: Dell, 1982.

Lorde, Audre. "Scratching the Surface: Some Notes on Barriers to Women and Loving." *The Black Scholar*, Vol. 9, No. 7, April 1978, pp. 31–35. Lesbian women.

Loulan, JoAnn. *Lesbian Sex*. San Francisco: Spinsters, Ink, 1984. Material on techniques and communication of ideas useful for all women.

Martin, Del, and Phyllis Lyon. "The Older Lesbian." In B. Bazow and R. Leighton, eds., *Positively Gay*. Mill Valley, California: Celestial Arts, 1979.

O'Connor, Dagmar. *How to Make Love to the Same Person for the Rest of Your Life and Still Love It*. New York: Bantam, 1986. A reassuring guide to a committed, yet adventurous, sexual relationship with the person you love by the director of a hospital-based sex-therapy program.

Olds, Sally Wendkos. *The Eternal Garden: Seasons of Our Sexuality*. New York: Times Books, 1985. The experience of sexuality from childhood through old age. Highly recommended.

Peterson, James, and Barbara Payne. *Love in the Later Years*. New York: Association Press, 1975.

Solnick, Robert, ed. *Sexuality and Aging*. University Park, California: Andrus Gerontology Center, University of Southern California, 1978. Excellent, thoughtful collection of articles about sex and aging. Includes nursing homes and health care.

Starr, Bernard, and Marcella Weiner. *The Starr-Weiner Report on Sex and Sexuality in the Mature Years*. New York: Stein & Day, 1981. Aging people speak for themselves.

Turner, Barbara F., and Catherine Adams. "The Sexuality of Older Women." In Elizabeth Markson, ed., *Older Women*. Lexington, Massachusetts: D.C. Heath/Lexington Books, 1983.

Zilbergeld, Bernie. *Male Sexuality*. Boston: Little, Brown, 1978. Good nonsexist book on male sexuality.

Other Publications

Sex Over Forty. Periodical. Order from S/40, P.O. Box 40428, San Antonio, TX 78229.

Sex and the Female Ostomate. Order pamphlet from United Ostomy Association, Inc., 2001 W. Beverly Blvd., Los Angeles, CA 90057. A discussion of sexuality for the woman who has had ostomy surgery.

Sex and Heart Disease. Order from your local chapter of the American Heart Association or write to the national center (see p. 467).

Audiovisual

Making It Last, a 45-minute videotape by Catherine Russo and Cheryl Qamar, is a rare look at sexuality in long-term lesbian relationships. With humor and honesty, women discuss the complexity of their sexual lives, including the impact of class and race differences, substance abuse, and histories of incest. An icebreaker for lesbian discussion groups and a useful guide for clinicians working with lesbian couples. Available for rental from Moonlight Productions, P.O. Box 105, W. Somerville, MA 02144.

Rose by Any Other Name by Judith Keller is an appealingly iconoclastic 15-minute film set in a nursing home that explores the lifelong need for affection, privacy, and sexual expression. Available for rental or sale (as film or videocassette) from Multi-Focus, Inc. (see below), or Pennsylvania State University (see General Resources, Audiovisual).

Where to Find Products Mentioned in Text:

Astro-lube Inc., P.O. Box 9788, North Hollywood, CA 91609. Sells Astroglide, an excellent lubricant.

Eve's Garden Ltd., 119 W. 57 St., Suite 1406, New York, NY 10019. Erotica and lubricants.

Good Vibrations, 3492 22 St., San Francisco, CA 94110. Vibrators and books, such as Joanie Blank, *Good Vibrations: The Complete Women's Guide to Vibrators*. San Francisco: Down There Press, 1984.

Multi-Focus, Inc., 1525 Franklin St., San Francisco, CA 94109, Tel. (800) 821-0514. Educational materials—books, films, videos, slides.

The Xandria Collection. Catalog of lubricants, vibrators, and other sex aids. Order from Lawrence Research Group, 1245 16 St., San Francisco, CA 74107.

BIRTH CONTROL FOR WOMEN IN MIDLIFE

Books and Other Publications

Bell, Susan, et al. "Reclaiming Reproductive Control: A Feminist Approach to Fertility Consciousness." *Science for the People*, Vol. 12, No. 1, 1980, pp. 6–9, 30–35. Available from Science for the People, 897 Main St., Cambridge, MA 02139.

Boston Women's Health Book Collective. *The New Our Bodies, Ourselves.* New York: Simon and Schuster, 1984. New edition of the classic women's health resource. See especially chapters on Anatomy and Physiology, Birth Control, Sexually Transmitted Diseases, and Abortion.

Corson, Stephen L., Richard J. Derman, and Louise B. Tyrer. *Fertility Control.* Boston and Toronto: Little, Brown, 1985. Good discussion of contraceptive-effectiveness issues.

Gordon, Linda. *Woman's Body, Woman's Right: A Social History of Birth Control in America.* New York: Penguin, 1977.

Hatcher, Robert A., Felicia Guest, et al. *Contraceptive Technology: 1986–1987.* 14th rev. ed. New York: Irvington Publishers, 1986.

Ory, Howard W. *Making Choices: Evaluating the Health Risks and Benefits of Birth Control Methods,* 1983. Order from The Alan Guttmacher Institute, 1360 Park Ave. S., New York, NY 10010. Includes comparisons of users by age.

Saunders, Jane. "Putting the Pill in Perspective." *WomenWise*, Spring 1983 (see General Health resources).

Seaman, Barbara. *The Doctor's Case Against the Pill.* New York: Dell, 1979.

Seaman, Barbara, and Gideon Seaman. *Women and the Crisis in Sex Hormones.* New York: Bantam, 1978. An excellent resource on the Pill, IUD, barrier methods, etc.

Wortman, J. "The Diaphragm and Other Intravaginal Barriers—A Review." *Population Reports*, Series H, No. 4, January 1976. Available from Population Information Programs, Johns Hopkins University, Baltimore, MD 21205.

Zones, Jane Sprague. "AIDS: What Women Need to Know." *The Network News* (see Health Resources), Vol. 11, No. 6, November/December 1986, p. 1. See pp. 94–95 for safe sex guidelines for women, reprinted from this informative article.

See General Health resources for organizations working in areas of women's health and reproductive rights.

CHILDBEARING IN MIDLIFE

Parenting

Books

Bing, Elisabeth, and Libby Coleman. *Having a Baby After Thirty: Reassurance and Professional Guidance for Couples Who Waited.* New York: Bantam, 1980.

Boston Women's Health Book Collective. *Ourselves and Our Children.* New York: Random House, 1978. An exploration of the whole experience of being a parent, including the decision to have a child, sharing parenthood with a partner and/or other(s), getting support, combining child raising with work outside the home, the shortage of child care, and other aspects of our society's lack of support for parenthood. Extensive bibliography on all aspects of parenthood.

Cohen, Judith Blackfield. *Parenthood After 30? A Guide to Personal Choice.* Lexington, Massachusetts: D.C. Heath/Lexington Books, 1985. Thoughtful and thorough. Includes extensive resource list.

Daniels, Pamela, and Kathy Weingarten. *Sooner or Later: The Timing of Parenthood in Adult Lives.* New York: W.W. Norton, 1982. Report on interview study and excellent discussion of issues around midlife parenting.

Mansfield, Phyllis Kernoff. *Pregnancy for Older Women: Assessing the Medical Risks.* New York:

Praeger, 1986. Compilation of recent research. Highly recommended.

Rothman, Barbara Katz. *The Tentative Pregnancy: Prenatal Diagnosis and the Future of Motherhood.* New York: Viking Penguin, 1986. Provocative discussion of the effect of pregnancy testing on the consequent decision to keep or abort a pregnancy and on the psychological experience of pregnancy and parenting.

Single Parenting

Books

Hall, Nancy Lee. *A True Story of a Single Mother.* Boston: South End Press, 1984. A Black woman's experience of single parenting.

Robinson, Susan, and H. F. Pizer. *Having a Baby Without a Man: The Woman's Guide to Alternative Insemination.* New York: Fireside/Simon & Schuster, 1985.

Lesbian Parenting

Organizations, Books, Audiovisual

Lesbian Mothers National Defense Fund, Box 21567, Seattle, WA 98111, Tel. (206) 325-2643. Provides information, emotional support and referrals to attorneys for custody disputes. Also provides information on artificial insemination.

Pies, Cheri. *Considering Parenthood: A Workbook for Lesbians.* San Francisco: Spinsters, Ink, 1985. Examines all aspects of the decision—social, economic, biological.

Choosing Children. A charming film depicting diverse lesbian families, beginning with such options as artificial insemination, adoption, and cooperation with gay men. Order from Cambridge Documentary Films, P.O. Box 385, Cambridge, MA 02139.

Pregnancy and Childbirth

Books and Other Publications

Baldwin, Rahima. *Special Delivery.* Millbrae, California: Les Femmes Publishing, 1979. Posi-tive discussions and descriptions of normal pregnancy, labor, and birth. Useful information if you are planning a home birth.

Boston Women's Health Book Collective. *The New Our Bodies, Ourselves.* New York: Simon and Schuster, 1984. See especially chapters on Pregnancy, Childbirth, Infertility, New Reproductive Technologies.

Brinn-Cassidy, Ginny, Francie Horner, and Carol Downer. *Women-Centered Pregnancy and Birth.* San Francisco: Cleis Press, 1984.

Health Letter, Vol. 4, No. 10. "What Is Amniocentesis?" Sante Fe Health Education Project, P.O. Box 577, Sante Fe, NM 87504-0577.

Inch, Sally. *Birthrights.* New York: Pantheon, 1984. A clear, systematic description of the few advantages and the many disadvantages of current obstetrical practices and drugs. A valuable factual tool for parents and childbirth educators.

Oakley, Ann. *Women Confined: Towards a Sociology of Childbirth.* New York: Schocken, 1980. A strong analysis of childbirth as a complex life event and a critique of the socialization of women and the medicalization of childbirth.

Odent, Michel. *Birth Reborn.* New York: Random House, 1984. A positive and affirming book that encourages women to listen to their own bodies.

Rothman, Barbara Katz. *Giving Birth: Alternatives in Childbirth.* New York: Penguin, 1984. Contrasts the medical model of childbirth with the midwifery model.

Sagov, Stanley, Richard Feinbloom, Peggy Spindell, and Archie Brodsky. *Home Birth: A Practitioner's Guide to Birth Outside the Hospital.* Rockville, Maryland: Aspen Systems Corp., 1983. A medical-practice group describes their own handling of pregnancy, labor, and birth. An essential book for prenatal-care providers and a reassuring guide for prospective parents.

Stewart, David, and Lee Stewart, eds. *Compulsory Hospitalization; Freedom of Choice in Childbirth?; The Five Standards for Safe Childbearing;*

also, *Safe Alternatives in Childbirth;* and *21st Century Obstetrics Now!* NAPSAC Publications, P.O. Box 267, Marble Hill, MO 63764. The proceedings from several conferences of the National Association of Parents and Professionals for Safe Alternatives in Childbirth. A multitude of interesting and useful articles.

Exercise and Nutrition for the Childbearing Year

Books

Balaskas, Arthur, and Janet Balaskas. *New Life.* Rev. ed. London: Sidgwick and Jackson, 1983. An exercise book that stresses relaxation, squatting, and changing positions during labor. Excellent drawings of the pelvis.

Brewer, Gail Sforza, ed. *The Pregnancy After 30 Workbook: A Program for Safe Childbearing No Matter What Your Age.* Emmaus, Pennsylvania: Rodale Press, 1978.

Goldbeck, Nikki. *As You Eat So Your Baby Grows.* Woodstock, New York: Ceres Press, 1977. A lot of basic nutrition information discussed in a simple, understandable way.

Noble, Elizabeth. *Essential Exercises for the Childbearing Year.* 2nd ed. Boston: Houghton Mifflin, 1982. Easy to understand, informative, well illustrated. Includes detailed discussions of the pelvic floor, and of the physiological reasons for doing specific exercises.

Williams, Phyllis. *Nourishing Your Unborn Child.* Rev. ed. New York: Avon, 1982. Basic information on good nutrition, including scores of recipes.

Infertility

Menning, Barbara Eck. *Infertility: A Guide for the Childless Couple.* Englewood Cliffs, New Jersey: Prentice-Hall, 1977.

Resolve, Inc., 5 Water St., Arlington, MA 02174, Tel. (617) 643-2424. Provides information and support and referral to specialists for men and women with infertility problems. Resolve can review with you the appropriateness of recom-

mended medical tests and treatment for infertility.

New Reproductive Technologies

Arditti, Rita, Renate Duelli Klein, and Shelly Minden, eds. *Test Tube Women.* Boston: Pandora Press, Routledge and Kegan Paul, 1984. This book's many and varied articles provide a strong feminist insight into new reproductive technologies and other issues, such as testing during pregnancy.

Corea, Gena. *The Mother Machine.* New York: Harper & Row, 1985.

Adoption

Organizations

Concerned United Birthparents
P.O. Box 396
Cambridge, MA 02238
A support organization for women who have given up babies for adoption. Lobbies for rights of adoptive children and birth parents to information.

International Concerns Committee for Children
911 Cypress Drive
Boulder, CO 80303
Tel. (303) 494-8333
Researches and provides information and support for orphan children in many countries. Publishes an annual listing of foreign adoption resources for U.S. citizens, "The Foreign Adoption Report," and also a listing of children available for adoption by U.S. adoptive families.

OURS, Inc.
3307 Hwy. 100 N., Suite 203
Minneapolis, MN 55422
Tel. (612) 535-4829
A national organization providing problem-solving assistance and information to adoptive and prospective adoptive families. Special groups consist of single parents, families who adopt physically or emotionally challenged children, and families who adopt children from ethnic backgrounds that differ from their own. OURS will provide information about local

groups if you send them a stamped self-addressed envelope.

Books and Other Publications

Gay, Kathlyn. *The Rainbow Effect.* New York: Franklin Watts, 1987. The author discusses the adaptability of adoptive parents and finds their children have high self-esteem and generally do well.

Gilman, Lois. *The Adoption Resource Book: A Comprehensive Guide to All the Things You Need to Know.* New York: Harper & Row, 1977.

Ladner, Joyce A. *Mixed Families: Adopting Across Racial Boundaries.* Garden City, New York: Anchor/Doubleday, 1977. The author cautions that white parents may be naive about the racism their adopted children may encounter. She advises teaching children about their heritage and preparing them for racism and prejudice.

Martin, Cynthia D. *Beating the Adoption Game.* La Jolla, California: Oak Tree Publications, 1980.

Plumez, Jacqueline Hornar. *Successful Adoption.* New York: Harmony Books, 1982.

Stepparenting

Organizations, Books, Audiovisual

Step-Family Association of America
    602 East Joppa Rd.
    Baltimore, MD 21204
    Tel. (301) 823-7570
Self-help groups for parents and children. Membership ($45.00) includes newsletter and attendance at local group if one exists in your community. Or you can get help to start one. Newsletter only, $14.00 per year.

Getzoff, Ann, and Carolyn McClenahan. *Stepkids: A Survival Guide for Teenagers in Stepfamilies: (and for Stepparents Doubtful of Their Own Survival).* New York: Walker & Co., 1985. Written from the teenager's point of view, this book can be helpful to parents and stepparents.

Keshet, Jamie. *Love and Power in the Step-Family.* New York: McGraw-Hill, 1986.

Stepparenting: New Families, Old Ties. A 25-minute film by Henry and Marilyn Felt. Interviews with stepparents and scenes from a stepparent support group. For stepparents and professionals. Polymorph Films, 331 Newbury St., Boston, MA 02115.

MENOPAUSE: ENTERING OUR THIRD AGE

Organizations

Women's Association for Research in Menopause (W.A.R.M.)
    128 E. 56 St.
    New York, NY 10022
W.A.R.M.'s purposes are to raise funds to support increased research about menopause, to promote public education and dispel the many myths about menopause, and to facilitate the formation of support groups.

Books and Articles

Clay, Vidal S. *Women: Menopause and Middle Age.* Pittsburgh, Pennsylvania: KNOW, Inc., 1977. One of the earlier helpful books on menopause. See especially the chart on the comparison of medical and nonmedical therapies for problems in menopause and aging, pp. 88–89.

Davis, Dona Lee. *Blood and Nerves: An Ethnographic Focus on Menopause.* St. John's, Newfoundland, Canada: Institute of Social and Economic Research, Memorial University of Newfoundland, 1983. This book examines the experiences of menopause of the women in a Newfoundland fishing village and also contains many cross-cultural references.

Gognalons-Nicolet, Maryvonne. "The Crossroads of Menopause: A Chance and a Risk for the Aging Process of Women." In Elizabeth W. Markson, ed., *Older Women.* Lexington, Massachusetts: D. C. Heath/Lexington Books, 1983, pp. 37–48. Comparison of the experiences of French and American women at midlife.

Greenwood, Sadja. *Menopause Naturally: Preparing for the Second Half of Life.* San Francisco: Volcano Press, 1984. A simply written and well-balanced book by a woman physician who has gone through menopause. Has chapters on osteoporosis, exercise, nutrition, and estrogen-replacement therapy. The chart showing the types of hormones and other drugs in the commonly prescribed hormonal preparations is very useful.

Lock, Margaret, guest ed. "Anthropological Approaches to Menopause: Questioning Received Wisdom." Special issue of *Culture, Medicine and Psychiatry*, Vol. 10, No. 1, March 1986.

Millette, Brenda, and Joellen Hawkins. *The Passage Through Menopause: Women's Lives in Transition.* Reston, Virginia: Reston Publishing Company, Inc. (A Prentice-Hall Company), 1983. A well-researched and well-documented paperback written by nurses for women and health care providers.

Nissim, Rina. *Natural Healing in Gynecology: A Manual for Women.* New York and London: Pandora, 1986. Describes the use of herbs, trace elements, and diet in ensuring the proper functioning of the body and in the treatment of gynecological disorders. Includes suggestions for the use of herbs for endometriosis and heavy bleeding.

O'Donnell, Mary, et al. *Lesbian Health Matters.* A publication of the Santa Cruz Women's Health Center, 250 Locust St., Santa Cruz, CA 95060, 1979. A unique resource for anyone concerned about women's health from a lesbian point of view. The chapter on menopause is useful for all women.

Parlee, Mary Brown. "Reproductive Issues, Including Menopause." In Grace Baruch and Jeanne Brooks-Gunn, eds. *Women in Midlife.* New York: Plenum Press, 1984, pp. 303–13. A review of past work and plea for more psychological research on women at midlife.

Reitz, Rosetta. *Menopause: A Positive Approach.* New York: Penguin, 1979. An indispensable resource supportive of menopause as a natural event.

Research on the Menopause. World Health Organization, Technical Report Series 670, Geneva, Switzerland, 1981. Available from WHO Publications Centre, 49 Sheridan Avenue, Albany, NY 12210. $7.05 including postage. Contains a summary and reference list of earlier research. The expert committee's recommendations for research, such as whether the health systems in developing countries are meeting the needs of women, and what the long-term effects of hormone use are, are still relevant.

Seaman, Barbara, and Gideon Seaman. *Women and the Crisis in Sex Hormones.* New York: Bantam, 1978. Slightly dated but still an excellent resource on the hazards of using sex hormones.

Voda, Ann M., Myra Dinnerstein, and Sheryl R. O'Donnell. *Changing Perspectives on Menopause.* Austin, Texas: University of Texas Press, 1982. A collection of articles that treats menopause as a subject for serious scholarly research, attempts to identify past errors, and develops new methodologies.

Weideger, Paula. *Menstruation and Menopause.* New York: Knopf, 1976. Historical and cultural background of myths and taboos of menopause.

Other Publications

Menopause Today. Rev. ed., 1985. Planned Parenthood Federation of America, 810 Seventh Ave., New York, NY 10019. Tel. (212) 541-7800. Bulk rates available. 8 pages.

Menopause: A Natural Process. 1982. San Francisco Women's Health Center. Now available from the Women's Midlife Resource Center, 1825 Haight St., San Francisco, CA 94117. Tel. (415) 221-7417. $2.00.

Menopause: A Self-Care Manual. Rev. ed., 1987. Santa Fe Health Education Project, P.O. Box 577, Santa Fe, NM 87504-0577. $4.20 includes postage. Bulk rates available. Also available in Spanish. 51 pages.

About Menopause. Rev. ed., 1985. Channing L. Bete Co., South Deerfield, MA 01373. Tel. (413) 665-7677. Bulk rates available. 15 pages.

The Menopause Time of Life. 1983. U.S. Department of Health and Human Services, PHS (NIH Publication No. 83-2461). 20 pages.

Voda, Ann. *Menopause, Me and You. A Personal Handbook for Women.* Salt Lake City, Utah: College of Nursing, University of Utah, 1984. Pamphlet can be ordered from: Ann M. Voda, 25 South Medical Drive, Salt Lake City, UT 84112. $4.95 for a single copy. Bulk rates available. Has a section on osteoporosis. 46 pages.

Slide/Tape Shows

Menopause: A Time of Transition. Produced by Planned Parenthood, Education Dept., 1660 Bush St., San Francisco, CA 94109. Tel. (415) 441-5454 (TTY). Describes value of good nutrition, exercise, and vitamins, as well as conventional "treatment of symptoms."

My Menopause. Produced by Planned Parenthood of Rochester and Monroe County, Inc., 114 University Road, Rochester, NY 14605. Tel. (716) 546-2595. Gives a good overview of menopause, but emphasizes estrogen-replacement therapy.

RELATIONSHIPS IN MIDDLE AND LATER LIFE

Organizations

Abused Women's Aid in Crisis
  G.P.O. Box 1699
  New York, NY 10116
  Tel. (212) 686-3628
Offers assistance to abused women and families. Serves as a national clearinghouse to provide information and referrals to inquiries from across the United States.

American Association of Marriage and Family Counselors
  225 Yale Ave.
  Claremont, CA 91711
Write to them for referrals to counselors in your area.

Federation of Parents and Friends of Lesbians and Gays, Inc.
  P.O. Box 24565
  Los Angeles, CA 90024

Newsletter and referrals to local parents' groups. Literature includes a short, simple pamphlet translated into Chinese, Spanish, French, and Japanese.

Grandparents'-Children's Rights, Inc.
  5728 Bayonne Ave.
  Haslett, MI 48840
  Tel. (517) 339-8663
Clearinghouse of information on state laws. Provides referrals to local self-help groups whenever possible.

National Association for Widowed People
  P.O. Box 3564
  Springfield, IL 62708
Offers widowed persons and their families a better understanding of the problems in dealing with grief and loneliness.

National Coalition Against Domestic Violence
  2401 Virginia Ave. NW, Suite 306
  Washington, DC 20037
NCADV is a national grass-roots membership organization of battered women's shelter and service providers and concerned individuals. Provides information on domestic violence, referrals and technical assistance to local groups.

Parents Without Partners
  7910 Woodmont Ave., Suite 1000
  Bethesda, MD 20814
Chapters in most large cities provide social opportunities for single parents and their children. Newsletter and magazine cover single-parent concerns.

Theos Foundation
  Penn Hills Mall, Suite 410
  Pittsburgh, PA 15235
  Tel. (412) 243-4299
Through meetings and one-to-one mutual aid, helps younger and middle-aged widowed persons to accept, after grieving, the death of a spouse and adjust to the change, set new goals, renew personal identity, and create a new life. Eight-issue publication: Survivors' Outreach Series.

Widowed Persons Service c/o American Association of Retired Persons (see General Resources).

RESOURCES

Books and Other Publications

Adelman, Marcy. *Long Time Passing: Lives of Older Lesbians.* Boston: Alyson Publications, 1987.

Battered Women's Directory. 9th ed. 283 pp. Betsy Warrior, ed. Order from: Directory—Terry Mehlman, Box E-94, Earlham College, Richmond, IN 47374, $12.00. Highly recommended. This directory includes articles with helpful information and support to battered women and their friends. Exhaustive list of resources throughout the United States and worldwide.

Bell, Roseann P., Bettye J. Parker, and Beverly Guy-Sheftall, eds. *Sturdy Black Bridges: Visions of Black Women in Literature.* Garden City, New York: Anchor/Doubleday, 1979. See especially Mary Burgher, "Images of Self and Race in the Autobiographies of Black Women." Issues of survival, creativity, and Black womanhood.

Bell, Ruth, and Leni Zeiger Wildflower. *Talking with Your Teenager.* New York: Random House, 1983. A guide to approaching difficult topics. Parents' counterpart to *Changing Bodies, Changing Lives*, a book for teens by the same authors.

Belovitch, Jeanne, ed. *Making Remarriage Work.* Lexington, MA: D.C. Heath/Lexington Books, 1987.

Block, Joel, and Diane Greenberg. *Women and Friendship.* New York: Franklin Watts, 1985.

Boston Lesbian Psychologies Collective, eds. *Lesbian Psychology: Explorations and Challenges.* Urbana and Chicago: University of Illinois Press, 1987. A pioneering anthology which captures the experiences of contemporary American lesbians. The articles, which were presented at a conference, focus on identity, relationships, community, and therapy.

Brans, Jo. *Mother, I Have Something to Tell You: Understanding Your Child's Chosen Lifestyle.* New York: Doubleday, 1987. How mothers cope when their children make choices different from their own.

Caine, Lynn. *Widow.* New York: Morrow, 1974. The author shares her experience of loss and makes a new beginning.

———. *What Did I Do Wrong? Mothers, Children, Guilt.* New York: Arbor House, 1985

Cherlin, Andrew J., and Frank Furstenburg, Jr. *The New American Grandparent: A Place in the Family, a Life Apart.* New York: Basic Books, 1986.

Coleman, Emily, and Betty Edwards. *Brief Encounters: How to Make Relationships Rewarding Even Though They May Not Last Forever.* Garden City, New York: Anchor/Doubleday, 1980.

Cowan, Connell, and Melvin Kinder. *Smart Women, Foolish Choices: Finding the Right Men and Avoiding the Wrong Ones.* New York: Signet/New American Library, 1985.

Fairchild, Betty, and Nancy Hayward. *Now That You Know: What Every Parent Should Know About Homosexuality.* New York and San Diego: Harvest/Harcourt Brace Jovanovich, 1979. Helpful book includes personal experiences and information on how to start Parents of Gays groups.

Flanner, Janet. *Darlinghissima: Letters to a Friend.* New York: Random House, 1985. Personal account of a long-standing lesbian relationship.

Getzoff, Ann, and Carolyn McClenahan. *Stepkids: A Survival Guide for Teenagers in Stepfamilies: (and for Stepparents Doubtful of Their Own Survival).* New York: Walker & Co., 1985. Written from the teenager's point of view, this book can be helpful to parents and stepparents.

Gilligan, Carol. *In a Different Voice: Psychological Theory and Women's Development.* Cambridge: Harvard University Press, 1982. A scholarly book that helps women appreciate their abilities in fostering and preserving relationships.

Gross, Zenith Henkin. *And You Thought It Was Over: Mothers and Their Adult Children.* New York: St. Martin's, 1985. Based on questionnaires sent to 500 midlife women and interviews with a smaller number, the author describes the continuing importance of the relationship between mothers and their grown children.

Hull, Gloria T., Patricia Bell Scott, and Barbara Smith, eds. *All the Women Are White, All the Blacks Are Men, But Some of Us Are Brave*. Old Westbury, New York: Feminist Press, 1982. Collection of articles on Black women, especially lesbian relationships, politics, and work.

Jolly, Constance. "Purple Balloons on Market Street." *Broomstick*, Vol. 8, No. 6, January–February 1986, pp. 3–8. Inspiring story by a mother about a lesbian daughter's coming out. Includes suggested readings.

Jongeward, Dorothy, and Dru Scott. *Women as Winners: Transactional Analysis for Personal Growth*. Reading, Massachusetts: Addison-Wesley, 1976. Personal development for women/relationships.

Kiley, Dan. *The Wendy Dilemma: When Women Stop Mothering Their Men*. New York: Avon, 1984. How to become self-directed and assertive while still enjoying relationships with men.

Kimball, Gayle. *The Fifty-Fifty Marriage*. Boston: Beacon Press, 1983. Relationships in marriage. Ways to achieve egalitarian relationships illustrated through stories of couples.

Kornhaber, Arthur. *Between Parents and Grandparents*. New York: St. Martin's, 1986.

———, and Kenneth Woodward. *Grandparents, Grandchildren: The Vital Connection*. Garden City, New York: Anchor/Doubleday, 1981.

Lenz, Elinor. *Once My Child, Now My Friend*. New York: Warner, 1982.

Lerner, Harriet Goldhor. *The Dance of Anger*. New York: Harper & Row, 1985. Helpful book by a therapist on anger in relationships.

LeShan, Eda. *Learning to Say Good-by: When a Parent Dies*. New York: Avon, 1976.

McConnell, Adeline, and Beverly Anderson. *Single After 50: How to Have the Time of Your Life*. New York: McGraw-Hill, 1980.

Morrison, Toni. *Sula*. New York: Knopf, 1974. Novel about a lifelong friendship between two Black women.

Nicarthy, Ginny. *Getting Free: A Handbook for Women in Abusive Relationships*. Seattle: Seal Press, 1982. Includes exercises to help women examine their options and make decisions with more objectivity.

Nye, Miriam Baker. *But I Never Thought He'd Die: Practical Help for Widows*. Philadelphia: Westminster Press, 1978.

Pogrebin, Letty Cottin. *Among Friends: Who We Like, Why We Like Them, and What We Do with Them*. New York: McGraw-Hill, 1986.

Polikoff, Nancy. *The Custody Handbook: A Woman's Guide to Child Custody Disputes*. 1984. Women's Legal Defense Fund, 2000 P St. NW, Suite 400, Washington, DC 20036. $4.00.

Powell, Barbara. *Overcoming Shyness: Practical Scripts for Everyday Encounters*. New York: McGraw-Hill, 1979. Beginning new relationships.

Powell, Mary Clare. *The Widow*. Order from Mary Clare Powell, Institute for Women and the Future, P.O. Box 1081, Northampton, MA 01060. Photo essay of the author's mother as a widow building a new life.

Rafkin, Louise. *Different Daughters: A Book by Mothers of Lesbians*. Pittsburgh, PA: Cleis Press, 1987.

Raymond, Janice G. *A Passion for Friends: Towards a Philosophy of Female Affection*. Boston: Beacon Press, 1986.

Reese, Lyn, Jean Wilkinson, and Phyllis Koppelman, eds. *I'm On My Way Running: Women Speak of Coming of Age*. New York: Avon, 1983. Primarily about younger women. See Chapter 4 on mother-daughter relationships.

Rodgers-Rose, La Frances, ed. *The Black Woman*. Beverly Hills, California: Sage Publications Inc., 1980. Articles on work, marriage, family roles, attitudes, and relationships.

Rubin, Lillian. *Just Friends: The Role of Friendship in Our Lives*. New York: Harper & Row, 1985. Engaging report on the importance of friendship, a frequently undervalued relationship.

Sarton, May. *The Magnificent Spinster.* New York: W. W. Norton, 1985. About a fifty-year-long friendship between women.

Schneider, Nina. *The Woman Who Lived in a Prologue.* Boston: Houghton Mifflin, 1980. Portrait over time of a woman in many roles—wife, mother, lover, grandmother.

Silverman, Phyllis. *Widow-to-Widow.* New York: Springer Publishing, 1985. Reports on self-help groups for widows.

Simon, Barbara Levy. *Never Married Women.* Philadelphia: Temple University Press, forthcoming 1987.

Switzer, David K., and Shirley Switzer. *Parents of the Homosexual.* Philadelphia: Westminster Press, 1980. Enlightening and compassionate from a religious perspective.

Tessina, Tina B., and Riley K. Smith. *How to Be a Couple and Still Be Free.* North Hollywood, California: Newcastle Publishing, 1980.

Triere, Lynette, with Richard Peacock. *Learning to Leave: A Woman's Guide.* New York: Warner Books, 1982.

Walker, Alice. *In Search of Our Mothers' Gardens.* New York: Harcourt Brace Jovanovich, 1983. See especially the title article and "Brothers and Sisters."

Westoff, Leslie Aldridge. *Breaking Out of the Middle-Age Trap.* New York: New American Library, 1980. Midlife change.

Witkin, Mildred Hope, with Burton Lehrenbaum. *45 and Single Again.* New York: Dembner Books, 1985. Addressed to women who face the trauma of losing a valued mate through divorce or death. Coping with issues such as love, sex, finances, and grown children, and with the process of starting a new life.

Yglesias, Helen. *Starting Early, Anew, Over and Late.* New York: Rawson Wade, 1978.

HOUSING ALTERNATIVES AND LIVING ARRANGEMENTS

Organizations

Adaptive Environments Center
  Massachusetts College of Art
  621 Huntington Ave.
  Boston, MA 02115
  Tel. (617) 739-0088
Provides information and workshops on adapting housing and workplaces for special needs.

American Association of Retired Persons (AARP) (see General Resources) offers materials on housing. Free booklets include *Housing Options for Older Americans,* 1984, 42 pp., large type; and *Your Home, Your Choice: A Workbook for Older People and Their Families,* 1984, 32 pp. (Requests should be addressed to AARP, Attention: Housing.) Slide shows, along with written materials for presenters, are available from the Program Scheduling Office (write to AARP, Department AW).

National Institute of Senior Housing
  c/o National Council on the Aging, Inc.
  (NCOA) (see General Resources)
The National Institute of Senior Housing is a unit of NCOA that addresses the growing need for independent housing adapted to the special needs and interests of older Americans.

National Policy Center on Housing and Living Arrangements for Older Americans
  University of Michigan
  College of Architecture and Urban Planning
  2000 Bonisteel Blvd.
  Ann Arbor, MI 48109
Information available on alternative arrangements for independent living.

National Trust for Historic Preservation
  1785 Massachusetts Ave. NW
  Washington, DC 20036
  Tel. (202) 673-4000

Women's Institute For Housing and Economic Development, Inc.
  179 South St.
  Boston, MA 02111
  Tel. (617) 423-2296

A national nonprofit corporation that assists groups with housing and business development through information referrals as well as intensive project assistance. The Institute has published a useful 48-page pamphlet, *A Development Primer: Starting Housing or Business Ventures by and/or for Women*. Although it was written for community-based, grass-roots organizations, it could also be a catalyst and tool for individual women to form partnerships and develop housing for themselves and others. Cost $7.00. Also available, *A Manual on Transition Housing*, 1986.

See other organizations listed throughout Resources section. Many other organizations concerned with issues of older people may also have materials on housing.

Books and Other Publications

Gold, Margaret. *The Older American's Guide to Housing and Living Arrangements*. Published by the Institute for Consumer Policy Research, Consumers Union, 256 Washington St., Mount Vernon, NY 10553, Tel. (914) 667-9400, 1984. $14.00, 115 pp., with appendix. Comprehensive and efficiently organized, it contains realistic descriptions of advantages and disadvantages for a range of housing options. Helpful in setting personal priorities.

Hayden, Delores. *The Grand Domestic Revolution: A History of Feminist Designs for American Homes, Neighborhoods and Cities*. Cambridge, MA: MIT Press, 1981. Historic view of women in communities.

————. *Redesigning the American Dream: The Future of Housing, Work, and Family*. New York: W.W. Norton, 1984.

Hochschild, Arlie Russell. *The Unexpected Community: Portrait of an Old Age Subculture*. Berkeley, California: University of California Press, 1978. An ethnographic study of a community which developed in lower-income senior citizens' housing demonstrates the importance of peer relationships to elders.

Phillips, Alice H., and Caryl K. Roman. *A Practical Guide to Independent Living for Older People*. Seattle: Pacific Search Press, 1984. Written by two active older women. Specific and clear, with extensive resources. Large type.

Safety for Older Consumers. A home-safety checklist available from the U.S. Consumer Product Safety Commission, Washington, DC 20207, Tel. (800) 638-2772.

Shahan, Lynn. *Living Alone and Liking It*. New York: Harper & Row, 1981. Not specifically for older women, but useful in gaining a fresh perspective and seeing positive aspects to living alone.

Tone, Teona, and D. Sclar. *Housemates: A Practical Guide to Living with Other People*. New York: Ballantine, 1985.

Special Housing Programs for Women

The Susan B. Anthony Memorial Unrest Home. For more information write to Mary and Jan, Rte. 1, Box 215, Millfield, OH 45761.

The Crone's Nest, 207 Coastal Hwy., St. Augustine, FL 32084. A proposed intergenerational community that will provide long-living women with an alternative to traditional retirement options.

Quest, Box 31, Montreal, WI 54550. The Midwest's and perhaps the nation's first shared housing program for gay and lesbian senior citizens and retirees. Write to them for current information.

Home Equity Conversion Information

Organizations

American Bar Association
Commission on Legal Problems of the Elderly
1800 M St. NW
Washington, DC 20036
Tel. (202) 331-2200

National Center for Home Equity Conversion (NCHEC)

110 East Main, Room 1010
Madison, WI 53703
Tel. (608) 256-2111
Ask for brochure and copies of their newsletter.

Articles

"Credit Roulette: Home Equity Loans May Put Homes in Peril." *AARP News Bulletin*, Vol. 28, No. 5, May 1987.

Shared Living

Publications

Is Homesharing for You? A Self-Help Guide for Homeowners & Renters. 1983. National Shared Housing Resource Center, Inc., 6344 Greene St., Philadelphia, PA 19144, Tel. (215) 848-1220. $3.00. For individuals who have no access to match-up programs or prefer to seek a home-sharing arrangement independently.

Living With Tenants—How to Happily Share Your House With Renters for Profit and Security. The Housing Connection, P.O. Box 5536, Arlington, VA 22205. $7.00.

Shared Living—An Individual Planning Guide. 1982. Action for Boston Community Development, Inc. (ABCD), 178 Tremont St., Boston, MA 02111, Tel. (617) 357-6000. $2.00. Takes readers through a step-by-step process in establishing their own shared-living arrangements.

Shared Living...What Is It? Would I Like It? 1982. ABCD (see above). $2.00. Large type. Describes different types of small shared-living arrangements, who might choose them and why, and examines ownership or rental styles and managerial responsibilities.

Streib, Gordon F., and Mary Ann Hilker. *An Experiment in Shared Living for Older People: A Description and Guide for Action.* 1980. Center for Gerontological Studies, University of Florida, Gainesville, FL 32604. $5.00. Authors describe Share-A-Home, the first organization to promote group housing.

Condos and Co-ops

National Association of Housing Cooperatives
2501 M St. NW
Washington, DC 20037
Tel. (202) 887-0706

Condominium Buyers Guide. National Association of Home Builders, 15th and M St. NW, Washington, DC 20005, Tel. (202) 822-0200.

Questions and Answers About Condominiums. U.S. Department of Housing and Urban Development. 53-page booklet from the U.S. Consumer Information Center, Pueblo, CO 81002.

Accessory Apartments and ECHO Housing

Hare, Patrick H. *Accessory Apartments: Using Surplus Space in Single Family Housing.* 1981. American Planning Association, 1313 E. 60 St., Chicago, IL 60637. $10.00. Relevant zoning issues and sample language for a zoning amendment to permit accessory apartments.

———. *ECHO Housing.* Available from AARP (see General Resources).

Continuing Care and Retirement Communities

American Association of Homes for the Aging. *National Continuing Care Directory* (an AARP book). Glenview, Illinois: Scott, Foresman. Provides basic information on some 400 continuing-care communities.

A Consumer Guide to Life Care Communities. National Consumers League, 815 15 St. NW, Suite 516, Washington, DC 20005. Tel. (202) 639-8140. $3.00.

The Continuing Care Retirement Community: A Guidebook for Consumers. American Associations of Homes for the Aging, 1129 20 St. NW, Suite 400, Washington, DC 20036. Tel. (202) 296-5960. $2.00. Checklist of facts and examples of contracts for CCRCs.

The Directory of Retirement Communities in the United States. Published by the Institute of Gerontology, University of Michigan, Ann Arbor, MI 48109. This listing of 2,300 retirement communities is in many public libraries.

Independent Living Research Utilization (ILRU) Project
  3233 Weslayan
  Houston, TX 77027
  Tel. (713) 960-9961
ILRU is a national center for information, training, and technical assistance in the field of independent living. Write for a publication list including a list of independent living programs which is updated quarterly. Their comprehensive survey of independent living programs, the *Annotated Registry of Independent Living Programs*, is currently being revised and will provide information on services, eligibility, clients' ages, location, and other material.

Home Care

See Resources—Caregiving.

WORK AND RETIREMENT

Organizations

American Association of Retired Persons (AARP) (see under General Resources). Their Institute for Lifetime Learning helps older persons pursue educational and career changes.

American Civil Liberties Union (see Resources —Money Matters). The ACLU publishes a series of useful inexpensive books on workers' rights, such as *The Rights of Women* and *The Rights of Employees*. Ask for their list of titles.

American Federation of State, County and Municipal Employees
  1625 L St. NW
  Washington, DC 20036
This union has provided leadership in the fight for pay equity and is a good source of information and support for women workers.

Coalition of Labor Union Women
  15 W. Union Square
  New York, NY 10003
  Tel. (212) 242-0700

Offers programs and resources for employed women, including a committee for older and retired women workers. Ask for their pamphlet on organizing women workers. The CLUW Center for Education and Research is located at 2000 P St. NW, Suite 615, Washington, DC 20036. Tel. (202) 296-3408.

Displaced Homemakers Network
  1411 K St., #930
  Washington, DC 20005
  Tel. (202) 628-6767
Over 900 programs serving displaced homemakers nationwide. The national network will put you in touch with the services nearest you. Their programs include job clubs specifically designed to make job hunting a group project instead of the lonely and frustrating burden that it usually is. In such activities as peer counseling (one person acting as a sounding board for the other) women draw on their life experience to help someone else with similar problems.

Elderhostel
  100 Boylston St., Suite 200
  Boston, MA 02116
  Tel. (617) 426-7788
Short-term campus-based educational experiences for older adults. Three seasonal catalogs.

Gray Panthers (see General Resources) has done excellent work toward abolishing mandatory retirement.

National Commission on Working Women
  1325 G St.
  Washington, DC 20005
  Tel. (202) 737-5764
Committed to promoting the rights of working women, they are especially concerned with ageism, and they provide information about employment rights as well as facts about older working women.

National Committee on Pay Equity
  1201 16 St. NW, Room 222
  Washington, DC 20036
  Tel. (202) 882-7304
Offers information and support on pay equity, including a pamphlet "Women of Color and Pay Equity" published in collaboration with the National Institute for Women of Color.

9 to 5 National Association of Working Women
   1223 Huron Road
   Cleveland, OH 44115
A national association of women office workers. Membership dues based on income include a bimonthly newsletter and discounts on publications such as books and pamphlets on automation, stress, and occupational health and hazards.

Older Women's League (OWL) (see General Resources) has a Task Force on Women and Work and publishes "Gray Papers" on a variety of topics, including women and work. Their pamphlet *Older Women and Job Discrimination: A Primer* (1984) is indispensable to women fighting unfair treatment at work and is a bargain at $1.50. The pamphlet discusses kinds of discrimination and contains a list of Equal Employment Opportunity Commission (EEOC) field offices.

Retired Senior Volunteer Program (RSVP). Jointly funded by the Federal Government and local communities, RSVP's purpose is to enable older persons to use their time, experience, and skills to benefit their communities. Look in your phone book under Elder Services—Volunteer Opportunities, or check with your area Agency on Aging.

Volunteer—The National Center for Citizen Involvement
   P.O. Box 4179
   Boulder, CO 80306
   Tel. (303) 447-0492
Seeks to encourage more Americans to become volunteers. Acts as a clearinghouse for volunteer programs. Maintains a network of 300 affiliated voluntary action centers.

U.S. Department of Labor
   Bureau of Labor Statistics
   441 G St. NW
   Washington, DC 20212
   Tel. (202) 523-1239
An excellent source of general statistical information on working women.

Books

Allen, Jeffry G., and Jess Gorkin. *Finding the Right Job at Midlife.* New York: Simon and Schuster, 1985. For women and men coping with fear of younger competitors. Layoff survival kit and how to recognize signs of a coming layoff.

Anzalone, Joan, ed. *Good Works: A Guide to Careers in Social Change.* New York: Dembner Books, 1985. Lists 600 organizations in the U.S., their starting salaries and contact persons. Regional and topical index.

Berman, Eleanor, ed. *Re-Entering: Successful Back-to-Work Strategies for Women Seeking a Fresh Start.* New York: Crown, 1980.

Better Late Than Never: Financial Aid for Re-entry Women Seeking Education and Training. Women's Equity Action League (see General Resources), 50 pp. $10.00. May be found in libraries and college financial aid offices.

Bolles, Richard Nelson. *The New Quick Job-Hunting Map.* Berkeley, California: Ten Speed Press, 1985.

———. *The 1986 What Color Is Your Parachute.* Berkeley, California: Ten Speed Press, 1986. Job-hunting and career-changing guidebook. Detailed and cheerful advice.

Brudney, Juliet F., and Hilda Scott. *Beyond the Gray Horizon: Job-keeping and Job-seeking When You Are Over Fifty.* New York: Simon and Schuster, forthcoming. Interviews with 150 women and men about the growing difficulties faced by older workers.

Catalyst. *Upward Mobility: A Comprehensive Career Advancement Plan for Women Determined to Succeed in the Working World.* New York: Holt, Rinehart & Winston, 1981.

———. *When Can You Start? The Complete Job Search Guide for Women of All Ages.* New York: Macmillan, 1981.

Chastain, Sherry. *Winning the Salary Game.* New York: Wiley, 1980. Indispensable tool for demystifying salary negotiations.

Committee on an Aging Society, Institute of Medicine and National Research Council. *America's Aging: Productive Roles in an Older Society.*

Washington, DC: National Academy Press, 1986. Research and analysis of the role of older volunteers.

Fillmore, Mary D. *A Foot in the Door: Women MBAs in the Eighties.* Boston: G. K. Hall, 1987. Provocative assessment of the pros and cons of an MBA degree for women's chances for advancement in organizations. Includes an excellent chapter on starting one's own business.

Groneman, Carol, and Mary Beth Norton, eds. *To Toil the Livelong Day: America's Women at Work, 1780–1980.* Ithaca, New York: Cornell University Press, 1987.

Kenan, Regina, Susan Klitzman, Lin Nelson. *Resource Guide on Women's Occupational and Environmental Health.* 1987. National Women's Health Network (see General Health resources).

Malos, Ellen, ed. *The Politics of Housework.* New York: Schocken, 1980. Anthology includes the groundbreaking article of that same title by Pat Mainardi.

Matthaei, Julie A. *An Economic History of Women in America: Women's Work, the Sexual Division of Labor, and the Development of Capitalism.* New York: Schocken, 1982. Historical and contemporary perspectives on women's work in the labor force and in the home.

Mendelsohn, Pam. *Happier by Degrees—The Most Complete Sourcebook for Women Who Are Considering Going Back to School.* New York: Dutton, 1980.

Miller, Luree. *Late Bloom: New Lives for Women.* New York: Paddington Press, 1979. Women find new directions at midlife, especially in education, creativity, and work.

Moore, Lynda L., ed. *Not as Far as You Think: The Realities of Working Women.* Lexington, MA: D.C. Heath/Lexington Books, 1986. Useful, up-to-date articles on such issues as women as bosses, and older women working for younger women.

Ruddick, Sara, and Pamela Daniels, eds. *Working It Out: 23 Women Writers, Artists, Scientists,* *and Scholars Talk About Their Lives and Work.* New York: Pantheon, 1977.

Scollard, Jeannette B. *The Self-Employed Woman: How to Start Your Own Business and Gain Control of Your Life.* New York: Simon and Schuster, 1985. A step-by-step guide to starting and managing one's own business, with attention to problems and issues that women are likely to face.

Sher, Barbara, with Anne Gottlieb. *Wishcraft: How to Get What You Really Want.* New York: Ballantine, 1979. How to learn about yourself and what you want. How to get help for brainstorming, networking, and support.

Shields, Laurie. *Displaced Homemakers: Fighting for a New Life.* New York: McGraw-Hill, 1981. An exciting account of women's struggles to win recognition for displaced homemakers and to establish new lives. Available from Older Women's League (see General Resources). $7.00.

Shuman, Nancy, and William Lewis. *Back to Work: How to Re-enter the Working World.* New York: Barron's, 1985. Practical basic advice. Includes descriptions of new automated equipment a woman reentering the business world might encounter for the first time.

Stolz, Barbara Ann. *Still Struggling: America's Low-Income Working Women Confronting the 1980s.* Lexington, Massachusetts: DC. Heath/Lexington Books, 1985. In a scholarly yet eminently readable piece of work, the author analyzes the complex web of social and individual factors that can keep women poor.

Szinovacz, Maxine, ed. *Women and Retirement: Policy Implications of Recent Research.* Beverly Hills, California: Sage Publications, 1982.

Walshok, Mary Lindenstein. *Blue Collar Women: Pioneers on the Male Frontier.* New York: Anchor/Doubleday, 1981.

Editors of Working Woman, with Gay Bryant. *The Working Woman Report: Succeeding in Business in the 80s.* New York: Simon and Schuster, 1984.

Other Publications

How to Get College Credit for What You Learned as a Homemaker or Volunteer. Educational Testing Service, Princeton, NJ 08540.

Shea, Beverly. "Late Bloomers: They Got Their First Jobs at 50." *Ms.*, November 1985.

Wilkinson, Carroll Wetzel. "Work: Challengers to Occupational Segregation." In Mary McFeely, ed., *The Woman's Annual*, No. 5. Boston: G. K. Hall, 1986, pp. 149–67. Article focuses on female pioneers in nontraditional jobs, especially blue-collar jobs. Includes an extensive bibliography.

MONEY MATTERS: THE ECONOMICS OF AGING FOR WOMEN

Organizations

American Association of Retired Persons (AARP) (see General Resources)

American Civil Liberties Union
132 W. 43 St.
New York, NY 10036
Publishes a series of helpful books on legal and financial issues such as *The Rights of Single People; The Rights of Gay People;* and *The Rights of Crime Victims*. Write for their literature list.

Center for Popular Economics
P.O. Box 785
Amherst, MA 01004
Tel. (413) 545-0743
Each summer faculty from the University of Massachusetts at Amherst conduct week-long intensive workshops for activists to help them understand how the economy works. Scholarships available.

Developmental Disabilities State Protection and Advocacy Agencies. These agencies, in each state, help protect your legal rights if you should become disabled. They will advocate for you with the Social Security system and in cases of job discrimination. A social service agency can put you in touch with the office in your state.

Gray Panthers (see General Resources). The Panthers publish useful material on older women's economic and financial problems and chapters often organize around economic issues affecting older women.

National Community Action Agency Directors Association
1411 K St. NW, Suite 1010
Washington, DC 20005
Tel. (202) 737-9895
Community Action Program (CAP) agencies are antipoverty programs. They often provide services for low-income elders and can help you find out if you are eligible for public assistance. The national office can help you find the CAP agency nearest you.

National Federation for Consumer Credit
8701 Georgia Ave., Suite 507
Silver Spring, MD 20910

Nolo Press
950 Parker St.
Berkeley, CA 94710
Publishes a newsletter which helps the lay reader deal with legal issues. Also publishes sourcebooks, workbooks, and computer software about benefits, entitlements, wills, and other financial and legal matters. Write for their list.

Older Women's League (see General Resources). OWL publishes pamphlets on various economic issues including one on no-fault divorce and "Women and Pensions."

Organization for the Enforcement of Child Support
119 Nicodemus Road
Reiserstown, MD 21136
Tel. (301) 833-2458
Works with all branches and levels of government to improve the child-support enforcement

system. Educates legislators, courts, and the public on the problems involved in collecting child support, makes people aware of their rights under current child-support laws. Send $2.00 for initial mailing. Newsletter by donation.

The Social Investment Forum
    Franklin Research and Development
    711 Atlantic Ave., 5th floor
    Boston, MA 02111
Ask for their directory, *Social Investment Services: A Guide to Forum Members*. Socially responsible investment opportunities, advisers, investment funds, including community-targeted programs and socially responsive tax shelters.

The Women's Foundation
    3543 18th St.
    San Francisco, CA 94110
    Tel. (415) 431-1290
Raises money to fund women's and girls' projects in Northern California. Special focus on women over forty and women over sixty.

Periodicals

Dollars & Sense. 38 Union Square, Somerville, MA 02143. Explains in everyday language current economic issues and trends from an activist's perspective. Covers women's issues often, but not exclusively.

Goodmoney. 28 Main St., Montpelier, VT 05602. Looks at traditional and alternative investments. A newsletter for social investing that uses a minimum of technical language.

Insight. 711 Atlantic Ave., 5th fl., Boston, MA 02111. Analyzes the impact of social issues on the financial and economic environment. An advisory letter for social investing.

Money. Box 2519, Boulder, CO 80322. Overview of current financial problems facing individuals and families. Written in understandable language; often includes a case study.

Progress. Women for Economic Justice, 145 Tremont St., Boston, MA 02111. Quarterly publica-

tion discussing economic issues of concern to women, such as pay equity, welfare, and economic literacy.

Books and Other Publications

Bove, Alexander A., Jr. *Joint Property*. New York: Simon and Schuster, 1982. See especially Chapter 7, "Joint Bank Accounts—the Poor Man's Will," and Chapter 12, "Avoiding Probate Through Joint Accounts and Other Bad Ideas."

Burts, Bettina. *The Political Economy of Women*. New York: Harper & Row, 1985.

Card, Emily. *Staying Solvent: A Guide to Equal Credit for Women*. New York: Holt, Rinehart & Winston, 1985. How to handle sex discrimination in obtaining consumer credit.

Chesler, Phyllis, with Jane Goodman. *Women, Money, and Power*. New York: Morrow, 1976. An excellent book probing the attitudes and institutions that keep women afraid of money.

Domini, Amy L., and Peter D. Kinder. *Ethical Investing: How to Make Profitable Investments Without Sacrificing Your Principles*. Reading, Massachusetts: Addison-Wesley, 1986. Highly recommended.

Harrington, Geri. *The Health Insurance Fact & Answer Book*. New York: Harper & Row, 1985. Tells how to shop for health insurance; examines the gap between Medicare and health insurance and looks at sex-discrimination issues.

Harwood, Norma. *A Woman's Legal Guide to Separation and Divorce in All 50 States*. New York: Scribner, 1985.

Hughes, Theodore E., and David Klein. *A Family Guide to Estate Planning, Funeral Arrangements, and Settling an Estate After Death*. New York: Scribner, 1983.

Jehle, Faustin. *The Complete & Easy Guide to Social Security and Medicare*. Madison, Connecticut: Fraser, 1983. Explains how these systems work, how to calculate the benefits you are entitled to, and how to obtain them.

Kingson, Eric R., Barbara A. Hirshorn, and Linda K. Harootyan. *The Common Stake: The Interdependence of Generations.* A report of The Gerontological Society of America debunking the myth of competition between generations for public funds. Available from Seven Locks Press, P.O. Box 27, Cabin John, MD 20818.

Lasson, Kenneth, and the Public Citizen Litigation Group. *Representing Yourself: What You Can Do Without a Lawyer.* New York: Farrar, Straus & Giroux, 1983.

Matthaei, Julie. *An Economic History of Women in America.* New York: Schocken, 1982. Fascinating discussion of the changing definitions of women's work and its effect on family patterns and the concept of "femininity."

Olson, Laura Katz. *The Political Economy of Aging.* New York: Columbia University Press, 1982. How class, sex, and race shape our experience of old age. Alternative social policies toward the aging.

On the Other Side of Easy Street: Myths and Facts About the Economics of Old Age, 1987. A single free copy is available from the Villers Foundation, 1334 G St. NW, Washington, DC 20005, Tel. (202) 628-3030. Additional copies $5.00 each.

Porter, Sylvia. *Sylvia Porter's New Money Book for the 1980s.* Garden City, New York: Doubleday, 1979. An encyclopedia of personal finances.

Quinn, Jane Bryant. *Everyone's Money Book.* New York: Delacorte, 1979. Starts with the basics. Detailed but easy to follow.

Rix, Sara E. *Older Women: The Economics of Aging.* This and other excellent publications are available from Women's Research and Educational Institute, 1700 18 St. NW, Suite 400, Washington, DC 20009. $5.50. Packed with data on the financial situation of older women.

Sidel, Ruth. *Women and Children Last: The Plight of Poor Women in Affluent America.* New York: Viking Penguin, 1986. Excellent chapter on poor older women, but summary chapters mainly concerned with younger women and children.

"Social Security: A Woman's Issue," recently updated by the Seattle/King County chapters of OWL and NOW analyzes Social Security as it affects women of all ages. Write to Social Security Book, 1115 19th Ave. E., Seattle, WA 98112. Single copy $1.50. Ten or more copies at reduced rates.

Status Report on Displaced Homemakers in the U.S., 1987. Order from Displaced Homemakers Network (see p. 448). Full report $16.50; summary $3.00.

Storey, James R. *Older Americans in the Reagan Era.* Washington, DC: Urban Institute Press, 1983.

Supplemental Social Security Income: The Promise and the Performance. SOS Education Fund, 1201 16 St. NW, Suite 222, Washington, DC 21136. Single free copy; bulk rates available.

Takas, Marianne. *Child Support: A Complete Up-to-Date Authoritative Guide to Collecting Child Support.* New York: Harper & Row, 1985.

Warschaw, Tessa Albert. *Rich Is Better.* New York: Doubleday, 1985. Takes a brisk approach to the intersection of money and psychological issues in women's lives, with good sections on divorce and using financial experts effectively. The emphasis on individual initiative obscures the fact that women's poverty is part of a pervasive economic system.

Webster, Bryce, and Robert L. Perry. *The Complete Social Security Handbook.* New York: Dodd Mead, 1983. Very clear, with a good chapter on women.

Weitzman, Lenore. *The Divorce Revolution: The Unexpected Social and Economic Consequences for Women and Children in America.* New York: Free Press, 1985.

Workbooks

These books contain worksheets for budgets, insurance and retirement planning, credit analysis, net worth, and helpful discussions about using the data. (Interestingly, all were written by women.)

Levin, Elizabeth. *Your Personal Financial Fitness Program*. Revised ed., 1987. Facts on File Publications, 460 Park Ave. S., New York, NY 10016, Tel. (800) 322-8755.

Phillips, Carole. *The Money Workbook for Women*. New York: Arbor House, 1982.

Sohl, Joyce D. *Managing Our Money: Workbook on Women and Personal Finances*. Service Center, General Board of Global Ministries, 7820 Reading Road, Cincinnati, OH 45237.

Curriculum

Facing Our Future is an education-for-aging program for midlife women available from the National Council on the Aging (see General Resources).

CAREGIVING

Organizations

Children of Aging Parents (CAPS)
  2761 Trenton Road
  Levittown, PA 19056
  Tel. (215) 547-1070
CAPS is a nonprofit volunteer organization that teaches coping skills, offers support, guidance, and referrals to appropriate professionals and agencies. CAPS actively helps start other, similar support groups, locally and across the country and overseas. Publishes a bimonthly newsletter, fact sheets, and manuals such as "Starting Self-Help Groups for Caregivers of the Elderly." They can make referrals to social service agencies in many communities.

The National Council on the Aging (see General Resources) has a Family Caregivers Program that provides literature and other resources including guidelines and ideas for caregivers' support groups and a manual providing a model for respite care.

National Women's Law Center
  1616 P St. NW
  Washington, DC 20036
  Tel. (202) 328-5160

If you provide care for a dependent member of your household at home, you may be eligible for tax relief. The NWLC gathers and provides information on the Dependent Care Tax Credit for Federal and state taxes.

Older Women's League (OWL) (see General Resources) has task forces on caregiving issues in many local chapters. These usually begin as study groups and move on to take action, such as organizing a conference and/or working for legislation and programs to provide support for caregivers. Write for their pamphlet *Till Death Do Us Part: Caregiving Wives of Severely Disabled Husbands*. Gray Paper #7, 1982. OWL members in California are at work on a book about caregiving to be titled *Women Take Care*.

Books

Bayless, Pamela J., ed. *Caring for Dependent Parents*. Research Institute of America, 90 Fifth Ave., New York, NY 10011. Well-written 58-page pamphlet covering long-term care of aging parents, including financial, legal, emotional, and psychological issues.

Cicirelli, Victor G. *Helping Elderly Parents*. Boston: Auburn House, 1981. Results of two studies sponsored by AARP (see General Resources) demonstrate the extent to which adult children support and care for elder parents. Results suggest that adult children serve as coordinators of other service providers and that there is a need for promoting self-help approaches for elders.

Dass, Ram, and Paul Gorman. *How Can I Help? Stories and Reflections on Service*. New York: Knopf, 1985. Accounts by volunteers tied together by the authors' reflections on such topics as natural compassion, social action, burnout. In one particularly useful section they discuss the importance of communicating trust and respect rather than self-righteousness in order to be an effective helper.

Hooyman, Nancy R., and Wendy Lustbader. *Taking Care: Supporting Older Women and Their Families*. New York: Free Press, 1986. An excellent book of strategies for coping. Reports on the various lifestyles of caregivers from nuclear families to gay and lesbian couples.

Lester, Andrew D., and Judith L. Lester. *Understanding Aging Parents*. Christian Care Books #8. Philadelphia: Westminster Press, 1980. Strong Christian viewpoint, but provides sound guidance for all readers.

MacLean, Helene. *Caring for Your Parents*. New York: Doubleday, 1986.

Portnow, Jay, and Martha Houtman. *Home Care for the Elderly: The First Guide for the Millions of Americans Caring for Elderly Loved Ones*. New York: McGraw-Hill, 1987. A doctor and nurse help home caregivers improve the quality of life of the ill or bedfast person. Includes nutrition and exercise, adaptive gadgets, personal hygiene, signs of illness, care for the bedfast, resources, and specialized help.

Rubin, Dianne. *Caring: A Daughter's Story*. New York: Holt, Rinehart & Winston, 1982. Honest account of one woman's feelings as a primary caregiver.

Silverstone, Barbara, and Helene K. Hyman. *You and Your Aging Parent: The Modern Family's Guide to Emotional, Physical and Financial Problems*. Rev. ed. New York: Pantheon, 1981. Comprehensive, well-written guide for anyone who is a caregiver or expects to be one.

Other Publications

Miller, Dorothy. "The Sandwich Generation: Adult Children of the Aging." *Social Work*, Vol. 26, September 1981, pp. 419–23.

Parent Care: Resources to Assist Family Caregivers. Gerontology Center, 316 Strong Hall, University of Kansas, Lawrence, KS 66045. An excellent newsletter of articles, book reviews, and other up-to-date information equally useful to family caregivers and professionals.

Rathbone-McCuan, Eloise. "Geriatric Day Care: A Family Perspective." *Gerontologist*, Vol. 16, 1976, pp. 517–21.

Robinson, Betsy. "Validation of a Caregiver Strain Index." *Journal of Gerontology*, Vol. 38, 1983, pp. 344–48.

Rubin, Shelley S. *Family Caregivers: The Invisible Network of Long-Term Care*. 1986. Provocative analysis of feminist and intergenerational issues in caregiving with proposed models for a progressive public policy to address these issues. Unitarian Universalist Service Committee, 78 Beacon St., Boston, MA 02108. $2.50 plus postage.

Silverman, A., C. Brahce, C. Zielinski. *As Parents Grow Older: A Manual for Developing Community-Based Support Groups for Families of Aged Persons*. Ann Arbor, Michigan: Institute of Gerontology, University of Michigan, 1981.

Sommers, Tish. "Caregiving: A Woman's Issue." *Generations*, Fall 1985, pp. 9–13.

"Who's Taking Care of Our Parents?" *Newsweek*, May 6, 1985.

Home Care

How to Hire Helpers: A Guide for Helpers and Their Families. Task Force on Aging, Church Council of Greater Seattle, 4759 15 NE, Seattle, WA 98105. $2.00; bulk rates available. Discounts for quantity purchases. Emphasizes the importance of developing a job description for the helper and offers a sample contract form and a checklist to use in interviews.

National Home Care Council, Inc.
A division of Foundation for Hospice and Home Care, Inc.
519 C St. NE
Washington, DC 20002
Tel. (202) 547-6586
Has many publications including *All About Home Care: A Consumer's Guide*, which was published with the Better Business Bureau. $2.00 plus stamped self-addressed envelope.

Home Health Aid Catalogs

Medical supply stores can help you get equipment and are aware of what Medicare and Medicaid will or will not pay for. Their catalogs offer ideas for helpful adaptive devices and their rental and purchase prices. Catalogs may also be available at rehabilitation hospitals, pharmacies that deal in home health equipment, and major catalog department stores. For example, the *Sears Home Health Aid Catalog* can be ordered from any Sears catalog store. In addition, there are small mail-order catalogs, such as *Comfortably Yours: Aids for Easier Living*, which includes a range of products and clothing to reduce discomforts stemming from minor conditions to serious illnesses. Write to them at 52 West Hunter Avenue, Maywood, NJ 07607. Or call (202) 368-0400. These catalogs offer many practical items that make it easier for someone disabled, for example, by crippling arthritis, to feed her/himself, pull up zippers, open bottles and perform many other daily chores that are otherwise difficult. (See section on adapting housing in the chapter Housing Alternatives, p. 157.)

To Find Help for Elder Relatives Who Live at a Distance

Agencies such as Family Service Agencies, Jewish Family Service, and Catholic Family Service in your community can refer you to agencies in your relative's community that are capable of providing services and keeping you in touch with your relative's condition and needs.

Family Services of America
  (Counseling and Referrals)
  11700 West Lake Park Drive
  Park Place
  Milwaukee, WI 53224
  Tel. (414) 359-2111
Agencies in forty states provide counseling for families of the elderly and make referrals to other services.

Audiovisual

My Father, My Mother, an award-winning documentary, presents four examples of families dealing with the aging of a parent. Unusually candid film and videotape spark identification and helpful discussion. Order from Terra Nova Films, Inc., 9848 S. Winchester Ave., Chicago, IL 60643, Tel. (312) 881-8491.

UNDERSTANDING, PREVENTING, AND MANAGING MEDICAL PROBLEMS

GENERAL HEALTH

Organizations

Black Women's Health Project of the National Women's Health Network
  450 Auburn Ave. #157
  Atlanta, GA 30312
  Tel. (404) 659-3854
Programs for education and advocacy on Black women's health issues.

Center for Medical Consumers and Health Care Information
  237 Thompson St.
  New York, NY 10012
  Tel. (212) 674-7105
Free medical library for the lay public with a strong women's health section. Visit the library when you are in New York. It does not have a phone service. The center publishes a monthly newsletter, *Health Facts*, $18.00 per year.

Exceptional Cancer Patients
  2 Church St. S.
  New Haven, CT 06519
  Tel. (203) 865-8392
Started for people with cancer but now assists people with any catastrophic illness. Offers counseling and support groups in New Haven and New York City. Has catalog of audio- and videotapes and books based on the concepts of Bernie Siegel integrating self-healing with standard medical treatment. (See his book under Books and Other Publications, following this section.)

Health/Pac (Health Policy Advisory Center)
  17 Murray St.
  New York, NY 10007
  Tel. (212) 267-8890

A progressive health activist organization. Membership provides a discount on its publications and *Health PACKETS*, a newsletter, *Inside Friends*, and a bimonthly magazine, *Health/PAC Bulletin*.

National Women's Health Network
1325 G St. NW, Lower Level B
Washington, DC 20005
Tel. (202) 543-9222
The only national membership organization devoted exclusively to women and health; publishes bimonthly newsletter, *The Network News*, and monitors Federal health policy affecting women.

People's Medical Society
14 E. Minor St.
Emmaus, PA 18049
Tel. (215) 967-2136
A nonprofit citizens' action group committed to better, more responsive, and less expensive medical care. For a $15.00 yearly donation, members receive a bimonthly newsletter plus discounts on publications such as *Take This Book to the Hospital with You*.

Public Citizens Health Research Group
2000 P St. NW
Washington, DC 20036
Works to change the political and social problems in the health field by monitoring government agencies and initiating legal action and legislative change. Publishes a bimonthly newsletter, *Health Letter*, $9.00 per year. Publication list of excellent books and pamphlets such as *How to Compile a Consumer's Directory of Doctors and Their Fees* and *Compiling a Guide to Medicare Fees*. Membership dues: $20.00 per year.

Women's Health Information Center
Boston Women's Health Book Collective
47 Nichols Ave.
Watertown, MA 02172
Tel. (617) 924-0271
Materials used in writing this book will be donated to the WHIC and will be available for public use. The Center's collection of books, periodicals, and clippings includes extensive materials on birth control, abortion, and reproductive rights. Information requests by mail or phone are answered for a nominal fee or donation to cover costs.

Women's Midlife Resource Center
1825 Haight St.
San Francisco, CA 94117
Tel. (415) 221-7417

Books

Barice, E. Joan, with Kathleen Jonah. *The Palm Beach Long-Life Diet. A Total Health Plan for Men and Women Over 50*. New York: Simon and Schuster, 1985.

Brody, Elaine. *Mental and Physical Health Practices of Older People*. New York: Springer Publishing, 1985.

Brody, Jane. *The New York Times Guide to Personal Health*. New York: Random House/Times Books, 1982.

Butler, Robert N., and Myrna I. Lewis. *Aging & Mental Health*. St. Louis, Missouri: C.V. Mosby, 1983.

Corea, Gena. *The Hidden Malpractice: How American Medicine Mistreats Women*. Rev. ed. New York: Harper & Row, 1985. Remains the most stunning investigative report on American medicine's shameful history with regard to women.

Egginton, Mary, Maryann Kunigonis, Joan Mintz, and Dorothy Roser. *An Older Woman's Health Guide*. New York: McGraw-Hill, 1984. For women over sixty-five.

Feltin, Marie. *A Woman's Guide to Good Health After 50*. An AARP Book. Glenview, Illinois: Scott, Foresman, 1987.

Haug, Marie R., Amasa B. Ford, and Marian Sheafor. *The Physical and Mental Health of Aged Women*. New York: Springer Publishing, 1985.

Kahn, Ada P., and Linda Hughey Holt. *Midlife Health: Every Woman's Guide to Feeling Good*. New York: Facts-on-File, 1987. The material in this book is based on the concerns expressed in a survey of the 51-year-old primary author's high school and college classmates.

Kaptchuk, Ted. *The Web That Has No Weaver.* New York: Congdon and Weed, 1984. Explains the differences between Western and Eastern medicine and contains an excellent explanation of acupuncture.

Lettvin, Maggie. *Maggie's Women's Book.* Boston: Houghton Mifflin, 1980. See especially the warm-ups for early-morning stiffness, pp. 54–8.

Lewin, Ellen, and Virginia Oleson, eds. *Women, Health and Healing.* New York: Methuen, 1985.

Linde, Shirley, and Donald J. Carrow, eds. *The Directory of Holistic Medicine and Alternate Health Care Services in the U.S.,* 1986. Lists more than 1,000 practitioners, associations, schools, and publications in the holistic health field. Health Plus Publishers, P.O. Box 22001, Phoenix, AZ 85028, $6.95.

Murphy, Lois B. *The Home Hospital: How a Family Can Cope with Catastrophic Illness.* New York: Basic Books, 1982. A moving account of the author's care at home of her husband, who suffered from Parkinson's disease.

Pitzele, Sefra Kobrin. *We Are Not Alone: Learning to Live with Chronic Illness.* New York: Workman, 1986. A useful handbook on chronic illness that includes chapters on pain, health care and rights, finding help, and other important subjects. The chapter on adaptive living strategies contains photos of useful gadgets.

Siegel, Bernie. *Love, Medicine, and Miracles: Lessons Learned About Self-healing from a Surgeon's Experience With Exceptional Patients.* New York: Harper & Row, 1986. Helpful for anyone facing a life-threatening disease, especially cancer or AIDS.

Table Manners: A Guide to the Pelvic Examination for Disabled Women and Health Care Providers. Planned Parenthood, Education Dept., 1660 Bush St., San Francisco, CA 94109, Tel. (415) 441-5454 (TTY). $4.00. Bulk rate available. How to provide sensitive care to women with physical, visual, and hearing disabilities. Includes alternative positioning, transfers to the examining table, and other considerations.

Ways, Peter. *Take Charge of Your Health. The Guide to Personal Health Competence.* Lexington, Massachusetts: The Stephen Greene Press, 1985.

Other Publications

Aches and Pains: A Practical Guide to Diseases and Their Outcomes for the Elderly and Their Families. A new bimonthly newsletter published by the National Foundation for Long Term Health Care, 1200 15 St. NW, Washington, DC 20005. $12.00 per year. Free sample copy available.

A Friend Indeed: for women in the prime of life. An excellent newsletter written by one woman, including an exchange of information and self-help from readers. Ten issues a year for $20.00; back issues, $3.00. Write: Janine O'Leary Cobb, P.O. Box 9, NDG Station. Montreal H4A 3P4, Canada, Tel. (514) 481-9886.

Golub, Sharon, and Rita J. Freedman, eds. "Health Needs of Women as They Age." Special issue of *Women and Health,* Vol. 10, Nos. 2 and 3, Summer/Fall 1985.

Healthsharing. Women's Healthsharing, Box 230, Station M, Toronto, Ontario M6S 4T3, Canada. A quarterly newsletter covering a wide range of women's health concerns.

National Institute on Aging publishes *The Age Page.* These have been compiled under the name *Help Yourself to Good Health* and are sponsored for publication by the Pfizer Corporation. Type is large and comfortably readable for older eyes. Many topics are covered including arthritis, foot care, etc. Single copies are available free from Expand Associations PFP, 7923 Eastern Ave., Suite 400, Silver Spring, MD 20901.

Off Our Backs, 1841 Columbia Road NW, Room 212, Washington, DC 20009. An excellent feminist newspaper with regular coverage of women's health issues. Monthly, $12.50 per year.

Santa Fe Health Education Project. *Health Letter.* P.O. Box 577, Santa Fe, NM 87504-0577, Tel. (505) 982-3236. An excellent health education series in English and Spanish. Each issue covers a single subject on one long page. Back issues and bulk rates available. Subscription price is $6.50 for 12 new issues.

WomenWise, New Hampshire Feminist Health Center, 38 S. Main St., Concord, NH 03301, Tel. (603) 225-2739. An excellent publication that covers a wide variety of topics on women and health. Quarterly, $7.00 per year.

PROBLEMS IN THE MEDICAL CARE SYSTEM

Organizations

National Health Law Program, Inc.
  2639 South La Cienega Blvd.
  Los Angeles, CA 90034
  Tel. (213) 204-6010
Provides technical assistance and training to lawyers and advocates from all over the country focused on issues concerning access to health care for low-income people. Publishes a newsletter, *Health Advocate*, eight times each year. Publication list is available.

See other organizations under General Resources and under General Health.

Books and Other Publications

Annas, George. *The Rights of Hospital Patients: The Basic Guide to a Hospital Patient's Rights*. New York: Avon, 1974. Still useful for discussion of basic issues.

Committee on an Aging Society. Institute of Medicine and National Research Council. *America's Aging: Health in an Older Society*. Washington, DC: National Academy Press, 1986.

Dallek, Geraldine, et al., eds. *The Best Medicine. Organizing Local Health Care Campaigns*. The Villers Foundation, 1334 G St. NW, Washington, DC 20005, 1984. Single copy plus updates $7.00; bulk rates available. A useful manual for organizing to change the health care system.

Ehrenreich, John. *The Cultural Crisis of Modern Medicine*. New York: Monthly Review Press, 1978. Shows the influence of medicine on a broad range of fundamental values and human experiences in the West.

Fisher, Arlene. "Surgery: Always Get a Second Opinion." *Redbook*, Vol. 168, No. 3, January 1987, pp. 94–95, 132–35.

Harrington, Geri. *The Health Insurance Fact & Answer Book*. New York: Harper & Row, 1985. Tells how to shop for health insurance, examines the gap between Medicare and other health insurance, and looks at sex discrimination issues.

Knowing Your Rights. A Program on Medicare's Prospective Payment System. American Association of Retired Persons (AARP), 1909 K St. NW, Washington, DC 20049. Stock number D12330. Includes a complete listing of the Peer Review Organizations (PROs) in each state.

McKinlay, John, ed. *Issues in the Political Economy of Health Care*. London: Tavistock Publications, 1984. Essays by prominent critics arguing that profit-seeking capitalism is responsible for a worldwide medical-industrial complex that has lost its humane outlook since World War II.

Mechanic, David. *From Advocacy to Allocation*. New York: Free Press, 1986. Examines the problems of increased medical expenditures in the U.S. and argues for the greater involvement of people in their own care and prevention, and other ways to prevent abuses. Contains a chapter on older people.

Minkler, Meredith, and Carroll L. Estes, eds. *Readings in the Political Economy of Aging*. Farmingdale, New York: Baywood Publishing, 1984.

Older Women's League. *Gray Paper: Health Care Financing and Midlife Women: A Sick System*, 1986, $3.00. See General Resources under Organizations.

Oleson, Virginia, and Ellen Lewin, eds. *Women, Health and Social Policy*. New York: Tavistock Publications, 1984.

Plough, Alonzo L. *Borrowed Time: Artificial Organs and the Politics of Extending Lives*. Philadelphia: Temple University Press, 1986. Using the example of subsidies for kidney dialysis and transplantation, the author describes the conflict in our system between our commitment to free enterprise and cost-saving, and the ideal of high-quality services. This is an important discussion as more and more new medical technologies are used.

Public Citizen Health Research Group. *Medical Records: Getting Yours*, 1986, $5.00. See General Health resources under Organizations.

Sidel, Victor W., and Ruth Sidel. *A Healthy State. An International Perspective on the Crisis in United States Medical Care*. New York: Pantheon, 1977. Shows what the planned systems of four other nations have accomplished. Makes suggestions for how a national health service in the U.S. based on centralized standards and local implementation could be more effective and socially just.

Skolnick, Barbara. *Prescription for Action: A Guide to Community Health Reform*. An AARP publication (see General Resources). To encourage actions in other communities, this publication describes projects undertaken by local groups who wanted to "cut the cost and keep the care."

Staying Alive! is a quarterly newsletter published by health advocates who believe that access to quality health care is a right, not a privilege. It focuses on issues in Massachusetts but may interest and inspire advocates in other states. CommonHealth, c/o House Officers' Assn., HO Building Mezzanine, Boston City Hospital, 818 Harrison Ave., Boston, MA 02118. $10.00 per year.

Swenson, Norma, Diana Laskin Siegal, and Paula Brown Doress. "Women, Health, and Aging." In Mary Feeley, ed., *Women's Annual, Number 5, 1984–85*. Boston: G. K. Hall, 1985, pp. 22–42.

NURSING HOMES

Organizations

American Association of Homes for the Aged
  1050 17 St. NW, Suite 770
  Washington, DC 20005

Tel. (202) 296-5960
The national organization of nonprofit long-term care facilities offers numerous publications and other information. They support resident empowerment and have often sided with consumers on quality-care issues.

American Health Care Association
  1200 15 St. NW
  Washington, DC 20005
  Tel. (202) 833-2050
The national association of mostly for-profit long-term care providers. Although necessarily provider-oriented, the organization seeks consumer input, emphasizes family involvement, and pressures its members to provide high-quality care. Its numerous useful publications include facility selection, residents' rights, access to facilities, and health care decision-making.

The Gray Panthers (see General Resources) have over 100 local chapters; many of these advocate on behalf of, or in conjunction with, nursing home residents and their allies.

National Citizens' Coalition for Nursing Home Reform (NCCNHR)
  1825 Connecticut Ave. NW, #417B
  Washington, DC 20009
  Tel. (202) 797-0657
This nonprofit, consumer-based organization of over 250 groups and 300 individual members is the best source of information, publications, and analyses from an advocacy point of view. NCCNHR's goal is to improve long-term health care and quality of life for residents. They coordinate many special projects and respond to proposed new or revised laws and regulations. Ask for their list of publications, a sample newsletter, and for referral to advocacy groups in your area.

National Coalition of Resident Councils
  3231 First Ave. S.
  Minneapolis, MN 55408
  Tel. (612) 827-8151
Provides information and ideas on resident council development and publishes a newsletter. Works closely with the National Citizens' Coalition for Nursing Home Reform.

State Residents' Organizations

Coalition of Institutionalized Aged and Disabled
  Lehman College, Building T-3, Room 113A
  Bronx, NY 10468
  Tel. (212) 584-0990
The New York State coalition of residents' councils provides assistance and training for organizing residents' councils and coordinates advocacy activities on behalf of members. Materials available include an excellent videotape, "Resident Council Organizing." Call or write for other materials and fees.

L.I.F.E. (Living Is For the Elderly)
  19 Campbell St.
  Woburn, MA 01801
  Tel. (617) 933-9109
The Massachusetts residents' organization. Organizes residents to advocate on their own behalf, individually and in groups, in their own facilities and communities as well as with policymakers. Regular meetings, conferences, and other events educate residents, families, and staff, and encourage residents' independence and competence.

Nursing Home Residents Advisory Council
  3231 First Ave. S.
  Minneapolis, MN 55408
  Tel. (612) 827-8151
The Minnesota residents' organization provides assistance in organizing resident and family councils, and connects residents to policymakers. Has guidebook and slide show on resident council organizing.

Books and Other Publications

Bausell, R. Barker, and Michael A. Rooney. *How to Evaluate and Select a Nursing Home*. Emmaus, Pennsylvania: People's Medical Society, 1984.

Horn, Linda, and Elma Griesel. *Nursing Homes: A Citizen's Action Guide*. Boston: Beacon Press, 1977. Although somewhat dated, still a good resource for information on organizing, laws and regulations, innovations in nursing homes, and other issues.

Institute of Medicine. *Improving the Quality of Care in Nursing Homes*. Washington, DC: National Academy Press, 1987. Useful for citizens'

groups striving for higher standards in nursing homes.

Kautzer, Kathleen. "Empowering Nursing Home Residents: A Case Study of the LIFE Organization." In Shulamit Reinharz and Graham Rowles, eds., *Qualitative Gerontology*. New York: Springer Publishing, 1987. An in-depth study of the Massachusetts nursing home residents' organization.

Langer, Ellen. *The Psychology of Control*. Beverly Hills, California: Sage Publications, 1983. A compilation of research suggesting that increased responsibility for decision-making and an enhanced sense of competence may counteract the effects of institutionalization.

Mendelson, Mary Adelaide. *Tender Loving Greed*. New York: Vintage, 1975. The original investigation into profit-taking excesses in the nursing home industry. The report is still very useful for anyone interested in reform. The book was written before the growth of consumer and resident advocacy groups in the mid- to late seventies and some of the problems described have since been addressed by new laws and regulations.

Quinn, Mary Jo. *Elder Abuse and Neglect*. New York: Springer, 1986.

Sarton, May. *As We Are Now*. New York: W. W. Norton, 1973. A moving novel with a shock ending about a woman's experience in a badly run nursing home.

Straus, Murray, Suzanne Steinmetz, and Richard Gelles. *Behind Closed Doors*. Garden City, New York: Doubleday, 1980. A book about elder abuse.

U.S. Department of Health and Human Services. *How to Select a Nursing Home*, 1980. Obtain from the Government Printing Office, Washington, DC 20402. $4.75 including postage.

Vladeck, Bruce. *Unloving Care*. New York: Basic Books, 1980. One of the most thorough analyses of the history and practice of long-term care. It traces policy and other changes from the early twentieth century. A useful reference book.

Audiovisual

Rose by Any Other Name, by Judith Keller, an appealingly iconoclastic film that explores the lifelong need for affection, privacy, and sexual expression in the context of relationships among nursing home residents. Available for sale or rental from Multi-Focus, Inc., 1525 Franklin St., San Francisco, CA 94109, Tel. (800) 821-0514.

Agencies and Services

Many of the agencies and services that can help you with problems ranging from discrimination at admission to residents' rights violations are hard to find. Following is a list of potential sources of help and suggestions for finding them in your area.

Nursing home ombudsprograms investigate complaints related to residents' rights or resident care. Look for the state agency with a name such as aging, elder affairs, or elder services. Local ombudsprograms can be found through the state agency or through your area agency on aging, or legal services office.

Legal services (See National Health Law Program on page 459 and General Resources under Organizations.)

Licensing agencies are generally responsible for promulgating and enforcing regulations, inspecting facilities, and investigating complaints, including abuse. They are usually located in agencies for health, public health, health and human services, etc.

Area agencies on aging (See General Resources.)

Consumer protection may be covered through your state's attorney general's office and/or a department or office of consumer affairs.

Medicaid is usually administered through a state welfare, public assistance, or social services agency. A Medicaid fraud unit often is part of the Medicaid division, and suspicions of fraud and discrimination should be reported to them.

State nursing home associations, or provider groups, exist in most states and can provide

varied information. They are usually affiliates of the American Health Care Association and the American Association of Homes for the Aged (see above under Organizations).

JOINT AND MUSCLE PAIN, ARTHRITIS AND RHEUMATIC DISORDERS

Organizations

The Arthritis Foundation
1314 Spring St. NW
Atlanta, GA 30309
Tel. (404) 872-7100
Publishes booklets such as *Arthritis, The Basic Facts*, and *Osteoarthritis, A Handbook for Patients, Living and Loving with Arthritis*, and a quarterly newsletter, *National Arthritis News*. Has developed guidelines for aquatic exercise programs in cooperation with the YMCA. Has prescription discount service for members. Check your phone book for local chapters, which may have additional pamphlets.

The National Institute of Arthritis, Musculoskeletal, and Skin Diseases (NIAMSD)
Information Officer
Building 31, Room 9A04
9000 Rockville Pike
Bethesda, MD 20891
Tel. (202) 496-3583
NIAMSD has publications. Write them for the address of the federally funded research and treatment center for arthritis nearest you. Also funds:

Arthritis Information Clearinghouse
P.O. Box 9782
Arlington, VA 22209
Tel. (703) 588-8250
Offers materials and bibliographies.

Books and Other Publications

American Medical Association. *Guide to Back Care*. Rev. ed. New York: Random House, 1984.

Arthritis Foundation, Arthritis Health Professions Section. *Self-Help Manual for Patients with*

Arthritis. 2nd ed., 1980, catalog No. 4081. Available from The Arthritis Foundation (see under Organizations) or from local chapters. Contains many suggestions for conserving energy and protecting joints, a bibliography, and more than 300 addresses to purchase self-help aids.

Berson, Dvera, with Sander Roy. *Pain-Free Arthritis.* New York: Simon and Schuster, 1978. At age sixty-five, Berson demonstrated the value of persistent exercise in water.

Carr, Rachel. *Arthritis: Relief Beyond Drugs.* New York: Harper & Row, 1981. Contains yoga techniques.

Fries, James F. *Arthritis: A Comprehensive Guide.* Rev. ed. Reading, Massachusetts: Addison-Wesley, 1986. Includes excellent brief descriptions of arthritis in nontechnical language.

Klein, Arthur C., and Dava Sobel. *Backache Relief.* New York: Random House/Times Books, 1985. Read this one first if you have back pain. Lists 25 often-mentioned ways to free yourself from back pain.

Krewer, Semyon, with Ann Edgar. *The Arthritis Exercise Book.* New York: Simon & Schuster/ Cornerstone Library, 1981. Offers preventive exercises for everyone and corrective exercises for those with arthritis.

Kushner, Irving, et al., eds. *Understanding Arthritis.* Published for the Arthritis Foundation by Consumers Union, Mount Vernon, NY, 1984. Especially good section on fibrositis.

Lettvin, Maggie. *Maggie's Back Book.* Boston: Houghton Mifflin, 1976. Useful when your back hurts. The author tells you how the exercise will ultimately be done, and then takes you through the steps to get there.

Lorig, Kate, and James F. Fries. *The Arthritis Helpbook.* Rev. ed. Reading, Massachusetts: Addison-Wesley, 1986. Developed with participants of arthritis self-management classes, this book explains what the doctor may not.

Root, Leon, and Thomas Kiernan. *Oh, My Aching Back.* New York: New American Library,

1985. Recommended by people who regularly do the exercises.

White, Augustus A., III. *Your Aching Back. A Doctor's Guide to Relief.* New York: Bantam, 1983.

Temporomandibular Joints

Organizations

Jaw Joints & Allied Musculo-Skeletal Disorders Foundation, Inc. (JJAMD)
   Forsyth's Research Institute
   140 Fenway
   Boston, MA 02115
   Tel. (617) 262-5200 Ext. 360 or (617) 266-2550
Membership, pamphlets, support groups, lectures and seminars. Starting state chapters.

Books and Other Publications

Ahlin, Jeffrey H. *Maxillofacial Orthopedics: A Clinical Approach for the Growing Child.* Chicago: Quintessence Publishing, 1984. Chapter 10 on TMJ is useful for adults also.

American Dental Association. *Temporomandibular Disorders.* 211 E. Chicago Ave., Chicago, IL 60611. Single copy available free.

Lupus

Organizations

American Lupus Society
   23751 Madison St.
   Torrance, CA 90505
   Tel. (213) 373-1335
Literature, media awareness, and fund-raising for research.

The Lupus Foundation of America, Inc.
   11921A Olive Blvd.
   St. Louis, MO 63141
   Tel. (314) 872-9036
A dues organization. Chapters offer medical referrals, educational materials, and counseling.

Books and Other Publications

Aladjem, Henrietta. *Understanding Lupus.* Rev. ed. New York: Scribner, 1985.

OSTEOPOROSIS

Books and Other Publications

DeLorey, Catherine. "Osteoporosis—Not Just for Older Women." *WomenWise,* Summer 1984, pp. 6–7 (see General Health resources, under Other Publications).

A Friend Indeed: for women in the prime of life. Entire issue, Volume III, No. 4, September 1985, is on osteoporosis (see General Health resources under Other Publications).

Greenwood, Sadja. *Menopause, Naturally.* San Francisco: Volcano Press, 1984. A simply written and well-balanced book by a woman physician. Has chapters on osteoporosis, exercise, nutrition, and estrogen replacement therapy.

Goulart, Frances S. *Nutritional Self Defense.* New York: Dodd Mead, 1984. A commonsense, helpful approach to nutrition.

Kamen, Betty, and Si Kamen. *Osteoporosis: What It Is, How to Prevent It, How to Stop It.* New York: Pinnacle Books, 1984. This is an extremely valuable aid to understanding the connection between nutrition and osteoporosis. Easy to read.

Midlife Wellness: A Journal for the Middle Years. Center for Climacteric Studies, University of Florida, 901 NW Eighth Ave., Suite B1, Gainesville, FL 32601. Four issues for $12.00. Written under medical auspices. Contains diverse materials about osteoporosis and menopause.

Notelovitz, Morris, and Marsha Ware. *Stand Tall: The Informed Woman's Guide to Preventing Osteoporosis.* Triad Publishing, P.O. Box 13096, Gainesville, FL 32604. An easy-to-understand explanation of the complex problem of osteoporosis.

"Osteoporosis. Part One: Screening Tests plus Prescription Drugs Blamed for Falls and Frac-

tures." *Health Letter,* Vol. 3, No. 5, May 1987, pp. 1–4; and "Part Two: Prevention and Treatment." *Health Letter,* Vol. 3, No. 6, June 1987, pp. 1–6. Excellent articles. The June issue contains information on the disintegration and dissolution times of various commercial calcium supplements. Public Citizen Health Research Group (see General Health resources under Organizations).

Porcino, Jane. *Growing Older, Getting Better: A Handbook for Women in the Second Half of Life.* Reading, Massachusetts: Addison-Wesley, 1983. Chapter on osteoporosis takes a strong stand against both estrogen and fluoride therapy.

Seaman, Barbara, and Gideon Seaman. *Women and the Crisis in Sex Hormones.* New York: Bantam, 1977. Has a chapter on osteoporosis containing an important history of the estrogen replacement therapy debates and information on nutrition and exercise.

Voda, Ann. *Menopause, Me and You: A Personal Handbook for Women.* Salt Lake City, Utah: College of Nursing, University of Utah. Has a section on osteoporosis. Pamphlet can be ordered from Ann M. Voda, 25 S. Medical Drive, Salt Lake City, UT 84112. $4.95 for a single copy. Bulk rates available.

DENTAL HEALTH

Organizations

American Dental Association
  Department of Public Information and Education
  211 E. Chicago Ave.
  Chicago, IL 60611
  Tel. (312) 440-2500
Many pamphlets available including *Periodontal Disease.* A single copy is free.

International Dental Health Foundation, Inc.
  11800 Sunrise Valley Drive
  Reston, VA 22091
Send $3.00 and a business-size self-addressed stamped envelope for information about the Keyes technique and referral to a dentist in your area trained in the technique.

Books and Other Publications

American Academy of Periodontology. *Consumers Guide to Periodontal Disease*. 211 E. Chicago Ave., Room 924, Chicago, IL 60611.

———. *Facts About Periodontal Disease, Edition II*. Address above.

American Dental Hygienists' Association. *A Beautiful Smile Is Ageless*. 444 N. Michigan Ave., Suite 3400, Chicago, IL 60611.

Denholtz, Melvin, and Elaine Denholtz. *How to Save Your Teeth and Your Money (A Consumers' Guide to Better, Less Costly Dental Care)*. New York: Van Nostrand Reinhold, 1980.

Finkelman, Ellen S., and Sharon Compton. "The Keyes Method of Alternative Periodontal Therapy: A Critical Review." *Dental Hygiene*, July 1985, pp. 302–5.

Mellberg, James R., et al. *Fluoride in Preventive Dentistry: Theory and Clinical Applications*. Chicago: Quintessence Publishing, 1983. Section on remineralization, pp. 51–9.

Non-Chew Cookbook. See Eating Well resources, under Cookbooks if you must eat soft foods.

Public Citizen Health Research Group. *Taking the Pain Out of Finding a Good Dentist*, 1975 (see General Health resources under Organizations). $1.00 plus handling.

URINARY INCONTINENCE

Organizations

Continence Restored, Inc.
 785 Park Ave.
 New York, NY 10021
Associated with Help for Incontinent People (HIP). Forming support groups with medically trained leaders. For information, send stamped self-addressed business-size envelope.

The Simon Foundation
 P.O. Box 815-M
 Wilmette, IL 60091
 Tel. (800) 23-SIMON

For a sample copy of *The Informer*, an informative and supportive quarterly newsletter, send a stamped self-addressed business-size envelope. Also publishes a list of urinary incontinence treatment centers.

Help for Incontinent People (HIP)
 P.O. Box 544
 502 Park Drive
 Union, SC 29379
 Tel. (803) 585-8789
  (803) 427-5434, after business hours
An international clearinghouse of information among lay people, medical professionals, industry, and social workers on services, treatments, and products available for people with incontinence. Publishes *The HIP Report*, a quarterly newsletter (annual subscription $5.00). A sample copy is available for $1.00 plus a stamped self-addressed business-size envelope. Also publishes *Resource Guide of Continent Aids and Services* for $3.00.

Books and Other Publications

Budoff, Penny Wise. "Urinary Tract Infections." Chapter 7, pp. 146–9. In *No More Hot Flashes and Other Good News*. New York: Putnam, 1983.

Farley, Dixie. "Incontinence Comes Out of the Closet." *FDA Consumer*, March 1987, pp. 5–9.

Fugh-Berman, Adriane. "Standard Bladder Infection Treatment May Bring On Interstitial Cystitis." *The Network News*, May/June 1985, pp. 4–5.

Gartley, Cheryle B., ed. *Managing Incontinence*. Ottawa, Illinois: Jameson Books, 1985. A pioneering book by the founder of The Simon Foundation offers experiences, advice, practical help, and encouragement for all those who live with or manage incontinence in themselves or others. Available from the foundation.

Hadley, Evan C. "Bladder Training and Related Therapies for Urinary Incontinence in Older People." *Journal of the American Medical Association*, Vol. 256, No. 3, July 18, 1986, pp. 372–9.

Kilmartin, Angela. *Cystitis: The Complete Self-Help Guide*. New York: Warner Books, 1980.

Lanson, Lucienne T. "Urinary System Disorders." In Patricia J. Cooper, ed. *Better Homes & Gardens Books: Women's Health & Medical Guide*. Des Moines, Iowa: Meredith Corp., 1981.

Lehman, Betsy A. "At Long Last, Help for the Incontinent." *The Boston Globe*, April 13, 1987.

"More Accurate Measures of Incontinence Replacing Bonney Test." *Ob. Gyn. News*, January 1984, pp. 15–31.

Robertson, Jack R. "Endoscopic Examination of the Urethra and Bladder." *Clinical Obstetrics and Gynecology*, Vol. 26, No. 2, June 1983, pp. 347–58.

Stanton, Stuart L. "What is the place of urodynamic investigations in a district general hospital?" *British Journal of Obstetrics and Gynaecology*, February 1983, pp. 97–9. Describes a typical program in England where they pay much more attention to incontinence than in the United States.

Staskin, David R. "Operations for the Treatment of Genuine Stress Incontinence in Female Patients." *The Informer*, Winter 1986, p. 1 (newsletter of The Simon Foundation).

"Symptoms Best Guide to Surgery for Urinary Stress Incontinence." *Ob. Gyn. News*, January 1984, pp. 1–14.

West, Joanne. "Urinary Problems Resulting from Hysterectomy." *HERS Newsletter*, April 1983, pp. 3–4.

Witherington, Roy. "Stress Urinary Incontinence: A Practical Protocol for Dx and Tx." *Geriatrics*, Vol. 37, No. 5, May 1982, pp. 38–43, 47.

Products

For products to aid bladder control, look in drug stores, medical supply stores, in novelty mail-order catalogs, and in catalogs such as Sears, Roebuck and Company's *Home Health Care Products*. Watch the ads for new products.

Freshette, 7415 Stewart & Gray, Downey, CA 90241, sells a small "urinary director" developed for the American Women's North Pole Expedition through which a woman can urinate without squatting or undressing.

HYSTERECTOMY AND OOPHORECTOMY

Organizations

HERS (Hysterectomy Educational Resources and Services)
   422 Bryn Mawr Ave.
   Bala Cynwyd, PA 19004
   Tel. (215) 667-7757
Provides information and counseling for women who have had hysterectomies and for those to whom hysterectomy has been recommended. Sponsors conferences in other cities. Quarterly newsletter, $15.00 per year.

Books and Other Publications

Budoff, Penny Wise. *No More Menstrual Cramps and Other Good News*. New York: Putnam, 1980. In her section on "precancerous conditions" she gives a description of the uterus from its healthy state to various diseased states and the chances of such conditions becoming cancerous. Helpful to avoid surgery but is uncritical of medication.

———. *No More Hot Flashes and Other Good News*. New York: Putnam, 1983. More of the same material as previous book but with a new section on ovarian tumors and ovarian cancer. Same caution regarding medication.

Cutler, Winifred B., Celso-Ramón García, and David A. Edwards. *Menopause, A Guide for Women and the Men Who Love Them*. New York: W. W. Norton, 1983. This book written by a team of researchers contains a well-documented chapter on hysterectomy. Easy-to-read language and new discoveries that are helpful.

Keyser, Herbert H. *Women Under the Knife*. Philadelphia: George F. Stickley Co., 1984. A gynecologist exposes some of the unethical, money-oriented practices of his colleagues in performing unnecessary D&Cs and hysterectomies. His emphasis is more on protecting younger women from such abuse, and he also fails to mention anything about adverse after-effects of the surgeries he denounces.

Lauersen, Nils. *Listen to Your Body.* New York: Simon and Schuster, 1982. A health-care guide by a gynecologist that contains vital information about myomectomy. (Not to be confused with his earlier book, *It's Your Body,* which contains some outdated information about sex after a hysterectomy.)

Mendelsohn, Robert. *Malpractice—How Doctors Manipulate Women.* Chicago: Contemporary Books, 1981. In the chapter "What Do You Need Your Uterus for Anyway?" Dr. Mendelsohn blasts medicine's condescending attitude toward women.

Morgan, Susanne. *Coping with a Hysterectomy.* New York: Dial, 1982. A highly recommended pioneer work that gives good suggestions for avoiding unnecessary surgery. Author is a sociologist who herself had a hysterectomy.

Network News. The March/April 1984 issue entitled "Midlife and Older Women: Taking Responsibility for Our Own Health" contains information about hysterectomy. The issue is available by sending $1.00 plus postage to the National Women's Health Network (see p. 457).

Stokes, Naomi Miller. *The Castrated Woman: What Your Doctor Won't Tell You About Hysterectomy.* New York: Franklin Watts, 1986. Takes a strong stand against hysterectomies but doesn't give much information about other health or medical actions to avoid them.

Wigfall-Williams, Wanda. *Hysterectomy: Learning the Facts, Coping with the Feelings, Facing the Future.* New York: Michael Kesend, 1986. Contains some useful information but does not strongly enough oppose unnecessary hysterectomies.

Audiovisual

Sudden Changes. The Cinema Guild, 1697 Broadway, New York, NY 10019, Tel. (212) 246-5522. Rental or purchase. Emphasis in myomectomy discussion is on younger women.

HYPERTENSION, HEART DISEASE, AND STROKE

Organizations

American Heart Association
  National Center
  7320 Greenville Ave.
  Dallas, TX 75231
  Tel. (214) 373-6300
Check your telephone directory or contact the National Center for the chapter nearest you. Publications available from local chapters include *An Older Person's Guide to Cardiovascular Health,* 1983; *Sex and Heart Disease,* 1983 (a short, nonsexist treatment of a sometimes sensitive topic); *Why Do They Behave That Way?* 1983 (a short description of possible behavior traits of a stroke victim. Helpful to family and patient).

Books and Other Publications

CASS Principal Investigators and Their Associates. "Myocardial Infarction and Mortality in the Coronary Artery Surgery Study (CASS) Randomized Trial." *The New England Journal of Medicine,* Vol. 310, No. 12, March 22, 1984, p. 750.

Cousins, Norman. *The Healing Heart: Antidotes to Panic and Helplessness.* New York: W. W. Norton, 1983. A personal account combining information about the technology of coronary care with the power of positive thinking.

Kahn, M. Gabriel. *Heart Attacks, Hypertension, and Heart Drugs.* Emmaus, Pennsylvania: Rodale Press, 1987. Contains good information about drugs.

Ornish, Dean. *Stress, Diet and Your Heart.* New York: Holt, Rinehart & Winston, 1982. A report of a study on heart disease and how we can prevent it through exercise and diet.

Public Citizen Health Research Group. *Heart Valve.* Information packet, $4.00. (See General Health resources under Organizations.)

Weisfeldt, Myron. *The Aging Heart*. New York: Raven Press, 1980.

CANCER

Organizations

American Cancer Society (ACS)
4 W. 35 St.
New York, NY 10001
Tel. (212) 736-3030

See the telephone directory for your local and state chapters. Chapters have lists of local community resources, home care items for loan, transportation services, and public education programs including literature, films, and speakers. ACS offers two short-term programs of one-to-one visits by a person with the same kind of cancer: *Reach to Recovery* for women with breast cancer, and *CanSurmount* for people with any other kind of cancer. Also has two group rehabilitation and support programs: one for people who have had a laryngectomy (removal of the voice box) and the second for people with ostomies, in cooperation with the United Ostomy Association. Offers a support group for people with cancer: *I Can Cope*.

American Institute for Cancer Research
500 N. Washington St.
Falls Church, VA 22046
Tel. (703) 237-0159

Booklets on fiber, fat, and dietary guidelines to lower cancer risk are available free. Publication list.

Cancer Information Service (CIS)
Tel. (800) 4-CANCER

CIS is a program of the National Cancer Institute (NCI), which provides information, referral, and free publications about cancer. Also operates PDQ (Physician Data Query), a computerized information base developed by NCI that provides information on standard and experimental treatments for more than 80 types of cancer.

Encore support and exercise groups for women who have had mastectomies. Contact your local YWCA.

Exceptional Cancer Patients (see General Health resources under Organizations).

Make Today Count
P.O. Box 222
Osage Beach, MO 65065
Tel. (303) 348-1619

Sponsors support groups in many communities for people with cancer.

National Cancer Survivors Network
P.O. Box 4543
Albuquerque, NM 87196
Tel. (505) 268-7388

A new national networking organization for individuals and groups with peer support as a primary part of the program.

United Ostomy Association, Inc.
2001 W. Beverly Blvd.
Los Angeles, CA 90057
Tel. (213) 413-5510

Quarterly newsletter, $10.00 per issue. Over 600 chapters in North America. Local dues average $15.00 per year, which entitle members to the national quarterly, local bulletin, other literature, and meeting notices.

The organizations listed above mainly present the views of established medical practice. For organizations that advocate alternative therapies, see Linde and Carrow (p. 458). See also the Boston Women's Health Book Collective, *The New Our Bodies, Ourselves*. New York: Simon and Schuster, 1984, p. 551.

DES Action, 2845 24 St., San Francisco, CA 94110 and Long Island Jewish Hospital, New Hyde Park, NY 11040.

Books and Other Publications

American Academy of Dermatology. *It's Never Too Late to Stop Skin Cancer*. Includes information on sunscreen products. Send a stamped self-addressed envelope to the Academy at Box 561, Dept. BG, New York, NY 10156.

American Cancer Society. *Cancer Facts and Figures*. Published annually. Available from your local chapter or the National Office (see above).

Bailer, John C. III, and Elaine M. Smith. "Progress Against Cancer?" *The New England Journal of Medicine*, Vol. 314, No. 19, May 8, 1986, pp.

1226–32. An important article that presents data showing we are losing the war against cancer and argues for more emphasis on research for prevention than for treatment.

Beattie, Edward J., Jr. *Toward the Conquest of Cancer*. New York: Crown Publishers, 1980.

Boyle, Robert H. *Malignant Neglect: Known or Suspected Cancer-Causing Agents in Our Environment and How by Controlling Them We Can Control the Spread of Cancer Itself*. New York: Random House, 1980.

Clarke, Juanne Nancarrow. *It's Cancer: The Personal Experiences of Women Who Have Received a Cancer Diagnosis*. Toronto: IPI Publishing Ltd., 1985.

Corbett, Thomas H. *Cancer and Chemicals*. Chicago: Nelson-Hall, 1977.

Doll, R. and R. Peto. "The Causes of Cancer: Quantitative Estimates of Avoidable Risks of Cancer in the U.S. Today." *Journal of the National Cancer Institute*, Vol. 66, 1981, pp. 1191–1308.

Durant, John. "The Problem of Nausea and Vomiting in Modern Cancer Chemotherapy." *CA*, January/February 1984, p. 2.

Epstein, Samuel. *The Politics of Cancer*. New York: Anchor/Doubleday, 1979.

Fredericks, Carlton. *Winning the Fight Against Breast Cancer: The Nutritional Approach*. New York: Grosset & Dunlap, 1977.

Glassman, Judith. *Cancer Survivors and How They Did It*. New York: Dial, 1983.

Glucksburg, Harold, and Jack Singer. *Cancer Care: A Personal Guide*. Baltimore: Johns Hopkins University Press, 1980.

Gorbach, Sherwood L., et al. *The Doctors' Anti-Breast Cancer Diet*. New York: Dial, 1983. Rationale and recipes for a low-fat diet.

Henderson, I. Craig, and Jay R. Harris. "Breast Cancer: Current Trends in Diagnosis and Treatment." In R.G. Petersdorf, et al., eds. *Harrison's Principles of Internal Medicine. Update VII*. New York: McGraw-Hill, 1986, pp. 181–208.

If You've Thought About Breast Cancer... Kensington, Maryland: Women's Breast Cancer Advisory Center, Inc., 1985. Booklet on breast cancer detection and treatment. Free on request from the Cancer Information Service, Tel. (800) 4-CANCER.

Kushner, Rose. *Alternatives: New Developments in the War on Breast Cancer*. (Formerly published as *Why Me?*) Cambridge, Massachusetts: Kensington Press, 1984.

Langone, John. "Cancer: Cautious Optimism." *Discover*, March 1986, pp. 36–45. Summary article on investigational immune-system activators for treating cancers.

LeShan, Lawrence. *You Can Fight for Your Life: Emotional Factors in the Treatment of Cancer*. New York: M. Evans, 1977.

Lettvin, Maggie. *Maggie's Woman's Book*. Boston: Houghton Mifflin, 1980. Contains section on exercises for lymphedema of the arms.

Levy, Sandra M. *Behavior and Cancer*. San Francisco: Jossey-Bass, 1985. Includes a review of the literature on how behavior influences the development of cancer and how the risks can be reduced.

Locke, Steven E., ed. *Psychological and Behavioral Treatments for Disorders Associated with the Immune System: An Annotated Bibliography*. New York: Institute for the Advancement of Health, 1986. Contains references on meditation, relaxation, imagery, psychotherapy, and hypnosis as cancer therapy.

Lorde, Audre. *Cancer Journals*. New York: Spinsters, Ink, 1980. A Black lesbian feminist poet's personal experiences with breast cancer and mastectomy.

Lynch, Dorothea, and Eugene Richards. *Exploding into Life*. New York: Aperture Foundation in association with Many Voices Press, 1986. Aperture Foundation, 20 E. 23 St., New York, NY 10010. A powerful and sometimes disturbing diary and photo record of a thirty-four-year-old woman with fatal breast cancer. Describes the struggles she and other people with cancer have with the medical system.

Morra, Marion, and Eve Potts. *Choices: Realistic Alternatives in Cancer Treatment*. Rev. ed. New York: Avon, 1987. Thorough and clearly written overview of conventional medical procedures involved in diagnosis and treatment of cancer.

Moss, Ralph W. *The Cancer Syndrome*. New York: Grove Press, 1982. Discusses the political climate that inhibits alternatives to the currently accepted cancer treatments, indicting both the National Cancer Institute and the American Cancer Society for irresponsibility.

Mullen, Barbara D., and Kerry A. McGinn. *The Ostomy Book*. Palo Alto, California: Bull Publishing Co., 1980. A vivid personal experience that includes much practical information.

National Cancer Institute. *The Breast Cancer Digest: A Guide to Medical Care, Emotional Support, Educational Programs, and Resources*, 1984. Office of Cancer Communications, National Cancer Institute, Bethesda, MD 20003. Free on request from the Cancer Information Service, Tel. (800) 4-CANCER.

National Research Council. *Diet, Nutrition, and Cancer*. Washington, DC: National Academy Press, 1982.

Reports from the 1985 Women and Cancer Conference are available from the National Women's Health Network (see General Health resources under Organizations). Papers available on breast cancer, food and cancer, reproductive cancers, medical practices that could cause cancer, and living with cancer. Prices $6.00 to $15.00.

Shapiro, Sam, et al. "Prospects for Eliminating Racial Difference in Breast Cancer Survival Rates." *American Journal of Public Health*, Vol. 72, No. 10, October 1982, pp. 1142–5.

Siegel, Bernie. *Love, Medicine, and Miracles*. (See General Health resources under Books and Other Publications.)

Simone, Charles B. *Cancer and Nutrition*. New York: McGraw-Hill, 1983.

Simonton, Carl, et al. *Getting Well Again: A Step-by-Step Self-Help Guide to Overcoming Cancer for Patients and Their Families*. New York: Bantam, 1978. A discussion of methods by which the mind can influence the body both for health and toward disease.

United Ostomy Association. *Sex and the Female Ostomate*. 1982. (See Organizations, this section.)

Wainwright, Sonny. *Stage V: A Journey Through Illness*. Berkeley, California: Acacia Books, 1984. A personal account of living with breast cancer.

White, Kristin. *Diet and Cancer—There Is a Connection*. New York: Bantam, 1984.

DIABETES

Organizations

American Diabetes Association (ADA)
   National Service Center
   1660 Duke St.
   Alexandria, VA 22314
   Tel. (800) 232-3472
Diabetes Forecast, a bimonthly magazine with articles on every topic of interest from careers to cookery, insulin to insurance, pregnancy to parenting and peer support groups is provided with membership in ADA. A publication list and *Diabetes '87*, a quarterly newsletter, are free. To join ADA or obtain a complete list of ADA materials, contact your local ADA affiliate or the National Service Center.

Diabetes Center, Inc.
   P.O. Box 739
   Wayzata, MN 55391
   Tel. (800) 848-2793 toll-free
Distributes the materials of the International Diabetes Center including *Fast Food Facts: Nutritive Values for Fast Food Restaurants*, *Gestational Diabetes*, and a free quarterly newsletter, *Living Well with Diabetes*.

Sugarfree Center, Inc.
13715 Burbank Blvd.
P.O. Box 114
Van Nuys, CA 91401
Tel. (800) 972-2323 toll-free. Answers questions about diabetes on (818) 994-1093.
Publishes *Health-O-Gram*, a newsletter and catalog for information and products of use to diabetics.

Books and Other Publications

American Diabetes Association. *Guide to Good Living*. An A-to-Z guide for integrating good diabetes management into the life-style of the 1980s.

_____. *Diabetes in the Family*. Englewood Cliffs, New Jersey: Prentice-Hall, 1982. A comprehensive reference for newly diagnosed diabetics and for those who have had diabetes for some time, and their families. A handbook on all aspects of diabetes: diagnosis, treatment, psychosocial impact, and the future of research.

_____. *Exchange Lists for Meal Planning*. Includes "new" foods such as kiwi fruit and tacos. $1.75

American Diabetes Association and American Dietetic Association: *The Family Cookbook and Nutrition Guide*. Englewood Cliffs, New Jersey: Prentice-Hall, Vol. 1 (1980) and Vol. 2 (1984).

Bierman, June, and Barbara Toohey. *The Diabetic's Sports and Exercise Book*. Philadelphia: Lippincott, 1977.

_____. *The Diabetic's Total Health Book*. Los Angeles: Jeremy P. Tarcher, 1980.

_____. *The Woman Diabetic*. Los Angeles: Jeremy P. Tarcher, 1986.

Folkman, Jane, and Hugo [Holly] Hollerorth. *Guide for Women with Diabetes Who Are Pregnant or Plan to Be*. Joslin Diabetes Center, One Joslin Place, Boston, MA 02215, 1985. $24.50. Teaching guide for women themselves.

Jovanovic, Lois, and Charles Peterson. *The Diabetes Self-Care Method*. New York: Fireside/ Simon & Schuster, 1984.

Krall, Leo, ed. *Joslin's Diabetes Manual*. Philadelphia: Lea Febinger, 1985.

Off Diabetes Pills. Public Citizen Health Research Group, 1978 (see General Health resources under Organizations). Explains how these pills can cause serious health problems and emphasizes the importance of a proper diet as an essential part of diabetes therapy. $3.50 plus handling.

Pray, Lawrence. *Journey of a Diabetic*. New York: Simon and Schuster, 1983.

Sims, Dorothea F. *Diabetes: Reach for Health and Freedom*. St. Louis: C.V. Mosby Co. and American Diabetes Association, 1984.

Sims, Dorothea F., and Ethan A. H. Sims. *The Other Diabetes*. Alexandria, Virginia: American Diabetes Association, rev. ed. forthcoming, 1987. A paperback on Type II diabetes describing causes, treatment, and psychosocial aspects of self-care.

GALLSTONES AND GALLBLADDER DISEASE

Organizations

American Digestive Disease Society
7720 Wisconsin Ave.
Bethesda, MD 20814
Tel. (301) 652-9293
Disseminates information about specific digestive disorders, including dietary recommendations. Provides physician referrals and personal counseling to members. Sponsors GUT-LINE, a telephone call-in information service. Publishes *Living Healthy*, a monthly periodical, "Person to Person" brochures, and dietary plans for special conditions including gallbladder disorders. Subjects covered in the publications include gallbladder, diverticulosis, hiatal hernia/esophagitis, diarrhea and constipation, gas and heartburn, and other digestive problems.

National Digestive Diseases Information Clearinghouse
  1255 23 St. NW, Suite 275
  Washington, DC 20037
  Tel. (202) 296-1138
Part of the National Institutes of Health. Provides fact sheets, resource lists, directories of lay and professional groups, and an annotated listing of educational materials on a variety of subjects related to gallbladder function, digestion, food allergies, and related subjects.

VISION, HEARING, AND OTHER SENSORY LOSS ASSOCIATED WITH AGING

Vision

Organizations

American Foundation for the Blind
  15 W. 16 St.
  New York, NY 10011
  Tel. (212) 620-2172
National private organization with five regional offices. Provides information and services. Catalog of special products.

Commission for the Blind. In each state.

Division for the Blind and Physically Handicapped
  Library of Congress
  Washington, DC 10542
Publishes *The Directory of Library Resources for the Blind and Physically Handicapped*. Anyone who is unable to read or use standard printed materials as a result of a temporary or permanent visual or other limitation may receive services, such as talking books, magnifiers, Braille materials, Kurzweil reading machines, large print and Braille typewriters, etc. Not every library provides these services, so check first to see what is available at yours. For more information, call toll-free, (800) 424-8567. When you apply, bring a brief written description of your limitation from a professional, such as a physician, nurse, or optometrist. Or a professional librarian may recommend these services.

National Association for Visually Handicapped
  22 W. 21 St., 6th floor
  New York, NY 10010
  Tel. (212) 889-3141
  Western states, Alaska, and Hawaii:
  3201 Balboa St.
  San Francisco, CA 94121
  Tel. (415) 221-8753
Serves the partially sighted (not totally blind), their families, and professionals with counsel, information, and referral. Offers large-print loan library free of charge through the mail, literature, and adult discussion groups in New York City and San Francisco. Dues $35.00 per year.

VISION Foundation, Inc.
  818 Mt. Auburn St.
  Watertown, MA 02172
  Tel. (617) 926-4232
In Massachusetts only, a toll-free number, (800) 852-3029. A consumer-run, self-help organization that provides information and support for people with low vision, newly blind people, and those with progressive eye conditions. Support groups are offered for mixed ages and for elders, and telephone buddies are assigned for those who are homebound. Referrals are made throughout the U.S., but the National Self-Help Clearinghouse (see p. 423) may have a more up-to-date list of local groups outside of Massachusetts.

Books and Other Publications

Independent Living Aids, 11 Commercial Court, Plainview, NY 11803, Tel. (516) 681-8288; TTY: (516) 681-8289.

Dickman, Irving. *Making Life More Livable: Simple Adaptations for the Homes of Blind and Visually Impaired Older People.* New York: American Foundation for the Blind, 1983. Large print. $5.00. Describes simple, inexpensive adaptations that can be made in the homes of older people to allow them to carry on everyday activities despite poor or deteriorating vision.

Penner, Jonathan. *Going Blind.* New York: Simon and Schuster, 1975. A middle-aged male professor tries to conceal his oncoming blindness. Fiction.

Public Citizen Health Research Group. "Cataracts." *Health Letter*, Vol. 3, No. 3, March 1987, pp. 1–6. (See General Health resources under Organizations.)

Rosenbloom, Alfred, Jr., and Meredith W. Morgan, eds. *Vision and Aging: General and Clinical Perspectives.* New York: Professional Press/Fairchild Publications, 1986.

Schaeffer, Susan Fromberg. *Mainland.* New York: Linden Press/Simon & Schuster, 1985. A novel about a woman struggling with vision loss along with midlife issues.

Smith, Margaret M. *If Blindness Strikes: Don't Strike Out—A Lively Look at Living with a Visual Impairment.* Charles C. Thomas, Publisher, 2600 S. First St., Springfield, IL 62794–9265, 1984. $32.75. Concentrates on the common problems that confront a person who is losing his or her sight. Offers practical solutions and shows how the reader can take control of his or her own life. Includes a chapter for family members and a resource list. Available on tape from Readings for the Blind, Inc., 29451 Greenfield, Suite 116, Southfield, MI 48076. Four-track (five cassettes) $7.50, two-track (nine cassettes) $13.50. Available on loan from The National Library Service for the Blind and Physically Handicapped. Cassette (RC 21060); Braille (BR 5858).

Weisse, Fran A., and Mimi Winer. *Coping with Sight Loss. The VISION Resource Book.* No date. Vision Foundation (see Organizations, this section). Large print.

Winer, Mimi. "Self-Help Programs for People with Sight Loss." *Journal of Visual Impairment and Blindness*, Vol. 76, No. 10, December 1982, pp. 393–7.

Hearing

Organizations

American Association of Retired Persons (AARP) (see General Resources). Ask for their pamphlet, "Have You Heard? Hearing Loss and Aging."

The American Speech-Language-Hearing Association (ASHA)
  10801 Rockville Pike, Dept. AP
  Rockville, MD 20852
The professional, scientific, and accrediting organization representing 45,000 speech-language pathologists and audiologists.

American Tinnitus Association
  P.O. Box 5
  Portland, OR 97207
  Tel. (503) 248-9985
Information and referral to worldwide network of clinics and self-help groups. Research and education.

National Association for Hearing and Speech Action
  Same address as ASHA above.
  Tel. (800) 638-8255 toll-free
A consumer affiliate of ASHA set up to handle specific questions about communication problems and how to find professional assistance. Publishes literature on communication disorders. Provides information on insurance coverage for consumers and a directory of sites, such as libraries, community centers, and religious centers around the country equipped with assistive devices for the hearing-impaired.

Better Hearing Institute
  5021 Backlick Road
  Annandale, VA 22003
  Toll-free Hearing Helpline: (800) EAR-WELL

Division for the Blind and Physically Handicapped
  Library of Congress
  Washington, DC 10542
Publishes *The Directory of Library Resources for the Blind and Physically Handicapped.* Anyone who needs special help because of a physical limitation, including hearing impairment, may apply for use of such aids as amplifiers and telecommunications devices for the deaf, including teletypewriters that enable deaf persons to make or receive telephone calls, and TV decoders that provide close-captioned access to TV programs. Not every library provides these services, so check first to see what is available at yours. For more information, call toll-free, (800) 424-8567. When you apply, bring a brief writ-

ten description of the limitation from a professional, such as a physician, nurse, or audiologist. Or a professional librarian may recommend these services.

Gray Panthers
(see General Resources)
Advocacy organization working for a national health care program. They have also done research and advocacy on legislation regarding hearing aids.

Office of Scientific and Health Reports
National Institute of Neurological and Communicative Disorders and Stroke
Building 31, Room 8A-06
Bethesda, MD 20205
Ask for their pamphlet, "Hearing Loss: Hope Through Research," and other publications.

SHHH (Self-Help for Hard-of-Hearing People, Inc.)
7800 Wisconsin Ave.
Bethesda, MD 20814
Tel. (301) 657-2248
A self-help organization for hard-of-hearing people and their families. Local groups meet regularly, offering understanding, information, and self-help strategies for people ages six to ninety-eight. Dues include a bimonthly magazine, advisory services, and special programs.

Books and Other Publications

Becker, Gaylene. *Growing Old in Silence: Deaf People in Old Age*. Berkeley and Los Angeles: University of California Press, 1980. An anthropological study of aging among the lifelong deaf provides a positive view of social support through interdependence.

Dalton, Phyllis I. *Library Service for the Deaf and Hearing Impaired*. Phoenix, Arizona: Oryx Press, 1985. $39.50.

Hearing Loss: Hope Through Research. U.S. Dept. of Health and Human Services, NIH Publication No. 82–157, January 1982.

Hypothermia

Organizations

National Center for Accidental Hypothermia
P.O. Box 797
Portland, ME 04104–0797
Tel. (207) 871-7436
Materials available include an excellent pamphlet, "Accidental Hypothermia: A Winter Hazard for the Old," and a list of companies that produce low-reading thermometers.

Articles

"Hypothermia." In the American Medical Association, *Family Medical Guide*, p. 723. New York: Random House, 1982. See also "First Aid" on p. 809, which warns: *Do not give alcohol*.

Rango, Nicholas. "Exposure-Related Hypothermia Mortality in the United States, 1970–79." *American Journal of Public Health*, Vol. 74, No. 10, October 1984, pp. 1159–60.

Siwolop, Sana. "Why Women Get Cold." *Savvy*, June 1985, pp. 70–1.

Products

A regular mercury thermometer may detect a low temperature only if it has been shaken down to its lowest point. Usually the occurrence and severity of the hypothermia can be determined only by using a low-reading or subnormal thermometer, or a rectal probe.

Smell and Taste

Fact Sheet: Smell and Taste Disorders. NIH Pub. No. 86-2655, December 1985. Prepared by the National Institute of Neurological and Communicative Disorders and Stroke. For additional information about research supported by the NINCDS, contact:
Office of Scientific and Health Reports
NINCDS
National Institutes of Health
Building 31, Room 8A-06
Bethesda, MD 20892
Tel. (301) 496-5751

MEMORY LAPSE AND MEMORY LOSS

Organizations

Alzheimer's Disease and Related Disorders Association (ADRDA)
National Headquarters
70 E. Lake St.
Chicago, IL 60601
Tel. (800) 621-0379; in Illinois (800) 572-6037
Organizational newsletter also contains informative articles. Also has pamphlets, and state and local chapters that sponsor support groups and lists of community resources.

American Geriatrics Society
10 Columbus Circle
New York, NY 10019

American Association for Geriatric Psychiatry
230 N. Michigan Ave., Suite 2400
Chicago, IL 60601

Gerontological Society
1835 K St. NW
Washington, DC 20006

American Academy of Neurology
4015 W. 65 St.
Minneapolis, MN 55435
Tel. (612) 920-3636

National Council on the Aging
600 Maryland Ave. SW, West Wing 100
Washington, DC 20024
Tel. (202) 479-1200

Books and Other Publications

The American Journal of Alzheimer's Care and Related Disorders. 470 Boston Post Road, Weston, MA 02193. Quarterly covering major areas of interest to caregivers and professionals.

Blodgett, Harriet E., Evelyn Deno, and Virginia Hathaway. *For the Caregivers: Caring for Patients with Brain Loss,* 1986. $2.00 Metropolitan Council, 300 Metro Square Building, Seventh and Roberts Sts. St. Paul, MN 55101. Excellent pamphlet that provides emotional support and practical advice for the caregiver.

Butler, Robert N., and Myrna I. Lewis. *Aging and Mental Health.* New York: New American Library, 1983.

Cohen, Donna, and Carl Eisdorfer. *The Loss of Self: A Family Resource for the Care of Alzheimer's Disease and Related Disorders.* New York: W. W. Norton, 1986. Contains many personal accounts by persons with Alzheimer's disease and their relatives. Practical and readable without being simplistic.

Heston, Leonard L., and June A. White. *Dementia: A Practical Guide to Alzheimer's Disease and Related Illnesses.* New York: W. H. Freeman & Co., 1983.

Inoue, Yasushi. *Chronicle of My Mother.* New York: Kodansha International Ltd., 1982. Moving account of a woman's gradual mental decline.

Mace, Nancy L., and Peter V. Rabins. *The 36-Hour Day: A Family Guide to Caring for Persons with Alzheimer's Disease, Related Dementing Illnesses, and Memory Loss in Later Life.* Baltimore: Johns Hopkins University Press, 1981. Excellent guide for anyone caring for an older person with memory loss, disorientation, and/or increased dependence.

Noyes, Lin E. *What's Wrong With My Grandma.* Distributed by ADRDA, Northern Virginia Chapter, 200 E. Broad St., Apt. No. 1, Falls Church, VA 22046. $2.50. Tel. (403) 534-8466. Illustrated booklet to help children understand Alzheimer's disease.

Powell, Lenore S., and Katie Courtice. *Alzheimer's Disease: A Guide for Families.* Reading, Massachusetts: Addison-Wesley, 1983.

Reisberg, Barry. *A Guide to Alzheimer's Disease: For Families, Spouses, and Friends.* New York: Free Press, 1984.

Safford, Florence. *Caring for the Mentally Impaired Elderly.* New York: Henry Holt, 1986. Sound, innovative, and informative.

475

U.S. Department of Health and Human Services. *Alzheimer's Disease Handbook*, Vol. I. San Francisco: Aging Health Policy Center, University of California, April 1984.

West, Robin. *Memory Fitness Over 40*. Gainesville, Florida: Triad Publishing, 1985. Includes practical ways to improve memory.

DYING AND DEATH

Organizations

Compassionate Friends
  900 Jorie Blvd.
  Oak Brook, IL 60522
  Tel. (312) 323-5010
Self-help organization offering friendship and understanding to bereaved parents—to support and aid parents in the resolution of their grief, and to foster the physical and emotional health of the bereaved parents and their other children.

Concern for Dying
  250 W. 57 St.
  New York, NY 10107
  Tel. (212) 246-6962
Literature available on legislation concerning dying and death. A free copy of the Living Will form will be provided upon request. Publishes *Concern Newsletter* quarterly.

Continental Association of Funeral and Memorial Societies, Inc.
  2001 S St. NW, Suite 530
  Washington, DC 20009
Federation of nonprofit consumer organizations fostering freedom of choice in funeral arrangements. Checklists, pamphlets, directories, and other publications. Write for addresses of local memorial societies that can help with preplanning.

Hemlock Society
  P.O. Box 66218
  Los Angeles, CA 90066
  Tel. (213) 391-1871
Books and articles on euthanasia and self-deliverance. Will provide a durable power of attorney for health care form. Newsletter available.

The Hospice Association of America
  214 Massachusetts Ave. NE, Suite 240
  Washington, DC 20002
Recently organized to be a voice for the grassroots hospice movement and to advocate for legislative changes that would permit more community-based hospices to participate in Medicare. Only 200 of 1,500 hospices have qualified to do so under the current restrictive legislation.

National Hospice Organization
  1901 North Fort Myer Drive, Suite 902
  Arlington, VA 22209
An organization formed to help primarily hospital-affiliated hospice programs deal with legislative, regulatory, and reimbursement issues. Publishes *The Hospice Journal*.

Older Women's League (OWL) (see General Resources under Organizations) offers a variety of resources on dying and death, such as their *Living Will Packet* (send $1.00), which includes a sample living will and durable power of attorney, flyer on wills and trusts, and a compilation of practical information on memorial services and burial. Other publications include *Taking Charge of the End of Your Life: Proceedings of a Forum on Living Wills and Other Advance Directives*, July 1985; and *Death and Dying: Staying in Control to the End of Our Lives*, Gray Paper, 1986, $3.00.

Society for the Right to Die
  250 W. 57 St.
  New York, NY 10107
  Tel. (212) 246-6973
A nonprofit organization working for the recognition of the individual's right to die with dignity. Distributes living will forms appropriate for each state, supports judicial and legislative action, publishes a newsletter and various other materials, provides referrals and legal counseling on the status of living will laws in each state.

Suicide Prevention

Check your phone directory's community services section or listings for local hot lines run by the Samaritans or local mental health agencies. Or write to either of the following:

American Association of Suicidology
2459 S. Ash St.
Denver, CO 80222
Tel. (303) 692-0985
Provides referrals to suicide prevention services throughout the United States.

The Samaritans of the USA
55 Jackson St.
Lawrence, MA 01840
Tel. (617) 688-6607
Provides referrals on the East Coast of the United States and in some countries abroad.

Widowhood—Families and Relationships resources, pp. 442–5 for books and organizations.

Books and Other Publications

Becker, Ernest. *The Denial of Death*. New York: Free Press, 1973. The thesis of this book is that the fear and denial of death is the mainspring of all human activity—activity largely designed to overcome our fear by denying in some way that death is our final destiny.

Deciding to Forgo Life-Sustaining Treatment: Ethical, Medical, and Legal Issues in Treatment Decisions. President's Commission for the Study of Ethical Problems in Medicine and Biomedical and Behavioral Research. Washington, DC: Government Printing Office, 1983. (Special edition available for $5.00 from Concern for Dying. See p. 476.)

Editors of Consumer Reports. *Funerals: Consumers' Last Rights: The Consumers' Union Report on Conventional Funerals and Burial...and Some Alternatives, Including Cremation, Direct Cremation, Direct Burial and Body Donation*. New York: W. W. Norton, 1977.

Euthanasia: A Decade of Change. Excerpts from Annual Conferences 1968–1977 available from Concern for Dying (see p. 476).

"Funerals." *Modern Maturity*, December 1984/January 1985, p. 16.

Grollman, Earl. *Concerning Death: A Practical Guide for the Living*. Boston: Beacon Press, 1974.

Articles addressing the practical issues of death in our lives.

———. *Explaining Death to Children*. Boston: Beacon Press, 1967.

Humphrey, Derek. *Let Me Die Before I Wake: Hemlock's Book of Self-Deliverance for the Dying*, available from Hemlock Society (see p. 476).

Kübler-Ross, Elisabeth. *On Death and Dying*. New York: Macmillan, 1969. Classic presentation of the theory that dying persons move through stages from denial to acceptance.

———. *Death: The Final Stage of Growth*. Englewood Cliffs, New Jersey: Prentice-Hall, 1975. Essays chiefly centered on what the dying teach about the value of life.

Levine, Steven. *Meetings at the Edge: Dialogues With the Grieving and the Dying, the Healing and the Healed*. New York: Doubleday, 1984.

———. *Who Dies? An Investigation of Conscious Living and Dying*. New York: Doubleday, 1982.

Little, Deborah. *Home Care for the Dying*. New York: Doubleday, 1985. Highly recommended.

Maheady, Joseph, and Rita Reimer. *Comparative Analysis of State Statutes Recognizing a Patient's Right to Die a Natural Death*. Washington, DC: Congressional Research Service, 1985.

Mitford, Jessica. *The American Way of Death*. New York: Fawcett, 1979. Classic exposé of the burial and funeral businesses. Has sparked some reforms.

Morgan, Ernest. *Dealing Creatively with Death: A Manual of Death Education and Simple Burial*. Burnsville, North Carolina: Celo Press, 1984.

Munley, Ann. *The Hospice Alternative: A New Context for Death and Dying*. New York: Basic Books, 1983. This book is strongest in those sections in which the author empathically describes the inner struggles of dying persons and their loved ones. It is unfortunately too uncritical of the policies and politics that have hampered the hospice movement from accomplishing its purposes.

Nelson, Thomas C. *It's Your Choice: The Practical Guide to Planning a Funeral.* AARP Books, 1982. $5.00, from AARP Books, Dept. CATA, 400 S. Edward St., Mount Prospect, IL 60056.

Reimer, Rita. *Legal Analysis of the Right to Die.* Washington, DC: Library of Congress, 1985.

Rollin, Betty. *Last Wish.* New York: Linden Press/Simon & Schuster, 1985. Author tells of her terminally ill mother's decision to stop treatment and commit suicide. Though quite ill, her mother remained in charge throughout.

Sarton, May. *A Reckoning.* New York: W.W. Norton, 1981. A novel that celebrates caring and connection, and honors the process of dying itself, which the protagonist experiences as "ripening."

Saunders, Dame Cicely, and Mary Baines. *Living With Dying: The Management of Terminal Diseases.* New York: Oxford University Press, 1983. Home health care for the dying.

Pastan, Linda. *The Five Stages of Grief. Poems.* New York: W.W. Norton, 1978. A moving account of dark times by a woman whose poetry allows the reader to feel many facets of the mourning process.

Robertson, John. *The Rights of the Critically Ill.* New York: Bantam, 1983.

Silverman, Phyllis. *Helping Women Cope with Grief.* Beverly Hills, California: Sage Publications, 1981.

Slagle, Kate Walsh. *Live with Loss.* Englewood Cliffs, New Jersey: Prentice-Hall, 1982. Practical, compassionate techniques for coping with many kinds of loss and moving through grief to growth.

Special Committee on Biomedical Ethics. *Values in Conflict: Ethical Issues in Hospital Care.* Chicago: American Hospital Association, 1985.

Wanzer, Sidney H., et al. "The Physician's Responsibility Toward Hopelessly Ill Patients." *The New England Journal of Medicine,* Vol. 310, No. 15, April 12, 1984, pp. 955–9.

Weizman, Savine G., and Phyllis Kamm. *About Mourning: Support and Guidance for the Bereaved.* New York: Human Sciences Press, 1985. Written for mental health workers, but contains helpful, sensitively written information for the general reader.

Wentzel, Kenneth. *To Those Who Need It Most—Hospice Means Hope.* Boston: Charles River Books, 1981. A general introduction to the philosophy of hospice care.

Worden, J. W., and William Proctor. *Personal Death Awareness.* Englewood Cliffs, New Jersey: Prentice-Hall, 1976.

Zoza, Victor, and Rosemary Zoza. *A Way to Die.* New York: Knopf, 1980.

CHANGING SOCIETY AND OURSELVES

See General Resources for organizations that advocate for women and elders. See also organizations listed under specific chapters.

Books and Other Publications

Cheatham, Annie, and Mary Clare Powell. *This Way Daybreak Comes.* Philadelphia: New Society Publishers, 1985. The authors traveled 30,000 miles to talk with American women in all walks of life about creating new institutions and changing old ones by valuing nurturance and cooperation, and living as one with others and with the natural world.

Durr, Virginia Foster. *Outside the Magic Circle.* Birmingham, Alabama: University of Alabama Press, 1985. Memoirs, beginning in the 1930's, of a "proper Alabama lady" who stepped outside the privileged circle into which she was born to challenge the cruelty of racial segregation.

Flexner, Eleanor. *Century of Struggle: The Woman's Rights Movement in the United States.* New York: Atheneum, 1973. A history of women's fight for equality in education, work, and voting rights.

Giddings, Paula. *When and Where I Enter.* New York: Morrow, 1984. Historical account of Black women in social reform movements in the United States.

McAllister, Pam, ed. *Reweaving the Web of Life: Feminism and Nonviolence*. Philadelphia: New Society Publishers, 1982. Explores women's commitment to nonviolent means of change.

"Older, Wiser, Stronger: Southern Elders." Special Issue of *Southern Exposure*, Vol. XIII, No. 2–3, March–June 1985. Order from Southern Exposure, P.O. Box 531, Durham, NC 27702. Fascinating and original compilation of elder activism in the South.

Philbier, Marianne, ed. *The Ribbon: Celebration of Life: The Remarkable Ribbon Around the Pentagon, A Unique Worldwide Plea for Peace*. Love Books, 50 College St., Asheville, NC 28801, 1985.

Self-Advocacy Organizing, a manual for people with disabilities, describes step-by-step how to start self-advocacy groups, organize successful meetings, recruit members, get publicity, raise funds, pick issues, and win. In large print or on tape. Price: $6.00 for consumers; $10.00 for agencies; bulk rates available. Order from Massachusetts Coalition of Citizens with Disabilities, 18 Williston Road, Brookline, MA 02146, Tel. (617) 734-7277.

Presses

New Society Publishers
 Life Center Association, Inc.
 4722 Baltimore Ave.
 Philadelphia, PA 19143
Publishes a variety of self-help manuals for social change activists on such subjects as working collectively, feminist leadership, empowering ourselves in the nuclear age, and consensus decision-making. Their publications include Virginia Coover, Ellen Deacon, et al., *Resource Manual for a Living Revolution*, 1985, which includes innovative decision-making techniques; and Joanna Rogers Macy, *Despair and Personal Power in the Nuclear Age*, 1983.

INDEX

In this index, a boldface page number is used to indicate the major discussion of the topic. An italic r refers to the Resources section; an italic n refers to a footnote.

estrogen *(cont.)*
286, 299, 308–9, 347
smoking and, 266
estrogen-positive cancer (ER+),
346, 347
estrogen-receptor-negative cancer,
347
estrogen-receptor test, 345, 346
"ethical will," 11
ethnic factors:
in breast cancer, 342, 344
in cancer, 330
in diabetes, 351
in gallbladder disease, 358
in glaucoma, 367
in hypertension, 109, 314
in lactose intolerance, 264
in nursing homes, 232
in osteoporosis, 263–64, 267
in strokes, 314
in tooth loss, 267
Evans, John S., 343*n*
evening primrose oil, 118*n*, 344
Exceptional Cancer Patients, 456*r*
excisional biopsy, 333, 345
exercise and movement, 3, 6, 7, 26,
62–76, 329
for abdominal muscles, 63, **73–74**,
248, 250, 288
abnormal reactions to, 72
aerobic, **65–66**, 68, 254, 261, 317
anaerobic, 65–66
angina pectoris and, 316
arthritis and, 64, 71, 245, 254
belly dancing, 41
bicycling, 64, **68–69**, 254
for bladder control, 72–74, 284–
85, 286, 287, 288, 291
blood sugar and, 355
bone density and, 62, 66, 68, 72,
74, 266
clothing for, 72
dancing, 14, 41, 64, **69**, 70, 266,
310
depression and, 33, 62, 63, 310
diabetes and, 353, **355–56**
digestion and, 63, 71
disabilities and, 64, 70–73, 245
energy and, 62, 63
excessive, 264
for eyes, 366–67
for feet, 247
for fibrositis, 255
for hands and fingers, 253
heart disease and, **317**, 323
hypertension and, 315
insomnia prevented by, 33

joint pain and, 244, 245, 246, 252,
253
limitation on, **70–73**, 285
martial arts, 7, 13
menopause and, 119
osteoporosis and, 47, 66, 72, **74**,
261, 264, 265, 266, 271, 272, 310
passive, 252
for pelvic muscles, 63, **73–74**, 111,
285, 288
precautions for, **72**, 250
pregnancy, **110–11**, 439*r*
for pubococcygeal muscle, **73–74**
for rehabilitation, 323
resources, 432*r*–34*r*, 439*r*
for scoliosis, 251
smoking and, 25
stress reduced by, 14–15, 31, 33
stretching, 63, 65, 244, 248, 250,
254
swimming, 62, **68**, 70–71, 119,
245, 250, 254, 255, 258, 266, 286,
310, 324
Tai Chi, 70
walking, **68**, 250, 254, 255, 258,
266, 271, 272, 285, 287, 310
weight-bearing, 266
weight gained by, 66
for weight loss, 49
yoga, 3, 34, **70**, 245, 251, 310
exercise testing for heart disease,
319
eyes:
blinking of, **366**
care of, 354, 356, **366–67**, 370–71
diseases of, **367–71**
dry, 121, 298, 366
examination of , 354, 366, 367,
370–71
exercises for, 366–67
hemorrhage in, 353
nutrition for, **367**
operations on, 370
pain in, 252, 370
palming of, **366–67**
self-help for, **366–67**
tearing of, 366
see also vision loss

face-lifts, 41, 42
fainting:
in heart attack, 319
low carbohydrate intake and, 48
Fair Employment Practices Agency,
167
fallopian tubes, 298, 306
cancer of, 299

ligation of, 103, 104, 295
removal of, 308
false unicorn, 124
family members, **127–36**
abuse of elderly by, 234
caregiving by, **198–212**, 234, 235,
387, **390–91**, 455*r*–56*r*
death of, **128**, 393, 394–95, 396,
398, 399, 400, 401–2, 406
friends as, 127, **128–29**
grandchildren as, **133–36**, 154,
382, 394
grown children as, **129–36**
health insurance coverage of, 226
housing shared by, 153–55, 156
love of, 127, 128, 238
in nursing home councils, 239–41
Family Services of America, 456*r*
Farmers Home Administration, 149
fasting, 8, 265, 266
fat, body, 57
diabetes and, 47, 317, 351
estrogen produced by, 266, 285,
301
corticosteroids and, 256
distribution of, 47, 64, 66, 87, 317
heart attacks and, 317
hypertension and, 317
menstruation and, 264
osteoporosis and, 264, 266
strokes and, 317
see also obesity
fat, dietary, 351
gallbladder disease and, 359, 361
hydrogenated, 54
importance of, 55, 56–57, 58, 60,
110, 318
mono-unsaturated, 54–55
reduction of, 53, 54–55, 286, 301,
317, 329, 340, 344, 359–60, 361
saturated, 54, 317, 359
unsaturated, 54, 317
fat, in blood, 48, 316, 351, 356
fatigue, **9–10**, 62, 117, 122, 298, 303,
352, 384
"fat phobia," 46
fat-soluble vitamins, 34, 57
fatty acids, essential, 55, 56–57,
118*n*
antiinflammatory effect of, 256,
258
FDA, *see* Food and Drug
Administration, U.S.
FDIC (Federal Deposit Insurance
Corporation), 190
fear:
of aging, xxiv, 3, 79

Motrin, 303
"Mourning to Do" (Sarton), 388–89
mouth, dryness of, **276–77**, 279, 292
mouth cancer, 22, 279, 328
mouthwashes, **276**
Ms., 88
MSG (monosodium glutamate), 55
MTBE (methyl tertbutyl ether), 363
multi-infarct dementia, **383–84**, 385
multiple sclerosis, 286
muscles:
    flexibility of, 244
    glycogen in, 351
    inflammation in, 244, 253
    loss of tissue from, 260
    pain in, 243, **244**, 253
    spasms in, 244, 246, 247, 263
    swollen, 244, 253
    weak, multi-infarct dementia as
        cause of, 383
    weak, urinary incontinence caused
        by, **284–85**, 310
    see also specific muscle groups
music, stress reduced by, 15
myelogram, 250
myocardial infarction, *see* heart
    attack
myofascial pain syndrome, 255
myomas, *see* fibroid tumors
myomectomy, 225, 300, **301–2**
myotherapy, 246

nadolol, 315
naproxen, 303
Narcotics Anonymous, 428r
nasal cancer, 279, 336
National Academy of Sciences, 53,
    58
National Action Forum for Midlife
    and Older Women, 409
National Anorexic Aid Society, 429r
National Association for Hearing
    and Speech Action, 473r
National Association for Lesbian
    and Gay Gerontology, 418r
National Association for Visually
    Handicapped, 472r
National Association for Widowed
    People, 442r
National Association of Alcohol and
    Drug Abuse Directors, 427r
National Association of Gay
    Alcoholism Professionals, 426r
National Association of Housing
    Cooperatives, 447r
National Autopsy Assistance
    Network, 386n

National Cancer Survivors Network,
    468r
National Catholic Women, 210
National Caucus and Center on the
    Black Aged, 418r
National Center for Accidental
    Hypothermia, 414r
National Center for Health
    Statistics, 108
National Center for Home Equity
    Conversion, 447r
National Citizens' Coalition for
    Nursing Home Reform
    (NCCNHR), 231–32, 233, 237,
    238, 239
    address of, 460r
National Coalition Against Domestic
    Violence, 442r
National Coalition of Resident
    Councils, 239, 460r
National Coalition on Older
    Women's Issues, 418r
National Commission on Working
    Women, 448r
National Committee on Pay Equity,
    167, 448r
National Community Action Agency
    Directors Association, 451r
National Council of Jewish Women,
    418r
National Council of Negro Women,
    409, 413, 418r–19r
National Council of Senior Citizens
    (NCSC), 413, 419r
National Council on the Aging
    (NCOA), 413, 454r, 475r
    address of, 418r
National Council on Alcoholism,
    Inc., 426r–27r
National Digestive Diseases
    Education and Information
    Clearinghouse, 428r, 472r
National Federation for Consumer
    Credit, 188, 451r
National Health Law Program, 459r
National Hearing Aid Society, 377
National Home Care Council, 455r
National Hospice Organization, 476r
National Housing Law Project, 148n
National Institute of Arthritis,
    Musculoskeletal and Skin
    Diseases, 462r
National Institute of Neurological
    and Communicative Disorders
    and Stroke, 474r
National Institute of Occupational
    Safety and Health, 41

National Institute of Senior Housing,
    445r
National Institute on Aging, 458r
National Institutes of Health
    Consensus Conference on
    Estrogen Replacement Therapy
    (1979), 360
National Institutes of Health
    Consensus Development
    Conference (1984), 268
National Interfaith Coalition on
    Aging, 419r
National Organization for Women
    (NOW), 409, 413, 419r
National Pacific/Asian Resource
    Center on Aging, 419r
National Policy Center on Housing
    and Living Arrangements for
    Older Americans, 445r
National Self-Help Clearinghouse,
    372, 423r
National Senior Citizens' Law
    Center (NSCLC), 413, 419r
National Trust for Historic
    Preservation, 147, 445r
National Urban League, 146
National Women's Health Network
    (NWHN), 413, 457r
National Women's Law Center, 454n
National Women's Political Caucus
    (NWPC), 413, 419r
Native American women:
    aging as viewed by, 4
    death as viewed by, 398
    gallbladder disease among, 358
    menopause among, 117
nausea:
    cancer treatments as cause of,
        336, 337, 338
    fluoride as cause of, 271
    glaucoma as cause of, 370
    in heart attack, 319
    hormone therapy as cause of, 270
NCCNHR, *see* National Citizens'
    Coalition for Nursing Home
    Reform
NCOA, *see* National Council on the
    Aging
NCSC (National Council of Senior
    Citizens), 413, 419r
neck problems:
    polymyalgia rheumatica, 256
    prevention of, **247–48**, **252**
needle biopsies, needle aspirations,
    333, 345
negative nodes, 346
Network, 418r

PAULA BROWN DORESS is a coauthor of *Our Bodies, Ourselves, Ourselves and Our Children*, and a series of articles on sex education and censorship. As a founding member of the Boston Women's Health Book Collective, she has lectured on a variety of women's health issues. As coordinator of the "Women Growing Older" chapter in *The New Our Bodies, Ourselves*, Paula became aware of the need for more information by and about older women and conceived the idea for *Ourselves, Growing Older*. Paula was among the first to develop a curriculum for and teach women's studies courses at the college level. She holds a master's degree in Women's Studies and is working toward a Ph.D. in Community Psychology with a research focus on women's issues.

DIANA LASKIN SIEGAL holds a master's degree in Public Administration and has worked for health departments and programs in Kansas and Massachusetts. A pioneer member of the first class to graduate from Brandeis University, she has never had a job that someone else held before. She has been involved in starting many health planning and public health programs, including the Cancer Information Service. Always a consumer advocate and an activist, she has served on many committees, boards, and political campaigns. Currently she is a consultant and lecturer on older women's health issues and is active in the Older Women's League. *Ourselves, Growing Older* is her first book.

THE MIDLIFE AND OLDER WOMEN BOOK PROJECT is the group that came together to work on *Ourselves, Growing Older*. See the Preface for more about the Book Project.

THE BOSTON WOMEN'S HEALTH BOOK COLLECTIVE is a nonprofit organization devoted to education about women and health. Their many projects include a Women's Health Information Center, open to the public; extensive distribution of materials to women and organizations in the United States and other countries; the publication and distribution of a Spanish-language edition of *Our Bodies, Ourselves* (*Nuestros Cuerpos, Nuestras Vidas*); and distribution of a videotape about teenage pregnancy. Upon publication of *Ourselves, Growing Older*, the Collective will become the repository of this project's books and files and will add the area of women and aging to the considerable list of topics on which it can provide information to the public. Tax-deductible donations (made payable to BWHBC) are welcome to help support the work of the Collective. Send to 47 Nichols Street, Watertown, MA 02172.

Books by the Boston Women's Health Book Collective:

Our Bodies, Ourselves
Ourselves and Our Children
Our Jobs, Our Health (coauthored with the Massachusetts
    Coalition for Occupational Safety and Health)
The New Our Bodies, Ourselves